THE OXFORD HANDBOOK OF
PUNK ROCK

THE OXFORD HANDBOOK OF
PUNK ROCK

Edited by
GEORGE McKAY
and
GINA ARNOLD

OXFORD
UNIVERSITY PRESS

Oxford University Press is a department of the University of Oxford. It furthers
the University's objective of excellence in research, scholarship, and education
by publishing worldwide. Oxford is a registered trade mark of Oxford University
Press in the UK and certain other countries.

Published in the United States of America by Oxford University Press
198 Madison Avenue, New York, NY 10016, United States of America.

© Oxford University Press 2025

All rights reserved. No part of this publication may be reproduced, stored in
a retrieval system, or transmitted, in any form or by any means, without the
prior permission in writing of Oxford University Press, or as expressly permitted
by law, by license, or under terms agreed with the appropriate reproduction
rights organization. Inquiries concerning reproduction outside the scope of the
above should be sent to the Rights Department, Oxford University Press, at the
address above.

You must not circulate this work in any other form
and you must impose this same condition on any acquirer.

CIP data is on file at the Library of Congress

ISBN 978-0-19-085956-5

DOI: 10.1093/oxfordhb/9780190859565.001.0001

Printed by Marquis Book Printing, Canada

Contents

Foreword ix
  GEORGE MCKAY AND GINA ARNOLD
List of Contributors xvii

1. "Enjoy It, Destroy It?" 40 Years of Punk Rock Scholarship 1
   LUCY WRIGHT

PART ONE: RECONSIDERING PUNK ROCK

2. The Punk Worlds of Liverpool and Manchester, 1975–1980 27
   NICK CROSSLEY

3. Riot Grrrl: Nostalgia and Historiography 45
   ELIZABETH K. KEENAN

4. Punk as Folk: Continuities and Tensions in the UK and Beyond 72
   PETE DALE

5. "This Is Radio Clash": First-Generation Punk as Radical Media Ecology and Communicational Noise 86
   MICHAEL GODDARD

6. Art School Manifestos, Classical Music, and Industrial Abjection: Tracing the Artistic, Political, and Musical Antecedents of Punk 100
   MIKE DINES

PART TWO: OH BONDAGE, UP YOURS! GENDER AND PUNK

7. Danger, Anger, and Noise: The Women Punks of the Late 1970s and Their Music 115
   HELEN REDDINGTON

8. "We're Just a Minor Threat": Minor Threat and the Intersectionality of Sound 133
SHAYNA MASKELL

9. Let's Talk about Sex: Punk, Rap, and Reproductive Health 148
JESSICA A. SCHWARTZ

10. Queer and Feminist Punk in the UK 166
KIRSTY LOHMAN

PART THREE: IDENTITY IS THE CRISIS, CAN'T YOU SEE

11. "Don't Be Afraid to Pogo": Latinx Punk in LA 187
MARLÉN RÍOS-HERNÁNDEZ

12. Queer Punk, Trans Forms: Transgender Rock and Rage in a Necropolitical Age 202
CURRAN NAULT

13. Guilty of Not Being White: On the Visibility and Othering of Black Punk 217
MARCUS CLAYTON

14. Punk and Aging 231
ANDY BENNETT

15. Identity? How 1970s Punk Women Live It Now 245
LUCY O'BRIEN

PART FOUR: SAFE EUROPEAN HOME: FROM THE PROVINCIAL TO THE INTERNATIONAL

16. "I Don't Care about London": Punk in Britain's Provinces, circa 1976–1984 265
MATTHEW WORLEY

17. Punk in Russia: From the "Declassed Elements" to the Class Struggle 281
IVAN GOLOLOBOV

18. The "New Flowers" of Bulgarian Punk: Cultural Translation, Local
    Subcultural Scenes, and Heritage   295
    ASYA DRAGANOVA

19. Iberian Punk, Cultural Metamorphoses, and Artistic Differences in
    the Post-Salazar and Post-Franco Eras   314
    PAULA GUERRA

20. Punk in Belfast, Northern Ireland: Critical Perspectives on the
    Troubles and Post-conflict "Peace"   332
    JIM DONAGHEY

PART FIVE: NEAT NEAT NEAT? STYLE, SOUND, MEDIA

21. From Punk to Poser: T-Shirts, Authenticity, Postmodernism, and the
    Fashion Cycle   359
    MONICA SKLAR AND MARY KATE DONAHUE

22. Kicks in Style: A Punk Design Aesthetic   379
    RUSS BESTLEY

23. The Art of Slouching: Posture in Punk   397
    MARY FOGARTY

24. World's End: Punk Films from London and New York, 1977–1984   418
    BENJAMIN HALLIGAN

25. Sound Recordists, Workplaces, Technologies, and
    the Aesthetics of Punk   438
    SAMANTHA BENNETT

26. Fanzine Scenes   452
    KEVIN C. DUNN

PART SIX: NEVERMIND: THE SHIFTING POLITICS OF PUNK

27. "Caught in a Culture Crossover!" Rock Against Racism and
    Alien Kulture   465
    JOE O'CONNELL

28. Rethinking the Cultural Politics of Punk: Antinuclear and Antiwar (Post-)Punk Popular Music in 1980s Britain — 481
GEORGE McKAY

29. Pussy Riot: Punk on Trial — 502
JUDITH A. PERAINO

30. You Ain't No Punk, You Punk: On Semiotic Doxa, Postmodern Authenticity, Ontological Agency, and the Goddamn Alt-Right — 521
DANIEL S. TRABER

31. Touch Me I'm Rich: From Grunge to *Alternative Nation* — 538
RYAN MOORE

32. Death in Vegas — 553
GINA ARNOLD

Index — 567

Foreword

GEORGE McKAY AND GINA ARNOLD

Steve Severin, bassist with Siouxsie and the Banshees, observed in 1994 that "the farther [punk] recedes into the distance, the more important in seems" (quoted in Lydon 1994, 188). Now approaching fifty years after punk rock, rather than the twenty of Severin's observation, it still demands critical attention. From "White Riot" to Riot Grrrl to Pussy Riot, *Never Mind the Bollocks* to *Nevermind*, DIY to never gonna die(t), the Slits to *We Are Lady Parts*, punk rock to punk studies, it has marked or stained—it marks or stains—our musical and cultural history and practice. So should that then be not "fifty years *after*" but "fifty years *of* punk rock"? It seems that, in spite of the Sex Pistols' bold declaration, "No future" (which also kind of meant "No past"), the musics and scenes of punk have had a future after all. In aspic throb punk confounds, even if its constancy may be its primary enduring gift of surprise. Like other incendiary and innovative rock and roll moments, punk had no pretensions to longevity, yet it (has) endured. Unlike other rock and roll bursts, punk wrapped itself in an attitude of rejection of the past and future alike, the former gestural and ahistorical, the latter gestural and potentially self-defeating. The gesture is the link, not empty but resonant and energizing, even if one might think it incorrect twice over. While for aging fans and subcultural adherents across many genres and scenes "music is about not only where they have been but also where they are going" (Bennett 2013, 32), it is a result of the culture of early punk's eschatological halo that such questions of futurity and longevity as are being discussed here are especially pertinent.

Since it now has its own past—a lengthy (for popular music) history—and a future—evidenced by its ongoing capacity to attract new adherents—punk needs and warrants its studies more than ever. This should not, though, be a hauntology: if punk had an originary impulse of rejection, whether generational or musical, what has become abundantly clear is that that impulse was not a one-off moment. It has spoken and appealed to subsequent generations as well (so: not one-off) and seemed somehow to keep speaking to early elements (not simply a moment). Intriguingly, as it accrued a past, this has not seemed to weigh it down. Its reflexivity and humor might have contributed here: If you are in a punk club pogoing to a song like "I Am a Cliché," perhaps when you become a cliché it's not quite so bad? (Singer Poly Styrene's solo spoken intro to the 1 min. 54 sec. song seeks to confirm its observation: "I *am* a cliché"—even though, of course, we may know that she of all punks was not: X-Ray Spex 1978.)

Many people—or some (it may depend a little on your editor)—place punk's origins in the United States, locating them in Michigan and dating punk as early as 1967, with the formation of Iggy Pop's band the Stooges. After that (the story goes), the sound, the style, and even individual band members wafted east to New York City, where punk rooted itself in the Bowery at the club CBGB, with bands including but not limited to the New York Dolls, Television, Blondie, and the Ramones, and from there it jumped the Atlantic where it underwent a form of meiosis—with each cell division, or band, creating a new set of genetic material. We can probably think of punk's high period as circa 1976–1984, and then with developments and revivals, and the kinds of multiple musical and cultural spin-offs expected of a *bricolage* form and practice, that contribute to longer-term influence and legacy. Internationally, it has a longevity and visibility, which may be as much on account of its DIY (Do It Yourself) narrative, and its anti-authoritarian attitudinality, as on its actual music and sounds. Although many successful punk bands have signed to major labels and played the commercial live music venue circuits, DIY became and remains a central tenet of punk, and that requires unpacking. DIY is generally punk's "most prevalent core value" (Moran 2010, 62), while for Kevin Dunn the source of punk's "opportunity for personal empowerment" rests in its connection of "an anti-status quo disposition with a DIY ethos" (Dunn 2016, 58); its progenitors in 1950s skiffle and subsequent influence on 1980s rave culture are acknowledged (McKay 1998). But let us also note, potentially more critically, that, in the term's meanings, DIY can be individualistic or noncollective (Yourself), entrepreneurial (Do It), and either vaguer or wider than punk (It). And let us note altogether more critically that recent scholarship has begun "to challenge the standard critical narrative of punk as originary DIY culture," as well as to argue that DIY more broadly might benefit from a dose of "depunking" (McKay 2024).

As for its longevity, there is strength in the suggestion that "if punk can never quite give up the ghost, perhaps that's because we are still trawling through the political and economic wreckage that prompted its emergence in the first place" (Brown et al. 2013, 1). Also, punk was never simply a new rock and roll burst, could never be restricted to mere music: its broader cultural innovation, impact, and influence—from fashion to graphic design, enterprise to its (cloaked) entrepreneurship, its sometimes radical politics to its perhaps less tangible features such as ways of walking and talking, or attitudinality—contribute to and help explain its enduring significance. A few years ago, when one of the editors of this volume was working on the subject of disability and music, in an essay he set and answered a question to himself, for his readers: "Does punk matter (any more, decades later)? Curiously, I think, it has begun to speak more to me in my fifties than at any other time since my contumacious teens in the late 1970s." He thought about punk rock's "new meaningfulness" to him with surprise, but also with something like gratitude. "[A]s I aged," he wrote, "I looked for a culture that would help me understand, embrace, maybe even emblazon my own body thing, as my condition ... deteriorated, and I found one in, of all places, the memory of that mad music and mismovement of my own youth" (McKay 2016, 239–240). In a time of personal crisis, corporeality spinning out of control, he reached for something "in, of all places," punk rock. That "of all places" stands out: it is the signifier of surprise, yes, but also the acknowledgment of weight. It turns out that punk *did* still matter, as perhaps any other old punk who still carried the flame could have told him all along.

Both editors were there, in fact: as teenage punks in the crowd, one saw the Pistols on their penultimate UK gig on December 24, 1977, the other three weeks later on the US tour, January 14, 1978, the very final band gig (until reunion tours decades later; that particular editor made it her business to see their first gig back, in Finland, as well). So what? Does *that* matter, or signify? Of course, it speaks to as well as confirms a continuing sense within punk of authenticity, which may be both critically useful and restricting: useful as it can offer a way in to the minutiae, or the grand energy, of a distant scene or moment; restricting as it might overframe punk within subjective experience and the unreliable fractures of memory. In either instance, as a sort of opening statement, it begins by situating punk understanding historically, and, while some of what can be called punk studies has aimed to uncover its lost or forgotten scenes, bands, or events from "back in the day," we have sought out careful, reflexive, or revisionist histories, and also, equally importantly, explorations of the trajectories, continuities, developments, and tensions in the decades of punk that followed.

But those memories and emotions of teenage gigs, which were sonic and performative twists of feelings of alienation and belonging, should not be discarded upon articulation: it may well be those that have made a book like this happen, for better or worse, enabled or forced us in our editorial labor. Thus, while our small statement of "autoethnographic insider status" coupled with "firsthand knowledge of events" is a kind of "membership badge," in Alistair Gordon's terms (2014, 192–194)—with the exclusory potential that entails—it is also an explanation of motivation and a fragment of material history. Here (Figure 1) is another (re/membership) badge, or button, which is a very, very minor part of punk's materiality. It was made around 1979 or 1980, by an editor's younger sister for her late-teenaged older brother. Although apparently lacking conscious design consideration, it is in fact a pure punk product: DIY, handwritten in best caps., off-center, amateur, ephemeral, faded Day-Glo green background. It says punk, and it is. Its observational statement is really a private sibling communication, not intended for public gaze—after all, anyone outside would know his subcultural identity from his clothing or walking or hair, and why would anyone want or expect to read his name? Yet the sister looked at her brother, the girl looked at George, and found somehow that he was not just *a* punk but *was punk*. The full stop may infer the unarguable nature of the statement, but also or instead speak to its finality. But that present tense, unchangeable *and* encompassing, is mesmerizing. Of course, as Andy Medhurst observed twenty or so years (like Severin) after punk, "'I was there' is . . . a difficult badge to dislodge" (1999, 219). Yet Medhurst kind of wore it himself, proudly and reflexively, in his still resonant chapter about punk and "punctum"—intense memory and autobiography as critical positionality—if you *were* there, and it is now nearly half a century later, that is worth a pause, a reflexive comment, an essay, a memoir, an *Oxford Handbook* even. The farther it recedes, the more important it is. Also, though, if you *are* there—because you never really went away, possibly, or because you are in or of one of punk's more recent or current manifestations—some of the essays here show how those positions matter too.

FIGURE 1. DIY punk badge/pin/button, c. 1979, UK. George McKay personal archive (ephemera).

"Boredom," the song by Buzzcocks recorded (so the single picture sleeve tells us) as played "live" in the studio in Manchester in 1976, and released on one of the very first independent punk labels, New Hormones, is generally widely lauded for its cultural significance and witty innovation. For instance, as Robin Murray nicely captures it in a 2016 *Clash* magazine interview with Buzzcocks' Steve Diggle, "its two-note guitar solo [was] a two-fingered salute" to the inflated, indulgent rock scene of the time (Murray 2016). Diggle himself remembers the impact "Boredom" had: "Just that one word summed up the music thing, and society at the time. Within three minutes it changed people's lives—or minds. . . . It brought them to life. It changed everything" (quoted in Murray 2016). Of course, the sleeve also tells us that the solo is an overdub—so, not quite a "live" studio recording. The repeated E-B solo ends on an A both times—so, not two notes, but three. The final A of the same solo played for the second time is the song's last note, and it is, surprisingly perhaps, sonically treated with a touch of echo. Boredom repeats: bah-dum, bah-dum. (Rhythmically, this famous punk guitar anti-solo is not really boring either: its three-beat pattern interrupts the straight four of the song, a cross-rhythmic motif that injects tension and then resolution.) It is an interesting performance of boredom that also begins to constitute the punk discourse of boredom.

Of course, boredom may beget creativity, may be one of its essential preconditions, or at least "a motivating force/catalyst for action" (Mann and Cadman 2014, 166). But there is more to punk boredom, for it is also a social critique ("that one word summed up . . . society at the time"), as much as a group marker (the repeated "boring boredom" in "I Am a Cliché": X-Ray Spex 1978; see also Worley 2017, 111–114). And perhaps, if we think we need awkwardly to acknowledge that, sometimes, well, punk itself might be boring, the response is not to adapt (Theodore) Sturgeon's Law about science fiction, that it "is indeed ninety-percent crud, but . . . *ninety-per cent of* everything *is crud* . . . —cars, books, cheeses, hairstyles, people and pins" (Sturgeon 1957, 49; emphasis in original). Intriguingly, writing in a 1950s science fiction zine, Sturgeon is rather punkily tilting at the "smarmy" disdain toward science fiction in the establishment literary circles of the *Saturday Review* and the *New Yorker*. We would not say 90 percent of punk is boring, but we would seek to align with the critical positionality Sturgeon adopts against the cultural mainstream, especially when found in the smaller publication of a zine. We would use Sturgeon to suggest that, as all those "flowers in the dustbin" (Sex Pistols 1977) suggest, *punk may even be a 100 percent crud product*, in moments of its self-articulation and its loud questioning of cultural value alike. If punk is boring, it is because, as "Boredom" (Buzzcocks 1977) taught us early on, it is *about* boredom. Being about boredom is one of the things that makes punk interesting. We think this book is full of other interesting things, too—indeed, we confidently state that the chapters to follow are *not boring*, for their concern is with how a culture made half-a-century-plus (perhaps quite a lot plus) of flawed material, experience, and politics out of boredom.

In terms of the intellectual organization of the book, punk has been a movement that rewires artistic, aesthetic, ideological, and political boundaries, influencing its practitioners and its critics alike. This book thematically structures punk's strands of influence not primarily along geographical or chronological lines but by interrogating its significance in music, style, performance, identity formation, cultural impact, politics, and theory, as well as arguing for its lasting influence, its creative and innovative possibilities, and its currency. It charts and assesses the significance of punk rock across its musical, cultural, and political spheres, and offers a timely re-evaluation of its significance. We can think of a *long punk rock*, which includes looking at the "high" punk years, of course, but also at some key pre-punk sounds and activities, and with a focus on what *Social Text* has called punk's "afterlives" or even "afterburns" (Brown et al. 2013, 1, 7). Thus, we admit we are only slightly surprised to be thinking about punk's proto-presence and enduring legacy being staged across at least four but quite feasibly as many as six or seven decades. That's quite a career, in either or both nounal and verbal terms. The approach is interdisciplinary, drawing on the now quite extensive scholarship about punk and related scenes and movements from media and cultural studies, music, history, sociology, and art. Music and sounds, attitudinality and identity, culture and media/film, fashion and design, DIY and "indie" modes of (self-)organization, protest, youth and aging, documentary and memoir, cultural theory—these are fields in which punk's enduring impact can be traced. For punk has been enormously generative. (Today there are punk festivals and punk museums, meaning that it may be a living and heritage culture at the same time.)

Our essays seek to capture and interrogate the burst of energy and ideas from long-standing and early career punk researchers alike. The essays herein speak to a range of positions in a range of voices; there is not a house style to the critical textuality of this collection, but there is an insistence from all on its sharpness. Punk in academia has, it seems to us, sometimes permitted, maybe even encouraged, a kind of overwriting: punk scholarship is one of those pop fields replete with enthusiasts and celebrants, and—can we say this?—this has been sometimes to the detriment of its critical gaze. This may be partly because writers drawn to it are often highly sympathetic to it, themselves once or now punks. It may partly be a reflection of its cultural terrain and gesturality: art-theory- and fashion-informed, stylistically avant-garde, eschatological and scatological, juvenile and wise. It may, if we are being kinder, partly be in response to punk's knowing performativity. Thus, punk and its studies have *sometimes* been surprisingly orthodox as a cultural and critical field. Above all else, we and our contributors have tried not to follow or uncritically repeat that orthodoxy. It is vital to note that contributors identify and explore core punk contradictions. These include, for example, its antiwar messages alongside not only its aggressive sounds but also its (often gendered) violence, its claimed antiracism alongside its dominant whiteness, its energy and attitudinality as a youth culture for an aging demographic, or its intermittent but persistent flirtations with populism and nationalism. We do claim a semantic and social richness for the culture, which may be celebrated but must be relentlessly critiqued. Lest we be thought of as trying to diminish the energy and attitudinality that might set not only punk but also, at its best, punk scholarship apart, let us be clear that we view these as among its most remarkable characteristics, and possibly its most valuable ones. Within them we can locate its praxis, its politics, its generosity even, all of which may be encapsulated in—well, here's a letter, here's a second, here's a third, now form a band, daub a slogan, change the world—after all, what's the point in being here, on this page, otherwise?—DIY.

Following an introductory chapter that offers a critical review of the development of punk scholarship over the decades, the book is structured in six sections that loosely group together sets of essays thematically. We do not want to overstress the structural integrity of these sections here, for it is in the spirit of interdisciplinary dialogue—punk's untidy seams and productive bricolage—to expect chapters to speak or leak across, or even demolish, any borders we might set. The sections are most useful primarily as a way of handling our wealth of material. Part One contains chapters that invite readers to reconsider punk rock, both in terms of alternative critical and theoretical approaches, and in thinking about some of its significant pre-lives. (So: a *hint* of chronological rationale here.) Parts Two and Three look at the importance of punk in constructing versions of identity, including how those negotiate aging, as well as its liberatory *and oppressive* practices. With a set of geographical case studies, Part Four critically charts ways in which punk spaces have spread, provincially *and* internationally, the case studies being culturally and historically situated. Part Five looks at questions of punk's wider cultural and media resonance. Finally, the chapters that form Part Six offer critical explorations of the sometimes uncomfortable shifting politics of punk across the decades, and how the music has played these out.

We will not overstate it, but we will state it: there has been some pushback against a project like this. There is a view, from some in punk studies and others in the wider punk scene itself, that the academic press–branded product of an elite university will always seek to recuperate something like punk and drain its irruptive energy or potential. For them, the very notion of an *Oxford Handbook of Punk Rock* sticks and stalls in the first two words: Oxford—home of scions and prime ministers, fast-tracked from private schools; Handbook—authoritative guide and manual on how-to-do punk and DIY. A less DIY production process would be difficult to envisage (except for academic publishing's standard lack of professional remuneration for the labor of *all* its authors): to take one instance, copyediting outsourced by transatlantic organization to agency workers in India seems to speak more of hegemonic globalization than DIY. But such tracing of *complicity* is not at all new in punk, and was indeed part of its founding discourse and its founding drama. We can think of it as a rich culture of multiple complicities: a complex folding together of accomplices intent on doing something objectionable. If there is a charge against the book, we accept and refuse it: if we are to be among punk's late-to-the-party enthusiastic undertakers, we bring with us what we consider to be a prickly set of sharp writing and thinking that seeks always to do the culture's richness, ideas, contradictions, and problems justice. (Nor is complicity distant from academia, for there is a critical complicity familiar to all who work in the neoliberal university.) Like Burns's nursèd wrath, perhaps, our attitude and purpose as editors has been *kept warm* by the residual heat of those teenage Pistols gigs, and, even—pushing it—*that's why we were at them*.

Viv Albertine of the Slits has explained that in her groundbreaking 2014 memoir *Clothes, Clothes, Clothes. Music, Music, Music. Boys, Boys, Boys*, she carefully put the word "punk" in quotation marks whenever she used it, because she always felt that the term was one that had not been adopted by herself or anyone in her scene. This makes sense. The earliest US practitioners of what would later be labeled punk—the MC5, the Ramones, the New York Dolls, Iggy Pop, and others—would not have recognized themselves as being part of a cohesive, singular, descriptive label; nor, in truth, did the British incarnation. The Clash, the Sex Pistols, the Damned, Buzzcocks, Siouxsie and the Banshees, the Raincoats all sound wildly different from one another, and arguably even unlike what many people today consider "punk." (Here we can glimpse its mutability over decades, as well as both its inventiveness and lack thereof.) From this perspective, then, rather than being a sound, punk was (is) an attitude or perspective; perhaps more accurately one can observe that it developed into a worldview. It has international recognition and impact, after all, across a range of cultural fields. As Pussy Riot's Masha Alyokhina said in 2016, in response to a question about whether the word *punk* described her art: "You are talking about genres. Like Human Rights or Music or Theater is genres, but punk is a way of life for me" (quoted in Peraino, this volume).

Punk as a way of life. We hope that this volume is able to capture and critically interrogate aspects of that. But, in the relentless spirit of inquiry that punk warrants, is such a claim, and especially its inference that this is why punk matters, an adequate argument? It explains why punk matters to the person for whom it is a way of life (it matters because it matters to me), and there is evidence of that position in our collection—which can extend to offering an academic rationale for the research: punk studies matters because punk matters to me. But punk is also a cultural method; a repertoire of sounds, gestures, styles; a problematic of discourse; passing juvenilia; a prop or compensation; a (re)fillable adjective (punk golf, punk management, punk archaeology, etc.); a limited palette; a surprise even in its predictability; a plurality of contradictions; troubling and violent; a yes-slash-no-slash-fuck-you to life and art; both music and anti-music—any of these may be less than (the claim of) a way of life, but no less vital or energizing for that. Hey ho, let's go.

REFERENCES

Albertine, Viv. 2014. *Clothes, Clothes, Clothes. Music, Music, Music. Boys, Boys, Boys: A Memoir.* London: Faber and Faber.

Bennett, Andy. 2013. *Music, Style, and Aging: Growing Old Disgracefully?* Philadelphia: Temple University Press.

Brown, Jayna, Patrick Deer, and Tavia Nyong'o. 2013. "Punk and Its Afterlives: Introduction." *Social Text* 31, no. 3: 1–11.

Buzzcocks. 1977. "Boredom." *On Spiral Scratch EP.* New Hormone Records.

Dunn, Kevin. 2016. *Global Punk: Resistance and Rebellion in Everyday Life.* New York: Bloomsbury.

Gordon, Alastair. 2014. "Distinctions of Authenticity and the Everyday Punk Self." *Punk and Post-Punk* 3, no. 3: 183–202.

Lydon, John. 1994. *Rotten: No Irish, No Blacks, No Dogs.* With Keith and Kent Zimmerman. London: Hodder and Stoughton.

McKay, George, ed. 1998. *DiY Culture: Party and Protest in Nineties Britain.* London: Verso.

McKay, George. 2016. "Punk Rock and Disability: Cripping Subculture." In *The Oxford Handbook of Music and Disability Studies*, edited by Blake Howe, Stephanie Jensen-Moulton, Neil Lerner, and Joseph Straus, 226–245. New York: Oxford University Press.

McKay, George. 2024. "Was Punk DIY? Is DIY Punk? Interrogating the DIY/Punk Nexus, with Particular Reference to the Early UK Punk Scene, c. 1976–1984." *DIY, Alternative Cultures and Society* 2, no. 1: 94–109. https://journals.sagepub.com/doi/full/10.1177/27538702231216190.

Medhurst, Andy. 1999. "What Did I Get? Punk, Memory and Autobiography." In *Punk Rock: So What? The Cultural Legacy of Punk*, edited by Roger Sabin, 219–231. London: Routledge.

Moran, Ian P. 2010. "Punk: The Do-It-Yourself Subculture." *Social Sciences Journal* 10, no. 1: 58–65.

Murray, Robin. 2016. "You Know the Scene: Buzzcocks: Steve Diggle on Punk, *Spiral Scratch*, and the DIY Revolution." *Clash* magazine (August 2), https://www.clashmusic.com/features/you-know-the-scene-buzzcocks.

Sex Pistols. 1977. "God Save the Queen." In *Never Mind the Bollocks Here's the Sex Pistols.* Virgin Records.

Sturgeon, Theodore. 1957. "On Hand: A Book." *Venture Science Fiction* 1, no. 5 (September): 49–51. https://archive.org/details/Venture_v01n05_1957-09_Gorgon776/mode/1up.

Worley, Matthew. 2017. *No Future: Punk, Politics and British Youth Culture, 1976–1984.* Cambridge: Cambridge University Press.

X-Ray Spex. 1978. "I Am a Cliché." In *Germfree Adolescents.* EMI Records.

Contributors

Gina Arnold is a US-based scholar and professor and the author of four books on popular music and society. Her first, *Route 666: On the Road to Nirvana* (St. Martin's/Picador, 1993), chronicled the rise of the band Nirvana through the punk-derived independent underground scene of the 1980s; her latest, *Half a Million Strong: Crowds and Power from Woodstock to Coachella* (University of Iowa Press, 2018), is a study of the historical underpinnings of large rock festivals, their problems with race and gender, and their use-value as non-utopian spaces where ideological changes can be viewed in the making. A former rock writer for *Rolling Stone*, *Spin*, and many other newspaper and magazine outlets, her interest in punk stems from having attended the last Sex Pistols concert at Winterland in 1978. She holds a PhD from Stanford University in Modern Thought & Literature and teaches rhetoric and writing, media theory, and critical race studies at various universities in the San Francisco Bay Area.

Andy Bennett is a professor of cultural sociology in the School of Humanities, Languages and Social Science at Griffith University, Australia. He has written and edited numerous books, including *Music, Style and Aging: Growing Old Disgracefully?* (Temple UP, 2013), *Music Scenes: Local, Translocal and Virtual* (co-edited with Richard A. Peterson; Vanderbilt UP, 2004), and *Popular Music and Youth Culture: Music, Identity and Place* (Palgrave, 2000). He is a faculty fellow of the Yale Center for Cultural Sociology, an international research fellow of the Finnish Youth Research Network, a founding member of the Consortium for Youth, Generations and Culture, and a founding member of the Regional Music Research Group. Bennett is also founding co-editor-in-chief (with Paula Guerra) of the Sage journal *DIY, Alternative Cultures and Society* (2023–).

Samantha Bennett is professor of music and Associate Dean Higher Degree Research at the Australian National University, and Chair of the International Association for the Study of Popular Music. Her co-authored book with Eliot Bates, *Gear: Cultures of Audio and Music Technologies*, is forthcoming from the MIT Press. She is the author of two further monographs, *Modern Records, Maverick Methods: Technology and Process in Popular Music Record Production 1978–2000* (Bloomsbury, 2018) and *Peepshow*, a 33 1/3 series edition on the album by Siouxsie and the Banshees (Bloomsbury, 2018). She is also a co-editor of *Critical Approaches to the Production of Music and Sound* (Bloomsbury, 2018) and *Popular Music, Stars and Stardom* (ANU Press, 2018). Samantha has published numerous book chapters on the technological, sound recording, and production aesthetics of recorded popular music, and her journal articles are published in *Popular*

Music, *Popular Music and Society*, the *Journal of Popular Music Studies*, and *IASPM@ journal*, and her technical papers are published in the *Journal of the Audio Engineering Society*.

Russ Bestley is a reader in graphic design and subcultures at London College of Communication. His areas of interest include graphic design, popular culture, alternative music scenes and subcultures, comedy and humour. His books *Visual Research* (2004, 2011, 2015, 2022) and *The Art of Punk* (2012) have been published internationally in several languages. His book, *Turning Revolt Into Style: Punk Graphic Design in the UK*, is forthcoming from Manchester University Press. He recently designed a critically acclaimed autobiography by Pauline Murray, *Life's A Gamble*, for Omnibus Press. Russ is lead editor of the academic journal *Punk & Post-Punk*, series editor and art director for the Global Punk book series published by Intellect Books, and a founding member of the Punk Scholars Network. In 2013, he established the Graphic Subcultures research hub at the LCC, before going on to form the University of the Arts London-wide Subcultures Interest Group in 2022. hitsvilleuk.com.

Marcus Clayton is a writer who grew up in South Gate, California, and who holds a masters of fine arts from California State University at Long Beach. He is currently pursuing a PhD in literature and creative writing at the University of Southern California, focusing his studies on the intersections between Latinx literature, Black literature, and punk rock. He is an executive editor for *Indicia Literary Journal* and has previously taught English composition at several Southern California colleges. Published work can be seen in the *Los Angeles Review of Books*, *The Adroit Journal*, *Apogee Journal*, and *DUM DUM Zine*, among many others. In his free time, he can also be found screaming and playing loud guitar in a local LA punk band, *tudors*.

Nick Crossley is a professor of sociology and cofounder/codirector of the Mitchell Centre for Social Network Analysis at the University of Manchester, UK. He has published on a range of topics in sociology, including social theory, embodiment, social movements, and social networks. In his recent work he has been pioneering a relational approach to sociology. This was originally a matter of pure theory, culminating in the book *Towards Relational Sociology* (Routledge, 2011). More recently, however, he has been developing these ideas in the context of music sociology, with a particular focus on his first musical love: punk. He has a number of publications focusing on UK punk, including *Networks of Sound, Style and Subversion: The Punk and Post-Punk Worlds of Manchester, London, Liverpool and Sheffield, 1975–1980* (Manchester UP, 2015). This book focused in particular upon the social networks of the early UK punks and post-punks, and the network focus was also developed in the co-edited collection, with Siobhan McAndrew and Paul Widdop, *Social Networks and Music Worlds* (Routledge, 2015). His latest book, *Connecting Sounds: The Social Life of Music* (Manchester UP, 2020), seeks to extend these ideas, looking at a variety of relational dynamics in music, including but not restricted to social networks. In his spare time Nick is teaching himself saxophone, and in his imagination he has played in X-Ray Spex, as well as the classic lineups of both Theatre of Hate and Spear of Destiny.

Pete Dale studied at Sunderland Polytechnic, UK, 1989–1992. On graduating, he played in several indie/punk underground bands (Pussycat Trash, Red Monkey, Milky Wimpshake) and set up the cult DIY label/distributor Slampt, which ran very successfully between 1992 and 2000. Taking up school teaching in 2001, Pete completed an MA in music (2005) and then a PhD at Newcastle (2010) while simultaneously working as a teacher. He took an early career fellowship at Oxford Brookes in 2012, subsequently becoming Senior Lecturer in Music at Manchester Metropolitan University from 2013 to 2021. At present, Pete is lecturer in music education at the University of York. His monographs include *Anyone Can Do It: Tradition, Empowerment and the Punk Underground* (Ashgate, 2012), *Popular Music and the Politics of Novelty* (Bloomsbury, 2016), and *Engaging Students with Music Education: DJ Decks, Urban Music and Child-Centred Learning* (Routledge, 2017). Pete was associate editor of the journal *Punk & Post-Punk* until 2022 and is a founding member of the Punk Scholars Network.

Mike Dines is a British musician, writer, scholar, publisher, and avid supporter of Portsmouth Football Club. He founded Itchy Monkey Press with the publication of the anarcho-punk novella *The Darkening Light* (2014), followed by *Tales from the Punkside* (2014), *Some of Us Scream, Some of Us Shout* (2016), and *And All Around Was Darkness* (2017) with Greg Bull. As a scholar he has written widely on subcultures and popular music, most recently co-editing *The Aesthetics of Our Anger: Anarcho-Punk, Politics, Music* (Autonomedia/Minor Compositions, 2016), *Punk Pedagogies: Music, Culture and Learning* (Routledge, 2017), and *The Punk Reader: Research Transmissions from the Local and the Global* (Intellect, 2019). His current writing takes him in the direction of punk and spirituality with the co-edited collection, *Beatified Beats: Exploring the Spiritual in Popular Music* (Bloomsbury, 2020), as well as several new volumes on the contemporary global punk scene. He is currently a lecturer in music at Middlesex University.

Jim Donaghey has been a punk for most of his life by now. He has been researching punk scenes, culture, and politics in various global contexts for over a decade, with a particular focus on Indonesia, France, Kosovo, and Ireland. He currently works as a research fellow at Ulster University, UK, leading an Arts & Humanities Research Council-funded research project titled 'Failed States and Creative Resistances: The Everyday Life of Punks in Belfast, Banda Aceh and Kosovo'. Jim is co-editor, with Will Boisseau and Caroline Kaltefleiter, of The Anarchism and Punk Book Project, which has published two volumes thus far: *Smash the System! Punk Anarchism as Culture of Resistance* (2022) and *DIY or Die! Do-it-Yourself, Do-it-Together and Punk Anarchism* (2024), both on Active Distribution. Jim continues to live the rural punk dream in a wee toon near the North Coast.

Mary Kate Donahue is from Bethesda, Maryland, USA, and is a recent graduate in fashion studies from the University of Georgia. She won a competitive college-wide undergraduate research award for her work on punk and merchandising with Monica Sklar. She is pursuing a career in fashion merchandising in New York City.

Asya Draganova is a popular music culture researcher and lecturer from Sofia, Bulgaria, based at Birmingham City University, UK. She is also a guitar player and singer and writes new music reviews for *The Arts Desk* website and *The I* newspaper. Asya is the author of *Popular Music in Contemporary Bulgaria: At the Crossroads* (Emerald, 2019). Her research and publication topics include subcultural scenes in postcommunist Europe, popular music heritage, heavy metal, and the Canterbury Sound. Asya is part of the editorial team of the journal for experimental writing on music *Riffs* and co-leads the popular music research cluster at the Birmingham Centre for Media and Cultural Research. She is also an avid fencer and enjoys writing poetry and abstract painting.

Kevin C. Dunn is a professor in the Department of Political Science at Hobart and William Smith Colleges in Geneva, New York, USA. He is author of several books, including *Global Punk: Resistance and Rebellion in Everyday Life* (Bloomsbury, 2016) and, with Pierre Englebert, *Inside African Politics* (2nd ed., Lynne Rienner, 2019). His nonacademic publications include regular contributions to the music zine *Razorcake*.

Mary Fogarty is an associate professor in the Department of Dance at York University (Toronto, Canada). She is currently editor of *IASPM Journal* and president of IASPM-Canada (International Association for the Study of Popular Music). She was in a punk band in high school in Thunder Bay and recorded on a compilation for Meathead Records. Subsequently, her passion became hip-hop culture, and most of her research and publications stem from her experiences as a b-girl (breaking practitioner). She is currently the Graduate Program Director in MA and PhD dance studies, where she supervises work on popular culture topics.

Michael Goddard is a reader in film, television, and moving image at Goldsmiths, University of London, UK. He has published widely on international cinema and audiovisual culture as well as cultural and media theory. In terms of the latter, his most significant contribution is the monograph *Guerrilla Networks: An Anarchaeology of 1970s Radical Media Ecologies* (Amsterdam University Press, 2018), the culmination of his media archaeological research to date. His previous book, *Impossible Cartographies* (Wallflower Press, 2013), was on the cinema of Raúl Ruiz. He has also been doing research on the fringes of popular music, focusing on groups such as The Fall, Throbbing Gristle, and Laibach, leading to the two co-edited collections on noise published by Bloomsbury: *Reverberations: The Philosophy, Aesthetics and Politics of Noise* (2012) and *Resonances: Noise and Contemporary Music* (2013). He is currently working on a book on the British postindustrial group Coil and a research project on emo music, mental health, and early social media.

Ivan Gololobov is a lecturer in politics and Russian studies at University of Bath, UK. He has authored and co-authored a number of publications on Soviet and Russian punk, music, and artistic underground in Russia and the Soviet Union, including *Punk in*

Russia: Cultural Mutation from the Useless to the Moronic (Routledge, 2014) and punk-oriented articles in *Sociological Research Online* and *Punk and Post-Punk*. He has organized series of events on Russian punk in Pushkin House (London). He regularly comments on politically committed and protest movements in Russia on BBC World Service, *New Statesman*, and other media outlets. He is also a founding member of a Russian avant-punk band The Zverstvo, and a member of Bristol-based sports and social club Easton Cowboys & Cowgirls.

Paula Guerra is a professor of sociology at the University of Porto, Portugal, and a researcher at the Institute of Sociology of the same university. Paula is an adjunct associate professor of the Griffith Centre for Social and Cultural Research in Australia. Her research is on the sociology of culture, of youth, and arts. She is the founder/coordinator of the Network All the Arts: Luso-Afro-Brazilian Network of the Sociology of Culture and the Arts. She is the founder/coordinator of KISMIF (kismifconference.com and kismifcommunity.com), member of the Board of the Research Network of Sociology of Art of ESA, and chair of IASPM Portugal. Paula has been a visiting professor at numerous international universities. She is a member of the editorial council of several national and international journals, as well as editor and reviewer of several articles and books on a national and international level. She is the founding co-editor-in-chief (with Andy Bennett) of the Sage journal DIY, *Alternative Cultures and Society* (2023–). paulaguerra.pt.

Benjamin Halligan is the director of the Doctoral College of the University of Wolverhampton, UK. His publications include *Michael Reeves* (Manchester UP, 2003), *Desires for Reality: Radicalism and Revolution in Western European Film* (Berghahn, 2016), and *Hotbeds of Licentiousness: The British Glamour Film and the Permissive Society* (Berghahn, 2022). Halligan has co-edited nine books: *The Fall: Art, Music and Politics* (Ashgate, 2010), *Reverberations: The Philosophy, Aesthetics and Politics of Noise* (Bloomsbury, 2012), *Resonances: Noise and Contemporary Music* (Bloomsbury, 2013), *The Music Documentary: From Acid Rock and Electro-Pop* (Routledge, 2013), *The Arena Concert: Music, Media and Mass Entertainment* (Bloomsbury, 2016), the late David Sanjek's *Stories We Could Tell: Putting Words to American Popular Music* (Routledge, 2018), *Politics of the Many: Contemporary Radical Thought and the Crisis of Agency* (Bloomsbury, 2021), *Diva: Feminism and Fierceness from Pop to Hip-Hop* (Bloomsbury, 2023), and *Adult Themes: British Cinema and the X-Rating in the Long 1960s* (Bloomsbury, 2023) benjaminhalligan.com.

Elizabeth K. Keenan completed her doctorate in ethnomusicology at Columbia University, USA. She has published on a variety of topics related to feminism and popular music in *Women and Music, Journal of Popular Music Studies, Oxford Handbooks Online, Archivaria*, and *Current Musicology*, as well as two chapters in Julia Downes's collection *Women Make Noise: Girl Bands from Motown to the Modern* (Supernova, 2012). Her first novel, *Rebel Girls*, was published by Inkyard Press in 2019.

Kirsty Lohman is an independent scholar now based in Glasgow, UK. She is editor of the Community Development Journal and a multidisciplinary DIY artist and crafter. Her academic work focuses on queer and trans community organizing, and tackles issues of place, space, and subculture. Her first book is *The Connected Lives of Dutch Punks: Contesting Subcultural Boundaries* (Palgrave Macmillan, 2017). She has played in feminist, anarcho, and queer punk bands Not Right, Die Wrecked, and Fear and Slothing; contributed to zines, including *Not Right* (issues 1–7), *Revolt* (issues 1–4), and *Riot Grrrl UK 2013*; and ran Coventry's feminist punk night Revolt and Leamington Spa's queer punk festival Femmington Spa Fest. kirstylohman.com.

Shayna Maskell is an assistant professor in the School of Integrative Studies at George Mason University, USA. She received her PhD from the American Studies Department at the University of Maryland. Her forthcoming book *Politics of Sound: Race, Class, and Gender in Washington DC Hardcore Punk 1978–1982* (University of Illinois Press) retheorizes how and why cultural forms, such as music, produce and resist politics and power. Her areas of research include popular and youth culture, music, social media, and social justice. She has published in the *Journal of Popular Music Studies* and has contributed a number of chapters in collections on music and sound. Shayna previously taught for over a decade at institutions such as the University of Southern California, California Institute of the Arts, University of Maryland, and Corcoran College of Art and Design. Her classes often focus on intersectionality and the ways in which concepts of self and society are constructed through a multitude of popular texts.

George McKay was a punk in the 1970s. He is a professor of media studies at the University of East Anglia, UK. His research interests are in popular music from jazz to punk to festivals, social movements and cultural politics, disability, and gardening. Among his books are *Senseless Acts of Beauty: Cultures of Resistance since the Sixties* (Verso, 1996), the edited volume *DIY Culture: Party and Protest in Nineties Britain* (Verso, 1998), *Glastonbury: A Very English Fair* (Gollancz, 2000), *Community Music: A Handbook* (co-edited with Pete Moser; Russell House, 2004), *Circular Breathing: The Cultural Politics of Jazz in Britain* (Duke UP, 2005), *Radical Gardening: Politics, Idealism and Rebellion in the Garden* (Frances Lincoln, 2011), *Shakin' All Over: Popular Music and Disability* (Michigan UP, 2013), the edited volume *The Pop Festival: History, Media, Music, Culture* (Bloomsbury, 2015), and, with Emma Webster, *Music from Out There, In Here: 25 Years of London Jazz Festival* (2017). He was a founding editor in 2002 of the Routledge journal *Social Movement Studies*. George has been a member of several EU-funded research projects on countercultures, music, and festivals, including Society & Lifestyles (2006–2008), Rhythm Changes (2010–2012), and CHIME (2015–2017). He was Arts and Humanities Research Council Leadership Fellow for its Connected Communities program (2012–2019). georgemckay.org.

Ryan Moore teaches sociology at San Francisco State University, USA, and is the author of *Sells Like Teen Spirit: Music, Youth Culture, and Social Crisis* (NYU Press, 2010). He has published widely on issues related to popular music, subcultures, youth, and social inequality.

Curran Nault is an assistant professor in radio-television-film at the University of Texas at Austin, USA, and is the author of *Queercore: Queer Punk Media Subculture* (Routledge, 2018). His scholarship on grassroots queer artivism has been published in *Jump Cut*, *Feminist Media Studies,* and the *Journal of Film and Video*, among others. Curran is also the founder and artistic director of the queer transmedia festival OUTsider, and is a producer on the documentaries *Before You Know It* (PJ Raval, 2013) and *Call Her Ganda* (PJ Raval, 2018).

Lucy O'Brien is the author of *She Bop: The Definitive History of Women in Popular Music* (Jawbone, 2020), now in its fourth edition; *Lead Sister: The Story of Karen Carpenter* (Nine Eight, 2023), *It Takes Blood and Guts*, with Skin (Simon & Schuster, 2021), *Madonna: Like an Icon* (Pan, 2018), and in-depth biographies of Dusty Springfield (Michael O'Mara Books, rev. edn 2019) and Annie Lennox (Sidgwick and Jackson, 1991). She has been a music writer since the 1980s, contributing to *NME, Q, Mojo, The Sunday Times, The Guardian,* and *The Quietus*. She co-produced the BBC Radio 2 series She Bop (2002) and Righteous Babes (1998), a Channel 4 television film about rock and new feminism. Her PhD was on women's participation, agency, and power in popular music. And back in 1979–1980, she played in all-girl punk band The Catholic Girls. She teaches at London College of Music, University of West London. Her areas of research are subcultures, feminism, life-writing, and memoir. lucyobrien.co.uk

Joe O'Connell is a lecturer in music at Cardiff University, UK. His PhD research examined notions of authenticity in the presentation of politically engaged performers in Thatcherite Britain, taking in Rock Against Racism, Live Aid, and Red Wedge, alongside studies of Billy Bragg and Crass. He has also published ethnographic research on the UK math rock scene, with a specific focus on identity and scene formation through interrogation of performers' experiences of the ArcTanGent festival, an event that has played a key role in strengthening a nationwide math rock community. Joe also continues to cultivate designs upon rock stardom with his band Rough Music.

Judith A. Peraino is a professor of music at Cornell University, USA. Her publications include articles on medieval music, Blondie, David Bowie, PJ Harvey, Mick Jagger, and early synthpop. Her discovery of a tape of unknown songs created by Lou Reed for Andy Warhol was reported on by the *New York Times*, the *Washington Post*, and *Rolling Stone* among other news outlets, and is detailed in the article "I'll Be Your Mixtape: Lou Reed, Andy Warhol and the Queer Intimacies of Cassettes," published in the *Journal of Musicology*. She is the author of two books: *Listening to the Sirens: Musical Technologies of Queer Identity from Homer to Hedwig* (University of California Press, 2006) and *Giving Voice to Love: Song and Self-Expression from the Troubadours to Guillaume de Machaut* (Oxford UP, 2011), and the co-curator for the exhibition Anarchy in the Archives, featuring materials from Cornell's Punk Collection. Her gallery tours for this exhibit and on-stage interviews with Masha Alyokhina (Pussy Riot) and John Doe and Exene Cervenka (X) are available on YouTube.

Helen Reddington played bass in a punk band in Brighton, UK, in 1977. This led to a seven-year musical career under the moniker of Helen McCookerybook, with both The Chefs and Helen and the Horns recording sessions for John Peel's BBC Radio 1 show. Later she wrote film soundtracks and was a songwriting facilitator on housing estates in South London, before moving into academia; she now works as an independent researcher. Her 2007 book *The Lost Women of Rock Music: Female Musicians of the Punk Era* (Ashgate) was her response to the fact that there were no histories of *women* punk musicians in university libraries. In 2021, she published *She's at the Controls: Sound Engineering, Production And Gender Ventriloquism in the 21st Century* (Equinox), in a response to the frequently-asked question "Why are there so few female producers?" Her film *Stories from the She-Punks: Music with a Different Agenda* (co-directed by Gina Birch of The Raincoats) adds to the history of women's punk bands, and she toured the UK with Doc'n'Roll in 2019. Helen continues to play live and releases music now as a solo artist. She also works as a documentary illustrator. mccookerybook.com.

Marlén Ríos-Hernández is an assistant professor of Chicana and Chicano Studies at California State University, Fullerton. She was a UC President's Postdoctoral Fellow at the University of California, Los Angeles, USA, in the Department of Chicana and Chicano Studies, and is co-organizer of the University of California at Riverside Punk Conference—a biennial gathering of punks from all backgrounds at UCR. She is currently drafting her book manuscript and (re)committing to social justice organizing in the Los Angeles area.

Jessica A. Schwartz is an associate professor of musicology at the University of California, Los Angeles, USA. Jessica works on creative dissent, anti-imperialism, and non-oppositional musical resistances. Jessica's forthcoming book, *Radiation Sounds: Marshallese Music and Nuclear Silences* (Duke UP), explores the ways in which Indigenous musicians from the Marshall Islands use songs to remediate histories of and damages from US nuclear weapons testing. Jessica has published on music, gender, and militarism in journals such as *Women & Music*, *American Quarterly*, and *Music & Politics*, and is co-editing a collection of essays with Noriko Manabe, *Nuclear Music* (Oxford UP). Their current research explores the intersections of (invisible) disability, (nonbinary) gender, and (mixed) ethno-racial categorizations mediated through punk experimental practice. And Jessica plays noise-punk guitar.

Monica Sklar is a professor of fashion history and merchandising and museum curator at the University of Georgia, USA. She is the author of *Punk Style* (Bloomsbury, 2013), vice-president of technology of the Costume Society of America, and an active writer, presenter, and public speaker on subculture and design. She is also a longtime participant in underground scenes, including punk and hardcore, booking fests and shows, playing in bands, writing for zines, and collecting punk's style history.

Daniel S. Traber is a professor of English at Texas A&M University in Galveston, Texas, USA. He is the author of *Culturcide and Non-identity across American Culture* (Lexington, 2017) and *Whiteness, Otherness, and the Individualism Paradox from Huck to Punk* (Palgrave, 2007). His work has appeared in journals such as *Cultural Critique*, the *Journal of Popular Culture*, the *Hemingway Review*, *American Studies*, and *Popular Music and Society*.

Matthew Worley is a professor of modern history at the University of Reading, UK, and co-founder of the Subcultures Network, an interdisciplinary research group exploring youth culture, popular music, and social change. Articles on the politics and contextualization of punk have been published in journals such as *Britain and the World*, *Contemporary British History*, *History Workshop*, *Popular Music*, and *Twentieth Century British History*. He is the co-editor with Mike Dines of *The Aesthetic of Our Anger: Anarcho-Punk, Politics and Music* (Minor Compositions, 2016) and, with the Subcultures Network, *Fight Back: Punk, Politics and Resistance* (Manchester UP, 2015), *Ripped, Torn and Cut: Pop, Politics and Punk Fanzines from 1976* (Manchester UP, 2018), and *Let's Spend the Night Together: Sex, Pop Music and British Youth Culture, 1950s–80s* (Manchester UP, 2023). His monograph *No Future: Punk, Politics and British Youth Culture, 1976–84* was published by Cambridge UP in 2017. His latest book, *Zerox Machine: Punk, Post-Punk and Fanzines in Britain, 1976–1988*, was published by Reaktion Press and University of Chicago Press in 2024.

Lucy Wright is an artist based in Leeds, UK. Following a stint in academia, she shifted her practice to contemporary art spaces, working at the intersection of folklore and activism. Recent works include Ritual Bitchual, Oss Girls, Non-Fertility Rituals, and her newly invented tradition, Dusking. Lucy is a visiting fellow in Folklore at University of Hertfordshire, UK. She is the author of the *Folk is a Feminist Issue* manifesta. lucywright.art.

CHAPTER 1

"ENJOY IT, DESTROY IT?" 40 YEARS OF PUNK ROCK SCHOLARSHIP

LUCY WRIGHT

Introduction: Punk Beginnings

THE year 1976 was a defining one for punk rock. It saw the release of the first UK punk single (the Damned's "New Rose") and debut performances by the Clash and Buzzcocks. It was the year of the Ramones' "Blitzkrieg Bop," and the Sex Pistols' controversial appearance on Thames Television's *Today* program, now widely credited with lighting the touch paper for a generation of bored teenagers. Less than two years later, punk was pronounced dead, a short-lived youth subculture, at least in mainstream consciousness (see, for example, Savage 1992, 423). Commonly described as a "breach" (Marcus 1989, 3), a "rupture" (Hebdige 1979, 107), and even an "explosion" (Home 1995, 23) in everyday life and culture, the confrontational—and frequently transformational—phenomenon of punk rock has proved to be fertile soil for writers and scholars. Projects aimed at understanding and mapping the scene have taken place within academic tomes (from early work by Hebdige 1979 and Laing 1985 through to the dedicated academic journal *Punk and Post-Punk*), popular music papers (see Savage 1992; Arnold 1997), hastily photocopied (fan)zines and books created and disseminated by enthusiasts and participants (see O'Hara 1999; Perry 2009), as well as a slew of musicians' memoirs and autobiographies (e.g., Albertine 2014; Gordon 2015; Hynde 2016). In fact, forty years since the first outing of punk rock music, writers are turning to the subject in ever-growing numbers—the following were published in a *single* year: Czezowski and Carrington 2017; Doe and DeSavia 2017; Ingham 2017; Gimme Danger 2017; Lloyd 2017; Marcade 2017; Marr 2017; Nault 2017; Nilan 2017; Tyler 2017; Worley 2017; Zeisler 2017. This literature review provides an overview of some of these varied accounts, from 1976 on.

However, punk literature cannot be viewed as distinct from punk rock subculture (see Worley 2017, 36). Punk writers have not only documented punk subcultures, but influenced and shaped them, too.[1] Dick Hebdige famously cautioned that commentators (he cites "sociologists and interested straights") "threaten to kill with kindness the forms which we seek to elucidate" (1979, 140), or as the Slits might have put it, "enjoy it, destroy it" (1979). But whether or not punk literature can be added to the list of possible suspects in punk's purported demise (the continued interest in both punk music and punk writing, only heightened in its regular anniversary years, suggests otherwise), it is undeniable that any summary of punk rock literature also inevitably contributes to a process of circumscribing and delimiting punk activities. The corpus of writing on punk scenes is frequently criticized for placing too little emphasis on punk rock music (Medhurst 1999; Letts and Nobakht 2007, 13–14; Trainer 2016), while an emphasis on oral testimony and a historicized approach is felt by some to fail to capture the breadth and longevity of many punk scenes (e.g., Medhurst 1999; Turrini 2013; Worley 2017) as well as more recent ideas about the pluralities of subcultural experience (Hannerz 2015, 3). Others point to an irony inherent in seeking to assimilate the history of punk rock music "as 'works' into a canon" (Gelbart 2011, 271), not least in light of its high-profile "No future" or "No (more) heroes" axioms, while others argue for a greater diversity of authorial voices (see Reddington 2012, 16). In spite of this, or perhaps because of it, commentators generally agree that punk rock requires *more* exegesis, not less. As Matthew Worley suggests, punk may already have "catalogued and reported" aspects of its history and legacy, but "it rarely explained" them (2017, 19). The aim of this review, then, is to draw out some of the most pertinent themes from across the spectrum of punk scholarship, and to explore ways in which punk rock has—to date—been conceived and conceptualized.

Punk Politics

With ostentatious specificity and in provocative detail, Greil Marcus pins a hyperbolic point: "At a certain time, beginning in late 1975, in a certain place—London, then across the UK, then spots and towns all over the world—a negation of all social facts was made, which produced the affirmation that anything was possible" (1989, 7). That punk was felt to represent a distinctly new musical—and political—epoch is reflected in the subculture's much-vaunted "year-zero attitude to tradition and the past" (Medhurst 1999, 224), and a high value is placed on novelty and the disruption of mainstream norms by members of punk subcultures (Worley 2017, 7), not least in their active pursuit of alternative modes of music production and distribution (Frith 1981). However, many writers also highlight punk's referentialism to a range of older popular music forms, including folk (Dale 2012) and blues (Rapport 2014), as well as its parallels with other youth movements, including—perhaps counterintuitively—1960s hippies (Frith 1981, 51; McKay 1996) and 1950s Teds (Savage 1992, 11). Punk scholarship embodies these tensions, frequently torn between the desire to accentuate punk's distinctiveness

(Marcus 1989; Heylin 1993) and a drive to assert its position within a "'family' of rock music" (Laing 1985, 102) or tradition of avant-garde performance (Marcus 1989). Perhaps for this reason, the notion of year zero, though widely criticized, retains currency, if only as an indicator of the subculture's aspirational stance against straightforward canonization and normalization (Osgerby 1999; Dale 2012; Court 2015).[2]

For many, punk rock and politics are indivisible (see McKay 1999; Greene 2012). Punk subcultural practices are typically characterized not just by musical expression but by a spirit of rebellion, which combines "revolutionary rhetoric with pop culture" (Savage 1992, 5; see also Wilkinson et al. 2017, 397).[3] First-wave punk—in the UK at least—was said to be propelled by a politics of boredom (Frith 1981, 127; Worley 2017, 112), tapping into "a reservoir of social discontent" (Home 1995, 20), and achieving rapid popularity among perceivedly "disaffected" young people (Heylin 2008, 7). Roger Sabin suggests that punk was commonly understood as "a cultural and political 'movement'" with the potential to effect "a basic shift in the zeitgeist" (Sabin 1999b, 5).[4] Strongly identified with broadly anarchist ideals of Do It Yourself (DIY) and individual freedom—embodied most closely in the anarcho-punk movement of the late 1970s and 1980s—the global spread and enduring appeal of punk has promoted participants' continued involvement with myriad social causes, including those around class and gender equality, antiwar movements, and environmental consciousness. However, some writers have questioned the integrity of punk's political engagement (Osgerby 1998; Medhurst 1999; Cobley 1999), suggesting the genre's radical credentials have been overstated (Dale 2012, 30). At the same time, and in stark contrast to its generally leftist connotations, other scholars have explored links between punk and fascism (Sabin 1999a; Steinholt 2012; Worley 2017), arguing that the history of punk politics leaves room for significant—and problematic—ambiguity.

Most commentators agree that punk's primary political association is with anarchism (or some form of it). Indeed, the Sex Pistols' debut single, "Anarchy in the UK," was declared by manager Malcolm McLaren as "a statement of self-rule, of ultimate independence, of do-it-yourself" (quoted in Marcus 1989, 9), a sentiment perhaps given added credibility by McLaren's oft-quoted links to the Situationists (e.g., Marcus 1989; Savage 1992).[5] Despite this somewhat bombastic tone setting, many punk scenes continue to emphasize participation (the notion that "anyone can do it"; Dale 2012), accessibility ("no heroes"—see Idol 2015, 114) and "seizing the technical means of music production" (Frith 1981, 158),[6] although the extents to which these ideals have been met remains the subject of debate (see Bennett 2013, 170). For some scholars, the perceived superficiality of first-wave punk's anarchism provided a catalyst for the subsequent emergence of anarcho-punk, with bands such as Crass, Flux of Pink Indians, and the Subhumans in the UK, and Black Flag and the Dead Kennedys in the US (see Gosling 2004; Glasper 2014; Dines and Worley 2016). Anarcho-punk aimed to more fully realize anarchist thought and practice via self-organized, "underground" networks for the creation and distribution of music, and attempts to develop sustainable modes of living, distinct from the mainstream (see McKay 1996; Berger 2006). As Tim Gosling writes, "[w]hereas the Sex Pistols would proudly display bad manners and opportunism in their dealings with 'the establishment,' the anarcho-punks kept clear of 'the establishment' altogether, working in opposition to it instead" (2004, 170). For others, however, the appeal to anarchism of punk more broadly provides a conceptual backbone to the subculture's often disparate activities, helping to link the acts of the first wave to the many iterations of punk that were to follow it (Reddington 2012, 1).

Despite these generally anarchist associations, punk has also been critically linked to right-wing, even fascist, ideologies. In the UK, the controversial decision of some early punks (including famously, Siouxsie Sioux) to wear swastika-emblazoned clothing[7] was understood by some to have created a pervasive "miasma of fascism" around the genre (Savage 1992, 483), prompting important questions about the scene's attitudes to race. Roger Sabin argues that punk left "ample space for right-wing interpretation," which included "overtly racist aspects" (1999a, 199). In particular, he suggests that punk reveled in a sense of political ambiguity, attracting fans with far-right interests and creating "a legacy for the fascist music scene of the post-punk era" (199). Examples of such ambiguity contained within the punk subculture include the complex symbiotic relationship between punk and skinhead scenes (see O'Hara 1999, 47) and the working-class-inflected right-wing sympathies of Oi! (Worley, 2013), which would gain a national reputation for being "a music for racists, if not a music of racism" (Laing 1985, 112). Similarly, in Russia, the short-lived involvement of Grazhdanskaya Oborona frontman Yegor Letov with the National Bolshevik Party in the 1990s may have "ignored the Russian context," as Yngvar Steinholt suggests, while a negative—if not altogether justified—association with racism has "severely delayed research on punk rock in Russia" (2012, 402).

Other scholars argue that punk's political acuity—in any direction—has been overstated (see Worley 2017, 139). Simon Frith argued that first-wave "punk consciousness was just a new variation of an established gesture or teenage bravado" (1981, 158), debunking the romantic claim that the genre spoke for and of "working class" struggle, or what Savage calls punk's "cult of proletarianism" (1992, 54). At the same time, Dale comments that in addition to the demonstrably political acts, many punk bands demonstrated "little or no interest in politics" (2012, 23), while Worley notes the reticence of some punks to express straightforward political allegiances, commenting that "card-holding affiliations were rare" (2017, 144). Perhaps with this in mind, Dale goes on to ask if "punk's politics [is] part of its style or is there something politically substantial in punk?" (2012, 30). Indeed, the ready subsumation of (aspects of) punk into mainstream cultural frameworks is typically viewed as indicative of a loss of political integrity or effectiveness (see Home 1995, 17), though many scholars believe that punk retains its essential resistance to dominant hegemonies *despite* attempts to normalize it. O'Hara suggests that "[r]ebellion is one of the few undeniable characteristics of Punk" (1999, 38), highlighting some of the ways in which punk participants have championed a range of political and social causes (129). In a similar way, Dunn's view of punk as the embodiment of a "progressive cultural politics" (2012, 234) finds support in recent ethnographic studies by Erik Hannerz (2015) and Andy Bennett (2013), which found that punk participants continued to align themselves with activist practices, commonly listing squatting, hunt sabotage, and environmental protest among the activities in which they were, or had been, implicated (Bennett 2013, 175). Although some scholars suggest that punk's politics have become increasingly individualistic rather than socially motivated (e.g., straight edge punk and "positive" punk—see O'Hara 1999, 123; Dale 2012, 2), Paula Guerra argues that punk's continued oppositional stance remains effectual, being "based on shared individuality" (2014, 120). However, Dale suggests that while punk may have offered a platform for "the post-1968 politics of the Left; . . . it has not provided a vanguard for the militant empowerment of the subaltern class" (2012, 91).

Perhaps with this in mind, Wilkinson et al. call for a greater clarity on the impacts of punk politics, concluding that further research is required "to trace not only . . . [punk's] political associations and connotations, but to specify the particular cultural, social and political spheres in which their impact has had a greater or lesser effect" (2017, 410).

Punk Identities

With its notionally libertarian underpinning, punk rock places significant emphasis on individuality and the rights of the individual (e.g., Robb 2006, 411; Beer 2014, 28). Perhaps for this reason, issues of identity (e.g., Andes 1998; Davis 2006; Ambrosch 2016) and, to a lesser extent, the body (Bloustien 2003; Church 2013; McKay 2015) represent dominant themes in punk criticism. Typically portrayed as an egalitarian music scene that embraces a heterogeneity of identities and bodily practices (Frith 1981; Dale 2012), punk is often felt to actively challenge, subvert, and even "re-programme" mainstream identity norms (Ambrosch 2016, 258), including and in particular those around gender (e.g., O'Brien 1999, 2002; Reddington 2012; Albertine 2014), sexuality (Ambrosch 2016; Nault 2017), race (Sabin 1999a; Traber 2001; Gilroy 2002; Malott and Peña 2004; Traber 2007; Ramírez-Sánchez 2008; Duncombe and Tremblay 2011), and disability (Waltz and James 2009; Church 2013; McKay 2009, 2015). Sometimes collectively described as a "community of misfits" (O'Hara 1999, 165), punk is also understood as a distinct subcultural identity (Rivett 1999; Cobley 1999; Bennett 2013; Hannerz 2015), the appeal and influence of which extends beyond the punk rock movement into, for example, parts of academia (Dunn 2008; Beer 2014; Parkinson 2017). Other writers, however, suggest that punk's apparently progressive identity politics are often more aspirational than effective (O'Brien 2002, 136, 160; Hannerz 2015, 198), noting that positive developments are frequently less well manifested in scholarship, where there remains a conspicuous paucity of female, homosexual, disabled, and nonwhite punk writers (see Bennett 2013; Ambrosch 2016). At the same time, the scene's own problematic violent undercurrents are highlighted by Reddington (2012, 112), Bennett (2013, 127), and more broadly by Ogg (2013).

Recent years have witnessed a long overdue assessment of the role of women in punk rock, both as constituent members of the first waves of the 1970s and 1980s (O'Brien 1999, 2002; Reddington 2012) and later as instigators of the feminist-inflected[8] Riot Grrrl movement of the 1990s and early 2000s (particularly in the US: see Downes

2007, 2012; Marcus 2010; Huber 2010; Kaltefleiter, 2016).[9] More frequently associated with "the 'healthy' masculinity of 'white working class youth'" (Home 1995, 117), Lucy O'Brien has argued that the early British punk scene "was not an easy place to be if you were a woman" (2002, 136). Indeed, early journalism—including Mark Perry's unequivocal statement that "punks are not girls"—demonstrates that female participation could be actively contested (Perry 2009). Despite this, Helen Reddington suggests that punk has represented a unique space for many women, providing "unprecedented access to a voice and platform" (2012, 118; see also O'Brien 2002; Albertine 2014). Others comment that punk fashions offered a radical alternative to mainstream norms of femininity (Marcus 2010), permitting women to experiment with "power, anger, aggression—even nastiness" (O'Brien 2002, 133). However, writers such as Frith (1981, 242) and O'Brien (2002, 160) have questioned any lasting influence of punk on gender equity in music, suggesting that its impacts were short-lived and limited in scope. Nevertheless, O'Brien suggests that punk helped redefine 1960s feminism and "still has an impact on the way women operate, not just in music, but culture generally" (1999, 198).

Issues around punk and race have also received increased attention in the decades since Dick Hebdige's suggestion that punk be understood as "a white 'translation' of black 'ethnicity'" (1979, 64). Earlier accounts focused primarily on relationships between punk and reggae (e.g., Hebdige 1979; Frith 1981; Laing 1985; Savage 1992; see also Cogan, 2012), emphasizing the significant crossover between the two musics in the UK first wave (Frith 1981, 163). Although sonic disparities between the two musical forms were readily acknowledged (Hebdige 1979, 68), the widely perceived affinity of punk and reggae participants could be attributed to the two musics' oppositionality and Otherness in the context of mainstream British society (see Laing 1985, 40). Much has been made of this alliance—not least at the high-profile Rock Against Racism movement, tours, and carnivals (Gilroy 2002; Dawson 2005; Goodyer 2009; Rachel 2016; Renton 2019), though Sabin's relatively early contribution argued punk's majority-white subculture toed an uneasy line in regard to racism (1999a, 205).[10] Later commentators have sought to address the "co-cultural" experiences of Muslim punks (e.g., Murthy 2010, 2013; Fiscella 2012; Nilan 2017) and black punk participants (Ramírez-Sánchez 2008; see also Duncombe and Tremblay 2011; Malott and Peña 2004), perhaps most succinctly addressed in James Spooner's documentary about the US Afro-punk scene (2003). While punk rock remains predominantly white, black punks have worked hard to address the latent prejudices of the scene (see Duncombe and Tremblay, 2011, 13), and Ramírez-Sanchez concludes that while black punk participants sometimes report feeling "pushed to the margins of their scenes" (2008, 97), punk can also function as an important space to rediscover black identity (2008, 98). The privileges of whiteness have been acknowledged (Duncombe and Tremblay 2011) and discussed (Schilt 2014).

Although race and the subcultural participation of women represent growing scholarly concerns, relatively less has been written on the subject of punk and disability. McKay argues that "punk and post-punk enfreakment" "opened up new cultural spaces and corporeal expectations" for disabled performers and fans alike (2013, 11). David Church suggests that "the genre's rough, open and unfinished musical style evokes qualities similarly associated with disabled bodies" (2013, 31), while Heylin has noted the influence of the disabled performer Ian Dury on John Lydon's stage persona (2008, 81). McKay makes a similar point, arguing that punk fashions demonstrate a fascination with "certain sartorial markers or even generators of disability," listing straitjackets, bondage trousers, and fetish wear as examples (2015, 232), while pogoing—the style of dance most often associated with punk—might be read as "a further display of a kind of incompetence, an inelegant, if thoroughly energetic solo reaction of body to music" (231). He goes on to suggest that the inclusion of disabled people in punk narratives potentially "disrupts subcultural theory," constituting a "new body language of punk performance" (237–238). Also significant, but somewhat under-recognized, are issues around punk sexualities (Nault 2017, 2). Although much was made of punk's supposed "asexuality" (particularly during the first wave: see Hebdige 1979, 123; O'Brien 1999, 194), as well as the "cross-dressing" of the proto-punk outfit the New York Dolls (Savage 1992, 62), mainstream punk literature has arguably been slower to recognize the significance of "queercore" from the mid-1980s on, and its role in advocating for the LGBTQ punk community (see Arnold 1997, 159–171; DeChaine 1997; du Plessis and Chapman 1997; O'Hara 1999; Taylor 2012; Nault 2017). At the same time, Schilt argues that punk's intersectionality is widely neglected, despite representing a pivotal issue for the Riot Grrrl movement (2014).

Finally, punk can be perceived as an identity in its own right, potentially offering "an alternative to the institutionalized or passé identities of the status quo" (Laing 1985, 131). Miriam Rivett described punk as "a process through which, by direct participation, identities are formed" (1999, 33), while early media representations warned parents about the "cultish nature" of the movement, which "embodied a threat beyond routine teenage rebellion" (Cobley 1999, 173–174). While most accounts focus on punk as a youth subcultural identity (such as Fox 1987; Frith 1981; Andes 1998; Epstein 1998; Glass 2012), Andy Bennett has written extensively about the specific experiences of punks and the aging process, suggesting that many older punks view their continued role in music scenes as concerned with "preserving the punk aesthetic and passing this on to the next generation" (2013, 131). Similarly, Joanna R. Davis speaks of the ways in which punk identities shift over the course of a lifetime, suggesting that a "synthesized identity" enables both incorporation of the aging self and the negotiation of a new one within the subculture (2006, 64). Outside of punk rock music, punk identity markers and DIY practices have led to thinking about what Bennett calls "DIY-oriented career paths" as part of the entire life cycle (Bennett 2013, 98), while a small number of scholars—"edupunks" (Parkinson 2017, 114) or "punkademics" (Furness, 2012)—have found in punk an opportunity to reimagine the way academic work is conducted (see Beer 2014, 33). However, Duncombe and Tremblay warn of the pitfalls of presuming the presence and applicability of a "universal subcultural citizenship," arguing that "insisting that punk was more important than race didn't change the still-sizeable degree of privilege Whites derived in mainstream and punk culture as a result of their skin colour, language, and so forth" (2011, 10, 11).

Punk Materialities

In his seminal text of the punk era, *Subculture: The Meaning of Style*, Dick Hebdige writes that "[i]n punk, alienation assumed an almost tangible quality.[11] It could almost be grasped" (1979, 28). Indeed, the vibrant and highly recognizable material cultures of punk rock—including its distinctive fashions, graphic arts, and DIY publishing practices—can be readily glimpsed in much punk criticism, despite a surprising paucity of dedicated studies.[12] Many commentators have followed Hebdige, understanding the "cacophonous fashions" worn by many participants (Davis 2006, 64), and the tabloid-influenced designs of Jamie Reid and peers (Garnett 1999), as visual manifestations of the anger and oppositionality of the scene (Bennett 2013, 168; Idol 2015, 52; Worley 2017, 77).[13] However, there is also a tendency to view punk style—particularly its fashion—as the superficial end of the punk project, with pointed references to the genre's theatricality (see Home 1995, 10; Cobley 1999, 171; O'Brien 2002, 132), and to its propensity to become diluted, for example, through co-option by the commercial fashion industry (Rivett 1999, 37; Laing 1985, 124). While ethnographic studies of punk scenes indicate that the assumption of a punk identity is commonly signaled by an (often dramatic) transformation of personal appearance (see Fox 1987; Hannerz 2015), many also insist that punk should not be understood as a purely stylistic entity, emphasizing instead the movement's political—and (less frequently) musical—significance (Robb, 2006, 1; Letts and Nobakht 2007, 13–14; Guerra 2014, 111). Nonetheless, Wilkinson et al. caution that a tendency to privilege "the theoretical" has tended to result in the neglect of punk's material history, placing distance between punk as conceptualized by scholars and punk as experienced by participants (2017, 406).

Hebdige argued that punk style could be understood as a series of "refusals," at the first level embodying participants' rejection of mainstream societal structures (1979, 132). Writing at the tail end of UK punk's first wave, he suggested that "[n]o subculture has sought with more grim determination than the punks to detach itself from the taken-for-granted landscape of normalised forms, nor to bring down upon itself such vehement disapproval" (19).[14] Coined "confrontation dressing" by fashion designer Vivienne Westwood (quoted in Hebdige 1979, 107), punk fashion remains characterized by an aesthetics of "abjection" (Cobley 1999, 175) and a commitment to "wearing its political dissatisfactions on its sleeve" (Bennett 2013, 168). In adopting specific styles—which included (infamously) the safety pin in the ear or cheek (Reddington 2012, 155), the Mohican- or Mohawk-style haircut (Fox 1987, 355), and fetish clothing made from rubber and plastic (Hebdige 1979, 70)—Hebdige felt that punks created for themselves an ontological Other, distinct from the mainstream (65), whose "constant state of assemblage, of flux," constituted a second level of refusal. Punk fashion "invites the reader to 'slip into' 'significance' to lose the sense of direction, the direction of sense" (126). By contrast, Laing contended that punk style quickly ossified, coming to stand in for the subculture before any discernible political stance (1985, 95; see also Dale 2012, 1).[15]

Compounded by the crossover between punk and the mainstream fashion market—a process that began in the fledgling days of Malcolm McLaren and Vivienne Westwood's Kings Road, London, boutique (see Savage 1992; Heylin 2008)—he observed that 'the punk look solidified into a uniform, suitable to join the ready-made clothing advertisements in the music press (Laing 1985, 109).

The exploration of tensions between punk style and its commodification is evident throughout the literature (see Rivett 1999, 37; Moore 2004, 233; Smith 2009, 41). Although clothing functioned as "'entry level' to punk" for many participants (Cartledge 1999, 145), the popularity and mass replicability of the punk image is perceived by many as a double-edged sword (see Bloustien 2003, 55). "Punk changed everything. Not just our trousers," writes John Robb (2006, 1), invoking the common connection between (punk) style and (social) substance (see also O'Hara 1999, 9). At the same time, notional hierarchies of "subcultural capital" (Thornton 1995) institute a materials-led dialectic between inauthentic and "true" punks (Laing 1985, 124), which generally attributes greater value to DIY garments than to mass-produced, shop-bought items (see Albertine 2014, 130) and permanent or semi-permanent bodily modifications over more temporary visual expressions (Fox 1987, 355). In spite of the ambivalence of some writers on punk styles, however, firsthand accounts, in particular by female punks, disabled punks, and punks in non-Western contexts, suggest that fashions—regardless of their provenance—retain a transformative potential, on both a personal and societal level (see O'Brien 1999, 187; McKay 2015, 232; Hayton 2017, 362). At the same time, greater attention toward the heterogeneities of subcultural experience (Hannerz 2015) has begun to challenge ideas about the uniform punk aesthetic. As Reddington notes calmly, "there is photographic evidence that [early] punk gigs belonged to variously dressed performers and audiences from different ethnic, cultural and demographic backgrounds" (2012, 155).

In addition to its controversial fashions, the enduring appeal and relevance of punk's material cultures are also revealed in a growing number of works documenting the popular phenomenon of self-published punk fanzines or zines (Triggs 2004, 2006; Piepmeier and Zeisler 2009) as well as punk visual art practices (Yedgar and Sladen 2007; Bestley and Ogg 2012). That punk's material signifiers appear more readily transferable than its musical outputs is supported by Teal Triggs's persuasive analysis of the ways in which the iconography of zines has been widely co-opted by mainstream design and advertising that seek to trade on an "association with 'punk authenticity'" (2006, 69). In this way, she suggests, zines constitute a "graphic language of resistance" that is readily understood outside of the context of punk rock subculture. Marcus also speaks of punk as "a new set of visual and verbal signs" (1989, 69), attempting to trace the movement's lineage through avant-garde art movements including Dadaism, Lettrism, and Situationism. Robert Garnett, too, proposes that punk was able to penetrate the dual worlds of "high" and "low" art, perhaps even contributing to the dissolution of such unstable boundaries (1999). But while increased recognition is a crucial step forward, a lack of extensive scholarly engagement to date with the genre's graphic and material incarnations poses the question of whether punk's visual histories are mistakenly felt to speak for themselves (as in the coffee-table books that typically eschew written exegeses): Has punk denied analysis?

Punk Spaces

Perhaps counterintuitively, given its lyrical and attitudinal stance of alienation (Hebdige 1979; Worley 2013), punk rock is closely linked to various aspects of place. Punk is understood to emphasize local concerns and small-scale cultural production (Gosling 2004; O'Connor 2008), but it is also a global or at least hemispheric phenomenon, "a transatlantic insurrection" (McKay 1999, 69). Typically associated with urban (Hebdige 1979) and suburban spaces (Culton and Holtzman 2010; Trainer 2016), its forms are sometimes characterized as issuing directly from "the street" (Baron 1989) and are periodically subject to censorship and prohibition (see Savage 1992 on the UK; Hayton 2017 on East Germany), but punk participants have also worked to create dedicated punk venues (Debies-Carl 2014; Lloyd 2017), to reclaim existing sites (Guerra 2014), and to re-envisage the spatial organization of gigs (Fonarow 2005). Indeed, punk venues are a constitutive part of punk's *structures of feeling*, elements that encapsulate the cultural movement (Wilkinson et al 2017, 400). In addition to occupying physical, lived spaces, punk is also described as a conceptual or "formative space" that has "shaped the engagement of many with the world" (Wilkinson et al. 2017, 411).

Many—especially popular—histories have focused on the large, high-profile punk scenes in London and New York (consider Savage 1992; McNeil and McCain 2016; Marcade 2017). While these locations are jointly considered to be the primary—and originary—centers of the punk rock movement, a tendency toward monocultural approaches (Savage 1992; Robb 2006; McNeil and McCain 2016) has led to discursive tussles over punk's "definitive" birthplace and progenitors. In 1993 Clinton Heylin, for example, argued that New York punk typically received less scholarly attention than the British scene, despite the fact that "American punk predates British punk" (1993, xi). He suggested that the high visibility and iconic status of the Sex Pistols (and thus the London scene of which they were a leading part) eclipsed the perceived contribution of "American bands like the Stooges, the Modern Lovers and the Dolls," on whom later punk musicians would draw "second-hand" (1993, xiv). However, other accounts suggest that UK punks—not least the Sex Pistols' manager, McLaren—were well aware of their US (and UK) ur-punk forebears (see Laing 1985, 24; Letts and Nobakht, 2007, 82), sometimes viewing British punk (or perhaps specifically punk Englishness; see Adams 2008) as a conscious response to the reported Americanization of cultures. As Mark Perry urged readers of the first issue of *Sniffin' Glue* zine in 1976: "Let's build our own bands up instead of drooling over the New York scene" (2009). Other writers resist lionizing the chronological imperative, presenting punk in terms of its "transregionality" (Slobin 1993), suggesting that the genre emerged with approximate simultaneity in multiple places worldwide (see Guerra 2014, 112).

Although descriptions of punk in London and New York during the 1970s continue to dominate the majority of punk print space, a growing interest in provincial punk scenes in the UK and US (such as Smith 2015; Crossley 2015; Doe and DeSavia 2017) and in international punk subcultures can be identified in some—especially more recent—literature (see Greene 2012 on Peru; Hannerz 2015 on Sweden and Indonesia; Trainer 2016 on suburban Australia; Draganova and Blackman 2019 on Bulgaria). In part, this reflects a drive to better represent punk as both a local and global phenomenon (Smith 2015, 497), as well as an attempt to document the subculture's enduring appeal across the decades. As Simon Frith notes, punk's ethos of small-scale, independent networks and "demystified" production contributed to "an astonishing expansion of local music-making"(1981, 159), resulting in a diverse—and contemporary—"translocal" music community worldwide (Bennett and Peterson 2004, 8). Some provincial scenes are understood to possess distinct characters and influence; for example, the UK-based Manchester scene is felt to have helped usher in a new era of post-punk and new-wave music in the 1980s (Smith 2009; Crossley 2015), while globally, punk-rock practices have been employed to protest against unpopular governments (Willems 2014; Wiedlack 2016) and to enact solidarity with other subcultural groups, particularly in the midst of repressive political regimes (Hayton 2017). With this in mind, Yngvar Steinholt (2012, 404) points to the abilities of (particularly non-Western) punks to adapt the genre to meet local needs and expectations, while Erik Hannerz (2015, 5) cautions against assumptions that non-Western and non-Anglophone punk expressions are derivative or second-rate.

Significantly, the increasing diversification of what we can think of as the parochial or provincial punk literature sheds light on punk experiences outside of the dominant London and New York scenes. Small towns are typically described as more socially conservative than their metropolitan counterparts, rendering adoption of a punk identity highly visible—and thus potentially more controversial—by comparison (Cobley 1999, 171). This situation is even more acutely felt by punks who do not conform to the expected (that is, straight, white, male) model of subcultural participation; for example, Lucy O'Brien writes of the isolation of being "the only girls doing [punk] for miles around" (2002, 83). However, despite its obvious practical challenges, regional punk scenes are often admired for their resourcefulness (Letts and Nobakht 2007, 89) and perceived lack of "corruption" by mainstream and commercial forces (Hayton 2017, 363). Parochial or provincial punk activities are sometimes described as being necessarily more "DIY" than their better-connected inner-city and/or Western equivalents. Perhaps for this reason, a number of punk acts have sought to emphasize the (typically underprivileged) place origins of their music, with McKay noting that a significant number of band names reference specifically suburban locations (1999, 57), while Matthew Worley writes that the "local references" deployed by Oi! bands constituted a "focus for working class identification" (2013, 632). Hebdige seems to take this further, arguing in addition to punk's appeals to "recognisable locales," many lyrics also involve "a denial of place . . . celebrating the blank, expressionless, rootless" (1979, 65). This is not so much suggestive of topophilia (Tuan 1990), but rather acts as an engaged critique of the often unsatisfactory conditions of everyday life—and potentially a vision to improve upon it.

Punk participants also carve out their own discreet places to meet and perform (Marcus 1989, 75; Dale 2012, 2). Performance spaces are central to many punk histories and mythologies, with a number of recent publications centered on specific venues, such as the Roxy club in London (Marko 2007; Czezowski and Carrington 2017) and CBGB in New York (Lloyd 2017). This emphasis is perhaps unsurprising, given punk's track record of public censorship and prohibition.[16] Punk's perceived subversiveness (see Smith 2015, 491) and associations with violence and antisocial behaviors (O'Hara 1999, 45–46; Steinholt 2012, 413) have led to significant practical difficulties in securing and maintaining places to meet—as Billy Idol remarked of the birth of the Roxy in 1976: "Starting our own venue was the only option" (2015, 70). The resultant grass-roots involvement with punk venues often contributes to a strong sense of cultural ownership: Jeffrey S. Debies-Carl draws attention to the affective attachments formed with performance spaces through regular attendance and participation (2014), while Helen Reddington suggests that punk venues are indissoluble from punk practices themselves, writing of The Vault in Brighton that "the grim aesthetics... had an effect on the type of music and behaviour that emanated from it" (2012, 80). However, the important role of self-organized, communal spaces does not necessarily reflect a cohesive or shared punk vision; as Hannerz writes of a punk festival in Sweden, "many participants here despise other participants present for the kind of punk they represent" (2015, 2).

Finally, at the intersection with punk politics and identities, punk can be understood as a "formative space" in which new ideas and ways of living can be modeled and explored (Wilkinson et al 2017, 411). The subcultural punk "underground" is typically conceived as ideologically opposed to what Greil Marcus described as "the official pop space" (1989, 75), and indeed some punk venues and events are run along consciously ideological lines, sometimes attempting to dissolve the barriers between performers and audience (Marcus 1989, 38), and/or resisting hierarchical concert billing (Dale 2012, 27). Such ideals have been achieved with varying degrees of success in different aspects of the punk subculture; for example, the spatial organization of gigs was a particular concern for the Riot Grrrl scene of the early 1990s, with feminist acts such as Bikini Kill making significant efforts to draw out girls and young women from the sidelines at punk venues and into more active positions at the front of—and on—the stage (Marcus 2010). This desired potential for punk to embody an egalitarian and accessible ideology extends well beyond the concert stages. Bennett suggests that punk provides an ongoing conceptual "space for the nurturing of a critical sensibility" (2013, 175), while Kevin Dunn argues that "[i]n the face of the alienating process of specialisation and professionalization, punk offers resources for participation and access" (2008, 198). However, if the emergence of punk in the 1970s was understood by some as the brokering of a new cultural and ideological space, then for others its existence was fragile and transitory; as Robert Garnett writes, "the moment of punk passed not simply because it was recuperated, reified or processed by the culture industry; it passed because the space within which it operated was closed down" (1999, 17).

Conclusion: Punk Legacies

The "death" of punk rock was widely reported—eulogized as early as 1977 in some parts of the popular music and alternative press (Anon 1977), and relatively accepted by 1978 (see Marcus 1989, 39; Savage 1992, 477; Laing 1985, 106).[17] Claims that the movement had been tainted by commodification (see Arnold 1997; Rivett 1999, 37; Reddington 2012, 163), or had come to represent "a parody of itself" (Reynolds 2005, xvii), were—and continue to be—commonplace explanations. However, many writers have challenged such a dismal narrative of punk's purported demise, pointing to acts such as the Slits (Albertine 2014; Cogan 2012) and the Clash (Green and Barker 2000; Gelbart 2011; Gilbert 2009), who continued to perform long after the movement's apparent end date. Others focus on subsequent transmutations of the genre, which include post-punk (Hesmondhalgh 1997; Reynolds 2005; Mankowski 2014; Crossley 2015; Butt, Eshun, and Fisher 2016; Wilkinson 2016), new wave (Lull 1982; Fryer 1986; Coon 1997; Joynson 2001), hardcore (O'Hara 1999; Haenfler 2006; Cisar and Koubek 2012), Riot Grrrl (Downes 2007; Huber 2010; Angell 2010; Marcus 2010; Dunn and Farnsworth 2012; Darms and Fateman 2013), grunge (Heylin 2008; Prato 2010; Strong 2011a, 2011b), and even rave culture (McKay 1998; Hill 2002; Reynolds 2005, 525). Still others suggested that punk remained intact alongside later incarnations, "alive and well . . . one of those subcultures that travels successfully in a globalised world" (Ron Eyerman, quoted in Hannerz 2015, iv; see also Bennett 2006, 2013). For this reason, critical understanding is split on whether punk in the twenty-first century represents a living tradition (Dale 2012), an exercise in nostalgia (Medhurst 1999; Smith 2009; Turrini 2013), and/or a sociohistorical artifact (Savage 1992; McNeil and McCain 2016). Despite this, most commentators agree that further work should be done to fully understand punk and its legacies; as Matthew Gelbart suggests, "[p]unk may be normalised but (luckily) it is not yet fully digested" (2011, 271).

While much continues to be written on punk's first wave, relatively less attention is typically paid to the acts of the immediate post-punk period or to the punk-inflected genres, such as hardcore and grunge, that followed (see critique by Reynolds 2005, iv; Butt et al. 2016, 8).[18] For some commentators, this was attributable to a perceived compromise in the later movements' "purity" and relevance (see Moore 1999; Wilkinson et al. 2017, 405),[19] although Simon Reynolds argues that punk's "most provocative repercussions" took place "long after its supposed demise" (Reynolds 2005, xvi). For other writers, there remains some disagreement about how "post-punk" should be defined. Reynolds, for example, differentiates between the "populist 'real punks'"—including those involved in the Oi! movement—for whom punk represented the *vox populi*, and the distinct "post-punk genre," which was characterized by an "imperative to constant change" and attempts to create a "break with tradition" (2005, xvii). "It was at this point," Reynolds writes, "that punk's fragile unity between working-class kids and arty, middle-class bohemians began to fracture" (xvii). O'Hara (1999), by contrast, uses "post-punk" as an umbrella term to describe any and all punk-identifying cultures that followed the initial popularity of the first wave. This definition includes, of course, the majority of punk activities taking place over the past four decades; as TV Smith noted—over three decades ago—"[w]e are in a 'post-punk' world" (quoted in Laing 1985, 1).

Despite growing recognition of the importance of post-punk histories, some writers—and participants—argue that punk rock should be approached as an ongoing and parallel (as opposed to antecedent) musical form. "Not everyone tired of punk," writes Crossley. "Punk worlds continued to form and grow even in those places where vibrant post-punk worlds were emerging" (2015, 165). Indeed, punk's prophesied "absence of permanently sacred signifiers" (Hebdige 1979, 115) now reads as overstatement, not least because, as Laing noted, "[w]hether or not punk rock was dead after 1978, punks themselves weren't" (1985, 109). However, although punk continues to play a role in popular music subcultures worldwide, a long-term interest in punk rock music—particularly among aging music fans (see Bennett 2006, 2013)—is sometimes dismissed as nostalgia, undermining the "no futures" paradigm (see Savage 1992, 55; Sabin 1999b, 5). Andy Medhurst writes that "[g]etting nostalgic about punk is worse than a contradiction in terms, it's a kind of betrayal, trading in punk's forensic nihilism for rose-coloured cosiness" (1999, 224; see also Smith 2009, 81, 191). But Bennett (2013, 131) contends that many older punks continue to play an active role in punk scenes, often viewing their role as one of safeguarding punk ideologies and aesthetics for future generations of punk fans. Dale, too, characterizes punk as a living tradition that continues to empower its increasingly cross-generational participants to "feel that a new politics, culture and society are possible" (2012, 215; see also Hannerz 2015).

Terminological debates aside, a marked increase in publications in the years leading up to the fortieth anniversary of punk rock (e.g., Wilkinson 2016; Lloyd 2017; Ingham 2017) suggests a continued appetite for (re)evaluating the influence of punk.[20] One commonly proposed legacy is the recent expansion of "DIY" activities and practices, from political activism to knitting to careers (e.g., McKay 1998; Gauntlett 2011; Bennett 2013). Indeed, some scholars suggest that it is this broad legacy—more than its music—that constitutes punk's primary cultural contribution. As Marcus wrote in 1978, "[t]he Sex Pistols left behind more history than music" (in Marcus 1999, 21).[21] In a related way, Bennett suggests that punk participants' "ongoing engagement with the socioeconomic fallout of a post-industrial society" represents its most crucial legacy (2013, 177), while Garnett has argued that the present "space between academic high art and the realm of popular culture" was one of the primary results of the punk rock movement (1999, 19). However, not all of punk's legacies are straightforwardly benign. Reddington suggests that despite women's increased participation in punk and post-punk scenes, "[a] phenomenal amount of energy went into preventing it from having any lasting influence," noting that many commentators sought to "belittle and forget those who were part of it all" (Reddington 2012, 194). Garnett, too, suggests that while DIY could be a liberating prospect, it also elided neatly with the Thatcherite philosophy of "'getting on your bike' and self-improving your way out of Giro city" (Garnett 1999, 27), potentially paving the way for the embrace of neoliberal agendas. As McKay has noted of the Crass artist Gee Vaucher superimposing Margaret Thatcher's head onto Johnny Rotten's body: *"It's all in the hair!* Dyed blonde on dyed blond. Two radicals moving in one space, each wrapped in a Union Jack while changing the nation" (2016, 76; emphasis in original).

And what of punk literature? I asked earlier if punk, in its gesture and attitude, had denied or resisted analysis. Plainly not, as the scope of this review and indeed a collection such as *The Oxford Handbook of Punk Rock*, should testify. For Reynolds, the demise of post-punk in 1985 or so also signaled a foundering of punk writing: "More than musical inspiration per se, what began to sink into a coma was the discourse *around* music" (Reynolds 2005, 518). Referring primarily to music journalism, Reynolds was not, it seems, commenting necessarily on the broader critical writing about punk, including academic. However, if his purpose was to draw attention to the continued absence of grand narratives in later punk writing—as scholars prefer to limit their engagement to specific periods or geographical locations—this would be a pertinent reminder of the potential value of expansive and inclusive discourse. Similar publications are commonly dogged by a lack of authorial diversity, with the voices of writers who are not male, white, straight, or able remaining marginal in many accounts of the genre (see Reddington 2012, 16), though there have been shifts here in recent years. Others argue that punk literature would do well to refocus its attention on punk rock *music*, with Gelbart surmising that efforts to "normalise" punk into an aesthetic and cultural discourse have contributed to a neglect of punk sounds (2011, 233; see also Rapport 2014, 44). However, he concedes that this normalizing process also "offers at least the potential to do the opposite, to become more open and thoughtful" (Gelbart 2011, 270), or as Worley puts it, to "re-historicise punk beyond its media moment" (2017, 23). These offer, perhaps, a hint at the future directions of punk scholarship. Parallels are increasingly drawn between the social and political conditions that formed the backdrop to the first-wave punk era and those of the present day; as Letts and Nobakht write, "[t]he current climate feels as if punk never happened" (2007, 215; see also Butt et al. 2016, 19). Perhaps punk rock music—and subsequently punk criticism—might have a role to play outside of popular music studies, offering the benefit of its historical positioning to influence wider political debate.

Acknowledgments

The research for this chapter was undertaken as part of the Arts and Humanities Research Council Connected Communities program project, Participatory Arts and DIY Cultures, at the University of East Anglia, UK, on which I was a Senior Research Associate, 2017–2018. I am grateful for the AHRC's support.

Notes

1. Perhaps the most compelling example is taqwacore (Fiscella 2012), a Muslim subgenre of punk rock whose emergence as a lived music scene was inspired directly by a fictional account by Michael Muhammad Knight (2007).

2. In an attempt to unpick this issue, Pete Dale coined the term "new-sense" to describe punk's evocation of "strongly apparent novelty" and "appearance of ostentatious newness" (2012, 90).
3. Indeed, for some scholars, punk can (even should) be approached as a primarily political—as opposed to musical—phenomenon (see Laing 1985, xi on Hebdige 1979).
4. In the US, punk was conceptually linked to an avant-garde tradition that included the Situationist International and their specific interpretation of anti-authoritarian Marxism (see Marcus, 1989), although some scholars have argued that first-wave American punk was less consciously political than its UK counterpart (Fox, 1987, 345).
5. Both McLaren's involvement and the conflation of Situationism and anarchism have been challenged, not least by Court (2015).
6. This DIY ethos also includes nonmusical practices, including writing (particularly zines; see Triggs 2006), fashion (Cartledge 1999) and art (Garnett 1999).
7. The anarcho-punk band Crass received criticism for their on stage uniform of all black clothes, and for their "crypto-fascist" logo (Berger 2006, 104).
8. Lucy Toothpaste has suggested that female punks of the first wave were generally loathe to self-describe as feminists, "because I think they thought the feminist label was too worthy"; however, she concludes that "[p]unk made women feel they could compete on equal terms to men" (quoted in Savage 1992, 418).
9. In addition to scholarly works, a number of popular autobiographies, most notably by the Slits' Viv Albertine (2014), as well as Chrissie Hynde of the Pretenders (2016), Kim Gordon of Sonic Youth (2015), and Carrie Brownstein of Sleater Kinney (2015), have helped to raise the public profile of female punk artists, highlighting their contributions to the scene (see Reddington 2012, 5, 153).
10. For example, Daniel Traber writes of the problematic "self-marginalization" of punk participants, for whom crossing the border into Otherness might be read as "a commodification of the Other that aestheticizes identity for capital in a symbolic economy of signification" (Traber 2001, 50). In a similar way, in his case for hearing punk as blues, Evan Rapport argues that as an extreme manifestation of the rock project, punk "depends on an association of blackness with particular kinds of blues resources, and then the processes of white appropriation, transformation and obfuscation of those resources" (2014, 61).
11. It is perhaps no accident that the metaphor of tearing "the cultural fabric" is common to descriptions of the emergence of first-wave punk (Home 1995, 23; Bennett 2013, 151; Worley 2017, 3).
12. A continued emphasis on the aesthetic (and aestheticized) aspects of the punk experience is reflected in the relative prevalence of photographic collections documenting the subculture's striking visual history (see, for example, Connolly and Cheslow 1988; Cervenka 2002; Ercoli 2004; Lens and Friedman 2008; Ingham 2017).
13. Punk style is arguably the material counterpart of punk rock music (see Albertine 2014, 131).
14. Fox argues that in the US, a reduced emphasis on class politics and youth unemployment led to an even closer connection between punk and style (1987, 345).
15. Laing writes that "[a]s punk established itself, so bondage trousers plus spiky hair, chains and pins came primarily to denote a punk identity, rather than . . . the refusal of meaning so central to Hebdige's claims" (1985, 95).
16. It is well-known, for example, that the Sex Pistols were banned from many mainstream music venues during 1976–1977—as well as blanked in the UK single charts—but punk

fans were also prohibited from gathering in public spaces in East Germany during the 1980s (Hayton 2017, 365), and, more recently, Pussy Riot were jailed for their "punk prayer" in a Moscow cathedral in 2012 (Willems 2014).

17. Although the precise date differs between accounts, most writers link punk's collapse to the break-up of the Sex Pistols, with whom the movement in Britain was also felt to have begun.
18. Several authors have commented on the tendency of historians to overemphasize the activities of the first wave—in particular the role of the Sex Pistols (Court 2015)—to the detriment of later punk incarnations (see Home 1995, 30; O'Hara 1999, 11).
19. Others, such as Laing, recalled that punk acts were sometimes encouraged to rebrand themselves in order "to evade the stigma" of punk rock in the early post-punk period, and as such, punk histories might omit those who later chose to disassociate with the term (1985, 37).
20. As well as anniversary tours, reunions and re-releases, and dedicated books and articles, the swell of interest around punk rock also included exhibitions and documentary films. For example, efforts to commemorate punk took place at a host of UK institutions during 2016, including the Roundhouse, the British Library, and Paul Smith fashion boutique in London, as part of a year-long Heritage Lottery Fund–supported festival celebrating "40 years of subversive culture."
21. Indeed, one possible critique of the present canon of punk literature is that scholars have taken this sentiment too much to heart, tending to neglect punk rock music itself (Reynolds 2005, xv).

References

Adams, R. 2008. "The Englishness of English punk: Sex Pistols, subcultures, and nostalgia." *Popular Music and Society* 31(4): 469–488.

Afro-Punk. 2003. Directed by J. Spooner.

Albertine, V. 2014. *Clothes, Clothes, Clothes. Music, Music, Music. Boys, Boys, Boys.* London: Faber.

Ambrosch, G. 2016. "'Refusing to be a man': Gender, feminism and queer identity in the punk culture." *Punk & Post Punk* 5(3): 247–264.

Andes, L. 1998. "Growing up punk: Meaning and commitment careers in a contemporary youth subculture." In J. S. Epstein, ed. *Youth Culture: Identity in a Postmodern World*. Malden, MA: Wiley, 212–232.

Angell, K. 2010. "Archiving grrrl style now." *Feminist Collections: A Quarterly of Women's Studies Resources* 31(4): 16–19.

Anon. 1977. "Punk is dead." *International Times* (February), 6.

Arnold, G. 1997. *Kiss This: Punk in the Present Tense*. New York: St. Martin's Griffin.

Baron, S. W. 1989. "Resistance and its consequences: The street culture of punks." *Canadian Journal of Sociology* 14(3): 207–237.

Beer, D. 2014. *Punk Sociology*. Basingstoke, UK: Palgrave Macmillan.

Bennett, A. 2006. "Punk's not dead: The continuing significance of punk rock for an older generation of fans." *Sociology* 40(2): 207–237.

Bennett, A. 2013. *Music, Style, and Aging: Growing Old Disgracefully?* Philadelphia: Temple University Press.

Bennett, A. and Peterson, R. A., eds. 2004. *Music Scenes: Local, Translocal, and Virtual.* Nashville: Vanderbilt University Press.

Berger, G. 2006. *The Story of Crass.* London: Omnibus.

Bestley, R. and Ogg, A. 2012. *The Art of Punk.* London: Omnibus.

Bloustien, D. 2003. "'Oh bondage, up yours!' Or here's three chords, now form a band: Punk, masochism, skin, anaclisis, defacement." In D. Muggleton and R. Weinzierl, eds. *Post-Subcultures Reader.* Oxford: Berg, 51–63.

Brownstein, C. 2015. *Hunger Makes Me a Modern Girl: A Memoir.* London: Virago.

Butt, G., Eshun, K., and Fisher, M., eds. 2016. *Post-Punk Then and Now.* London: Repeater.

Cartledge, F. 1999. "Distress to impress? Local punk fashion and commodity exchange." In Sabin 1999b, 143–153.

Cervenka, E. 2002. *We're Desperate: The Punk Rock Photography of Jim Jocoy 1978–1980.* New York: Power House Books.

Church, D. 2013. "Punk will tear us apart: Performance, liminality and filmic depictions of disabled punk musicians." In M. E. Mogk, ed. *Different Bodies: Essays on Disability in Film and Television.* Jefferson, NC: McFarland, 28–39.

Cisar, O. and Koubek, M. 2012. "Include 'em all? Culture, politics and a local hardcore/punk scene in the Czech Republic." *Poetics* 40(1): 1–21.

Cobley, P. 1999. "Leave the capitol." In Sabin 1999b, 170–185.

Cogan, B. 2012. "Typical girls?: Fuck off, you wanker! Re-evaluating the Slits and gender relations in early British punk and post-punk." *Women's Studies* 41(2): 121–135.

Connolly, C. and Cheslow, S. 1988. *Banned in DC: Photos and Ancedotes from the DC Punk Underground.* Washington, DC: Sun Dog.

Coon, C. 1997. *1988: The New Wave, Punk Rock Explosion.* London: Orbach & Chambers.

Court, B. 2015. "The Christ-like antichrists: Messianism in Sex Pistols historiography." *Popular Music & Society* 38(4): 416–431.

Crossley, N. 2015. *Networks of Sound, Style and Subversion: The Punk and Post-Punk Worlds of Manchester, London, Liverpool and Sheffield, 1975–80.* Manchester, UK: Manchester University Press.

Culton, K. R. and Holtzman, B. 2010. "The growth and disruption of a 'free space': Examining a suburban Do It Yourself (DIY) punk scene." *Space and Culture* 13(3): 270–284.

Czezowski, A. and Carrington, S. 2017. *The Roxy Our Story: The Club That Forged Punk in 100 Nights of Madness, Mayhem and Misfortune.* London: Carrczez.

Dale, P. 2012. *Anyone Can Do It: Empowerment, Tradition and the Punk Underground.* Aldershot, UK: Ashgate.

Darms, L. and Fateman, J. 2013. *The Riot Grrrl Collection.* New York: Feminist Press.

Davis, J. R. 2006. "Growing up punk: Negotiating aging identity in a local music scene." *Symbolic Interaction* 29(1): 63–69.

Dawson, A. 2005. "'Love music, hate racism': The cultural politics of the Rock Against Racism campaigns, 1976–1981." *Postmodern Culture* 16(1): 1–13.

Debies-Carl, J. S. 2014. *Punk Rock and the Politics of Place: Building a Better Tomorrow.* London: Routledge.

DeChaine, D. R. 1997. 'Mapping subversion: Queercore music's playful discourse of resistance. *Popular Music and Society* 21(4): 7–37.

Dines, M. and Worley, M., eds. 2016. *The Aesthetic of Our Anger: Anarcho-Punk, Politics and Music.* Colchester, UK: Minor Compositions.

Doe, J. and DeSavia, T. 2017. *Under the Big Black Sun: A Personal History of L.A. Punk*. Boston: Da Capo Press.

Downes, J. 2007. "Riot Grrrl: The legacy and contemporary landscape of DIY feminist cultural activism." In N. Monem, ed. *Riot Grrrl: Revolution Girl Style Now*. London: Black Dog, 12–49.

Downes, J., 2012. "The expansion of punk rock: Riot Grrrl challenges to gender power relations in British indie music subcultures." *Women's Studies* 41(2): 204–237.

Draganova, A. and Blackman, S. 2019. "A howl of the estranged: Post-punk and contemporary underground scenes in Bulgarian popular music." In P. Guerra and A. Bennett, eds. *DIY Cultures and Underground Music Scenes*. London: Routledge, 230–242.

Duncombe, S. and Tremblay, M., eds. 2011. *White Riot: Punk Rock and the Politics of Race*. London: Verso.

Dunn, K. 2008. "Never mind the bollocks: The punk rock politics of global communication." *Review of International Studies* 34(1): 193–210.

Dunn, K. 2012. "'If it ain't cheap, it ain't punk': Walter Benjamin's progressive cultural production and DIY punk record labels." *Journal of Popular Music Studies* 24(2): 217–237.

Dunn, K. and Farnsworth, M. S. 2012. "'We ARE the Revolution': Riot Grrrl Press, girl empowerment, and DIY self-publishing." *Women's Studies* 41(2): 136–157.

Epstein, J. S., ed. 1998. *Youth Culture: Identity in a Postmodern World*. Malden: Wiley.

Ercoli, R. 2004. *Legends of Punk: Photos from the Vault*. San Francisco: Manic D Press.

Fiscella, A. T., 2012. "From Muslim punks to taqwacore: An incomplete history of punk Islam." *Contemporary Islam* 6(3): 255–281.

Fonarow, W., 2005. "The spatial organisation of the indie music gig." In K. Gelder, ed. *The Subcultures Reader*. 2nd ed. London: Routledge, 360–369.

Fox, K. J. 1987. "Real punks and pretenders: The social organisation of a counterculture." *Journal of Contemporary Ethnography* 16(3): 344–370.

Frith, S. 1981. *Sound Effects: Youth, Leisure and the Politics of Rock 'n' Roll*. New York: Random House.

Fryer, P. 1986. "Punk and the new wave of British rock: Working class heroes and art school attitudes." *Popular Music and Society* 10(4): 1–15.

Furness, Z., ed. 2012. *Punkademics: The Basement Show in the Ivory Tower*. Wivenhoe, UK: Minor Compositions.

Garnett, R. 1999. "Too low to be low: Art pop and the Sex Pistols." In Sabin 1999b, 17–30.

Gauntlett, D. 2011. *Making Is Connecting: The Social Meaning of Creativity, from DIY and Knitting to YouTube and Web 2.0*. Cambridge: Polity.

Gelbart, M. 2011. "A cohesive shambles: The Clash's *London Calling* and the normalization of punk." *Music and Letters* 92(2): 230–272.

Gilbert, P. 2009. *Passion Is a Fashion: The Real Story of the Clash*. London: Aurum.

Gilroy, P. 2002. *There Ain't No Black in the Union Jack: The Cultural Politics of Race and Nation*. 2nd ed. London: Routledge.

Gimme Danger. 2017. Directed by J. Jarmusch. Dogwoof.

Glasper, I. 2014. *The Day the Country Died: A History of Anarcho Punk 1980-1984*. Oakland: PM Press.

Glass, P. G. 2012. "Doing scene: Identity, space and the interactional accomplishment of youth culture." *Journal of Contemporary Ethnography* 41(6): 695–716.

Goodyer, I. 2009. *Crisis Music: The Cultural Politics of Rock Against Racism*. Manchester: Manchester University Press.

Gordon, K. 2015. *Girl in a Band: A Memoir*. London: Faber.

Gosling, T. 2004. "'Not for sale': The underground network of anarcho-punk." In Bennett and Peterson 2004, 168–183.

Green, J. and Barker, G. 2000. *A Riot of Our Own: Night and Day with the Clash*. London: Phoenix.

Greene, S. 2012. "The problem of Peru's punk underground: An approach to under-fuck the system." *Journal of Popular Music Studies* 24(4): 578–589.

Guerra, P. 2014. "Punk, expectations, breaches and metamorphoses: Portugal, 1977–2012." *Critical Arts: A South-North Journal of Cultural & Media Studies* 28(1): 111–122.

Haenfler, R. 2006. *Straight Edge: Hardcore Punk, Clean-Living Youth, and Social Change*. New Brunswick, NJ: Rutgers University Press.

Hannerz, E. 2015. *Performing Punk*. New York: Palgrave Macmillan.

Hayton, J. 2017. "Crosstown traffic: Punk rock, space and the porosity of the Berlin Wall in the 1980s." *Contemporary European History* 26(2): 353–377.

Hebdige, D. 1979. *Subculture: The Meaning of Style*. London: Routledge.

Hesmondhalgh, D. 1997. "Post-punk's attempt to democratise the music industry: The success and failure of Rough Trade." *Popular Music* 16(3): 255–274.

Heylin, C. 1993. *From the Velvets to the Voidoids: A Pre-Punk History for the Post-Punk World*. London: Penguin.

Heylin, C. 2008. *Babylon's Burning: From Punk to Grunge*. London: Penguin.

Hill, A. 2002. "Acid House and Thatcherism: Noise, the mob, and the English countryside." *British Journal of Sociology* 53(1): 89–105.

Home, S. 1995. *Cranked Up Really High: Genre Theory and Punk Rock*. Hove, UK: Codex.

Huber, J. L. 2010. "Singing it out: Riot Grrrls, Lilith Fair, and feminism." *Kaleidoscope: A Graduate Journal of Qualitative Communication Research* 9(1): 65–85.

Hynde, C. 2016. *Reckless*. London: Ebury Press.

Idol, B. 2015. *Dancing with Myself*. New York: Simon & Schuster.

Ingham, J. 2017. *Spirit of '76: London Punk Eyewitness*. Brooklyn, NY: Anthology Editions.

Joynson, V. 2001. *Up Yours! A Guide to UK Punk, New Wave and Early Post Punk*. Wolverhampton, UK: Borderline Productions.

Kaltefleiter, C. K. 2016. "Start your own revolution: Agency and action of the Riot Grrrl network." *International Journal of Sociology & Social Policy* 36(11/12): 808–823.

Knight, M. M. 2007. *The Taqwacores*. London: Telegram Books.

Laing, D. 1985. *One Chord Wonders: Power and Meaning in Punk Rock*. Rev. ed. Oakland: PM Press, 2015.

Lens, J. and Friedman, G. 2008. *Punk Pioneers*. New York: Universe.

Letts, D. and Nobakht, D. 2007. *Culture Clash: Dread Meets Punk Rockers*. London: SAF Publishing.

Lloyd, R. 2017. *Everything Is Combustible: Television, CBGB's and Five Decades of Rock and Roll: The Memoirs of an Alchemical Guitarist*. Mount Desert, ME: Beech Hill.

Lull, J. 1982. "Popular music: Resistance to new wave." *Journal of Communication* 32(1): 121–131.

Malott, C. and Peña, M. 2004. *Punk Rockers' Revolution: A Pedagogy of Race, Class, and Gender*. New York: Peter Lang.

Mankowski, G. 2014. "Pop manifestos and nosebleed art rock: What have post-punk bands achieved?" *Punk & Post Punk* 3(2): 159–170.

Marcade, P. 2017. *Punk Avenue: Inside the New York City Underground, 1972–1982*. New York: Three Rooms.

Marcus, G. 1989. *Lipstick Traces: A Secret History of the Twentieth Century*. Cambridge: Secker & Warburg.

Marcus, G. 1999. *In the Fascist Bathroom: Punk in Pop Music, 1977–1992*. Cambridge, MA: Harvard University Press.

Marcus, S. 2010. *Girls to the Front: The True Story of the Riot Grrrl Revolution*. New York: Harper Perennial.

Marko, P. 2007. *The Roxy London WC2: A Punk History*. London: Punk 77 Books.

Marr, J. 2017. *Set the Boy Free: The Autobiography*. London: Arrow.

McKay, G. 1996. *Senseless Acts of Beauty: Cultures of Resistance since the Sixties*. London: Verso.

McKay, G., ed. 1998. *DIY Culture: Party and Protest in Nineties Britain*. London: Verso.

McKay, G. 1999. "'I'm so bored with the USA': The punk in cyberpunk." In Sabin 1999b, 49–67.

McKay, G. 2009. "'Crippled with nerves': Popular music and polio, with particular reference to Ian Dury." *Popular Music* 28(3): 341–366.

McKay, G. 2013. *Shakin' All Over: Popular Music and Disability*. Ann Arbor: University of Michigan Press.

McKay, G. 2015. "Punk rock and disability: Cripping subculture." In B. Howe, S. Jensen-Moulton, N. Lerner, and J. Straus, eds., *The Oxford Handbook of Music and Disability Studies*. Oxford: Oxford University Press, 226–243.

McKay, G. 2016. "Gee Vaucher's punk painting as record sleeves." In S. Shukaitis, ed. *Gee Vaucher: Introspective*. Colchester, UK: Firstsite/Minor Compositions, 66–78.

McNeil, L. and McCain, G. 2016. *Please Kill Me: The Uncensored Oral History of Punk*. New York: Grove.

Medhurst, A. 1999. "What did I get? Punk, memory and autobiography." In Sabin 1999b, 219–331.

Moore, R. 2004. "Postmodernism and punk subculture: Cultures of authenticity and deconstruction." *Communication Review* 7(1): 305–327.

Moore, S. 1999. "Is that all there is?" In Sabin 1999b, 232–236.

Murthy, D. 2010. "Muslim punks online: A diasporic Pakistani music subculture on the Internet." *South Asian Popular Culture* 8(2): 181–194.

Murthy, D. 2013. "'Muslim Punk' music online: Piety and protest in the digital age." In K. Salhi, ed. *Music, Culture and Identity in the Muslim World: Performance, Politics and Piety*. Abingdon, UK: Routledge, 162–179.

Nault, C. 2017. *Queercore: Queer Punk Media Subculture*. London: Routledge.

Nilan, P. 2017. *Muslim Youth in the Diaspora: Challenging Extremism through Popular Culture*. London: Routledge.

O'Brien, L. 1999. "The woman punk made me." In Sabin 1999b, 186–198.

O'Brien, L. 2002. *She Bop: The Definitive History of Women in Rock, Pop and Soul*. London: Continuum.

O'Connor, A. 2008. *Punk Record Labels and the Struggle for Autonomy: The Emergence of DIY*. Lanham, MD: Lexington Books.

Ogg, Alex. 2013. "For you, Tommy, the war is never over." *Punk and Post-Punk* 2(3): 281–304.

O'Hara, C. 1999. *The Philosophy of Punk: More Than Noise!!* 2nd. ed. Edinburgh: AK Press.

Osgerby, B. 1999. "Chewing out a rhythm on my bubble-gum: The teenage aesthetic and genealogies of American punk." In Sabin 1999b, 154–169.

Osgerby, W. 1998. *Youth in Britain: Since 1945*. Malden: Wiley.

Parkinson, T. 2017. "Being punk in higher education: Subcultural strategies for academic practice." *Teaching in Higher Education* 22(2): 143–157.

Perry, M. 2009. *Sniffin' Glue and Other Rock 'N' Roll Habits: The Essential Punk Accessory*. London: Omnibus.

Piepmeier, A. and Zeisler, A. 2009. *Girl Zines: Making Media, Doing Feminism*. New York: New York University Press.

du Plessis, M. and Chapman, K. 1997. "Queercore: The distinct identities of subculture." *College Literature*, 24(1): 45–58.

Prato, G. 2010. *Grunge Is Dead: The Oral History of Seattle Rock Music*. Toronto: ECW Press.

Rachel, Daniel. 2016. *Walls Come Tumbling Down: The Music and Politics of Rock Against Racism, 2 Tone and Red Wedge, 1976–1992*. London: Picador.

Ramírez-Sánchez, R. 2008. "Marginalization from within: Expanding co-cultural theory through the experience of the Afro Punk." *Howard Journal of Communications* 19(2): 89–104.

Rapport, E. 2014. "Hearing punk as blues." *Popular Music* 33(1): 39–67.

Reddington, H. 2012. *The Lost Women of Rock Music: Female Musicians of the Punk Era*. 2nd ed. Sheffield: Equinox.

Renton, David. 2019. *Never Again: Rock Against Racism and the Anti-Nazi League, 1976–1982*. Abingdon, UK: Routledge.

Reynolds, S. 2005. *Rip It Up and Start Again: Post-Punk 1978–84*. London: Penguin.

Rivett, M. 1999. "'Punk writing' and representations of punk through writing and publishing." In Sabin 1999b, 31–48.

Robb, J. 2006. *Punk Rock: An Oral History*. London: Ebury Press.

Sabin, R. 1999a. "I won't let that dago by: Rethinking punk and racism." In Sabin 1999b, 199–218.

Sabin, R., ed. 1999b. *Punk Rock: So What? The Cultural Legacy of Punk*. London: Routledge.

Savage, J. 1992. *England's Dreaming: Sex Pistols and Punk Rock*. London: Faber.

Schilt, K. 2014. "'The punk white privilege scene': Riot Grrrl, white privilege and zines." In J. Reger, ed. *Different Wavelengths: Studies of the Contemporary Women's Movement*. London: Routledge, 39–56.

Slits, The. 1979. "Instant Hit." On *Cut*. 12″ album. Island Records.

Slobin, M. 1993. *Subcultural Sounds: Micromusics of the West*. Hanover, NH: Wesleyan University Press.

Smith, M. E. 2009. *Renegade: The Lives and Tales of Mark E. Smith*. London: Penguin.

Smith, P. 2015. "Holidays in the sun: The Sex Pistols at the seaside." *Popular Music & Society* 38(4): 487–499.

Steinholt, Y. B. 2012. "Siberian punk shall emerge here: Egor Letov and Grazhdanskaia Oborona." *Popular Music* 31(3): 401–415.

Strong, C. 2011a. *Grunge: Music and Memory*. Farnham, UK: Ashgate.

Strong, C. 2011b. "Grunge, Riot Grrrl and the forgetting of women in popular culture." *Journal of Popular Culture*, 44(2): 398–416.

Taylor, J. 2012. *Playing It Queer: Popular Music, Identity and Queer World-Making*. New ed. Bern: Peter Lang.

Thornton, S. 1995. *Club Cultures: Music, Media and Subcultural Capital*. Cambridge: Polity.

Traber, D. S. 2001. "'White minority': Punk and the contradictions of self-marginalisation." *Cultural Critique* 48(1): 30–64.

Traber, D. S. 2007. *Whiteness, Otherness, and the Individualism Paradox from Huck to Punk*. New York: AIAA.

Trainer, A. 2016. "Perth punk and the construction of urbanity in a suburban city." *Popular Music* 35(1): 100–117.

Triggs, T. 2004. *"Generation Terrorists": The Politics and Graphic Language of Punk and Riot Grrrl Fanzines in Britain 1976-2000*. PhD diss., University of Reading.

Triggs, T. 2006. "Scissors and glue: Punk fanzines and the creation of a DIY aesthetic." *Journal of Design History* 19(1): 69.

Tuan, Y.-F. 1990. *Topophilia: A Study of Environmental Perceptions, Attitudes, and Values*. New York: Columbia University Press.

Turrini, J. 2013. "'Well I don't care about history': Oral history and the making of collective memory in punk rock." *Notes: Quarterly Journal of the Music Library Association* 70(1): 59–77.

Tyler, K. 2017. *Smashing It Up: A Decade of Chaos with the Damned*. London: Omnibus.

Waltz, M. and James, M. 2009. "The (re)marketing of disability in pop: Ian Curtis and Joy Division." *Popular Music* 28(3): 367–380.

Wiedlack, K. 2016. "Pussy Riot and the Western gaze: Punk music, solidarity and the production of similarity and difference." *Popular Music & Society* 39(4): 410–422.

Wilkinson, D. 2016. *Post-Punk, Politics and Pleasure in Britain*. Basingstoke, UK: Palgrave Macmillan.

Wilkinson, D., Worley, M., and Street, J. 2017. "'I wanna see some history': Recent writing on British punk." *Contemporary European History* 26(2): 397–411.

Willems, J. 2014. "Why 'punk'? Religion, anarchism and feminism in Pussy Riot's *Punk Prayer*." *Religion, State and Society* 42(4): 403–419.

Worley, M. 2013. "Oi! Oi! Oi! Class, locality, and British punk." *Twentieth Century British History* 24(4): 606–636.

Worley, M. 2017. *No Future: Punk, Politics and British Youth Culture, 1976–1984*. Cambridge: Cambridge University Press.

Yedgar, A. and Sladen, M. 2007. *Panic Attack! Art in the Punk Years*. London: Merrell.

Zeisler, A. 2017. *We Were Feminists Once: From Riot Grrrl to CoverGirl, the Buying and Selling of a Political Movement*. New York: Public Affairs.

PART ONE

RECONSIDERING PUNK ROCK

CHAPTER 2

THE PUNK WORLDS OF LIVERPOOL AND MANCHESTER, 1975–1980

NICK CROSSLEY

Accounts of the origins of UK punk invariably focus upon bands and events in London, particularly the early exploits of the Sex Pistols. This is understandable and faithful to the facts (Crossley 2015). However, punk did not remain concentrated in the capital for long (Crossley 2015; Glasper 2004). Bigger towns and cities across the UK quickly spawned their own local punk "worlds." Moreover, the politics and DIY ethos of punk became infused, in some cases, with a self-conscious regionalism and rejection of the dominance of London.

This was nowhere more evident than in Manchester, whose early response to developments in London allowed some of its bands, particularly Buzzcocks and Slaughter and the Dogs, to figure among the pioneering first-wave UK punk bands, alongside the Pistols, and whose participants often recount, with relish, the ways in which Manchester punk departed from that of London, at least as they see it. For example:

> You didn't need bondage trousers and spikey hair to be a Punk in Manchester, it was more a question of your attitude. Everybody got their clothes from the Salvation Army or antique clothing markets. Coming to London to see the Ramones in June I was astounded at how fashion oriented it was.
>
> (Malcolm Garrett, quoted in Savage 1991, 405)[1]

Likewise, many accounts of the city's most celebrated independent record label, Factory, observe that a key motivation for its formation was the desire to avoid kowtowing and indeed even traveling to London. Manchester was as good as anywhere, if not better, in the eyes of its punk "movers and shakers," and for them doing it yourself, whatever else it meant, meant not deferring to or being dependent upon London.

In this chapter I discuss the emergence and structure of Manchester's punk world, along with that of Liverpool. Rivalry between Liverpool and Manchester, the two biggest cities in the northwest of England, thirty-five miles apart and joined by the M62 motorway, is and was at least as intense as that between Manchester and London, fueled by the rivalry between their respective celebrated football teams. In relation to punk and its development, however, we find considerable cooperation between movers and shakers in the two cities and a regular to and fro of traveling artists and audience members. The love of punk trumped intercity rivalry for the most part, and the two local punk worlds evolved in symbiosis, distinct but connected and concatenating to form the core of a bigger, regional (Northwest) punk world.

The largest part of the chapter is divided between a historical reconstruction, which tracks the movement of punk from London to Manchester and Liverpool, discussing early developments, protagonists, and institutions in the two cities, and a brief dissection, drawing upon the techniques of social network analysis (SNA), of the networks constitutive in some part of these two seminal UK punk worlds and, to a lesser extent, connecting them to one another (for an introduction to SNA, see Borgatti et al. 2012; Scott 2000; Wasserman and Faust 1994). Before I begin, however, it is necessary to briefly define and discuss some of the key concepts that I draw upon, and to explain the significance that I attach to networks.

Punk?

Tracking the development of punk within and across two cities inevitably begs the question of what is being tracked. What was and is punk? This question has two parts. There is the matter of how punk should be demarcated from other, similar "things"; whether, for example, this or that band should be regarded as punk? In addition, however, there is the issue of the kind of "thing" punk was and is. Is punk, following Hebdige (1988), a "subculture"? Is it, following Straw (1991), a "scene"? Or is it something else? And what do we mean by "subculture," "scene," etc.? These are not trivial questions, because we cannot trace or explain the development of punk if we do not know what we are tracing the development of and what we should be looking for as signs of its development.

The proper sociological response to the demarcation question is to defer to participants in the situation under study, accepting, where they disagree, that the boundaries of punk were and are fuzzy and contested. It is not for the sociologist to arbitrate between competing definitions of "punk," not least because those definitions and applications are part of the very "stuff" of which punk is composed. The existence of punk depends, among other things, upon processes of labeling and boundary construction on behalf of interested parties. Debate and disagreement about what punk is, at least from a sociological perspective, is part of what punk is, and should be regarded as such rather than foreclosed with what would inevitably be just one more definition for insiders to dispute. If punk has no neat boundary, which certainly was the case back in the late 1970s, and probably still is, than we must approach and analyze it as such.

It is sometimes claimed that the punk label in Britain was coined by Caroline Coon in an article published in the weekly music magazine *Melody Maker* in August 1976. In this article Coon profiled two Manchester bands, Buzzcocks and Slaughter and the Dogs, alongside the Sex Pistols, as well as several other London and some US bands (Coon 1976). In fact, the label was used earlier, in the *New Musical Express* (*NME*) in February 1976, in a review of a Sex Pistols gig by Neil Spencer, to which I will return (Spencer 1976). As is evident in his review, Spencer borrowed the term from the United States, where a number of artists were being categorized as "punk" and where a related zine titled *Punk* had been launched in 1975. More important than the origin of the term for present purposes, however, is the fact that Coon both attached the label to a cluster of British bands and put it into circulation within UK rock music circles, where it was appropriated by other journalists and quickly—following further publicity, not least the Bill Grundy incident[2]—entered general usage, allowing many thousands of young people, excited by the songs, bands, and characters with whom it was associated, to embrace it as an identity.

Punk Worlds

The punk label gave a groundswell of previously unnamed activity a symbolic existence, and its appropriation and subsequent use by both insiders and outsiders played a key role in the processes of boundary construction and identification which maintained that symbolic existence. However, punk was more than a label. It had a social as well as symbolic existence. This brings us to the second of the two questions above, regarding the type of "thing" that punk was and is. In previous work, building upon the work of Becker (1982) and others influenced by him (Finnegan 1989; Gilmore 1987, 1988; Martin 2005, 2006), and arguing against prevailing conceptions of "subculture" and "scene," I have formulated a concept of "music worlds," taking the early UK punk world as a principal example of what I mean by this (Crossley 2015). This is not the place to reiterate this discussion, but a few words on the "world" concept are necessary.

"Art" is sometimes equated with objects, such as paintings, musical scores, and (stretching the definition of "object") performances. However, Becker (1974, 1982) insists that these objects only take on and retain the status of "art" in virtue of ongoing human interactions within and between (often intersecting) sets of artists, audience members, and what he calls "support personnel," meaning promoters, producers, engineers, critics, journalists, archivists, and the many others who mediate between artists and audiences and more generally enable what those involved regard as "art" to happen. Objects are cocreated and iteratively constituted and reconstituted as art within social interaction. Art is collective action, for Becker, and an art (and by extension music) world encompasses all participants to this action, including artists, audiences, and support personnel, alongside the aforementioned objects; the places and events where art is done; corporate actors[3], such as record labels; and all of the many and various relationships between these elements. It is, to invoke a concept I return to, a network.

Contemporary music worlds have local, translocal and/or virtual dimensions (Emms and Crossley 2018). The Liverpool and Manchester punk worlds were each local, for example, but contact between them combined them within a translocal world. Indeed, both were important nodes in a wider translocal network of punk worlds in the UK during the late 1970s. The UK punk world comprised multiple local networks, each with its own cluster of bands, zines, labels, and venues, but each of these local networks was connected to certain others by flows of, among other things, traveling bands and audiences, records, tapes, and zines. Moreover, local networks were further connected by their common ties to key movers and shakers at the national level, including journalists on the weekly music press; entrepreneurs such as Geoff Travis, at Rough Trade, who forged distribution channels for punk's cottage industry of small independent record labels; and Radio One DJ John Peel, whose show, which was a key focus for punks across the country, championed many of these independent releases. The "virtual" aspect common to music worlds today was not possible at the birth of punk, of course. The Internet hadn't been invented. However, the flow of zines and both official and unofficial recordings through a human network played much the same role. Word got around, as did sounds and images, linking those attracted to and involved with them.

Defined thus, music worlds are always in-process. They are continually made and remade in the interactions of their participants. However, process does not preclude structure. A music world is a structure-in-process. Its structure has three dimensions.

Firstly, behaviors that are initially the outcome of contingencies, and are in that respect arbitrary, become settled conventions that shape interaction. Conventions play a crucial role in music worlds because they resolve "coordination problems" (Lewis 1969). By orienting to conventions, participants minimize uncertainty about what they are doing and reduce the need for lengthy and complex negotiation with collaborators. They do things "the way things are done" without further thought. Conventions run deep in music—"all the way down," according to McClary (2001)—and some, including those concerning tonal distances and scales, are shared across many music worlds. Others, however, concerning matters of dance, dress, audience appreciation, and musical style, are specific to particular music worlds and help to lend those worlds a distinct identity. Bands are candidates for the punk label, in some part, for example, on account of conventions they and their audiences variously adhere to and reject.

Secondly, "musicking," to borrow Small's (1998) term, typically draws upon and involves the pooling and exchange of a range of different resources, from skills (e.g., playing an instrument, operating a mixing desk, booking bands), through equipment and space (for rehearsal, recording, and performance), to money. And, importantly, the distribution of such resources is usually largely unvarying in the short term. As such, music worlds manifest a relatively stable division of labor and often center upon key resource holders. In the Liverpool and Manchester punk worlds, for example, we find entrepreneurs with resources they are prepared to invest in bands, whose investment was crucial, and who were constant and central figures in their respective worlds throughout the late 1970s and early 1980s.

Tony Wilson was perhaps the best known of Manchester's punk entrepreneurs, but there were others, including T. J. Davidson, whose rehearsal rooms (immortalized in Joy Division's video for "Love Will Tear Us Apart") were used by most of the better-known punk and post-punk bands at one time or another, and whose label released some of the work of Mick Hucknall's early band, the Frantic Elevators. In Liverpool, Roger Eagle and Ken Testi, who owned the city's key punk venue, Eric's (Testi also managed the band Deaf School), and Geoff Davies, who owned Probe, a record shop and label that became a hub in the Cartel distribution network,[4] were key movers and shakers, as were Bill Drummond and Dave Balfe, who founded Zoo Records and managed several key bands, as well as playing in bands themselves.

Thirdly, interaction between participants in a music world both draws upon and (re)generates a network, and this network has a structure. I want to very briefly elaborate upon this third aspect of structure before turning more squarely to Liverpool and Manchester.

Worlds as Networks

I have suggested in previous work that networks are an important element in the story of early UK punk (Crossley 2015). The formation of a punk world requires a "critical mass" of would-be participants—big enough to form the multiple bands, labels, zines, and so on necessary for a flourishing world; to make gigs and other events economically viable; and more generally to pool the resources necessary for the collective actions involved. Mass itself is not enough, however. Collective action entails that members of that mass combine and connect in a network.

Networks have no inevitable effects. Their structural properties vary, with differing consequences, and their impact is always mediated by context and the agency of those involved in them. However, compact and cohesive networks typically facilitate communication and thereby coordination of activities. Participants are in receipt of the same information and directions and are therefore "on the same page." They enable pooling and exchange of resources, allowing participants to find collaborators and thereby form bands, zines, labels, and so on. Moreover, cohesive networks often generate "social capital," in Coleman's (1990) sense; that is, norms of cooperation, mutual support, and trust that constrain network members but equally thereby enable forms of individual and collective action not otherwise possible. Finally, they often encourage competition between individuals whose awareness of the success of others both galvanizes their own efforts and encourages them to push at boundaries, in both cases vitalizing their music world. All of these effects were important in early UK punk (Crossley 2015).

How do such networks form? In a classic paper, Feld (1981) observes that individuals with similar tastes and interests are typically drawn, in virtue of their tastes and interests, to the same places and events ("foci"), increasing the likelihood that they will meet and form ties. The punks in any given town have an increased likelihood of knowing one another, for example, because they will tend to converge upon the same gigs, pubs, and record shops. Focal places and events generate networks by drawing likeminded individuals into proximity. And the effect is reciprocated. Places and events become focal in a music world in virtue of the reputation they enjoy within a network and the flow of gossip and information about them passing through the network. Networks and foci coevolve. But how did they do so in Manchester and Liverpool?

A Dispatch from the Capital and a Gig That Changed the World

On February 21, 1976, the *NME* published a gig review by Neil Spencer. The gig had taken place at London's Marquee on the 12th and the headline act had been the rising pub rockers Eddie and the Hot Rods. The review didn't mention them, however. It was entirely focused upon their support act. Headlined, "Don't Look Over Your Shoulder, but the Sex Pistols Are Coming," and accompanied by a picture of a short-haired singer with a confrontational stare, it described a shambolic but exciting performance by a band who were quoted claiming, "[W]e're not into music.... We're into chaos." Helping readers to place them, the article cited several bands whose songs the Pistols covered, including, importantly, the Stooges.

This was not the Pistols' first gig review. They had been dismissed in derisory terms in an earlier *NME* review of a performance at Queen Elizabeth College (London) on December 7, 1975 (Phillips 1975). The Pistols were largely unheard of outside of a very small London-based network before Spencer's review, however, and the significance of the review is that it caught the eye of readers outside of the capital who were bored with the UK's musical mainstream, looking for alternatives, and drawn for this reason to bands such as the Stooges. Spencer's review was a sign to these readers that something interesting was stirring.

In Devon, in southwestern England, the article contributed to the decision of Stooges fans Timothy Smith and Gaye Black to move to London. They became TV Smith and Gaye Advert, forming one of first-wave punk's best loved bands: the Adverts. Our concern here, however, is with the Northwest, and more particularly two students at Bolton College of Technology, a small college in a small town ten miles northwest of Manchester. Having, by chance, access to a car for the weekend, Peter McNeish and Howard Trafford decided to venture down south in search of the Sex Pistols, phoning the *NME* office in advance for help and staying with McNeish's friend Richard Boon. Pacing the King's Road they found SEX, the shop the Sex Pistols manager, Malcolm

McLaren, co-owned with Vivien Westwood. He was in and, luckily for them, the Pistols were playing two gigs that weekend. McNeish and Trafford attended both, were blown away by the experience, negotiated with McLaren for the Pistols to make a trip up north, and stepped up their ongoing efforts to form a band (which to that point had been modeled on the Velvet Underground and related US artists, including the Stooges).

The original plan was for the Pistols to play Bolton College, but a disastrous gig by McNeish and Trafford's own band on April 1 dissuaded the Student Union. It also convinced McNeish and Trafford that their own band was not ready to support the Pistols for the latter's first Northwest gig, which took place on June 4, relocated to the Lesser Free Trade Hall in central Manchester. An entire book, *The Gig That Changed the World*, is devoted to this event (Nolan 2006); *NME* voted it number one in their "100 Gigs You Should Have Been At" as recently as 2012 (see cover story, March 12), and it is widely joked that if everybody who claims to have been there actually was the audience would have filled Maine Road, the Manchester City football stadium. In fact, only twenty-eight tickets were sold in advance (Nolan 2007), and it is widely agreed that there were no more than sixty people present. It is also agreed, however, that many of the key figures in what in a short space of time would become Manchester's own thriving punk world were there, having had their interest aroused by Spencer's article. Peter Hook and Bernard Sumner (Joy Division) were there. Formative members of the Fall were there:

> We'd heard about them already through the music press, just as a group that did Stooges' cover versions. There was a photo of a guy with short hair and I was wondering what these "skinheads" were doing covering Stooges' songs, I wasn't really into the idea. I went along thinking I could heckle or something but I was really bowled over. I got my hair cut soon after, I could see that something was happening.
>
> (Martin Bramah, cited in Ford 2003, 16)

And so was the chair of the UK's New York Dolls fan club, Stephen Morrissey, in attendance on account of the association between the Pistols and the Dolls (McLaren had briefly worked with the Dolls in late 1975).

If attendance was small at the June 4 gig, the excitement and enthusiasm it created spread rapidly through attendees' personal networks, leading to an exponential increase for the three further gigs that the Pistols played in Manchester during 1976:

> I've no idea of the time difference between the first and the second show but I just get the feeling that we'd all run around and said "You've got to come, you've got to come..."
>
> (Paul Morley, cited in Nolan 2006, 72)

> I was evangelical about it, honestly. I told everybody about that band, everybody I encountered, about the Sex Pistols.
>
> (Ian Moss, cited in Nolan 2006, 72)

> Maybe it's only in a small city that you can have that kind of communication, that can take you from thirty-five people on June 4th to several hundred on July 20th. The word goes out, the word spreads.
>
> (Tony Wilson, cited in Nolan 2006, 71)

Punk, as Spencer had called it in his review, had acquired an audience in Manchester, and not only an audience. The Pistols inspired some among their audience to form bands, others to hurry along with the bands they were already in the process of forming, and some existing bands, including local glam rockers Slaughter and the Dogs, and their friends, Wild Ram (quickly renamed Ed Banger and the Nosebleeds), to punk up. Slaughter's singer, Wayne Barrett, already had green hair!

McNeish and Trafford, having changed their names to (Pete) Shelley and (Howard) Devoto, were ready to support the Pistols, alongside Slaughter and the Dogs, when the Londoners returned to the Free Trade Hall for their second Manchester gig on July 20. Their band, Buzzcocks, would become key figures in the vanguard of first-wave punk, releasing what many regard as the first DIY punk record, *Spiral Scratch*, on New Hormones, a label they formed with Richard Boon (who also managed Buzzcocks and promoted a variety of punk events around the city). The EP inspired many hundreds of punk bands across the country to follow suit.

Meanwhile, Peter Hook had bought a bass guitar the day after the June 4 gig, and he and Bernard Sumner began rehearsing the band that would become Warsaw, then Joy Division, and finally New Order. The Fall, too, whose members had been experimenting with performance poetry prior to punk, turned to music. And the trickle quickly became a flood, involving such bands and artists such as John Cooper Clarke, V2, the Worst, the Frantic Elevators, and the legendary (at least within Manchester) John the Postman—a Royal Mail employee whose drunken decision to storm the stage one night before a Buzzcocks performance, offering an a capella rendition of "Louie Louie," was to become a regular ritual, often included on the bill.

In addition, the collective effervescence triggered by the early Pistols gigs gave rise to zines (e.g., *Shy Talk* and *City Fun*), labels (e.g., Factory, Rabid, and TJM), and a number of focal punk venues and spaces. Like the inner circle of the London punk world, who congregated at Louise's, a lesbian bar in Soho, many of Manchester's pioneering punks took refuge in the more open-minded environment of a local gay bar, the Ranch. More important still, at least in the early days, however, was the Electric Circus.

A dilapidated heavy metal venue in the Collyhurst area of Manchester, the Electric Circus hosted the Pistols when they visited the city for the fated Anarchy tour of December 1976. Many venues pulled out of the tour following the Pistols' interview with Bill Grundy on December 1, 1976, and the moral panic that followed in its wake. The owners of the Electric Circus took a different view, however. Realizing that the kerfuffle, which included a ban on the Pistols at both the Free Trade Hall and Manchester's Palace Theatre, was bringing the band to the attention of every teenager in the land, and that every expression of moral outrage by parents and other authority figures was equivalent to a five-star review in the *NME*, they picked up some of the slack caused by gig cancellations, offering the Pistols two dates and advertising these shows under the banner "Banned from the Palace, Banned from the Free Trade Hall." The venue was closed in late 1977, on health and safety grounds, but the two Anarchy gigs in December 1976 established it as *the* punk venue in Manchester throughout 1977.

And not only Manchester. Neil Spencer's review, alongside Caroline Coon's aforementioned article and the moral panic following the Grundy interview, brought punk before the entire nation, exciting interest and provoking activity in all corners of the island (and over the water in Northern Ireland), but McNeish and Trafford's entrepreneurial efforts had given Manchester a head start in forming its own punk world. Along with the foresight of its owners in the face of punk's widespread condemnation, this gave the Electric Circus a head start in becoming a key venue for punk across the whole of northern England. A number of Liverpool's early punk pioneers, for example, have recounted their trips to the Electric Circus in the early days of punk, prefiguring a pattern of music-related travel between the two cities that would continue throughout the punk and post-punk eras.

Liverpool, too, was to acquire a focal venue fairly early in the history of UK punk, however, when Eric's, which opened in October 1976, hosting a wide range of musical styles, acquired a reputation within the city's emerging network of punks during 1977 and became a "go to venue," alongside the Electric Circus, for touring punk bands. Indeed, Eric's was arguably more widely celebrated than the Electric Circus nationally, and it had the advantage of being situated within what was effectively a wider bohemian enclave, alongside Probe (record shop) and the Liverpool School of Language, Music, Dream and Pun: a converted warehouse that provided a rehearsal space for musicians, a performance space for experimental theater, and an indoor bazaar (Aunt Twackies) whose stalls included O'Halligan's Tea Rooms, where local punks met to chew the fat, and a clothing stall run by Jayne Casey, who would front the most famous of Liverpool's early punk bands, Big in Japan.

This bohemian enclave preexisted punk's uptake in Liverpool, primarily servicing students from the Liverpool College of Art (Strachan 2010). However, some of its features, pre-1977, might qualify as proto-punk experimentation, and its main resident band, Deaf School, who were comparable to the more arty bands on London's pub rock circuit, such as Ian Dury's Kilburn and the High Roads, played a bit part in the London punk story. It was at a Deaf School gig at the Nashville (London) on August 2, 1975, that Mick Jones (later of the Clash) and Tony James (later of Chelsea and Generation X), who were at that time putting together their proto-punk band London SS, met Bernard Rhodes (who managed them and later, more famously, managed the Clash). It was only in the course of 1977, however, that this enclave took on a recognizably punky aspect.

The Sex Pistols first played in Liverpool, at Eric's, in October 1976. There does not appear to have been a "Free Trade Hall moment," however, and a projected second appearance for the Anarchy tour, at the Liverpool Stadium, was canceled, like many of the others. If there was a Free Trade Hall moment in Liverpool it was May 5, 1977, when the Clash first played Eric's. Aside from the performance itself, two events of considerable significance occurred in that space on that night. First, a number of

Eric's regulars decided to form a band. Big in Japan were always more infamous than famous—catalysts who provoked others into action rather than well-loved locals. Indeed, Julian Cope and others ran a campaign, with a petition in Probe, calling for them to be disbanded (the members of Big in Japan all signed). Along with the Spitfire Boys and the Accelerators, however, Big in Japan were the best known of Liverpool's early punk bands, and the band's members, individually and in various combinations, were to have a huge influence on the city's music throughout the post-punk and into the dance music eras.

The second momentous event occasioned by the Clash's appearance at Eric's was the meeting of Ian McCulloch (later of Echo and the Bunnymen), Pete Wylie (later of Wah!), and Julian Cope (later of the Teardrop Explodes), who would team up in a pre-fame supergroup, the Crucial Three. In itself the Crucial Three was a relatively unremarkable band. However, in pulling the eponymous three together and kick-starting their musical careers, it was hugely significant for Liverpool's local music world.

In addition, it illustrates a phenomenon that I noted on several occasions in my research into early UK punk: bands that achieve little in and of themselves, whose chemistry is not right, but that serve as a vehicle for launching important musical careers and help to establish a local sound by facilitating mutual influence between members who move on to more successful ventures. Big in Japan are another example of this. Indeed, bands and their membership were often short-lived and fluid in Liverpool. The constant factor wasn't this or that band, but rather a relatively stable population of musicians hooking up in different combinations: a musical network.

The Crucial Three and the later bands and projects of its members are probably better considered post-punk than punk, but that in itself is revealing of the punk story in northwestern England. Punk bands continued to form and flourish in Liverpool, Manchester, and their environs through the eighties and nineties, right up to the present day, where they still form and flourish (Watson 2019). However, many of those inspired early on by punk quickly tired of what they perceived to be its formula and the direction it was taking; choosing to use the opportunities it presented, the infrastructure and resources its collective effervescence had created, in the form of zines, venues, labels, and networks of audiences and artists, to do something different. As Julian Cope says of Liverpool:

> [T]he punk thing had this kind of built-in obsolescence. When I first got into the idea, in November 1976, I thought I was way too late. But new people were finding the scene all the time. Now we figured punk would be over in a couple of months. We wanted something new.
>
> (Cope 1994, 43)

Likewise, Linder Sterling (singer with Ludus and a visual artist responsible for many early Buzzcocks and Magazine record sleeves) on Manchester:

> The original punk thing ran out very quickly ... in its initial purity punk was probably just six months or so. ... with Howard [Devoto] being so articulate it happened early—this sense of 'It's not right, it's not right.'
>
> (quoted in Reynolds 2009, 219)

Indeed, Peter Saville, who was largely responsible for Factory's visual identity, including the celebrated sleeve designs of the best-known Joy Division records, claims that a corner had already been turned by the time of a farewell gig thrown for the Electric Circus in late 1977. Devoto, who had left Buzzcocks after *Spiral Scratch*, was premiering his new band, Magazine, and Saville, to his delight, could sense a change of direction:

> That night showed the way forward. ... There was a sense of shock, and then relief that some of the pre-punk strands some of us actually still liked—glam, avant-garde electronics, canonical quotation—were okay again.
>
> (quoted in Nice 2010, 20)

Back to Networks

The history of music worlds, such as the punk worlds of Liverpool and Manchester, is punctuated and to some extent driven by events: gigs, record releases, bands forming and splitting, venues opening and closing, and so on. However, these events are enabled by the existence of social networks connecting their protagonists—networks that these events simultaneously reproduce and transform. A music world exists because, and to the extent that, the critical mass of participants necessary for it are connected: communicating, coordinating, cooperating, and competing. In what follows I will reflect briefly upon the structure of this (always evolving) network in the Manchester and Liverpool cases.

In Figures 2.1 and 2.2 I visualize[5] the networks of the Manchester and Liverpool punk/post-punk worlds, respectively, for the period 1975–1980. Each node represents a key participant in the music world under consideration, as identified by me from available archives and secondary sources. The presence of a connecting line between two nodes indicates that those two participants collaborated on a music-related project during the stipulated period. Nodes are, in many cases, musicians, and collaboration between them often means playing in the same band. However, support personnel, such as managers, promoters, and sound engineers, played a crucial role in these music worlds, and they too are included in the network, linked to others in virtue of the various supporting roles they played in the organization of gigs or release of records. The artist/support role distinction is not straightforward because many of the most active participants in a music world play multiple roles, including both artist and support roles. And of course many

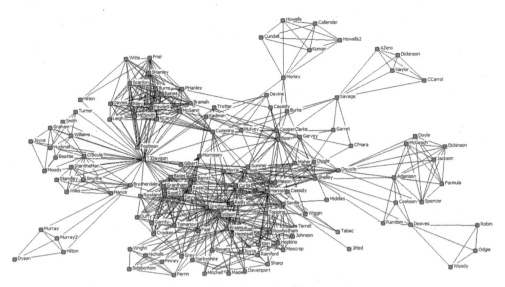

FIGURE 2.1. The Manchester Punk and Post-Punk World, 1975–1980.

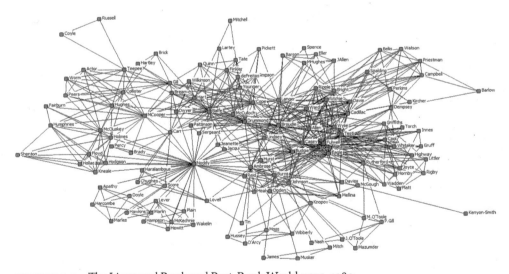

FIGURE 2.2. The Liverpool Punk and Post-Punk World, 1975–1980.

people offer one another piecemeal support when the occasion calls for it. However, focusing upon those who played a significant and named support role (irrespective of other roles they may have played), I was able to identify fourteen support personnel in Manchester and nine in Liverpool.

If the data had been available, I would also have included audience members. Audiences play a crucial role in music worlds, and there is no music world without an audience. However, it is much more difficult to obtain data regarding audiences, particularly in the historical case, and I was not able to do so. That said, artists and support personnel formed a significant chunk of the regular audience crowd.

The visualizations each compress five years into a single snapshot. For some purposes this would be problematic, and it is important to bear in mind that networks are always in-process. However, given that turnover does not appear to have been too great, they are useful. In what follows I offer a brief description of some of the key structural features of these two networks. They are surprisingly similar.

Each network has a similar number of nodes (Manchester = 129, Liverpool = 131). This was not intentional on my part. In each case I trawled the available archives in search of every key participant I could identify and only later discovered that there were almost exactly the same number in each case. Furthermore, they have an identical density when rounded to two decimal places. "Density" is the number of connections in the network (or between a subset of nodes) expressed as a proportion of the number there would be if every node was connected to each of the others. In the Liverpool network, for example, there are 131 nodes. If each one of them was connected to all of the rest that would add up to $\frac{131*130}{2} = 8,515$ connections. In fact, however, we observe 681 connections, giving a density of $\frac{681}{8,515} = 0.08$. Although the numbers of participants and ties for Manchester is slightly different, the density, as noted, is the same. Why it is the same is a question I cannot consider here, but it is interesting and suggests that musicking perhaps constrains density in some way.

Density, or rather high density, is often taken as a sign of the cohesion which, in turn, can engender the social capital referred to above. A density of 0.08, though we lack reliable benchmarks, seems relatively low and might suggest lack of cohesion. The density of the network as a whole is only one measure of cohesion, however, and can for various reasons be misleading. Other measures point to much greater cohesion in each of the two networks. Each participant in the Manchester network is connected, on average, to 10.85 others, for example, and the figure (technically "average degree") is 9.82 for Liverpool. Furthermore, the average density for these personal networks (technically, the "clustering coefficient") is 0.79 in each case. In other words each participant is, on average, connected to ten others, and in each case most of those ten (79 percent) are connected to one another. This *is* conducive to the development of social capital.

Note also that each network forms a single "component"; that is, every node in each of the two networks is at least indirectly linked to every other node in their network by a "path" comprising other nodes and the connections between them. This is important because it suggests that resources, including information and gossip passing through the network, can reach everybody. Moreover, the average path length connecting pairs of ties (measured in numbers of relations involved ("degrees") is 2.75 for Manchester and 2.62 for Liverpool. This means that such goods do not have far to travel and can therefore traverse the network quickly and with minimal degradation. Both networks are compact.

Not everybody is equal within the network, however. According to several of the different measures of centrality afforded by SNA, for example, some nodes are more central than others. Interestingly, the most central are often support personnel. I found those who play a major support role to be significantly more central in the network, statistically and again by a number of different measures, than those who do not (Crossley 2015). This is not surprising, but it is important. Support personnel are central in music worlds because there are relatively few of them; they own and control scarce and sought after resources, including skills, equipment, and often money; and artists, who are more numerous in the network, therefore have an incentive to seek them out and connect to them.

Beyond individual differences in centrality, moreover, we find a core-periphery structure in each of the networks.[6] That is, each contains a subset of nodes (the core) who are particularly densely connected to one another by comparison with the rest (the periphery). In a classic core-periphery structure, such as we find in each of our cases, the density between core and periphery, while much lower than that within the core, is higher than that within the periphery, indicating that, while the core form a cohesive subgrouping, the periphery do not. In the Manchester network, whose core-periphery structure is visualized in Figure 2.3, the core comprises 22 percent of nodes and has a density of 0.5, compared to 0.06 in the periphery and 0.7 between core and periphery. In Liverpool the core involves 28 percent of nodes with a density of 0.52, compared to 0.04 for the periphery and 0.08 for core-periphery relations.

The significance of core-periphery divides is context-specific, but in these cases, I suggest, it points to the existence of an elite "in-crowd" within each punk world. This

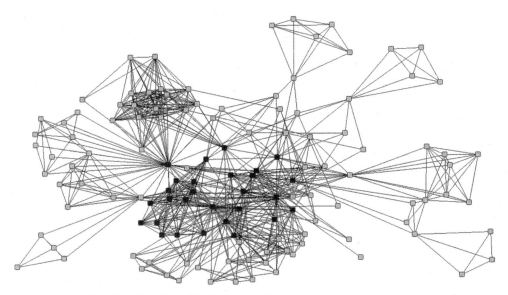

FIGURE 2.3. The Core-Periphery Divide in Manchester.

(core nodes are shaded in black)

interpretation is supported by the archives and secondary literature, where references to in-crowds abound. I cannot be sure that the cores I have identified correspond to the in-crowds referred to in firsthand accounts, but the general sense that there was an in-crowd in each case suggests that this may be what I am detecting. There was a hierarchical divide in each world between a core "in-group" and more marginal participants on its periphery.

A Tale of Two Cities

There is much more that could be done to analyze the two networks, and indeed to analyze the punk worlds of Liverpool and Manchester more generally (Crossley 2015). I will turn now, however, to relations between the two cities. They exist on a number of levels. Firstly, the archives indicate that audiences in each of the two cities traveled to see bands in the other and, as a consequence, became friends. Julian Cope, Ian McCulloch, and Dave Pickett (Liverpool) were huge fans of (Manchester's) the Fall, for example, with Cope claiming that they saw the band twenty-eight times in 1978. This inevitably resulted in friendships both with the band and with the Mancunian audience. Fall singer Mark E. Smith recalls this period:

> We used to have a right laugh.... Mac [McCulloch] used to write songs like, "You Don't Notice Time on the New Bury Road." I went up to stay at Mac's in Liverpool once and their idea of fun was him and Cope and about ten other guys walking around looking like David Bowie, talking about records, in the pouring rain.
> (quoted in Fletcher 1987, 17)

As does John the Postman:

> There was a lot of cross-fertilisation between the Liverpool and Manchester scenes.... I knew Julian Cope, Wylie, Ian McCulloch. They used to go and see the Fall; they were big Fall fans.
> (quoted in Haslam 2000, 135)

In addition, as noted, Liverpool punks often traveled to the Electric Circus during 1977 because it tended to attract most of the punk acts. And moving in the other direction, Paul Morley (2008) recalls running buses from Manchester to Liverpool so that Mancunian punks could see bands at Eric's.

These relations were further consolidated by relations between entrepreneurs in the two cities. Eric's co-owner, Roger Eagle, for example, was originally from Manchester, where he had run the Twisted Wheel, a well-known club in the northern soul world, and he retained contacts in Manchester, not least with Tony Wilson and T. J. Davidson. When Wilson, along with Alan Erasmus and Peter Saville, sought to plug the gap created by the closing of the Electric Circus with a new club, the Factory, he consulted Eagle to learn about what might be involved. Moreover, their friendship facilitated a pairing of Eric's and the Factory; bands would sometimes be booked to play both clubs over consecutive nights. And Wilson's television show, *So It Goes*, which afforded many punk bands (including the Sex Pistols) their first television appearance, was recorded at Eric's on a number of occasions. Wilson was an infamously proud Mancunian, to the point of belligerence, and as with many Mancunians this involved a sense of rivalry with Liverpool, but in his case this was playful and tempered with a love of his Northwest neighbors.

These business links allowed for some mobility of bands. Liverpool's Orchestral Manoeuvres in the Dark recorded their first single, "Electricity," on (Manchester's) Factory records, at Wilson's instigation and following an introduction by Eagle, for example. Conversely, T. J. Davidson was able to put (Manchester's) Mick Hucknall in contact with (Liverpool's) Roger Eagle, who subsequently briefly managed Hucknall's band, the Frantic Elevators, and made Hucknall a regular DJ at Eric's. As Hucknall has recalled:

> [W]e spent a lot of time rehearsing in that Mathew Street part of [Liverpool] . . . then I'd stay on and DJ in the evenings. . . . There was a whole scene around Probe Records; everyone knew everyone. I was pleased to be in Liverpool. . . . We got to know a lot of the Liverpool bands.
>
> (quoted in Strachan 2010, 139)

It is difficult to resist the speculation, given Eagle's aforementioned importance in the northern soul world, that this relationship played a part in influencing Hucknall's later work with Simply Red. Whether or not this is so, however, the more general point is that the Liverpool and Manchester worlds were connected and there was movement and influence between them. The two local worlds were bridged, forming a translocal world.

Conclusion

Having originally formed within a small network in London, punk sparked the formation of a network of further local worlds across the UK, including some that proved very influential. Each of these worlds itself comprised a network of participants whose contribution as artists, audience members, and in a variety of support roles generated punk music and culture at a local level. Such worlds are always evolving, but they comprise relatively enduring (social) structures. They are structures-in-process. In this chapter I have offered a brief account of Liverpool and Manchester worlds, paying particular attention to their network structure.

Punk generated networks because it brought those excited and animated by it together, encouraging the formation of bonds. As collective action, however, it equally depended upon networks, with the communication, coordination, cooperation, and competition they enable and encourage. Liverpool and Manchester each had their own network, but they too were networked, in a translocal punk world, and of course they were only two of many nodes in the much wider, translocal network that was UK punk.

Collective action implies collaboration but not necessarily equality. Examining the network structures of Liverpool and Manchester we find evidence of structural cohesion and compactness, which is conducive to coordination and the generation of social capital, but also evidence of core-periphery divides, pointing to the existence of in-groups, which are also alluded to in the archives. Importantly, moreover, we find that "support personnel" were particularly central to these networks, a skew attributable to their ownership and control of resources essential for successful music-making.

Notes

1. In fact, photographs from the time suggest that Manchester had its fair share of spikey-haired, bondage-trousered punks, too.
2. On December 1, 1976, the Sex Pistols were interviewed on a London-area teatime television show. Their interviewer, Bill Grundy, encouraged them to "say something shocking," which they duly did, prompting outrage in the national press and a moral panic about punk.
3. A corporate actor is an organization staffed by human beings, but whose decisions, actions, and often resources are irreducible to the mere aggregation of those individuals (see Hindess 1988).
4. An important network for distributing independent record releases during the early 1980s.
5. I have performed all network visualizations and measurements in this paper using UCINET and related Netdraw software (Borgatti et al. 2002).
6. There are several ways of testing for and finding core-periphery structures. For present purposes I used the categorical optimizing algorithm available in the UCINET software package.

References

Becker, H. 1974. "Art as Collective Action." *American Sociological Review* 39, no. 6: 767–776.
Becker, H. 1982. *Art Worlds*. Berkeley: University of California Press.
Borgatti, S., M. Everett, and L. Freeman. 2002. *UCINET for Windows: Software for Social Network Analysis*. Cambridge, MA: Analytic Technologies.
Borgatti, S. P., M. G. Everett, and J. Johnson. 2012. *Analysing Social Networks*. London: SAGE.
Coleman, J. 1990. *Foundations of Social Theory*. Cambridge, MA: Belknap Press.
Coon, C. 1976. "Punk Rock: Rebels against the System." *Melody Maker*, August 7, 1976, 24–25.
Cope, J. 1994. *Head-On/Repossessed*. London: Element.
Crossley, N. 2015. *Networks of Sound, Style and Subversion: The Punk and Post-Punks Musical Worlds of Manchester, London, Liverpool and Sheffield 1976–1980*. Manchester, UK: Manchester University Press.
Emms, R., and N. Crossley. 2018. "Trans-Locality, Network Structure and Music Worlds: Underground Metal in the UK." *Canadian Review of Sociology* 55, no. 1: 111–135.

Feld, S. 1981. "The Focused Organization of Social Ties." *American Journal of Sociology* 86: 1015–1035.
Finnegan, R. 1989. *The Hidden Musicians: Music-Making in an English Town*. Cambridge: Cambridge University Press.
Fletcher, T. 1987. *Never Stop*. London: Omnibus.
Ford, S. 2003. *Hip Priest*. London: Quartet.
Gilmore, S. 1987. "Coordination and Convention." *Symbolic Interaction* 10, no. 2: 209–227.
Gilmore, S. 1988. "Schools of Activity and Innovation." *Sociological Quarterly* 29, no. 2: 203–219.
Glasper, I. 2004. *Burning Britain*. London: Cherry Red.
Haslam, D. 2000. *Manchester, England*. London: Fourth Estate.
Hebdige, D. 1988. *Subculture: The Meaning of Style*. London: Routledge.
Hindess, B. 1988. *Choice, Rationality and Social Theory*. London: Unwin Hyman.
Lewis, D. 1969. *Convention*. Cambridge, MA: Harvard University Press.
Martin, P. 2005. "The Jazz Community as an Art World: A Sociological Perspective." *Jazz Research Journal* 2. https://journals.equinoxpub.com/JAZZ/article/view/1715.
Martin, P. 2006. "Musicians' Worlds." *Symbolic Interaction*, 29, no. 1: 95–107.
McClary, S. 2001. *Conventional Wisdom: The Content of Musical Form*. Berkeley: University of California Press.
Morley, P. 2008. *Joy Division: Piece by Piece*. London: Plexus.
Nice, J. 2010. *Shadowplayers*. London: Aurum.
Nolan, D. 2006. *The Gig That Changed the World: I Swear I Was There*. Shropshire, UK: Independent Music Press.
Nolan, D. 2007. *Bernard Sumner*. Shropshire, UK: Independent Music Press.
Phillips, K. 1975. "Review of All Night Christmas Ball at Queen Elizabeth College." *New Musical Express*, December 7, 1975, 27.
Reynolds, S. 2009. *Totally Wired*. London: Faber and Faber.
Scott, J. 2000. *Social Network Analysis: A Handbook*. London: SAGE.
Small, C. 1998. *Musicking*. Middletown, CT: Wesleyan University Press.
Spencer, N. 1976. "Don't Look over Your Shoulder, but the Sex Pistols Are Coming." *New Musical Express*, February 21, 1976, 31.
Strachan, R. 2010. "Liverpool's 1970s Bohemia." In *The Beat Goes On*, edited by M. Leonard and R. Strachan, 124–142. Liverpool: Liverpool University Press.
Straw, W. 1991. "System of Articulation, Logics of Change." *Cultural Studies* 53: 368–388.
Wasserman, S., and K. Faust. 1994. *Social Network Analysis*. Cambridge: Cambridge University Press.
Watson, J. 2019. "The Persistence of Punk Rock: A Statistical Network Analysis of Underground Punk Worlds in Manchester and Liverpool, 2013–2015." PhD diss., University of Manchester.

CHAPTER 3

RIOT GRRRL
Nostalgia and Historiography

ELIZABETH K. KEENAN

Introduction

As the 1990s slide away from the contemporary moment into history, feminist and popular music scholars alike have singled out Riot Grrrl, a loose coalition of feminist bands and zine writers, as a germinal moment of the third wave of feminism, a move that has numerous implications in terms of musical and political positioning. Riot Grrrl began in 1990 in Olympia, Washington, with bands such as Bikini Kill, Bratmobile, Excuse 17, and Heavens to Betsy, who produced raw, often intentionally amateurish punk music, filled with a DIY ethos. The movement quickly found momentum in a time when a burgeoning alternative scene intersected with the mainstream, and when other women musicians in alternative music received recognition for their feminist politics.[1] Like participants in other punk subcultures, Riot Grrrl musicians and their fans produced fanzines that merged music and politics,[2] and like other feminist counterpublics,[3] the movement specifically reached out to girls as their audience, with slogans such as "Revolution Girl Style Now"[4] and "Every Girl is a Riot Grrrl."[5]

Although academics and journalists frequently invoke the phrase "Riot Grrrl movement,"[6] Riot Grrrl started less as a movement than as a rough coalition of female-oriented punk bands reacting to the conditions of the time, with its initial participants citing Susan Faludi's *Backlash*, watching race riots in Washington, DC, and facing discrimination from their male peers as reasons they started bands.[7] In the summer of 1991, members of the bands Bikini Kill and Bratmobile[8] moved temporarily to Washington, DC, which had a similarly political punk scene,[9] and soon more Riot Grrrl bands and zines cropped up there. Washington, DC, was also the first place that Riot Grrrl meetings—consciousness-raising, girl-only spaces for discussing music and politics—were held, beginning in July 1991. In addition, the year was a watershed year for punk and alternative music, and Riot Grrrl musicians, especially Bikini Kill, received an intense amount of media attention as "the next big thing" among many other women musicians. While, for a number of reasons, including a media blackout instituted in 1992,[10] Riot Grrrls never crossed over into the mainstream in the ways that other women in alternative rock music did, the movement's legacy has spread far past its initial reach.

Since about 2010, Riot Grrrl has re-entered the public consciousness in ways that draw on nostalgia, but also display a desire to craft feminist histories of a social movement whose work is not yet complete. In both popular culture and in academic spaces, Riot Grrrl has become a central, defining moment for third-wave feminism, particularly that which emphasizes images of the body, sexuality, and personal narrative. From reunion tours for bands like Bikini Kill and Sleater-Kinney,[11] to documentary films,[12] to academic conferences[13] and museum retrospectives,[14] to the establishment of an archival presence,[15] the Riot Grrrl resurgence has helped to establish the movement as an essential founding moment both in the history of third-wave feminism and in the history of women in punk rock. In fact, for reasons explored in this essay, Riot Grrrl has assumed an even greater presence in the emerging historical narrative of the third wave than more popular contemporaneous alternative musicians who identified as feminists, such as Liz Phair, Hole, Seven Year Bitch, and L7, or women who promoted empowerment discourses within hip-hop and R&B, such as Queen Latifah, TLC, and En Vogue.

In the process of historicizing the movement, both academics and journalists have at times glorified Riot Grrrl's political force at the expense of accuracy, while at other times they have struggled to add nuance to critiques, particularly around race, class, and elitism, that have followed Riot Grrrl from its beginnings. Remembering the movement, too, has been for some a call to political action, while for others it is a cataloging of disappointments, a midlife assessment of feminist progress in a time when women's rights are once again under siege. As theorist Svetlana Boym (2002, 3) notes, "Nostalgia is not always about the past; it can be retrospective but also prospective. Fantasies of the past determined by the needs of the present have a direct impact on the realities of the future." How one remembers Riot Grrrl, then, has as much to do with the present and future as it does with the past. Drawing on feminist historiography and theories of nostalgia, this essay questions the political nature of remembering Riot Grrrl in the present day and addresses the juncture where the now-popular production of 1990s nostalgia intersects with the important project of feminist historiography of the third wave.

Recent History and the Problem of Nostalgia

The specter of nostalgia looms over any project that addresses recent history, but it presents a particular problem for popular music studies. In his 2011 book *Retromania*, the journalist Simon Reynolds argues that, during the second half of the twentieth century, nostalgia became so bound up with popular culture that it became a site of commercialism, rather than reflection. Reynolds acknowledges that nostalgia can be used as a progressive force, but warns against the perils of "retro," or this most derivative form of nostalgia. For Reynolds, "retro" takes objects from the immediate past and recycles them in ways that "neither idealize nor sentimentalize the past, but seeks to be amused and charmed by it" (Reynolds 2011, xxx). While Reynolds's argument often feels overly simplistic and as if it separates out the "serious" aspects of popular music from the consumer culture in which it is enmeshed, it does describe a particular kind of youthful embrace of past musical and fashion styles, including Riot Grrrl. As this essay will explore, the nostalgia around Riot Grrrl often contains specific political goals for its most invested participants, who are attempting to ensure its legacy as a musical and political movement, but it exists in a "retro" world, where, as Reynolds notes, recent history is often part of a consumerist culture. To Reynolds's point, Riot Grrrl nostalgia has frequently appeared in fashion magazines aimed at audiences too young to have experienced Riot Grrrl firsthand. In June 2009, *Nylon* magazine—a fashion magazine aimed at women in the 18–25 age range—featured a spread of Riot Grrrl–inspired beauty tips; the magazine then rehashed a similar story online in 2015 (see Korn 2015). In 2017, Erica Euse, a writer for *Vice*'s i-D vertical, interviewed me for an article about Riot Grrrl hairstyles (see Euse 2017). The range of dates in these examples illustrate that retro-90s looks in general, and Riot Grrrl in particular, became a go-to sign of fashionable rebellion for younger women during the 2010s, at the same time that Riot Grrrl became solidified within the less commercial spaces of archives, art exhibits, documentaries, and academic conferences. This tension underlies the ways that the concept of "Riot Grrrl" is treated in pop culture and academic spaces: the "retro" environment makes it easy to look at Riot Grrrl as a bunch of cute-but-angry girls wearing Doc Martens, but many former Riot Grrrls are seeking to solidify their movement's place in history and to inspire the following generation.[16]

Beyond living in a "retro" culture and working with materials belonging to living interlocutors who have their own political agendas,[17] scholars who work with the history of the recent past face suspicions from their peers about the "objectivity" of their work. In the book *Doing Recent History*, Renee C. Romano notes that historians of the recent past are often criticized for lacking in "critical distance," whether for political positioning, an absence of a vaguely defined "hindsight," or a sense of accurate "pattern recognition": "Some theorists imply that it is nearly impossible to have sufficient detachment from the recent past simply because we are too close to it in time; those who are caught up in events or who experience them firsthand cannot understand the larger processes at work at the heart of the historical enterprise" (Romano 2012, 39). While Romano doesn't specifically call out "nostalgia" as one of the pitfalls here, one can easily see it as part of the lack of "sufficient detachment" that supposedly objective history requires. But, as Romano argues, "given today that few scholars contend that there is any such a thing as an absolutely true account of the past, then the challenges that recent historians face in positioning ourselves in relation to politicized events are no different than those who study more distant, but politically charged, pasts" (38).

If there is no "true" past, then what become important are the stories we tell, who we center in those stories, and what kind of critique we make in the telling. The feminist historian Joan Wallach Scott noted in the introduction to her classic collection of essays, *Gender and the Politics of History*, that feminist scholarship *is* feminist politics that "makes critical analysis of the past and present a continuing operation; the historian can interpret the world while trying to change it" (Scott 1988, 6). This kind of critical analysis becomes even more important when writing about feminism itself. Clare Hemmings (2011) argues that feminists tend to create a narrative cycle of progress, loss, and return. These narrative cycles are everywhere in writing about Riot Grrrl, as they are in much feminist history, but also because they fit neatly into popular music's nostalgia and tropes of authenticity. It is my hope that in this essay, I will not fall into the trap of glorifying that cycle of progress, loss, and return, but instead examine the limits of a punk rock feminist movement in its time, as it has been historicized, and what that means for future scholarship.

Today, over twenty-five years after Rebecca Walker—who was not a Riot Grrrl, but the daughter of second-wave feminist Alice Walker—declared "I Am the Third Wave" in the pages of *Ms.* magazine (Walker 1992), we are in the beginnings of a move to establish a history of third-wave feminism. A similar process of remembering the second wave took place in the late 1980s, when books such as Alice Echols's *Daring to Be Bad: Radical Feminism in America 1967–1975* were published. In her Epilogue, Echols writes,

> Fundamental to feminism's decline in the political arena has been its failure to attract large numbers of younger women. As in the 20s—a decade to which the '80s bears some resemblance—feminists have discovered that many younger women are indifferent if not hostile to the women's movement. They are, in the words of one journalist, "postfeminist." Why has the women's movement, which so successfully voiced many women's concerns in the late '60s and early '70s failed to attract younger women? To some extent, feminism is the victim of its own success.
>
> (Echols 1987, 293)

A few years later, Susan Faludi's *Backlash* (1991) outlined the ways in which neoconservative politics—and not just feminism's success—helped to dismantle feminism as a movement. Both of these books examined the past, saw a present that left much to be desired, and, in part, imagined a future where the options would differ.

Scholars locating Riot Grrrl's place in the history of the third wave and in punk rock are invariably part of a feminist political project to ensure that women aren't erased. Included within a truly feminist political project, though, is an imperative not just to record "the true story of Riot Grrrl"[18] in an objectivist manner, but to also place Riot Grrrl within a framework that properly locates its scope at the time as well as the reasons it continues to resonate beyond its initial, small circle. For scholars trying to historicize the movement, that also means examining the intersections of power and identity that have allowed Riot Grrrl to take such a large place within the popular and scholarly narrative of punk rock and feminism since 1990, sometimes at the expense of other, equally influential women musicians (see Keenan 2015). Understanding Riot Grrrl requires confronting the movement's own failures, particularly along lines of race, class, and sexuality, but understanding the movement also demands that scholars examine their own motives, prejudices, and tastes when developing a historical narrative around third-wave feminism that foregrounds a movement driven largely by young, middle-class white women.

Riot Grrrl in the 1990s

One of the early articles on Riot Grrrl—and one of the few to feature prominent participation from self-identified Riot Grrrls, such as Kathleen Hanna and Tobi Vail of Bikini Kill and Allison Wolfe of Bratmobile—framed the movement as "a group of musicians and writers and friends who decided to aggressively co-opt the values and rhetoric of punk, 15 years later, in the name of feminism" (White 1992). As a movement that merged feminism and punk rock, Riot Grrrl cannot be separated into its parts, but must be situated in relation to both. After all, localized punk and alternative scenes and the nascent third-wave feminism responded to the same dominant conservative mainstream US culture of the 1980s and early 1990s. The Moral Majority, Ronald Reagan (and later George H. W. Bush), apartheid in South Africa, the lack of attention on the AIDS crisis, Rodney King's treatment by the LAPD, and threats to reproductive rights were all part of the environment that shaped early 1990s popular music, from punk to hip-hop.

While the kinds of political engagement and commentary varied from scene to scene, genre to genre, the two geographic scenes most associated with Riot Grrrl—Olympia, Washington, and Washington, DC—both relied on a sense of punk-inspired DIY community, although the music they produced sounded quite different. Within the landscape of independent music scenes in the late 1980s and early 1990s, Olympia's music scene, with a built-in audience of students from the Evergreen State University, was known for being relatively more welcoming toward women than many others. Women in Olympia participated in every aspect of music-making, from being in bands to booking shows to running record labels.[19] K Records' 1991 International Pop Underground Convention, a six-day music festival, opened with a "Girl Night"[20] meant to highlight women musicians. Members of Bikini Kill played the event, Bratmobile debuted their new line-up as a three-piece, and the event also featured the first performance of the band Heavens to Betsy.[21] Of the two scenes, Washington, DC, offered a more overtly developed political sensibility, partly due to being the nation's capital rather than a small college town and state capital. Fugazi—a band that Bikini Kill performed with fairly often—and its label Dischord shaped the scene into one that confronted national politics in numerous ways, from their song lyrics to the causes they raised money for and their performance venues, including public spaces, such as in front of the White House or the Supreme Court, which created political commentary in and of themselves.[22] During their time in Washington, DC, Bikini Kill and Bratmobile took part in these events as well as helped to establish a separate "girls-only" space through Riot Grrrl meetings, zines, and organizing, beyond their original activities in Olympia.[23]

Although Riot Grrrl had connections in these two scenes, the movement's goals were not limited by geography so much as constructed by ideology. As the bands toured, they would encourage girls in different cities to start their own Riot Grrrl chapters and hand out zines and copies of the ever-evolving Riot Grrrl Manifesto, a series of bullet points outlining the movement's reasons for existing, which originally appeared in the *Bikini Kill #2* zine in 1991.[24] *Sassy* magazine often honored Riot Grrrl zines for its "Zine of the Month" column, which gave girls far outside the two scenes access to the movement's literature for a little more than the cost of postage. In 1993, Bikini Kill toured the UK with English band Huggy Bear, solidifying Riot Grrrls's reputation as a far-reaching feminist youth movement.

This other element of Riot Grrrl—its feminism—was more specifically born of the conditions that Faludi outlines in *Backlash*, which intensified in the early 1990s. The Clarence Thomas confirmation hearings in 1992, in which an all-male panel graphically questioned Anita Hill in ways that seemed both invasive and incredulous, and Thomas was appointed anyway, served as a flame for Riot Grrrl,[25] but also for the much broader range of young feminists who would shape third-wave feminism.[26] Those hearings also inspired the "Year of the Woman," referring to the record number of women running for office in 1992.[27] Also serving as a push to action were anti-abortion protests and legislative efforts to restrict abortion, which inspired rock band L7's Rock for Choice as well as the massive pro-choice protest on the National Mall in April 1992 (see de Witt 1992). In the early 1990s, right-wing cultural critic Rush Limbaugh coined the term "feminazis" to describe any woman with even vaguely feminist ideas. Often, critics of feminism adopted the language of feminist critique in their attempts to dismiss the movement. "Postfeminist" authors such as Camille Paglia (1992) and Katie Roiphe (1994) argued that second-wave feminism had gone too far into a "victim culture." Paglia and Roiphe, in particular, dismissed feminist progress around sexual assault by reducing the concept of date rape to a white, middle-class complaint. Paglia argued that only middle-class white women care about date rape, writing that "it's not black or Hispanic women who are making a fuss about this—they come from cultures that are fully sexual and they are fully realistic about sex" (Paglia 1992, 57). While she comes across as stunningly racist, Paglia's dismissive attitude of sexual assault as a white, middle-class problem at times influenced journalist's accounts of Riot Grrrl.

Third-wave feminists, including but not limited to Riot Grrrls, responded to this pushback, but also sometimes absorbed the negative assumptions about second-wave feminism's range of beliefs and accomplishments.[28] As a movement, Riot Grrrls actively countered the early 1990s "postfeminist" narrative by using song lyrics, zines, and Riot Grrrl meetings to challenge sexual harassment, bring up issues of sexual assault and abuse, and offer support for victims of sexual assault and abuse. Like other branches of third-wave feminism, and like the second wave before it, Riot Grrrl struggled with issues of class and race. As a "revolution" for "every girl," Riot Grrrl often projected a type of girlhood solely available to white, middle-class teens, and did so within the context of punk rock, a genre that also most commonly hails a white, middle-class audience.

During Riot Grrrl's initial bloom, both mainstream rock music reporters and academics took notice of the movement's ties to a nascent, youth-oriented feminism, but in very different ways. Much of the mainstream cultural and rock music reportage and criticism of Riot Grrrl drew on the idea that its participants, as young, middle-class white women, were not experiencing "real" problems, or that Riot Grrrls were blowing these problems out of proportion.[29] Because the most prominent Riot Grrrls eschewed media interviews, many articles on Riot Grrrl often contained only outsider perspectives that at best provided inaccurate frameworks for the movement.[30] In general, articles on Riot Grrrl infantilized the movement, construing their emphasis on creating space for girls as a permanent childishness, while at the same time sexualizing it, erasing the anger and confrontation of Riot Grrrl performers. *Newsweek*, for example, positively noted that Riot Grrrls "may be the first generation of feminists to identify their anger so early and to use it," but then undercut this anger by describing Riot Grrrls as "sexy, assertive, and loud," and stating, "Riot Girl is feminism with a loud happy face dotting the 'i.'" Finally, *Newsweek* reminded its readers, "For all its deadly seriousness, this movement isn't just about anger, it's about fun" (*Newsweek* Staff 1992). Like most contemporary journalism about Riot Grrrl, *Newsweek* painted the sex-positive nature of the movement in overwhelmingly heterosexual terms, despite its connections to queer zine writers and queercore bands.[31]

Other contemporary news articles on Riot Grrrl illustrate the tendency to dismiss both the scope of Riot Grrrl and its emphasis on sexual assault and abuse in line with postfeminist critiques. For example, Emily White's *LA Weekly* article mentioned above mostly shows the movement in a favorable light, but falls in line with Roiphe and Paglia's ideas that younger feminists were altogether too concerned about rape:

> The continuous circling of these women around the image of the raped, violated body—whether in songs, writing, or conversations—makes their feminism very much of our time. Incest in particular has become a cultural obsession, our highest-rated horror the gothic violation of the "inner child." Yet unlike the TV talk shows and the pop psychology books, the Riot Girls don't wallow in "victimization" or even try to heal themselves. They don't use confession as a psychological tool but as a political tool, a form of propaganda. They aren't indulging their rape fear so much as identifying it as the ultimate oppression, a dictator that must be overthrown. The Riot Girls are reliving, or imagining, sexual abuse over and over as a way to bring their ranks together and to recognize each other as part of a subculture—a community sociologists have ominously labeled "rape culture."
>
> (White 1992)

Although White tries to distinguish what the Riot Grrrls are doing as separate from "victim culture," she portrays them as doing something potentially more problematic: instead of shedding light on a serious issue that affects their ranks, Riot Grrrls are using rape and sexual abuse to form a subculture.[32] Moreover, White sews doubt in both the fear of sexual assault ("indulging in their rape fear") and in the accounts of the girls themselves (they "are reliving, or imagining, sexual abuse"). This doubt falls in line with Roiphe's argument that women on college campuses were largely imagining the specter of rape, rather than naming a problem that already existed.

Missing from most of this popular journalism was a measured look at how Riot Grrrl dealt with issues of race and class.[33] Instead, issues of race and class were vaguely alluded to with terms like "suburban" and "affluent," instead of the more precise "white" and "middle class."[34] At times, this devolved into accusations of "elitism," in which Riot Grrrl bands ostensibly considered themselves to have greater feminist purity than other women musicians.[35] For example, Kim France's 1993 *Rolling Stone* article "Grrrls at War" listed five assumptions about the movement, including "they hate men" and "they're elitist." France portrays a sneering attitude for the Riot Grrrl—petulant, childish, and closed off, their decision to eschew media a sign of immaturity rather than one of protection. She also pits the movement against other female musicians, quoting Courtney Love as calling the movement "fascistic,"[36] and Kim Gordon complaining that, for women musicians, "Riot Grrrl has become a yardstick by which you're measured" (France 1993).

In contrast to the mainstream media accounts of Riot Grrrl, academia has long taken Riot Grrrl more earnestly, both as a punk subculture and as a type of feminism. Almost all of the early academic literature on Riot Grrrl was laudatory, in the same way as much early writing on punk as a subculture was. Joanne Gottlieb and Gayle Wald (1994) addressed the connections between the reclamation of "girl" identities, commodity culture, and youth subcultures in Riot Grrrl. In 1997, a watershed year for Riot Grrrl scholarship, Neil Nehring's *Popular Music, Gender and Postmodernism: Anger Is an Energy* examined the dismissive tone of musical critics toward Riot Grrrl (Nehring 1997); Mary Celeste Kearney connected the movement to 1970s lesbian separatist feminism (Kearney 1997); Marion Leonard addressed feminism and "girl culture" in zines (Leonard 1997); and Leslie Heywood and Jennifer Drake included two chapters related to Riot Grrrl in their edited volume *Third Wave Agenda: Being Feminist, Doing Feminism* (Heywood and Drake 1997).

In 1999–2000, academic endeavors intersected with popular history in the Experience Music Project's Riot Grrrl Retrospective, the first institutionally sponsored examination of the movement. The EMP's project brought together women from the movement for a series of oral history interviews, collected zines from its participants, and combined them with sound clips for the museum's very first exhibit, which premiered online. But, over the 2000s, Riot Grrrl went "underground," disappearing largely from both pop culture views and academia, with the exception of a few articles by Kristin Schilt, which were among the first to examine Riot Grrrl's limitations as a movement that largely hailed white, middle-class girls (Schilt 2003, 2004, 2005). Riot Grrrl slipped from ethnographic present into history, as its participants moved on to other things, like the early 2000s music festival Ladyfest,[37] or different bands, or careers in music journalism or the arts, or political activism. "Riot Grrrl," though—the idea of the movement as a lost opportunity for feminist authenticity—was just getting started.

Return of Riot Grrrl: Nostalgia and Authenticity

And then, around 2010, Riot Grrrl returned, once again in popular media and in academic spaces. And this time—at least for journalists and popular historians, if not academics—every girl was a Riot Grrrl. Even if they weren't.[38] That is, the varied story of women in alternative music in the early 1990s got flattened into Riot Grrrl, as did the origin of third-wave feminism. In her 2016 article on Riot Grrrl zines, Janice Radway argues that the "movement" part of Riot Grrrl may not usefully describe the early 1990s flourishing of "girl zines": "[T]he act of naming what happened in and around these bands as a movement, and as an autonomous one at that, with a certain coherence and 'organicity' and an identifiable trajectory, may narrow and fix the fluidities of social process too much and iron out complexities and contradictions that ought to be attended to with greater care" (Radway 2016, 3). I would like to build on Radway's observation, and offer an additional explanation: the broad category of "girl zines," like many of the activities of women in popular music in the early 1990s, have been conflated with the narrow activities of the "Riot Grrrl movement." That is, Riot Grrrl itself *was* a small, but fairly coherent, movement with a trajectory, but "girl zines" encompass a much broader swathe of participation than just Riot Grrrl. As in many other subcultures, Riot Grrrl musicians, zine writers, and fans were simultaneously invested in other, related subcultures. The process of telling the story of Riot Grrrl as *the* coherent movement—the yardstick by which all feminist musicians of the early 1990s are measured, per Kim Gordon—erases the activities of many other women, but it also relies on nostalgia to smooth out the narrative and reframe the critiques of the movement.

Unlike the early 1990s accounts of Riot Grrrl, where "elitism" stood in for "white and middle class," the present-day popular narrative uses the walls that Riot Grrrl built around itself—through a genre and political style that appealed to a certain type of girl, and by eschewing mainstream acceptance—to distill a problematic historical narrative that combines feminist authenticity and punk-rock authenticity. The current nostalgia-based story of the "Riot Grrrl movement" often goes like this: A group of angry young women use rock and roll and zines to kick-start a new generation of feminism, all on their own. Exploited in vicious articles in *Newsweek*, *Rolling Stone*, and *USA Today*, which focus on their fashion instead of their politics, they withdraw via media boycott, keeping their motives and politics still pure and their wallets appropriately empty. The exploitative media moves on to angry women as a selling point, and then to the Spice Girls, to market to even younger girls, and "girl power" ceases to contain meaning.[39] For example, Marisa Meltzer's *Girl Power: The Nineties Revolution in Music* describes Riot Grrrl in direct juxtaposition with the commercial, pop Spice Girls:

> The 2001 edition of the *Oxford English Dictionary*, that *eminence grise* of the English language, included the phrase "Riot Grrrl," which was given a rather bare-bones definition of "a movement expressing female resistance to male domination in society." Another phrase added that year was "girl power," which was described as "a self-reliant attitude among girls and young women manifested in ambition, assertiveness, and individualism." The distillation of a Riot Grrrl slogan "revolution girl-style now" into something more mainstream and palatable, girl power was, disturbingly, feminism without the activism—and it was a resounding success.
> We have the Spice Girls to thank for the world domination of the catchphrase.
>
> (Meltzer 2010, 72)

Later in that chapter, Meltzer continues:

> The simplification of punk rock, third wave feminist values to girl power was a shocking concept to the Riot Grrrl veteran Tobi Vail. "When I hear a Spice Girls song on the radio, it is profoundly alienating," she says. "I might be like, 'Wow, this is cool,' but then I go, 'Isn't it a little fucked up?' And am I crazy, or did I make this happen?" She asks an important question: Would the Spice Girls have existed without Riot Grrrl? On the surface, yes—a manufactured group singing about love and friendship was certainly nothing groundbreaking. But I don't believe their message of girl power would have existed without Riot Grrrl predating them by a few years. Whoever masterminded the Spice Girls' girl-power message in the mid-nineties conceivably heard or read about Riot Grrrl. (72)

Within this framework, the authenticity of punk rock collapses into the authenticity of feminism, and Riot Grrrl's quick destruction stands in for the destruction of an unproblematized feminist purity. In juxtaposing Riot Grrrl consistently with the Spice Girls, one becomes "true" feminism, while the other stands in for a sellout version. This image untroubles Riot Grrrl's own "true story"—to again borrow that phrase from Sara Marcus—and reduces third-wave feminism to a subculturally oriented musical style. By placing feminist authenticity in one early 1990s movement, it also divorces the third wave from its many other contributions, including, perhaps most importantly, its emphasis on understanding identity through an intersectional framework that takes into consideration class, sexuality, race, and ethnicity, among others, that could perhaps be better investigated through hip-hop feminism, which is almost always more commercially oriented (see Keenan 2015).

In an effort to establish Riot Grrrl as a lost opportunity of feminist politics, sometimes the nostalgia enmeshed in remembering the movement is less about 1990s nostalgia than about 1960s nostalgia.[40] For example, Susan Douglas's 2010 book *Enlightened Feminism* dismisses much of the third wave's cultural production. Douglas makes an exception when she describes Riot Grrrl, drawing a comparison with the second wave that positions both as substantive movements watered down by the media. She writes:

> The media responded to [Riot Grrrl] much as it had when radical feminism emerged in the late 1960s and early 1970s: attack, ignore, trivialize the political substance of the movement, decapitate the look or style of the movement from its substance, and use this new style to marginalize the movement and create new stuff to sell. While the immediate press response to Riot Grrrl was hostile, the movement's energy and its members' insistence on a new empowerment for girls was not ignored: within a few years we had "girl power" lipstick and an entire federal initiative, headed by Donna Shalala, labeled "girl power."
>
> (Douglas 2010, 45)

Douglas's trajectory confirms Riot Grrrl's relationship to the second wave, legitimizing it as feminism, while at the same time separating it from the supposedly problematic consumerism of the third wave, which Douglas refers to as "enlightened sexism." Douglas, however, does little to examine the complexities of the intersection of pop culture and politics, instead dismissing the rest of the third wave: *Buffy* and *Xena* are bad, and we don't even want to hear about *Gossip Girl*. Her position on recent pop culture is deeply ironic, considering she once argued that the highly commercial music of girl groups deeply influenced the second wave (see Douglas 1994).

The role of nostalgia for third-wave feminists, such as Meltzer and Marcus, operates slightly differently. In an interview in *Slate* magazine, Marcus and Meltzer debated nostalgia and its role in their work. In particular, Marcus positioned her book away from nostalgia, while critiquing Meltzer's more commercial orientation:

> Sara Marcus: I think the '90s were an unusual estuary: Some underground culture was flowing into the mainstream and hadn't yet been completely diluted or transformed by it. And a vibrant, cohesive, self-sufficient, actual underground existed for people who weren't satisfied with the crossover acts. The '90s were something special that we haven't seen since, which contributes to and flavors the upswing in nostalgia that we're seeing now.
>
> I would never deny you the pleasure of your flannels and babydolls, Marisa, but I think '90s nostalgia is problematic . . . the major animating value of the era and of Riot Grrrl was DIY: Create your own art, culture, and communities rooted in the realities of your life and what affects you in the here and now. Nostalgia for a bygone era kind of misses the point.
>
> (Marcus and Meltzer 2010)

Marcus's critique of nostalgia, while simultaneously declaring the early 1990s a unique era for the underground and for feminist politics, allows her to assign nostalgia to Meltzer's work, which extends much further into the 1990s, and, therefore, away from the supposedly purely feminist moment of Riot Grrrl.

In an interview I conducted with her, however, Meltzer argued that nostalgia could be a motivating force:

> So for me, nostalgia has always been something that empowers me. It's very easy to look back at a certain era, and be like, those days were perfect, but I really try not to end there. I feel like I've gotten some criticism of the book with it being overly nostalgic. And I certainly don't hide that part of myself. I don't think anyone should feel bad about feeling nostalgic. I think it's a pretty universal emotion.
>
> .... It's funny to me, because I think some reviews of the book have said I'm way too embracing of everything, and everything was perfect. I actually think the book was really critical. There were so many problems. I think Riot Grrrl was at its heart pretty elitist. You had to have a lot of access. You had to find out about that music, somehow. And even though they got a lot of mainstream publicity, you had to figure out how to find the zines. You had to get the courage to go to these intimidating, all-ages punk clubs, especially if you were a girl who hadn't been part of the punk scene and it was your first show, or something like that. You know, if you wanted to make a zine or start a band, there's a certain barrier to entry in terms of skill set, and organization, and money, and the kinds of peers and family that recognize those as important uses of your time.[41]

Meltzer's simultaneous belief that nostalgia can mobilize political actions and that Riot Grrrl was elitist at first seems contradictory. However, she recognizes the limits of Riot Grrrl in terms of class, and how those limits disappointed Riot Grrrl's claim to inclusion.

Meltzer's stance on nostalgia bumps up against how Marcus positions *Girls to the Front*. Unlike Meltzer, Marcus holds that her project is history, not nostalgia, but, she admits, it wouldn't be published if it didn't resonate with 1990s nostalgia in the marketplace:

> SARA MARCUS: My book is clearly mobilizing nostalgia in a certain way. I've always had the thought that those of us who had come of age in the 1990s could get back in touch with the idealism we had, with the bravery . . . I was talking with a friend of mine about my irritation with '90s nostalgia, and he said, but pardon me, but isn't your whole book about that? And I was like, yes, no, yes, no! It's not the same at all.
> EK: How do you think about it as different?
> SM: I think about it as being really nonpresent and about idealizing a particular time, where there's not a real gesture toward what can we bring in the current space? What can we abstract from this thing that we feel warmly toward to enrich our current life?[42]

Like Meltzer, Marcus views her work as a potentially politically motivating cultural product, and part of her desire to write her book was to recapture the feelings of the early 1990s and turn them into a present-day activism. Nostalgia, for her, is merely a starting point.

Notably, much of the past decade's popular resurrection of Riot Grrrl loses the critiques of the movement's relationship to race and class. For example, Marcus's *Girls to the Front* offers a detailed account of a handful of Riot Grrrl's participants. Based on dozens of interviews with well-known Riot Grrrls such as Kathleen Hanna of Bikini Kill and Allison Wolfe, Erin Smith, and Molly Neuman of Bratmobile, as well as lesser-known women who contributed to the organization of Riot Grrrl chapters around the country, such as zine writer Christina Woolner. However, in her choice of time frame, Marcus reinforces the standard notion that Riot Grrrl belonged to only white, middle-class girls. By starting in 1990 and ending in 1993, and telling mainly the stories of women involved in that first generation, Marcus continues the framework of Riot Grrrl's violation by the mainstream media. In particular, this time span leaves out Riot Grrrl chapters in the San Francisco Bay Area and Los Angeles, both of which featured a significantly more diverse population in terms of race and class, both of which could challenge the standard easy dismissal of Riot Grrrl along race and class, and both of which suggest another meaning for the "true" story of the Riot Grrrl revolution. Erasing these critiques not only forgets the contributions of women of color, but also guarantees that a feminism drawing on Riot Grrrl will replicate its mistakes.

In her important 2012 essay, "Riot Grrrl, Race, and Revival," Mimi Thi Nguyen argues that the forming historiography of Riot Grrrl relies on tropes of intimacy, cultivated in semi-public spaces such as zines, that allowed white participants to bond over their shared oppression through consciousness-raising type confessions:

> This subculture of intimacy and self-referentiality borrowed its structure for transformation from consciousness-raising, and the notion that the deeply oppressed had radical knowledge stemming from their specific social positions. . . . The raising of consciousness did not aim to end structural determinations, and instead ossified its categories of class or gender as an absolute reality to predict social expression (such as the commonplace claim that working-classness manifested loud, straightforward, and therefore truer speech). But how then could experience yield revolutionary knowledge about race, where the dominant experience was whiteness?
>
> (Nguyen 2012, 179)

The intimacy of zine writing, Nguyen argues, operates as a barrier to women of color, who are expected to offer education for the benefit of white women—a "proximity without intimacy." Nguyen ties this problematic Riot Grrrl tendency to use women of color as an educational moment in the early 1990s to the ongoing nostalgic formulation of Riot Grrrl historiography: "I worry that Riot Grrrl retrospectives will take the form of a story of the loss of a more utopian moment of feminist intimacy, into which race is either a disruption (generating bad feelings) or an intervention (feeling bad to assure that we are good) and otherwise contained as such" (190). Instead, Nguyen argues that bad feelings about the past, rather than contained as a single moment of intervention, should be something that force us to "acknowledge that feminist futures cannot look like the feminist past" (191). The next section of this essay will address how Riot

Grrrls—including Nguyen herself—are attempting to craft Riot Grrrl's legacy, for better or for worse, in a political landscape where, much like the early 1990s, women's rights are once again backsliding.

CRAFTING A LEGACY: ARCHIVES AND ABSENCES

Although Nguyen warns against characterizing Riot Grrrl as a lost utopian moment, for many of its participants, it *does* represent a loss—if not of a utopia exactly, then of feminist potential, as both Meltzer and Marcus remind us. Riot Grrrls—and third-wave feminists more broadly—developed their political movements during a time of backlash against women's rights. Now, at midlife, they once again see this backslide, and they question what happened then, and what they can do now. In his book *Cruising Utopia: the Then and There of Queer Futurity*, Jose Esteban Muñoz argues for "a backward glance that enacts a future vision," a sense of utopian politics that are enacted by remembering the potential of past situations (Muñoz 2009, 4). Muñoz uses Frank O'Hara's poem "Having a Coke With You" as an example of a quotidian desire to simply *be* in a homosexual relationship, as a point of reference, where he sees "the past and the potentiality imbued within an object, the ways it might represent a mode of being and feeling that was not quite there but nonetheless an opening. . . . Such utopian feelings can and regularly will be disappointed. They are nonetheless indispensable to the act of imagining transformation" (9). In the poem, the act of sharing a Coke in a public space offers a bittersweet desire for the ordinary that gay couples couldn't have at the time O'Hara wrote the poem. Muñoz's ideas about queer futurity and looking backward can be applied to the process of remembering feminist histories, or the histories of other social movements whose work remains incomplete. It is possible to imagine in Riot Grrrl a moment where young women's anger had the potential to shape public discourse about sexuality, the body, and autonomy. At the same time, in the case of Riot Grrrl and third-wave feminism, we must hold in our minds the thought that those incomplete social movements, those disappointed utopian moments, are incomplete and disappointed *because* they were not inclusive and did not take into account relationships of power, and so they couldn't bring about sustained change.

For some of the most prominent Riot Grrrls, this midlife reassessment of their contribution to third-wave feminism led to the desire to document and preserve their movement by establishing formal archival collections in institutions, namely the Riot Grrrl Collection at New York University's Fales Library and Special Collections.[43] The establishment of a feminist archive signals recognition of the movement's significance, but it comes with both the opportunity to shape the historical narrative and the risk of replicating the very things that hampered the movement's potential, namely a focus on the activities of its white, middle-class, heterosexual members.[44] An archive is always made of people who are asked to participate, people who wish to participate, and people who are considered "important." After all, in order to establish an archive in the first place, an institution must see value in the materials it will preserve. In short, it is a space that can replicate structures of power very easily, depending on what considerations drive the acquisitions.

Of the collections that make up the Riot Grrrl Collection, Kathleen Hanna's papers have been the most heavily publicized, as they initially formed the core of the collection.[45] The establishment of the collection began as a conversation between Lisa Darms, who was then the senior archivist at Fales Library, and Hanna, the former singer of Bikini Kill, who had gone on to perform in Le Tigre and, more recently, Julie Ruin.[46] Darms viewed the establishment of a Riot Grrrl archive as key for preserving feminist history, but also something marketable, like Fales's Downtown Collection. In the time since, she's been proven right: the Riot Grrrl Collection represents less than one half of one percent of the total archival holdings at Fales, but it is already being using by about 15 percent of Fales patrons (Keenan and Darms 2013). In considering the archive as a repository of materials of significance for Riot Grrrl, Darms acted as a gatekeeper for the kinds of feminist history that will be written in the future as memories fade and oral histories become no longer possible. Her role as archivist determined whose papers made it into the collection and whose received priority for preservation and cataloging, which also determined when they would be available to scholars. Since its inception, the archive has expanded rapidly: from the core of Becca Albee, Molly Neuman, and Kathleen Hanna, all Riot Grrrl musicians, it has grown in scope to include a more wide-ranging group of materials.[47]

As the initial donation that founded the collection, the Kathleen Hanna Papers deserve some discussion here in order to shed light on the acquisition process. Darms and Hanna's friendship dated back to when they met in a photography class at Evergreen. Years later, shortly before Darms began working at Fales, the two attended an event there. In an interview, Hanna told me:

> I made a joke because Marvin [J. Taylor, Director of Fales Library and Special Collections] was talking about how they have the Richard Hell collection. And I was like, they should take my stuff. They should do some kind of Riot Grrrl collection, and I could get rid of my stuff in my basement. But I was kidding, and I remember thinking, am I as big as Richard Hell? Is my stuff really important? All of the sudden, and I had never really thought about it before. And I had been keeping all this stuff because I knew I should. But it was really funny and I was thinking, if they have Richard Hell's stuff, why wouldn't they have mine?[48]

The question here—"Is my stuff really important?"—goes right along with the midlife assessment that many other Riot Grrrls have talked about. What started as a joke soon became a concrete possibility when Darms became an archivist at Fales. As Hanna told me in 2010, she carefully went through her papers to remove anything embarrassing, and she, too, acknowledged the role that nostalgia played in constructing her own archive. She started thinking about it after her last band broke up, and she was reassessing her career. She had a desire to "create a legacy that I had control of. I remember a lot of those times as really being very naïve and constantly surprised at the attention we were getting."[49]

Hanna edited her contribution to Fales over a period of six months, during which she returned her 1990s filing cabinet to its "original" state. In our interview from August 2010, Hanna told me that most of the materials in the filing cabinet had since moved to a tub in her basement, and more recent, useful items were in the cabinet. Along with an intern, who was getting her MLS, Hanna went through her zine flats and ephemera, carefully selecting the materials for Fales. She deliberately included things that she had hesitated to publish in zines at the time, including lengthy 100-page zines that would have cost far too much to photocopy, let alone ship. But she also excised personal writings that she thought would bring up old grudges or disputes, some of which are outlined in Marcus's book. The end result, while extensive and certainly one of the most comprehensive in the Riot Grrrl Collection, nonetheless forms a legacy she could have control of, to reference Hanna's own words.

At the same time, even selected to craft a certain narrative of her life, Hanna's papers offer insight into the creative process and political development of Riot Grrrl in ways that a zine collection cannot. Instead of just final products, Hanna's papers contain rough drafts of both song lyrics and writing for zines, zine flats, mock-ups for album artwork, and notebooks that track Hanna's thoughts of what Riot Grrrl could or should be.[50] On the first page of her "Riot Grrrl Test Patterns" notebook, from roughly the summer of 1991, Hanna outlines what the movement should be, noting that some of the big questions for the movement were about race ("How can we make our scenes less white in both numbers and ideology?") but also about engaging with women outside punk ("How can we best support/educate non-punk feminists? Should we?").[51] That both of these are on par as large issues for Hanna speaks to the fact that Riot Grrrl faced both the constant issue of feminism—that is, how to be a movement that extends beyond the white, middle-class—and the fact that Riot Grrrl would have a great deal of trouble reaching beyond that white, middle-class audience if they drew boundaries around themselves as punk feminists.[52] A few pages later in the notebook, Hanna writes: "RG is dedicated to anti-racist work in THEORY + PRACTICE and thus MUST HAVE women of color among its elite."[53] Hanna lists possible meetings with different groups to "dialogue" how to be antiracist and more inclusive, but the notebook doesn't document whether these meetings happened, or what they produced. Even further, on a page outlining a Riot Grrrl meeting, she writes that outreach should include a number of groups, including "sexual assault and domestic violence survivors, girls of color, girls with no $$$, differently abled girls, high school girls, older women, lesbians, mainstream feminists," and, she noted, "zines by/for marg.[inalized] girls ARE A MUST as a way to educate each other + not repeat the same old things."[54] From what Hanna writes in the "Riot Grrrl Test Patterns" notebook, questions about broadening Riot Grrrl's scope formed a vital part of its formation, and the movement had a genuine, serious interest in outreach. But, as Nguyen pointed out in her 2012 essay, the framework here relies on girls of color—and other marginalized girls—educating white Riot Grrrls, instead of being seen as equals in the movement.

I bring up the materials from the Kathleen Hanna Papers not only because they demonstrate how Riot Grrrls addressed inequality and thought about inclusion in their movement, but also because they connect to another issue in the archive itself: that the materials reflect the women who were considered significant within the movement, who have decided to donate their materials, and who had the resources and foresight to preserve their correspondence, zines, and other ephemera. Although women of color did participate in Riot Grrrl, many of them were not the members of the "elite" that Hanna mentions. At first, the archive contained mostly well-known women musicians and zine-makers who had gone on to successful careers in the arts, such as Hanna, Molly Neuman, Tammy Rae Carland, and Sheila Heti, all of whom made sense for institutional inclusion, but all of whom were white.[55] The lone exception in the initial group of acquisitions was the Ramdasha Bikceem Riot Grrrl Collection. Bikceem had been a skater and Riot Grrrl, whose zine *Gunk* offered a critical look at race within punk space, including an essay in *Gunk* #4 detailing her experiences at the 1992 Riot Grrrl Convention in Washington, DC.[56] The issue of Bikceem being the only black voice—indeed, the only person of color—in the archive replicated a situation that the zine writer was familiar with. Bikceem told the journalist Gabby Best (2015), "I just hesitate to talk about Riot Grrrl like this because I become a footnote all the time, for reference." That is, Bikceem becomes the "go-to" example of a woman of color within Riot Grrrl, both in articles about the movement and within the archive itself.

The absence of other women of color became more obvious when Darms announced a book project based on the archive, containing facsimiles of flyers, posters, photographs, and excerpts of zines. When Darms asked her Twitter followers what they would like to see included in the book,[57] Daniela Capistrano, founder of the POC Zine Project, responded offering assistance in finding zines by people of color.[58] Although Darms said she was happy to have Capistrano's help, her book drew only on the items donated to the Riot Grrrl Collection, which were limited. The Twitter conversation would lead to a collaboration between Darms, Capistrano, and Mimi Nguyen, and result in a significant acquisition of zines by people of color for the Riot Grrrl Collection. Nguyen's donation—copies of zines that she had solicited from women of color in the 1990s for her compilation zine *Race Riot*—is unusual for its criticism of Riot Grrrl and punk subcultures within its original zine content and in her donor statement. Nguyen's donor statement is filled with ambivalence about the efficacy of her donation in terms of the historiography of Riot Grrrl. She raises concern that "inclusion and incorporation might be made to cover over more troubling queries about *how* women of color are included, incorporated, or otherwise made visible" in archives and retrospectives in "such a way that contains their critique and segregates it from the story of the movement's contribution."[59] At the same time, Nguyen suggests that, rather than seeing women of color as intervening in Riot Grrrl or punk, the materials she donated point to not a side story in Riot Grrrl movement, but *the* story of encounter and contest, exchange and challenge—denoting not the singularity of Riot Grrrl movement, but its slide by other feminisms, fracturing and multiplying into other worlds.... Those other histories of people of color—here represented in the materials we donate together—are not an interruption into a singular scene or movement but the practice of another, co-present scene or movement that conversed and collided with the already-known story, but with alternate investments and forms of critique.[60]

Nguyen's suggestion of thinking about the histories of people of color not as an interruption to a larger, white movement but as the practice of another, co-present scene that "collided with an already-known story" has implications for how other scenes interacted with Riot Grrrl as well. Most prominently among these is queercore, which overlapped with Riot Grrrl in practice and in participants, but which early journalism about Riot Grrrl overlooked and which continues to be a footnote in the historiography of Riot Grrrl. Unlike people of color, though, white queer writers and musicians are not underrepresented in the movement or in the archival record of the movement, but somehow, despite that, their queerness is a less visible part of the historiography of Riot Grrrl than would be expected.[61] Some of the most prominent zine writers identified as lesbian or queer. These include Tammy Rae Carland, creator of the zine *I (heart) Amy Carter* and who later ran Mr. Lady Records, and Donna Dresch, creator of the zine *Chainsaw*, founder of the Chainsaw Record label, and member of the all-lesbian queercore band Team Dresch. Around the time that he was preparing his donation to Fales, Matt Wobensmith, the founder of the zine and independent record label Outpunk, told me, "Riot Grrrl and queercore were the same scene. The bands hung out together and were on the same labels."[62] Among the compilations Wobensmith put out were *There's a Fag in the Pit* and *There's a Dyke in the Pit*, the latter of which included Bikini Kill. While many historiographers talk about sexuality within Riot Grrrl, particularly in terms of sexual trauma and abuse, few have thoroughly addressed the queerness of the movement and how queer sexualities shaped Riot Grrrl's feminism.

The Place of Music in Riot Grrrl Historiography

The final section of this chapter turns to the place of music, which is underrepresented in both the historiography and in the archive. Riot Grrrl's music gets very little attention in popular histories, and most of the academic writing on Riot Grrrl has focused on political and personal zines rather than the movement's musical impact (Radway; Leonard 1997, 2006; Schilt 2003, 2004; Piepmeier 2009; Downes 2012; Nguyen 2012; Eichorn 2013). Zines are, after all, a place where Riot Grrrls' politics become visible, both through the kinds of personal, intimate confessions that Nguyen addresses and through the more deliberate political statements, like the Riot Grrrl Manifesto. Beyond the appeal of the medium itself, zines are also more easily available to researchers: in addition to Fales's Riot Grrrl Collection, there are also significant zine collections at the Sallie Bingham Center at Duke University and the Zine Library at Barnard College.[63] Even within the Riot Grrrl Collection at Fales, which is specifically *not* a zine archive, many of the individual donors have provided only zines, rather than video or audio recordings, correspondence, or other ephemera.[64] The emphasis on zines as political tracts doubly obscures music's place in Riot Grrrl, first by ignoring discussions about music in zines, and second by treating the music as an add-on to the movement, rather than its impetus. So where is the music, and how does it relate to the politics?

Overall, the archive has few audio and video recordings. Included in the Kathleen Hanna Papers, for example, is a selection of Bikini Kill performances, but they were given to Hanna by Mark Anderson, a member of the DC punk scene; they also contain performances by Fugazi and Nation of Ulysses, two all-male bands from Washington, DC. The contrast between Fugazi and Bikini Kill is worth noting here. In 2011 Fugazi began making available over eight hundred performances from the band's decade-long history; anyone can download these shows—all of which are given a description and a grade—for a suggested payment of $5. With Hanna's band Bikini Kill, this option is impossible. Bikini Kill, like others associated with the Riot Grrrl movement, often refused to allow unknown photographers to take their pictures, and audio and video recordings were seen as potential violations of a safe space created for teenage girls. As a result, recordings of the band's performances are difficult to obtain. This absence of audio and visual documentation makes it difficult to analyze what drew many fans to the band and others, such as Bratmobile and Excuse 17—such as their unrelenting, chaotic performances, deliberately amateurish style, and dialogue with the audience.

The music does deserve greater attention, though, as it formed the impetus of the movement, and, perhaps more than any other iteration of punk over the past thirty-some years, integrated its DIY ethos into its music. One Riot Grrrl told me, off the record, "The music wasn't that great, and that wasn't the point." Although I disagree with her about the quality of Riot Grrrl's music, she reveals another truth: Riot Grrrl's amateurism was a way of luring young women to feminism *and* to playing music. Seeing a Riot Grrrl band exchanging instruments mid-set, and trying out a new song they had just learned, offered a different kind of experience of feminism—the ability to not feel the weight of expectation to be *good* at something. But, like many other musicians who started out in punk bands, members of Riot Grrrl bands have gone on to have long, critically acclaimed careers in indie rock music in bands like Le Tigre and Sleater-Kinney that also engaged in politics through their music. For the performers and their fans, Riot Grrrl's musical contribution is a starting point, and not an ending point, for how music and politics intersect over time.

In closing, I would like to bring in the 2019 Bikini Kill reunion, as another reason to reconsider Riot Grrrl's musical legacy and importance. The shows, in New York City and Los Angeles, sold out within seconds, illustrating that the band still had an audience eager to hear its music. According to the members of Bikini Kill, who long resisted the idea of a reunion, these concerts were not a way to revel in their legacy or to cash in on 1990s nostalgia, like so many other '90s bands. Instead, as Tobi Vail explained to Pitchfork's Jenn Pelly, the songs have become more relevant to her since the 2016 presidential election:

> Among a charged punk songbook that often reads like it was written yesterday, Vail particularly mentions the guttural *Pussy Whipped* cut "Lil Red," an intense recasting of Little Red Riding Hood in which Hanna sings, "Here's my life, why don't you take it / Here's my cunt, why don't you rape it." "Remember when everyone thought Trump wasn't going to get elected because that video came out of him talking about grabbing the pussy?" Vail asks. "That just seems like the response."
>
> "I don't think any of us were interested in doing some kind of nostalgic exercise, but the songs need to be out there—and personally, we feel like playing them. So it's a way to keep these songs alive," she adds. "We'll be in practice, and I'll just be playing drums and I'll get chills thinking about how the lyrics speak to what's happening today, or somebody will start crying while we're playing a song. In the course of our band, that feeling probably wore off towards the end. But now we're feeling it"
>
> (Pelly 2019)

Mark Twain once said that history may not repeat but it rhymes, and Vail speaks to the kinds of rhymes in history that move beyond nostalgia to a reevaluation of how the past colors the present. In Vail's case—and for many of Bikini Kill's fans—the music itself has a lot to say in the current political moment, in which a president was elected despite numerous credible accounts of sexual assault, and when a woman testified that a potential Supreme Court justice had attempted to rape her, and, again, he was confirmed. It is definitely worth scholars' time to pay attention to not just what the zines—or even the song lyrics—say, but also how the music offered girls an outlet for their frustration, anger, fear, rage, joy, confusion, etc. That is, scholars need to pay attention to why the songs give Vail the chills or move her to cry, even now, and why so many fans feel the same way.

Placing a stronger emphasis on music in the historiography, though, does not mean losing sight of the critiques of women of color, or of the failure of Riot Grrrl as a feminist movement to practice an intersectional feminism. By this, I do not mean only reiterating that punk rock—within the United States at least—has largely been a white, middle-class phenomenon, or suggesting that the music, too, offers a space for analysis of race and class, and the position from which one speaks.[65] Rather, addressing the music would help to create a more holistic picture of Riot Grrrls' successes and failures as a movement, as well as a more nuanced view of Riot Grrrl bands' connections to their contemporaries and their influences on younger musicians. For example, as a movement of "angry girl musicians," Riot Grrrl offers much to examine around the types of expressions of emotion available (or not available) to different types of women through popular music, and how seriously different listeners might receive those emotions.[66] Until Riot Grrrl's music enters into the historiography more fully, scholars will forge at best an incomplete picture of the movement's relationship to its historical setting and will fail to understand why, however imperfect and contested, it continues to be compelling in the popular imagination.

Notes

1. Although some women musicians at the time, such as PJ Harvey and Juliana Hatfield, eschewed the "feminist" label, others embraced it. The musicians from L7, for example, were behind the creation of Rock for Choice and partnered with the Feminist Majority.
2. For more on Riot Grrrl zines, see Radway (2016); Eichorn (2013); Nguyen (2012); Dunn and Farnsworth (2012); Piepmeier (2009); Schilt and Zobl (2008); and Kearney (2006).
3. For more on Riot Grrrl and third-wave feminism as a counterpublic, see Keenan and Darms (2013).
4. Bikini Kill's first cassette-only demo EP used "Revolution Girl Style Now" as its title, and the slogan was part of the intro to the band's song "Double Dare Ya."
5. Although meant to be inclusive, the slogan has come under fire for flattening out girls' experience. See Nguyen (2012).
6. Janice Radway (2016) has argued that the "movement" aspect of Riot Grrrl is problematic, in that it tends to corral all "girl zines" of the 1990s under the umbrella of "Riot Grrrl," when they reflect a much broader array of participants, politics, and tastes.
7. *Riot Grrrl* #1, summer 1991.
8. Members of each band had connections to the area beyond the music scene itself. Bratmobile's Molly Neuman and Bikini Kill's Kathleen Hanna had grown up in the greater Washington, DC, area.
9. The Washington, DC, punk scene featured politically active bands such as Fugazi and Nation of Ulysses, the DIY record label Dischord, and the Positive Force DC activist collective. Fugazi's Ian MacKaye would record Bikini Kill's first EP.
10. The media blackout is mentioned in many contemporary articles on Riot Grrrl, including Emily White's "Revolution Girl-Style Now!" (White 1992). However, in *Girls to the Front: The True Story of the Riot Grrrl Revolution*, Sara Marcus (2010) shows that the decision was not initially uniform or evenly enforced.
11. Bikini Kill's 2019 reunion shows in Los Angeles and New York City sold out within seconds. Although Sleater-Kinney is not a "Riot Grrrl band" per se, its members Corin Tucker and Carrie Brownstein started their musical careers in Riot Grrrl bands Heavens to Betsy and Excuse 17, respectively.
12. Sini Anderson's 2013 film *The Punk Singer* focuses on Kathleen Hanna's career as an artist and her struggle with Lyme disease.
13. Just two examples are Sarah Lawrence College's "The Message Is in the Music: Hip Hop Feminism, *Riot Grrrl*, Latina Music, and More," March 6, 2010, and the University of Limerick's "Riot Grrrl Symposium," April 16, 2013.
14. The *Alien She* touring exhibit focused on artists whose visual art practices were influenced by Riot Grrrl; it appeared in various locations from 2014 to 2016, including the Miller Gallery at Carnegie Mellon University, the Yerba Buena Center for the Arts in San Francisco, and the Orange County Museum of Art in Newport Beach, California. Riot Grrrl zines and art also appeared in the Museum of Modern Art's "Looking at Music 3.0," February 16–May 30, 2011.

15. The Riot Grrrl Collection, which is located within the Fales Library and Special Collections at New York University and includes the papers of both prominent and lesser known participants in Riot Grrrl, opened its doors to researchers in 2010. Since then, it has expanded its scope to include Riot Grrrl–adjacent materials, such as the archive for the Ladyfest 2000 music festival in Olympia, Washington. Additionally, in 2000, Sarah Dyer donated her zine collection to what became the Bingham Center Zine Collections at the Sally Bingham Center for Women's History and Culture at Duke University. The Bingham Center Zine Collections now include over 4,000 zines.
16. During Bikini Kill's 2019 reunion tour, Kathleen Hanna told audiences that the band decided to reunite because their music was relevant again during the Trump administration: "I'm singing these songs for you, but I'm also singing them because I need them."
17. For more on the concerns of working with an expanding archive, see Keenan and Darms (2013).
18. A reference to Sara Marcus's framework for her 2010 book.
19. For example, from 1989 to 1999, Candace Pedersen owned one half of Olympia's K Records.
20. The evening's full, official name was "Love Rock Revolution Girl Style Now."
21. Other performers that night included Jean Smith of Mecca Normal, Kicking Giant, 7 Year Bitch, Lois Maffeo's band Courtney Love, and Rose Melberg of Riot Grrrl band Tiger Trap.
22. Bikini Kill would participate in one of Fugazi's larger public-space events, on July 25, 1992, in front of the Supreme Court. In addition to bands, the event featured civil rights speakers and was meant to draw attention to the perceived rightward swing of the Supreme Court.
23. The Riot Grrrl Collection at Fales Library features numerous artifacts that illustrate the evolution of Riot Grrrls' ideals throughout the summer of 1991 in Washington, DC. Both the Kathleen Hanna Papers and the Molly Neuman Riot Grrrl Collection contain drafts of writing that would appear in zines of the time, as well as personal correspondence, that show the process of honing Riot Grrrl's goals and philosophies.
24. Each bullet point of the manifesto starts with "BECAUSE," including "BECAUSE we know that life is much more than physical survival and are patently aware that the punk rock 'you can do anything' idea is crucial to the coming angry grrrl rock revolution which seeks to save the psychic and cultural lives of girls and women everywhere, according to their own terms, not ours."
25. In 2018, many would find a similar anger in the confirmation hearings for Brett Kavanaugh, in Christine Blasey Ford's testimony that Kavanaugh had assaulted her in the early 1980s when they were both high school students. "Broken," a song on Sleater-Kinney's 2019 album *The Center Won't Hold*, addresses Blasey Ford's testimony.
26. Third-wave feminism encompasses a wide range of philosophies and political perspectives. For more on the third wave in general, see Gillis, Howie, and Munford (2004); and Henry (2004). For more on how third-wave feminism intersects with popular music, see Keenan (2010, 2015).
27. See the US House of Representatives web page "Women on the Campaign Trail," https://history.house.gov/Exhibitions-and-Publications/WIC/Historical-Essays/Assembling-Amplifying-Ascending/Women-Decade/ (accessed November 15, 2019).
28. For more on generational frameworks in feminism, see Henry (2004). For a critique of generational frameworks, see Hemmings (2011).
29. I want to be very specific here in noting that this critique was made by white writers, from a position of more power, about Riot Grrrl, and not women or girls of color who felt Riot Grrrl excluded them as participants. Critiques by women of color from within and

outside Riot Grrrl tended to highlight concerns about white privilege and the unexamined prejudices that white participants in Riot Grrrl held, but are not in service of dismissing concepts such as harassment or date rape.

30. Many articles distanced Riot Grrrl from earlier feminism, such as those in *Newsweek*. But had the journalists had access, they would perhaps have learned that many of the early Riot Grrrls had second-wave feminist mothers, including Allison Wolfe, whose lesbian feminist mother had started a women's health clinic in Olympia.
31. Some of the most prominent zine writers and musicians identified as lesbian or queer, which will be discussed in more detail later in this essay.
32. It's worth noting that White misuses the term "rape culture" here. "Rape culture" does not mean a group of victims speaking about their abuse, but a culture in which rape and sexual abuse are normalized and excused, not called out.
33. An exception is White's "Revolution Girl-Style Now!" (1992), which noted that "until the Riot Girls address the socioeconomic basis of their movement—the way their somewhat privileged lives have given them the time and the freedom to express their rage, have given them enough economic power to desire other types of power—their force will be limited."
34. An example of this coding is Lauren Spencer's "Grrrls Only," *Washington Post*, January 3, 1993.
35. The idea that Riot Grrrls were elitist along taste lines only works if one does not read Riot Grrrl zines. See, for example, Radway (2016).
36. France notes that this quote is part of a *Melody Maker* editorial that Love penned. However, France uses Love's words to paint a larger picture of Riot Grrrls as enemies of other female musicians.
37. For more on Ladyfest, see Keenan (2008).
38. For an account of how music journalists apply the term "Riot Grrrl" both retroactively and to contemporary bands outside the scope of the movement, see Zoladz (2011).
39. This argument also underpins Schilt (2003), in which the epigraphs move from Riot Grrrl to the Spice Girls.
40. A condensed version of Douglas's view of the third wave appears in Keenan (2015).
41. Interview with the author, May 28, 2010.
42. Interview with the author, June 14, 2010.
43. This location seems like it falls into the "elitism" trap that has followed Riot Grrrl from the beginning, but, at the same time, few places offer both institutional security and public access. See Eichorn (2013).
44. For a thorough explanation of archival theory in relation to the Riot Grrrl Collection, see Eichorn (2013).
45. The *Village Voice* provided some of the earliest coverage, which featured a photo of Darms with Hanna's filing cabinet, giving a sense of physicality to the materials in the archive. See Soloski (2010).
46. Darms is also my friend and a colleague with whom I have published a paper. Eichorn writes thoughtfully on Darms's personal connections to many of the archive's donors in her chapter on the Riot Grrrl Collection in Eichorn (2013).
47. These include Teresa Carmody's Ladyfest Collection; the Mimi Thi Nguyen Zine Archive, in collaboration with PoC Zine project; and Matt Wobensmith's Outpunk Archive.
48. Interview with the author, August 17, 2010.
49. Interview with the author, August 17, 2010.
50. For a more detailed analysis of the Kathleen Hanna Papers, see Downes (2014).

51. "Riot Grrrl Test Patterns" notebook in the Kathleen Hanna Papers, Fales Library and Special Collections, New York University, New York, MSS.271, Box: 2, Folder: 22.
52. In her chapter on the Riot Grrrl Collection, Eichorn argues that subcultural theory insufficiently addresses Riot Grrrl, because "the scope and range of radical literatures, critical theory, and avant-garde works included and referenced in Hanna's files in the Riot Grrrl Collection suggests that at least at its point of origin, Riot Grrrl was already far too self-reflexive and entangled in the institutions and industries it sought to occupy and critique to be understood simply through a framework of youth dissent" (2013, 112). While Eichorn makes a good point about the scope of influences for Riot Grrrl, her analysis gives short shrift to subcultural studies, which has long outgrown the framework of "youth dissent," and ignores the ways that Riot Grrrl's participants filtered their influences through the language of punk subculture.
53. "Riot Grrrl Test Patterns."
54. "Riot Grrrl Test Patterns."
55. Although the donors in this list are white, some of their collections contain materials by people of color.
56. An excerpt of this essay can be found in Darms (2013).
57. Lisa Darms, @lisa_deee, "I'm making final selections for my @FeministPress book of Riot Grrrl ephemera: zines, flyers, and more! What would you love to see included?," August 2, 2012, https://twitter.com/Lisa_Deee/status/231110146707836929?s=20.
58. Daniela Capistrano, @POCZineProject, ".@LisaDarms @FeministPress Let us know if you need suggestions for #pozcines for your riot grrrrl book. Happy to assist," August 3, 2012, https://twitter.com/POCZineProject/status/231254929577218048?s=20.
59. Mimi Nguyen, "Fales Library Donation Statement," January 13, 2012, https://poczineproject.tumblr.com/post/40517982011/poczp-news-mimi-collection-donation-statement-fales.
60. Nguyen, "Fales Library Donation Statement."
61. It's worth noting that Mary Celeste Kearney (1997) made a similar observation that the mainstream media coverage of Riot Grrrl, but, outside Kearney's writing on Riot Grrrl, it remains an issue within the academy as well.
62. Interview with the author, December 10, 2010.
63. For more on these zine collections, see Eichorn (2013).
64. Significantly, the only mention of music in the press around the Riot Grrrl Collection is Kathleen Hanna's tapes for *Julie Ruin*, an album that she wrote between Bikini Kill and Le Tigre. Along with the eight-track tapes, Hanna donated the eight-track player on which it was recorded, so that musicologists would have access to the recordings; but so far, Darms hasn't found any way of giving researchers access to the tapes while preserving them.
65. At the same time, there is definitely room for a critical analysis of how Riot Grrrl addressed race in songs such as Bikini Kill's "White Boy," Bratmobile's "Polaroid Baby," and Heavens to Betsy's "White Girl."
66. I am thinking here of the recent discussions around female anger after the 2016 election. See, for example, Brittany Cooper, *Eloquent Rage: A Black Feminist Discovers Her Superpower* (New York: St. Martin's Press, 2018); Soraya Chemaly, *Rage Becomes Her: The Power of Women's Anger* (New York: Simon & Schuster, 2018); and Rebecca Traister, *Good and Mad: The Revolutionary Power of Women's Anger* (New York: Simon & Schuster, 2018).

References

Best, Gabby. 2015. "Alternatives to Alternatives: the Black Grrrls Riot Ignored." *Vice*, August 3, 2015. https://www.vice.com/en_us/article/9k99a7/alternatives-to-alternatives-the-black-grrrls-riot-ignored.

Boym, Svetlana. 2002. *The Future of Nostalgia*. New York: Basic Books.

Darms, Lisa, ed. 2013. *The Riot Grrrl Collection*. New York: Feminist Press.

de Witt, Karen. 1992. "Huge Crowd Backs Right to Abortion in Capital March." *New York Times*, April 6, 1992. https://www.nytimes.com/1992/04/06/us/huge-crowd-backs-right-to-abortion-in-capital-march.html.

Downes, Julia. 2014. "'We Are Turning Cursive Letters into Knives': The Synthesis of the Written Word, Sound and Action in Riot Grrrl Cultural Resistance." In *Litpop: Writing and Popular Music*, edited by Rachel Carroll and Adam Hansen, 89–105. Farnham, UK: Ashgate.

Douglas, Susan. 1994. *Where the Girls Are: Growing Up Female with the Mass Media*. New York: Three Rivers Press.

Douglas, Susan. 2010. *Enlightened Feminism: The Seductive Message That Feminism's Work Is Done*. New York: Times Books.

Dunn, Kevin, and May Summer Farnsworth. 2012. "'We ARE the Revolution': Riot Grrrl Press, Girl Empowerment, and DIY Self-Publishing." *Women's Studies* 41, no. 2: 136–157.

Echols, Alice. 1987. *Daring to Be Bad: Radical Feminism in America 1967–1975*. Minneapolis: University of Minnesota Press, 1987.

Eichorn, Kate. 2013. *The Archival Turn in Feminism: Outrage in Order*. Philadelphia: Temple University Press.

Euse, Erica. 2017. "Revisiting Riot Grrrl's Perverse Love of Infantilized Hair: How Baby Barrettes and Pigtails Came to Symbolize a New Kind of Feminism." *Vice*, June 22, 2017. https://i-d.vice.com/en_us/article/7xbvga/revisiting-riot-grrrls-perverse-love-of-infantilized-hair.

Faludi, Susan. 1991. *Backlash: The Undeclared War against Women*. New York: Crown.

France, Kim. 1993. "Grrrls at War." *Rolling Stone*, July 8–22, 1993.

Gillis, Stacy, Gillian Howie, and Rebecca Munford, eds. 2004. *Third Wave Feminism: A Critical Exploration*. New York: Palgrave Macmillan.

Gottlieb, Joanne, and Gayle Wald. 1994. "Smells Like Teen Spirit: Revolution and Women in Independent Rock." In *Microphone Fiends: Youth Music and Youth Culture*, edited by Andrew Ross and Tricia Rose, 250–274. New York: Routledge.

Hemmings, Clare. 2011. *Why Stories Matter: The Political Grammar of Feminist Theory*. Durham, NC: Duke University Press.

Henry, Astrid. 2004. *Not My Mother's Sister: Generational Conflict and Third-Wave Feminism*. Bloomington: Indiana University Press.

Heywood, Leslie, and Jennifer Drake, eds. 1997. *Third Wave Agenda: Being Feminist, Doing Feminism*. Minneapolis: University of Minnesota Press.

Kearney, Mary Celeste. 1997. "The Missing Links: Riot Grrrl—Feminism—Lesbian Culture." In *Sexing the Groove: Popular Music and Gender*, edited by Sheila Whiteley, 207–229. London: Routledge.

Kearney, Mary Celeste. 2006. *Girls Make Media*. New York: Routledge.

Keenan, Elizabeth K. 2008. "'Who Are You Calling "Lady"?' Femininity, Sexuality, and Third-Wave Feminism." *Journal of Popular Music Studies* 20, no. 4: 378–401.

Keenan, Elizabeth K. 2010. "If Liz Phair's *Exile in Guyville* Made You a Feminist, What Kind of Feminist Are You? Heterosexuality, Race, and Class in the Third Wave." *Women & Music* 14: 45–71.

Keenan, Elizabeth K. 2015. "Intersectionality in Third-Wave Popular Music: Sexuality, Race, and Class." In *Oxford Handbooks Online*. https://www.oxfordhandbooks.com/view/10.1093/oxfordhb/9780199935321.001.0001/oxfordhb-9780199935321-e-36?rskey=acbqJV&result=1.

Keenan, Elizabeth K., and Lisa Darms. 2013. "Safe Space: the Riot Grrrl Collection." *Archivaria* 76 (Fall 2013): 55–74.

Korn, Gabrielle. 2015. "6 Rad Spring Looks for Rebel Girls." *Nylon*, March 25, 2015. https://nylon.com/articles/spring-beauty-punk-makeup.

Leonard, Marion. 1997. "'Rebel Girl, You Are the Queen of My World': Feminism, 'Subculture,' and Grrrl Power." In *Sexing the Groove: Popular Music and Gender*, edited by Sheila Whiteley, 230–256. London: Routledge.

Marcus, Sara. 2010. *Girls to the Front: The True Story of the Riot Grrrl Revolution*. New York: Harper Perennial.

Marcus, Sara, and Marisa Meltzer. 2010. "Exile from Grrrlville: What Happened to All the Angry Powerful Women in '90s Rock?" *Slate*, February 11, 2010. https://slate.com/human-interest/2010/02/a-discussion-about-liz-phair-riot-grrrls-and-other-90s-women-in-rock.html.

Meltzer, Marisa. 2010. *Girl Power: The Nineties Revolution in Music*. New York: Faber and Faber.

Muñoz, Jose Esteban. 2009. *Cruising Utopia: The Then and There of Queer Futurity*. New York: New York University Press.

Nehring, Neil. 1997. *Popular Music, Gender, and Postmodernism: Anger Is an Energy*. Thousand Oaks, CA: SAGE.

Newsweek Staff. 1992. "Revolution, Girl Style." *Newsweek*, November 22, 1992. https://www.newsweek.com/revolution-girl-style-196998.

Nguyen, Mimi Thi. 2012. "Riot Grrrl, Race, and Revival." *Women & Performance: A Journal of Feminist Theory* 22, no. 2–3: 173–196.

Paglia, Camille. 1992. *Sex, Art, and American Culture: Essays*. New York: Vintage Books.

Pelly, Jenn. 2019. "How Bikini Kill Got Together." *Pitchfork*, April 26, 2019. https://pitchfork.com/thepitch/how-bikini-kill-got-back-together/.

Piepmeier, Alison. 2009. *Girl Zines: Making Media, Doing Feminism*. New York: New York University Press.

Radway, Janice. 2016. "Girl Zine Networks, Underground Itineraries, and Riot Grrrl History: Making Sense of the Struggle for New Social Forms in the 1990s and Beyond." *Journal of American Studies* 50, no. 1: 1–31.

Reynolds, Simon. 2011. *Retromania*. New York: Farrar, Straus and Giroux.

Roiphe, Katie. 1994. *The Morning After: Sex, Fear, and Feminism on Campus*. Boston: Back Bay Books.

Romano, Renee C. 2012. "Not Dead Yet: My Identity Crisis as a Historian of the Recent Past." In *Doing Recent History: On Privacy, Copyright, Video Games, Institutional Review Boards, Activist Scholarship, and History that Talks Back*, edited by Claire R. Potter and Renee C. Romano, 23–44. Athens, GA: University of Georgia Press.

Schilt, Kristin. 2003. "'A Little Too Ironic': The Appropriation and Packaging of Riot Grrrl Politics by Mainstream Female Musicians." *Popular Music and Society* 26, no. 1: 5–16.

Schilt, Kristin. 2004. "'Riot Grrrl Is...': Contestation over Meaning in a Music Scene." In *Music Scenes: Local, Translocal, and Virtual*, edited by Andy Bennett and Richard A. Peterson, 115–130. Nashville, TN: Vanderbilt University Press.

Schilt, Kristin. 2005. "'The Punk White Privilege Scene': Riot Grrrl, White Privilege, and Zines." In *Different Wavelengths: Studies of the Contemporary Women's Movement*, edited by Jo Reger, 39–56. New York: Routledge.

Schilt, Kristen, and Elke Zobl. 2008. "Connecting the Dots: Riot Grrrls, Ladyfests, and the International Grrrl Zine Network." In *Next Wave Cultures: Feminism, Subcultures, Activism*, edited by Anita Harris, 171–192. New York: Routledge.

Scott, Joan Wallach. 1988. *Gender and the Politics of History*. New York: Columbia University Press.

Soloski, Alex. 2010. "Revolution, Girl-Style—Shhh!" *Village Voice*, April 6, 2010. https://www.villagevoice.com/2010/04/06/revolution-girl-style-shhh/.

Walker, Rebecca. 1992. "Becoming the Third Wave." *Ms.*, January 1992, 39–41.

White, Emily. 1992. "Revolution Girl-Style Now! Notes from the Teenage Feminist Rock 'n' Roll Underground." *LA Weekly* 14, no. 32 (July 10–16, 1992). https://www.chicagoreader.com/chicago/revolution-girl-style-now/Content?oid=880507.

Zoladz, Lindsay. 2011. "Not Every Girl Is a Riot Grrrl." *Pitchfork*, November 16, 2011. https://pitchfork.com/features/article/8710-not-every-girl-is-a-riot-grrrl/.

CHAPTER 4

PUNK AS FOLK

Continuities and Tensions in the UK and Beyond

PETE DALE

Introduction

PUNK and folk are associated at least closely enough for "folk punk" to be a well-established (if loose) category. In some popular sources (such as *Wikipedia*), that category would seem to stretch to almost anything punky that is played on an acoustic guitar. The English singer-songwriter Patrik Fitzgerald's output from the late 1970s might be claimed by some as a starting point for the genre (or, perhaps better, subgenre/hybrid-genre) of folk punk. For the kind of folk purists associated with the organization in London that champions traditional music, the English Folk Dance and Song Society (EFDSS), and the affiliated Cecil Sharp House, however, the songs of someone like Fitzgerald would doubtless be considered a far cry from their objects of interest, even though they were mostly a single voice accompanied by an acoustic guitar. The International Folk Music Council's 1954 concession to "continuity, variation, and selection" remains a watershed moment in the history of folkloristics across the world (IFMC 1955). Nevertheless, it seems certain that a song like Patrik Fitzgerald's "Buy Me, Sell Me" (1978a) would contain far too much of the second of these elements (variation from folk tradition) and too little of the first (continuity of tradition) to be allocated the title of "folk song" by many within the EFDSS and the like.[1] Most punks, meanwhile, have very limited interest in Morris Dancing, based on my experience.

Punk and folk are not the same thing, then, though there are some shared elements. In this chapter, I begin by discussing the main similarities and continuities, which include amateur approaches to music-making, broadly leftist tendencies, and collective music-making. I then explore some important tensions. First, regarding the tensions between punk and folk, I challenge punk's and so-called post-punk's claim to "year zero" novelty, showing that there is always something (a good deal, indeed) being carried forward musically from the past. The critique of the folk ideal for its efforts to present or preserve a pure tradition is well established, thus I spend little time discussing it.[2] Critique of punk's frequently modernist tendencies is less common, however, and I therefore focus more on this: punk, I argue, is very much a tradition. Furthermore, the traditions of punk continue well past 1984, despite a tendency in some quarters to delimit post-punk to that year, or even to restrict punk, in the UK at least, to the 1970s.[3] Punk, over decades now, has carried forward the past through repeated "re-births" (Dale 2012) in the form of punk subgenres such as anarcho-punk, cutie, Riot Grrrl, math rock, and many more. Nevertheless, rhetoric around a novelty that, tautologically enough, could arrive from nowhere (from "the void," one might say if one wanted to invoke Badiou, as Simon Reynolds, for example, repeatedly has) remains common to some punk-related discourses, as well as in broader discussions of the state of popular music.[4]

Having discussed the broadly aesthetic question of novelty in relation to both punk and folk, I move to attempt a disambiguation of the politics of punk from the politics of the folk tradition(s). Both are often leftist, granted, but the latter links more strongly to socialist traditions (songs in favor of the unions, invocations of essentially Marxist ideals, and so forth), while punk's shifting relation with anarchism, sometimes strongly articulated, is well known. The punk rhetoric around anarchism marks it out as having a different trajectory from the typical tendency found in leftist folk. (Both folk and punk have nationalist and right-wing undercurrents, of course, a fact that is beginning to be more researched. The classic early study is Sabin 1999; see also Worley 2017; Raposa 2012; and Duncombe and Tremblay 2011.)

My third exploration of key differences between folk and punk centers on the specific detail of collective and individual agency and creativity in each. Collective music-making occurs in both punk and folk contexts, admittedly, with a degree of dispersal of creative work in both. However, it can be argued that folk music, through its floor-singing tradition, does more to ensure that "anyone can do it" than punk typically does. Yet, and at the same time, folk musicians often want to develop their playing as a craft within a "musicianly" milieu, whereas punk can still privilege unskilled and spontaneous music-making by inspired individuals.

Who Put the Folk in Punk?

As I have detailed in *Anyone Can Do It* (Dale 2012), claims to a similarity between folk and punk are quite common, as these examples illustrate: "Structurally, there isn't a whole lot of difference between some punk music and folk music—three chords, verse and chorus" (Andy Sheie, quoted in Farseth 2001, 166); "For me, Hardcore is Folk Music" (Ed Ivey of Rhythm Pigs, quoted in Blush 2001, 43); "the Ramones 'I Wanna Be Sedated' is what folk music is really all about" (Neil Gaiman, in Millar 2006); "the traditional sing-alongs of the 1960s folk revival and early punk sensibilities two decades later" can be linked due to the key element of "participation" (Drew 2004, 76); US folksinger Lead Belly "was the first punk rocker" (attributed to Kurt Cobain, quoted in True 2006, 147); and so forth. As I showed, Penny Rimbaud of leading punk band Crass has claimed his band's work as "modern folk music," with punk in general being "people's music for the people by the people" (a description which many also, or instead, would apply to folk) (Rimbaud 1998, 96). David Hesmondhalgh, meanwhile, has linked the punk-related "indie" scene to "folk revivalism" (1999, 56).

More recently, John Encarnacao (2013) has made an interesting contribution to the broad topic in *Punk Aesthetics and New Folk: Way Down the Old Plank Road*. Encarnacao's understanding of what constitutes folk is simultaneously narrower and broader than my own. He has little interest in the "revival of folk that was often preservationist in its ideals"—a scene he associates with the "second" folk revival of the 1950s and 1960s (the earlier folk song revivals, of ca. 1890–1920 in the UK and the 1930s and 1940s in the US, figure minimally in his book). Instead, Encarnacao prefers the 1960s' "idiosyncratic" musicians and "more diverse mixture" of rock-influenced folk-associated music: Dylan and so forth (Encarnacao 2013, 75). This allows him to sweep a huge range of music into the bracket of folk: Tim Buckley, the Incredible String Band, even Pink Floyd. To be fair, Encarnacao is explicit as to the breadth of his definition: "I will use the term 'folk' to denote acoustic tendencies and the use of traditional, pre–Tin Pan Alley song forms and techniques in rock practice." He is interested in folk within "the discourse of rock music," in other words (8). Encarnacao is careful in the language used to articulate his scope; for example, he takes pains to emphasize that some of the punk-associated "new folk" he discusses will only "carry connotations of folk music for *some listeners*" (11; emphasis added). Many other listeners, I suggest, would find his argument that John Fahey's 1968 *The Voice of The Turtle* album evokes "[p]unk aesthetics... on several levels" (90) contentious, but he is probably on good ground in regards to at least some listeners.

Overall, Encarnacao's research differs from my own in that he is more keen to emphasize the continuities between folk and punk than to explore the tensions between them. The similarities he finds largely echo the quotations offered above. Punk uses the "spirit of inclusion and spontaneity of folk music"; it "has been handed down to people living through the second half of the twentieth century and into the next *as* folk music." There are "ideological aspects common to folk and punk." These include "constructions of authenticity" around being "'natural,' 'unmediated,' 'small' and 'informal'" (all can be interrogated), and which yet retain "continuing power" in vernacular discourse and music-making practice (Encarnacao 2013, 2, emphasis in original, 41, 27). From the outset, Encarnacao is keen to emphasize the "preference for the hand-made" and the use of "rhetorics that celebrate the amateur and communal in preference to demonstrations of instrumental technique and technological mastery." With good reason, he associates these with both folk and punk, but he also finds that this "dichotomy" (amateurism versus mastery of technique/technology) is "unsustainable" (1).

Building from all of the folk/punk continuities so far in this chapter, I prioritize three elements as being notable similarities between folk and punk. First, amateur and typically "low-tech" approaches to music-making are common to both fields. The idea that "anyone can do it" is common in folk and punk discourses, while guitars (electric in punk, acoustic in folk, typically) are far more common than, say, synthesizers. Each field holds faith with the idea that something exciting happens when a beginner picks up a guitar.

Second, Encarnacao is certainly correct that there are common ideological trajectories. I would say, further, that the ideological tendency in question tends to be broadly leftist (especially in more recent periods of the punk tradition). Consider the Campaign for Nuclear Disarmament (CND), for example. George McKay has suggested that "a soundtrack of jazz and folk" was important for the "subcultural politics" of CND's Aldermaston protest marches in the late 1950s (2005, 47), while Jon Savage has asserted that Crass "sowed the ground for the return of serious anarchism and the popularity of CND in the early eighties" (1991, 598). During the national UK Miners' Strike of 1984–1985, it was not only folkies like Dick Gaughan who raised money for the strikers' families, but also innumerable punk bands at their benefit gigs (see Glasper 2006). Since the 1980s, the "alternative lifestyles" that can be recognized with a still extant festival scene ("New Age travelers," as some will label them) tend to be soundtracked by traditional music, punk (and punk-related) music, and, often in the far corner of the field, EDM of one kind of another. For decades, both punk and folk have raised money for, and raised spirits within, the Left, and leftist sentiments are recognizable within the lyrics of countless folk and punk songs.

The third element of similarity I prioritize between punk and folk is collective music-making. An editorial complaint from the folk magazine *The Living Tradition* in 2006 was that folk enthusiasts are "increasingly being treated as music consumers rather than music-makers," due to "the majors . . . [and the] big music business" (quoted in Dale 2012, 43). The tone here strongly recalls that of the fanzines of the punk movement. Punks and folkies make music, of course, but, more importantly, there is an expectation that participants will do it *together*. This might mean the singalong of a folk session or the collective release of intermingling bodies at a punk gig. It might involve membership of or regular attendance at one of the folk clubs that still exist in pub backrooms up and down the UK, or it might mean creating a "DIY space" that claims to be "autonomous." On several levels, punk and folk encourage enthusiasts to get involved, and that involvement takes place in dedicated non-elite musical spaces—this is a key commonality.

I hope that I have shown in this section that a discourse exists that associates punk with folk. Many of the comparisons are very reasonable. It is also the case, nonetheless, that the two fields are far from being synonymous. Indeed, there are important tensions between punk and folk, and it is to these that I now turn, beginning with the question of tradition in relation to perceived-to-be-striking innovation.

Tradition versus Novelty

The folk idea of a pure tradition—a reliable and identifiable collection of cultural products that should be kept free from the corruption of modern mores, that is—has been widely challenged (Boyes 1993; Harker 1985). As Richard Middleton has shown, the distinction that J. G. Herder made in the late eighteenth century between *das Volk* (the folk-singing people) and *der Poebel* (the "shrieking mob," as Herder put it) demonstrates that conceptions of "folk culture" were politically problematic from a very early stage (Middleton 2003, 252). As noted earlier, mid-twentieth-century acknowledgement that the maintenance of a pure tradition would be impossible is reflected in the International Folk Music Council's 1954 resolution that variation would inevitably take place. By the later 1950s, A. L. Lloyd and Ewan MacColl were further challenging orthodox sensibilities by treating the nineteenth-century songs of industrial workers as folk material, rather than assuming that folk songs must derive from rural and ancient contexts. Eric Hobsbawm and Terence Ranger's *The Invention of Tradition* (1983) further undermined the view of traditions more broadly as pure and reliably fixed entities. Specifically within folk music, Georgina Boyes's *The Imagined Village* (1993) interrogated the orthodoxies that emerged from the EFDSS in the twentieth century.

The world of folk, then, eventually tuned in to the idea that traditions are always in flux, always developing, and never perfectly identifiable or pure. Regrettably, however, the converse and fundamentally modernist idea that, shall we say, *tradition can be fully escaped* has not been challenged quite as rigorously, I would assert. On the contrary, the works associated with high modernism, and the values that effectively prompted their creation, still tend to get prioritized and are rarely critiqued in a strong way.

It is perhaps not surprising, therefore, that a quite glib modernism can be found often in the vernacular discourses of punk and (so-called) post-punk musics. Talk of "year zero" in punk has been quite common; indeed, singer Billy Bragg (a highly important figure in the crossing of punk with folk) has gone as far as to argue that the phrase was applied to a "Stalinist" extent in the heyday of UK punk (quoted in Robb 2006, 530). Dave Thompson echoes the commonplace idea: "What made punk so exceptional as a cultural force was that it came out of nowhere," and thus "had no precedent, no past and ... no parallel" (2004, 7). As noted already, Reynolds is the strongest advocate for modernist tendencies in punk and post-punk alike, as signaled by book titles alone: *Rip It Up and Start Again* (2005) and *Retromania* (2011). We should also note that concerns about the possibility for new directions for punk/post-punk in the future are also voiced by contemporary enthusiasts of this music. For one example, consider the title alone of a 2014 *Noisey* online article: "Punk Needs New Ideas: The current state of punk is actually great. It's just been done before" (Sailer 2014).

The idea that punk was radically novel, and that it needs to maintain aesthetic novelty, remains strong today, then. I am broadly in agreement with Marshall Berman's declaration that punk bands "are modernists whether they know it or not" (1992, 45). Punk tends to hope "to break the windows and leap to freedom," whereas folk musicians, if we can stretch the metaphor, are generally inclined to leave the windows intact—and perhaps use the door to get out, or just open the windows for a sniff of freedom (46). Folk traditions morph, inevitably, but a distinct repertoire and a performance style have been kept alive, nonetheless, retaining a wide popularity. Many forms of punk are highly consistent in their musical content once a formula has been established: "D-Beat" sounds like this, "ska punk" sounds like that, and most acculturated listeners know which subcategory of punk a particular band can best be placed within. Clearly, however, a rhetoric around absolute novelty has been strong in punk from the 1970s to the present. Even though punk creates a tradition, there are always dissenting voices who say this is not what punk should be doing. Not all those involved in or commenting on punk say that it has to have radical novelty to be valuable, then, but many do.

A major issue with this modernism-recalling (intermittent) preference for absolute novelty in punk ("rip it up and start again") is that punk and post-punk *always* carried forward existing musical elements. There have always been essentially "traditional" elements in play in punk. "Punk rock" grows from the rock tradition, obviously; post-punk, even as it reacts against the reification of punk, grows from not only punk itself (a negation that, as a negation, already contains aspects of the thing it would negate within it), but also the broader twentieth-century traditions of modernism and avant-gardism (see Marcus 2001). Following a Derridean line, we might add that such an "always already" is necessarily the case in every creative event; from Kandinsky to Throbbing Gristle, the shock of the new will always mix with the ring of familiarity precisely because, as Derrida has emphatically put it, "everything begins before it begins" (2006, 202). Take, say, the song "New Rose" by the Damned, generally understood to have been released as the UK's first punk single, in 1976. I agree with producer Nick Lowe that this music was "startlingly original" in its day—the title even tells us as much, for it is "new" and it has risen ("rose"); nevertheless, it was simultaneously "an ancient story somehow told in a brand new way," according to Lowe (quoted in Dale 2016, 82). Such is always the structure, according to post-structuralism: the new is always supplementary to (that is, conjoined to but not fully part of) that which preexists it. What Derrida calls the "trace"—the strictly non-present but felt to be discernible track or path we might otherwise call "tradition"—is always in play: no avant-gardist can escape it but, simultaneously, no traditionalist can bring it fully in to view, for it is always already an absent presence.

Marxism versus Anarchism

Not every folk singer is a Marxist, by any means; most, indeed, are not. Nevertheless, there have been a number of powerfully socialist individuals, some of whom have been Marxists, within the folk field: Woody Guthrie, Pete Seeger, Alan Lomax, A. L. Lloyd,

Ewan MacColl, Irwin Silber, Jack Elliott of Birtley, Leon Rosselson, and others. Topic Records, a central plank in recorded music of the mid-twentieth-century folk revival in the UK, emerged from the communist-affiliated Workers' Music Association. Folk songs relating to the struggles of workers are innumerable. There are strong reasons, then, to suggest that there has a been a long-held and strong affiliation between folk music and socialism; quite a number of folk singers and folk songs, it turns out, are Marxist.

Similarly, not all punks and punk bands are anarchists, and yet anarchy has been talked about a great deal by punk fanzines, punk bands, and in punk songs. The debut single by the Sex Pistols, "Anarchy in the UK," is the era-defining example, of course, but countless songs by, notably, Crass are also of pivotal influence via their development of anarcho-punk (see Glasper 2006; Cross 2010; Dines and Worley 2016). Even as the Clash are often claimed as a socialistic group, it is fair to say that their politics aligned more with the squatting-orientated counterculture that members were involved in than any traditional leftism. It is reasonable, overall, to argue that punk in the 1970s and beyond tends to be anarchistic at least at the level of rhetoric.

To what does this broad-brush difference of political tendency between folk and punk speak? In part, I would suggest, it reflects a broad contrast within "leftism," at least in the UK, between the middle decades and the latter end of the twentieth century. Leftist folk singers and folk songs were often concerned with the experience of workers; punk songs have often been hostile even to the idea of work as such. Returning to the example of Patrik Fitzgerald, we can note his lyrical statement in 1978 that "I don't know what your Daddy would say if he knew your friends refused to work," gleefully adding "Up the Revolution! And up your Dad!" In the same song, furthermore, Fitzgerald comments that we get "a Labour government, then a Conservative government, then a Labour government, then a Conservative government, then a Labour government, etcetera etcetera etcetera" (Fitzgerald 1978b). Arguably, such anarchistic rejection of the postwar consensus means that punks like Fitzgerald were anti-political rather than being truly leftist: rather than calling for solidarity among workers, punks seem to have taken the Sex Pistols' "We don't care!" as their only value (Sex Pistols 1977a). In some cases, this would be true: early punk often did have strongly nihilistic tendencies, from LA to London. However, it is clear that many other groups, from Crass to the Clash to Fugazi, had a fairly strong social conscience. Note, for example, that Fitzgerald attacks internationalists who are fighting "irrelevant battles" in regard to "children in Chile" and such like, on the grounds that, in our "own backyard," "some of us are having a hard, hard time" (1978c). Overall, we can find a broadly leftist agenda in much punk if we understand leftism to entail a socially conscious focus on the plight of the disadvantaged as well as a resistance to the dominant order. Furthermore, this social tendency grew in the 1990s and into the twenty-first century; punks have formed a very significant constituency within the anti-globalization "black bloc," for example.

Are the political differences between folk and punk simply a reflection of larger social forces in which socialism and Marxism fell from favor just as unemployment rose sharply in the UK during the 1970s? It is significant, perhaps, that one of the most overtly socialist punk-informed acts, Billy Bragg, is often placed within a folk bracket and, furthermore, has drawn parts of his repertoire from Woody Guthrie, Leon Rosselson, Dick Gaughan, and the like. A "punk," etymologically speaking, can be assigned as a worthless person; even the worker is not so low, socially speaking.

Perhaps, then, the rise of punk and the declining popularity of folk does reflect broad social changes across the last fifty years. In Marxist terms, we might suggest that a change in the economic base has been enacted by the increase in manufacturing automation, the increased globalization of capitalism, and so forth; this, in turn, has brought a change in the cultural "superstructure," one expression of which can be found in the arrival of punk as a movement. As unemployment in the West rose, the punk replaced the worker as the alienated victim of the capitalist system, in short. Yet this kind of explanation is too tidy. For one thing, folk music always had its, shall we say, rugged individualists alongside those who were more conventionally socialist. We can note, for example, that Joe Hill (whose left-wing songs have come to be categorized as folk) was a Wobblie, a member of the International Workers of the World, an organization that many see as anarchist or anarcho-syndicalist. Perhaps more tellingly, in an influential moment within the documentary *Don't Look Back*, Bob Dylan is informed that the press are referring to him as an anarchist.[5] Obviously, anarchism does not begin with punk, but we can also note that, even within the narrower context of popular music, anarchistic tendencies are easily recognizable at numerous points prior to 1976.

Yet I argue that relatively few individuals who identify (or have identified) as punks would take a universalist and Marxist view as opposed to favoring the spontaneity of an anarchist trajectory of resistance to the dominant order. By contrast, quite a few agents within folk music have been prepared to follow an orthodox Marxist trajectory. For many punks, socialism, communism, and Marxism seem to have been regarded as part of the historical problem, whereas anarchist orientations seem to offer new and exciting possibilities. For this reason, the political questions I have explored in this section do relate to the question of tradition and novelty I explored in the last section. I shall return to this comparative point in the conclusion.

Collective versus Individual Creativity

Arguably, folk and punk are subcultural genres in the twenty-first century. Subcultures always involve collective agency on several levels, and genres are created by groups, not isolated individuals. As we have seen, both punks and folkies have often been leftists of some stripe, and leftism must surely entail collective agency on some level. There is no doubt, then, that both folk and punk have a collective character of sorts. However, the mode of creativity differs between punk and folk in important ways. Punk groups often create their music through a broadly mutual exploration of sonic possibilities, sometimes using instruments with which they have somewhat limited experience. The classic early punk claim was that individual x saw band y and decided to form a band, even though they had never considered playing music before. Such tales may well be apocryphal: the ever-growing literature on punk shows that many individuals (Joe Strummer of the Clash, who spoke of his epiphany at seeing the Sex Pistols; Billy Bragg, who has described the first time he saw the Clash as deeply inspiring; and so forth) were already either trying to learn to play instruments, or had actually already formed bands, before they encountered the punk band that spurred them further on. Nonetheless, punk certainly did embolden many fans to go further than they otherwise might have, and "beginners" to do more than just begin. Often the new activity involved a group adventure in which the rudiments of music were deduced, rather than being learned. Sometimes these rudiments were then finessed so that the group could find its own "sound"—one only has to listen to particular records to see that something like this seems to have identifiably occurred. Take "Jigsaw Feeling" by Siouxsie and the Banshees (1978), for example: the tritone that arises near the outset of the opening bass line (A to D#) is very unlikely to have been an accident arising from total lack of awareness of the rudiments of harmony. The strong use of dissonance in this song, and in countless comparable pieces of music from the punk/post-punk field, is much more likely to have represented an attempt to go "out there" into the perceived-to-be-radical world of dissonance.[6]

Such a mode of creativity is rather different from the folk process as normally conceived. A folk musician can be a beginner, of course; indeed, it is the neophyte musicality of folk song that often seems to have attracted the ear of musically trained individuals, resulting in a form of primitivism in its appeal to some. However, the IFMC's emphasis on continuity, variation, and selection indicates central preoccupations for folk music at least since the 1950s. Folk music is a repertoire; that repertoire shifts over time and sometimes "performances can, in fact, become so highly individual that the question will arise whether the singer can be said to have 'composed' a new song," as Ruth Crawford Seeger put it. Nonetheless, it is telling that Seeger seeks to downplay such individual significance by stating that any "invention" or "composition indeed" involved is best understood "mainly as added increment to a current stock or repertoire" (2001, 7). Selection and variation, in other words, are always subservient to continuity, without which there can be no folk tradition. To summarize, where folk emphasizes continuity, punk often (though not always) prefers *dis*continuity. We have already explored this to an extent. My focus in this section is the way this impacts on issues around the collective and the individual. We can relate this to openness to amateurism, on the one hand, and professionalism, on the other.

We have seen in several quotations cited so far that both punk and folk are supposed to be welcoming to amateurs, and there is much truth in that. Yet it is important to acknowledge that many of the UK's mainstream punk bands of the 1970s did have strongly competitive tendencies, a fact that a more celebratory account of DIY perhaps overlooks. Nevertheless, from the 1970s onward, individuals from punk bands have written fanzines praising other bands, organized gigs for and/or lent equipment to other bands, shared knowledge about how to make a record, and so forth. Punk bands, at the DIY level, tend to help each other make a start in music; as things become more professionalized and commercially successful, higher levels of competition are more likely to encroach, but at the grass roots, punk typically allows people to simply have a go.

Processes are similar in the folk field. In the grass-roots environment of, for example, a pub session where floor singers take turns to perform, the environment can be very welcoming. Sam Richards, for example, has argued that in the 1970s folk scene, which he experienced in the UK, it was assumed that "everyone had an equal right to do a floor spot once in a while" (1992, 74). This even included, Richards insists, "a chap in Exmouth who was practically tone deaf and utterly embarrassing to listen to." "While no bones were made about who were considered good singers," he argues, "those whose experience of singing was limited were rarely openly criticised for having a bad voice, a quiet voice, or anything else" (81, 74). It is here that we find a small but nonetheless notable difference between the folk scene's attitude toward amateurs and that which is, in general, typical of the punk scene. In the folk environment, amateurs are encouraged to perform even if and when they lack ability; however, technical mastery is valued highly, and amateurs are typically hungry to advance their skill just as professional folk musicians have done. In a punk context, by contrast, lack of technical prowess can be a badge of pride and technical mastery scorned.[7]

To put it briefly as well as generally, the folk musician works at musicianship in order to express one's individuality within a tradition. The punk musician (and scare quotes could be added to "musician" here, for many will argue that punk is not about being musicianly at all) rejects tradition in the hope of finding a radical individuality. This attempt at a radical individuality, I would argue, links back strongly to punk's modernist tendencies, as well as, less strongly but nonetheless significantly, to punk's political sensibilities, where working-class consciousness gives way to something more like social anarchism. I conclude with a discussion of how all this knits together to make *folk not quite the same as punk*, despite the range of interesting similarities.

Conclusion

Encarnacao and others are right to compare folk and punk: there are many similarities, and punk is something of a modern folk tradition in a certain sense. It is a tradition in sartorial terms, with punks generally being recognizable as a spectacular subculture. It is a tradition in musical terms because, although there has been variation across a wide range of punk subgenres, there are certain recognizable musical features that mark punk as, in essence, a musical genre. It is folk-like because the music has been transmitted orally across, at this point, a few generations, because the songs have given voice (often a dissenting voice) to many who otherwise might get little chance to express themselves, and because it is generally resistant to modern technology in music.

Some punk music is designed to maintain a traditional sound—"old school punk" gives a clue in the name in this regard, for example. Some punk music, however, is more modernist in its intent, as I have shown in this chapter: punk and post-punk music are seen to have been radically new, and it is often assumed that such music must retain radical novelty in order to retain value and/or political significance. From a Derridean perspective, the idea that punk and post-punk could have achieved a novelty *ex nihilo* is problematic. The risk of such a Derridean critique is to forget that punk, at various points for various listeners over more than four decades, has *felt* radically new. Punk often gives (young) people a new sense of radical possibility, and sometimes this new sense leads them to cause a nuisance (pun intended) for "the authorities" and "the system" (two favorite targets of punk rhetoric).

Folk music, by contrast, in my view, gives little or no new sense to the struggles of the Left. Many of the songs are concerned with workers' struggles and experiences, often historically set, but the sentiments are not presented as a reaction to radically shifting social realities and are not accompanied by shockingly new-sounding music. The Sex Pistols' cries about "no future for you" (1977b) and that "anarchy for the UK / it's coming some time maybe" (1976) seem to have felt like bold and highly relevant statements about life in Britain three decades after the end of World War II, set to music that clearly excited a huge number of listeners. Were the Sex Pistols serious anarchists? (Short answer: no.) Even Crass, renowned for a certain puritan seriousness of outlook, famously joked that their knowledge of anarchist theory was loose enough that they could have mistaken Bakunin for a brand of vodka (McKay 1996, 83; see also Donaghey 2013). However, punk's talk of anarchism resonated with many young people at a time when the traditional socialist Left, to which many folk musicians adhered, provoked cynicism.

Were the ostensibly post-Marxist and anarchistic Left, and the punks who formed part of the newest strand of the New Left, really all that different from the more traditional Left that many folk musicians remained faithful to? I think they probably wanted much the same thing—peace, and an end to exploitation, for a start, say—and it is important to note that the "traveler" scene of the 1980s onward tended to combine folk, punk, and, since the 1990s, electronic dance music (EDM), as well as, in this author's experience, stalls and workshops at festivals that span Marxism, anarchism, eco-consciousness, and more. This does not mean that folk and punk, and Marxism and anarchism, amount to the same thing. There are important tensions that can be explored at the micro level (the essentially artistic question as to whether individuals can best express themselves through radical novelty that breaks from groups and from collectivities, or by working within the confines of a collective tradition, for example) or at the macro level (geopolitical developments since 1945, say). Modernism, which I have argued punk recalls, may be a valuable thing we should hope will return, and traditionalism, which folk relies upon if it relies upon anything, might be preferable for the future of art and music. This chapter has not attempted to come down heavily on one side or the other regarding such matters. Moreover, my intention is to encourage at least hesitation and consideration before punk is claimed as simply "the new folk music" or some such thing, for there are complexities at work that cloud such a claim and that are intriguing, rewarding, and socially engaged facets of such rich popular music cultures.

NOTES

1. When I presented a paper titled "Punk as Folk" at the 2007 British Forum for Ethnomusicology annual conference (a significant bastion of traditional sensibilities vis-à-vis what folk can be said to be), I found significant hostility to the idea that punk could be defined in relation to folk (see Boyes 1993 for an understanding of the restricted sense of what folk music and culture can be said to be, as propounded by Cecil Sharp and the EFDSS).
2. See Boyes 1993 for a sustained critique of folk purism, or, for a more hostile account still, Harker 1985. For an attempt at a rebuttal of the "Harker-Boyes thesis," see Gregory 2009. For a critical yet sympathetic view of folk purism, see Gammon 2008.
3. To invoke the dominant example with regard to so-called post-punk, consider Simon Reynolds's *Rip It Up and Start Again* (2005). The tendency to delimit punk to the 1970s has reduced in recent years, but for a long time the common historical assumption about punk was that "it" happened in the late 1970s and ended when the Sex Pistols broke up in 1978. Key contemporary historical accounts such as Matt Worley's *No Future* have explicitly sought to avoid "ahistorical rememberings of punk circa 1976–78," and instead "to re-historicise British punk beyond its media *moment* through to . . . 1984" (2017, 23; emphasis in original). This realization, that punk actually retained great significance in the decades since the Sex Pistols were active, rather than ossifying and stagnating as a fixed subcultural object, has grown in recent years. See, for example, Kevin Dunn's *Global Punk*, which is emphatic that "despite repeated claims that 'punk is dead,' punk has become a global force that . . . changed the world and continues to do so" (2015, 9); see also Dale 2012. Beyond academia, the texts on punk by Ian Glasper are excellent "oral history"-type guides to the development of punk across the 1980s and 1990s (such as Glasper 2006).
4. For complaints about a perceived lack of progression in pop music in general (featuring some specific detail on latter-day punk and post-punk), Simon Reynolds's *Retromania* (2011) is the most strident example; see Reynolds 2011, 54, 428, for invocations of Badiou. For scholarly discussion of the broader issue of novelty and popular music, see Dale 2016 and Loss 2017. For a handwringing discussion of the perceived lack of newness in contemporary popular music, see countless newspaper articles and other journalistic discussions. The assumption that music has to be new to be good seems almost unshakeable in most quarters today, I would assert, very often including discourses in and around punk (see Sailer 2014).
5. Dylan's response to this—"'give the anarchist a cigarette!,' he declares with bemusement"—would eventually provide the name for a book by the countercultural musician and writer Mick Farren, *Give the Anarchist a Cigarette* (2001).
6. Steve Severin, who played the bass part under discussion, lists albums by Captain Beefheart, Glenn Branca, and Steve Reich among his Top Ten favorite records, indicating a clear taste for nonstandard music (Severin n.d.).
7. Regarding pride in lack of technical prowess, consider the self-consciously boring two-note guitar "solo" in Buzzcocks' landmark punk song "Boredom" (1977).

References

Berman, M. 1992. "Why Modernism Still Matters." In *Modernity and Identity*, edited by Scott Lash and Jonathan Friedman, 33–58. Oxford: Blackwell, 33–58.

Blush, S. 2001. *American Hardcore: A Tribal Account*. Los Angeles: Feral House.

Boyes, G. 1993. *The Imagined Village: Culture, Ideology and the English Folk Revival*. Manchester, UK: Manchester University Press.

Cross, R. 2010. "'There Is No Authority but Yourself': The Individual and the Collective in British Anarcho-Punk." *Music and Politics* 4, no. 2: 1–20.

Dale, P. 2012. *Anyone Can Do It: Empowerment, Tradition and the Punk Underground*. Aldershot, UK: Ashgate.

Dale, P. 2016. *Popular Music and the Politics of Novelty*. London: Bloomsbury.

Derrida, J. 2006. *Spectres of Marx: The State of the Debt, the Work of Mourning and the New International*. Translated by Peggy Kamuf. London: Routledge.

Dines, M., and M. Worley, eds. 2016. *The Aesthetic of Our Anger: Anarcho-Punk, Politics and Music*. Colchester, UK: Minor Compositions.

Donaghey, J. 2013. "Bakunin Brand Vodka: An Exploration into Anarchist-Punk and Punk-Anarchism." *Anarchist Developments in Cultural Studies* 1: 138–170.

Drew, R. 2004. "'Scenes': Dimensions of Karaoke in the United States." In *Music Scenes: Local, Translocal, and Virtual*, edited by Andy Bennett and Richard A. Peterson. Nashville, TN: Vanderbilt University Press, 64–79.

Duncombe, S., and M. Tremblay, eds. 2011. *White Riot: Punk Rock and the Politics of Race*. London: Verso.

Dunn, K. 2015. *Global Punk: Resistance and Rebellion in Everyday Life*. New York: Bloomsbury.

Encarnacao, J. 2013. *Punk Aesthetics and New Folk: Way Down the Old Plank Road*. Aldershot, UK: Ashgate.

Farren, M. 2001. *Give the Anarchist a Cigarette*. London: Jonathan Cape.

Farseth, E. 2001. *Wipe Away My Eyes: Underground Culture and Politics*. Minneapolis: Abandoned House.

Gammon, V. 2008. "'Many Useful Lessons': Cecil Sharp, Education and the Folk Dance Revival, 1899–1924." *Cultural and Social History* 5, no. 1: 75–97.

Glasper, I. 2006. *The Day the Country Died: A History of Anarcho-Punk, 1980–1984*. London: Cherry Red.

Gregory, D. 2009. "Fakesong in an Imagined Village? A Critique of the Harker-Boyes Thesis." *Canadian Folk Music* 43, no. 3: 18–26.

Harker, D. 1985. *Fakesong: The Manufacture of British "Folksong," 1700 to the Present Day*. Milton Keynes, UK: Open University Press.

Hesmondhalgh, D. 1999. "Indie: The Institutional Politics and Aesthetics of a Popular Music Genre." *Cultural Studies* 13, no. 1: 34–61.

Hobsbawm, E., and T. Ranger, eds. 1983. *The Invention of Tradition*. Cambridge: Cambridge University Press.

IFMC (International Folk Music Council). 1955. *Journal of the International Folk Music Council* 7.

Loss, R. 2017. *Nothing Has Been Done Before: Seeking the New in 21st Century American Popular Music*. London: Bloomsbury.

Marcus, G. 2001. *Lipstick Traces: A Secret History of the Twentieth Century*. London: Faber.

McKay, G. 1996. *Senseless Acts of Beauty: Cultures of Resistance since the Sixties*. London: Verso.

McKay, G. 2005. *Circular Breathing: The Cultural Politics of Jazz in Britain*. Durham, NC: Duke University Press.
Middleton, R. 2003. "Locating the People: Music and the Popular." In *The Cultural Study of Music: A Critical Introduction*, edited by Martin Clayton, Trevor Herbert, and Richard Middleton, 251–262. New York: Routledge.
Millar, M. 2006. *The Good Fairies of New York*. Brooklyn, NY: Soft Skull.
Raposa, A. 2012. "30 Years of Agit-Prop: The Representation of "Extreme" Politics in Punk and Post-Punk Music Graphics in the United Kingdom from 1978 to 2008." PhD diss., University of the Arts, London.
Reynolds, S. 2005. *Rip It Up and Start Again: Postpunk 1978–1984*. London: Faber.
Reynolds, S. 2011. *Retromania: Pop Culture's Addiction to Its Own Past*. London: Faber.
Richards, S. 1992. *Sonic Harvest: Towards Musical Democracy*. Oxford: Amber.
Rimbaud, P. 1998. *Shibboleth: My Revolting Life*. Edinburgh: AK Press.
Robb, J. 2006. *Punk Rock: An Oral History*. London: Ebury.
Sabin, R. 1999. "'I Won't Let That Dago By': Rethinking Punk and Racism." In *Punk Rock: So What? The Cultural Legacy of Punk*, edited by Roger Sabin, 199–218. London: Routledge.
Sailer, B. 2014. "Punk Needs New Ideas: The Current State of Punk Is Actually Great. It's Just Been Done Before." *Noisey*, November 13, 2014. https://noisey.vice.com/en_au/article/r3z8j8/punk-needs-new-ideas.
Savage, J. 1991. *England's Dreaming: Sex Pistols and Punk Rock*. London: Faber.
Seeger, R. C. 2001. *The Music of American Folk Song*. Suffolk, UK: Boydell & Brewer.
Severin, S. n.d. "My Top 10 Favourite Albums." *Louder Than War*. https://louderthanwar.com/steven-severin-my-top-10-favourite-albums/.
Thompson, D. 2004. *Wheels Out of Fear: 2-Tone, the Specials and a World in Flame*. London: Soundcheck.
Wikipedia. n.d. "Folk Punk." https://en.wikipedia.org/wiki/Folk_punk.
Worley, M. 2017. *No Future: Punk, Politics and British Youth Culture, 1976–1984*. Cambridge: Cambridge University Press.

Discography

Buzzcocks. 1977. "Boredom." On *Spiral Scratch*. New Hormones Records. 7" EP.
Damned. 1976. "New Rose"/"Help!" Stiff Records. 7" single.
Fitzgerald, P. 1978a. "Buy Me, Sell Me." On *Safety Pin Stuck in My Heart*. Small Wonder Records. 7" EP.
Fitzgerald, P. 1978b. "Ragged Generation for Real." On *The Paranoid Ward*. Small Wonder Records. 12" EP.
Fitzgerald, P. 1978c. "Irrelevant Battles." On *The Paranoid Ward*. Small Wonder Records. 12" EP.
Sex Pistols. 1976. "Anarchy in the UK"/"I Wanna Be Me." EMI Records. 7" single.
Sex Pistols. 1977a. "Pretty Vacant." On *Never Mind the Bollocks . . . Here's the Sex Pistols*. Virgin Records. 12" album.
Sex Pistols. 1977b. "God Save the Queen." On *Never Mind the Bollocks . . . Here's the Sex Pistols*. Virgin Records. 12" album.
Siouxsie and the Banshees. 1978. "Jigsaw Feeling." On *The Scream*. Polydor Records. 12" album.

CHAPTER 5

"THIS IS RADIO CLASH"
First-Generation Punk as Radical Media Ecology and Communicational Noise

MICHAEL GODDARD

Introduction

MULTIPLE attempts have been made to characterize first-generation London punk rock, whether in early accounts in terms of subcultural style (Hebdige 1979), or as an intervention into the recording industry (Laing 1985). More nuanced later accounts have noted punk's influence on cultural spheres as diverse as contemporary art, fashion, film, and popular music, as well as attempting to capture its cultural politics (see Sabin 1999). However, more can be said about punk as radical media—and not only because its proliferation was inseparable from a range of alternative media practices, from Xerox and (fan)zine production, to alternative radio, to DIY recording practices. More than this, punk was itself a form of media, operating less aesthetically than communicationally, as a way of channeling resistant energies to dominant forces and expressing both this domination and resistance via lyrics, artwork, texts, performances, fashion, and both print and audiovisual media. This chapter will examine these dynamics, focusing on the Clash, whose explicit presentation of themselves in media terms, especially as a form of pirate radio or "alternative world service," was only a more explicit expression of tendencies within punk more generally. The Clash can also be seen as a prime example of punk "selling out" in terms of signing early to a major record label, in this case CBS Records, and arguably becoming nothing more than a hardworking rock band before disintegrating altogether. Nevertheless, they maintained the aim of providing alternative modes of communication, such as engaging with a range of black musics, incorporating other media forms (especially radio), and presenting guerrilla struggles in the developing world, such as those of the Sandinistas in Nicaragua, to audiences who may have had little idea where a country like Nicaragua even was.

This chapter will argue that in relation to dominant communication media such as newspapers, radio, and television, punk rock operated as a form of noise, though less in the literal sense, since noisy forms of rock music were already well established, but in the sense of communicational noise, as an excess of the standard requirements for rock music communication. More than just "ineptness" in relation to professional recordings and instrumental prowess (Hegarty 2007), punk was a short-circuiting of mainstream media channels operating both by an alternative production of media and the production of events unassimilable by the mass media, especially radio and television.

In order to do this, it is necessary to explain briefly what is meant here by the term "media ecology." First developed from the work of Marshall McLuhan by Neil Postman and others (see Postman 1987), media ecology was initially seen as an attempt to explain how human experience and society is increasingly shaped by technology and modes of information and communication. However, more recent formulations of media ecology by Matthew Fuller and others (see Fuller 2005) have taken a less anthropocentric but more dynamic approach, seeing in media ecologies potentially transformative assemblages of agents, practices, and technologies that are neither necessarily humanist nor technologically determinist. If ecology can be expanded beyond the strictly physical environment to also encompass social relations and phenomena of subjectivity, as Felix Guattari suggested in *The Three Ecologies* (2000), then media ecology is a way of grasping expressive media not merely as representations, or technically determined practices, but as constitutive of worlds that articulate subjectivities with technologies, social practices, and specific environments in ways that are every bit as dynamic as an organic ecosystem.

This approach is useful where it comes to understandings of punk for its ability to go beyond the limits of semiotic approaches to punk, strongly evident in Hebdige's study of subcultural style, and to some extent in Laing's book, while at the same time more generative of a theoretical understanding of punk than purely historical or journalistic approaches like those of Savage (1991) or Heylin (2008), or similar accounts of the Clash, in particular those of Grey (1995), Gilbert (2004), or Andersen and Heibutzki (2018). This approach will focus neither on the meaning or style of punk, nor on narrating its development and the biographies of key individuals and groups, but rather on the material relationships between its constitutive elements—recorded music, live performances, pirate radio, posters, flyers, fanzines, and fashion, among others—with the idea that all of these elements taken together constitute a media ecology, in relation to the sociopolitical environment of late-1970s Britain and, more specifically, London. This is not to criticize these other accounts of punk, all of which have their merits and have informed the current scholarship on punk rock to this day. However, what this chapter will try to show is that punk was not only a phenomenon associated with specific modes of media production and circulation, but was itself a form of radical media, perhaps more so than a genre of music, which it has only become retroactively. To develop this idea, the focus will be mainly on the Clash's recorded music, and on relations with mainstream media and with the urban environment, while acknowledging that live performances, fashion, and album art were also essential components of the band's media ecology.

This approach will also mean taking a view of punk in proximity to contemporaneous social and political movements, such as Italian and German Autonomy movements, as I have argued elsewhere (Goddard 2018, 160–173). This is not to claim that punk was a similar political movement, or even any mutual influence, so much as a resonance based on shared practices such as squatting, the refusal of work, and the disturbance of dominant norms of both political organization and communication (see also Milburn 2001). There were also more local movements around squatting and against racism taking place, especially in West London since the mid-1960s, both of which had marked influences on punk, and especially on the Clash. Jon Savage writes about these scenes in *Goodbye to London* (Proll 2010), edited appropriately enough by former Red Army Faction member Astrid Proll who came to London to escape police attention in West German and immediately engaged with this squatting scene. According to Savage, "the whole area around Notting Hill, Gate, Ladbroke Grove, and Portobello Road . . . has been a seismograph of London life for much of the twentieth century" (Savage 2010, 16), citing phenomena from mid-1960s swinging London and *Performance* (Cammell and Roeg 1970) to the Angry Brigade, the Notting Hill Carnival, and, of course, the Clash themselves, alongside the local squatting scene that made many of these phenomena possible. In a sense, punk fit right into this sixties underground legacy and took it full circle, providing "a focus for a new generation who react against the sixties, even if they are continuing that work in a new guise" (Savage 2010, 16). For these reasons, this approach also sees UK (and especially London) punk as specific and markedly different from punk as it had developed earlier in the United States. As Roger Sabin has argued, "if we accept that one of the key defining elements of punk was an emphasis on class politics then it could only have begun in one time and one place—Britain in the late 1970s. . . . [T]he UK's economic recession can be seen as a catalyst . . . the quality of the experience in America was different, and much less politicised" (Sabin 1999, 3).

The Media Ecology of the Clash, Radio, and Punk Communication

Despite the above caveat about personal biographies, it is worth reiterating at this point that there were aspects of the background of members of the Clash that were quite distinct and fed into the nature of their musical activities and the subsequent modes of media communication they adopted. This has been chronicled extensively in several accounts of the band, including those of Gray and Gilbert, the latter giving the Clash's three principal personae their own chapters, as well as devoting quite a few pages to their manager. Joe Strummer (born John Mellor) had an idiosyncratic background, which was both middle class and initially quite itinerant, as his father, who was born in India and only acquired British citizenship shortly before Strummer's birth, worked for the Foreign Office, and was posted to such places and Ankara, Cairo, and Mexico City (see Gilbert 2004, 6–8; Gray 1996, 88–91). While Strummer was eventually packed off to boarding school in Surrey at the age of nine, such a background was, on the one hand, embarrassingly middle class in the London punk milieu, but, on the other hand, also unusually international, arguably feeding into the subsequent lyrics of the Clash, which were considerably more internationalist than other punk bands, while still attuned to the specific environment of London and specifically the West London area comprising Maida Vale, Kilburn, Notting Hill, and especially Ladbroke Grove, the area in London that Strummer would wind up in after dropping out of art school.

This area was not only important for the punk scene of the 1970s, but had already been so for the radical counterculture of the 1960s, which is one of the reasons it contained a vibrant squatting and generally alternative scene, as epitomized by the Powis Square address of the character Turner, played by Mick Jagger in *Performance* (Cammell and Roeg 1970). Even more significantly for the subsequent development of the Clash, this part of London was also the home of the Notting Hill Carnival from 1965, the biggest event in the UK to celebrate black British and Caribbean diasporic culture and especially music, that would have a decisive influence on the Clash's early lyrical content and musical style, not only in "White Riot," but also songs like "1977" and "(White Man) in Hammersmith Palais."[1] This environment was inscribed in the name of his pre-Clash pub rock/rhythm and blues band the 101ers, which referred to the address of the Maida Vale squat where Strummer was living in 1976, from where he recruited the other band members of the 101ers.

Mick Jones and Paul Simonon had more working-class London origins, with connections with Ladbroke Grove, although the former grew up more in South London and the latter only spent part of his teenage years in the area, after an earlier childhood spent in Brixton. Famously, Jones's grandmother had a flat in Westbourne Park in a tower block overlooking the Westway, as reflected in the title of the Don Letts documentary, *From the Westway to the World* (2000), which nicely sums up both the local anchoring and global aspirations of the group imaginatively spanning from Ladbroke Grove to the farthest reaches of global rebel struggle. As Jon Savage put it in Ballardian "hyper-realist" terms in *England's Dreaming*:

> From his grandmother's nineteenth-floor flat on the Warwick and Brindley estate, Clash guitarist Mick Jones had an eagle's eye view of a whole stretch of inner London: Harrow Road, North Kensington and Paddington, dominated by the elevated Westway, and blocks like the massive Trellick Tower that looms over the whole of Portobello Road and Ladbroke Grove. This was their stretch, marked, where the Westway passes over the Harrow Road by the grafitto THE CLASH, that remained there, fading slowly, for years after the group's vigorous life was over.
>
> (Savage 1991, 233)

As for Simonon, he was often overlooked in interviews and early histories of the Clash and considered either as a pretty boy, reticent, or even a bit thick (see Gray 1996, 67). According to Viv Albertine, who was both going out with Jones and sharing her squat with Simonon at the time, "Paul is as handsome as a film star, like Paul Newman and James Dean rolled together, and he's nice to girls, not chauvinistic. He's a bit tongue-tied and bashful but can afford to be, his looks do all the talking. It's Paul who comes up with the new band name, The Clash, from a newspaper headline" (Albertine 2014, 89). Not only was he responsible for the name the band adopted, but also their early look. This included the Jackson Pollock–style splattering of their clothes and the stenciled slogans taken from both their own and contemporary reggae lyrics, as seen on the cover of the "White Riot" single, and giving the band from the outset a militant and confrontational appearance. As Gilbert points out, whereas Mick Jones only went to art school in the disappointed hope of finding others to form a rock band with, Simonon was really drawn to being an artist, and in fact would continue his artistic activities beyond the career of the Clash (see Gilbert 2004, 48–54 ff.).

Into this mix, and indeed facilitating it in the first place, was the key role of their manager Bernie Rhodes. Rhodes was a long-term associate of Malcolm McLaren, with whom he shared a Jewish background and work in the rag trade, although his origins were less middle class, having grown up in an orphanage. Together with McLaren and Vivienne Westwood, he was the co-designer of the infamous "You're gonna wake up one morning and *know* what side of the bed you've been lying on," with its polarized list of "loves" and "hates," including many of the key themes that would be taken up in UK punk. This was, in Savage's words,

> an accidental sequence so meticulous and complete that it holds in one small patch of cloth stands that would unravel over the next few years. The "hates" mainly comprise the dead culture of the time: pompous rockers, faded rebels, repressive institutions, "a passive audience." The "loves" include sex professionals, renegade artists, hard Rockers, IRA terrorists, working class heroes and, well hidden, the first printed mention of "Kutie Jones and his SEX PISTOLS."
>
> (Savage 1991, 83–84)

Given Rhodes's often noted tendency toward left-wing rants, he is likely the author of a good portion of these lists, and certainly claimed later on to have been the one to put the Sex Pistols together, in the sense of "discovering" John Lydon and introducing him to McLaren, Steve Jones, and Paul Cook, even if McLaren subsequently rejected him having any involvement with managing the group. Certainly Gilbert supports this view of his significance, quoting Paul Simonon: "You can't overestimate Bernie's importance, he set up the whole punk scene, basically" (Simonon in Gilbert 2004, 78). In response to McLaren's dismissal, Rhodes decided to create his "own" punk band; approaching ex-members of the high-turnover proto-punk band London SS, including Mick Jones, Paul Simonon, and Keith Levene, the latter of whom would soon be ejected from the mix. Certainly, Rhodes was the one who hooked up Jones and Simonon with Joe Strummer, who was enjoying some modest success as singer of the 101ers, although the former later claimed to have already had their eye on him as the best front man around. Arguably, Rhodes can be seen as the creator of the Clash more so than McLaren as having created the Sex Pistols. One point on which almost everyone involved agrees is the pivotal role Rhodes played in getting the Clash to write songs about everyday issues that affected them, like unemployment and the urban environment, although from the beginning this extended beyond their immediate environment of West 11 and London to more global issues.

The classic example of this reorientation is the song "I'm So Bored with the USA," from the Clash's first album in 1977. This began life as a Mick Jones song about an ex-girlfriend ("I'm so bored with you"), which Strummer creatively misheard, giving the song an entirely new lyrical content: "Never mind the stars and stripes / Let's print the Watergate Tapes." Not only did the song show an awareness of US imperialism, but also was critically engaged with US television culture, namechecking *Starsky and Hutch* and *Kojak*, as well as US detective series in general. Other early songs did, however, make specific references to West 11, such as "London's Burning" (1977): "I'm up and down the Westway, in and out the lights . . . I can't think of a better way to spend the night." As the local fanzine writer Tom Vague put it, "[this] is as close as you're going to get to authentic socio politico [sic] urban angst in a pop song outside of early Motown. It's obviously a Speed song as Strummer puts it 'We'd take amphetamines and storm around the bleak streets with nothing to do but watch the traffic. That's what 'London's Burning' is about'" (Vague, 1997, n.p.).[2] These associations of the Clash with the urban environment of London, W10 and 11, and more specifically the Westway have been explored by Conrad Brunström, who emphasizes the mythical and contradictory nature of the notion of speeding on the typically traffic-bound Westway: "Nuzzled under the Westway, an unusable arterial road (especially for a young, unemployed demographic), The Clash declare that the freedom of the open road—a frankly American cultural import—is both inescapable and impossible at the same time" (Brunström 2019, 163).

In addition to car headlights, tower blocks, amphetamines, and the Westway, a key referent in the song is again television, which in punk circles was synonymous with the boredom of contemporary urban experience, presented here as the new religion: "Everybody's sitting 'round watching television" (The Clash, "London's Burning"). This was to become prevalent throughout punk culture, influencing the names of bands (Television Personalities, Alternative TV, the Adverts), performers (TV Smith), and innumerable song lyrics. There is certainly no lack of television and advertising references in the Clash, especially in their third album, *London Calling*, in tracks like "Koka Kola" or "Lost in the Supermarket," although more in the sense of advertising and consumer culture. Even when talking about US imperialism, militarism, or rebellion, there is often a sense of the world as mediated via televisual imagery, as reflected often in their music videos. Songs like "Tommy Gun," with its focus on urban guerrillas, or the apocalyptic imagery of the track "London Calling" are mediated by the "Nine o'clock news" ("Tommy Gun," 1978) and media rumors that have to be confirmed via direct experience: "You know what they said / Well some of it was true" ("London Calling," 1979).

However, this latter track contains another key media reference in its title and lyrical reference to being "at the top of the dial," namely to radio, which was an obsessive theme throughout the Clash's career to the extent that they can be usefully understood as constituting a form of pirate radio alternative world service, an idea the Strummer in particular was especially interested in. In fact, around 1980, this was actually considered a possible activity for the band in the *Combat Rock* period, even if it would remain only an imaginary one (see Gray 1996, 389–390).

In early Clash songs, commercial radio was an object of critique, as especially evident on the blistering single "Capital Radio One" (1977), which begins with a derisive reference to the "Dr. Goebbels Show," and continues to denounce the content of the eponymous radio station's programming: "They don't make the city beat / They make all the action stop," singling out the station's music manager, Aiden Day: "He picks all the hits to play / To keep you in your place all day." What is even more interesting in this song, however, is its awareness of the legacy of 1960s pirate radio and the gap left by its demise: "Now all the stations are silenced / 'Cause they ain't got a government license." This is a far more focused and cogent media critique than the Clash's not entirely consistent denouncing of US popular culture, and also points to the ways the band were positioning themselves as an alternative mode of radio. It would also be complemented by critical engagement with the music industry, including the highly self-referential "Complete Control" (1977), one of several Clash tracks that critically references their own recording contract: "They said we'd be artistically free / When we signed that bit of paper" (taking the unusual step of using a single to criticize their own record label, CBS, for releasing "Remote Control" (1977) as a single against their wishes. Ironically enough, in 1999 Joe Strummer would become a radio DJ for the BBC World Service, playing an eclectic range of world musics, as featured extensively in the Julien Temple documentary *Joe Strummer: The Future Is Unwritten* (2007), but as several interviewees, such as Bono, indicate in the film, the Clash were already "an atlas," an alternative world service alerting British youth not only to what was taking place in central London, but also in the Middle East or, famously, the revolution in Nicaragua, to which the Clash dedicated their fourth studio album.

Seeing the Clash in terms of radio makes sense of their extensive "pirating" of other musical styles, such as reggae and later jazz, blues, rockabilly, funk, and hip-hop, whether in the form of cover versions or their own synthetic versions of these different styles of largely black music. As opposed to the narrow horizons of commercial radio, the Clash had eclectic listening tastes and were expert in reinterpreting these styles for a punk audience—not merely speeding things up and draining their content of any virtuosity, as became typical for punk cover versions, but honing their essence and at times generating entirely new resonances, whether for Vince Taylor's rockabilly "Brand New Cadillac" (1959), the upbeat rock and roll of the Bobby Fuller Four's "I Fought the Law" (1966), or contemporary reggae tracks like Willie Williams's "Armagideon Time" (1979) or Toots and the Maytals' "Pressure Drop" (1969). The Clash were not content with creating a hybrid musical style between a variety of other musical forms and their own via cover versions, they wanted also to reinterpret these styles in original recordings, such as their own eccentric versions of jazz ("Jimmy Jazz," 1979), soul and reggae ("Rudie Can't Fail," 1979) or hip-hop ("The Magnificent Seven," 1980). However, it was one of their earlier singles' appropriation of reggae that resulted in a truly exceptional piece of music that addressed the situation of black and white youth, informed by the experience of attending a reggae night at the Hammersmith Palais, in West London. This is done through the staging of a collision of the very musical styles referred to in the lyrics. Critical of the reggae on offer that night when there were "many black ears here to listen" ["(White Man) in Hammersmith Palais," 1977], the song goes on to critique the posing of new punk bands with a clear dig at the Jam: "fighting for a good place under the lighting . . . Turning rebellion into money,"[3] Spiraling outward to both the need and impossibility of effective youth rebellion due to the imbalance of forces, the song returns to the Palais, with the singer just looking for fun like anyone else. This incredible journey through black and white musics and their shortcomings is conducted in a musical idiom that opens with anthemic rock chords that are then replaced with a reggae rhythm throughout most of the rest of the track, but the rock idiom makes a return in a short bridge lamenting the lack of "roots rock rebel." Then, at the end of the track, there is a veritable hybridization of reggae, rock, and punk, with even some harmonica thrown in, embodying in a single track the eclectic musical styles that would later be explored on albums like *London Calling*. It is as if the band are proposing to tackle the social divisions of black and white youth by creating a musical amalgam adequate to both, and thereby constituting the "roots rock rebel" missing from that night at the Palais. The music critic Bill Wyman, who considers this song the finest one to be recorded by the band, describes it in the following terms: "The journey we'd been on was an extraordinary one—expectations challenged, dashed, and then trumped musically and thematically. That's what the band did in their best songs, and that's sort of what Strummer and Jones ended up doing with their band, which, for a time, blew a hole in the radio and were everything a rock band could be" (Wyman 2017, n.p.).

This brings us back to "London Calling," that broadcast to the boys and girls of far-away towns, calling them "out of the cupboard" despite the apparently apocalyptic conditions. This is not only explicitly modeled on a radio broadcast—"This Is London Calling" was a station identification on BBC World Service, also used during World War II—but also suggests it is on a national if not international scale, calling on youth to follow the lead of London and resist dominant powers and, specifically, the "nuclear era" ("London Calling," 1979). This would become the template for the Clash's mode of addressing their increasingly global audience, especially on *Sandinista!*, where entire sides of the triple album are presented in the form of a radio broadcast, with Mikey Dread as resident DJ. This radio address would be reprised on their final album, *Combat Rock*, in the humorous track "Know Your Rights" (1982) opening with the lines "This is a Public Service Announcement / With guitars," and arguably reaches an apotheosis in "Straight to Hell" (1982), which presents devastating scenes from Vietnam, England, and the United States of the after-effects of war, colonialism, and industrial decline in a form of poetic documentary reportage on the global dispossessed: "It could be anywhere / Most likely could be any frontier, any hemisphere." But the equation of the Clash with radio was most directly and forcefully expressed in the earlier single "This Is Radio Clash."

"This Is Radio Clash" exists in two nearly identically titled versions on each side of the original 7-inch release, both making reference to the use of radio during the Cuban revolution. On the B-side the track (here titled "Radio Clash") begins with the lyrics "This is Radio Clash / Resuming all transmissions / Beaming from the mountaintop / Using aural ammunition," and even more explicitly in the more well-known version form on the A-side: "This is Radio Clash from Pirate Satellite / Orbiting your living room, cashing in the bill of rights / Cuban army surplus or refusing all third lights." This hip-hop-style track is at once an ode to the prevalent culture of beat boxes and ghetto blasters the group encountered in New York, and a fantasy of constituting a form of guerrilla radio, against militarism, napalm, and ghettoization, seducing its listeners with "audio ammunition." While embodying one of the major paradoxes that pervades Clash lyrics (and, indeed, perhaps even the band's name), namely couching anti-militarism in terms that are themselves militaristic, it perhaps provides the most complete vision of the Clash as pirate, guerrilla radio, taking on world issues from Vietnam and its aftermath to the nuclear umbrella, advocating a sound that "is brave and wants to be free"— perhaps the most direct articulation of the entire ethos of the Clash across the band's extraordinary trajectory from "White Riot" to "Rock the Casbah." In the music video for the song, this is presented as a veritable global pirate media ecology encompassing ghetto blasters combining radio and cassettes, satellite transmissions "interrupting all programmes," seemingly on both radio and television, with New York graffiti and hip-hop breakdancing as a backdrop linking the Clash with black music culture in this new urban context (see Figure 5.1).

The later track "Rock the Casbah" can be seen as a humorous companion broadcast to "Radio Clash," proposing a Middle East solution based on "that crazy casbah jive" that affects even the jet pilots who pick it up through the "cockpit radio blare" and start wailing to the infectious beat rather than dropping bombs. In a cruel irony, perhaps reflecting the ambivalence around militarism inherent in the Clash's rebel stance (especially evident in their preference for combat clothing as well as in their rebel lyrical themes), this infectious pop song would become the music of choice for US fighter pilots in the Gulf War, something that Joe Strummer found devastating. However, of more importance than this often-critiqued rebel stance was the Clash's explicit self-positioning as a source of noisy interference with dominant messages, which quickly dispensed with the need to be necessarily accompanied by noisy music in a conventional sense.[4] The Clash instead generated communicational noise, whether via the interference between previously distinct musical styles, or the use of music to resist and short-circuit dominant messages from capitalist consumerism and control to youth militarization and incipient fascism. Listeners were encouraged *not* to "hear the call up [and] act the way you were brought up" ("The Call-Up," 1980), or "start wearing blue and brown and working for the Clampdown" ("Clampdown," 1979). Instead, they were offered another call, a rebel call that welcomed the losers and dispossessed, from petty criminals in the West End ("The Card Cheat," "Jimmy Jazz," 1979) or Brixton ("Guns of Brixton"), to "ragged

FIGURE 5.1. The Clash imagined as global pirate radio in *Clash on Broadway* (Letts 2001), a previously unreleased film included as a DVD extra on Don Letts's documentary *The Clash: Westway to the World*.

armies, fixin' bayonets to fight the other line" ("Spanish Bombs," 1979), to the panoply of the global dispossessed addressed in "Straight to Hell." As Wyman puts it in his account of the merits or otherwise of all 139 songs by the Clash in *Vulture*: "Strummer had an instinctive impulse to support whoever was being persecuted at any given time, even if the person deserved it" (Wyman 2018), and the Clash as a group can be seen as running media interference to short-circuit the operations of power and support the freedom of both individual and collective rebels through a "brave sound" that "wants to be free."

Conclusion: Punk as Communicational Noise

Too little attention has been paid to punk as a complex media phenomenon, crossing between recorded music, film, television, fashion, graphic arts, music journalism, flyers and posters, live performance, and records and cassettes, and produced out of and through the confluence of these various technical media as a distinct and contagious media ecology that would ultimately have global effects. More specifically, out of this range of available media in a specific urban sociocultural environment, punk was able to construct an intense reflection of both the reigning dominant forces and the resistance to them via a rebellious range of mediated performances, from new modes of urban dress and behavior, to aggressive live performances, to the generation of a range of artifacts extending well beyond the music itself (films, posters, record covers, and homemade cassettes are only part of this extensive archive). In all of these arenas, punk, in relation to existing norms of rock music, operated very much in terms of noise, as has been argued here more explicitly in relation to the Clash. This is not only in the obvious sense of producing "noisy" music, since psychedelic rock and heavy metal before punk were both exemplars of noise, sometimes produced more effectively than in punk. Punk, however, was noisy in a communicational sense precisely for its failure to meet a set of what had become standard requirements for rock music communication; namely, technical proficiency and macho prowess over one's instrument, professional standards of recording and live performance, and appropriate behavior of fans and consumers. In all these levels of what Paul Hegarty (2007, 89-90) qualifies as punk's "ineptness," noise was generated in relation especially to the stadium virtuosity of progressive rock, leading him to affirm the Sex Pistols' *The Great Rock and Roll Swindle* despite, or rather because of, its obvious flaws and inauthenticity as a greater punk album than *Never Mind the Bollocks* (95–97).[5] This position flies in the face of writers like Savage, Laing, or Greil Marcus, who celebrate tracks from the latter, such as "Holidays in the Sun," as sophisticated works of punk rock originality and brilliance, as opposed to the lacklusterly performed bad cover versions of the former, expressly designed to promote McLaren's version of the Sex Pistols as his own fraudulent creation—a version of events John Lydon would only be able to correct through the formation of the decidedly post-punk Public Image Limited.

But punk noise was not limited to ineptness in relation to rock norms, nor the refusal to produce a quality product, even where it came to rebellion (something that bands like the Clash would certainly depart from). Rather, punk noise was a short-circuiting of mainstream media channels, both by producing punk's own forms of media and especially by presenting the mass media with messages and content it was unable to easily assimilate. The 1976 Bill Grundy "obscenity" live television interview with the Sex Pistols and its subsequent tabloid amplification is one example of this, but on a smaller scale so was the refusal of the Clash to go on *Top of the Pops*, leading their single "Bankrobber" to be presented in the form of interpretive dance, courtesy of the chart program's resident dance troupe Legs and Co. While this could be seen as one of Bernie Rhodes's pointless and counterproductive provocations, it also expressed a legitimate objection to faking a live performance via lip-syncing and a refusal to participate and perform as a commercial media standardized product. The Clash *did* appear in movies both during their existence (*The Punk Rock Movie* [Letts 1978]; *Rude Boy* [Hazan and Mingay 1980]) and in retrospective documentaries like *Westway to the World* (Letts

2000), and also made music videos. Many of these remixed materials from earlier films and music videos and tended to emphasize both the authenticity of live performances and their rebel image, often expressed via an at times outlandish sense of fashion and style. What is especially evident through these audiovisual representations of the band is an oppositional response to dominant media representations, often presented in the form of televisual collage, and the constitution of noise in relation to this media environment. This is especially evident in the "This Is Radio Clash" video, which makes use of much of the material Letts shot in New York for the unfinished film *Clash on Broadway* (Letts 2001).

At its best, punk was a disturbance to norms of both media communication and the music industry, by being popular enough to be in the charts while remaining unpresentable in terms of both radio airplay and televisual representation. At the same time it forced a reluctant music industry to engage with material that was directly critical of its practices, as in the Clash's "Complete Control" or the Sex Pistols' even more direct "EMI" (1977). In this sense, punk functioned not only as literal, musical noise, or the sociological, subcultural noise identified by cultural studies accounts like Hebdige's, but also as communicational, media noise, short-circuiting dominant modes of representation and opening spaces for alternative modes of expression.

Notes

1. Other Clash tracks, like "The Prisoner" (1978), "Clash City Rockers" (1977), "All the Young Punks" (1978), and "Last Gang in Town" (1978), make more general London and urban references, but always centered on the specific environment of West 11.
2. Tom Vague would continue his fanzine activities well beyond the punk era and especially embraced the Situationist practice of psychogeography, but in a much more vernacular mode than both the Situationists or the English literary progeny like Iain Sinclair. In Vague's case this would be centered on West 11, and in one psychogograpically themed issue of *Vague* he give a hilarious account of an awkward encounter with "the actor, Joe Strummer" in a newsagent in the area, in which he congratulates Strummer for his performance in *Misery Train* [sic]. See Vague 1993, 6–8.
3. A similar criticism was applied to the Clash by the anarcho-punk band Crass, who also perceived the guerrilla posturing of the Clash while bankrolled by a major record label as hypocritically turning rebellion into money.
4. This perception of the Clash's rebel stance as hypocritical is especially evident in the work of Clinton Heylin, which draws on earlier suspicions of the Clash due to their perceived class origins, their selling out by signing early to a major label, and the sense that their rebellion was a pose behind which lay quite conventional aspirations to rock success. Heylin adopts an especially sneering tone in relation to both the Clash and their manager that is often more irritating than informative. See Heylin 2008, 190–192ff.
5. This argument was essentially adopted from Stewart Home's *Cranked Up Really High* (1996), which takes issue with the importance for punk of groups like the Sex Pistols and the Clash as well as critics like Marcus and Savage.

References

Albertine, Viv. 2014. *Clothes, Clothes, Clothes. Music, Music, Music. Boys, Boys, Boys: A Memoir*. London: Faber.

Andersen, Mark, and Ralph Heibutzki. 2018. *We Are the Clash: Reagan, Thatcher, and the Last Stand of a Band That Mattered*. New York: Akashic Books.

Brunström, Conrad. 2019. "'Up and Down the Westway' or 'Live by the River'? Britishness, Englishness, London and The Clash." In *Working for the Clampdown: The Clash, the Dawn of Neoliberalism and the Political Promise of Punk*, edited by Colin Coulter, 161–177. Manchester, UK: Manchester University Press.

Fuller, Matthew. 2005. *Media Ecologies*. Leonardo Series. Cambridge, MA: MIT Press.

Gilbert, Pat. 2004. *Passion Is a Fashion: The Real Story of the Clash*. London: Aurum.

Goddard, Michael. 2018. *Guerrilla Networks: An Anarchaeology of 1970s Radical Media Ecologies*. Amsterdam: Amsterdam University Press.

Gray, Marcus. 1996. *Last Gang in Town: The Story and the Myth of the Clash*. New York: Henry Holt.

Guattari, Félix. 2000. *The Three Ecologies*. Translated by Ian Pindar and Paul Sutton. London: Continuum.

Hebdige, Dick. 1979. *Subculture: The Meaning of Style*. London: Methuen.

Hegarty, Paul. 2007. *Noise/Music: A History*. London: Continuum.

Heylin, Clinton. 2008. *Babylon's Burning: From Punk to Grunge*. Harmondsworth, UK: Penguin.

Home, Stewart. 1996. *Cranked Up Really High: Genre Theory and Punk Rock*. Hove, UK: Codex Books.

Laing, Dave. 1985. *One Chord Wonders: Power and Meaning in Punk Rock*. Oakland, CA: PM Press. Revised edition published 2015.

Milburn, Keir. 2001. "When Two Sevens Clash: Punk and *Autonomia*." Unpublished conference paper, *The Free Association*, http://freelyassociating.org/when-two-sevens-clash-punk-and-Autonomia/.

Postman, Neil. 1987. *Amusing Ourselves to Death*. London: Methuen.

Proll, Astrid, ed. 2010. *Goodbye to London: Radical Art and Politics in the 70's*. Ostfildern, Germany: Hatje Cantz Verlag.

Sabin, Roger, ed. 1999. *Punk Rock: So What? The Cultural Legacy of Punk*. London: Routledge.

Savage, Jon. 1991. *England's Dreaming: Sex Pistols and Punk Rock*. London: Faber.

Savage, Jon. 2010. "London Subversive." In Proll 2010, 12–31.

Vague, Tom. 1993. "W11 Days: Notes From the Portobello Style Underclass." In *Vague 24: The West 11 Days of My Life*. London: Aldgate Press.

Vague, Tom. 1997. "Punk Reggae Party: The Sound of the Westway." In *Vague 28: Grove Massive Psychogeography Report: More Notes from the Portobello Style Underclass*, edited by Tom Vague. London: Aldgate Press.

Wyman, Bill. 2017. "All 139 the Clash Songs Ranked from Worst to Best: Death or Glory?" *Vulture*, October, 2017. https://www.vulture.com/2017/10/all-139-the-clash-songs-ranked-from-worst-to-best.html.

Filmography

Cammell, Donald, and Nicolas Roeg, dirs. 1970. *Performance*. London: Goodtimes Enterprises, Warner Brothers.

Hazan, Jack, and David Mingay, dirs. 1980. *Rude Boy*. London: Buzzy Enterprises, Michael White Productions.
Letts, Don, dir. 1978. *The Punk Rock Movie*. London: Sun Video.
Letts, Don, dir. 2000. *The Clash: Westway to the World*. London: 3DD Entertainment.
Letts, Don, dir. 2001. *Clash on Broadway*. Previously unreleased short film. Released as DVD extra to *The Clash: Westway to the World* (DVD), 2001. London: Sony Entertainment.
Temple, Julien, dir. 2007. *Joe Strummer: The Future is Unwritten*. London: Parallel Film Productions, FilmFour, Sony BMG.

Discography

The Bobby Fuller Four. "I Fought the Law." On *I Fought the Law*, 1966.
The Clash. "1977." On *The Clash*, 1977.
The Clash. "All the Young Punks." On *Give 'em Enough Rope*, 1978.
The Clash. "The Call Up." On *Sandinista!*, 1980.
The Clash. "Capital Radio One." On *Capital Radio* (EP), 1977.
The Clash. "The Card Cheat." On *London Calling*, 1979.
The Clash. "Clampdown." On *London Calling*, 1979.
The Clash. "Clash City Rockers." Single, 1978.
The Clash. "Complete Control." Single, 1977.
The Clash. "Guns of Brixton." On *London Calling*, 1979.
The Clash. "I'm So Bored with the USA." On *The Clash*, 1977.
The Clash. "Jimmy Jazz." On *London Calling*, 1979.
The Clash. "Know Your Rights." On *Combat Rock*, 1982.
The Clash. "Koka Kola." On *London Calling*, 1979.
The Clash. "London's Burning." On *The Clash*, 1977.
The Clash. "London Calling." On *London Callingv*, 1979.
The Clash. "Lost in the Supermarket." On *London Calling*, 1979.
The Clash. "Last Gang in Town." On *Give 'Em Enough Rope*, 1978.
The Clash. "The Magnificent Seven." On *Sandinista!*, 1980.
The Clash. "The Prisoner," Single B-side, 1978.
The Clash. "Remote Control." On *The Clash*, 1977.
The Clash. "Rock the Casbah." On *Combat Rock*, 1982.
The Clash. "Rudie Can't Fail." On *London Calling*, 1979.
The Clash. "Spanish Bombs." On *London Calling*, 1979.
The Clash. "Straight to Hell." On *Combat Rock*, 1982.
The Clash. "This Is Radio Clash," Single, 1981.
The Clash. "Tommy Gun." On *Give 'Em Enough Rope*, 1978.
The Clash. "(White Man) in Hammersmith Palais." Single, 1978.
The Clash. "White Riot." Single, 1977.
Sex Pistols. "EMI." On *Never Mind the Bollocks, Here's the Sex Pistols*, 1977.
Vince Taylor. "Brand New Cadillac." Single, 1959.
Toots and the Maytals. "Pressure Drop." On *Sweet and Dandy*, 1969.
Willie Williams. "Armagideon Time." Single, 1979.

CHAPTER 6

ART SCHOOL MANIFESTOS, CLASSICAL MUSIC, AND INDUSTRIAL ABJECTION

Tracing the Artistic, Political, and Musical Antecedents of Punk

MIKE DINES

"It is the early seventies," writes Jon Savage in the opening sentences of *England's Dreaming: Sex Pistols and Punk Rock* (1991). "All the participants of what will be called Punk are alive, but few of them know each other." Soon, he notes, they will assemble in a "network of relationships as complicated as the rabbit warren London slums of [Charles] Dickens's novels. The other beginnings of Punk—the musical texts, vanguard manifestos, pulp fictions—already exist, but first we need the location, the vacant space where, like the buddleia on the still plentiful bombsites, these flowers bloom" (Savage 1991, 3). Savage's depiction of punk as a subcultural overspill formed from art school manifestos, musical and artistic experimentation, and risqué political ideologies raises two very important issues around, first, the origins of punk, and second, the means through which those origins are portrayed. In other words, while Savage's ideas may highlight the complex social, political, and aesthetic trajectory of punk, his rhetorical prose-style language adds to the mythologizing of both its formation and transformation.

This chapter explores the origins of punk through three different case studies, beginning with an exploration of the influence of the Situationist International (SI) on the punk ethos and aesthetic. This section will draw upon the polarizing views of, in particular, Greil Marcus and Stewart Home, raising questions about the extent to which the SI influenced key progenitors of first-wave punk (in this case Malcolm McLaren and Jamie Reid) and whether any such influence is echoed by those who saw themselves as part of a wider punk "scene." Second, this chapter looks at the musical and artistic trajectory of the anarcho-punk band Crass and, in particular, the contemporary classical music tradition that informed the work of Penny Rimbaud et al., from the late 1960s to the formation of Crass in the 1970s. It will provide an overview of related musical ensembles before Crass, in particular the avant-garde ensemble Exit, charting Crass's creative process through their influences from Fluxus, an experimental art-music movement founded in the 1960s, and other contemporary classical practices. Third, the chapter will then turn to the artistic influences of Neil Megson, later to be known as Genesis P-Orridge. Here, emphasis will be placed upon a timeline of artistic and political activities by P-Orridge, from his time in school, through his forming of COUM Transmissions in the early 1970s, to the early days of the innovative musical ensemble Throbbing Gristle (TG), formed in 1975.

Through the examination of these three key protagonists in punk, questions will be raised about the cultural, musical, and artistic antecedents of punk. Punk was not a "year zero" phenomenon, but instead evolved from a cultural milieu rich with the overspill of the experimental art scene of the 1960s and early 1970s counterculture. Although some of these trajectories are increasingly mythologized—not least in the Situationist-inspired artwork of the Sex Pistols—it is clear that punk evolved from a continuing undercurrent of subversive ideology and action, not least in the influence of contemporary classical music and the emerging industrial scene from the early 1970s.

The Sex Pistols, Punk, and Situationism

For Savage, then, the story of the relationship between the SI and punk begins in the late 1960s, and Malcolm McLaren's friendship with the artist Jamie Reid at Croydon Art School. The writer notes how they instigated a sit-in to support the May 1968 events in France, a two-month period that had begun through a series of student occupation protests and soon swept across the country in the form of civil unrest. For Savage, the events in France signified "a generation claiming its political rights," where protest turned from a political act into "aesthetic style," and where "the violent intensity of pop that had flooded the world from 1964 was translated into a public demonstration of the utopian promise: that the world could be transformed" (Savage 1991, 27). Importantly, the noticeable demands and promise of 1968 were found in the posters and graffiti that adorned Paris. "Their cryptic phrases were the perfect medium for this mediated revolt—novel, easily packageable and paradoxical," writes Savage, "phrases like 'Demand The Impossible' or 'Imagination Is Seizing Power' inverted conventional logic: they made complex ideas suddenly seem very simple" (28).

Although the Croydon sit-in eventually dissipated, Savage contends that it was key in McLaren becoming aware of the subversive aesthetic and ideology of the SI, which would inform his managerial career with the New York Dolls and the Sex Pistols. As evidence, Savage draws upon McLaren's own words: "I'd heard about the Situationists from the radical milieu of the time.... You had to go up to Compendium Books. When you asked for the literature, you had to pass an eyeball test. Then you got these beautiful magazines with reflecting colour covers in various colours: gold, green, mauve." He continues, "the text was in French: you tried to read it, but it was so difficult. Just when you were getting bored, there were always wonderful pictures and they broke the whole thing up. They were what I bought them for, not the theory" (quoted in Savage 1991, 30).

Savage's comments regarding the influence of the SI on punk echo those of Greil Marcus. Writing in *Lipstick Traces: A Secret History of the Twentieth Century* (1990), Marcus not only attempts to trace a subversive thread back to the student revolts of the 1960s (or indeed even to the formation of the SI in the 1950s), but also as far back as 1534 and to the Dutch heretic John of Leydon. "The question of ancestry is culture is spurious," he writes, "every new manifestation in culture re-writes the past, changes old maudits into new heroes, old heroes into those who should have never been born" (Marcus 1990, 21). To illuminate such a lineage, "in the 1920s in literary America it was Herman Melville; in the rock 'n' roll 1960s it was Mississippi bluesman Robert Johnson of the 1930s. In 1976 and 1977, and the years to follow, as symbolically remade by the Sex Pistols, it was perhaps Dadaists, Lettrists, Situationists, and various medieval heretics" (21–22). *Lipstick Traces* therefore,

> grew out of a desire to come to grips with the power of "Anarchy in the UK" as music, to understand its fecundity as culture; it may be that the key to those questions is not that the Sex Pistols could have traced their existence to the [Lettrists'] gift, but that, blindly, they returned the gift—and in a form those who first offered it, aesthetes who would have been appalled to see their theories turned into cheap commodities, would never recognise.
>
> (Marcus 1990, 23)

England's Dreaming and *Lipstick Traces* are key texts in the mythologizing of the relationship between punk and the SI, particularly in both their resolve to demonstrate the SI's influence on the aesthetic and ideological trajectories of punk. In sharp contrast to both Savage's and Marcus's texts, Stewart Home contends that "PUNK ... came out of nowhere and was heading straight back there. What was punk if not a media hype? It was empty, shallow and trivial—and that was its greatness" (Home 1996, 20; emphasis in original). He explains, "[W]hen I was fourteen and first got into PUNK in 1976 I didn't know anything about the Situationists, I was too young and ignorant, they wouldn't have interested me. I hadn't even heard of Dada until one of the Sunday papers ran a feature comparing the PUNK phenomena to events at the Cabaret Voltaire. PUNK was much sound and fury, signifying nothing" (20; emphasis in original. See also Home 1991). In his critique of the English language Situ-inspired punk pamphlet "The End of Music" by Dave W, Home argues that Dave W overestimates the influence of "specto-Situationist theory, both on punk and in general. This is perhaps not surprising, since at the time the text was produced he was part of the miserable milieu centred on Guy Debord and the Champ Libre publishers in Paris" (Home 1991, 81–82).

The answer lies somewhere in the middle ground. If punk "may be best understood as a cultural process of critical engagement rather than a specific musical or sartorial style" (Worley 2017, 11), then one could gauge the influence of the SI, and other intellectual influences upon punk, in the context of an artistic and ideological "milieu." In other words, one can think of punk "as a source of pathways to a set of literatures, ideas and music that give the audience and the artists a sense of worth that is based on being challenged and stretched by the art in question" (Webb 2007, 105). While one should not overestimate the influence of the Situationists on punk, therefore, one must not disregard the influence of the broader counterculture upon punk, and in particular the confrontational politics that often accompanied earlier incarnations of protest. Even if many (perhaps most) punks were unaware of the intricacies of SI theory (or indeed of the SI at all), it would certainly be problematic to overlook the richness and flow of countercultural ideas more broadly.

Connections can become entrenched as "causalities" over time due to repeated use. A number of significant contributors to the establishment of what was to become known as "punk" in the UK (including McLaren, Reid, Clash manager Bernie Rhodes, and others) certainly had at least a passing knowledge of the activities and writings of the Situationist International in the late 1960s, though at that time the SI would rarely have been seen in isolation from other avant-garde art and/or political movements, and would more likely have formed part of the late 1960s and early 1970s countercultural zeitgeist. Like the previous generation's adoption of the *image* of Che Guevara's revolutionaries as hippie icons—when in practice the freaks would never have been tolerated in post-revolutionary Cuba—we have witnessed a retrospective association between punk in the UK and the radicalism of late 1960s France, yet this is one that, I argue, becomes more tenuous the more it faces critical scrutiny. One could argue that British pop art had at least equal influence, particularly for punk artists and designers—and those studying at art colleges in London, Leeds, Newcastle, and beyond (see Frith and Home 1987; Walker 1998).

Interestingly, it is a debate that endures. In Richard Cabut and Andrew Gallix's *Punk is Dead: Modernity Killed Every Night* (2017), punk remains uncritically within a Situationist framework, while Brian James Schill's *This Year's Work in the Punk Bookshelf, Or, Lusty Scripts* (2017) takes punk intellectualism to a new level, drawing upon writers and philosophers such as Charles Baudelaire, G. W. F. Hegel, and Friedrich Nietzsche to find new meanings in punk (see Schill 2017, 129). For Tom Vague, in *Anarchy in the UK: The Angry Brigade* (1997), it is not just a question of tracing the avant-garde antecedents of punk, but of critically thinking about what these together might have gone on to produce: "[W]hether the Sex Pistols and punk rock actually count as a revolution or a Situationist intervention is open to debate. . . [S]uffice to say the punks probably unwittingly recuperate the bits of Situationist theory that filter down to them, and leave themselves wide open to their recuperation by Thatcher and the yuppies." On the plus side (perhaps), he concludes, "the unconscious hooliganism side of it was not to be missed" (Vague 1997, 135).

CRASS, ANARCHO-PUNK, AND CLASSICAL MUSIC

If McLaren and Reid's story begins at Croydon Art School, then the story of anarcho-punk band Crass begins in a 1960s commune in Epping Forest and the formation of the experimental ensemble the Stanford Rivers Quartet. Placing an emphasis on the experimental creative process, anarchist musician and later Crass member Penny Rimbaud describes how, "[i]nspired by the Bauhaus artists and composers such as [Luciano] Berio and [Edgard] Varèse, our early work investigated the relationship between sound and visual imagery." He continues, "out of this [the Stanford Rivers Quartet] developed a method of notation, which used markings on graph paper to determine time, pitch and volume, the resultant scores appearing more like painting than music" (quoted in Berger 2008, 28). These remarks are echoed by anarchist artist Gee Vaucher, who describes writing music

> with colours and shapes. We did it on a regular bar system of music writing but you'd have, say, for the violin, I'd do a red line, that maybe started off thick and maybe end up thin at the end of the bar. And you'd know that red would maybe mean something to that musician—it might be anger or it might be heat. And it would be a very thick sound because it was covering maybe two bars. But the shape would waver. So you'd interpret this and play. (quoted in Berger 2008, 28)

Through graphic scores, Rimbaud, Vaucher, and the other members of the quartet developed a personalized musical notation that gave cohesion and unity to their early work. This continued and developed further in their art/sound/event ensemble Exit: "By placing a grid/graph over any image," notes Rimbaud in the sleeve notes to Exit's *The Mystic Trumpeter*, "we were able to translate it into sound" (Exit 2013). Employed by composers since the 1950s, and perhaps most notable in the works of John Cage, Karlheinz Stockhausen, and Cornelius Cardew, the graphic score added an aleatoric or indeterminate effect toward performers' interpretations. This meant that a notated work was unique in each performance, with an element of spontaneity and improvisational interpretation.

Another artistic movement that influenced the various experimental ensembles that would lead to Crass was the international grouping of processual art known as Fluxus. Formed in the early 1960s by the American artist George Maciunas, members of Fluxus included Yoko Ono, George Brecht, and Dick Higgins. Influenced by John Cage's music composition course at the New School for Social Research in New York, the aims of the Fluxus movement were outlined in their Manifesto: "PROMOTE A REVOLUTIONARY FLOOD AND TIDE IN ART," "Promote living art, anti-art, promote NON ART REALITY to be grasped by all peoples, not only critics, dilettantes and professionals" (quoted in Phillpot n.d.) "We were part of the Fluxus movement," Gee Vaucher has remembered, "and . . . we were affected by street theatre—by the idea of taking something out of the four walls and off the canvas" (quoted in Berger 2008, 33).

Although Fluxus remains a complex movement, two key concepts are useful here. The first involves what the musician George Brecht calls "event scores." Here, Brecht looked to explore the complex relationship between art and life using everyday objects and "events" to create a "performance." The "score" did not involve notation as such, but instead contained instructions for the performer. In his *Drip Music (Drip Event)*, for instance, the score simply reads, "For a single or multiple performance. A source of dripping water and empty vessel are arranged so that the water falls into the vessel." The second concept involves the instruction-like compositions of the musician La Monte Young. Alongside Brecht's "events," Young was interested in the spontaneity and singularity of the moment. In his *Compositions 1960*, for instance, Young placed further emphasis on the performer(s) and location in order to interpret his compositions with #5, asking the performer to "Turn a butterfly (or any number of butterflies) loose in the performance area. / When the composition is over, be sure to allow the butterfly to fly away outside" (quoted in Nyman 2003, 84).

In this extraordinary artistic world of innovations and experimentations, it may be no surprise that the Stanford Rivers Quartet would give way to another experimental avant-garde ensemble, Exit. Whereas the repertoire for the Quartet was generally notated (albeit using graphic scores), Exit was altogether more influenced by the Fluxus "event": "To call the line up fluid would be an understatement," writes George Berger in his band biography of Crass; "people were free to come and go as they pleased, even during performances" (Berger 2008, 30). Rimbaud also suggests other influences for Exit. "Taking on-board the ideas of free jazz," he writes, "we became increasingly dependent on improvisation, but rather than reflecting the cultural roots of American jazz . . . the results showed more affinity to European classical modernism" (quoted in Exit 2013 sleeve notes). Exit began playing regular shows, with events lasting up to three hours, and featuring extended improvisations Rimbaud describes as "almost Messianic in scale" (quoted in Exit 2013 sleeve notes).

Soon, Exit were appearing at the festival of contemporary music called the International Carnival of Experimental Sounds, or ICES 72. Playing at London's Roundhouse, Exit were to share the stage with the likes of John Cage, Terry Riley, and Cornelius Cardew. Exit performed on Sunday, August 20, 1972, their set lasting just under an hour. Ten musicians were involved, including Rimbaud on drums, voice, and electronic effects, and Vaucher on stripped-down upright piano. The recorded performance was finally released in 2013, as *The Mystic Trumpeter*, a reference to the poem by Walt Whitman whose work was read aloud prior to the Exit performance. Incidentally, one could also argue that it is a reference to the English composer Gustav Holst, whose "The Mystic Trumpeter" (1904) had also set the Whitman work to music. In Exit's performance, one can hear the symbiotic relationship between performers common in the work of Cardew and others: the democratization of the performing space as a means of co-operation, of listening and responding to those players around you.

But how far were the anarcho-punk sounds of post-Exit Crass influenced by the (contemporary) classical tradition? The Fluxus-inspired "events" that saw the multimedia, undetermined, atonal performances of Exit informed the experimentalist musical repertoire of Crass, in particular through the complex relationship between musical soundscapes and the political. One need only turn to Crass's *Penis Envy* (1981), for instance, a work that contains lyrics solely delivered by female vocalists. (It would be one of Crass's surprises that the main male lead vocalist, Steve Ignorant, does not feature on this album.) The experimental unpredictability of the work lies partly in singer Eve Libertine's comment that "the previous record was [the rather relentless and hardcore] *Stations [of the Crass]*. People would want more of that, so we'd do something different" (quoted in Berger 2008, 199). What is interesting about the album is not just the philosophical lyrical content ("Where Next Columbus"), or the powerful feminist message ("Bata Motel" and "Smother Love," for instance), but also the vocal delivery and its context within an expanding soundscape. Placed as the last song on Side A, "What the Fuck" begins with the sound of a turntable needle being scratched over the vinyl, followed by the recording of whispering, murmuring voices. In the background, a woman's voice is heard articulating the beginning of the track proper. The spoken nature of the vocal delivery, the stabbing, biting vocal delivery accompanied by the atonal soundscape, reminds one of Schoenberg's *Sprechstimme*, a technique used in compositions such as *Erwatung* (1909) and *Pierrot Lunaire* (1912). Linked to operatic recitative, *Sprechstimme* is a method of spoken singing, where the tonal quality of the speech is heightened or lowered according to musical notation. The method of delivery resonated with an expressionist agenda that informed Schoenberg's work at the time: an expressionism that looked inward to the angst and fear that lay within the unconscious mind. Schoenberg wished to avoid what he termed "traditional forms of beauty," instead using new modes of musical expression to convey feelings (quoted in Sadie 1991, 244).

That said, there is, perhaps, one piece in the Crass repertoire that resonates compellingly with the influence of the avant-garde and the modern classical music tradition. This is *Yes Sir, I Will* (1983), specifically influenced by the pacifist composer Benjamin Britten and his *War Requiem* (1962). Like *Penis Envy*, *Yes Sir, I Will* is a set—one could say suite—of related songs, presented in an album format. Britten's contribution to the Requiem tradition is unique, not only in recasting the Requiem Mass in a contemporary sound, but also through its inclusion of the poetry of Wilfred Owen alongside traditional liturgical text. One needs only to compare Britten's work to those of his nineteenth-century predecessors, most notably Berlioz, Verdi, and Faure. Here, it is evident that Britten not only continues this tradition—there is inclusion of liturgical text—but also reworks the musical form and structure (Wilfred Owen's text for instance in the Dies Irae) into a contemporary musical setting. Beyond form and structure, Britten also recasts the role of Requiem as a stark reminder of the horrors of war. Here, he recasts the Requiem into a complex musico-drama that provides a subtle reproval of violence.

Yes Sir, I Will recasts the role of punk agitators in the much the same way that Britten laments for peace in his *War Requiem*. Up until the Falklands War in 1982, Crass had been systematic in their condemnation of a postwar, capitalist Britain, from their early release of *The Feeding the Five Thousand* to their feminist-charged *Penis Envy* (1981). As their development as a political, musical, and artistic critique of the newly emerging Thatcher government of the 1980s saw them move from the safety of swiping at subcultural predecessors, the desperate cries from the dissonant, almost nonformulaic musical material of *Yes Sir, I Will* reflects the hopelessness and anguish of a community now lost within a far wider political arena. The appeal to individuality—the safe existence—of Crass within the subcultural confines of punk rock is now gone, and the band are encountering far wider issues *outside* of this subcultural realm.

The creative trajectory of Crass, from their earlier roots in avant-garde musical and performance ensembles to being a foundational icon of anarcho-punk, raises questions of creative ownership. As McKay (1996, 76) notes, Crass comprised "around nine male and female musicians, artists, film-makers and activists," but emphasis is often placed upon the leading role of Rimbaud and, to a lesser degree, the artist Gee Vaucher and Steve Ignorant. (I acknowledge that, effectively, in aiming to trace classical and avant-garde influences on anarcho-punk, I have myself stressed the contributions of Rimbaud and Vaucher over other members.) Relatively little is heard from some of those who were central in the aesthetic and political articulation of Crass, including N. A. Palmer, Phil Free, and Pete Wright; and, although these individuals may have distanced themselves from the "Crass" name, one must be careful in placing Rimbaud as a sole spokesperson for essentially what many saw as an anarchist-commune and collective creative practice.[1]

THROBBING GRISTLE, EXPERIMENTAL NOISE, AND PERFORMANCE ART

As Crass were influenced by the avant-garde, so too were Throbbing Gristle, seen by many as the key protagonists of industrial music (see Reynolds 2005, 30–31; Hegarty 2007, 105; Encarnacao 2019, 75). Their aesthetic lay in the "confrontation, degradation, mutual abjection, shared violence, unlimited expression of taboo subjects and acts" (Hegarty 2007, 108–109), as Genesis P-Orridge et al. disrupted the normative popular music aesthetic through harsh noise, tape cut-ups, the use of non-instruments, and the incorporation of visuals, often of pornography or graphic violence. Alongside other acts and artists, such as Cabaret Voltaire, Monte Cezazza, and NON, Throbbing Gristle used popular music as a means of breaking new ground in performance and composition.

Key to the narrative is the enigmatic figure of P-Orridge, who even in his early days as a schoolboy in the English midlands in the 1960s was already conceiving of "street happenings"—that is to say, here is further evidence of (1960s) countercultural influence on (1970s) punk rock. Going under the name of "The Knights of the Pentecostal Flame," he recalled how he and some friends "scattered small cards with evocative [haiku-like] words written on them all over town, inside cafés, bookshops, etc." Influenced by the "cut-ups" of Brian Gysin and William Burroughs, "all the cards picked up also 'wrote' a long poem, but one that nobody would ever see or hear complete" (P-Orridge, quoted in Cuzner, 2017). At university in Hull, he was introduced to a world of new ideas and art from John Cage and Aleister Crowley to Andy Warhol and the Velvet Underground. Soon he was dropping out to live in a north London art commune, where, in Cosey Fanni Tutti's words, there was a sense of "life as art, communal creativity, everyone [as] an artist, costumes, rituals, play, artworks, scavenging for art materials, street theatre, rejection of conventions, and the advocation of sexual liberation" (Tutti 2017). Significantly, it was during this time that the idea of the pre–Throbbing Gristle music and art collective COUM Transmissions came to P-Orridge.

COUM's early events remain important artistic and musical starting points in the group's developments, not least the 1969 performance of "Clockwork Hot Spoiled Acid Test," at Hull University students' union. This was inspired by, and a mash-up happening of, Ken Kesey's Merry Pranksters (and Tom Wolfe's 1968 account of their activities, *The Electric Kool-Aid Acid Test*) and Anthony Burgess's 1962 dystopian novel *A Clockwork Orange*. Their support act slot for the space-rock psychedelic band Hawkwind in Bradford in 1971 included a "'John Smith from Bridlington' singing while stood on a surf board balanced on buckets of water" (Cuzner 2017). Two years later, COUM were invited by Hull Arts Centre to perform at their commemoration of the UK joining the EEC. Here, they performed several pieces, including "Ministry of Anti-Social Insecurity," where the group installed a mock border control desk in the city's Ferens Art Gallery, complete with fake forms. By now their reputation was growing and they were included in a film for Granada Television as part of the Manchester Arts Festival. Here, "COUM member Fizzy Paet, dressed as a roller-skating clown, was seen to marry Tremble, Cosey [Fanni Tutti]'s dog, in a derelict church. A brass band, Morris dancers and coloured food are said to also have featured in the surreal ceremony" (Cuzner 2017).

Relocating back to London, COUM became part of a touring exhibition, FLUXshoe, drawing—as had pre-Crass EXIT—on the experimental, radical art-group tactics and ideas of Fluxus. Here, COUM performed a number of works, including "Snail Trail," where "P-Orridge crawled from one Nottingham venue to the next under a plastic sheet while secreting a trail of stickers," to sending John Lennon a Blackburn phone directly drilled with holes to embody the lyric "four-thousand holes in Blackburn, Lancashire" from the Beatles' "A Day in the Life." The following years saw COUM take advantage of the extensive art networks in London, and the performance of "Orange and Blue," a piece questioning gender roles and stereotyping, and fetishistic "Couming of Youth" where Cosey and P-Orridge's performance included, in his words, "this thing of spitting at each other and then licking all the spit off, and then licking each other's genitals, and then having sexual intercourse while her hair was set on fire with candles" (quoted in Cuzner 2017).

But it is the 1976 Institute of Contemporary Arts, London, exhibition Prostitution that remains the most notorious COUM event, and the one closely linked to punk. The more music- than performance art-oriented aspect of COUM would be explored in a kind of band, named Throbbing Gristle, that would play not a concert but a "disconcert" (quoted in Reynolds 2005, 224). The provocations of the exhibition have been outlined elsewhere (see Savage 1991, 250–253), especially Sir Nicholas Fairbairn's infamous "wreckers of civilization" comment and the subsequent headline in the Daily Mail. Accompanying performance by LSD (aka the punk band Chelsea), the transvestite guards, the used tampons, and a stripper, there was also a performance of Throbbing Gristle, born from the musical wing of COUM, opening the exhibition. With the flyer for the event listing them as performing "Music from the Death Factory," Throbbing Gristle's set included "Slug Bait," and "Very Friendly," the former live recording ending up on the band's first album, The Second Annual Review (1977). "Slug Bait," in particular, highlights "the banality [and] artlessness of P-Orridge's voice: its nasal taunting [and its] capacity to introduce gruesome subject matter completely dispassionately" (Encarnacao 2019, 79–80). Among those in the audience for the anti-performance of Throbbing Gristle at the ICA were some of the new young punks, including Siouxsie Sioux and Steven Severin of the Banshees.

This being their third performance, for some, Throbbing Gristle, and the emerging Industrial scene, were influenced by an ideology akin to that of the Italian Futurists (including some aesthetic fascination with fascism), representing a "set of attitudes towards society, art and technology" embodied within popular music "with machine-like rhythms" (Encarnacao 2019, 76). According to Encarnacao,

> In Throbbing Gristle specifically we can see and hear traces of many artistic traditions, some acknowledged by the group, others not so, including various trajectories of experimental art, the non-linear techniques of William Burroughs, the "any sound can be music" philosophy of John Cage, and the immersive sensory experience of progressive rock groups such as Pink Floyd and Hawkwind.
>
> (Encarnacao 2019, 76)

One might legitimately ask, Where is the punk in this? Yet alongside the likes of Patti Smith, Devo, and Pere Ubu, Throbbing Gristle held a unique space in the punk canon, one categorized by a post-hippie, pre-punk aesthetic and ideology. For others, in a forerunner to punk, the confrontational aesthetic of the band also contained an important message: a statement of taboo-breaking intent. Furthermore, Throbbing Gristle encompassed a conscious move away from the artistic to a musical aesthetic which coincided with the emerging punk scene. As such, the band rapidly pushed the punk format past its parameters in terms of musical amateurism and lyrical content. This may be their most significant contribution to punk—that they immediately went beyond it, almost before it had even happened. They made punk old when it was barely new. After all, Genesis P-Orridge had challenged the new DIY claims of punk in 1977: referring to the punk fanzine–distilled mantra of "here's three chords . . . now form a band," he complained and explained to the music press:

> [But i]t starts with chords. They're saying "Be like everyone else, you gotta learn to play." [But y]ou can start with *no chords*. Why not just say, "Form a band and it doesn't matter what it sounds like or whether you even make a noise, if you just stand there silent for an hour, just do what you want."
>
> (quoted in Reynolds 2005, 230; emphasis in original)

Simon Reynolds has observed of Throbbing Gristle that, "[i]n terms of being shocking, punk was pretty tame in comparison" (quoted in Leland 2018): after all, where punks spat, P-Orridge and Cosey in performance spat at each other, then licked it off, and then went well beyond that.

COUM had already been noticed by the music industry, with Virgin Records in particular taking an interest early on, leading to the *Melody Maker* publishing its first article on the band, a sole interview with P-Orridge. Moreover, according to Tutti's recent autobiography, P-Orridge forged conscious links with the punk movement through his friendship with Mark Perry of *Sniffin' Glue* fanzine and the band Alternative TV, and his relationship with Soo Catwoman. P-Orridge and Soo were courting a number of record labels so as to secure a record contract, much to the chagrin of the other band members who wanted to "refocus away from anything punk" (quoted in Tutti 2018, 226). Finding direct links between COUM, Throbbing Gristle, and punk may remain a task of historical and aesthetic reraveling, but in some performative practices, common venues, and audience crossovers—as well as more standard industry DIY approaches such as the use of independent record labels—we can see influences and productive informed tensions.

Conclusion

Through the examination of three key sets of protagonists in punk—McLaren and Reid, anarcho-punk band Crass, and Throbbing Gristle, this chapter has charted different journeys toward the emergence of punk in the 1970s. From the manifestos of the art school Situationists to the contemporary classicism of Crass and the auto-didactical experimentation of Genesis P-Orridge, it is clear that punk is a subculture with a rich set of social, cultural, musical, and artistic antecedents. Punk was not a "year zero" phenomenon; whether it had a future or not, it definitely had a past. There are similarities between all three case studies, not least in their protagonists having an active involvement in the experimental art scene of the 1960s and early 1970s counterculture. One sees a trajectory that may leave behind those who, as Stewart Home (1996) has noted, had no idea of the Situationists, nor of the Fluxus-influenced compositions of George Maciunas and others. While the Sex Pistols-McLaren-Reid-Situ axis has been well enough mapped and even mythologized, there may be other opportunities to recast punk's sense of self: not least in the case of contemporary classical music, or the radical employment of not three chords but "no chords" and the cultural confrontation in industrial music and performance. The mythologizing of punk invites us to consider the ontological fluidity of subversive and radical ideas. Punk has often been thought and written of as a beginning of an era, a "year zero" that energetically gathered up the many threads of (among others) Situationism, countercultural idealism, and anarchist thought, positing them in the music of the Sex Pistols, Crass, or Throbbing Gristle, and many others. Yet, as this chapter has aimed to show, it is not punk that did the "gathering"; rather, the undercurrent of the subversive runs like a thread through each era. Thus, punk is simply another disruptive episode in a long line of insurrectionary politics, social thought, and musical/artistic expression.

Note

1. Tension around control in the archive can be glimpsed in bassist Pete Wright's disagreement over the reissue from 2010 onward of Crass's albums, an endeavor tellingly perhaps, for us, titled the Crassical Collection. As well as including new artwork from Vaucher and bonus tracks, each album was digitally remastered by Rimbaud. In Wright's view, however, the Crass stuff "should remain 'of its time'" (quoted in Wright 2013, 5), noting how, "when the band was going, we operated a consensus form of decision making, leaving each person with a veto" (quoted in Wright 2013, 7).

References

Berger, George. 2008. *The Story of Crass*. London: Omnibus Press.
Cabut, Richard, and Andrew Gallix. 2017. *Punk Is Dead: Modernity Killed Every Night*. Alresford, UK: Zero Books.
Cuzner, Russell. 2017. "Primal Evidence: The Strange World of the COUM Transmissions." *The Quietus*, January 27, 2017. https://thequietus.com/articles/21586-coum-actions-cosey-fanni-tutti-genesis-p-orridge.
Encarnacao, John. 2019. "Throbbing Gristle's Early Records: Post-Hippie/Pre-Punk/Post-Punk." In *Mute Records: Artists, Business, History*, edited by Zuleika Beaven, Marcus O'Dair, and Richard Osbourne, 71–86. London: Bloomsbury.
Exit. 2013. *The Mystic Trumpeter*. CD. London: Exitstencil Press.
Frith, Simon, and Howard Horne. 1987. *Art into Pop*. London: Methuen.
Hegarty, Paul. 2007. *Noise/Music: A History*. London: Bloomsbury.
Home, Stewart. 1991. *The Assault on Culture: Utopian Currents from Lettrisme to Class War*. Stirling, UK: AK Press.
Home, Stewart. 1996. *Cranked Up Really High: Genre Theory and Punk Rock*. Hove, UK: Codex.
Leland, John. 2018. "Genesis P-Orridge Has Always Been a Provocateur of the Body. Now She's At Its Mercy." *New York Times*, November 9, 2018. https://www.nytimes.com/2018/11/09/arts/music/genesis-p-orridge-throbbing-gristle.html.

Marcus, Greil. 1990. *Lipstick Traces: A Secret History of the Twentieth Century*. Cambridge, MA: Harvard University Press.

McKay, George. 1996. *Senseless Acts of Beauty: Cultures of Resistance since the Sixties*. London: Verso.

Nyman, Michael. 2003. *Experimental Music: Cage and Beyond*. Cambridge: Cambridge University Press.

Phillpot, Clive. n.d. "Fluxus: Magazines, Manifestos, Multum in Parvo." http://georgemaciunas.com/about/cv/manifesto-i/.

Reynolds, Simon. 2005. *Rip It Up and Start Again: Postpunk 1978–1984*. London: Faber.

Sadie, Stanley, ed. 1991. *The Norton Grove Concise Encyclopaedia of Music*. New York: W. W. Norton.

Savage, Jon. 1991. *England's Dreaming: Sex Pistols and Punk Rock*. London: Faber.

Schill, Brian James. 2017. *The Year's Work in the Punk Bookshelf, Or, Lusty Scripts*. Bloomington: Indiana University Press.

Tutti, Cosey Fanni. 2017. "'I Smeared Gen in Flour and Paste and Whipped Him Hard': An Extract from Cosey Fanni Tutti's Book." *Guardian*, March 14, 2017. https://www.theguardian.com/music/2017/mar/14/i-smeared-gen-in-flour-paste-and-whipped-him-hard-an-extract-from-cosey-fanni-tuttis-book.

Tutti, Cosey Fanni. 2018. *Art Sex Music*. London: Faber.

Vague, Tom. 1997. *Anarchy in the UK: The Angry Brigade*. Stirling, UK: AK Press.

Walker, John A. 1998. *Art and Outrage: Provocation, Controversy and the Visual Arts*. London: Pluto Press.

Webb, Peter. 2007. *Exploring the Networked Worlds of Popular Music: Milieu Cultures*. London: Routledge.

Worley, Matthew. 2017. *No Future: Punk, Politics and British Youth Culture, 1976–1984*. Cambridge: Cambridge University Press.

Wright, Pete. 2013. "Crass Journal: a Record of Letters, Articles, Postings and E-mails, February 2009–September 2010 concerning Penny, Gee and Allison's *Crassical Collection*." http://www.crassicalcollection.com/crass.pdf.

PART TWO

OH BONDAGE, UP YOURS! GENDER AND PUNK

CHAPTER 7

DANGER, ANGER, AND NOISE

The Women Punks of the Late 1970s and Their Music

HELEN REDDINGTON

> We were revolutionaries as far as I was concerned and we were on a mission and what was going on outside was really just irrelevant.
> —Gina Birch, The Raincoats, 2000 (author's interview)

AFTER the libertarian sexual and social politics of 1960s Britain, a period in time when the British economy was thriving, there was a stark change in the 1970s. Despite the Sex Discrimination Act of 1975 theoretically promoting equality in the workplace for women and men, increasing unemployment meant that the idea of women potentially competing for "men's jobs" was not well received. The 1970s generation of young people experienced entirely different employment prospects than those of their parents, who had been able to find work relatively easily. Those adults who had survived the experience of growing up in wartime were anxious that their children should reap the financial, social, and moral rewards of victory, and, crucially, that they should show gratitude for their good fortune. Trade unions were powerful in the 1970s and reflected masculine aspects of an economy based on heavy industries such as coal mining, shipbuilding, and steel manufacture, all of which began to decline further throughout the decade. Certainties like the consistency of the royal family, fixed gender roles, and abiding by the law were increasingly focused on as the economy became more fragile (see Thornett 1998; Beckett 2009; and Sandbrook 2019 for contrasting historical accounts of the late 1970s and early 1980s in Britain).

Danger

Many young people in Britain in the mid-1970s had simply ceased to believe in the metanarrative of postwar industrial capitalism; they clustered into tribes and subcultures, often with music at their heart. The Teds were a throwback to the Teddy Boys of the 1950s, focused around American music of the rock 'n' roll decade, and bands playing covers or pastiches of their musical style (Darts, Shakin' Stevens); they often had reactionary viewpoints commensurate with their retro clothing style. The skinheads listened to Ska music, and ironically, given that this music originated in Jamaica and that early British skinhead culture involved both black and white youths, in the late 1970s developed right-wing views and involved themselves in racist violence. The "straights" did not appear to focus on any type of music, but they could also be violent, sometimes appearing to see themselves as moral arbiters. Football hooligans mainly concentrated on internecine fighting; most English football teams had "firms" of football hooligans who clashed violently at matches, and who also served as foot soldiers for the newly developing extreme-right National Front. They were also a threat to members of other subcultures. The hippie lifestyle still appealed to some young people, and they were sometimes politically active, often as anarchists involved in the squatting movement.

Postwar tribal divisions were identified and analyzed in research by the Birmingham Centre for Contemporary Cultural Studies in 1975, and published in book form just before the advent of the punk subculture. The resulting book, *Resistance through Rituals*, remains the most thorough account of the variety of youth groupings in the postwar landscape that preceded it (Hall and Jefferson 1975; see also Willis 1978; Hebdige 1979; McRobbie 2000). Visually, the roots of punk style combined everything potentially offensive, from fetish literature to references to the IRA (Irish Republican Army) (York 1980, 137); sonically, challenging lyrics and loud volumes combined to create distinctive "shock effects" (Laing 1985, 69–102).

Perhaps in part because of their novelty, punks were disliked by all of these contemporary youth subgroupings; it was in this subculture that women protagonists became significant, and this factor added to the reasons why the others should want to conflict with them. The punk subculture encouraged (or allowed) women to take on active roles as photographers, such as Caroline Coon (also a journalist for *Melody Maker*); artists, such as Gee Vaucher (a member of the Crass community, whose work formed the group's distinctive record sleeves and posters); stylists and fashion designers, such as Linder Sterling (the Manchester-based designer of the Buzzcocks' collage-based artwork, designer of the original meat dress, and a musician herself) and Vivienne Westwood (designer of punk clothing for the SEX shop in King's Road); journalists and fanzine makers, such as Julie Burchill (journalist for the *NME* [*New Musical Express*]), Vivien Goldman (journalist for *Sounds*), Lucy Toothpaste (founder of the fanzine *Jolt*), Liz Naylor and Cath Carroll (of Manchester's *City Fun* fanzine); and, at the epicenter of the punk scene, rock musicians. This last category was particularly significant, because rock and pop music had been extremely stratified along gender lines—the rebellion that rock preached had always been predominantly *male* rebellion up to this point—but now there were bands such as the Slits, who subverted dress codes by wearing torn "little-girl" dresses and who subverted rock music by using both musical instruments and voices in challenging ways; the Raincoats, who sported jumble-sale chic and whose lyrics and music reflected the heart of the new feminist approach to gender relations (among other subjects); and the Au Pairs, who sang about everything from the "troubles" in Ireland to sexual problems, while rejecting glamorous clothing.

Previously in pop and rock music, women's power had been expressed in a number of different ways: through powerful rock and soul vocalists such as Janis Joplin and Tina Turner; more "introverted" protest singers such as Joni Mitchell and Joan Baez (whose strength was channeled through their lyrics); and highly trained and emotionally expressive pop singers such as Aretha Franklin, Diana Ross, or the British entertainers Dusty Springfield and Petula Clark. Actual protest music by women had generally been gentle, a slipping-by of subversive political messages carried by an acoustic guitar, often with a male Svengali figure, or at best enabler, attached (e.g., Joan Baez/Bob Dylan, Joni Mitchell/Graham Nash). Strong and assertive lyrically, but ultimately measured in approach, the music apparently did not readily challenge the male hegemony of rock music. It was Vivien Goldman who, in 1976, first identified the sudden influx of women rock bands onto the London live music scene, in an article in the national musical weekly *Sounds* titled "The Other New Wave" (Goldman 1976). She included heavy metal (Painted Lady), punk (the Slits), and jazz-flavored artists (Mother Superior) in her article, and she was at the forefront of writing about the new rock-instrument-playing sorority on the live circuit who derived empowerment from actually playing the instruments themselves (18–20). Previously, such activity was rare, and even rarer when accompanied by an attitudinality or pose.

Many male punk bands had names that were "menacing . . . still steeped in Hell's Angels male pathology," according to Lesley Woods, singer and guitarist with the Birmingham band the Au Pairs (author's interview, July 2010). All-male bands such as the Sex Pistols, the Clash, the Stranglers, and the Damned all referenced the darker side of life in their names. But even bands featuring female musicians and singers were not immune: the Slits, the Castrators, Shanne Bradley's band the Nipple Erectors, and Chrissie Hynde's early, short-lived (understandably) band the Moors Murderers, named after a pair of notorious 1960s child killers, also contributed to an overall impression of deviation, and often threat. It is worth considering the frequent and aggressive use of the swastika and other Nazi imagery that was also part of early punk, not least as this impinged on female artists. Siouxsie and the Banshees in particular claimed to use the swastika as a symbol of resistance; in some interviews, the band explained that the swastika was worn specifically to upset what they felt was their parent generation's glorification of the Second World War (see Whiteley 2000, 109). Yet the perceived ambivalence toward Nazism was disturbing to many in the punk community, and with retrospect has been regarded as overt anti-Semitism (see Sabin 1999, 208). But just as a literal reception of fetish-wear was deliberately de-recuperated by the media, the even more inflammatory resurrection of the swastika as an emblem of youth revolt played in to the hands of the far-right National Front, who in turn reappropriated it as a tool for recruiting some of the young punks and many skinheads into their ranks. Ironically, the overtly pacifist and feminist Vi Subversa of Poison Girls was among those women punk musicians whose gigs were disrupted by violent National Front skinheads. In 1979, *NME* interviewed her about clashes between National Front skinheads and young aggressive men from the Socialist Workers' Party at a Poison Girls gig. Subversa responded, saying, "There are a lot of young people about, and a lot of other people who are trying to colonise their energies—vultures who see us as a kind of prey." Four days after the interview, neo-fascist thugs broke up one of their gigs at the Theatre Royal Stratford, attacked the band, and destroyed their equipment. The *NME* subsequently reported, illustrating punk's capacity to frame socio-musical debates within questions of gendered violence, that "[l]ater the band issued a statement that violence stems from male power games and asked for help in formulating ways of combating this that did not involve violence" (Lock 1979, 30).

The assertiveness and aggression shown by some women punks did not protect them from being attacked; equality with their male peers meant that they too got beaten up for looking and sounding extraordinary, and this threat was amplified if you were in a band. From interviews conducted by the author, it is apparent that the more female members a band had, the more likely they were to be assaulted; the all-female Slits in particular elicited as much physical aggression as they did fear or ridicule, simply by the way they dressed and behaved in public. Confrontation came not only from rival subcultures like the skinheads, but also from "normal" men, as guitarist Viv Albertine explains:

> It felt violent all the time wherever you were.... The skinheads didn't differentiate between men and women; they'd happily beat up a girl. Then you got the normal thing: kerb crawlers, dirty old men. I was flashed at all the time.
>
> (author's interview, 2010)

The Slits were attacked constantly, and have summed up most clearly the real danger experienced by women punks who lived the life offstage as well as on it:

> ARI: If boys were rebellious, it was OK, they're boys, they *can* be rebellious. But if it was women, that was like a totally different situation. It was a different planet. It was so taboo—we absolutely threatened the world. It's easy to be a woman who's all dressed up on stage and looking punky and rebellious on stage, and then when they come off the stage they look all dainty and camouflaged again. Let them walk around in all the real shit the way we did at the time....
>
> I was stabbed for looking the way we looked. Some disco guy stabbed me, some John Travolta guy.
>
> TESSA: She had loads of layers of clothes on and he came up behind her with a knife and said, "Here's a Slit for *you*." But she had so many layers of clothes on, she was OK, she was only scratched.

ARI: And by the time we turned round he had gone. There's no way we could go to the police, are you kidding me? Do you think people like us could go to the police at the time? We were harassed by police as well.

(author's interview, February 2006; see also Street-Howe 2009, 62)

Lucy O'Brien (of the Southampton band the Catholic Girls) reports her all-female band being chased after a gig by a group of skinheads, who objected to them being "girls" playing music. After having bottles thrown at them when they were on stage, the band took refuge in their van, and they were finally rescued by the police who had been alerted by people living nearby. At other Catholic Girls gigs, "there were regular cries of: 'fuckin' cows, who do you think you are?" (O'Brien 1999, 193). June Miles-Kingston, drummer with The Mo-Dettes, would confront skinheads directly:

When they used to come up on stage or throw things, I'd come down the front with the sticks and say look, pack it up, shut it up and just deal with it. They gain respect for you then. It's like anything: if the bully pushes and pushes, you've gotta push back, and then they stop. We ended up becoming such good friends with the skinheads that they became our followers, and two of them became our roadies. They had Mo-Dettes tattoos.

(author's interview, 2006)

The problem of violence against women in punk music *audiences* was often just as bad as it was for the bands, even (or especially) when the bands playing were all-female. Paul Du Noyer reported the "unimpressive yobbery" of the audience at a Mo-Dettes gig at the Marquee, where fireworks and stink bombs were let off after a stage invasion (1980, 41), while Lucy Toothpaste reported skinheads in the audience pushing women to the back and sides of Dingwalls at a gig by the Bodysnatchers (1980, 13).[1]

Shanne Bradley of the Nipple Erectors experienced opposition from within the punk subculture itself, reporting several instances of being threatened by male members of other punk bands:

When I first was trying to play the guitar someone came and just cut the strings off to stop me playing. People just used to laugh if you were a girl trying to play guitar; they just didn't take you seriously. It just made me more determined and angry.

(author's interview, 2010)

This was in addition to being chased by Teddy Girls and even heckled by hippies at gigs; from stories such as these one can glimpse the remarkable level of female determination that was necessary in order to participate in music-making during this time. New sources of conflict and violence seemed to appear constantly; for instance, at the 1980 Stonehenge People's Free Festival, it was the Hell's Angels who assaulted the punks. No matter how much Poison Girls decried "the system of gang warfare" from these largely male youth factions (including the left wing), this did not stop them from attacking the punk bands, sometimes viciously (Cross 2014, 127).

Hostility toward female bands of this era was not confined to Britain; in America the Mo-Dettes experienced a woman exposing herself to them in Miami, threats of violence from Californian Guardians of Morality in Orange County, plus Hell's Angels approaching a car in which they were sleeping to leer at them through the windows (Grabel 1980, 24). Belonging to a British punk subculture just triggered trouble for female bands. As Lesley Woods of the Au Pairs said in 2010, "[Our generation] got the tail end of the guys at school, the geography teachers who would cane you . . . the corporal punishment. I think we got the aftermath of the postwar years." She was attacked with a baseball bat "for opening my mouth" (author's interview). This generation of women had become used to being assaulted, looked down on, and marginalized. For those who overstepped the male mark too frequently, there was always the weapon of sexual violence to put a stop to it. The author's study of 2012 documents some of this (Reddington 2012, 67–75), but many of the women punks interviewed at the time quite understandably did not wish to cast themselves as victims of rape. However, it is notable that since the publication of *The Lost Women of Rock Music*, five additional rapes that happened at the time have been reported to the author by the original interviewees who had been reluctant at the time to talk about what had happened to them. Balancing the positive aspects of punk (such as empowerment and access to male space for women in the subculture) against the negative ones (such as sexual assault) is an understandable response to a female historian's discourse. An element of trust in the nature of the published narrative probably led to these discussions, which happened separately over a number of years.

Anger

Less commonly focused upon are the acts of *female* aggression in the punk community. Sometimes, these were conducted in self-defense, but sometimes they could be just as much an overreaction and just as provocative as acts of violence by men. Violence and abuse have always been part of women's lives; punk turned fear of violence inside out and encouraged expressions of female assertiveness both on- and offstage, potentially making women objects of fear rather than objects of desire. This was particularly apparent during the early days of punk in London, when punk belonged to a relatively small coterie of people whose overheated lifestyles occasionally clashed. For instance, Vivienne Westwood is reported as having starting fights at gigs by band manager Nils Stevenson (Colegrave and Sullivan 2001, 115) and also by John Lydon, whose disparaging dismissal of Westwood's fight at a gig at London's Nashville Rooms in 1976 demonstrates his feelings about her at the time:

There was supposedly a fight, this big symbol of early punk rock violence. It was just a load of people falling all over the place. Vivienne smacked some girls. It was nonsense—fisticuffs and handbags really. The pictures of that fight make it look a lot worse than it was. It was a bunch of silly bitches squabbling.

(Lydon et al. 1994, 102)

The participants in punk subculture were deviant in the traditional sense in their unwillingness to relate to hegemonic rules, and in their grouping together they validated their own rules (see Becker 1963, 81). Within the subculture itself, punk girls amplified behaviors that Angela McRobbie and Jenny Garber identified as resistant in teenage girls in situations where men were dominant: groups of girls giggling together as defensive, and inappropriate sexual titillation as aggressive (1975, 178). As an example of this, the music journalist Ian Penman was greatly disturbed by a performance by the Slits in Liverpool where the band parodied their sexuality to the point where it became "a teasing, inverted approximation of the norm" (Penman 1979, 35). Ari from the Slits had a sense of mischief that sometimes spilled over from self-protection to provocation; at an early gig at The Roxy in Covent Garden, London, she tried to unplug the microphone leads as X-Ray Spex were performing, according to Poly Styrene (Denom 1977, 48), and allegedly jabbed the father of Bazooka Joe's bass player in the eye with a pen (Colegrave and Sullivan 2001, 206). Her chutzpah was admired by Nils Stevenson, who reported on it: "Last night at The Roxy she attacked Paul Cook with a knife. It left a huge hole in the back of a leather jacket he stole from Malcolm. But I love the sound The Slits make—*their gigs are as unpredictable as Ari's mood swings*" (1999, 97; emphasis added). At a Slits gig at the Coventry Theatre reviewed in the fanzine *Guttersnipe*, a local writer described an effective response to being spat at:

They all started spitting and Ari told them to stop. She told one of the audience to come and get on the stage and when he did she gobbed a greenie right on his face. "Good one Ari" he almost fell off the stage with shock I don't know what he was expecting [*sic*].

(*Guttersnipe*, Issue 7, 1979)

BBC Radio 1 DJ John Peel, who was at the forefront of championing punk music nationally, appeared to be grudgingly impressed by his first meeting with Palmolive in a 1977 *Sounds* article titled "Arthritic pogoer hit by Slit": "she approached as I was deep in conversation with one of the Celtic gents who runs the Rock On stall in Soho Market, and banged our heads together" (Peel 1977, 11). Peel mentions that the band is about to record a session for his show; he appears to have taken the incident entirely in his stride. Here we can begin to sense the level of admiration for the toughness of women punk musicians that runs through many of their male contemporaries' descriptions of their aggressive behavior. In his diaries, Nils Stevenson, manager of Siouxsie and the Banshees, reports almost as a matter of course the ways that Siouxsie protected herself on and off the stage:

Siouxsie co-headlines the Music Machine with Richard Hell. . . . Some little bastard headbuts [sic] me and runs away. He can't be more than fifteen. It fucking hurts though. Spend much of the evening trying to find him, but to no avail. I don't know how Siouxsie copes with playing to these arseholes, screaming to see her tits, grabbing her legs and gobbing at her. I get immense pleasure when she raps one of the wankers with the mike stand or kicks someone on [sic] the head who's too amorous, though they probably like it. (1999, 107)

At a major industry Christmas party in 1979, remembered Stevenson, he and Siouxsie "bump into [ex-drummer] Kenny Morris there. Naturally it all ends in tears. Siouxsie throws the first punch and then I steam in" (1999, 124).

Even the mature performer Vi Subversa was continually troubled by the violent element of punk and the ways it made her feel, and was particularly affected by the aggression of the audiences in what became anarcho-punk—ironically, with its strong emphasis on nonviolence—at the beginning of the 1980s. As she told Lucy Whitman in an interview in feminist magazine *Spare Rib* in 1981,

My conflict with that is what to do with my anger, I have fantasies where I want to kill people who I think are totally destructive and have too much power and do too much damage. But I've always wanted to change the war economy, which breeds war.

(quoted in Whitman 1981a, 32)

Subversa's approach was probably informed by the fact that she, even as a child, "got into trouble with the authorities" (Bayton 1998, 55). Punk provided a forum for angry women just as much as for men. Liz Naylor, of the band the Gay Animals and later the editor of the fanzine *City Fun*, was expelled from school at the age of fifteen and committed to a secure unit. As she says,

I remember being interviewed and I was wearing a man's suit, albeit fucked up, and I had this spiky hair; I cut it myself with bald patches. And the people who interviewed me saw my behavior and dress as deeply sociopathic, and dwelt a lot upon it. And I thought, "Well, I'm a punk." I was an "Other." I think it was a big gathering-together of people who regarded themselves as freaks.

(author's interview, 2000)

For many women musicians, there was an overall rejection of what it meant to be a woman, in particular a girly-girl. Gaye Black from the Adverts discussed her ambivalence about her gender, and the conflicts that occurred at the band's first two gigs, with journalist Sue Denom in *Spare Rib*:

I wanted to be a male pop star when I was little, I didn't want to be a soppy girl singer. . . . [A]t The Roundhouse some guy at the front yelled out "Why don't you learn to play." I got really angry and screamed at him to fuck off, I felt like chucking the bass at him and telling him to do better.... The violence was horrible at the first gig we did, I had to go off stage. But at the next one even when things were going OK, a woman came up and threw beer all over me. That's what upset me; I wouldn't have minded if it had been a guy.

(quoted in Denom 1977, 48)

Arlene Stein gives a very clear description of how it *felt* to be a female fan of male rock music, and not wanting to grow up to suffer the same passive fate that she perceived her mother to have done:

I didn't necessarily want to be a guy, or even want to date one, but I did fantasize, perhaps unconsciously, about possessing their power. If my embrace of rock was at least partly a revolt against my mother, it was also a revolt against the gender system that trapped her.

(Stein 1999, 221)

It is not surprising that girls then did not want to grow up to be women; the journey of a 1970s girl into adulthood for most was focused on being attractive enough to snare a husband, and then settling down and raising a family, putting the husband and family's needs to the forefront and effectively ceasing to exist as a human being in one's own right. Being involved in a punk band was therefore far more significant for the young women musicians than it was for the men.

Caroline O'Meara's comment on the Raincoats could be applied to many of the women punk bands: "[T]hey used the public forum of rock discourse to open the closed worlds of the home and women's emotional life to expression in rock" (2003, 303). Not only this; these bands highlighted the distance between the different roles women were expected to play. In both exposing authentic private thoughts and, for some women, bringing clothing associated with deviant male sexuality into their visual display, the subversion in the music was all the more powerful. Part of this process involved a redefinition of the word "camp," which had been so carefully and perceptively discussed by Susan Sontag in 1964 (see Sontag 1982). The gender play of the male pop groups of the 1970s had engaged with traditional camp in its co-optation of the feminine dress of the time; the chaotic and liberated redefinition of what it meant to be a punk girl or a punk woman, with its constantly shifting style and content, made the recuperation and commercialization of their music almost impossible. There was much to resist; the female journalist Robbi Millar, writing in *Sounds* about sexism in rock lyrics in 1970s heavy metal, reports a woman reader cutting out all the "girly" photos and sending them back, and,

[a]lthough I make a living from this magazine, I can't help but find some of its contents—especially those ghastly captions in Jaws which label women as "dogs," "boilers" and other inferior beasts—distressingly cruel. The attempt is at a certain breed of deprecation-cum-humour, but the results, though possibly funny

in an office atmosphere, translate into cold print as contemptuous anti-woman propaganda.

(Millar 1980, 32)

By that time even the patience of some women performers had apparently worn out, with Barbara Gogan of the Passions

declaring that she really gets a buzz slagging off men from the stage.... "All the best rock has been about people's anger.... It's all to do with people's emotions being reflected in the music and how genuine those emotions are. Obviously you're going to sing and play better about something you believe in, or you've experienced."

(Pearson 1980, 27, 28)

NOISE

Dick Hebdige's definition of subcultures as "represent[ing] 'noise' (as opposed to sound)" (1979, 90) uses our sense of hearing as a metaphor for the abrasive effect that these groups had on culture and society. In Hebdige's view, punks were

dramatizing what had come to be called "Britain's decline".... The punks appropriated the rhetoric of crisis which had filled the airwaves and the editorials throughout the period and translated it into tangible (and visible) terms.

(1979, 87; emphasis in original)

The ways that the female punk bands were written about by most rock critics at the time did much to propagate the reaction from punk audiences in general to their activities. As Kembrew McLeod notes, the approval or disapproval of rock critics was implicit in the type of descriptive language they used to "influence who feels comfortable enough to come out and play—and how certain cliques form" (2002, 93).

Just as with their male equivalents, there was nothing pretty about the way women sang in punk bands. In punk songs the energy of danger was processed into music that was sonically uncomfortable and disturbing; it echoed the desire of the Futurist art movement to cause disruption in society through violent sound. Although Futurism had itself been a misogynist movement, the first statement of their 1909 manifesto, "We intend to sing the love of danger, the habit of energy and fearlessness," perfectly describes the music made by women punks (Italian Futurism website). Rather than being overwhelmed by the maleness of the subculture and both the hegemonic and subcultural aggression aimed at them, punk women in bands fought for their territory using sound for their gender's own "war with the status quo" (Reynolds and Press 1995, 23), and contributed to the reinforcement of punk as an oppositional community by providing a female version of the rock music that women audience had often previously felt an affinity to, despite the sexist lyrics of most male rock songs (see Reddington 2012, 187–190). In this respect, they took the process that Valerie Walkerdine (1997) writes of, where young girls subvert and create their own empowered meanings from pop music that seems almost designed to repress them, to its logical conclusion.

In 1981, Simon Frith documented his realization, at a gig by the all-female band the Mistakes, that women's voices were not directed at the male ear:

> As a man, I've always taken it for granted that rock performances address male desires, reflect male fantasies in their connections of music and dance and sexuality. The first time I saw a women's band perform for women I was made physically uneasy by the sense of exclusion. (1988, 155)

Punk women's self-penned songs often veered between music and noise, especially vocally, where tempered screams battered pointed and fearless lyrics into the heads of their audiences. An alternately delighted and horrified Charles Shaar Murray wrote of singer Poly Styrene that she

> could only sing in tune if it was an emergency of the highest priority, screamed "1-2-3-4!" at the beginning of her every song whatever its actual pace and tempo happened to be, fronted a band who produced—alternately as well as simultaneously—some of the most exhilarating and horrible noises of a period memorable for both exhilarating and horrible noises. (1980, 30)

In another example, Graham Lock reports hearing Vi Subversa's voice "crackle with power or shriek in anguish" (1979, 25), while, according to Jon Savage,

> *No woman had made these noises before.* For the Slits, the result was a maelstrom of over-amped guitar and sheet-metal drumming and, amid the chaos, musicians creating their own order. By the autumn, the "armed playground chants" . . . had become full-blown streetfights, anarchic and threatening. (1991, 418; emphasis added)

Male reviewers struggled with the vocabulary needed to describe this new way of communicating songs. The sounds of women's voices in rock and pop had historically been subject to the control of men as producers and gatekeepers and aimed at them as listeners, as Frith has noted (1988). Holly Kruse observes, tongue-in-cheek, an almost spiritual dimension to this: "[R]ock is governed by a more or less transcendental aesthetic, which, it therefore follows, only men can comprehend" (2002, 136). Many audiences were having difficulty in understanding what was happening, as the unabashed anger expressed in these voices was an unfamiliar sound. It is notable that Savage describes the Slits as "musicians"; many other rock journalists, who were overwhelmingly male, could not bring themselves to do this. Adrian Thrills attempted to rationalize the sound of their music in his *NME* review of their first album, *Cut*, in 1979:

> The Slits see their album as an extension of their volatile personalities. Where they are confused and confusing, their record is confused and confusing—and often better for it. Where they are forthright and assertive, their record is likewise. (1979, 28)

In his review of *Cut*, Paul Morley also pinpointed Up's apparently limited vocal technique, writing that she "snaps and talks, compressing spiteful, sore words into extreme approximations of melodies" (1979, 27). In the same review, he describes the singing style of Siouxsie on the Banshees' *Join Hands* album as "conceited, over-exerted vocals; I like them, other people find them unlistenable." Later, he describes a version of their "The Lord's Prayer" as "a superfluous exercise in banal improvisation with defective chanting and ranting" (27). Together, these comments by Morley function as a kind of "negging," where guarded praise focused on the identity of the person doing the praising is tempered by harsh criticism. Siouxsie has explained that the Banshees highlighted and celebrated the fact that they were *not* trained musicians: "[T]alking about breaking down walls and actually doing things are quite different things. In our naivety, we started making this noise that was ours" (quoted in Savage 1991, 419). In fact, there *were* skilled musicians among some of the female-driven groups: Ari Up was a trained classical piano player, Ana Da Silva and Pauline Murray had both been folk singers before punk began, and Lesley Woods had been a guitarist and singer with an older male band before being in punk bands. As we have seen, there was a tendency by male rock critics to assume that the "noise value" (Hegarty 2009, 95) of the female bands was accidental, rather than deliberate, "social disruption" (in Jacques Attali's term; quoted in Hegarty 2009, 95). Posing the question "Is amateurishness the same as ineptitude, though?," Hegarty notes that "[s]kill becomes a judgement, not a craft" (2009, 99). There was a simple desire by many female punk groups *not to sound like their male predecessors* that was often misunderstood, with the resulting music often assumed to be the accidental result of complete lack of skill. The lack of technical ability praised and capitalized upon by male bands was regarded as an asset for them; the same lack in female bands was often regarded as an emblem of inferiority.

A "special understanding" of the sonic identity of female bands manifested itself in work by other journalists writing about other bands. For instance, Caroline O'Meara, while describing the Raincoats' singing, observes that "punk's embrace of the ugly" sometimes becomes entangled with the idea of "uniquely feminine" music, taking issue with a comment made by the journalist Graham Lock, where Lock claimed to understand the band's specifically female sound that other male audience members did not, at a point where the band had been touring and recording regularly and had actually developed considerably beyond their initial amateur status (2003, 301). Ana Da Silva rejects Lock's simple definition of their sound, explaining the way the music "embodied the very issues discussed in the lyrics," and, according to O'Meara, the "discomfort" in the way Da Silva and Gina Birch used their voices was integral to the music (2003, 311). Birch also sited the sound of the band firmly in the desire to express how they felt, rather than to impress their audiences:

I think I despised anything that wasn't what I was doing because what I was doing was a revolution. We were revolutionaries as far as I was concerned and we were on a mission and what was going on outside was really just irrelevant.

(author's interview, June 2000)

This sense of revolutionary agency in the construction of female presence in punk music, effectively singing themselves into a collective existence, was acknowledged by Greil Marcus, who described the Raincoats as

not exactly singing "as themselves," not in the way rock 'n' roll has led us to understand the idea. They are not, as would Joni Mitchell or John Lennon, singing to refine an individual sensibility or to project a personality or a persona onto the world. Rather, they are singing as factors in the situations they are trying to construct. (1993, 178)

This successful approach of this new, explicitly female sonic identity was also noted in Lynne Hanna's review of a gig by the Slits in 1980, under the heading "Dancing up the Warpath":

The Slits onstage frequently lift their music straight out of the rock sphere into a species of female performance art.... [S]ince their early days they have come to represent a proud, radical rock feminism which means that their music is now almost inseparable from a fully-fledged philosophy. (1980, 55)

Hanna takes inspiration from this performance, delighting in the anarchy of the band's musical and performative approach, whose "savagely sparse" music she regards as an antidote to "the turgid pomposity and grim determination of so much rock music which relentlessly labours some pseudo-revolutionary point for the allotted hour and obligatory two encores."

In *One Chord Wonders*, Dave Laing wrote about the way women punks used their voices. He identified two main styles of rock and pop vocals as "confidential" and "declamatory" modes of singing, and argued that punk singing was almost exclusively declamatory (1985, 73–74). In his hearing, this declamatory mode was practiced by Poly Styrene, Siouxsie, Ari Up, Pauline Murray of Penetration, and many others. The emphasis was not on craft, but on feeling and marking out of territory. Laing describes Styrene using falsetto whoops reminiscent of those used in soul music, describing an X-Ray Spex performance in which the sax echoes the defiance "in Poly Styrene's vocal stance" (1985, 78). Styrene challenged reviewers as much as the Slits did, although her visual style might have seemed less confrontational. In 1977, Chas de Whalley was torn between trying to categorize her as a sexual being and feeling threatened by her onstage persona, referring patronizingly at first to "pretty Poly's husky cockney accent and music hall shriek," and later to the gig as a "sonic attack" (1977, 14). In another (extraordinary) *Sounds* review from the same year, which forms an interesting counterpoint to Laing's more measured description of the interplay between Styrene's vocals and Lora Logic's saxophone, Tim Lott (1977) attempted to defang the impact of the band by pouring patronizing comments on both singing and playing: "I like it when Poly screams nice and flat and duets with that whining sax from the totally docile looking saxophonist whose name you'd forget, and I have." Echoing the writing of other male journalists who respond to the fact that these women performers do not appear to be trying to please them, he understands the band while simultaneously appearing to hedge his bets:

> I thought they were hugely exciting. I know they were, in fact, because even the man who had blood pouring out of his wrists and the Irishman branding a broken glass looked excited now and then, which proves that it was at least violent music, and that's important, isn't it?
>
> (Lott 1977, 40)

Using the volume and timbre of their voices as an aural weapon was a very effective way of disrupting the accepted ways of sounding like a woman (or girl) in rock and pop. Although feisty girl group music of course had been in the air and was undoubtedly an inspiration throughout the late 1960s and early 1970s when the punk generation was growing up, featuring as it did "untrained" timbres, the sound of that music had been a girlhood mediated according to male taste: though undoubtedly spirited, singers like Janis Joplin, Tina Turner, and other pop screamers were sexual in their delivery and had a strong appeal to men. Women punk singers displayed in their delivery and subject matter a sense of agency that had hitherto been missing from women's pop music. Their vocal styles, where volume and expression were to the forefront, were designed to disrupt and convey aggression. Detached from its subculture, even a recorded punk song that has been through the mediation of a producer can sound harsh and uncompromising to ears untrained in its reception, as the author discovered in the 1990s when playing "Oh Bondage, Up Yours" to a group of music students who were hearing the track for the first time; they appeared to be appalled by the aggression in the track, which they could not engage with aurally despite being familiar with the work of artists such as Tori Amos.

Female punk singers often used an open-larynxed "belt-quality" similar to that of Ethel Merman. In style they had completely detached themselves from the aesthetics normally expected of women's music, and through sheer volume they broke through a boundary of decorum that had historically constrained women speakers as well as singers—as Anne Karpf has observed, "[t]he literature extolling silence in women is voluminous" (2006, 156). It almost seemed as though, through surprise tactics, a critique and readjustment of the whole function of womanhood had been created through the instrument of punk, which seemed to speak or to sing

> the language of contradiction, dialectical in form as well as content: the language of the critique of the totality, of the critique of history. Not some "writing degree zero"—just the opposite. Not a negation of style, but the style of negation.
>
> (Debord 1995, 143–144)

Guy Debord would note that the *content* of the dialectic was also of great importance; lyrically, many bands directly addressed specific women's and young people's issues, from the Slits' "Typical Girls," the Raincoats' "Off Duty Trip" (about a rape by a soldier), Penetration's "Don't Dictate," the Au Pairs' "Come Again" (which was censored by the BBC), The Vital Disorders' "Let's Talk about Prams," the Chefs' "Thrush," and the Ettes' "Rape Victim." One of the most powerful examples of the dramatizing of women's experiences in song was made by the Bodysnatchers, an all-female band that grew out of punk and which, despite hailing from London rather than Coventry, are usually bracketed within the Two Tone movement. Lucy Toothpaste described the impact on the audience of "The Boiler" in the leading feminist magazine *Spare Rib*:

> "Boiler" tells the tale of a girl who goes out to a gig with a boy; when she says she doesn't want to go to bed with him, he gets angry; she is upset by the quarrel and tried to make it up, and he forces her into an alley and rapes her. It's very disconcerting at a live performance, because you've been dancing around to all their other numbers, and you suddenly find you're dancing to a horror story.
>
> (Toothpaste 1980, 13)

The song ends in female screaming, and in the *Spare Rib* interview, band members discuss whether the description of the success of the rape is appropriate; men laugh at the defeat of the protagonist, they say, but the song illustrates men's attitudes. Ultimately, the music of women punk bands took advantage of the openness of the original punk scene, using the "big energy" and "big noise" (Vi Subversa, quoted in Bayton 1998, 200) of punk to carve out their own distinct sonic identities across the spectrum, from mainstream punk (Penetration and X-Ray Spex), to the avant-garde (Slits and Raincoats). The extraordinary effect of the subculture was its valorization of women who chose to play angry and subversive loud music in the sort of rock line-ups that had previously been the exclusive territory of adolescent males. Writing on the subversive elements of these bands, Whitman states that in traditional rock music, "the resistance usually finds its expression in the rhythm (especially when it's syncopated), and the capitulation in the harmonies" (1981b, 21), and it is in the disruption of this aesthetic "norm" through the introduction of noise and disorder that women's punk music found its identity; as Viv Albertine has written of when she heard recordings of the Slits for the first time (their 1977 Peel session): "I'm amazed at the ferocity of the music. We sound like we have enough energy to conquer the world" (2014, 190).

Conclusion

As we have seen, through participation in writing and performing punk songs, and through being punks themselves, women were full participants in the British punk subculture in the late 1970s and beyond. Punk made noise a woman's weapon, yet this was still resisted especially at the beginning by male journalists. The moral panic caused by women punks within the moral panic of punk itself, a moral panic within a moral panic, was too much for the music industry to recuperate, and by the early 1980s the energy generated by the early punk women bands dissipated: there was nowhere for them to go. It was almost as though young people's energy and aggression had become co-opted by Prime Minister Margaret Thatcher (elected in 1979), and channeled into the Falklands War, with popular music returning to an unchallenging gendered and commercialized narrative of young people's experiences and emotions (Reddington 2012, 131–156). Punk women had created, lived, and commented on a subversive cultural process that is accurately summed up by Jacques Attali in his reflection on music in society, as a practice "capable of making its audience conscious of a commonality—but also of turning its audience against it" (1985, 28). As Savage ruefully noted in 1983:

> Punk's furious belligerence was a direct response to the cultural and social vacuum it appeared to face under the Callaghan government. Now we have the strong, rigidly masculine government of Thatcher, it's not surprising to find feminine values being reasserted in pop music, not least the quasi-feminine image of the love object, whatever the gender.
>
> (Savage 1983, 23)

It would be more than another decade before assertive and loud women's music-making again came to the notice of the British music press, when the socially active and feminist Riot Grrrl movement spread to Britain from its roots in the United States. Many Riot Grrrl bands took inspiration from the likes of the Slits and the Raincoats, whose legacies are once more being celebrated at the time of writing, through organizations such as London's *Loud Women*, which have found that even in the twenty-first century, noisy women's bands still need powerful representation in order to carve out performance space in the world of rock music.

Note

1. This issue of women's space at gigs was eventually addressed head-on by Riot Grrrl bands more than a decade later. For instance, Kathleen Hanna of the band Bikini Kill insisted on men clearing space for women in the mosh pit at their gigs after reports of assaults on women fans. This "girls to the front" policy allowed women to feel respected and welcome at gigs by female bands in the 1990s (see LeBlanc 1999; Leonard 2007).

References

Albertine, V. 2014. *Clothes, Clothes, Clothes. Music, Music, Music. Boys, Boys, Boys.* London: Faber.

Attali, Jacques. 1985. *Noise: The Political Economy of Music.* Minneapolis: University of Minnesota Press.

Bayton, M. 1998. *Frock Rock: Women Performing Popular Music*. Oxford: Oxford University Press.
Becker, H. 1963. *Outsiders: Studies in the Sociology of Deviance*. New York: Free Press.
Beckett, A. 2009. *When The Lights Went Out: What Really Happened to Britain in the Seventies*. London: Faber.
Colegrave, S., and C. Sullivan, eds. 2001. *Punk: A Life Apart*. London: Cassell.
Cross, R. 2014. "'Take the Toys from the Boys': Gender, Generation and the Anarchist Intent in the Work of Poison Girls." *Punk & Post-Punk* 3, no. 2: 117–145.
Debord, G. 1995. *The Society of the Spectacle*. New York: Zone Books.
Denom, S. 1977. "Women in Punk." *Spare Rib* 60 (July 1): 48–51.
De Whalley, C. 1977. "Oh Bondage! X-Ray Spex Have Got It All Tied Up! Puns Chas de Whalley Up Yours! Sez Poly Styrene." *Sounds*, October 22, 1977, 14–15.
Du Noyer, P. 1980. "Mo-Dettes, Marquee." *New Musical Express*, July 19, 1980, 41.
Frith, S. 1988. *Music for Pleasure*. London: Polity.
Goldman, V. 1976. "The Other New Wave." *Sounds*, December 11, 1976, 18–20.
Grabel, R. 1980. "Exposed! To by Women Threatened! By Men Leered At! By Hells Angels." *New Musical Express*, October 18, 24–25.
Hall, S., and T. Jefferson, eds. 1975. *Resistance through Rituals: Youth Subcultures in Post-war Britain*. London: Routledge, 2006.
Hanna, L. 1980. "Dancing up the Warpath." *New Musical Express*, October 25, 1980, 55.
Hebdige, D. 1979. *Subculture: The Meaning of Style*. London: Methuen, 1991.
Hegarty, P. 2009. *Noise/Music: A History*. London: Continuum.
Italian Futurism. https://www.italianfuturism.org/manifestos/foundingmanifesto/.
Karpf, A. 2006. *The Human Voice: The Story of a Remarkable Talent*. London: Bloomsbury.
Kruse, Holly. 2002. "Abandoning the Absolute: Transcendence and Gender in Popular Music Discourse." In *Pop Music and the Press*, edited by S. Jones, 134–155. Philadelphia: Temple University Press.
Laing, D. 1985. *One Chord Wonders: Power and Meaning in Punk Rock*. 2nd ed. Oakland: PM Press, 2015.
LeBlanc, L. 1999. *Pretty in Punk: Girls' Gender Resistance in a Boy's Subculture*. New Brunswick, NJ: Rutgers University Press.
Leonard, M. 2007. *Gender in the Music Industry: Rock, Discourse and Girl Power*. London: Routledge.
Lock, G. 1979. "Poison Girls Come Out to Play." *New Musical Express*, November 24, 1979, 25.
Lott, T. 1977 "X-Rays Are Harmless Claims Critic." Review of X-Ray Spex/Eater/Wire at The Vortex. *Sounds*, August 20, 1977, 40.
Lydon, J., with K. Zimmerman and K. Zimmerman. 1994. *Rotten: No Irish, No Blacks, No Dogs*. New York: St. Martin's Press.
Marcus, G. 1993. *Ranters and Crowd Pleasers: Punk in Pop Music 1977–92*. New York: Doubleday.
McLeod, K. 2002. "Between a Rock and a Hard Place: Gender and Rock Criticism." In *Pop Music and the Press*, edited by S. Jones, 93–113. Philadelphia: Temple University Press.
McRobbie, A. 2000. *Feminism and Youth Culture*. London: Palgrave Macmillan.
McRobbie, A., and J. Garber. 1975. "Girls and Subcultures." In Hall and Jefferson 1975, 177–188.
Millar, R. 1980. "Sexism Is No Joke." *Sounds*, September 20, 1980, 32.
Morley, P. 1979. "Nursery Rhyme Gothic?" *New Musical Express*, September 1, 1979, 27.
Murray, C. S. 1980. "Poly Unsaturates." *New Musical Express*, October 25, 1980, 30.
O'Brien, L. 1999. "The Woman Punk Made Me." In *Punk Rock: So What? The Cultural Legacy of Punk*, edited by R. Sabin, 186–198. London: Routledge.

O'Meara, Caroline. 2003. "The Raincoats: Breaking Down Punk Rock's Masculinities." *Popular Music* 22, no. 3: 299–313.
Pearson, D. 1980. "Women in Rock: Cute, Cute, Cutesy Goodbye." *New Musical Express*, March 29, 1980, 27–31.
Peel, J. 1977. "Arthritic Pogoer Hit by Slit." *Sounds*, September 24, 1977, 11.
Penman, Ian. 1979. The Slits at Eric's, Review. *New Musical Express*, January 13, 1979, 35.
Reddington, H. 2012. *The Lost Women of Rock Music: Female Musicians of the Punk Era.* Sheffield, UK: Equinox.
Reynolds, S., and J. Press. 1995. *The Sex Revolts: Gender, Rebellion and Rock 'n' Roll.* London: Serpent's Tail.
Sabin, R. 1999. "'I Won't Let That Dago By': Rethinking Punk and Racism." In *Punk Rock: So What? The Cultural Legacy of Punk*, edited by R. Sabin, 199–218. London: Routledge.
Sandbrook, D. 2019. *Who Dares Wins: Britain 1979–82.* London: Allen Lane.
Savage, J. 1983. "Androgyny: Confused Chromosomes and Camp Followers." *The Face* 38 (June): 20–23.
Savage, J. 1991. *England's Dreaming: Sex Pistols and Punk Rock.* London: Faber.
Sontag, S. 1982. *A Susan Sontag Reader.* Harmondsworth, UK: Penguin.
Street-Howe, Z. 2009. *Typical Girls: The Story of the Slits.* London: Omnibus.
Stein, A. 1999. "Rock against Romance: Gender, Rock 'n' Roll and Resistance." In *Stars Don't Stand Still in the Sky*, edited by K. Kelly and E. McDonnell, 215–227. London: Routledge, 215–227.
Stevenson, Nils. 1999. *Vacant: A Diary of the Punk Years 1976–1979.* London: Thames and Hudson.
Thornett, A. 1998. *Inside Cowley: Trade Union Struggle in the 1970s: Who Really Opened the Door to the Tory Onslaught?* London: Porcupine Press.
Thrills, A. 1979. "Up Slit Creek." *New Musical Express*, September 8, 1979, 28.
Toothpaste, L. 1980. "Bodysnatchers." *Spare Rib* 100 (November): 13.
Walkerdine, V. 1997. *Daddy's Girl: Young Girls and Popular Culture.* London: Macmillan.
Whiteley, S. 2000. *Women and Popular Music: Sexuality, Identity and Subjectivity.* London: Routledge.
Whitman, L. 1981a. "Take the Toys from the Boys." Interview with Vi Subversa. *Spare Rib* 113 (December): 31–32.
Whitman, L. 1981b. "Women and Popular Music 1976–1981: A Partial Enquiry." *Spare Rib* 107 (June): 6–8, 20–21.
Willis, P. E. 1978. *Profane Culture.* Princeton, NJ: Princeton University Press, 2014.
York, P. 1980. *Style Wars.* London: Sidgwick and Jackson.

CHAPTER 8

"WE'RE JUST A MINOR THREAT"

Minor Threat and the Intersectionality of Sound

SHAYNA MASKELL

HARDCORE, an evolution of mid-1970s American and British punk, continued in the musical tradition of stripping, shredding, and reconstituting rock 'n' roll for the sociopolitical times. It was a reaction to the commercialized, diluted, and increasingly lifeless mainstream punk, as well as the other genres of music that punks disdained. This new hardcore sound was characterized primarily through the amplification of punk's original elements: volume, speed, brevity, simplicity, and intensity. The instrumentation remained modest and accessible—drums, bass, guitar, and vocals—and the level of musicianship proudly persisted as crude. While the West Coast is often credited as the birthplace of hardcore punk, Washington, DC, was where hardcore found its true self; indeed, today hardcore still "implies a sound, style and aesthetic coming out of early 80s DC" (Blush 2010, 149).

If DC was the cultural lodestone of hardcore, then Minor Threat were the high priests. In their 1981 iteration, Minor Threat boasted Ian MacKaye on vocals, Jeff Nelson on drums, Brian Baker on bass, and Lyle Preslar on guitar. Coming from pockets of differing neighborhoods in Washington, Minor Threat were inspired to pick up instruments, sing into microphones, and write lyrics without any formal musical education. What they did have was passion, angst, and feelings of alienation and isolation, both personally and politically, which found articulation through sound. It was, like hardcore in general, the sound of a new generation. As MacKaye himself notes, "it was the manifestation of youth. It was fast, it was loud, it was unpredictable" (Rachman 2007).

The band's 1981 EP, *Minor Threat*, embodies that hardcore spirit. Clocking in at nine minutes and twenty seconds, with only eight tracks, *Minor Threat* became the blueprint for the DC hardcore sound; with precision and technical tightness, the album combines the rebellion of traditional rock 'n' roll with a heretofore unknown velocity and intensity of sound. Their abrupt blurs of sonic eruption zip by and transmogrify what rock, not to mention punk, meant. Their rebellion sounded different: it was angry, loud, dissonant, warped, and a bit out of control. It also sounded like the band themselves—male, white, and middle class. Despite—or perhaps because of—the revolutionary sound of hardcore, *Minor Threat* constructs a hardcore sound that often reflects, though sometimes subverts, conventional constructions of gender, class, and race. This chapter will explore the ways in which Minor Threat the band, and *Minor Threat* as an album, sonically reproduce and disrupt of the politics of sound.

THE GENDERING OF *MINOR THREAT*

Compete, compete, do it for the boys
Empty barrels make the most noise
You're always on the move
You've always got something to prove
　　　　　　　　　—"Small Man, Big Mouth," *Minor Threat* (1981)

While scholars agree that music is inherently gendered—that is, that there are no innate qualities to understand why a certain instrument, pitch, timbre, volume, or frequency evokes a sense of femininity or masculinity (or for that matter, racial, sexual, or geographic attributes)—they also concur that there is indeed a culturally constructed gender of sound. In part, the gender of sound is founded on the history of music itself, and the way certain music, instruments, and sounds have been historically and culturally linked to men and manhood. Such a history includes the homogeneity of the music industry; from production to creation and performance, music has been near unilaterally associated with and ruled by males. With, of course, some exceptions, male voices, male sounds, and male productions dominated every major musical genre for decades, simultaneously creating a sense of gender neutrality when it comes to music. However, sound is anything but neutral.

Minor Threat, and the music they created—both lyrically and sonically—were not immune from the construction of gender through sound. Indeed, much of their 1981 eponymous album acts to reinforce and replicate socially formed understandings of masculinity. Their use of the guitar and drums, tempo and vocals, as well as the lyrics of many of the album's songs, emphasize and reproduce the traditional role of males as dominant, aggressive, strong, and powerful, underpinning traditional gender roles and the binary between male and female. On the other hand, aspects of

Minor Threat also work to subvert gender norms, particularly through the introduction of the song "Minor Threat," as well as the brevity and minimalism of the album's composition.

Instruments as material objects, and the accompanying sounds they generate, do not have any fundamental or inherent meaning. Instead, "the instrument is used to invest the body of the performer with meaning, to confer upon it a unique identity whose authentic, natural appearance works to conceal its reliance upon artifice and technology" (Waksman 1999, 5). However, scholars have indeed understood instruments as having, if not gendered features, then at least gender appropriateness, which has translated into school-aged children choosing instruments based primarily on their perceived gender (Wych 2012). High-pitched and delicate-sounding instruments are often associated with femininity—the flute, violin, and clarinet, for example—while the louder, brass instruments, percussion, and guitar are linked to masculinity.

The electric guitar, in particular, is often analogous to the construction of masculinity—loud, powerful, aggressive, and dominating—and is also inextricably linked to the males who play and perform on this "technophallus" (e.g., Jimi Hendrix, Keith Richards, Jimmy Page), which is frequently understood as an extension of the male body (Waksman 1999). The electric guitar symbolizes domination and men "wield [this] technology to display their transcendence of nature, and their power to order the world according to their will" (5). Moreover, the electric guitar can be understood like the male-female binary, a corollary to the acoustic guitar, which is constructed as passive and subdued within the cultural realm assigned to women.

Minor Threat's Preslar reinforces this culturally constructed gender assigned to the electric guitar, creating a powerful and often penetrating sound on the band's eponymous album. Take "Seeing Red," where Preslar's uncompromising, beefy guitar playing starts and stops in short, staccato bursts of phrases in the song's opening refrain, teasing the listener with restraint and anticipation of what is to come. This release is quick in coming, with Preslar's guitar playing screeching and thrashing under a veil of distortion, speed, and volume for the remainder of the (less than two-minute) song. Even when the guitar acts as part of the melody, as it does in "Small Man, Big Mouth," Preslar's playing invokes a live-wire adrenaline bolt that works to echo and reinforce the enraged vocals of MacKaye. Moreover, the speed of Preslar's playing in a song like "Straightedge," and the concomitant control and mastery it takes to play guitar at that tempo, speaks to the guitar as a simultaneous threat (given its near-frenzied pace), and as restraint (given the skill it takes to play that pace), placing the male guitarist as the wielder of power: the power to unleash strength and force, and the power to control it. In this way, Preslar reinforces the construction of gendered sound, insofar as his guitar playing evokes both technical musical prowess and the sonic threat of strength and force, both of which are linked to masculinity.

Drums have also culturally acted as a foreboding and intimidating musical indication of masculinity. Historically, men played drums in preparation for battle, and contemporaneously, men battle in drum contests to prove their manliness, advancing the culturally constructed male characteristics of competitiveness and belligerence (Kartomi

1990). Sonically, the cavernous, throbbing backbeat of the drums suggests an aesthetics of domination and power, its rhythmic tension and anticipation suggest an undertone of sexuality, and how the drums are played is habitually referred to as an attack, with the bite or snap of the cymbal, tom-tom, or snare—further symbols for traditional masculinity.

Such a masculinized portrayal of the drums is reinforced by Jeff Nelson's playing on *Minor Threat*. While "Filler" starts with the punctuation of a guitar riff and the slow and low plucking of the bass, five seconds into the track Nelson's militant-like drum roll explodes, acting as palpable partner, a musical two of a one-two punch, with the previously discussed antagonism of the guitar. The same combative drumroll is introduced a mere second after the bass in "I Don't Wanna Hear It," four seconds into an electric guitar interval in "Screaming at a Wall," and repeatedly during the chorus for "Bottled Violence." In these tracks, the speed and aggression of the electric guitar, with its high-pitched metallic sound, are compounded and magnified by the deep, ominous, and equally-as-fast drums. Songs that begin with this bellicose drumroll —and the rest of the tracks that do not—still expose the trashing, frenzied drumming of Nelson, who attacks the drums with a ferocity that is intertwined with the assault of the electric guitar, creating a sonic onslaught that suggests a violent masculinity. In part, the violent undertones of Nelson's drumming stem from the physicality of the actual technique, which demands a near-continuous right-left-right-left thumping, with added force to the fulcrum on impact, allowing the drumstick to bounce multiple times on the drum head. The material force of Nelson sonically translates into metaphorical force.

The analyses of these songs suggest that it is not just the instruments that are played that speak to the gendering of hardcore sounds, but also the *way* these instruments are played. Indeed, specific compositional elements of these songs also have gendered implications, including that of tempo. According to Sergeant and Himonides (2016), listeners associate a faster tempo with a more controlled objective, dramatic, assertive, and masterful sentiment and significance. A slower tempo, on the other hand, conjures more sensitive, calm, reflective, and submissive implications. Clearly, these connotations are connected with specific (conventional) gender roles, with masculinity linked to authority, power, and forcefulness (fast tempo), and femininity to passivity, tranquility, and sensitivity.

Hardcore in general, and Minor Threat specifically, exemplifies masculinity through a lightning-fast tempo. With precision and technical tightness, *Minor Threat* combines the rebellion of traditional (historically masculine) rock 'n' roll with chaotic velocity and intensity of sound. Bassist Baker batters his instrument. Nelson's drumming is like an unending fistfight—pummeling, pounding, and walloping at hyper-speed, until the listener feels pulverized by his sheer force and momentum. The music writer Michael Azerrad (2001), in describing Minor Threat, stated: "The band's adrenalized rhythms, fierce attack, and surprisingly tuneful songs set them apart from anybody since."

We can more precisely understand the light-speed tempo of Minor Threat by examining the songs through beats per minutes (bpm), which is the standard for evaluating tempo. "Minor Threat" clocks in at 166 bpm, "Seeing Red" is 169 bpm,

"Bottled Violence" comes in at 186 bmp, "Straight Edge" and "Filler" are at a wild 189 bpm, and "I Don't Wanna Hear it" goes to 190 bmp.[1] As a contrast, we can look at the top songs on the Billboard charts in 1981, the same year as *Minor Threat*: Rick Springfield's "Jesse's Girl" clocks in at 119 bmp, Kim Carnes's "Bette Davis Eyes" is 117 bmp, and the Pointer Sisters' "Slow Hand" is 111 bmp. In this way, the breakneck tempo of Minor Threat acts as a signifier of masculinity, performing the culturally constructed masculine traits of authority, power, and strength.

However, the subversion of gender roles can also be understood in the simplicity of Minor Threat's compositions. While the minimalism of these songs will be further discussed as it relates to the performance of class, such austereness can also be understood as a function of gender. Incorporating the punk rock credo of "three-chord democracy," Minor Threat used the same guitar chords—in the same order—nearly exclusively: E/B/G/D/A/E. Indeed, seven of the eight songs in Minor Threat use the exact same progression.[2] Moreover, there are three instruments used in the album: guitar, bass, and drums.[3] Such simplicity has been connected to listeners' perceptions of masculinity. Sergeant and Himonides (2016) have found that the larger the number of musicians that are a part of the song, and concurrently the higher tonal density produced by a larger number of instruments, the more likely the song is perceived as masculine. Given tonal density can be translated into anthropomorphic characteristics of fullness, compactness, and strength, Minor Threat's lack of tonal density works to undermine the stereotype of masculinity. At least compositionally, Minor Threat sonically undercut the image of power-laden, formidable, and intense masculinity.

However, other elements of Minor Threat's music continue to reinforce a hypermasculinity, particularly through the vocal stylings of MacKaye. Like hardcore vocalists in general, MacKaye relies more on vocal expression through yelling than melodic singing. But MacKaye's vocals are really the gold standard of hardcore, expressing outrage, disdain, disbelief, wrath, and righteousness through his hoarse, throat-popping screaming and sarcastic spoken asides. With no formal vocal training, MacKaye takes vocal intensity and dissonance to another level, using his voice as a weapon to inflict feelings of pain, frustration, and sheer primitiveness—a prototypical construction of masculine rage. In "Filler," he howls out the first line, "What happened to you?," drawing out the last word over three seconds, before flinging out the last word of the chorus ("filler") in a fully enunciated two-syllable punch of a yelp. Indeed, this vocal style was a signature of MacKaye, who "spouted his lyrics like a frantic drill sergeant, halfway between a holler and a bark" (Azerrad 2001, 129). In "Seeing Red," the chorus is yelled with such resolve and exigency that MacKaye's voice sounds nearly hoarse; when he expels the line "Red / I'm seeing red" the listener can almost visualize the strain on his throat and envision the snapping of his vocal chords. His guttural roughness demands attention and invokes alarm—in the connotative tone and texture of his voice, but also in the tangible bodily harm it could cause. And when MacKaye roars "You built that wall up around you / And now you can't see out / And you can't hear my words / No matter how loud I shout" in "Screaming at a Wall," his jarring, strident yelps embody the lyrics he is singing; his ear-splitting shouts are a plea to listen, while the volume of the sound and the intensity and texture of his voice are an aural demand for the listener's attention.

This attention is a demand given and allowed for by MacKaye's masculinity—his low pitch and belligerent modulations speak to the authority, confidence, and dominance attributed to men (Puts et al. 2007; Dey et al. 2012). In small part, this vocal connotation can be attributed to MacKaye's use of the natural minor scale in his singing, which tends to have a bleaker, heavier sound, with a more dissonant and melancholy quality. However, it's also dependent on culturally constructed ideas of gender. Imagine if a woman was screaming, screeching, and emoting at an ear-piercing volume—she would be characterized as shrill, unladylike, and tuneless. Interestingly, the use of MacKaye's emotional brand of singing could be understood as feminine, for females alone are constructed as not only having, but also being able to express, emotions. In this way, MacKaye seems to blur the gendered norms of singing. However, there are two caveats to this subversion. First, the emotions that MacKaye expresses are positioned solidly within the construction of manhood: anger, bitterness, frustration—these are culturally approved emotions for men, rather than women. Second, it is the privilege of masculinity—expressed in part by this command and authority of yelling—that offers refuge from any overt gender reversal. That is, MacKaye is "safe" to express emotions because he does so in a way that is masculine.

Finally, we can evaluate the lyrics of *Minor Threat* as primarily fortifying a conventional construction of masculinity, in large part by reinforcing the typical traits of masculinity, as well as the binary between genders, with some examples of subversion of these norms. Three of the eight tracks on the album—"Screaming at a Wall," "Seeing Red," and "I Don't Wanna Hear It"—echo the vocal characteristics of MacKaye by promulgating the hypermasculine image of manhood as destructive, brutish, and barely (if at all) contained aggression. These lyrics imply a corporeal anger ("I'm gonna knock it all down / Any way that I can / I'm going to scream / I'm going to yell / I don't have to use my hands"), an implied violence ("You better reinforce those walls / Until you don't have no room to stand / Cause someday the bricks are gonna fall / Someday I'm gonna use my hands"), a simmering rage ("My looks, they must threaten you / To make you act the way you do / Red, I'm seeing red"), and outright hostility ("Shut your fucking mouth / I don't care what you say"). These lyrics, and their masculinized sonic and linguistic expression of anger, is always and already joined to the cultural construction of manhood. Customarily, "anger in men is often viewed as 'masculine'— it is seen as 'manly' when men engage in fistfights or act their anger out physically" (Dittman 2003, 52), a sentiment that is reiterated and validated not just by the traditional social and familial model, but also by the inundation of this representation by popular culture.

"Filler," on the other hand, works to reinforce the existing binary structure between men and women, primarily through the heteronormative function of the relationship discussed in the lyrics. In the song, MacKaye laments the loss of his friend to a woman, saying, "Was she really worth it? / She cost you your life / You'll never leave her side / She's gonna be your wife / It's in your head / FILLER / You call it romance / You're full of shit." In this song, masculinity is tied not only to heterosexuality, but also to a specific gender role within that heterosexuality. Specifically, the lyrics embolden the "whipped man" stereotype—that a male who is thought to be controlled or dominated by his girlfriend has lost his masculinity. In this way, not only is masculinity linked directly to the idea of power and independence, it is also predicated on what it is not—that is, femininity.

Yet some of the lyrics on *Minor Threat* work to subvert the cultural constructed tropes of masculinity, even when they acknowledge and replicate those stereotypes. For example, "Small Man, Big Mouth" destabilizes the image of the strong, burly dude as authoritative and commanding. MacKaye sings, "Compete, compete, do it for the boys / Empty barrels make the most noise / You're always on the move / You've always got something to prove," which recognizes the image of masculinity as one situated in competition, loudness, and establishing—and reestablishing—one's masculinity constantly. However, MacKaye is clearly criticizing these norms through his sarcastic rallying cry ("Compete, compete, do it for the boys," which sounds like a mocking cheerleader) and his mocking assertion that these big, hulky men have no substance ("Empty barrels make the most noise"). MacKaye seemingly has a similarly paradoxical take on the appearance-based construction of masculinity, particularly through the construct of height. In the second verse of the song he asks, "What are you fighting for? / Is it because you're five foot four?" This taunt clearly links to the Westernized cultural mandate for men to be tall, and the feelings of insecurity that it would evoke if a man failed to live up to that expectation. At the same time, and in the next verse, MacKaye sings, "You laugh at a man when he tries / You're trying to make up for your size," which indicates his criticism of such a stereotype. That is, MacKaye condemns the subject for laughing at failure (another expectation of masculinity—success) and implicitly argues that it is the subject's own insecurity with his failed expectations that leads him to exploit another man's. Thus, MacKaye at once concedes and undercuts the high and near-impossible expectations of masculinity demanded by young men, and simultaneously demonstrates the impact of those standards.

The Paradoxical Performances of Class in *Minor Threat*

> *Minor Threat was an after-school hobby for some relatively over-privileged kids from Washington, D.C.*
> —Brian Baker, guitarist for Minor Threat

> *We really didn't think about starting a record label. We just wanted to put out our record. That was our goal...*
> —Jeff Nelson, drummer for Minor Threat, on starting Dischord Records

As the French theorist Pierre Bourdieu contended, within the realm of cultural production, "nothing more clearly affirms one's 'class,' nothing more infallibly classifies, than taste in music" (1981, 18). By differentiating taste in music, one is able to reaffirm one's status in the hierarchy of social order, and, at the same time, perpetuate the control associated with the dominant preference of music. Musical preference, then, is an indicator of class because of its association with a specified set of cultural knowledge (implying an analogous set of economic, social, and educational knowledge) and an assertion of status because of that class. Music, in this regard, is always classed.

Minor Threat as a band, and *Minor Threat* as an album, are similarly classed, though the construction and performance of that class is complicated and contradictory, in both the music and the members themselves. On the one hand, the music of the band speaks to a working-class ethos, incorporating language that is antithetical to the elite and composing and playing songs that forgo and revile excess and musical idolatry. Yet, on the other hand, the members of Minor Threat, and their positionality as not only one of the most revered hardcore bands of all time, but also as the seeds of Dischord Records, an independent and still-thriving DC-based record label, cannot escape the construction of an upper-classed privilege.

Considered obscene, and by some even blasphemous, swearing, particularly publicly, has a strong historical and cultural association with social class. Indeed, the word *vulgar* literally means "common," and most often profanity emerged from lower-class transliterations of words (Mohr 2013). The list of expletives in the songs of Minor Threat is fairly extensive—fuck, shit, crap, pissed off, asshole—second only to the number of songs in which these swear words appear. In *Minor Threat* they appear in "Filler," "I Don't Wanna Hear it" (sample lyric: "I don't wanna hear it / Know that you're full of shit / Shut your fucking mouth / I don't care what you say"), "Small Man Big Mouth," and "Minor Threat."

To a certain extent, of course, the depth and breadth of these words is merely a reflection of the anger and frustration these band members were feeling; but more significantly, and more complicated, is what that anger is directed at and how it's directed. The repeated use of profanity, particularly in the recorded, public forum of music, is a literal and figurative "fuck you" to conventional, upper-class linguistic and social values, which cherish public propriety, verbal cleverness, and adherence to their constructed version of proper behaviors, and which look down on open displays of anger, coarse language, and an ignorance or outright ignoring of what is deemed common decency. Aligning themselves linguistically with the working class, Minor Threat's joyous, continuous, and liberal use of expletives in their songs acts as a performance of classed identity.

Simultaneously, Minor Threat embodied and embraced the spirit of punk rock—raw, minimalistic, loud, and fast. And such a spirit was decidedly and intentionally classed. Their sound is unfussy and simple, with only the fundamental use of chords played by teens still learning to play their instruments. Not only do Minor Threat's songs rely on just three instruments,[4] but their songs nearly exclusively use a simple verse-and-refrain structure. This simplicity is an aural declaration of restraint; if intros, bridges, and codas were musically illustrative of the excess of the upper class, then a basic verse-chorus-versus-chorus arrangement typified working-class austerity. Moreover, Minor Threat's self-titled album is a total of nine minutes and twenty seconds long (the two longest songs last a minute and forty-two seconds, and the shortest is forty-six seconds). This succinctness of songs speaks to the repudiation of glut and to the ideals of asceticism and frugality. As MacKaye explains, "I will say what is exactly on my mind, and do it in 32 seconds" (Rachman 2007). Trimming the fat of decadence, the bands' minimalism of lyrics and sound serve as a class statement against excess.

These songs were also a clear statement within the class-grounded field of music. Indeed, the division between upper-class taste and working-class ethos was embodied in the late 1970s by the musical bifurcation between conventional aesthetic-touting progressive rock and its heretic counterpart, punk rock. Staidly in the corner of musical orthodoxy, progressive rock extolled musical innovation, idolized musical expertise through its reverence to and obsession with lengthy musical solos, and, in doing so, attempted to elevate its sounds to the status of art. On the other hand, Minor Threat specifically, and punk rock more generally, acted as the heretic, as "the culture of working-class. . . banal, simple-minded . . ." (Frith 1981, 214). Punk's roots—in both American proto-punk and Britain's initial formulation of punk rock—explicitly attempted to enact a working-class aesthetic, at once reinforcing the stratification of musical taste as class status and challenging the boundaries of what music could and should sound like.

While Minor Threat explicitly resisted the social and musical expectations of upper-class privilege by embracing a sonic idealization of the working class (in their compositional simplicity, aesthetic of minimalism, and profanity), they could also not escape the trappings of their class-based and music-entrenched privilege. This privilege can be understood in two ways, both situated within the realm of recording.

There is, simply in the ability to and act of recording sound—of producing music for mass consumption—an inherent, if often invisible, privilege. The phonograph itself was "conceived as a privileged vector for the dominant speech, as a tool reinforcing representative power and the entirety of its logic . . . to preserve a representation of power, to preserve itself" (Attali 1985, 92). Despite this attempt at total social control, recordings, from political speeches to telephone conversations, the phonograph, and its competitor, the gramophone, offered a revolutionary reimaging of cultural and public space. By virtue of its function—the capacity for reproduction and repetition—the recording of sound, specifically that of music, brought about significant changes in the maintenance of cultural systems of power.

First, individuals who possess the ability to record are endowed with a unique form of power and control. The fact that their words, ideas, speeches, and sounds are considered (by those seemingly omniscient and omnipotent cultural forces) important enough to be recorded necessarily creates a power differential, a hierarchy based on those who are recorded and those who are not. The act of memorialization that is integral in recording, with its implicit value judgment, elevates, if not idolizes, both the content of the sound (whether it is music, comedy, or speeches) and the producers of that sound. Recorded sound becomes an "essential symbol of a privileged relation to power . . . [of] social status, and order, a sign of one's relation to others" (Attali 1985, 100).

Second, and correspondingly, this hierarchy is also a function of the other radical aspect of recording, mass distribution. Recording artists draw significant portions of their power from their sheer ability to reach and influence huge swathes of society. Of course, this dissemination process also affects the sound consumers are exposed to in profound, and interrelated, ways. The sharp lines of social class, particularly in terms of musical consumption, which had previously been limited to (price- and class-exclusive) concerts and performances, were blurred and rearranged. A person who could not afford the expensive luxury of attending the symphony could now purchase that same performance for a fraction of the price. In this way, the recording of music helped democratize the consumption of sound. This democratization then led to a flattening of disparities in cultural capital, whereby musical knowledge and experience is, to a certain extent, not wholly contingent on class. In turn, this acts as a part of the function of the collective experience of listening to recorded music; no matter where in the country (or city or town or world) one is, no matter what gender, race, sexuality, or age one is, everyone is hearing the exact same sounds, the exact same tempos, timbres, pitches and phrasings.[5] The recording process, therefore, is a necessarily cyclical and paradoxical process: it broadens the culturally constructed social class of musical consumers, but also concentrates the number of people able to and responsible for the formation and content of this cultural capital.

Minor Threat's capability and success with recording albums can be seen, then, as both privilege and as a meaningful expression of agency. At the same time, the circumstances surrounding the recording processes of Minor Threat were significantly different, intentionally so, then that of major label artists. The do-it-yourself (DIY) aspect of their recording, including the funding of their own albums and the establishment of their own label, Dischord Records, worked as a symbol of concurrent privilege and an attempt to subvert the economic domination of the recorded music industry. The label started as so much of the DC hardcore punk scene did—under cultural and economic duress. As MacKaye recalls, "In L.A. you hear 'record label' and 'getting signed.' You don't hear that in Washington" (Andersen and Jenkins 2009, 55). Without a label to put out their music, Nelson and MacKaye's first band, Teen Idles, pooled together their funds from playing shows from the previous year to produce a record (*Minor Disturbance*) and create Dischord. And while the record label was born of necessity, it quickly became MacKaye and Nelson's[6] sociopolitical and musical mouthpiece, a way to release DC hardcore albums that no other label would touch, while at the same time deemphasizing the monetary aspects of the music industry. Dischord embraced music as a de-commodified form of art.[7] With the consolidation of the music industry into only a handful of firms, and musical diversification permissible only at the whim of these companies, innovation was hamstrung by concerns about money and "sellability" (Lopes 1992).

Their label, then, was a personal, though ultimately political, tactic in the valuation of music over the valuation of profit. The record label shunned the normal division of labor of the music industry, distributing and selling its recordings solely through mail order or direct sales to record stores, in an effort to free bands in the production and content of their punk albums. In the true spirit of the DIY ethos, each and every album was hand-created, with Dischord house members folding song lyric sheets, putting together album sleeves, taking mail-order sales, and shipping them out to individuals.

At the same time, however, contained in their DIY label was the implicit acknowledgement of and respect for the consumption-based tenet of ownership and the corollary privilege of agency. Dischord, in an attempt to nullify the insidious effects of ownership industry practices, refused to either market its bands or sign contracts that would create intellectual property. Certainly, this was an admirable and important approach, given the industry's history of commandeering. However, it should also be understood within the context of social control—of power fashioned from freedom and the privilege of agency.

Dischord, then, acts as a tool of emancipation from the strict monetary and creative confines of the music industry. Yet that emancipation, that ability to control the creation, production, and distribution of one's own self and music, is in itself a privilege. Dischord's assumption of the creative and financial processes of their own bands is a seizure of the privileged instrument of control. In doing so, the label, and the bands that it represents, enacts a curious paradox of the class-and-status formula. By destabilizing conventional music industry practices, including the financial motive for music and the perilous battle for proprietary rights, Dischord actually reinforces the traditional capitalistic and consumption-driven ethos of ownership, and with it the attending virtues of agency and control. Perhaps ironically, these qualities acted to propel MacKaye and Nelson, and all of Dischord, into an upper social echelon, one where ownership, the ability for self-representation, and freedom of creative control necessarily indicate a privilege the label was in no way seeking.

Minor Threat and Race

I'd heard the lore and heard the tapes and was totally intimidated by this incredible band . . . grown men who were really playing their instruments. They were real musicians and we were kids.
—Brian Baker, bassist for Minor Threat, on Bad Brains

Any discussion of class and gender as categories of sociopolitical influence and identity cannot, and should not, be extricated from an understanding of their intersection with race. This is even more particularly the case in Washington, DC, whose label as the "Chocolate City" not just coexisted with, but was often parallel to, its massive class stratification. Indeed, the origins of DC hardcore sprouted up amid these racial and class-based divides, nestled within a city whose powerful and elite were nearly monolithically male. MacKaye, a fifth-generation Washingtonian, lived in the primarily black neighborhood of Capitol Hill until he was a young boy, when a break-in and devastating assault on a family relative spurred the family to move to the working-class Irish and Italian neighborhood of Glover Park. He and Nelson both attended Woodrow Wilson High School, which, despite its affluent surroundings and high rate of college-bound graduates, was racially diverse, with Caucasians being in the minority. Wilson provided the breeding ground for MacKaye and his punk brethren, in its encapsulation of the contradictions found within Washington, DC. The high school was itself a seeming paradox—its racially mixed population was avidly achievement-oriented but also heavily involved in drugs and drinking. Like the lower-class students attending the wealthy high school, the punks felt as if they did not quite belong.

MacKaye and Nelson, along with their fellow Minor Threat band members, found their place within the burgeoning hardcore punk scene, which was led by Bad Brains. It was this friendship, between Minor Threat and the relatively elder statesmen of Bad Brains, that greatly influenced the playing style and emotive ascetics of the former, prompting a noteworthy, if merely subconscious, identification of a white punk band with African American musical identity. The tutorship and influence of Bad Brains on Minor Threat is well documented. After Bad Brains had returned from New York broke, the Teen Idles invited the band to use their equipment and practice space; their musical power was an instant inspiration. Baker notes that the band's influence was "absolutely enormous," particularly on the somewhat antithetical hardcore aesthetic of technical prowess. As MacKaye recalls, "Here we are making this racket and complaining how shitty our equipment is, and then they would pick up our very same shit and play this amazing music. It was like another world" (Andersen and Jenkins 2009, 55).

As musical descendants of Bad Brains, Minor Threat continued the African American tradition of musical exceptionalism in the face of white musical appropriation. More specifically, the bebop-inspired technical exclusivity that Bad Brains sustained and recreated in punk rock acted as a template for their all-white disciples (Maskell 2015). The technical skills of Minor Threat, according to *Washington Post* music critic Howard Wuelfing, experienced "a quantum leap . . . I was blown away to see that they could pay with such speed and not have the structure of the song melt underneath. The difference . . . was Bad Brains. They set the example of how to play extremely fast but with extreme precision." Nelson agrees, noting how the band "influenced us incredibly with their speed and frenzied delivery" (Andersen and Jenkins 2009, 55).

Similarly, Minor Threat emulate Bad Brain's musically racial undertones with their incorporation of breakdowns in their songs, a musical interlude virtually unheard of in any other form of hardcore. Minor Threat's "Screaming at a Wall" includes a breakdown (:50–1:05) that, in conjunction with Bad Brains' original use, sets these two hardcore bands apart from every other punk sound. While Bad Brains incorporates this musical style into hardcore in order to demarcate their black selves from the white punk scene, Minor Threat, on the other hand, take on this particular form of "blackness" with their performance of this racially tinged musical segment.[8]

Furthermore, Minor Threat connected to the feelings of ostracization and marginalization that impelled the African American music of the blues. MacKaye recounts how being a punk in the sociocultural context of Washington "meant you were a magnet for getting shit. You saw how people acted. You kind of understood what it was like to be a black in America, to be just judged by the way you looked" (Andersen and Jenkins 2009, 65). Just as Bad Brains channeled that prejudice, and the accompanying anger and frustration, into their hardcore punk in the same musical tradition of the blues, so too did Minor Threat. Says MacKaye, "For me it's a total emotional outlet. I think the function of music is... the blues" (*Maximum Rocknroll* 1983). To be black was to be consigned to a lower social status; the same was true, to a significantly lesser extent, of being punk. The black "blues" of punk offered Minor Threat a vehicle to express that pain.

At the same time, however, it is undeniable that the whiteness of the band members offered a form of privilege not granted to their Bad Brains colleagues. While their status as punks conferred a considerable psychological, and sometimes physical, burden to the band members, their skin color still allowed for the privilege of invisibility. Clearly, we are unable to gauge what affect the bands' race had on the reception and influence of their music; however, just as plainly, we must consider the historical freedom granted to whites, particularly within the field of music—to criticize, to challenge, to evoke passion rather than fear. This whiteness also acted as permission, or at least conventionality, to enter an already-white punk scene.

Conclusion

The production of music has always contained weighty cultural implications, particularly in the construction of gender, race, and social class status. *Minor Threat* is no different. While this author does not mean to suggest that the band members were intentionally or even consciously recreating sonic representations of whiteness, masculinity, or codes of class, their music and their positionality within the sociopolitical landscape still performs such encoding. Hardcore in general, and Minor Threat in particular, contended with the same conundrum that every resistance-based movement faces, whether it be musical, social, or linguistic: the limitations of defiance and the inevitability of assimilation. No one can resist every social, political, and cultural convention, and no one can do so all the time. At any given moment we are resisting some form of hegemony and consenting and accepting another. Just as Minor Threat should be recognized and celebrated for their challenge to the contemporary musical and sociocultural mores of the day, they should also be understood through the lens of sociocultural complicity in their music. In this way, Minor Threat is both revolutionary and conventional. While upsetting sonic standards, their music also worked to reinforce, in many ways, the traditional music-based aesthetics of gender, class, and race.

Notes

1. The one exception on *Minor Threat* is "Small Man, Big Mouth," which is 99 bpm.
2. "I Don't Wanna Hear It" has a slightly different chord progression: F#/E/F#/B/E.
3. By 1983's *Out of Step*, Minor Threat had incorporated a second guitar, bringing the instrumentation to four.

4. Four instruments by the time of 1983's *Out of Step*, which incorporates two guitars for the first time.
5. This is not to say, of course, that those differences in identity don't affect the interpretation or appreciation of the music. Clearly, divergences in social and personal histories shape not only what genres of music one is more likely to consume, but also *how* one will consume and use said music; however, this doesn't nullify the fact that the music itself never varies.
6. Teen Idles' Nathan Strejcek was also a part of the creation of Dischord; however, by the time the label moved to its still-permanent address in Arlington in 1981, he was more and more disillusioned with the label, ultimately retreating completely.
7. And still does—Dischord Records continues to be the premier independent label in and for Washington, DC, releasing only local bands, and shipping their vinyl worldwide.
8. This is not to suggest that the bands intentionally or consciously attempted to perform blackness. However, that does not exclude them from still borrowing this form of Otherness. Just as Elvis and other early rock 'n' rollers, as well as blues-based revivalist white artists, did not deliberately appropriate a black sound, and with it, a cultural legacy, the link between race and sound, and the concurrent cultural connotations, still exists.

References

Andersen, M., and Jenkins, M. 2009. *Dance of Days: Two Decades of Punk in the Nation's Capital*. New York: Akashic Books.

Attali, J. 1985. *Noise: The Political Economy of Music*. Minneapolis: University of Minnesota Press.

Azerrad, M. 2001. *Our Band Could Be Your Life: Scenes from the American Indie Underground, 1981–1991*. Boston: Little, Brown.

Blush, S. 2010. *American Hardcore: A Tribal History*. Port Townsend: Feral House.

Dey, A., D. Feinberg, and J. Kim. 2012. *Effect of Voice Pitch on Comprehension of Content*. Conference presentation, McMaster University, Dept. of Psychology, Neuroscience and Behaviour.

Dittman, D. 2003. "Anger across the Gender Divide." *Monitor on Psychology* 34, no. 3: 52. https://www.apa.org/monitor/mar03/angeracross.

Frith, S. 1981. *Sound Effects: Youth, Leisure and the Politics of Rock 'n' Roll*. New York: Pantheon Books.

Kartomi, M. 1990. *On Concepts and Classifications of Musical Instruments*. Chicago: University of Chicago Press.

Lopes, P. 1992. "Innovation and Diversity in Popular Music, 1969–1990." *American Sociological Review* 57: 56–71.

Maskell, S. 2015. "Noise as Power." In *Music at the Extremes: Essays on Sounds Outside the Mainstream*, edited by Scott Willson. Jefferson, NC: McFarland.

Maximum Rocknroll. No. 8, September 1983.

Mohr, M. 2013. *Holy Sh*t: A Brief History of Swearing*. New York: Oxford University Press.

Puts, D. A., C. R. Hodges, R. A. Cárdenas, and S. J. Gaulin. 2007. "Men's Voices as Dominance Signals: Vocal Fundamental and Formant Frequencies Influence Dominance Attributions among Men." *Evolution and Human Behavior* 28, no. 5: 340–344.

Rachman, Paul, dir. 2007. *American Hardcore: The History of American Punk Rock 1980–1986*. Sony Pictures Classics.

Sergeant, D. C., and E. Himonides. 2016. "Gender and Music Composition: A Study of Music, and the Gendering Of Meanings." *Frontiers in Psychology* 7: 411.

Waksman, S. 1999. *Instruments of Desire: The Electric Guitar and the Shaping of Musical Experience*. Cambridge, MA: Harvard University Press.

Wych, G. M. 2012. "Gender and Instrument Associations, Stereotypes, and Stratification: A Literature Review." *Update: Applications of Research in Music Education* 30, no. 2: 22–31.

CHAPTER 9

LET'S TALK ABOUT SEX
Punk, Rap, and Reproductive Health

JESSICA A. SCHWARTZ

THE song "Oh Bondage Up Yours!" by the X-Ray Spex (1977) links, through female bondage and the control of bodily practices, sex to consumerism to mindlessness, through lyrics that invoke chain stores and chain smoking, chain gangs and chain mail, and sex slavery in general. The intervening chorus, "Oh bondage! Up yours! / Oh bondage! Come on!," screeched by then teenaged singer Poly Styrene, reveals the denigration of the entrapped body to the entrapped mind, enabling "little girls" to be perpetuated through the mail-order capitalist system. This punk song prompts reflection on the relationship, then, between the possible liberatory role of thinking, feeling, and hearing while female, as well as the right of refusing to be seen. It recalls to my mind conversations about the formation of corporate male professionalism through the (often racialized) bodies of women, such as gynecology, where men would look into women and dissect their bodies rather than listening to their voices and voice issues.

"Oh Bondage Up Yours," juxtaposed with images of a stethoscope, might remind us that little girls are to be seen *and heard* as a matter of policing. They are to be listened to, their insides monitored, while the hierarchical distance between the doctor and female patient is reproduced. When we listen to how "little girls" *are heard* as well as seen—*as bodies, partitioned and dismembered*, this paper argues, we can move beyond the myth of the spectacle as distance (the optics of being seen) and sonorous as proximity and begin to think about participatory democracy through acts of being seen and heard, as a matter of self-determination, which is central to decolonization projects. By exploring how female punk and rap collectivities use humor to engage in conversations about sex, sexuality, and women's reproductive systems—again, systems tightly controlled in male-dominated capitalist society—from nondominant (nonhegemonic) gendered and women of color's perspectives, this chapter will demonstrate an overlooked approach to pedagogical humor in punk and hip-hop, which can be read through selections from Salt-N-Pepa (1986) and the Yeastie Girlz (1988). These groups paved the way for other female collectives that continue to use humor to spread messages and spark conversation, and also, to be blunt, encourage self-determined sex talk.

In order to begin the project of dismembering the heteropatriarchy through musical-historical commentary, I will begin by discussing a New York–based female-trio musical project that I was in, called Lady Bits, that drew from punk and slam poetry, as part of the hip-hop/rap culture. Its pedagogical impetus was humor, and its musical message was sent by drawing attention to the way that women's bodies, historically, could be sentenced to death for their reproductive "issues." I will then situate the broader conversations, from "Oh Bondage Up Yours!" through the 1980s to the 2010s, with reflections on the social conservatism of this era and the work of Lady Bits. From there, I turn to the 1980s and offer concluding thoughts on female trios, musical messages, and confronting the stigma of women's health through humor and DIY (do-it-yourself). Ultimately, the ear, I argue, must also be considered as a reproductive organ.

The practice of reading the female body as part of biomedical corporate advance has its roots in Enlightenment-based, colonial politics, through which women were pathologized, particularly women of color and lower-class women. The stethoscope, which was inspired by the flute, offered a type of scopic health that persists in the tying and binding of gynecological practice and female reproduction that persists in male-dominated fields. The stethoscope, as Jonathan Sterne (2003) notes, was invented by René Laennec in 1816. Laennec, a flute player, was trying to come up with a way to do exams, in particular, on lower-class women, without having to be too close to them; that is, without having to touch their breasts while doing pulmonary exams. This was done not out of respect, but out of disgust for the female and, in particular, the marginalized lower-class body that infectious disease was mapped onto. The flute, in this essay, rather than a symbol of femininity, becomes one that is articulated to men that have used it to compose ways of listening to women's bodies, as an extension of the ear as a reproductive organ. The link between masculinist listening patterns and capitalist reproduction through the bondage of women's bodies and the importance of talking about sex in the public sphere and in DIY spheres, per punk and rap, are shown to be crucial reroutings of hierarchical procedures.

Women's voices and spaces for talking and sharing their health concerns are of primary importance to the possibility of emancipatory work, I believe, through which the body-and-mind (in a non-Cartesian holistic entanglement, or what we can call the thinking body) is afforded the space to breath, think, and feel its position in sexual, gendered, and societal respects. It is routed through the nineteenth century with Freudian psychoanalysis and the figure of the sexually dissatisfied female, the hysteric whose expression is one of histrionics and can thus be discounted, reinforcing how little girls are to be seen and not heard. The nineteenth-century practices of Freudian psychoanalysis, we should recall, are also linked with the talking cure and the ear. Freud himself had a complex relationship with music, such that he famously maintained a distance from its persuasions.[1] Moreover, he felt that music, given its "ephemerality," was difficult to study and observe, to diagnose and classify (cultural historian Michelle Duncan, in Johnson 2017).

In many ways, such a treatment of music can show how, from the time period of the 1970s, during the height of the women's movement in the United States (that was decidedly whitestreamed) and in non-whitestreamed feminisms, music can circumvent the optical reduction of the feminine body, making it heard in subversive ways that are unlike "listening in" as per talk therapy or gynecology. I suggest that humor and other rhetorical and poetic compositional devices are important means of this subversion in the punk and rap feminist trios that I discuss here. For, as inviting as the sterile tables of OB/GYN offices are, humor is a helpful way to break down some of the fear, anxiety, and stigma surrounding women talking about (and) feeling, including touching, their bodies, which is really a knowing of or hearing of their bodies such that they can be and are heard and not controlled in the consumerist space of reproductive health, an area that men have controlled as constitutive of capitalist entitlements.

Punk and hip-hop music, or rap, while recognized for being politically charged, are not often considered in terms of their attention to health, and more specifically to female health or women's health practices. Mainstream representations of these musical arts show them to be male-dominated, aggressive, unhealthy (e.g., illicit drug use and abuse), and misogynistic to varying degrees. Such mainstream representations share the reckless dreams of privileged male orientations to the female body (and by extension the male body), in which sex has no repercussions and women are non-agentive in their sexuality. Moreover, punk and rap are often portrayed in ways that reinforce heteropatriarchal and heteronormative modalities through which sexualization and gendering processes take shape. This chapter seeks to reconsider the importance of punk and rap from the perspective of two female collectives in the 1980s—a period known for a particularly heteropatriarchal, conservative Reagan culture that inspired the male-dominated punk and rap cultures, such as hardcore and gangsta rap masculinities.

REFLECTIONS ON SOCIAL CONSERVATISM IN THE CONTEMPORARY ERA

In June 2022, the US Supreme Court overturned *Roe v. Wade*, the statue that guaranteed abortion protections for women, resulting in an alarming number of medical emergencies in states that have restricted women's reproductive healthcare. Few things could better exemplify social conservatism, and particularly the "traditional" heteropatriarchal, white dominance that is situated in the postwar, early Cold War period, in which women who had been working during World War II returned to the "private" or domestic space to make room for men in the public professions and the public sphere in the reorganization of postwar society. In US corporate culture, like Protestant culture, it was felt that the father-son model of reproduction was crucial to the spread of democratic, capitalist, and military culture in the globalizing mission of the West's lead superpower. In other words, the figure of a strong white man—an Uncle Sam—as head of state in the form of Truman or Reagan has always been a pattern of precarity for women and persons of color in the United States.

It was the Reagan culture of the 1980s that American punk and rap masculinities most vehemently responded to, with the creation and dissemination of Los Angeles suburban and Washington, DC, hardcore punk, of gangsta rap from South Los Angeles, and of hardcore rap music, including Public Enemy, a hip-hop group from Long Island, New York, that formed in 1982. I have elsewhere argued, with Scott Robertson, that hardcore punk and rap groups, such as the Dead Kennedys and Public Enemy, used artful forms of comedic dissidence to deal with the challenges of an increasingly individualized, market-driven society in the aftermath of the "long 1960s" (1954–1974) (Schwartz and Robertson 2018). Ultimately, we argued for a robust critical engagement with punk and rap's pedagogies of comedic dissidence that asks not only about the joke and the reveal, but also which bodies and lives become unintentional "butts" of jokes. How are the men and women showcasing comedic relief in terms of exploitations and resistances? Since we focused on pedagogy, the question demanded that educators should be inclusive of men, women, and cisgendered and noncisgendered musicians and intersectional positionalities. To this critical end, I want to extend this conversation and listen to the humor of two groups: Bay Area female punk trio the Yeastie Girlz (1988), and Queens, New York, female rap trio Salt-N-Pepa (with Spinderella) (1985).[2]

Punk is tied to the figure of the misfit, the outcast, and the rejected, disenfranchised of society. However, or perhaps because of this, (nonmainstreamed) punk is scene-based and community oriented, often with a DIY ethos that is distributed in media forms, from zines to songs. Hip-hop collectives, which emerged around the same time period of a deindustrializing, post–Vietnam War milieu in the United States, have also developed DIY means of community organizing and protections. Issues that society finds taboo and difficult to address, such as suicide and domestic abuse, have been importantly explored in these communities through DIY productions and organizations, many of which maintain underground status. The creativity of groups often stems from their empowerment in these scenes, since dominant society retains heteropatriarchal and white supremacist reinforcements of who should be seen and heard and which bodies deserve better healthcare. While men in punk are allowed to be seen as disheveled, unhealthy, pockmarked, and addicted, women are compelled to look healthy and well cared for—even as women's healthcare has become harder to achieve for most women. At the same time, women's healthcare has been "othered" or specialized, making it often more expensive and placing women in more precarious positions at the global and local levels.

The World Health Organization (WHO) defines health as "a state of complete physical, mental and social well-being and not merely the absence of disease or infirmity." Health and the media industry are linked, and health is an industry that is being marketed and sold to the public. But what is being sold, and how does this dialogue with what is being marketed and sold to women more aggressively, such as diet pills,

Botox for facial lines, and medications for Fibromyalgia, a largely female disease? In the Global North, women often have a longer life span than men, but the mortality rate flips with women who are socially marginalized, who have substance abuse disorders, who are homeless or runaways, or who have been imprisoned and experienced forms of violence. According to a study by Roger Aldridge and colleagues (2018), women in stigmatized groups and experiencing 'social exclusion' are have higher morbidity rates than socially accepted females of the same age. Because punk women are often not receiving normative healthcare, it is ironic that they bear a higher burden of seeming healthy in performance arenas.

I should note here that, given the normative terms of defining "health" in our society, which often comes from individual-based studies that create norms and deviations predicated on Western categories and diagnostic tools that have been conventionally developed by and for male scientists and biomedical workers, I have conflicting feelings about how punk, rap, and health, as such, intersect. Therefore, rather than propose any sweeping or conclusive socio-statistical statements in this chapter, I want to tackle the question of female marginalization through notions of health. What does "world health" mean when considering the expressive female figure of the outcast, the misfit, the dismembered, for example, per Freudian hysteria and patriarchal optical controls that extend to listening (or, in Freud's case, finding listening to music difficult)? Also, what do women sing about in terms of health, particularly with respect to their reproductive and sexual agencies, given the long-standing stigma around women simply *talking about sex* and *sexual reproduction*?

I will again stress that the *ear is a reproductive organ*, and the dismemberment of the female body under the scopic gaze of male doctors has afforded the attrition of such sites for feminine empowerment. Punk and rap have been modalities of rearticulations of bodies, which, when thinking about the larger body politic and the normalized male voice in the public sphere, is of crucial importance. Focusing on gendered processes of dismemberment, this paper asks questions concerning health, drugs, bodies, and musical subcultures, particularly with consideration of the historical and the contemporary health issues in the United States, which since the end of World War II has influenced concepts of "world health" and its globalization as part of a widespread democratization of health through body and political agency through voice. I am interested in intergenerational punk networks of women's experiences concerning health and healing, broadly, and the ways in which we can draw on DIY subcultural connections to not only resist but also refuse, in both senses of the word, our bodies for, yes, ourselves.

Punk and rap music emerged at a time of neoliberal advance and individuation from the collective spaces of protest of the 1960s. The 1960s activism took a new look at educational models of the 1950s, specifically those that were focused on individual learning, particularly the young math and science student engaging in the techno-scientific pursuits of the postwar era (1950s) at the expense of the arts and humanities. Punk and hip-hop, which had music as central to their subcultural collective organizations, offered alternative modes of educational belonging not founded on the ignorant school master or on a pedagogy of oppression and domination where grades rather than ethical engagement, debates, critical thinking, and expressive contoured relationality were what mattered.

Punk and hip-hop demanded a different approach, and there was an initial rage, a militancy that had humor as an ingredient. In the early formulations of punk hardcore and rap hardcore, humor was used in the service of creative dissent and messages to teach collectives—disenfranchised youth becoming collective—about politics and the political—and to politicize them. In other words, masculinist stances of anger and frustration with the status quo affectively communicated through different types of subcultural humor—satire, irony, hype—and provided youth with means of becoming more critical and thoughtful civilians, which was the initial aim of public education in the United States. The well-known male artists must be put alongside female punk and rap inspired by the increasingly masculine spaces to better understand the educational importance of these subcultural musics to women's health.

By understanding how women punk and rap trios were inspired by these groups, we can even more clearly hear the humor, satire, and cross-cultural styles as educational—as pedagogies of remembering, pushing back on dismemberment and bondage. I begin with a punk response to Western classical music education by Lady Bits, followed by listening to how the Yeastie Girlz and Salt-N-Pepa historicize and gender "talking about sex." I consider whether these trios "sound" more educational because of the delivery, at least in parts—they are talking, giving history or an injunction to talk; they are asking us to talk about our bodies, sexual practices, and reproductive rights, historically and culturally. These are also highly politicized, but because they are by women, they are not looked at as general education. Punk and rap music brought women's health into subcultural and, with Salt-N-Pepa, mainstream music in a satirical way, and this was at a time when much debate was circulating about abortion and HIV. The moral panic about censorship with the FCC can also be heard, but the women fight this censorship. And this can be shown as a historical process—I begin with a class on Western art music taught in the ivory tower.

Lady Bits: Reproductive Rights and Music Education

If listening practices reproduce hierarchies (i.e. treating ear, mouth, genitals as reproductive organs of the political body and body politic), then we need to take seriously musical education and the possibilities of educational reproduction in terms of societal reproductions. Can reproducing the ear, the sensorial body, be thought of in terms of reproductive rights, and, if so, how do we consider the privileges of hearing and listening—from stethoscope to radio to our classrooms—in terms of extending and expanding conversations on reproductive rights?

In 2012, I began a postdoctoral position at Columbia University. I was assigned a class called "Music Humanities," which is basically teaching the Western classical music canon—from Gregorian chant through contemporary composition. There were two female composers—Hildegard of Bingen and Clara Schumann. Hildegard did medieval chant and found her voice through God, which, in the context of the Western canon, is presented as the patriarchal God, and composed in one-line monotone, although when one delves into her story and oeuvre, her visions and story are much more complex and robust. However, within the context of the class, Hildegard and Schumann, the wife of Robert Schumann, who composed Romantic era heteronormative love songs with, to, and about her husband, were the two female figures in the conventionally canonic part of the class (there was space where women composers, and even female composers of color, are later included, but this is in the twentieth century). And, still, the narrative surrounding the female composers in earlier periods were situated in ways that put them in the service of male genius.

With the understanding that the canon, or "music history," as a historical discipline, was conventionally developed and taught in the service of Western supremacy, I felt a critical exercise would be to draw upon an anarchic feminist punk pedagogy to provincialize harmony along the lines of Dipesh Chakrabarty's *Provincializing Europe* (2000).[3] As I began to incorporate more "popular musics," I tried to show how *all* music was mediated through our contemporary societal milieu, meaning that we—as political bodies—were listening to Bach or Mozart with twenty-first-century ears that layered heavy metal and Freud in conversation about women, sexuality, and genders that were nonbinary and nonconforming, given the lack of attention to such issues in most of the canon. Moreover, the celebration of colonial takings in the canon, such as Orientalism, can be paired with readings of Edward Said's *Orientalism* (1978) to highlight the "othering" productions of colonialism that patronize the East through appropriations of culture tied to lineage and land that often appropriate women's bodies and voices as well.

Yet the critical reflection of punk pedagogy that I learned from participating in the Bay Area's punk community that revolved, in part, around 924 Gilman St. and the spaces for discussion that were afforded on heteropatriarchal power and the need not only to look at how subjugated populations were dismembered and exploited, but to also consider how to dismember power, were woefully absent, at least in my lesson plans when it came to European men and women's relations, which dialogue precisely with the treatment of colonized populations. Teaching music history by listening to male authorities needed to be reinverted to discuss women's agentive means as matters of their voices, and to show how their voices had been comprised through entitlements to their reproductive capacities in ways that aligned with the spread of global capitalism and entitlements to colonized populations' bodies and the bodies of persons thought unfit to protect or reproduce society, persons commonly considered "disabled" or "sensorially impaired." For all the diversity my classes, something that I feel is celebrated in different ways (but also hidden to a degree depending on the scene) in punk, shifting to being heard as thinkers rather than being listened to as we reproduced the European genius to whom we were subservient students would be an appropriate exercise. From the canon, if we were the ones being listened to in the hierarchical reproduction of society, and if the ear *is* a reproductive organ, then we needed to reproduce our own conversations and break some taboo formations. As the elder of the classroom, I showed students by doing this myself, drawing on my positionality and creative resources, namely the band with whom I had been performing since just before I began teaching Music Humanities, Lady Bits.

Lady Bits remains a fiercely non-whitestreamed feminist band with a punk rock 'n' roll vibe that is at once experimental and playful, hard and edgy, melodic and memorable.[4] Although I departed in 2014 to move across the country, it is during the period in which I was fortunate to play with this female trio about which I speak, for I drew inspiration from the two members (Krishanti, guitar and vocals; Erin, drums) I joined with in 2012, which I brought to my teaching, and from the content of my teaching, which I brought to the band. I began doing research on female composers, and I came across a number of women who simply were not part of the discussion. And I do not believe that it is simply because they were women, but rather because their works would, could, and have inspired conversations about the intersections of sex, music, and societal reproduction. Take, for example, Renaissance composer Maddalena Casulana, whose rich repertoire is often dissonant and powerful, and which deals with death and both feminine and masculine forms of sexuality. Another Renaissance composer is Ann Boleyn, the wife of King Henry the VIII, who was imprisoned in the Tower of London and then beheaded for not bearing a male child. While awaiting her death in the Tower, she wrote a song, "O Death, Rock Me Asleep" (1536).

For our first, self-titled album (2014), Lady Bits included our "cover" of "O Death Rock Me Asleep," which we called "FAB" (fuck ann boleyn). I used the score as inspiration to arrange the piece as a basis for Lady Bits' song. We kept the melody and chordal/modal progression, with some modifications (Figure 9.1). FAB's lyrics (Figure 9.2) share how we opted to draw largely on the content of the first verse and chorus of the sixteenth-century Tudor-era poem. I then used our version to teach my class about the original song and notions of reproductive surveillance and dismemberment from life itself. I offered the Lady Bits version for two reasons—I wanted the students to take a "classical" piece (Western art music, more broadly) and arrange it for themselves, and I wanted them to augment it with a historical talking piece that would be educational, like "Let's Talk about Sex," which has historical and topical import.

The historical commentary in "FAB" comes during Krishanti's breakdown in the instrumental decrescendo, when she delivers a slam poetry–style educational moment that relays the poem's misogynistic, patriarchal context. Her historical narrative concludes with the word "dick," which is a reference to King Henry the VIII. On the album, we opted to augment the word "dick" with delay, which sustains the message until it entangles with the return of the chorus. I used this moment to speak to resonant bodies and contemplated how King Henry's control of breath, body, and political power can be contemplated through his musical investments as an avid recorder

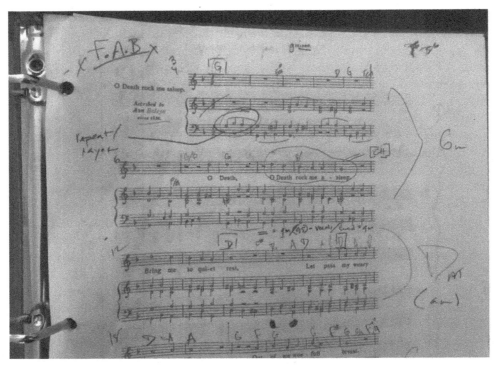

FIGURE 9.1. "O Death Rock Me Asleep," with FAB Arrangement Sketches (Author, 2012).

player. While I am in no way making generalizations about instrumentalists, the lesson is one in connections to technologies of power in control of the breath, the body, and the listening-in practices (e.g., René Laennec's stethoscope). Taking the space of the Musical Humanities course to "appreciate" Western music, to my mind, means to understand these aspects of power that move through economies of breath and body politics as instrumentalized differently at different historical nexuses. To model what I asked of the students, Lady Bits sonically and poetically assumed a critical stance on power by sounding solidarity with women's struggles, historically, and reshaping the king's historical body by lyrically (and studio production-wise) intimating the reproductive violence done to Ann Boleyn at the end of the breakdown.

Here, composite voices re-sound the ways in which sound reproduction is related to biological reproduction, which is related to societal reproduction and reproduction of hierarchies of power (and privilege). The musical commentary that weaves through complex issues concerning the politics, through the poetics, of bodies partitioned and body parts dismembered and censored, particularly in layered feminine registers over centuries, is, bluntly, one way to talk about sex. This historical commentary is also decidedly contemporary insofar as it brings up serious conversations about sexual violence, death, domestic abuse, and other means of controlling women through their reproductive means, including their voices and ovaries, for example.

fuck anne boleyn

bring me to quiet rest
let me pass my weary, guiltless ghost
out of my careful breast, toll on the passing bell
ring out my doleful knell

oh death, rock me asleep, rock me asleep
oh death, rock me asleep, rock me asleep
oh death, rock me asleep, rock me asleep
oh death, rock me asleep, rock me asleep

farewell my pleasures past
welcome my present pain
i feel my torment so incase that life cannot remain
there is no remedy

oh death, rock me asleep, rock me asleep
oh death, rock me asleep, rock me asleep
oh death, rock me asleep, rock me asleep
oh death, rock me asleep, rock me asleep

(breakdown)

1 - silence
2 - anne boleyn was born about 500 years ago
3 - she married the king of england, king henry the eight
4 - but she gave birth, to a daughter
5 - but that wasn't ok with king, so she tried again
6 - and had a miscarriage, but we all know that wasn't ok
7 - so she tried to give birth to a son but couldn't - so she ended up in the gallows
8 - and what do we know from this story? that king henry the eighth was a DICK

FIGURE 9.2. FAB Lyrics (emailed to author by Krishanti, 10/23/17).

Yeastie Girlz: Censorship and the Tampon Flute

The Yeastie Girlz 7-inch record *Ovary Action* was released on Lookout Records in 1988. The record contains ten songs with a Sprechstimme vocal delivery (no instruments) in tongue and cheek fashion. Dubbed "feminist rap," the band's name is a play on the Beastie Boys (New York, 1979), and the album title is a pun on the oft-misogynist labeling of women as overreacting or being hysterical, which is associated with the womb, and the action of women's reproductive organs—the ovaries. Being heard, as women, is often equated with being hysterical, and punk and rap offer outlets in which such labels, however antiquated society thinks they might be, can be shown to be still present in the microaggressions and popular culture of the extant patriarchal culture.

Hysteria, as explored by the (in)famous Sigmund Freud, was initially linked to dissatisfied female sexual desire. Elisabeth Bronfen (2014, ix) explains the current thinking: "It is commonly thought that hysteria as a psychosomatic ailment died out at the beginning of the twentieth century, and the fourth edition of the *Diagnostic and Statistical Manual* used by American psychiatrists and social workers accordingly no longer lists hysteria as a syndrome." However, tracing a line of critical feminist scholars from the late 1970s (e.g., Hélène Cixous, Catherine Clément), through the female performers of the 1980s, to the contemporary era (e.g. PJ Harvey, Madonna), in a similar trajectory to this paper's chronological arc, Bronfen shares how critical and performative tropes of the female histrionic hysteric have become staged to maintain hysteria, particularly with reference to "female subjectivity in a patriarchal culture," in academic mainstream conversations. For, as Bronfen explains, hysteria can manifest in various pathologies and forms of subjugation mapped onto women.[5]

Tracing a line from the Federal Communications Commission (FCC) to Freud (Freude), the Yeastie Girlz's *Ovary Action* (see Figure 9.3) can be situated within this commentary on the contemporary manifestations and impacts of routing women's voicings and expressivity through their ovaries to everyday acts of violence and censorship.[6]

Here, the ovaries are connected to the ear insofar as "hysteria" is concerned, for that which is expressed or voiced by women has been taken, historically, as a histrionics that can be helped or cured by managing women's genitals. The link between the ear, the mouth, and the reproductive organs, as matters of censorship at a political level, is made clear by the Yeastie Girlz first track on *Ovary Action* (Figure 9.4), which is titled "FCC,"

Yeastie Girlz, "Ovary Action" (Lookout! Records, 1988) Track Listing and Duration of Songs	
FCC	1:10
You Suck	1:28
Sperm Brain	1:00
Talkin' Shit	1:08
Orgasm Addict	1:00
Joyce	0:12
Put A Lid On It	1:25
Fuck Yerself	2:01
Sue Your Friends	1:30
Ode An Die Freude	1:27

FIGURE 9.3. Yeastie Girlz's *Ovary Action* track titles and durations.

FIGURE 9.4. Album cover art (front and back) of *Ovary Action* 7" record (Lookout Records, 1988).

a diatribe against the Federal Communications Commission. Below, I include the lyrics in full, since they introduce the group and carve a space in which they are "on the radio" or in which they need not be seen but rather can be heard. As they explain, they want to "talk about sex but [they're] not allowed."

> *"We're the Yeastie Girlz" (sung in chorus) "we're on the radio now" (sung solo) "We wanna talk about sex, but we're not allowed / Because the FCC is crackin' down hard. They want everything to sound just like a hallmark card / They won't even let us talk about number two / But I wonder what they call it when they get it on their shoe / We know what word they're using but we can't say it / (in chorus) because the FCC is full of bull shhhh / We're the Yeastie Girlz and we're here to say / (in chorus) that you better do something and right away / Yeah you better wake up and start using your head / Because your first amendment rights are just about dead / Well the FCC will tell you or haven't you heard / They think that freedom of speech is a dirty word / Well, the Yeastiez got a message for the people who agree / with the stupid regulations of the FCC / You think your kids will be corrupted if they hear about poo / Well, there's nothing wrong with them, we think the problem is you / Biology is neat, we like our bodies just fine / So if you're telling us it's dirty, well we say you're lying / They call it a free country but it feels like a prison / So write the Federal Communications Commission / Get your pen and paper ready because here's the address, 1919 M Street Northwest, Washington DC, 20036 / So, yeah, tell them that they're stupid, yeah, tell them that they're di. . . /. . . stroying our expression because they think it's outrageous / tell them that they're living in the dark ages / we're the Yeastie Girlz and we're here to say, we want the FCC to go away / yeah go away!*[7]
>
> —Lyrics to "FCC," the Yeastie Girlz's first song on *Ovary Action*.

The Yeastie Girlz come from the collective of 924 Gilman St. in Berkeley, California. Collectives offer dialogic spaces for the transmission of a pedagogy of comedic dissidence. The emergence of the collective, on December 31, 1986, was timely and offered a platform for the Bay Area feminist rap trio. The collective takes a decidedly "safe space" approach to membership. As you enter 924 Gilman St., there is a sign that, under the words "924 Gilman Collective," reads "No Racism, No Sexism, No Homophobia, No drugs, No alcohol, No violence, all ages volunteer run." For the collective to exist, then, a movement toward inclusivity was encouraged. With bands such as Green Day, Rancid, and The Offspring popularizing punk in the mid-1990s, it might seem as though punk continued to be a "boy's subculture." More particularly, these men were portrayed as straight (until later, when Green Day's singer and lead guitarist Billie Joe Armstrong came out as bisexual). Such mediation and circulation discounts the rich contributions of women and those advancing voices in the queer community through punk. With the Yeastie Girlz, we have an example of women taking a stand and expressing their viewpoints on a variety of issues—some broadly applicable (such as the song about the FCC) and others that deal with women's health and hygiene, for example.

Punk, in the 1980s, grew in popularity perhaps in response to the censorship. "For a decade of broadcasting that began with deregulation, the '80s wound up with the strongest shift towards governmental regulation of programming since the 1950s," *Los Angeles Times* writer Dennis McDougal explains in the 1989 article "Art in the Eighties: Censorship: A Decade of Tighter Control of the Arts" (Parachini and McDougal 1989). Since 1977, the Supreme Court has ruled that the FCC could ban "indecent" content, based on a case brought on by comedian George Carlin's "seven dirty words" monologue, about words that cannot be said on the air. This enabled the FCC a wide latitude of what "indecent" meant, and although the FCC maintained jurisdiction, it was tested to define "indecent" when some of the stations that were fined by the FCC joined together in a lawsuit against the FCC. However, in the midst of the lawsuit, "the FCC had found a staunch ally on Capitol Hill in Sen. Helms who authored a bill outlawing 'indecent' programming 24 hours a day. The bill was attached to an appropriations bill and, in the waning hours of the 1988 legislative session, was passed into law" (Parachini and McDougal 1989).

In 1985, the Parents Music Resource Center (PMRC) was formed. Famously founded by four women known as the "Washington Wives," including Tipper Gore, the center had the goal of increasing parental control of music, particularly music that was deemed violent, drug-related, or contained sexual content. They began the "Parental Advisory: Explicit Lyrics" label, and much of the music they targeted was classed and raced, such as heavy metal, rap, and punk. The PMRC was hotly debated and contested by punk and rap musicians in public venues, such as the *Oprah Winfrey Show*, with Dead Kennedys' lead singer, Jello Biafra, and the rapper Ice-T. Frank Zappa recorded the hearings and set them to music. The year prior, in 1984, the National Parent Teachers Organization (National PTA) adopted a resolution that encouraged record companies to adopt a rating system with which to gauge the amount of violence, sex, profanity, and vulgarity in the content or on the covers of albums. While, in 2001, the FCC defined indecency "as "material that, in context, depicts or describes sexual or excretory activities or organs in terms patently offensive as measured by contemporary community standards for the broadcast medium," the main issues around sexual activities and appropriateness to broadcast to a community revolve around who sets the standards and who defines "community" and the right to censor (Freedom Forum 2016). As with the Lady Bits song that critiqued royal regulation of reproduction, Yeastie Girlz use their concluding song to take aim at what they considered the "indecency" of the canonic fraternity that has been upheld in the Western community.

The final track, "Ode an die Freude," is a live performance lasting 11 minutes and 10 seconds. It is a cover of the "Ode to Joy" (Schiller) in Beethoven's Ninth Symphony, using the cardboard applicator of a tampon to perform the piece. This piece instrumentalizes the cardboard that women insert into themselves as a menstruation ritual, often taboo, in modern culture. The reappropriation, along with the re-sounding of Beethoven and Freud, as the foundational theorist to theorize women's hysteria and sexual unfulfillment, situate the feminist rap trio's work historically alongside, through the reconfiguration of, the male "artist," the seriousness of art, of fate, of listening, and of culture—as well as the male theorist of women who was unable to listen to music. The Yeastie Girlz drew upon this lineage to feminize and occupy the canon.

The dissonance thus resonates in this, the only instrumental song on the record, where we are taken back to the cultural listening-in device, the flute, that Laennec reappropriated to listen to women's chests. But here the women re-sound a comedic dissidence in the microtonal "pitchy" quality of the performance. The pitchy quality seems to weave in and out of the historical censors on talking about sex and reproduction, as well as health, from women's perspectives, from the music history to the restriction of voices, of music, on the radio and on television, which I will now turn to with Salt-N-Pepa. For these feminist trios draw on a non-whitestreamed version of feminism to critique masculine lineages and languages to listen-in to women and censor them, from Freud to the FCC.

SALT-N-PEPA

Formed in Queens, New York, in 1985, Salt-N-Pepa was one of the first all-female rap groups to form in the midst of 1980s censorship, which is complicated by issues of racialized violence that have also been censored and to which rap has often attested, such as with groups such as N.W.A and Public Enemy. Salt-N-Pepa brought their female perspective to this milieu; the group "[was] comprised of rapper Cheryl James (Salt), daughter of a bank manager and a transit worker; rapper Sandy Denton (Pepa), daughter of a nurse; and DJ Dee Dee Roper (Spinderella); James and Denton were raised in Queens, NY; both attended Queensborough Community College" (Encyclopedia.com 2018). The move to form a three-piece rap group made up of Black women was bold, because men dominated rap, and this led many women, most specifically feminists, to reject the entire genre. Salt-N-Pepa's music was brash and open. As Rob Hoerburger noted in a review in *Rolling Stone*, "Cheryl James, Sandy Denton, and Dee Dee Roper remain fixed on kicking rap in the pants.... In the best rap tradition, Salt-N-Pepa balance humor, arrogance and practicality" (Encyclopedia.com 2018). Hoerburger lists humor first, then arrogance, and then practicality. We translate this as Salt-N-Pepa's pedagogy of comedic dissidence, where practicality is code for pedagogy, arrogance is code for anti-masculinist narratives/assuredness, and humor can be translated to comedic reveal.

From the standpoint of learning objectives, Salt-N-Pepa orient listeners to their teachings that give women voice and room for critical debate about the actions of men and their feelings about relationships. They de-objectify themselves while, at the same time, paying attention to the difficult subject matter inscribed on them and their voices and bodies as Black women. The latter issue was increasingly important as MTV continued to make performers visible and categorize them into different racialized genres (e.g., *Yo! MTV Raps*) that reproduced gendered spaces. Salt-N-Pepa upheld the "fly girl" fashion, which can be read as a comical affront to masculinist voyeuristic tendencies when placed alongside their messages. Ethnomusicologist Cheryl Keyes discusses this aspect:

> By the mid-1980s, many female MCs began contesting the "fly girl" image because they wanted their audiences to focus more on their rapping skills than on their dress styles. Despite this changing trend, the female rap trio Salt-N-Pepa—Salt, Pepa, and Spinderella—nevertheless canonized the ultimate fly girl posture of rap by donning short, tight-fitting outfits, leather clothing, ripped jeans or punk clothing, glittering gold jewelry (i.e., earrings and necklaces), long sculpted nails, prominent makeup, and hairstyles ranging from braids and wraps to waves, in ever-changing hair coloring. Rap's fly girl image is, however, far more than a whim, for it highlights aspects of Black women's bodies considered undesirable by American mainstream standards of beauty (Roberts 1998). Through performance, Salt-N-Pepa are "flippin da script" (deconstructing dominant ideology) by wearing clothes that accent their full breasts and rounded buttocks and thighs, considered beauty markers of Black women by Black culture (Roberts 1998). Moreover, they portray via performance the fly girl as a party-goer, an independent woman, but, additionally, an erotic subject rather than an objectified one.
>
> (Keyes 2000, 260)

As erotic subjects, Salt–N–Pepa revealed male entitlements and female objectification and used their platform to marry conventional skit-based education on sexual health with the playful comedic tone of their rap vocal delivery and musical accompaniment (DJ Spinderella). An example of this is the single "Let's Talk about Sex" (1991). The song was released as a 7″ single. The cover has a comic aesthetic, already distancing the women from the somber or more serious tone of parental lectures. Rather than donning "fly girl" clothing, the women are dressed in more of a style of street fashion. These clothes also "flip the script," as Keyes noted, and are part of the larger "[deconstruction] of dominant ideology" that hierarchizes conversations about sex. Sex education is often the purview of high schools or middle schools—usually coupled with driver's education or sports (at least in the 1980s and 1990s). Men were often in charge of instructing students about sex, and men have dominated media representations about sex. Parental discussions concerning sex are less frequent as parents have less time to spend with their children, which is why these conversations have become necessary in the schools. Here, Salt-N-Pepa intervene in the dominant ideological structure of alienating sex ed in favor or a candid approach that engages the listener through women's voices.

"Let's Talk about Sex" was a Top 20 *Billboard* hit. "The song was significant because it was released during a time when the threat of HIV and AIDS were being broadcast on media networks across the country. The early 1990s was also a time of intensive education on the subject of sexually transmitted diseases and this song played a key role in educating young people about the dangers of unprotected sex" (Hess 2007, 204). Salt-N-Pepa's educational import is undisputed, but it is their aesthetic approach to mediation, like our previous examples, that takes education outside the schools to the collaborative space of musical creation, and then to the larger spaces of mass media dissemination. The video for "Let's Talk about Sex," in the analysis that follows, exemplifies a pedagogy of comedic dissidence that couples sound, visual, and cultural symbolism and metaphor to share the consequences of unprotected sex in humorous ways that are "self-enhancing," meaning that they are able to laugh at themselves talking about taboo subjects, such as sex, unplanned pregnancy, and STDs. This type of humor enables these difficult subjects to be broached in the first place.

The video begins with an image of a book titled "Talk Sex" being tossed into a trash can. After a flash image of a man breakdancing, the three women, dressed elegantly in black, begin a conversation. They are alone, together, and their talk is interspersed with active men breakdancing. Salt laughingly says, "Yo, I don't think we should talk about this," as she looks at Pepa and Spindarella, who scoffs, "Why not?" Salt, with a big smile on her face, turns to the camera, and directs her comment at us—the viewers: "People might misunderstand what we tryin' to say, you know?" Spindarella quickly says, "You know, but that's a part of life." We watch a frame where a man is duct-taped at a radio station, and Salt takes over—broadcasting Salt-N-Pepa's message. The women are dancing and go from being dressed in tight black dresses to street wear and even emulating construction workers. The women sing in chorus: "Let's talk about sex, baby. Let's talk about you and me. Let's talk about all the good things and the bad things that may be. Let's talk about sex. Let's talk about sex."

Part of Salt's verse is about message dissemination and injunction to have conversations and to learn: "Talk about sex on the radio and video. May will know / anything goes." The song continues as a dynamic interspersion of good humor mixed with political messages that are educational. When the tension and taboo crescendos, the women are shown as construction workers egging the men on—catcalling them—a play on what men do, but even this is done in a jovial manner to offset some of the gendered and sexed tension. And, provocatively, the background dancers are both men and women—and toward the end of the video, both men and women are lip-syncing—*everyone* needs to talk about sex, or they become, like the skeleton with the censored tape around its bony mouth, dead still and silent.

Conclusion

Rather than be listened to as objects, these trios talk about sex and reproduction across time, space, and cultural constructs, as something that is historically grounded in societal conventions that need to be disrupted and, perhaps, dismembered. In doing so, they offer embodied recollections of feminine power that resonate through punk and rap collectivities. By talking about sex and making space in the classroom, on the radio, and on MTV, these female trios situate the ear, music, and subcultural musics as subversive potentialities in ways that counter the female hysteric, given that talk is linked to speech, and yet they include the feminine voice in screams that are resonant of historically subjugated communities.

Notes

1. On the problematic of music within psychoanalysis, see Régnault (2010) and Johnson (2017).
2. Although outside of the general historical period of analysis, queercore bands like Pansy Division have developed their own satirical language based on challenging and confronting homophobia.
3. For a more thorough study of the discipline of history as Enlightenment construct to uphold colonialist notions of European supremacy in a secularizing world, see Chakrabarty (2000).
4. See Lady Bits at bandcamp, https://lady-bits.bandcamp.com.
5. Bronfen cites Mark S. Micale's urging for the inclusion of the male hysteric, which is an important conversation but one that is ultimately outside the purview of this chapter's exercise in women's health.
6. The inclusion of near-homonyms "Freud (Freude)" is meant to be a play on both Freud—as in Freudian psychoanalysis that the band rejects in terms of notions of "ovary reaction" (here, we can think about Sigmund Freud's problematic psychoanalytic labeling of women as "hysterical," once a medical diagnosis for insanity where the woman might be prescribed a hysterectomy, that is—removal of the cervix, uterus, and possibly ovaries. So, there is play on this history in terms of "ovary action" and "over reaction" perhaps the label of women by male doctors and/or the male doctors' over reaction when it comes to attempts to control women's reproductive movements or even expressivity around feelings, such as what could be construed as instances of feminine joy—"i.e. both consistent with ovary action."). The word play also references the band's repurposing of "Ode to Joy," playing it on a plastic "disposable" tampon and taking the toxic waste culture as a form of expression and community building. Again, I read this as resistant to the whole disposability of women's reasonable emotions and reproductive control.

7. "We don't actually say the word "dicks" here, we just let it be filled in by the listener because it rhymes with six from the FCC zip code, and then we merge the start of the word dicks into the word destroying . . . the point of the song was to be radio-safe while attacking the FCC." Jane Guskin commentary on the lyrics, personal communication, September 11, 2021.

References

Aldridge, Robert W., et al. 2018. "Morbidity and Mortality in Homeless Individuals, Prisoners, Sex Workers, and Individuals with Substance Use Disorders in High-Income Countries: A Systematic Review and Meta-Analysis." *The Lancet* 391, no. 10117: 241–250.

Bronfen, Elisabeth. 2014. *The Knotted Subject: Hysteria and Its Discontents*. Princeton, NJ: Princeton University Press.

Chakrabarty, Dipesh. 2000. *Provincializing Europe*. Princeton, NJ: Princeton University Press.

Encyclopedia.com. 2018. "Salt-N-Pepa." http://www.encyclopedia.com/people/literature-and-arts/music-popular-and-jazz-biographies/salt-n-pepa.

Freedom Forum. 2016. https://www.freedomforuminstitute.org/wp-content/uploads/2016/10/FirstReport.Indecency.Levi_.final_.pdf.

Hess, Mickey. 2007. *Icons of Hip Hop: An Encyclopedia of the Movement, Music and Culture*. Westport, CT: Greenwood Press.

Johnson, Stephen. 2017. "Breaking Free: Freud vs. Music." *BBC Sounds* (podcast). https://www.bbc.co.uk/sounds/play/b086t9qk.

Keyes, Cheryl L. 2000. "Empowering Self, Making Choices, Creating Spaces: Black Female Identity via Rap Music Performance." *Journal of American Folklore* 113, no. 449: 255–269.

Parachini, Allan, and Dennis McDougal. 1989. "Art in the Eighties: Censorship: A Decade of Tighter Control of the Arts." *Washington Post*, December 25, 1989. https://www.latimes.com/archives/la-xpm-1989-12-25-ca-781-story.html.

Régnault, François. 2010. "Psychoanalysis and Music." *The Symptom* 11 (Spring). http://www.lacan.com/symptom11/psychoanalysis-and.html.

Schwartz, Jessica A., and Scott Robertson. 2018. "Laughing All the Way to the Stage." In *Punk Pedagogies: Music, Culture, and Learning*, edited by Gareth Dylan Smith, Mike Dines, and Tom Parkinson. New York: Routledge.

Sterne, Jonathan. 2003. *The Audible Past: Cultural Origins of Sound Reproduction*. Durham, NC: Duke University Press.

CHAPTER 10

QUEER AND FEMINIST PUNK IN THE UK

KIRSTY LOHMAN

Introduction

Punk has long been an area for the culturally disenfranchised to experiment. Subcultural possibility has been shifted by a "do it yourself" (DIY) ethos, artistic norms that do not necessarily require high levels of proficiency, and an emphasis on participation over consumption. This is particularly important for groups including women and queer people, who are subject to systems of oppression and are marginalized in everyday life and in their subcultural endeavors.

This chapter focuses on contemporary DIY queer and feminist punk scenes in the UK to illuminate shifting cultural and subcultural norms. It builds on the works of Julia Downes (2009, 2012) to understand how queer and feminist punk scenes in the UK have—and have not—changed since her study took place. The chapter is based on formal ethnographic fieldwork (2017–2019), in addition to informal autoethnographic reflections (2013–2019) as part of my own participation in the scenes. It situates these scenes as part of a continuum of punk, particularly influenced by queercore and Riot Grrrl, but also as part of wider DIY creative cultures of inclusion and opportunity. Discussions, framed around the politics of inclusion, of musical and clothing aesthetics, and of punk economics, will uncover a trajectory of punk that centers around the inclusion of those otherwise marginalized in cultural production.

Queer and Feminist Punk, 1976–c.2010

Prior to punk, women and LGBTQ+ people had struggled to gain prominent roles in music-based youth subcultures in the UK, usually participating through style and fandom rather than as musicians, artists, or key scene innovators. Punk, however, had always provided space for punk women and queer people to be involved, often in prominent ways. Bands and musicians included X-Ray Spex, Tom Robinson Band, Jayne County, Buzzcocks, the Slits, and Poison Girls, to name but a few. Vivienne Westwood designed key elements of punk styles, and Jordan ensured that they were seen. Caroline Coon published about the subculture in the music press, and Linder Sterling pushed artistic boundaries (O'Brien 2012; Reddington 2012; Worley 2017). Early punk played with gender, sex, and sexuality. This was most notable through the (at the time, shocking) use of bondage gear, which was worn by punks regardless of gender or sexual identity and also manifested in English punks socialized in gay clubs across the country (Wilkinson 2015). The presence within punk of so many people who broke the mold of other (cisgender, heterosexual) male-dominated scenes enabled the empowerment of those who might otherwise feel marginalized in wider society (Downes 2012; Dunn 2016).

While the early punk scene in the UK did offer freedom of expression, it also replicated wider structural inequalities and oppressions. David Wilkinson (2015) details punk that harbored homophobic attitudes, and Helen Reddington (2012) discusses the sexism that women in punk had to navigate. Early punk remained dominated by white, heterosexual, cisgender men, and those who deviated from this were at risk of abuse and assault inside and outside the scene.

By the time punk had "gone underground" with anarcho- and hardcore punk in the 1980s (Clark 2003), patriarchal norms, deep-rooted homophobia, and misogyny solidified in the many scenes, particularly in North America (LeBlanc 1999). Women might not explicitly have been excluded from these more macho hardcore punk scenes, but they were placed in a situation where if they wanted to participate, they had to deal with a "trebled reflexivity":

> As punks, they counter the sartorial, vocational, and behavioural norms of the mainstream culture; as female punks, they counter the norms of feminine propriety, beauty and behaviour; as punk girls, in combining the discourses of punk and femininity, the[y] subvert the punk subversion, challenging the masculinist norms of the subculture.
>
> (LeBlanc 1999, 160)

Anti-sexist, anti-racist, and anti-homophobic discourses of "punk ideology" (see, for example, O'Hara, 1999), were not necessarily actualized in many punk scenes, but bigotry and abuse were experienced by many (Wald and Gottlieb 1993; Reddington 2012; Ensminger 2010). Women and/or queer people's broader subcultural participation and inclusion became more minimal and marginalized.

It was in North America that prominent breaking points were reached: in 1985 by LG(BTQ) people with queercore, and in 1991 by women and girls with Riot Grrrl. Participants and organizers in both scenes spoke and wrote about how they felt that their community was marginalized in wider punk scenes—targeted by homophobia and/or sexism. New communities would enable space for mutual support, and for queer and/or female punks to make connections with each other that were harder to find otherwise.

The queercore scene had its origins in Toronto, Canada (Nault 2017). In 1985, G. B. Jones and Bruce LaBruce launched the fanzine *J.D.s*, which critiqued both Toronto's macho punk scene and its liberal, assimilationist gay community. Neither of these scenes were welcoming to a wider spectrum of queer bodies (in terms of gender, sexuality, ability, and/or race). Jones and LaBruce later explained:

> The only difference is that at the fag bar, females have been almost completely banished, while at the punk club, they've just been relegated to the periphery, but allowed a pretense of participation (i.e. girlfriend, groupie, go-fer, or post-show pussy). In this highly masculinized world, the focus is doubly male, the boys on stage controlling the "meaning" of the event (the style of music, political message, etc.) and the boys in the pit determining the extent of the exchange between audience and performer.
>
> (Jones and LaBruce 1989, 27; see also Nault 2017, 19)

The fanzine started an underground buzz in Toronto that soon spread, first across North America, and then beyond. The queercore scene combined the radical anti-establishment politics of punk with the radical anti-heteronormative (and anti-homonormative) politics of queer (DeChaine 1997), to create a subcultural space for those who were unwelcome and unwilling to be part of other normative spaces and scenes.

Initially queercore was fanzine-led, opening up communication between queer punks locally and translocally. Importantly, *J.D.s* released a cassette tape with international contributions from queer punk bands, *J.D.s Top Ten Homocore Hit Parade Tape*, in 1990. Queer punks and their bands came out of the woodwork, coalescing, where numbers were greatest, into physical community-led scenes in larger metropoles, each taking on a different shape in their different contexts. In Toronto, queercore manifested a new queer (post-)punk scene; in San Francisco the fanzine *Homocore* pushed for space for queers within the wider hardcore punk scene (Fenster 1993). A proliferation of fanzines and compilation records inspired yet more queercore punk activity. These scenes were most active in the late 1980s and 1990s, yet their tendrils can be seen in events such as transnational Queeruption festivals (Brown 2007).

Riot Grrrl emerged around 1991 when groups of grrrls, many based in and around Olympia, Washington (USA), coalesced around fanzine writing, activist organizing, art, and punk music. Networks between "Riot Grrrl chapters" soon extended across the United States and beyond as more grrrls took up the methods of DIY punk organizing to create their own subcultural spaces. The infamous and influential Riot Grrrl Manifesto (1991) explained their motivations:

> BECAUSE us girls crave records and books and fanzines that speak to US, that WE feel included in and can understand in our own ways. . . . BECAUSE we don't want to

assimilate to someone else's (Boy) standards of what is or isn't "good" music or punk rock or "good" writing AND THUS need to create forums where we can recreate, destroy and define our own visions.... BECAUSE i believe with my holeheartmindbody that girls constitute a revolutionary soul force that can, and will, change the world for real.

Riot Grrrl's politics, aesthetics, and approach sparked a media frenzy, antithetical to the "ambiguous-by-design" approach of artists, bands, fanzine writers, and promoters (Schilt 2004, 124). Ultimately, this scrutiny, pressure, and misrepresentation was responsible for many of the original wave of bands splitting up (Schilt 2004). However, as with punk and queercore, the original Riot Grrrl movement had lasting global impacts: by the mid-1990s many women and girls who had never previously felt welcome or able to participate in punk, politics, or DIY subcultures were inspired to do just that.

Queercore and Riot Grrrl had global effects, drawing in more and more queer people and/or women. Amy Spencer (2008) has traced queercore's influences in the UK, from the first alternative gay club night Rock 'n' Doris held in Newcastle in 1989, through to the early 1990s, when club nights spread across England: from Manchester (Homocult) to London (Up To The Elbow; Vaseline, which later became Club V; and Homocrime). London was also the site of the world's first Queeruption in 1998.

The band Huggy Bear formed in Brighton in 1991. With a lack of easy access or information on what exactly American Riot Grrrls were doing, Huggy Bear shaped UK Riot Grrrl in a distinctly British way (Downes 2009). By 1992 the transatlantic gap narrowed: Huggy Bear collaborated with the most well-known of the Riot Grrrl bands from Olympia, joining Bikini Kill on tours and shared record releases. Rumors of the activities of the American Riot Grrrls spread across the UK, with Riot Grrrl "gangs" emerging in Leeds/Bradford, Aberdeen, Birmingham, Portsmouth, and London, among other locales (Ablaze! 2012).

In North America, queercore and Riot Grrrl were connected to punk and hardcore scenes through broader subcultural networks, with influences manifested in aesthetics. Each scene's broader context gave rise to its own distinct flavor: Toronto queercore was more punk/post-punk; San Francisco homocore was more hardcore; and Riot Grrrls in Olympia had links to the grunge scene in nearby Seattle. Queercore and Riot Grrrl were also connected to each other through overlapping rationales and audiences, and some bands described themselves as part of both scenes. Fifth Column and Team Dresch, for example, had members who identified as queer women and had access to queercore and Riot Grrrl (Nault 2017).

In the UK, these networks figured differently. Spencer (2008) explains how UK queercore was connected to the British indie scene, at a time when Britpop was rising to prominence. This was distinct from the more radical queer punk political networks of American and Canadian queercore—although those influences can be seen in the first Queeruption in London, which sat firmly within punk and squatting subcultures (Brown 2007). UK Riot Grrrl was distinct from UK queercore, lacking the overlaps seen in the North American scenes. Aesthetically, however, UK Riot Grrrl—like

UK queercore—was also heavily influenced by DIY indie and indie-pop scenes. Julia Downes explains that this was due to the more accepting and inclusive nature of indie-pop:

> Indie-pop audiences and bands tended to be more gender-balanced in relation to crust and anarcho punk music culture. Low key knowledge of riot grrrl circulated within these indie-pop communities and inspired young men and women to disrupt the everyday constitution of gender and sexuality in their immediate subcultural contexts. (2012, 211)

Riot Grrrl in the UK therefore manifested less as a reactionary response specifically to sexism and marginalization in (hardcore) punk, and more as an opportunity for greater girl gang–focused opportunities for (sub)cultural production.

The influence of Riot Grrrl can clearly be seen in the trajectory of UK scenes in the late 1990s, 2000s, and through to today, particularly in the proliferation of Ladyfest events and mentoring programs such as Rock Camps for Girls (Schilt and Zobl 2008; O'Shea 2014). The first Ladyfest in the UK was Ladyfest Scotland, held in Glasgow in 2001, one year after the first ever Ladyfest event in Olympia, and served as a "Riot Grrrl reunion" of sorts. Ladyfests (sometimes LaDIYfests) are women-focused DIY festivals that center art, creative and political workshops, and music, often with an aim to raise funds for women-focused charities. The structure is otherwise open, and Ladyfest collectives have emerged wherever there is an appetite to run an event. Between 2000 and 2010, thirty-two Ladyfests/LaDIYfests were held across the UK (O'Shea 2014). In their remit, ethos, and approach, Ladyfests sit within a feminist and Riot Grrrl paradigm.

More recent UK scenes draw on the aesthetics of both UK and US original Riot Grrrl, with some lighter indie-pop and other bands that have harder punk edges. We also see the (sometimes partial) erosion of divides between queercore and Riot Grrrl, with greater overlaps between aesthetics, bands, promoters, networks, and audiences, leading to the emergence in the 2000s of "DIY queer feminist (sub)cultures" (Downes 2009).

Who the Scenes Are For: Identity Politics, Boundaries, and Multiplicity

There are a myriad of contemporary punk scenes in the UK. Many of these scenes are queer-, feminist-, and/or people of color–focused, seeking to promote inclusion of people from social groups that might feel marginalized in broader punk scenes. Groups and collectives often focus on particular marginalized identities in order to push the boundaries for inclusion and participation in punk scenes. These include groups such as Decolonise Fest (London), Girl Gang Sheffield (and Leeds, Manchester, and Edinburgh), FemRock (Brighton), and Queerfest Nottingham (and Leeds). Other collectives are broader in terms of identity orientation, such as First Timers (London), which is for people who face any form of oppression within punk. The emphasis on people's identities (and their marginalizations) as a nexus of cultural organization is part of wider cultural trends that affect young people's self-perception, identities, and politics, as well as culture (see, for example, Lohman and Pearce 2020).

This emphasis on promoting the inclusion of marginalized identities is also a reflection of shifts in contemporary feminist understandings and praxis. Contemporary feminist thought is rooted in a recognition of previous movements' shortcomings, drawing particularly on black feminist critiques of middle-class, white-dominated approaches within second-wave feminism (Collins 1991; Davis 1983). Crenshaw's (1991) conceptualization of intersectionality, which recognizes the compounding effect of multiple forms of marginalization, has become common parlance among younger generations of feminists. Indeed, feminists in the UK now often firmly embed issues of identity and marginality within their terminology, defining themselves as "radical feminists, Marxist or socialist feminists, black feminists, trans-feminists and queer [feminists]" (Charles and Wadia 2018, 176).

There have also been demographic changes in the UK that affect notions of identity. Young people are increasingly likely to identify beyond normative cisgender and/or straight categories of gender and sexuality, and are also increasingly likely to dismiss more binary and monosexual forms of sexual and gendered identities (e.g., lesbian, gay, straight, transsexual) in favor of looser or more fluid identity (or anti-identity) labels (e.g., bisexual, queer, trans, nonbinary) (Pearce et al. 2019). In these shifts we see a mainstreaming of the approaches to queer identities, politics, and theory that informed queercore in the 1980s:

> These focuses of queer theory and identity politics—of deconstructing oppositional binaries and social categories of gender, sexuality, and heteronormativity; and of undercutting identity politics by instead focusing on the permeability and opening allowed by difference—underpin the strategies of subversion and resistance which queers employ in their everyday lives.
>
> (DeChaine 1997, 22)

The relationship between contemporary identity construction and politically informed cultural activities is therefore inherently linked to political understandings and activisms. Even in the names of many contemporary events (such as Loud Women, Bent Fest, and Decolonise Fest), identity is deeply integrated into the function of and rationale for many of the activities of queer and/or feminist punks today, raising questions about who these events are for (and who they are *not* for), as well as how the boundaries of identity are managed. This is a key context in which one sees the continued influences of Riot Grrrl and queercore today. Early punk provided a particularly "open" space, for society's outsiders and misfits, but this "space" narrowed as hardcore and some strands of anarcho-punk solidified hypermasculine punk norms. Riot Grrrl and homocore were both responses to this, for different (sometimes overlapping) audiences.

Queercore, was—in the original Toronto scene—created by and for the queer punks who felt excluded from mainstream gay *and* punk scenes. The scene that grew around the *Homocore* zine in San Francisco took a broader approach, laid out in their manifesto:

> You don't have to be gay; being different at all, like straight guys who aren't macho shitheads, women who don't want to be a punk rock fashion accessory, or any other personal decision that makes you an outcast is enough. Sexuality is an important part of it, but only part.
>
> (Jennings 1988)

This followed in the spirit of early punk scenes, promoting an explicit "openness": identifying as a sexual minority isn't required for participation. However, there were further *unintended* marginalizations in terms of those who did not feel that queercore was initially welcoming to them:

> Despite socially conscious and inclusive policies . . . queercore was, at least initially, white-centered. . . . Despite its blanched beginnings, queers of color eventually made inroads into the subculture, leaving a (b)lasting impact, . . . forcing the subculture to expand beyond its white, cisgender, able-bodied bubble. Exclusions continue to exist, but minority participants have not let them go unchallenged.
>
> (Nault 2017, 27)

Riot Grrrl, in some of its earliest incarnations, was radically *closed* rather than radically open: with many original US collectives and meetings "girl-only" (Marcus 2010). While Riot Grrrl and queercore both emerged in reaction to marginalization, many Riot Grrrls distinguished themselves by seeking an entirely separatist space, in which feminist discussions could safely take place away from any disruptive male presence. This was in keeping with a long history of "safe" woman-only spaces in Western feminist history, particularly the organizing tactics of women of color (Evans 1979). A number of US Riot Grrrl scenes were less prescriptive, with some male involvement in bands and in the scene: this occasionally caused tensions when bands with male members, such as Bikini Kill and Excuse 17, played in cities with a woman-only approach (Brownstein 2015). In the UK, Riot Grrrl was inclusive rather than exclusive. Many prominent UK Riot Grrrl bands, such as Huggy Bear, Comet Gain, and Coping Saw, had male members, and given the overlaps between Riot Grrrl and indie scenes, Riot Grrrl events were rarely closed to men; indeed, they often were explicitly mixed-gender spaces (Downes 2012).

As Riot Grrrls felt the pressure of media scrutiny in the mid- to late 1990s, critiques and tensions within the scene, as well as from outside, became more acute (Marcus 2010). Where it was ideally intended to be a space for all women and girls to feel safe to be creative and political, in practice a variety of aspects of how scenes operated were exclusionary and marginalizing. Riot Grrrl has been critiqued for both actively and passively excluding a variety of groups of people, including working-class women with less time and money to participate, women with disabilities whose access needs were not necessarily taken into account, and trans people kept away by gender essentialist and exclusive practices (Schilt 2003; Marcus 2010; Pearce 2012).

There has also been criticism of the approach to race and the overwhelming whiteness in many Riot Grrrl scenes. Mimi Nguyen locates in this the particular influence of a (white) liberal feminism and its understanding of race "that define[s] racism as ignorance, and ignorance as the absence of intimacy.... [W]e also know this in the familiar disavowal, 'I'm not racist, I have black friends,' which suggests that proximity is a social prophylactic against virulent racism" (2012, 181). This approach enabled "anti-racist" white Riot Grrrls to avoid examining and challenging their own dominance, so long as there was a degree of tokenistic diversity. Indeed, some white grrrls laid the "blame" for disruption and disbanding of original Riot Grrrl scenes with vocal Riot Grrrls of color (Nguyen 2012).

As later generations of feminist punks investigated the history of Riot Grrrl, they learned of and came to understand the failures of Riot Grrrl's—and queercore's—politics of inclusion/exclusion, with these critiques becoming common currency (Marcus 2010; Nguyen 2012). This dovetailed with rising awareness of theories of intersectionality as an analytical lens to understand how these scenes perpetuated marginalization. In contemporary queer and feminist punk scenes, there is a desire to keep these pitfalls from recurring. In the naming of the collectives and events, we see how these are often targeted toward particular groups of queer and/or feminist punks—be they loud women or grrrl gangs, bent or queer, or seeking to decolonize punk. However, the spaces that these collectives create usually *also* deliberately challenge the siloing of identities, instead seeking to pay attention to a range of marginalized experiences, their intersections, and the compounding effect of these experiences. This work is done in different ways, including, first, through booking bands, and second, through safe(r) spaces policies.

Organizers of contemporary UK DIY queer and/or feminist punk festivals often book a range of bands across a day or weekend, whose members represent a variety of marginalized identities. This ensures that representation, participation, and inclusion is front and center, which is intended to encourage marginalized punks to attend, and possibly also be inspired to take a more active role in cultural participation and production. This booking strategy often further encompasses a range of musical and aesthetic influences.

Moreover, event organizers explicitly work to ensure that a range of people can feel welcome in the audience. "Safe(r)" is used, rather than "safe," as a recognition that no space can be oppression-free. Safety work is undertaken in part through the use of safe(r) spaces policies that regulate event spaces. These policies usually set out a list of behaviors that will not be tolerated. Some DIY venues, including DIY Space for London and Wharf Chambers in Leeds, have their own safe(r) space policies and accountability processes, and where venues do not have such a policy, the event promoters will often institute one at the location for that night. The use of safe(r) spaces policies fits with a long tradition of organizing by marginalized groups. Over the last decade, the use of safe(r) spaces policies has become standard practice among younger generations of feminists. They work on multiple levels: by regulating who feels welcome in the scene, by explicitly communicating to members of various marginalized identities that they are welcome and should hope to feel safe here, by regulating behavior in the space, by empowering users of the space to challenge oppressive behaviors in the space, and by communicating to scene "outsiders" who disagree with the value of safe(r) spaces that this space is run differently from their subcultural norms.

While each space/promoter will institute their own policies, examples from Decolonise Fest and FemRock Fest are representative of many of the safe(r) spaces policies that are instituted:

> We will not tolerate racism, sexism, transphobia, classism, ableism, homophobia or fatphobia.
>
> (Decolonise Fest 2017)

> FemRock has a safer spaces policy against sexism, racism, homophobia, biphobia, queerphobia, transphobia and ableism. Any instances of the above will not be tolerated and you may be asked to leave the event.
>
> (FemRock 2018)

Through doing this, the promoters note a range of potential forms of oppression that work to marginalize their attendees (predominantly punks of color at Decolonise Fest, and mostly [largely white] women at FemRock), and recognize that action is needed to ensure that punks of color or women who face multiple forms of marginalization feel welcome; it is an enactment of intersectional politics, in other words. Decolonise Fest, moreover, uses its policy to explicitly extend space to punks who may be marginalized in one or multiple of the ways outlined, while still centering their primary aims: "White allies are welcome but remember this event will focus on people of colour" (Decolonise Fest 2017), and FemRock says: "[W]e believe gigs are something everyone should enjoy, so we say grrrls to the front///accessible venues for all" (FemRock 2018).

However, safe(r) spaces policies do not always achieve what they aim for; the policy alone is not adequate. Indeed, the very existence of Decolonise Fest, and of the broader DIY Diaspora Punx collective that runs this annual event, is itself a reaction to an enduring hold of liberal (white) feminism over (white) feminist and queer punk scenes. While intersectionality is often discussed in queer and feminist punk spaces, the attempted enactment of intersectional politics does not always move beyond tokenism. There are still fewer opportunities for punks of color to perform or otherwise be involved in events than for white punks, and racist microaggressions (Sue 2010) are still common in white-dominated queer and feminist spaces. Nguyen wrote in 2012 of her fears that later generations of feminist punks had not learned from Riot Grrrl's racial failings, and we see that this continues to be the case.

With queer and feminist punk scenes, particularly those with a politics of challenging marginalization, there is an ongoing cycle of new scenes emerging in reaction to established scenes. This is evident with older "waves" of queercore and Riot Grrrl, contemporary queer and feminist scenes, and, most recently, scenes that focus on decolonization. Rather than a siloing of culture based on identity, however, these scenes often exist alongside each other, allowing a greater variety of opportunity for marginalized groups. Queer folks were rarely explicitly *excluded* from 1980s hardcore punk, but with queercore they could additionally have access to a scene where they had more safety and more supportive opportunity. Similarly, punks of color are welcome throughout queer and feminist scenes, but are also entitled to their own, safe(r) subcultural spaces.

Aesthetics of the Scenes

Contemporary queer and feminist punk scenes in the UK mesh a variety of aesthetic influences. Subcultural aesthetics are expressed in a range of formats, including the graphic design of posters, record sleeves, and logos; fanzines; art; poetry; and spoken word. This section will focus on two major aspects of aesthetic importance: music and clothing styles. Musically, the contemporary scene draws on a broad range of aesthetics, with bands playing in a wide variety of styles. While some events might have a (musical) genre-specific focus, as with Synth Punk Fest LDN 2017, the majority of all-day or weekend events held within the queer and feminist punk scenes take a broader approach, showcasing a variety of genres. Clothing styles vary from scene to scene, and can be influenced as much by musical subcultural identities as by subcultural communication of social identity categories such as "queer."

Musical Aesthetics

The original Riot Grrrl and queercore scenes were shaped by their proximity and reaction to broader contemporaneous American hardcore punk scenes. Queercore, initially a disparate group of international punk bands connected by their queerness through fanzines, encompassed a range of punk/post-punk/hardcore aesthetics. Toronto's queercore scene was more broadly connected around post-punk, whereas San Francisco's homocore scene was embedded in hardcore punk. Original Riot Grrrl bands often drew on punk and rock in their musical aesthetics. In the UK both queercore and Riot Grrrl were shaped by influences from their North American originators in addition to their relationship to wider UK indie scenes, as Julia Downes has noted: "In Britain, Riot Grrrl tended to draw more influence and inspiration from indie-pop music culture . . . [and] typically infused optimistic 1960s pop elements into a fun, colourful and childish aesthetic" (2012, 211).

Music remains a driving force for contemporary UK queer and feminist punk scenes, although, as with previous scenes, creative involvement also includes a far broader range of mediums, including zines, poetry/spoken word, art, and film. In line with other punk and DIY scenes, there is a strong emphasis on cultural participation, rather than passive consumption, as a means of attaining subcultural capital (Thornton 1995; Lohman 2017). Indeed, these scenes exist largely *in order to* provide the space, encouragement, and tools for anyone who wants to, to be able to create. The DIY ethos combines with an understanding that standards of musical proficiency are—even within punk—used as patriarchal gatekeeping, with female musicians held to a higher standard than male musicians (Moore 2007). Therefore, the *form* that the music (or other artistic endeavor) takes is often a secondary consideration to the fact of its creation. This increases the reliance on a DIY approach within these scenes, exhibited both in musical style and in scene "economics" (see "Economics of the Scenes" below).

This DIY style and approach is most prominently exhibited by groups such as First Timers, a London-based collective that organizes an annual program of workshops and jam sessions, culminating in a festival at which new bands play. First Timers is part of a lineage of other Riot Grrrl–inspired movements such as Rock/Rock 'n' Roll Camp for Girls, but with a broader focus for targeted identities (Dougher and Keenan 2012). The aim is to demystify music, help people form bands, and provide a supportive, first live performance experience. First Timers emphasizes first-time involvement, particularly for those with marginalized identities, specifically

> people who are disabled (visible or non-visible), LGBTQIA+ folk, people of colour, and women. As well, we are here to support people who have never played in a band before // never played the instrument they've always wanted to learn before because of their class, race, gender, mental health, etc.
>
> (First Timers Fest 2019)

Bands that form through First Timers may then receive bookings from the promoters of other queer and/or feminist events, which can lead to success beyond DIY scenes. For example, Big Joanie formed and played their first gig at First Timers 2013. They have performed regularly at many events within the UK's queer and feminist punk scenes, and at the time of writing receive regular national radio play on BBC Radio 6 and were featured by BBC Music Introducing at SXSW 2019, in the United States.

The kinds of music played within the UK's queer and/or feminist punk scenes can be varied. Events often feature a broad range of acts. For example, Decolonise Fest 2017 featured bands with labels such as grunge soul, psychedelic, post-punk, jazz, doom, no wave, and experimental folk. Bent Fest 2017 included wonk pop, lo-fi synth, Riot Grrrl, d-beat, shoegaze, and anarcho-noise. While DIY approaches skew toward the lack of polish associated with guitar-based punk, they can also lead to musical diversity (Dunn 2008). This is heightened when queer and feminist identity politics bring together people with a range of different musical tastes, experiences, and proficiencies.

The events that form focal points for the scenes are typically curated less in relation to the musical cohesiveness of the gig, and instead foreground the politics of inclusion, thus providing a platform for bands whose members have identities that are marginalized within broader punk, DIY, and indie music scenes. This is similar to the

UK's "trans music scene" of the early 2010s, which was a subset of broader queer and feminist punk scenes that focused on trans identities, where events might include punk, opera, rock, hip-hop, comedy, burlesque, and spoken word. In this context, the multiplicity of identities present in the scenes can be linked to the multiplicity of musical styles. The "deconstruction" of identity norms (in terms of gender in the trans music scene, but equally applicable to other identity categories in broader queer/feminist music), is replicated in the "deconstruction" of subcultural norms of event organization and musical form (Pearce and Lohman 2019).

Contemporary queer and feminist punk and DIY scenes are certainly inspired by all that went before, in both the UK and North America. The majority of bands coalesce around punk and/or indie styles, playing with hardcore, post-punk, and/or poppier influences. However, the scenes contain musical aesthetics that span a wider genre-spectrum, making it harder to pin down a specific musical aesthetic.

The Aesthetics of (Queer) Style

Aesthetic norms vary between different sections of the scenes, particularly in terms of style and clothing. Style provides an(other) opportunity to trace the influence of prior scenes, given there is some degree of normalization coalescing around particular stylistic markers. Given the importance and complexity of style and clothing to aspects of gender presentation (especially with regard to queer genders and/or queer sexualities), it is useful to address the more feminist- and queer-leaning aspects of the scenes separately, despite the overlaps that exist in terms of bands, artists, and attendees, in order to better understand differences as well as similarities between them.

Feminist punk scenes coalesce around events such as Loud Women, FemRock, and the Girl Gangs of North England, and include bands such as Dream Nails, Charmpit, Skinny Girl Diet, the Ethical Debating Society, and ILL. Aesthetically, these scenes tend towards a style that exhibits an unabashed, aggressive femininity. Most often this takes the form of more normatively feminine clothing for musicians and audiences alike (skirts and dresses, with color palettes often using pink, red, and purple), with subcultural flair added through (fitted) band T-shirts, Dr. Marten boots, and the use of especially bright or dark shades in makeup. Performers also occasionally play with some of the more sexualized imagery and styles of early punk, as well as the explicit subversions of Riot Grrrl (e.g., writing feminist messages on exposed parts of the body, such as arms, legs, breasts, and stomachs).

Stylistically, these *feminine* punk presentations overlap with *queer femme* punk presentations (which can also commonly be found in contemporary UK scenes). Queer femme styles have the political goal of "failure or refusal to approximate patriarchal norms of femininity that [reserve] this gender expression for the sole use of cisgender, female-bodied, white heterosexual and able-bodied women" (Blair and Hoskin 2015, 231). However, such a reading risks reinforcing a binary distinction between queer and straight feminine-presenting punks, imbuing political agency only to the queers.

Instead, and in line with a contemporary broadening of understandings of femme identity beyond white, cisgender lesbians, we can similarly see how feminine punk presentations can operate as a subcultural, political, feminist intervention that resists culturally sanctioned gender norms (Blair and Hoskin, 2015). This is a femininity intended not for the male gaze, but rather for a predominantly feminist, female, subcultural gaze.

The aesthetics of queer punk scenes is a complex arena, tied to specific cultural and individual aspects of gender presentation and sexuality presentation, in which the gendered nature of a person's clothing may or may not directly communicate something about their gender and/or sexuality (or, indeed, the absence of either of these things). It is important to note that cisgender gay and bisexual men are in a minority within these scenes. Instead, the queer punks are predominantly lesbian and bisexual cisgender women—plus trans men, trans women, and nonbinary individuals who may or may not also identify as queer regarding their sexuality.

Norms of cisgender lesbian identity and presentation have shifted significantly since the mid-twentieth century, when a butch/femme dichotomy predominated within many—particularly working-class—Anglophone contexts (Feinberg 1993; Kennedy and Davis 2014; Rothblum 2010). This dichotomy seemingly stemmed from an inter-reliance between butches and femmes and an assumption that they only formed relationships with one another in a "mimicking" of heterosexual relationships, although experiences were more nuanced than this stereotype would suggest (Rifkin 2002). Contemporary lesbian identities and presentations are far more nebulous, with a broader spectrum of gender presentation being possible; moreover, there is more possibility of fluidity between "points" on the presentation continuum (Walker et al 2012; Mackay 2019). There is also a shift toward the recognition of gendered presentation being an expression of an individual identity rather than linked to one's partner (Blair and Hoskin 2015). However, within the UK's queer punk scenes, there are far more punks who present in butch-leaning and/or masculine-of-center styles, with styles commonly understood as "androgynous" typically coded as masculine. These queer punk styles are particularly influenced by hardcore punk, with (baggy) band T-shirts; denim, leather, or pleather jackets or vests often covered with band patches; Doc Martens; and a "color" palette dominated by black.

Trans attendees within queer punk scenes are similarly predominantly transmasculine (trans men and/or transmasculine nonbinary people), rather than transfeminine (trans women and/or transfeminine nonbinary people). This echoes a long history of marginalization for transfeminine people within Riot Grrrl (Pearce 2012), as well as within punk more generally (Namaste 2000). In this way, these queer punk scenes also propagate wider homonormative (and indeed, heteronormative) cultural norms in which masculinities are privileged and femininities pushed aside (Levitt et al. 2003; Serano 2007; Blair and Hoskin 2015). As previously described, more feminist-leaning events consciously provide space for women and femininity, sometimes explicitly stating that this includes trans women. However, they tend also to be cisnormative, providing a less welcoming space for transfeminine people to enter. As a consequence, transfeminine people remain underrepresented despite the intersectional political approaches common across these queer *and* feminist punk scenes.

Economics of the Scenes

The intersection of DIY, punk, indie, and feminist influences in queer and feminist punk scenes makes for an approach to subcultural economics that is wrought with tension. The DIY politics of punk, especially when filtered through years of anarcho-punk and hardcore organizing, can result in particularly strict dictums regarding the importance of doing everything "yourself"—from learning instruments, to putting on shows, to releasing records. This approach also comes with a strong anti-capitalist emphasis, in which money and economics are "bad," profit-making is particularly heinous (and loss-making acceptable), and those who "sell out" are no longer part of the scene (O'Hara 1999; Carella and Wymer 2019). These politics can be unworkable for many bands, unless they are able to rely on already having access to a degree of economic capital that can be "lost" to the scene; that is, enough money to pay for their own fuel or public transport, practice room hire, and recording costs that often will not be recouped. Subcultural activity can never be a wholly distinct world, and therefore requires some interaction with the capitalist system. This is especially the case today in the neoliberal Global North, where widespread attacks on squatting and alternative lifestyles mean that "living outside the system" has become increasingly difficult (Lohman, 2017).

Consequently, the politics of DIY scenes often rely on privilege and are less accessible to already marginalized people. Taking an "active" role in a subculture requires time to be spent on leisure and creative activities, away from the pressures of work and/or caring responsibilities (Bennet and Hodkinson 2012). Within Riot Grrrl circles of the 1990s, there was an awareness of and feminist challenge to how male-dominated hardcore punk operated to privilege those with existing financial means. This was particularly acute where the majority of shows were fundraisers, at which it was expected that bands and artists would not recoup their costs for performing in order to maximize charitable donations. Riot Grrrl events were still often fundraisers, but ensured that bands be reimbursed for their performances (Marcus 2010).

Contemporary queer and feminist punk scenes include people with various economic worldviews and politics. There are certainly anti-capitalist and anarchist punks who organize in line with hardcore punk norms, with a preference for anti-profit DIY models. These influences in the scenes are solidified through the regular hosting of events in anarchist spaces such as the Cowley Club in Brighton, and Wharf Chambers (previously The Common Place) in Leeds. Others involved with queer and feminist scenes call for the fair payment of artists, creatives, and those working to support the scene. These demands usually are argued from a position that, in following the logic of queer and feminist practices of inclusion, scenes should recognize and work against the exclusionary effects of economic marginalization. The argument follows that by holding to particular (patriarchal) approaches to putting anti-capitalist ideals into practice, the scene further exploits these individuals by relying on their time and free labor. Moreover, by providing payment for work within scenes, it provides "safety" from having to seek work outside the scenes in order to support living costs.

There are tensions around implementing the economics of feminist and queer politics within these scenes, with social media often operating as a battleground for "debate." However, there are also commonalities in how radical economic justice is sought at events. For example, entrance fees are usually held as low as possible, with many promoters offering "pay what you can" or free entry to those who otherwise can't afford it, operating on the basis of trust. Benefit shows and fundraisers are still key to the scene. For example, Loud Women shows raise money for women's charities, and multiple events have been held to support the Solidarity Not Silence campaign, raising legal costs for a group of women to "defend themselves against defamation claim made by [a] man in [the] music industry for statements that they made concerning his treatment of women" (Solidarity Not Silence, n.d.).

Contemporary queer and feminist punk scenes therefore continue in a long lineage of punk economics that practice DIY organizing, fundraising, and anti-capitalism. However, their approach is interwoven with feminist- and queer-influenced notions of economic justice that critique patriarchal anti-capitalist punk movements without necessarily forming a clear conclusion of how best to operationalize these politics.

Conclusion

This chapter has illustrated the many ways in which contemporary queer and/or feminist punk scenes in the UK are part of a long punk lineage, including important transatlantic influences. The focus on the politics of inclusion, of aesthetics, and of economics has been central to punk organizing practices throughout, but these aspects are particularly key to the trajectory of punk by and for queer people, and/or punk by and for women. This chapter has illustrated how queer and feminist punk scenes are an attempt to turn political ideology into political action through the medium of punk. Punk has always been about creating a space for the marginalized; we see here how the details of this have changed over time as more groups demand inclusion in punk, and create punk scenes that value and welcome, rather than exclude, them. No scene that aims for inclusion and diversity has been entirely successful on these terms, but with each new development, nuanced critiques of previous "failures" push the evolution of punk towards something better.

References

Ablaze!, K. 2012. *The City Is Ablaze! The Story of a Post-punk Popzine 1984–1994*. Leeds, UK: Mittens On.

Bennett, A., and P. Hodkinson. 2012. *Ageing and Youth Cultures*. London: Berg.

Blair, K. L., and R. A. Hoskin. 2015. "Experiences of Femme Identity: Coming Out, Invisibility and Femmephobia." *Psychology & Sexuality* 6, no. 3: 229–244.

Brown, G. 2007. "Mutinous Eruptions: Autonomous Spaces of Radical Queer Activism." *Environment and Planning A: Economy and Space* 39, no. 11: 2685–2698.

Brownstein, C. 2015. *Hunger Makes Me a Modern Girl: A Memoir*. London: Virago.

Carella, K., and K. Wymer. 2019. "'You Want Me to Surrender My Identity?': Laura Jane Grace, Transition, and Selling Out." *Punk & Post-Punk* 8, no. 2: 193–207.

Charles, N., and K. Wadia. 2018. "New British Feminisms, UK Feminista and Young Women's Activism." *Feminist Theory* 19, no. 2: 165–181.

Clark, D. 2003. "The Death and Life of Punk, the Last Subculture." In *The Postsubcultures Reader*, edited by D. Muggleton and R. Weinzierl, 223–236. Oxford: Berg.

Collins, P. H. 1991. *Black Feminist Thought: Knowledge, Consciousness, and the Politics of Empowerment*. 2nd ed. New York: Routledge, 2000.

Crenshaw, K. 1991. "Mapping the Margins: Intersectionality, Identity Politics, and Violence against Women of Color." *Stanford Law Review* 43, no. 6: 1241–1299.

Davis, A. Y. 1983. *Women, Race, and Class*. New York: Vintage, 2011.

DeChaine, D. R. 1997. "Mapping Subversion: Queercore Music's Playful Discourse of Resistance." *Popular Music & Society* 21, no. 4: 7–37.

Decolonise Fest. 2017. *Facebook: Decolonise Fest 2017*. https://www.facebook.com/events/129571150913030.

Dougher, S., and E. K. Keenan. 2012. "Riot Grrrl, Ladyfest and Rock Camps for Girls." In *Women Make Noise: Girl Bands from Motown to the Modern*, edited by J. Downes, 259–291. Twickenham, UK: Supernova.

Downes, J. 2009. "DIY Queer Feminist (Sub)cultural Resistance in the UK." PhD diss., University of Leeds.

Downes, J. 2012. "The Expansion of Punk Rock: Riot Grrrl Challenges to Gender Power Relations in British Indie Music Subcultures." *Women's Studies* 41, no. 2: 204–237.

Dunn, K. C. 2008. "Never Mind the Bollocks: The Punk Rock Politics of Global Communication." *Review of International Studies*, 34, no. S1: 193–210.

Dunn, K. C. 2016. *Global Punk: Resistance and Rebellion in Everyday Life*. New York: Bloomsbury.

Ensminger, D. 2010. "Redefining the Body Electric: Queering Punk and Hardcore." *Journal of Popular Music Studies* 22, no. 1: 50–67.

Evans, S. M. 1979. *Personal Politics: The Roots of Women's Liberation in the Civil Rights Movement and the New Left*. New York: Alfred A. Knopf.

Feinberg, L. 1993. *Stone Butch Blues: A Novel*. Los Angeles: Alyson Books, 2003.

FemRock. 2018. *Facebook: FemRock Fest 2018*. https://www.facebook.com/events/166128007417505.

Fenster, M. 1993. "Queer Punk Fanzines: Identity, Community, and the Articulation of Homosexuality and Hardcore." *Journal of Communication Inquiry* 17, no. 1: 73–94.

First Timers Fest. 2019. "DIY Space for London." https://diyspaceforlondon.org/first-timers-fest-2019/.

Griffin, N. 2012. "Gendered Performance Performing Gender in the DIY Punk and Hardcore Music Scene." *Journal of International Women's Studies* 13, no. 2: 66–81.

Jennings, T. 1988. "What the Fuck is HOMOCORE?" *Homocore* 1.

Jones, G. B., and B. LaBruce. 1989. "Don't Be Gay or, How I Learned to Stop Worrying and Fuck Punk in the Ass." *Maximumrocknroll* 69: 27.

Kennedy, E. L., and M. D. Davis 2014. *Boots of Leather, Slippers of Gold: The History of a Lesbian Community*. New York: Routledge.

Leblanc, L. 1999. *Pretty in Punk: Girls' Gender Resistance in a Boys' Subculture*. New Brunswick, NJ: Rutgers University Press.

Levitt, H. M., E. A. Gerrish, and K. R. Hiestand. 2003. "The Misunderstood Gender: A Model of Modern Femme Identity." *Sex Roles* 48, no. 3–4: 99–113.

Lohman, K. 2017. *The Connected Lives of Dutch Punks: Contesting Subcultural Boundaries*. Basingstoke, UK: Palgrave Macmillan.

Lohman, K., and R. Pearce. 2020. "Queering Community Development in DIY Punk Spaces." In *Arts, Culture and Community Development*, edited by R. Meade and M. Shaw. Bristol, UK: Policy Press.

Mackay, F. 2019. "No Woman's Land? Revisiting Border Zone Denizens." *Journal of Lesbian Studies* 23, no. 3: 397–409. doi:10.1080/10894160.2019.1565521.

Marcus, S. 2010. *Girls to the Front: The True Story of the Riot Grrrl Revolution*. New York: Harper.

Moore, R. 2007. "Friends Don't Let Friends Listen to Corporate Rock: Punk as a Field of Cultural Production." *Journal of Contemporary Ethnography* 36, no. 4: 438–474.

Namaste, V. 2000. *Invisible Lives: The Erasure of Transsexual and Transgendered People*. Chicago: University of Chicago Press.

Nault, C. 2017. *Queercore: Queer Punk Media Subculture*. New York: Routledge.

Nguyen, M. T. 2012. "Riot Grrrl, Race, and Revival." *Women & Performance: A Journal of Feminist Theory* 22, no. 2–3: 173–196.

O'Brien, L. 2012. *She Bop: The Definitive History of Women in Rock, Pop and Soul*. 3rd ed. London: Jawbone.

O'Hara, C. 1999. *The Philosophy of Punk: More Than Noise!* Edinburgh: AK Press.

O'Shea, S. 2014. "Embracing Difference in Feminist Music Worlds: A Ladyfest Case Study." In *Social Networks and Music Worlds*, edited by N. Crossley, S. McAndrew, and P. Widdop, 146–168. New York: Routledge.

Pearce, R. 2012. *Trans Grrrl Riot, Part 1: Was Riot Grrrl Transphobic?* https://ruthpearce.net/2012/08/22/trans-grrrl-riot-part-1-was-riot-grrrl-transphobic/.

Pearce, R., and K. Lohman. 2019. "De/constructing DIY Identities in a Trans Music Scene." *Sexualities* 22, no. 1–2: 97–113.

Pearce, R., D. L. Steinberg, and I. Moon. 2019. "Introduction: The Emergence of 'Trans.'" *Sexualities* 22, no. 1–2: 3–12.

Reddington, H. 2012. *The Lost Women of Rock Music: Female Musicians of the Punk Era*. 2nd ed. Bristol, UK: Equinox.

Rifkin, L. 2002. "The Suit Suits Whom?" *Journal of Lesbian Studies* 6, no. 2: 157–174.

Riot Grrrl Manifesto. 1991. *Bikini Kill* 2.

Rothblum, E. D. 2010. "The Complexity of Butch and Femme among Sexual Minority Women in the 21st Century." *Psychology of Sexualities Review* 1, no. 1: 29–42.

Schilt, K. 2003. "'A Little Too Ironic': The Appropriation and Packaging of Riot Grrrl Politics by Mainstream Female Musicians." *Popular Music & Society* 26, no. 1: 5–16.

Schilt, K. 2004. "'Riot Grrrl Is . . .': Contestation over Meaning in a Music Scene." In *Music Scenes: Local, Translocal and Virtual*, edited by A. Bennett and R.A. Peterson, 115–130. Nashville, TN: Vanderbilt University Press.

Schilt, K., and E. Zobl. 2008. "Connecting the Dots: Riot Grrrls, Ladyfests, and the International Grrrl Zine Network." In *New Wave Cultures: Feminism, Subcultures, Activism*, edited by A. Harris, 39–56. London: Routledge.

Serano, J. 2007. *Whipping Girl: A Transsexual Woman on Sexism and the Scapegoating of Femininity*. New York: Seal.

Solidarity Not Silence. n.d. "Women Facing Defamation Case for Speaking Up." Crowd Justice. https://www.crowdjustice.com/case/solidaritynotsilence/.

Spencer, A. 2008. *DIY: The Rise of Lo-Fi Culture*. London: Marion Boyars.

Sue, D. W. 2010. *Microaggressions in Everyday Life: Race, Gender, and Sexual Orientation*. Hoboken, NJ: John Wiley.

Thornton, S. 1995. *Club Cultures: Music, Media and Subcultural Capital*. Cambridge: Polity.

Wald, G., and J. Gottlieb. 1993. "Smells Like Teen Spirit: Riot Grrrls, Revolution, and Women in Independent Rock." *Critical Matrix* 7, no. 2: 11.

Walker, J. J., S. A. Golub, D. S. Bimbi, and J. T. Parsons. 2012. "Butch Bottom–Femme Top? An Exploration of Lesbian Stereotypes." *Journal of Lesbian Studies* 16, no. 1: 90–107.

Wilkinson, D. 2015. "Ever Fallen in Love (with Someone You Shouldn't Have?): Punk, Politics and Same-Sex Passion." *Keywords* 13: 57–76.

Worley, M. 2017. *No Future: Punk, Politics and British Youth Culture, 1976–1984*. Cambridge: Cambridge University Press.

PART THREE

IDENTITY IS THE CRISIS, CAN'T YOU SEE

CHAPTER 11

"DON'T BE AFRAID TO POGO"

Latinx Punk in LA

MARLÉN RÍOS-HERNÁNDEZ

At the 2018 Women of Rock Oral History Project launch party in Los Angeles, a panel of luminary punk-identified women were invited to perform and share their experiences being musicians in the rock genre. Alice Bag, one of the queer Chicana pillars of the early Hollywood punk scene from the late 1970s and front woman of the Bags, noticed a person weaving in and out of an audience comprising mostly of people of color and femmes, trying to get others to join them in a pit—that is, pushing one another in and out of a centrally located spot, usually in a violent, circular manner. Some fans pushed back, but most refused to comply, bothered by the forced invitation to pit. Since there was little momentum to start a mosh pit, Alice spoke into the microphone and encouraged the audience to pogo rather than pit. She demonstrated by explaining to the audience how the pogo—simply jumping up and down in place—was a type of dance her generation of punks would dance at shows. While the crowd got excited enough to try pogoing, I noticed the ease with which the audience slipped into trying to jump up and down. Bobbing heads in the dark morphed into a vertically jumping crowd of over thirty people pogoing in a collective effort to release the pressure valve that is their desire to dance to Bag's classics without having to pit.

The pogo's brief revival that night at the WOR launch party indicated the way that this dance can accomplish what institutional archives cannot: recreate moments and memories of belonging, in this case, for punks of color, women, and femmes within punk spaces in the absence of representation. While the pogo is largely attributed to the UK punk scene of the mid- to late 1970s, it serves this article as a loose starting point in the story of both the mosh pit and its role in the whitening of punk. The changed nature of punk can be seen through the pogo because that dance had a different valence, a more lighthearted and inclusive feeling. As acclaimed Chicana journalist Michelle T., thirty-three, from the 1990s Bay area scene, put it:

[The pogo] is a goofy move much in the same way like the running man . . . I think that having fun in punk has been kind of taboo for a really long time, like you're less serious if you express joy at a punk show . . . so like, punk has become less joyous . . . but we got into it because it was fucking fun. So if you pogo it's the acceptance that you look like an idiot. Like you do not pogo thinking you look cool. When you pogo, you have fully leaned into what a juvenile you are and goofball, right? You've leaned into the fool. And so the whole thing is, it's kind of like, I don't think punk embraces the fool anymore. And to us, punk fools are literally, you know, they're outdated people.[1]

Here, Michelle creates a new way to think about the genealogies of punk social dancing that for once addresses the unequivocal complexity of experiencing joy while being a woman of color in any punk scene. The outdated "fool" she is proposing, who is entangled with the pogo, is also a blunt gesture toward the gendered discrimination within punk dancing in which there is the pit, the masculine dance, with the pogo doubling as "the other," or the fool. There is an inclusive sentiment to the pogo that the pit lacks. Alice Bag's call to pogo during her set demonstrates precisely what Diana Taylor, in *The Archive and the Repertoire*, calls "cultural memory." Taylor explains that cultural memory is

a practice, an act of imagination and interconnection. The intermediary begins to imagine her heart—her memory. Memory is embodied and sensual, that is, conjured through the senses; it links the deeply private with social, even official, practices. Sometimes memory is difficult to evoke, yet it's highly efficient; it's always operating in conjunction with other memories . . . memory, like the heart, beats beyond our capacity to control it, a lifeline between past and future.

(Taylor 2003, 82)

Taylor's notion of cultural memory as a conjuring of the body's senses was exactly how some of the punks I spoke to for this project best explained how they remembered their punk scenes. For instance, Alex, forty, an artist, K-12 teacher, immigrant, and advocate/activist from the late 90s Berkeley/LA scene, cued up Fugazi's seminal song "Waiting Room"[2] to communicate her "frustration as a Guatemalan diaspora undocumented person and the frustration of watching all my peers move forward—go to college—while I remained in the 'waiting room' awaiting my legal status to change."[3] Alex's intimate connection to "Waiting Room," and its iconic opening lyrics aligns with the ways that other *punkera* women who spoke with me invoked challenging memories growing up punk by relying on their favorite aspects of punk rock, albeit a song, show, or a dance.

> I am a patient boy
> I wait, I wait, I wait, I wait
> My time is like water down a drain
> Everybody's moving, everybody's moving,
> Everybody's moving, moving, moving, moving
> Please don't leave me to remain[4]

Some women, during their *charlas* (chats), would raise their elbows in pitting-like fashion, forming their bodies in the shape of a "T," or sing bits and pieces of their favorite songs long archived in their throats, arms, and torsos, as a way to translate their memories from youth to help transport us to an event or show one was not present for. The consistent movement enacted during the *testimonios* as a tool of memory recovery included raising of elbows, gestures of pushing or shoving, or flipping off—all conclusive evidence that punk social dancing is not tethered to white male aggressive expressions within the mosh pit, but rather a deeper DIY negotiation of women's place and agency. These *testimonios* show how Latina and Chicana punks have made do with the dances they inherit, the white punk histories they both love and hate, and how they see the pit and how make it their own.

Clearly the pit and the pogo are bodily expressions of cultural memory, but a more pressing question this article grapples with is this: When and how did punk become white? Does the story of the mosh pit have anything to do with punk's whitening?

Utilizing what I call "intellectual dumpster diving," this article makes use of obsolete or unlikely ephemeral objects of memory recovery as intellectual archives. By sorting through *testimonio* and *charlas*[5] from Chicana and Latina[6] punks and early punk films predating 1979, when the pogo was still popular and widely performed at punk shows, I highlight a visual trajectory of the pogo's residency and expulsion within punk. I then recycle "The Slam" or the "Orange County Strut," utilizing the documentary *Another State of Mind* (1984), to help show the progression from the pogo to the slam and the racial, classed, and gendered divide with the arrival of hardcore, likening it to the process of gentrification. Finally, I locate in the debris from the tragic events of Woodstock '99, *the* event that completely rewrote punk culture and pitting as a patriarchal "men's only" space and dance. By gathering a mix of intergenerational *charlas* by *punkera* women and femmes on their thoughts and experiences with the mosh pit, and placing them alongside Taylor's "cultural memory," I piece together how the pogo is not only the mosh pit's queer predecessor, but also the missing link to help explain why punk continues to be seen as reserved for white people.

Exploring the history of the mosh pit offers a window into an alternative genealogy of punk historiography by way of its long-forgotten ties to the pogo. I argue that the erasure of the Los Angeles "punk of color" scene and queer Chicanx/Latinx/black youth from punk history can be mapped through the story of when and how the pogo was replaced by slamming and later the mosh pit. I position the Los Angeles punk scene of the late 1970s and early 1980s as a prime example of how the experiences of punk youth were deeply shaped by the conditions of possibility the pogo offered, creating a completely different scene than the ones more popularly archived as white, male, and devoid of queer people of color and women.

To be clear, it is not my intention to claim that all punk before 1980 was absent of racism, classism, homophobia, and sexism. Nor do I suggest that the arrival of punk from the beach cities in Southern California rejected any artistic collaboration between local punk scenes, as evidenced by some key texts mapping the history of early So Cal punk.

Influential texts such as *We Got the Neutron Bomb: The Untold Story of L.A. Punk*, *Under the Big Black Sun: A Personal History of L.A. Punk*, *Kids of the Black Hole: Punk Rock Postsuburban California*, and *Forming: The Early Days of L.A. Punk*, along with the many memoirs, autobiographies, and photo essays by early LA punk icons, all clearly tell the story of early LA punk as a complex site of youth counterculture. I regard this article as an homage to the early days of So Cal punk and a challenge to the overall lack of representation of punks that are of color, LGBTQIA+, and female-identifying within mainstream punk history. But the story of the mosh pit, while inculcated in punk culture as having been permanently present in punk, also needs dire revision from a queer Chicana feminist perspective.

Pogoing, the predecessor to moshing, is a physical dance consisting of jumping up and down with varying degrees of contact, usually danced by participants across a venue space. The pogo was a common form of punk dancing in the earlier days of punk and can be seen more prominently in *The Punk Rock Movie* (1980), *The Great Rock 'n' Roll Swindle* (1980), and the faux biography *Sid and Nancy* (1986). While these films were released in the early 1980s, much later then the scene's peak in the UK, they encapsulate how UK punk origins, including aspects of the pogo, have been viewed ironically. These films all depict the pogo as a series of transgressive movements layered with jumping up, down, and side to side, in a sea of colorful clothing, dramatic makeup, and spitting. In Don Letts's *The Punk Rock Movie* (1980), a film documenting a series of punk performances at the Roxy Club in 1977 during the UK punk scene, the pogo is introduced within the first three minutes, as it captures two English punk youth pogoing or skanking. One of them, a young woman, is seen skanking by herself in the same area that will later evolve into "the pit"—i.e., the front center of the stage. Dubbed over with the Clash's song "White Riot," this short scene of the young woman dancing alone and unabashedly exposing her breasts is proof of the once different positionality women could have at the front of the stage, long before Bikini Kill's call for "girls to the front." What is under the young woman's shirt for the viewer to see, and for the camera to record, replaces her V-sign without using her fingers: she opens her shirt over and over again as a crude gesture of outright punk femininity. For a brief moment, there is a type of feminine agency that has disappeared from the modern-day mosh pit. Quickly thereafter, two males interrupt her dancing by groping and molesting her, forcing her down to the ground. This occurs in the same space where the mosh pit eventually is born and eerily foreshadows the sexual assault cases and violent attacks against women at Woodstock '99, as this article will explore later.

A similar scene is enacted in Alex Cox's *Sid and Nancy* (1986), a film reimaging the tumultuous romantic relationship between Sex Pistols' bassist Sid Vicious and Philadelphia-born punk fan Nancy Spungen. While the film was released well after the peak of the UK scene, Sid and Nancy, as they are affectionately remembered, embody two of the most archived punk scenes in mainstream punk history—the UK and New York punk scenes. In *Sid and Nancy*, the pogo is shown in a variety of moments; however, it is during the Sex Pistols' Thames Riverboat show in 1977 that the pogo is particularly striking. During the Sex Pistols' performance of "Anarchy in the UK," a pregnant punk woman is seen in the pit area dancing amid pogoing punks on the boat. While the original footage of the Thames Riverboat show is different from the film's adaptation, which has been heavily critiqued by Sex Pistols' frontman John Lydon, who called the entire film "sadly sickeningly depressing" (Lydon, n.d.), the portrayal of the pogo, with a concert crowd pushing into each other and including the pregnant woman's participation, is still a filmed representation of women being central to punk dancing and what it may have been like to be a woman in a "mosh pit" before it was called such. It provides an image for punks of later generations to discover the Sex Pistols, and to a lesser extent to explore what happened to the pogo, at a time when there is no clear indication of the mosh pit anywhere. Each of these scenes foreshadows an exclusionary mosh pit.

"We Don't Need the English!"

At a Halloween party and backyard show in 2018, I watched a cover band performing a variety of iconic hardcore hits from Tony Hawk's *Pro Skater* video games—a series of video games that mostly my male friends and loved ones growing up mark as the game that introduced them to punk. Unlike my male friends, I did not grow up with Tony Hawk's *Pro Skater*, since that was strictly assigned as a boy's pastime and access to MTV was an upper-middle-class luxury I did not have until I arrived to college. But I had been regularly exposed growing up to elder women in Mexico in their *salas* dancing the night away to Los Hooligans and other bands from the golden era of *rocanrol*, where I pressed play on a CD player and I watched them do the vintage footwork of past eras. I had never seen older women's hips sway with arms extended out and jumping in place. Their circular thudding in the middle of a living room in my father's hometown in Hidalgo, Mexico, still remains, for me, the earliest incarnation of experiencing women being not only at the front, but also at the center, of the dance floor.

In truth, the act of jumping up and down is quite universal to just about any social dance across time. From the pogo, the slam, and finally the mosh pit, the attempt to draw out one single origin of the pogo proves to be messy at best. According to the writer Joshua Glenn (2011), *A Hard Day's Night* (1964), the mockumentary following the Beatles on a local tour in London, features the first images of the pogo as danced by Beatles fans. Ringo Starr is attending a party in which he is filmed dancing go-go style following an encounter with another male party attendee where both are see jumping up and down together. What is clearly a friendly poke at Ringo Starr's shorter height alongside a much taller dancer, Glenn maintains that the pogo was first invented in that moment, and this particular origin story is later reproduced over and over again, situating the UK at the epicenter of punk's creation.

But this is a version that is at best contingent on perspective. In her speech at the 2019 UCR Punk Conference, Alice Bag had this to say about the Bags' song and conference theme "We Don't Need the English!":

It really talking about a reaction to a magazine article where an English band dissed the L.A. scene and said that we were copying the English scene and just yesterday I was did an interview for *Remezcla* where the interviewer started asking me about all these male white bands and I said you know, I appreciate that those bands exist that they contribute as well but we have to take it back and acknowledge where they gathered their influences cos a lot of times, as Uhuru [member of Fuck U Pay US] said, they want you to claim the rhythm but not the blues. They want to take our influences or they do take our influences and if you ask these British rockers what they were listening to our music and by our music—I mean all our music. I don't mean one specific kind because all of our roots are there... it's a complex quilt. American music is not just one language and it is not just one style and for us to come back and find ourselves as punks through this Eurocentric lens really does a disservice to ourselves when we compare ourselves to British rockers or even white male rockers that's not who we are. (Bag 2019)

As Alice implied, when you change the perspective, the origin of the pogo can be found far away from the well-preserved archive of the Sex Pistols, and by turning to the music of my parent's generation, I found an alternative origin story in the Global South in Los Rockin Devil's, an early *rocanrol* group in Mexico in the 1960s, and their performance of "Es Lupe"[7] for a popular television program called "Discoteca Ofreon A Go-Go" (COMROCK85 2010). In this televised performance, Los Rockin Devil's are accompanied by a variety of backup dancers, including lead vocalist Blanca Estrada, wearing a knee-length A-line dress. The camera shifts to focus on a dark-skinned woman—a stark contrast to the overwhelming presence of white passing women—who dances in the "jerk" fashion. During this scene, the jerk turns into a nascent pogo via the two women dancing to stage right. One dancer of color specifically moves with more power in her form than the other white-passing dancer. Both are in fact representative of how Mexican youth are *supposed* to behave, in that their tightly structured form of arm and leg movements mimicking "the jerk" reveal a clean-cut and perhaps heterosexual version of the famous go-go dance, by way of the women individually and away from each other. Therefore, the featured dancers and the accompanying lead vocalist Francisco "Frankie" Estrada, who are socially permitted to jump up and down, provide cues that such behavior for 1960s Mexico is allowed for the oversexualized backup dancing body and the masculine lead.

By contrast, the dancing of the ideal Mexican woman of the 1960s, embodied by Blanca's rigid movements and subtle footwork, reveals the gendered and racialized pressures women had to face and negotiate within *rocanrol*. In some ways, it is no surprise that the pogo emerges here, amid the political and sexually repressive practices of the Mexican government onto *rocanrol*, for this very early version of the pogo offered the spontaneity of movement that is off-beat, syncopated, sexual, and very feminine. Just a few years before the infamous Tlaltelolco Massacre of 1968, where hundreds of unarmed students and community members were shot by Mexican armed forces, the pogo appears in the midst of a rising counterculture from the rebellious hips of young women in Mexico, via their creative take on "the jerk." "Es Lupe" shows how the jerk is necessarily sanitized for *rocanrol* in Mexico, just as the dance was sanitized and controlled after leaving black dance halls for white suburban America. The UK narrative, in which the pogo begins with the Beatles, leaves out such narratives.

Another instance in which the pogo exits the confines of the UK was in 1964 with Peru's Los Saicos. In 1964 Los Saicos released *Demolición*, which is credited by many punk historians, including Legs McNeil in a NOISEY documentary dedicated to Los Saicos, to have "invented punk rock" (NOISEY 2019). While there is virtually no filmed footage of Los Saicos live during their prime, footage of their brief tour in Latin America in 2003 demonstrates an audience pogoing through the entire song, as if performing a bodily form of cultural memory en masse for fans of Los Saicos long after their early careers (LimaPerú.TV 2013). During their performance of "Demolición," the pogo takes off in full swing, fueled by the electricity of the audience ready for the famous gritty yells by front man, Erwin Flores. The lone "YA YA YA YA YA YA!" sparks the crowd to jump up and down, and the accustomed opening of a pit is hardly noticeable.

White Punk as Property

These two indicators that the pogo was by no means restricted to Europe is just one more example of the erasure of POC punk participation in a long line of historically casting out punks of color from their own movements. In fact, the way that the role of non-European, black and brown punks has been pushed out of the history of punk can be likened to the process of gentrification, which is most often perceived as a relatively quiet process where changes to an entire landscape are made against the demands of the community being affected. *Gentrification* usually refers to raced and classed processes affecting the housing market, but it is an apt metaphor for what occurred in Los Angeles punk culture in the early 1980s due to venue closures, over-policing in the backyard scenes, and the takeover of hardcore in the 1980s, which overshadowed the more avantgarde and more artistically driven style of punk from before. Punk's ability to build space, to make *space* for itself, only to be subject to its own inevitable evacuation vis-a-vis its whitening *is* the gentrification process in microcosm. And it continues to plague punk even today.

Commodity consumption is one of the major factors that drive gentrification to help mask the economic duress communities of color are victimized by and the wealthy are beneficiaries of. Yet, in *There Goes the 'Hood: Views of Gentrification from the Ground Up*, Lance Freeman (2006, 3) reminds readers how depictions of gentrification as revenge on the underclass center the process as the leading star in the story of how a neighborhood is gentrified, when the stories of the residents must also take precedent. Freeman's call to consider the nuances of gentrification from the viewpoints of the people affected is what drives my idea that sound and dance have the capacity to change an entire subculture for the good, the bad, and the in-between.

Beyond the physical demolition or reinvestment into property, the threat and aftermath of gentrification also affects subversive soundscapes birthed from within affected communities, particularly queer, black, brown, immigrant, and additional POC working-class Angelinos during the late 1970s and early 1980s, as we see with the erasure of the pogo.

The term *gentrification* in this article refers to the process of bodily displacement by way of erasing culturally expressive forms such as dance, and the replacement of said forms with other types of dance and sound reserved for mainstream audiences, now stripped of feminist and queer political thought. Broader than a dance, the pogo signified a particular relationship between sound, community, and a sense of belonging—a *home* for the outsiders and their bands of misfit friends, and one that created space for queer Chicanx/Latinx/POC youth of color later forced to reckon with a new wave of punks wearing Swastika patches that served as eviction notices on their sleeves. The story of the pogo thus encompasses a brief window into the ways punks of color utilized the pogo to participate in punk in order to create space as a punk before 1980–1981. The band X said it best on an interview with NPR's *Fresh Air*, when singer Exene Cervenka explained how the pit formed following a trajectory of spontaneous punk dancing, which included the pogo, that blurred the lines between audience and performer, particularly during a time where punk was not yet under the scrutiny or rubric of what it meant to be "punk" (Doe et al. 2016). Delinking gentrification as exclusively spatial to include an analysis of space, social dance, and sound can help us understand how public access to the arts and music-making can be quickly demolished and replaced with new forms of expressive art doubling as modern-day eviction notices.

The eviction of the pogo reveals yet another gentrifying force that is not reduced to physical demolition but rather the palpable vibrational form of sound and dance—the mosh pit and early hardcore. Here, gentrification is not only sonic but very much racialized by way of who embraced the pogo during the early days of the Hollywood scene. When hardcore arrived in LA in the 1980s, former styles of punk were altered to conform to classed, gendered, and racialized standards of taste for white men—a process that included ridding itself of the pogo, via first the "slam" dance, and later the mosh pit. The slam, or "slamming," produced a new wave of punks that could consume punk, be punk, and expel punks before them who did not conform to the rubrics set by the music industry of the time, which was where many youth in the 1980s in Southern California learned to emulate punk culture.

Over time, value was grafted onto white punk narratives and historiography, and this only furthered access to punk by bourgeois white youth, especially by the early 2000s during the "Punk Renaissance." Eventually, the world was inundated with punk histories that removed the contribution of femmes, queers, and people of color (POC) within punk and hardcore. For instance, James Meredino's *SLC Punk!* (1998), a film my close group of mostly femme and gay friends in the mid- to early 2000s credited as having introduced them to punk culture far more than *Pro Skater* and *Decline of Western Civilization* (1981), tells the story of a group of white gutter or street punks in Salt Lake City in the early 1980s. But the fictional bourgeois punks in *SLC* defined punk as a temporal choice—a shorthand strategy to rebel against your (rich) parents by pretending to be poor—a stance only the rich can literally afford to take. For those of us who did not have punk elders, films like *SLC Punk!* led young brown femmes/queers like me to be punk by, unfortunately, enacting whiteness.

The pogo's replacement by the slam ushered in a new branch of punk called "hardcore," which produced a complicated hierarchy of taste and authenticity within punk culture based on race, class, and gender hardly seen before 1980, when affluent middle-class Orange County (OC) punks started visiting LA punk clubs in Hollywood. Professor Imani Johnson from Critical Dance Studies at the University of California, Riverside, has asked, "How does something accessible such as jumping up and down, a completely accessible type of movement, when possible to perform, allow for the opening of its own gentrification?" Oakland-born musician Dulcinea, fifty-one, comments:

> I feel like punk too just kind of ate itself. It just got, it's like a neighborhood getting gentrified or . . . or a culture being appropriated, or you know, anything like that. . . . If you think about the time when Alice Bag was in punk and playing, there were queers, there were women, there were all kinds of stuff happening, and then that was this short, golden era it seemed like. Then once it got into the media, and the more mainstream people who are, say, less creative and that just want to feed off other people, but has to somehow be superior, started to infiltrate the scene, right? And they changed it. They changed it and instead of the art side of things, the creative side of things was important, then it became just like the hate. The hate became the big thing. The hate and . . . just being, I don't know, what's the right word. I don't know, being physical and excluding people. Pushing out women. Pushing out gay men. Pushing out the Other. And then they just like, take it for their own and try to reclaim it.[8]

Here, gentrification takes the noisy and rapid shape of upper- to middle-class white Orange County hardcore punks from the beach cities introducing slamming and eventually pushing out the pogo—mirroring the co-optation of LA punk and finally cementing the story of US punk as white. Therefore, the genealogies of these punk dances demonstrate the ways that dance and sound together can produce the gentrification and expulsion of an entire scene and a people's history. In the story of moshing—a dance where predominantly young cis men gather in a circle, aggressively pushing into each other and forming what is later called the mosh pit—has become integral to the formation of punk history and culture, shaping how general audiences understand and pass on definitions of punk social dance.

THE POGO TO THE SLAM

While the pogo was still relatively aggressive by many accounts, according to the late MTV program *UltraSound*, pogoing began as a response to mainstream disco's "the bump" or "the hustle" (danhostler1985, 2011). Because of their complicated choreographed movements, which had to be memorized and repeated, these dances signified order and, more broadly, a celebration of US mass consumer culture that punks desired to resist. Though positioning the pogo as a direct response to disco can be deeply racialized—as disco initially was a queer, black, and brown musical movement before mass marketing brought it beyond underground urban dance clubs to the white suburbs—I would rather look to the pogo's embodiment of an era of punk in the United States, with a focused gesture to LA punk that existed before hardcore. Susana Sepulveda (2017) defines hardcore as an intensified version of 1970s punk coming out of the local beach cities and commemorated by white cis men, despite hardcore's queer and POC ties from earlier scenes, especially via LA. Unlike the earlier scenes that catered to poor whites and people of color, hardcore welcomed upper- to middle-class punks; hence, the process of how punk became white can be explained in part by the arrival of the slam dance.

Slam dancing, the predecessor to the mosh pit, is described by Joe Ambrose (2001) as the accompaniment to hardcore. While it can be recognized by its fast pace, it is also an expression of male youth aggression that includes a mix of the pogo, circle pitting, and stage diving. Slamming, unlike the pogo, is gendered as predominantly male and performed at the front and center of the stage. In his history of the mosh pit, Ambrose positions slamming as the main dance of the 1970s scenes, giving very little attention to the pogo. Slamming, however, as a variant of the pogo, was more violent and reflective of the anxieties and frustrations of upper- to middle-class white punks. It was a reactionary dance rooted in a bourgeois definition of boredom that punks before them could not afford, since boredom was, for them, rooted in poverty.

Ambrose's erroneous conflation of slamming and the pogo is challenged by various LA and OC punks, who have specifically pinpointed the moment they witnessed slamming taking over. Former Black Flag front man Ron Reyes, fifty-nine, remembers, from the *Decline of Western Civilization* filming days, "I knew that the early punk scene included Hispanics, women, gays you name it. That is one of the reasons I loved it so much and the main reason I left LA, quit Black Flag etc. cause the punk scene was starting to get overrun by angry white men (boys) and I had no love for the vibe that was emerging."[9]

In the chapter "Hard to the Core" from her pivotal memoir *Violence Girl*, Alice Bag (2011) recounts how the new wave of younger punks from the Southern California beach cities took over the scene and disinvested in punk as a creative and generally inclusive musical space. Just like Bag and Reyes, Jello Biafra of the Dead Kennedys also recognized that slamming helped sever the connection between audience and performer, writing the song "Nazi Punks Fuck Off" to call out the dance's connection between whiteness, hetero-masculinity, and violence that was rapidly and radically changing the scene. As he told the *Los Angeles Times* in 2012:

> I wrote that song in 1981, and at the time, it was aimed at people who were really violent on the dance floor; they didn't call it mosh pits yet. It began to attract people

showing up just to see if they could get in fights in the pit or jump off stage and punch people in the back of the head and run away. (Brown 2012)

As Bag, Reyes, and Biafra indicate, the pogo had ceased to serve as a conduit for community and home for its LA initiators. In an interview, Alice Bag recalled,

> I don't remember the exact moment when pogoing was replaced by moshing, there was a time when these co-existed but it was not a happy partnership. People who are pogoing still have their eyes on the band and are still listening to the music. I think people moshing are not usually watching the band they're into what's happening in the pit, it's like they're feeling the music in a different way.[10]

This coexisting tension between the pogo and the slam is also evidenced in *Another State of Mind* (1984), written, produced, and directed by Adam Small and Peter Stuart. This documentary mainly followed Social Distortion, Youth Brigade, and Minor Threat on tour in a used school bus across the United States and Canada, with brief stops in Baltimore, Chicago, Canada, Seattle, and DC in 1982. In it, the pogo takes place at the front of the stage throughout the parts of the film. Yet it is the interviews with two women that affirm how the pit is a reserved place for the men to let out their aggression. One punk shared, "You can get hurt, you can if you are a girl. So from a girl's point of view, I don't think slamming is advisable, or I don't even think it's . . . I think it's pretty stupid but it does it's a good thing it's a good way to get our aggressions out if you're a guy you can go out there and guys can usually handle it" (Small and Stuart 1984). Her interview is followed by another testimony of a woman who broke her leg while being the only woman slamming. The film *Clockwork Orange County* (2011), while featuring no women, motions to the slam as a gray area between violence and fun, even for punks from the 1970s.

While both the early LA and Orange County scenes were subject to gentrification, each bore witness to those shifts differently. For example, in the OC scene, specifically within the context of the infamous Cuckoo's Nest club, early punks dealt with police harassment, Nazi punks, and cowboys. The LA scene was met with very similar issues, including the embarrassing negation of the expulsion of queerness and race within punk that was indeed facilitated by not just Nazi punks but by hardcore itself, which literally straightened out punk from the moment the two scenes clashed in LA venues in the early 1980s. And once OC/beach punks found a home within the Hollywood scene, hardcore's sound materialized through slamming as a layered dance of classed expressions of boredom, antipathy, and anti-patriotism fueled by the Reagan administration—all aspects later exploited within mainstream US popular culture though the advent of televised talk shows during the late 1980s.[11]

By the 1990s, the mosh pit had made its home within punk, and as with the process of gentrification, its perch there was secured at the expense of the communities that came before it. Arguably, the material connection drawn between pitting and danger is really an association made by the tragic events at Woodstock '99, a festival that featured a plethora of bands that arguably had very little to do with punk, such as Limp Bizkit and Kid Rock. In the media, such as *The Daily Show with Jon Stewart*, the displays of aggression through the riots that occurred there were depicted as a *classed* display of protest against the festivals inflated food prices and dilapidated conditions for the concertgoers, who were characterized as mostly "idiot white suburban kids" (Stewart 1999). However, brief footage of the conditions for female concertgoers and the many instances of sexual assault within the muddy mosh pits at the festival are where the archive on the stark association of the danger of the mosh pit are captured for generations to come.

Nudity at Woodstock '99 came as a tradition followed by the first Woodstock in 1969, where displays of nudity were attempted signifiers of freedom of expression. But testimonies by women in the MTV coverage of the event illuminate the "over exuberance" of white men and the overall misogynist misconceptions around nudity, equating it to consent (MTV News 2009). MTV reported that "alongside the good-natured debauchery, there was an undercurrent of male aggression—young women were the all too frequent target." Then a young white woman interviewed during the same segment adds, "It was disgusting and I hate all men now." Sadly, the MTV coverage returns to footage of property damage and the limited access to water as the main complaints of the festival, after briefly mentioning that one arrest was made after the New York State Police was notified of the ongoing cases of sexual assault at the festival. In part because information about assaults in the Woodstock pits is very scant, excusing or normalizing groping or violence even in the modern-day pit is still part of the reoccurring undercurrent of the misogynist "good-natured debauchery" that protects rape culture within pits and continues to shape how femmes and queers of color have to negotiate their chances in a pit more than cis men do.

What We Do *Isn't* Secret

Truth be told, I miss being in a good pit. I miss the way the anticipation of the next song by the band I've been waiting to see for months or even years makes me put my tall can down and run to the center of the venue floor from the sides of the stage just to catch that first wave of adrenaline as the pit forms. Participating in pits are some of the few times I have felt completely free to both release my frustration with the status quo and express my love for punk. Yet reality sets in every time I get my concert ticket scanned at the entrance and take note of who is in the audience. While I know I'm there to see a band I like, I also know I am entering a space that generally does not recognize me as a punk. Sometimes I try to make nice with the white women that show up, and there's *always* one that joins the pit every time and comes back bloodier than the men, but even then, with another femme present, I still don't pit anymore. I am still brown—my other transgression. I know all the words, I own all the cassettes and CDs, and yet I still don't pit. Rather, I let the men hover around me like bodyguards, their "protection" a nonverbal reminder that the pit, or a punk show for that matter, is no place for a woman. It's ironic that the music I love, which is grounded in critiques of the state and celebrates nonconformity, has a material way, through the mosh pit, to ostracize the very groups of people that helped start punk to begin with—people of color. Today, the mosh pit has become a fabricated fantasy of white male aggression, one directly associated with whiteness and danger. But the lineage of the pogo, to the slam, then to the mosh pit shows that there is a stark difference between alternative genealogies and strategic static definitions of which dance came first and who embodied it.

Recently, I asked other Latinx/Chicanx punks about their thoughts about moshing and found a consensus regarding the role of the pit in their bodily experience within punk. Grace, twenty-one, from the queercore punk band GARBiTCH, said "punk may have been white but it's ours now . . . I stopped being afraid of the mosh pit as it is a spiritual act for me."[12] And Alex remarked,

> For me, the pit was wonderful, because it was a place where I could express my aggressions and frustrations in my life, in my family, as a woman of color, and as being treated as this servant in my own home, and having to display a submissive controlled behavior when I felt very angry, and I felt frustrated, and unheard. And suddenly, there's a place where I can go and be angry and pinwheel like a motherfucker, and no one's going to be angry. And just, I remember going in especially like, not all shows are like really hardcore shows, and just feeling the energy like getting in there and fucking pinwheeling and everybody just giving me room, like "give her room give her room!" and it was so awesome, because it felt like I was like, I don't know, it was spiritual. Primal, you know, in the way that I would say that our ancestors created those circles. Sorry, it makes me emotional, because as a person of color, we just didn't have places where we could be angry and frustrated.
>
> And so, suddenly, you have this place where no one's questioning you, no one's saying anything to you. And you can just be angry as you want to be, until you like, quench that like emotion inside of you. And we don't have to tell anybody where it comes from. For me, my rage came from being undocumented, from experiencing a different reality than my peers, and not knowing how to push and to rebel against it actively. So in a way, it was like rebelling against the experience that was forced upon me with this religious doctrine that my parents were like, making me live and then wanting to live a different reality. So yeah, for me the mosh was spiritual cleansing. And, yeah, I loved it. And like I said, if I fell, or somebody knocked me over, it was, it wouldn't take more than three seconds before I felt somebody pick me up. And that was the first time in my life that I felt that what my parents were teaching me was wrong.[13]

As Alex and Grace's testimonies indicate, the mosh pit is not exactly as exclusive to white cis-male punk as it purports to be. Although it surely remains a dangerously heteronormative space, it can serve multiple purposes for punks of color as well. There is no ignoring the archive we wear as queer punks on our bodies when we interrupt, push back, and disarm white punk narratives within our existence—which we do, every time we open up a pit or join one. As with the lost history of the pogo, which reveals a form of physical cultural memory that allows us to better understand punk's role in QTPOC communities, the mosh pit narrative also tells a story about inclusion, rejection, and the gentrification of an art form that deserves to be heard as well. What we do in the pit shouldn't stay in the pit. Like punk itself, it shouldn't be a secret.

Notes

1. Michelle T., phone interview with the author, April 19, 2019.
2. Fugazi is a post-hardcore punk band from Washington, DC, formed in the late 1980s. "Waiting Room" is from their self-titled 1989 album colloquially known as "the red album" or as *7songs*.
3. Alex, Interview with author, April 10, 2019.
4. Fugazi, "Waiting Room," recorded 1988. Inner Ear Studios, track 1 on *7songs*. Compact disc. Lyrics courtesy of Discord Records, © Fugazi, 1988.
5. The ethnographic practices in this article, which rely on the traditional question and answer format, also incorporate the notion of *charla*, loosely translated as "chat." This allowed for the informal and colloquial interactions between punks from neighboring communities as an example of what punk ethnography can be, because *charla* encouraged an exchange of stories from our respective scenes without having to provoke elitism. Such that, while being Institutional Review Board (IRB)-approved provoked immediate tensions between myself and people I spoke with during the interview process, I relied on the basics of mosh pit etiquette to help me negotiate how to uplift *punkera* stories or *testimonios* without harming the integrity of their agency within the very scene they critique and create every day.
6. Throughout this article, I knowingly oscillate between a variety of cultural, political, and racial descriptors to provide context for the people this article shares space with. This piece will identify punks within the scope of Latina, *punkera*, Chicana, Hispanic, Latino, of color, Chicanx, or Latinx to help broaden the scope of punk experiences this article pays homage to.
7. "Es Lupe" is a cover, in translation, of the McCoys' 1965 song "Hang on Sloopy."
8. Dulcinea G., phone interview with the author, May 20, 2019.
9. Ron Reyes, e-mail message to the author, April 28, 2019.
10. Alice Bag, e-mail message to the author, November 30, 2018.
11. To be clear, it is not the author's intention to suggest that all fans or musicians housed within hardcore, either in earlier or present forms of the style, are culpable of sexism, homophobia, racism, etc. Rather, in order to help punk fans digest the gritty nuances of what happed to the pogo in SoCal, I found it necessary to highlight how early hardcore, as it coalesced between LA, OC, and within the beach cities, did produce a set of permanent standards of authenticity within punk that still discriminates against femmes, queers, enabled folx, and people of color to this day. Whether that be via its own fans, its own musicians, or as a style of punk overall, this article attempts to give one possible answer to why hardcore is unfortunately so villainized yet revered.
12. Grace, personal interview with author, April 10, 2019.
13. Alex, interview with author, April 10, 2019.

References

Ambrose, Joe. *Moshpit Culture*. London: Omnibus Press, 2001.

Bag, Alice. 2011. *Violence Girl: East L.A. Rage to Hollywood Stage, a Chicana Punk Story*. Port Townsend, WA: Feral House

Bag, Alice. 2019. "We Don't Need the English: Punk and Its Afterlives." Keynote Speech, 1st Annual UCR PunkCon, Riverside, CA, May 4, 2019.

Brown, August. 2012. "Jello Biafra on 'Nazi Punks' and Hate Speech." *Los Angeles Times*, August 9, 2012. http://articles.latimes.com/2012/aug/09/entertainment/la-et-ms-jello-biafra-nazi-punks-hate-speech-20120809.

COMROCK85. 2010. "Los Rockin Devil's—Es Lupe." YouTube, April 4, 2010. https://www.youtube.com/watch?v=bOgtMuDIPU0.

danhostler1985. 2011. "MTV: Social History of the Mosh Pit 2002 PART 1." YouTube, February 21, 2011. https://www.youtube.com/watch?v=6okPRMlJufM

Doe, John, Exene Cervenka, and Dave Alvin. 2016. "A Personal History of L.A. Punk: 'It Was a Free-For-All for Outcasts.'" *Fresh Air*, NPR, Philadelphia, WHYY, May 2, 2016.

Freeman, Lance. 2006. *There Goes the 'Hood: Views of Gentrification from the Ground Up*. Philadelphia: Temple University Press.

Fugazi. *Waiting Room*. Dischord Records, June 1988.

Glenn, Joshua. 2011. "Origin of the Pogo." *Hilobrow*, June 22, 2011. https://www.hilobrow.com/2011/06/22/origin-of-the-pogo/

"Hang On Sloopy." The McCoys. Bang Records, 1965.

LimaPerú.TV. 2013. "Los Saicos Demolición en Lima Vive Rock 2013." YouTube, September 8, 2013. https://www.youtube.com/watch?v=bsiZHJYBEpg&index=17&list=RD-ahO_vGBdkg.

Lydon, John. n.d. "The 'Sid and Nancy' Film Is Not Factual. . . . It's Sadly Sickeningly Depressing." www.johnlydon.com/sidandnancy.html.

MTV News. 2009. "Woodstock Gets a Bit Out of Hand '99." MTV News, August 16, 2009. https://www.youtube.com/watch?v=8F3MnZyS8CM.

NOISEY. 2019. "Was Punk Rock Born in Peru?— Los Saicos—Noisey Specials." YouTube, August 12, 2019. https://www.youtube.com/watch?reload=9&v=tsdTKQb606Q.

Sepulveda, Susana. 2017. "Hardcore as 'Home': An Etymology of CORE through Chicana Punk Sound." *Sounding Out!*, September 4, 2017. https://soundstudiesblog.com/2017/09/04/hardcore-as-home-an-etymology-of-core-through-chicana-punk-sound.

Small, Adam, and Peter Stuart, dirs. 1984. *Another State of Mind*. DVD. Vancouver, Time Bomb.

Stewart, Jon. 1999. "WOODSTOCK '99 Fires." *The Daily Show with Jon Stewart*, Comedy Central, July 26, 1999. http://www.cc.com/video-clips/ak95or/the-daily-show-with-jon-stewart-woodstock--99-fires.

Taylor, Diana. 2003. *The Archive and the Repertoire: Performing Cultural Memory in the Americas*. Durham, NC: Duke University Press.

CHAPTER 12

QUEER PUNK, TRANS FORMS
Transgender Rock and Rage in a Necropolitical Age

CURRAN NAULT

In 1985 Toronto, nascent queer cultural troublemakers G. B. Jones and Bruce LaBruce promiscuously pooled punk practices of DIY cut-and-paste and rebellious antisocial rants with the queer provocations of explicit homo-porn pictures. The result was a zine that they mischievously monikered "*J.D.s*," denoting, among other things, "juvenile delinquents."[1] This effectively inaugurated "queercore" (née "homocore"), a queer punk scene known for its artistic irreverence and caustic critiques of homophobic hate in punk and shamed servility in the gay mainstream.

J.D.s emerged in a decade defined by an increasingly "out" and visible LGB (and sometimes inclusively "T") community, but also by a virulent backlash from more conservative corners. Within this incongruous context, *J.D.s*' decidedly anti-assimilationist queer politics and porn-punk aesthetics unfurled oppositionally alongside staggering statistics of gay bashings and an AIDS pandemic that produced more panic than altruistic action, especially in regard to its most pronounced, and already disparaged, subjects: sex workers, intravenous drug users, Haitians and other people of color and, of course, gay men.[2] Concocted years before ACT-UP (1987) and Queer Nation (1990) would take to the streets to angrily agitate against such grave, punitive prejudice, and before a newly minted "queer theory" carved its cutting-edge crevice into the academy with texts like Judith Butler's *Gender Trouble* (1990), queercore was already jostling LGBTQ+ politics toward radical horizons that are still being realized today. But, what starts as a revolution is often susceptible to regressive reinscription, and more than thirty years later, queercore has found its oppositional contours contravened.

Most recently, this queercore "identity crisis," namely the violation of its agitational politics and subcultural authenticity, has been fashioned in the form of some high-heeled shoes—Gucci's to be precise. That is, in early 2017, Gucci announced that it was releasing a series of ultra-chic shoes as an homage to "gay punk." In "reflecting the spirit of" gay punk, these shoes would be "fitted with multiple straps, studs and metal embellishments, including the Dionysus buckle." The title for this luxury line?

"Queercore," of course. Through a series of press releases, Gucci claimed that "queercore" was "lent" to them for their use. Queercore instigator G. B. Jones was quick to retort to this claim: "Queercore didn't 'lend its name' to Gucci for their shoes. I should know, I invented the term. They stole it, plain and simple. It's theft" (quoted in Gerdes 2017). For his part, queercore co-creator Bruce LaBruce lamented the "casual and clueless use of the term 'Queercore,'" asserting that the line of shoes, "has absolutely no connection to the movement whatsoever—not just politically, but in terms of style and spirit" (LaBruce 2017).

And so it goes that queer punk sedition is transformed into the latest trend in sellable footwear. Of course, this is not a new narrative. Radical subcultures, and in particular punk, have long found themselves targets of exploitation and capitalist commodification. Indeed, it was not long after punk first snarled its way onto the seventies scene that celebrated fashionista Vivienne Westwood started peddling punk looks on the store shelves of her shop SEX—*and*, it should not be overlooked, what Westwood was selling was not *just* punk, but (homo)sexual subculture, SEX's sartorial stylings being renegade repurposings of the underground attire of gay BDSM.[3] For, as Dick Hebdige famously opines in *Subculture: The Meaning of Style*, the "revolting style" of punk—it's "vulgar designs" and "nasty colors," which project anarchy, wildness, and noise—poses a symbolic threat to law and order, but one that is always in danger of incorporation, either through punk styles being transformed into mass-produced commodities (think of the purchasable "punk" products at Hot Topics in suburban malls) or through the ideological recasting of punk individuals as harmless and exotic by way of their easy-to-dismiss "strange looks" and "peculiar visions" (1979, 107).

The story of punk containment does not always end in acquiescence, however. Indeed in response to Gucci's grotesque gumption, LaBruce was rattled, but also persistent in preserving the still productive political possibilities of queercore in the face of such corporate cooptation:

> Queercore has to evolve to fight the new ultra-conservative, ultra-Right forces that have been activated by neo-liberal global policies. Queercore kids can't keep hanging on to the same old style strategies. What we need is a new, cohesive, revolutionary youth movement that consciously and consistently acts out against these reactionary forces, kids that resist the corporate exploitation of their artistic and political energy and that can use technology and global interconnectedness to fight the power. So in a weird way, maybe Gucci is doing Queercore a favor. It's time for a new kind of resistance.
>
> (LaBruce, 2017)

From the looks of the still-salient queercore scene, the new kids on the queer punk block could not agree more. Which is to observe that a new wave of queercore resistance is underway. No longer the age of AIDS hysteria and brutal bashings of gays (or at least not to the same scale), today's neoliberal[4]—and, I would say *necropolitical*[5]— environment has brought other issues to the fore. Trans survival in the face of increased hostilities is chief among these urgencies.[6] Not surprising then, looming large in the new queercore lineage are transgender/genderqueer artists who are raucously reacting to a modern set of gender troubles: depression in a cissexist society, death at the hands of transphobic assailants, and their ostracization to the outskirts of the LGB world.

More than an addendum, this new wave of transgender artists inspires reconsideration of the entire queercore field. For while it is true that trans folx are increasingly taking center stage, they have always been a vital component of the queercore scene. With this in mind, this essay recontextualizes and extends my earlier queercore writings in order to outline a neglected history of queercore, tracing the queercore sub-scene that we might call "transcore." This revised, trans-centered lineage extends from the foundational appearance of figures like Jayne County within the 1970s New York punk scene, to the popularity of *Hedwig and the Angry Inch* and Against Me! in the early 2000s, to the contemporary upsurge in angry, anti-normative transgender punk led by the likes of G.L.O.S.S. (Girls Living Outside of Society's Shit)—a band whose tactics of imagined violence in the face of necropolitical erasure may form the "new kind of [queercore] resistance" for which LaBruce politically pines. In the section that follows, I trace some punk precedents to our transgender times and end with a preliminary dive into contemporary "transcore" by way of G.LO.S.S. As this analysis ultimately attests, despite the gumption of Gucci's co-optive containment and similar exploitations, queercore is definitely not dead; indeed, it still has an axe to grind and further edges to explore.

Gender in the First Generation

To repeat, queercore began in 1985 with a zine: *J.D.s*. At the helm of this porn-punk provocation were two misfit malcontents living in a condemned apartment on Toronto's low-rent Queen Street. The first was the visual artist G. B. Jones, known for her dyke reworkings of Tom of Finland's swollen sexual sketches of gay male BDSM. The second was the film studies master's student and underground-filmmaker-to-be Bruce LaBruce. Although the pair were queer and punk, they felt equally out of place within both subcultures, at least as they were contemporaneously construed. When it came to punk, LaBruce had been the victim of a homophobic assault at the punk club Quoc Te in Toronto, and Jones, who was a member of proto-queercore outfit Fifth Column, was on the receiving end of the misogyny and mistreatment that had infiltrated the male-dominated punk scene of Toronto (and elsewhere).[7] And, when it came to gay and lesbian culture, in a decade of AIDS apathy and anti-LGBT assaults, Jones and LaBruce were aghast at the community's overwhelming shamed silence.

As an antidote to their alienation from punk, through *J.D.s*, Jones and LaBruce unleashed a queered take on the hyper-macho Toronto scene—proffered through compromising pictures of male punksters in various states of undress and stories satirizing the homoeroticism of such punk rituals as the male-on-male action of the mosh pit. And, as an antidote to the creeping conformity of the gay and lesbian mainstream, also through *J.D.*s, Jones and LaBruce openly ranted against establishment gays while conjuring sexually "unsafe" stories of life on the queer fringe. Across these instances, sex was *J.D.*s weapon par excellence, used to penetrate the tough hetero-masculine veneer of punk and to eschew the "family friendly" placations of homonormative[8] gays and lesbians.

From the start, however, gender was also central to *J.D.*s nonconformist affront to punk and gay/lesbian norms. After all, Jones's beef with the Toronto punk scene was as much about its pervasive male misogyny as it was about its homophobic hate. Equally, LaBruce's limp-wristed flamboyance, which he knowingly played to the hilt, was decidedly at odds with the muscled displays of hegemonic masculinity favored within commercial gay culture (then and now). Particularly pronounced was the duo's frustration with the separate spheres of gay and lesbian existence, encapsulated by a divided gay/lesbian bar scene. In response, queercore privileged cross-gender alliances, forging a cultural space that was not limited to just gay men *or* lesbians. As Toronto zinester (*Jane Gets a Divorce*) Jena Von Brücker relays:

> A women's bar was a women's bar, and a men's bar was a men's bar. And a guy couldn't get into The Rose [a lesbian bar] unless he was with women, and even then maybe not. They'd say, "no," they'd turn you away at the door. It was just ridiculous. (Personal interview)

Von Brücker continues by emphasizing the sexism that underpins this gendered segregation:

> It was like gay men hated women. There was this undertone of hostility. Not even an undertone, it was an overtone. It was like, "Eww, what are *they* doing here?" It was just gross... It's almost like, sometimes you can feel the hate between heterosexuals. You can feel the hate between the men and the women, except that they need each other. They have to find some way to get along on some level, even though they don't really want to. It's sort of like that, but they [gays and lesbians] don't need each other for anything. So, they were just completely polarized and there was a lot of animosity. (Personal Interview)

These comments reveal that gender trouble was a chief part of queercore's critique of the gay mainstream and that, by extension, *trans*gender trouble was also never far afield.

Indeed, one might even argue that transgender trouble paved the way for queercore. In point of fact, one of the original punksters in the New York scene, and a vital precursor to queercore, was the self-proclaimed "first transgender singer of rock," Jayne (formerly Wayne) County. As elaborated in my book *Queercore: Queer Punk Media Subculture*,[9] County was known for such gender-bending, in-your-face songs as "Are You a Boy or Are You a Girl?" and "Cream in My Jeans," as well as her joyfully unhinged live performances of these raucous button-pushers. For example, in 1972, County's short-lived band Queen Elizabeth played a notoriously wild gig at New York University.

As described in *Queercore*, swishing about a campus stage fully done-up with a pink baby doll nightdress and high-heeled shoes, County treated an increasingly shocked undergraduate student body to revved-up renditions of some of her greatest hits. During 'Goddess of Wet Dreams," she reportedly squirted the students with milk from a penis-shaped water gun, and during the feisty transgender anthem "It Takes a Man Like Me to Find a Woman Like Me," County scandalized onlookers further when she lifted her dress to reveal a rubber vagina, before madly fucking herself with a black double-ended dildo. An unamused college dean literally pulled the plug on the song mid-set—as a college dean might (County 1996, 88).

To interpret such scenes of gender mayhem, we might productively turn to Judith Butler (or *return*, as Butler's status as a "daddy" of queer theory may demand). In *Bodies that Matter*, Butler cites drag as a possible place where the incoherency of gender can be exposed, arguing that "[d]rag is subversive to the extent that it reflects on the imitative structure by which hegemonic gender is itself produced and disputes heterosexuality's claim on naturalness and originality" (2011, 85). Sarah Chinn elucidates:

> By performing gender in a hyperbolic, stylized way, drag queens don't simply imitate femininity, they reveal how women imitate femininity as well, and what hard work it is. Through parody, drag can expose the seeming naturalness of gender itself; it doesn't imitate an original, but reveals that there is no original, only layers of performance.
>
> (Chinn 1997, 300–301)

Donning plastic tasseled breasts, dresses made out of condoms, and platform shoes molded in the shape of erect penises, while yowling gender-twisting ditties like "Are You Man Enough to Be a Woman?," County is a quintessential example of gender performed "in a hyperbolic, stylized way." This is true even if County is also an *atypical* example of drag gender trouble, insofar as County's transgender identity stands out as exceptional within an archive of drag that has centered the cisgender. Which is to assert that, as claimed in *Queercore*, County's art and performances can be read as a revelation of gender fraud, her sonic and bodily acts carving a lawless space of spectacular gender/sexual confusion in the New York underground. Through her demented songs and performances, County became a subcultural legend, infusing the nascent punk scene with a fiery taste of gender fluidity and a queer flair for filth.[10]

Other transgender and gender-nonconforming folks soon followed suit, putting their own "beyond the binary" spins on the early punk scene, from the flagrantly androgynous "bulldagger swagger" of punk-turned-folkster Phranc (originally of synth-punk bands Nervous Gender and Catholic Discipline), to the genderqueer antics of queercore mainstay Vaginal Davis, whose zines (*Crude* [1976–1980], *Fertile LaToyah Jackson* [1982–1991], *Shrimp* [1993]), bands (Black Fag, !Cholita!, PME), and performance art (*The White to Be Angry*) combined barbed satire, warped gender and racial play, and uncouth theatrics into an agitational aesthetic that Jose Esteban Muñoz famously titled "terrorist drag" (1999, 100). Other early trans punk icons include Shawna Virago and the Deadly Nightshade Family, Christine Beatty of Glamazon, Jennifer Convertible, All The

Pretty Horses, and Silas Howard and Lynne Breedlove of Tribe 8 (discussed in the next section), all of whom left their gender-deviant mark on punk in the 1990s.

The fact that punk has always been a space for such gender variance, however provisionally (see note 11), is not that surprising, given the nonconformity of the punk aesthetic. The "revolting," "noisy," and "chaotic" style of punk, as identified by Dick Hebdige, has made the subculture particularly adaptable to unconventional gender displays—perhaps especially by women, who have found their choices circumscribed elsewhere. As Lucy O'Brien opines in "The Woman Punk Made Me," as hippie fashion, with its emphasis on freedom and experimentation (e.g., going barefoot and braless), became commodified and diluted in the 1970s, punk, with its decidedly unfeminine spikes, chains and rubberwear, emerged as a new option for women to rebel against oppressive beauty norms:

> To find fresh meanings as a woman [during this time of hippie fashion's incorporation] it was necessary to overturn the pastel shades of post-60s femininity and make an overt statement on a newly emerging, more aggressive understanding of female sexuality. Punk provided the perfect opportunity.
>
> (O'Brien 1999, 188)

Similarly, queer and trans theorist Jack Halberstam has written of punk as a space that allowed him to claim a genderqueer identity, and as more than just a phase; that is, as a space that allowed "girls" like him to extend their gender nonconformity into adulthood, circumventing pressures, exerted by patriarchal authorities and, more dubiously, conventional feminists, to "grow up" and become "normal" (i.e., straight) women: "While feminism has been preoccupied with producing strong women out of strong girls, subcultural forms like punk and riot grrrl have generated queer girls, often queer tomboys, with queer futures" (1993, 153). As Halberstam maintains, working against (gender) normative dress codes and conventional articulations of "adult behavior," punk productively offers "an alternative model" that "rejects [normative forms of] androgyny and binary gender systems, revels in girl masculinity, and encourages queer adulthoods (homo- or trans-sexual)" (176).

At the same time, as already noted, punk culture has, at its most malicious, been openly hostile to women, queers, and trans folx (see, for example, footnote 11 about the transphobic violence that Jayne County encountered in punk). Even queercore, although gender inclusive and, at times, subversive was, in its early years, a space primarily composed of cisgender dykes and fags. Tribe 8, discussed in the next section, is an important exception, however, whose use of imagined violence tactics paved a rough-edged road for transcore bands to traverse today.

TRIBE 8'S TRANSGENDER TIPPING POINT

Formed in San Francisco in 1991, Tribe 8 was an in-your-face band in the rowdiest of punk traditions, and it has since become a key reference point in the history of queercore—its legacy being solidified in the award-winning *Rise Above: The Tribe 8 Documentary* (2004), directed by Tracy Flannigan. Originally a self-proclaimed "dyke band," two of Tribe 8's most visible members, lead singer Lynnee Breedlove and guitarist Silas Howard, identify as trans men—with Howard having the current distinction of being one of the most coveted transgender directors working in film and television, with credits that include *By Hook or By Crook* (2001), *Transparent* (Amazon, 2014–), and *Pose* (FX, 2018–).

In *Queercore*, I discuss in detail their onstage antics as emblematic of imagined violence—one of the most potent political strategies within queercore. "Imagined violence," a concept that comes from Jack Halberstam's "Imagined Violence/Queer Violence" (1993), refers to the threat of violence, as opposed to its actualization, as a means for the marginalized to fend off hegemonic harm. In the 1990s, for example, Queer Nation adopted the slogan "Queers Bash Back!" as a warning to would-be attackers that gays and lesbians were no longer willing to turn the proverbial other cheek. Grounded in resistance to powerful white, straight, male, bourgeois domination, imagined violence is a rhetorical strategy—one that deliberately blurs the line between feigned and real violence in an effort to instill fear in objectionable others (Halberstam 1993, 188).

Take, for example, one of Tribe 8's most notorious gambits: Breedlove wearing a leather harness and strap-on dildo and using a knife to slice the dildo into pieces mid-set—fake blood spurting onto the audience in a grotesque spectacle of mock castration. This performance would occur during the song "Frat Pig," an anti-rape howler with the chorus, "Frat pig, it's called gang rape. Let's play gang castrate!" Allied with the principle of imagined violence, the ideological intent was fairly straightforward: to produce a fear of retaliation in would-be abusers. And also, as Breedlove explains, to allow for a palliative release of feminist frustration: "It's a cathartic ritual; it makes us feel like we are getting some kind of revenge" (quoted in Juno 1996, 42).[11]

Befitting the misogyny of their time, Tribe 8's tactics of imagined violence have been adapted by newer bands for the *trans*misogny of today. Bands like G.L.O.S.S have built on Tribe 8's use of imagined violence, while also swapping out their (trans)masculine theatrics in favor of a (trans)femme ferocity. Before we turn their way, however, I want to mention two trans-punk products that are more popular than button-pushing per se: the tentative trans-punk text *Hedwig and the Angry Inch* and the highly successful Against Me!, led by trans-rock icon Laura Jane Grace.

Transgender (R)Evolution (and Repression)

By the turn of the new millennium, queercore had expanded beyond its original outline within the rabblerousing pages of *J.D.s*. G. B. Jones and Bruce LaBruce were no longer on speaking terms following the surprise success of LaBruce's first feature, *No Skin Off My Ass*, in 1991—as Jones, who starred in the film and wrote part of the script, felt her contributions had not been fully acknowledged, and that LaBruce was effectively taking credit for a movement they had mutually manifested. Despite this kerfuffle, the Toronto scene was still banging along, with a new generation of queercore enthusiasts led by the likes of the artist Will Munro via his monthly queer-punk club night, Vazaleen. Meanwhile, Pansy Division, with their playful sexed-up songs, had brought queercore to the attention of a wider public, opening for Green Day in sold-out stadium arenas across the United States in 1993. Queercore was also attracting new audiences through large-scale events like Homo-A-Go-Go, created by Ed Varga, in Olympia, Washington and Queeruption, which occurred in various locales in Europe over the first decade of the 2000s.

The year 2001 also saw *Hedwig and the Angry Inch* make the leap from 1998 Off-Broadway musical to one of the most celebrated indie films of the year, garnering critical acclaim and Best Director and Audience Awards at the Sundance Film Festival, as well as a "Best Actor" Golden Globe nomination for director and star John Cameron Mitchell. Mitchell, who would go on to direct such films as the underground-inspired *Short Bus* (2006) and the Nicole Kidman vehicle *Rabbit Hole* (2010), had originated the role and cowritten the musical with the composer Stephen Trask, the music director and house band member at the New York club Squeezebox, where he performed with punk icons Debbie Harry, Lene Lovich, and Joey Ramone.

Hedwig tells the tale of a fictional punk rock band, the Angry Inch, fronted by an East German genderqueer singer named Hedwig, who undergoes a botched gender reassignment operation as a young adult, leaving her with the titular "angry inch." Years later, Hedwig finds herself in a relationship with a younger man, Tommy, becoming his mentor and musical collaborator, only to have Tommy steal her music and transform into an overnight sensation based on her talents. Building on these backstories, the majority of the film follows Hedwig and her band as they shadow Tommy's tour, exploring Hedwig's past and the complexities of her gender history.

A critical, but not immediate financial, success, *Hedwig* has, in the years since it was first released, become a cult phenomenon, generating new forms of queer punk fandom through its (trans)gendered subversions—just as *The Rocky Horror Picture Show* did for glam rock twenty-six years prior. Often referred to as one of the pivotal texts within the annals of both transgender and queer punk cinema history, *Hedwig* can perhaps also be said to have, in spectacular fashion, marked the turn from sexual to (trans)gender politics in queercore. Yet, despite its significance in the evolution of queercore, *Hedwig*'s gender politics are a matter of debate.

The film's unsettled (and unsettling) trans-punk politics are declared most vocally midway through the film, during the musical number titled "Angry Inch." The narrative intro to this song explains the reasons for Hedwig's character-defining botched surgery: To escape East Germany and be with the man she loves, Sergeant Luther Robinson, whom Hedwig meets while sunbathing just east of the Berlin Wall. Luther convinces Hedwig that s/he must undergo a sex change, as this will allow Hedwig to pass the medical exams required as part of the matrimonial process. Luther philosophizes: "To walk away, you've gotta leave something behind." Hedwig's mother agrees: "To be free, one must give up a little part of oneself."

Flash-forward to a dingy, all-you-can-eat diner in Baltimore. Hedwig is clad in zebra-stripe pants and a yellow tank top with "Punk Rock" scrawled across the front. Sneering through a song in front of a packed restaurant, Hedwig bemoans her "Barbie doll crotch" and "tits made out of clay," wildly careening from one side of the makeshift "stage" to the other, as the diner's customers recoil at the gruesome details of the bloody operation that produced her "one inch mound of flesh." Eventually, a burly man rises from his chair, yells "faggot" at Hedwig, and, in a sequence of stereotypical punk pugnacity, a brawl breaks out between the band and the crowd. Band members fly from the stage, one after the other, to join the melee—with the exception of Hedwig, who remains on stage, her furious delivery reaching a newly fevered pitch. Finally, Hedwig abandons the mic, and in a moment of surreal directorial fancy, starts to magically sail above the crowd, as if symbolically bypassing the Berlin Wall that trapped her young body on one side of the binary and that continues to imprison her as a gender-nonconforming adult.

Befitting its title, "Angry Inch" is indeed the angriest song on the soundtrack—unruly and ferocious, it spotlights the rage of a gendered misfit who belongs nowhere and within no clear bodily category. And if Hedwig's T-shirt was not an obvious enough clue, the song, with its three-chord thrash, is also the film's most discernibly punk song. Yet "Angry Inch" ultimately stands as a moment of trans-punk potential that is not fully realized. For one, punk quickly fades, as subsequent songs emphasize soft ballad hues and speak more of conventional themes of love and loss than dander and disgust. Trans legibility also dissipates, culminating in a finale in which a denuded Hedwig, stripped of her female signifiers, wanders off into the film's urban landscape. Read as a moment of self-acceptance and of facing the world unadorned, this finale intimates something other than transgender identification. Such an ambiguous relation to trans identification and politics suggested in these stripped-down closing shots is also evident in the song "Angry Inch" itself, as the primary target of Hedwig's punk rage is her own "deformed" body, rather than a transphobic society. Given Hedwig's disparaging description of her body, as well as her lack of agency and self-determination in undergoing her gender transition, her story appears at odds with typical transgender tales of "gender confirmation" and "coming out."

Such ambiguity has made the film a source of debate in subsequent years, with numerous academic essays seeking to come to terms with what remains opaque in the film—namely, whether Hedwig can even be properly identified as transgender. In "Gender without Genitals" (2013), Jordy Jones takes a harsh view of the film, claiming that it represents a misappropriation of trans identity, and that Hedwig is not, in fact, trans, for she has no desire to live her truth as a woman. Hedwig is instead a gay man—one who has been forced to live in body that the film articulates as disfigured and unwanted. As such, Jones positions *Hedwig* as a conservative text that erases authentic trans experience, while exploiting the trans body as an empty object for others to inhabit in order to work through their sexual and gender traumas. Taking a more ambivalent position, in "Transitions and Transformations," Karin Sellberg asserts that Hedwig is "both a homosexual man and a transsexual woman, and also neither"—believing these not to be mutually exclusive categories. Sellberg argues against Jones's strict definition of desire as the root of authentic trans definition, asserting, "If desire were considered a more transient concept, Hedwig certainly harbours a transsexual subjectivity" (2009, 78–79). Regardless of how one views Hedwig's "true" identity, however, or the underlying ideologies of the film, *Hedwig* remains one of the most well-known, if ultimately misclassified, trans-punk texts.

The other contender is Against Me!, a pop punk band that has been releasing albums since 1997. In 2012, Against Me! gained renewed attention when lead singer Laura Jane Grace came out as a trans woman. The band's subsequent 2014 album, *Transgender Dysphoria Blues*, which was a critical and commercial smash, explicitly tackles Grace's gender confirmation. Featuring such songs as "Drinking with the Jocks," a tongue-in-cheek parody of hegemonic masculinity, and "True Trans Soul Rebel," a wounded cry against transphobia and self-hate, the album stands as a watershed in trans-punk representation, even if its slick production diverges from the scrappier sounds of early queercore, raising questions of the albums proper placement on the pop-punk divide.

Powerful in her politics—both in song and in person—Grace has also found her edges blunted by commercial co-optation, performing in music videos with pop princess Miley Cyrus and appearing in an online video series for the tech giant AOL: *True Trans: With Laura Jane Grace*. Indeed, in an essay titled "True Trans Soul Rebel," Marta Kelleher (2017) laments Grace's appearance in *True Trans*, arguing that the series was carefully edited to make Grace appear traditionally feminine, and focused more on her domestic activities than her potent onstage performances. Thus, while *Hedwig and the Angry Inch* and Against Me! are two remarkable moments in the history of transcore ascendance, one must look elsewhere to find trans punk in the messier malcontent mold of the original DIY queercore scene.

TRANSGENDER ROCK AND RAGE IN A NECROPOLITICAL AGE

As noted earlier in this essay, the 1980s witnessed an increase in gay and lesbian visibility, but also an upsurge in the premature deaths of gay men from AIDS and homophobic beatings. Similarly, the early twenty-first century has seen a rapid increase in transgender visibility, especially within the realm of popular culture, from cinema (*Boys Don't Cry*, *All About My Mother*, *Hedwig and the Angry Inch*, *Transamerica*, *Tangerine*, *A Fantastic Woman*), to television (*Orange is the New Black*, *Transparent*, *Sense 8*, *Pose*), and culminating in the widely circulated "Transgender Tipping Point" and "I Am Cait!" magazine covers featuring the actress Laverne Cox and Olympian Caitlyn Jenner, respectively. As in the past, however, this increased visibility has gone hand-in-hand with staggering, and gradually rising, statistics of trans murder, with trans women of color being the most vulnerable to harm. The Human Rights Campaign, for example, documented the killings of twenty-one transgender people in the United States in 2015, twenty-three in 2016, twenty-nine in 2017, and twenty-two in the first few months of 2018 (see the Human Rights Campaign website for updated statistics). Other organizations, like GLAAD and the Transgender Law Center, have slightly different tallies, but the trend holds.

In our necropolitical age, there is also a sense that even those trans individuals who escape physical violence still find themselves subjected to brutalities of a more symbolic sort. Necropolitics is a concept coined by Achille Mbembe as a rejoinder to "biopower," conceived by Michel Foucault as a disciplinary mode of power centered on regulating life via the body, "an explosion of numerous and diverse techniques for achieving the subjugations of bodies and the control of populations" (2003, 140). Mbembe maintains that modern power is not so much concerned with life, but with making death, stipulating how some may live and others may die. Inferring more than a right to kill, necropolitics excavates an array of intensities that mark certain demographics for death, condemning persecuted parties to be the eternal walking wounded; it entails "new and unique forms of social existence in which vast populations are subjected to conditions of life conferring upon them the status of living dead" (39–40). Not confined to the catastrophic, necropolitics also occurs through what Lauren Berlant calls "slow death," or the "wearing out of a population and the deterioration of people in that population that is very nearly a defining condition of their experience and historical existence" (2007, 754).

In this necropolitical environment, in which trans individuals are a clear example of those who are literally and figuratively marked for death, transgender rage would seem to be a logical response—and punk the perfect outlet. Transgender historian Susan Stryker has, in fact, written about the political necessity of transgender rage, of the need to "harness the intense emotions emanating from transsexual experience—especially rage—and to mobilize them into effective political actions" (1994, 83). Noting the affinity between Frankenstein's monster and the trans body—both entities hegemonically construed as "unnatural" and "the product of medical science"—Stryker makes a case for laying claim to "monstrous identity" and wielding monstrous rage as a source of "transformative power" (84, 92). As Stryker avers, in a society that situates trans subjectivity as illegitimate and a violation of the natural order, "transgender rage furnishes a means for disidentification with compulsorily assigned subject positions" (92).

Such survivalist trans rage is on full display in what is arguably the gold standard of present day transcore: *Trans Day of Revenge* by G.L.O.S.S. (Girls Living Outside of Society's Shit). Fronted by the confrontationally named Sadie "Switchblade" Smith, G.L.O.S.S. formed in 2014 in Olympia, Washington, finding a fast following for their breakneck hardcore, arresting attention to radical politics, and insistence on punk authenticity—so much so that the band broke up at the height of their success in 2016, shortly after punk rock label Epitaph Records came calling with a financially lucrative offer. G.L.O.S.S. turned it down due to the label's association with Warner Bros., and promptly disbanded citing mental and physical fatigue.

Released that same year (2016), the malcontent mission of *Trans Day of Revenge* is immediately clear from its cover art. Situated at the bottom center, a human skull is flanked on both sides by switchblades and tubes of blood-red lipstick, collapsing signifiers of femininity into suggestions of ferocious fury and the possibility of attack. Adorning the sides, pink triangles conjure historical lineages of Nazi-era branding of gay men[12] and ACT-UP activism under the slogan "Silence Equals Death,"[13] placing transfeminism as the new frontier of LGBTQ+ action. Above the skull, hands with brightly painted fingernails engulf the title "Trans Day of Revenge," an appropriation of the commemorative "Trans Day of Remembrance" for much darker ends.[14]

The album itself is a short seven minutes of uncontained anger that begins with the fiery burst of "Give Violence a Chance": "When peace is just another word for death, it's our turn to give violence a chance!," screams Smith, simultaneously evoking the necropolitical denigration of marginal lives and "imagined violence" as a strategic solution. Intersectional invectives that "Black lives don't matter in the eyes of the law" follow, mixed with invocations of politicized punk purpose: "We scream just to make sense of things." Mere minutes later, the album crescendos with the title track, as Smith digs deeper into imagined violence and its refusal of "turn the other cheek" victimization, lamenting the killing of "Black trans women, draped in white sheets," with defiant demands to "break the cycle with revenge / Trans day of revenge!," and radical reminders to would-be-assaulters that "we are not as weak as we seem." If this "don't fuck with us" message of "Trans Day of Revenge" was not crystal clear, in an interview with *BitchMedia* Smith clarified her intent: "[I am] weaponizing a lifetime of anguish and alienation" (Berbenick 2015). In other words, far from the ameliorating tactics and "respectability politics" of the gay and lesbian mainstream and the greater acceptability of her queer punk elders, Smith remains deliberately on the outside, gathering her grievances, ready for the punk pounce.

CURRENT CONCLUSIONS

And so it goes that, in a time of exploitive grabs by Gucci brands, bands like G.L.O.S.S. remind the world of queercore's radical roots, while expanding the canon to include an ever-expanding roster of transgender takes. In our contemporary culture of gay tolerance, marriage and military rights, and *I Am Simon*–sized pop cultural fluff, gay punk may no longer have what it takes to keep the carnivorous capitalists at bay, but if the gall of G.L.O.S.S. is any indication, trans punk still holds the potential to rile the ultra-Right. G.L.O.S.S are also not alone. Musicians like +HIRS+, Downtown Boys, Shopping, Cute Puke, Vile Creature, Worriers, and CHRISTEENE—with transgender/genderqueer players, progressive politics, and rough rock edges—are also maintaining the scene's agitational allure. In addition, artists like Venezuela-based techno-punk artist Arca are transcending not only gender boundaries, but those of nation, genre and form as well. For example, Arca's most recent 2020 release, the curiously titled @@@@@, features just one sixty-two-minute track, defying logics of commercial appeal, dashing hopes of Spotify hits, and summoning a slippery, arguably trans, aesthetic of continuous flow. With such novel transcore interventions in mind, while I agree with Bruce LaBruce that "[i]t's time for a new kind of (queercore) resistance." I also know that this new kind of resistance is already here.

Notes

1. The name "*J.D.s*" was also a nod to Just Desserts, an all-night eatery where G. B. Jones and Bruce LaBruce first met, and, in its intentional ambiguity, a signifier for the popular post-punk band Joy Division; the favorite beverage of hard-drinking punks, Jack Daniels; and J. D. Salinger, whose blunt, outcast, youthful writing style was deliberately imitated in the pages of *J.D.s*.
2. While actual statistics on gay bashings in the 1980s and early 1990s are difficult to find, there were a number of high-profile cases that brought the practice to heightened community attention. These include the following (to name only a few): The beating of Rick Hunter and John Hanson by Minneapolis police outside the Y'all Come Back Saloon on January 1, 1982, while the officers repeatedly called the men "faggots." The drowning of Charlie Howard in Bangor, Maine, in 1984 for being "flamboyantly gay." The July 2, 1990, murder of Julio Rivera by two men who beat him with a hammer and stabbed him with a knife because he was gay. The demise of Houston-area banker Paul Broussard in 1991 after being beaten to death by ten homophobic men. The October 27, 1992, killing of US Navy Petty Officer Allen Schindler, who was murdered by a shipmate who stomped him to death in a public restroom in Japan. The rape and murder of trans man Brandon Teena in Nebraska in 1993. For more on the history of gay bashings in North America see, for example, *Hate Crimes: Confronting Violence against Lesbians and Gay Men*, edited by Gregory M. Herek and Kevin T. Berrill. For more on AIDS panic see, for example, Simon Watney's *Policing Desire: Pornography, AIDS and the Media*, and/or Douglas Crimp's *Melancholia and Moralism: Essays on AIDS and Queer Politics*.
3. For more on the intersections of SEX and gay culture, see my book *Queercore: Queer Punk Media Subculture*.
4. Neoliberalism refers to a modern form of liberalism that favors free-market capitalism. For more on neoliberalism, including its negative impact on queer culture, see Lisa Duggan's *The Twilight of Equality: Neoliberalism, Cultural Politics, and the Attack on Democracy*.
5. Necropolitics will be discussed in greater detail later in this essay, but essentially refers to the manner in which certain minority populations are marked for death within modern society.
6. The statistics on recent anti-trans violence are recorded later in this essay.
7. For more on the personal histories of G. B. Jones and Bruce LaBruce, see my *Queercore: Queer Punk Media Subculture*.
8. Homonormativity, a term popularized by Lisa Duggan in *The Twilight of Equality*, refers to the infiltration of traditional gender and sexual norms into gay and lesbian society, establishing an intra-community hierarchy with upwardly mobile, coupled, monogamous,

cisgender gay white men on top, and transgender, genderqueer, and intersex folks on the bottom, along with queers of color, the non-monogamous, and various subcultural practitioners, such as sadomasochists.

9. This is an abbreviated, updated version of my analysis of Jayne County in *Queercore: Queer Punk Media Subculture*. For more on County's queercore legacy, see this book.
10. This is not to claim that Jayne County was unequivocally accepted within the punk scene. A dramatic example of transphobia occurred during a County performance at CBGB in New York City in 1976. In the middle of her set, singer Dick Manitoba of the Dictators verbally attacked County, calling her a roster of homophobic insults. County, ticked off at a man who had, the night before, heckled Debbie Harry with cries of "Slut!," hit Manitoba in the shoulder with a metal microphone stand as he climbed on stage. An intense brawl ensued, which resulted in sixteen stitches and a broken collar bone for Manitoba, and landed County in jail. For more on this incident, see Legs McNeil's and Gilliam McCain's *Please Kill Me*.
11. This is an abbreviated, updated version of my analysis of Tribe 8 and imagined violence in *Queercore: Queer Punk Media Subculture*. For more on Tribe 8 and imagined violence, see this book.
12. In the WWII Nazi concentration camps, interred gay men were identified by a pink triangle patch that was sewn onto their shirts.
13. In the 1980s, ACT-UP reappropriated the pink triangle as their organizational symbol, along with the phrase "silence equals death."
14. The Trans Day of Remembrance is observed annually on November 20 as a way to memorialize trans people who have been murdered.

References

Berbenick, A. 2015. "Queer Hardcore Punks G.L.O.S.S. Talk Origins, Empowerment, & Their First Big Tour." Bitch Media, September 8. https://www.bitchmedia.org/article/queer-hardcore-punks-gloss-talk-origins-empowerment-their-first-big-tour.

Berlant, L. 2007. "Slow Death (Sovereignty, Obesity, Lateral Agency)." *Critical Inquiry* 33, no. 4: 754–780.

Butler, J. 1990. *Gender Trouble: Feminism and the Subversion of Identity*. New York and London: Routledge.

Butler, J. 2011. *Bodies That Matter: On the Discursive Limits of Sex*. New York: Routledge.

Chinn, S. E. 1997. "Gender Performativity." In *Lesbian and Gay Studies: A Critical Introduction*, edited by A. Medhurst and S. R. Munt. London: Cassell.

County, J. 1996. *Man Enough to Be a Woman: The Autobiography of Jayne County*. New York: Serpent's Tail.

Crimp, D. 2002. *Melancholia and Moralism: Essays on AIDS and Queer Politics*. Cambridge, MA: MIT Press.

Duggan, L. 2003. *The Twilight of Equality: Neoliberalism, Cultural Politics, and the Attack on Democracy*. Boston: Beacon Press.

Foucault, M. 1978. *The History of Sexuality*. Vol. 1. New York: Pantheon Books.

Gerdes, S. 2017. "Founder of Gay Punk Movement Accuses Gucci of Stealing Queer Culture." *Gay Star News*, March 27, 2017. https://www.gaystarnews.com/article/activists-accuse-gucci-stealing-queer-culture/#gs.7kswuFw.

Haritaworn, J., A. Kuntsman, and S. Posocco. 2014. "Introduction." In *Queer Necropolitics*, 1–28. New York: Routledge.

Halberstam, J. 1993. "Imagined Violence/Queer Violence: Representation, Rage and Resistance." *Social Text* 37: 187–201.

Halberstam, J. 1999. "Oh Bondage Up Yours!: Female Masculinity and the Tomboy." In *Sissies and Tomboys: Gender Nonconformity and Homosexual Childhood*, edited by Matthew Rottnek. New York: New York University Press.

Hebdige, D. 1979. *Subculture: The Meaning of Style*. London and New York: Routledge.

Herek, G. M., and K. T. Berrill. 1991. *Hate Crimes: Confronting Violence against Lesbians and Gay Men*. Thousand Oaks, CA: SAGE.

Jones, J. 2013. "Gender without Genitals: Hedwig's Six Inches." In *The Transgender Studies Reader*, edited by S. Stryker and S. Whittle, 449–468. New York: Routledge.

Juno, Andrea. 1996. *Angry Women in Rock*. Vol. 1. New York: Juno Books.

Kelleher, M. 2017. "Laura Jane Grace: 'True Trans Soul Rebel.'" *Gender Forum* 61: 53–65.

LaBruce, B. 2017. "Could Gucci's Clueless Co-opting of Queercore Inspire New Resistance?" *Huffington Post*, March 29, 2017. https://www.huffingtonpost.com/entry/could-guccis-clueless-co-opting-of-queercore-inspire-new-resistance_us_58dbd3cce4b0546370641db2.

Mbembe, A. 2003. "Necropolitics." *Public Culture* 15, no. 1: 11–40.

McNeil, L., and G. McCain. 2006. *Please Kill Me: The Uncensored Oral History of Punk*. New York: Grove Press.

Muñoz, J. E. 1999. *Disidentifications: Queers of Color and the Performance of Politics*. Minneapolis: University of Minnesota Press.

Nault, C. 2018. *Queercore: Queer Punk Media Subculture*. New York: Routledge.

O'Brien, L. 1999. "The Woman Punk Made Me." In *Punk Rock: So What?: The Cultural Legacy of Punk*, edited by Roger Sabin. New York: Routledge, 186–198.

Sellberg, K. 2009. "Transitions and Transformations." *Australian Feminist Studies* 24, no. 59: 71–84.

Stryker, S. 1994. "My Words to Victor Frankenstein above the Village of Chamounix: Performing Transgender Rage." *GLQ* 1, no. 3: 237–254.

Watney, Simon. 1987. *Policing Desires: Pornography, AIDS and the Media*. Minneapolis: University of Minnesota Press.

Personal Interviews

Breedlove, Lynnee. Personal Interview, July 21, 2010.

Von Brucker, Jena. Personal interview, September 28, 2010.

CHAPTER 13

GUILTY OF NOT BEING WHITE
On the Visibility and Othering of Black Punk

MARCUS CLAYTON

> Nothing is more punk rock than surviving in a hungry sea of white noise.
> —Hanif Abdurraqib (2017)

PUNK inherently celebrates equality and inclusivity with its brash sea of noise, yet punks of color are continually left drowning in those waters. At the forefront of the genre is the push against the establishment and its many forms—governmental interference in community lives, capitalistic greed, gender and sexual inequality, and racism—but when viewed through the lens of a punk of color, those pushes do not register any physical progression. Instead, the ideas behind punk rock utilize the usurpation of POC (people of color) ideals without worrying about the physical labor of being othered. In return, POC are given consolation acknowledgment in the punk rock canon: hyphenated inclusion and categorization akin to that of a special attraction. While these attempts to rectify the exclusion of POC within the punk canon are quasi-admirable, the feeling of condescension is impossible to escape. One should look at the term "Afropunk" in this mode: while the term represents a beautiful sect of punk rock that celebrates the noise and voices within the black community, its creation feels needless in the grand scheme of music.

Please note, this is not to say Afropunk is needless as its own entity. Its needlessness stems from the necessity behind its genesis. Think about the Black Lives Matter movement: while the movement has spawned an outreach that has allowed visibility within black communities in response to the frequent police shootings targeting black citizens, and has allowed black people to feel a sense of safety in knowing their identities are being acknowledged through this social outlet, the movement is still one generated by the needless ignorance, betrayal, and violence toward black individuals by the white community. Having to state "Black Lives Matter" is not a proclamation of pride and celebration of culture, but a survival tactic done in the hopes of protecting said *black lives* from further violence by the ignorant and privileged white populace. The Black Lives Matter movement now acts as a form of acknowledgment for the black community and a celebration of a fog now finally lifting from the way that some human beings were (and are) being treated, but its roots are firmly stemmed in violence and erasure, from the white populace forcing black lives out of the lexicon of American life. As the writer Claudia Rankine (2014, 135) has said, "Because white men can't police their imagination, black men are dying." The fact that a movement needed to be born and named in order to retain human dignity within a marginalized community speaks volumes about the needless dominance of white culture. The Black Lives Matter movement now successfully amplifies black voices within the global discourse of justice, but it cannot be forgotten that it was the displacement of blacks by white violence that necessitated the call to action—and the same is true of black voices in punk.

This is why the ideas surrounding such punk genres as Afropunk need to be interrogated: much like the Black Lives Matter movement, Afropunk was not created to celebrate culture so much as it was made to reclaim space stolen by whites. While it is perfectly understandable that Afropunk has generally brought more light to the punk aesthetic within the black community, as well as to other marginalized and POC groups, one should also understand that such labels simply plant white punks further within the foundation of punk, despite their only being a partial piece of the genre's construction. The alteration of "punk" with the prefix "Afro-" only alerts listeners to a mutation of punk; that is, to a form of the genre that reads as "unnatural" or "outside of the status quo of punk." In fact, black voices in punk, just like black lives within humanity, are not a mutation, and they certainly are not an addendum to a musical genre that revels in the ideas of rebellion, systematic change, and a dismantling of hierarchy. In a world where a genre like punk—a genre filled with anger over systematic injustices—is created after a decade rife with racial tensions and civil rights movements, it is laughable to think of punk without a black presence.

The truth is that blackness in punk predates punk. Being that the genre is meant to represent a push against injustices, a push for the intolerance of complacency within societal normalcy, and a tangible representation of the phrase "fuck the man" as a push for direct confrontations with the status quo, then people of color have always been enacting the punk rock ideal by existing in contention with the racial hierarchy created by whites. One could consider the entirety of the civil rights movement—from Rosa Parks taking a seat of her choosing on a bus to demonstrate the freedom she should *not* have to fight for, to Fred Hampton's proclamation and reiteration of his revolutionary and proletariat status to separate himself from law enforcement (Hampton 1969)—as punk, for the actions of black Americans during this time went against the status quo, fought injustices, and refused to stay quiet during times of unrest. When people were attacked by guard dogs or high-velocity fire hoses, they stood right back up and kept fighting. This is the very ethos of punk rock: being loud during a time when those abusing power demand quiet. The conversion of sorrow into anger, into an energy that can be maintained and used to create social upheaval in the name of equality is exactly what punk wants to do and why it breathes. Yet very little of these revolutionary ideals are ever attributed to black cultures within the confines of punk rock.

In fact, the way that punk has always been attributed to white bands and artists merely repeats an earlier act of theft—more sound taken from black culture and recontextualized for a white audience: rock and roll. Typically, Elvis Presley is considered the main culprit behind this claim, wearing his influences very heavily on his sleeve when he first gained notoriety. Albeit more of a symptom of osmosis articulated into 1950s rock songs, there is still no denying that the privilege that Presley's music received allowed the sounds of black angst into the mainstream without exposing white audiences to blacks. Shortly before Elvis became famous, Ray Charles rose to prominence with a brash take on rhythm and blues that would eventually transform into rock and roll (Fong-Torres 1973). But if one compares the reception Charles and Presley received when it came to airplay, one sees the genesis of white capitalization and acceptance within rock music—a reception that blacks would neither share nor profit on, and which would result in blacks receiving the leftover backlash in the coming years.

In 1957, Presley's appearance on the *Ed Sullivan Show* was demarcated for its sexual perversion within Presley's dance moves—he swung his hips around, which network censors feared would make female viewers too hot and bothered, apparently. His performance of "Don't Be Cruel," a rock song that expresses feelings of unrequited longing, was stricken with an act of censorship where the cameras were panned above his hips to avert any attention from his genitalia. The live audience can still be heard swooning during the performance, signaling his hips have swung despite the camera's view, and a sly smile is seen over his face, knowing he has gotten away with something (Television Academy Foundation 2017). To many viewers at home, this was indicative of the rock and roll spirit, a rebellion that ignited decades of weaponized music. However, the mere fact that he was still shown on television *at all* shows a preference of a white face leading such revolutions. It was a safe choice to have a familiar white face that the media could contort with impunity. Should the mask of a rebellious singer grow tiresome, Presley would have simply had to stop swinging his hips to be considered "acceptable" by a different audience. If his smile got too sardonic, the cameras could have easily panned away from his teeth, just as they did from his hips. Thus, regardless of how progressive the sound and moves of Elvis Presley seemed, he and his music were still manicured and presented in flavors that were never as biting as the sounds invented by black musicians. By contrast, when Ray Charles released his single, "What'd I Say" in 1959, it was outright banned from radio stations, both white and black—dismissed even by the black community for being blasphemous and disrespectful to the ideals of the church (Evans 2005). In that way, Ray Charles's music could be described as proto-punk, because it upset the church—and rebellion against religion, especially when it is so closely tied to one's own culture, should be celebrated as an act of punk.

Few people would point to Ray Charles as an original punk, in part because his music does not conform to what we think of when we hear the word. But a similar act of erasure in punk's origin story—or rather, it's replacement and co-option by a whiter object—also occurs in its musical formation, where once again the "why" gets lost in the "who." Although the origins of punk are often disputed between the UK and the USA, the band most often credited with being "the godfathers" of punk are Michigan-based garage band the Stooges. Not only were the heavy and fast noises produced from the self-titled record *The Stooges*, *Fun House*, and *Raw Power* harnessed to evolve music into a crystalized ball of fury known as punk, but the aesthetic of singer Iggy Pop's destructive on-stage persona influenced punks to synthesize music and violence both on stage and off. Pop was well-known for cutting himself, acts of nudity, and physical involvement with the audience, though what often gets forgotten is that the music and the stage persona were often out of sync. The albums themselves worked to display the Stooges as a cohesive unit of what would soon become punk, but many remember the Stooges' early shows more for the antics and the mutilation. A performance in 1968 at the rock club *Mothers* in a small Michigan town saw the Stooges play a set cut short by Pop's indecent exposure, and another set at the Goose Lake International Music Festival saw Pop command an audience to destroy a fence and incur a scene so chaotic that the bassist, Dave Alexander, was too frightened to continue playing, resulting in his firing by Pop himself. These scenes of destruction are synonymous with the Stooges' legacy and are intertwined with what is perceived as the punk legacy. However, the music itself—the aggressive musical notes and abrasive messages interwoven with the lyrics—are rarely the primary point of celebration. It is the violence that whites tie to the punk aesthetic, leaving little room for politics and musicality—such as the time, in 1974, when Pop's performance ended in several lacerations after he asked the audience, "Do you want to see blood?," and had guitarist Ron Asheton (dressed in a Nazi suit, no less!) whip him on the chest until blood was drawn. These scenes of destruction are synonymous with the Stooges and are intertwined with what is now perceived as the punk legacy (Rolling Stone 2016).

This has subsequently become the white version of punk, wherein artists who are not bound by racial limitations on their actions are able to push boundaries of what is "acceptable" and utilize trauma and violence as theatrics meant to represent their role as societal outcasts. Minus the theatrics, Death, another band from Michigan who predate the Stooges, has many more claims to the title "godfathers of punk." This black trio was composed of brothers, who formed the band in their bedroom in 1971, and created an aura of magnetism in their chaotic sounds that matched the Stooges' musicality as well as Iggy Pop's stage antics. Though the band had some of the same aural qualities of the Stooges, Death did not need to utilize violent imagery to convey the underlying ideas of punk rock. Instead, it was their heavy guitars, thumping bass, and high-speed drumbeats that conjured the feeling of rebellion and community.

At that time, black bands were relegated to performing funk-influenced work as dictated by mainstream radio, so the mere presence of three black brothers playing what was perceived to be "white music" recontextualized what it meant to be a musician and actively erased the notion that music—especially heavy music—was race-specific. In much the same way that the Stooges' approach to stage presence often frightened concertgoers, Death's musicianship itself was enough to stop people from the black community in their tracks during performances, as a rock sound permeating from black voices left people stunned. Bassist and vocalist Bobby Hackney has said of Death's performances, "We were in the inner city, on the east side, in the black community. Most of the bands were doing stuff like Al Green, Earth Wind & Fire, the Isley Brothers. Being in the black community and having a rock band . . . [a]fter we got done with a song, instead of cheering and clapping, people would just be looking at us" (Thompson 2010).

Even the name of the band had punk overtones, acting as a subversion of the very definition of Death—a moment of mourning for the absolute end of life. According to songwriter David Hackney, it was meant to ring positively, to look at the word and associate it with a revolutionary sound that would bring energy and life to the modern youth culture (Covino 2012). Death's lyrics especially ring loud in terms of political unrest, as much of their music stayed focused on ideas pertaining to captivity, distrust, and persevering despite societal setbacks. In songs such as "Politicians in My Eyes," which was one of the few songs made widely available during their initial run, there is a punk pivot being made to lambast the insincerity of politicians with the general public while trying to maintain privatized riches for themselves. These kinds of words easily fit into the modern punk rock mode of juxtaposing tones between biting sarcasm and urgent political discourse. The words urge the listener to know that politicians do not care about the public, and that the very act of pretending to care about the lives they are in charge of is an act of fashion to keep up façades in the political world.

Although Detroit area musicians have heard of them, no real dues were paid to this band until the end of the 2000s, as many viewed Death's sound and message to be too outlandish, and the very name "Death" caused their potential record label to drop them. Michigan-born Jack White of the White Stripes has said of the band, "The first time the stereo played 'Politicians in My Eyes,' I couldn't believe what I was hearing. When I was told the history of the band and what year they recorded this music, it just didn't make sense. Ahead of punk, and ahead of their time" (Letts 2005). But it did make sense. Black performers were not expected, wanted, or meant to play rock music, let alone punk rock. At this point, the rhythm and blues stylings crafted by the likes of Ray Charles, as well as Little Richard, Fats Domino, and Lead Belly, were almost completely adopted by white musicians as their own. This left black music to nurture the likes of funk, soul, and eventually hip-hop, announcing those genres to be where black music must be crafted and nurtured. In the end, Death has been left out of an origin story of punk—one that prefers to default toward the white bands from the Detroit area.

Death is not even the only all black proto-punk band to help shape how the punk genre sounded. Today, Death's legacy gets rewritten as the "punk band who was black first, or at least before Bad Brains," but the same could be said for the 1970s Philadelphia quartet Pure Hell. Here is another punk band relegated to the "proto-punk" section of history to make more room for the Sex Pistols and Ramones. Pure Hell suffered from the same lack of commercial viability and nonadherence to stereotypical "black" music—famously refusing to sign to any label in the 1970s due to the pressures to play more funk or soul, or simply "danceable," music that they have gone on record as saying they had no kinship with. With the refusal to fall in line with mainstream expectations, their name disappeared from the punk rock canon, save for a cover of Nancy Sinatra's "These Boots Are Made For Walkin,'" which was seen as more of a novelty than as impactful (although the idea of mutating the pop sensibilities of a white American musical standard has more punk essence than can be seen on some entire albums) (Pure Hell 1978b).

Death, Pure Hell, and Bad Brains are the best-known punk and proto-punk bands that featured black musicians, so it's sad enough that they are not given more credit. The biggest shame about their exclusion from the punk canon, however, is not only how well they fit into the mold of punk, but how much of a better fit they can be compared to their white counterparts—musically, stylistically, aesthetically, and so on. For example, the cover of the Ramones' first album (as well as *Rocket to Russia*) sees the band standing in front of a graffitied brick wall, all wearing leather jackets and torn jeans, and generally displaying faces of discontent and angst (Ramones 1977). To many, this is the image of punk rock: tough guys dressed in dark colors to reflect displeasure with "normal" society. To this day it stands as the standard for the punk rock ethos as well, representing the minimalistic and the gritty side of punk rock. The black-and-white overtone contributes to this idea, drowning the photo of color to perpetuate the dreariness in the music, eliminating the players' skin tone to create an omni-punk—to read these four as *any* teenager with angst. Objectively, this is a fantastic representation of punk. That said, should one look to the vinyl release of Pure Hell's only record, *Noise Addiction*, one will be treated to an even more fierce representation of punk rock. Some ideas stay the same: leather jackets, worn-out jeans, and the look of displeasure upon the faces of each member. But now, behind them is a metallic door—material arguably tougher than brick and impossible to graffiti—and to the top and bottom of the band members is their name and album title written in a font akin to medieval scrawling, a font that signifies rougher times and harsher landscapes. The color is drained from this photo as well, distorting discernable differences within items in the photo (Pure Hell 1978a). The band in this photo, nonetheless, is still black. They are still discernably black, and white teenagers (according to mainstream record companies and Jim Crow laws) can never relate to black punks.

Pure Hell singer Kenny Gordon has mentioned never wanting to be remembered simply as a black band, but only as a band from the original run of punk bands from the 1970s, and he is not alone in this desire (George 2018). When Bad Brains hit the scene in the late 1970s, many considered them pioneers for a couple of very important reasons: one being the creation of a sped-up version of punk rock later known as "hardcore," and the other being that they were an all-black Rastafarian band playing music primarily associated with whites. Once again, this attention (while well-deserved for what Bad Brains did for the landscape of punk) focused on primordial status rather than qualitative musicianship. But the unfortunate truth is that black punk, even now, is *seen* as a sensational moment in music history that deviates from what punk is "meant" to be, despite how much blackness has permeated punk rock from its very start. There are many disputes over the origins of punk, even now, but none of these disputes mention race. Instead, the types of arguments often focus their attention on "authenticity," struggles of class status, and the fetishization of violence. These obsessions were on full display at a March 2019 screening of a newly released docuseries simply titled *Punk*. An all-white panel of punk rock musicians and aficionados, including Henry Rollins, L7's Donita Sparks, and Duff McKagan of metal band Guns N' Roses, gathered with the intention to speak on the series. The panel quickly devolved into a sparring contest between the Sex Pistol's front man, John Lydon (Johnny Rotten), and the Ramones' second drummer, Marky Ramone, over the authenticity of their devotion to punk. On one side, Lydon rallied against the class status of suburban-bred Black Flag and called their music "boring" because of their upbringings, to which Henry Rollins simply retorted with a smirk, saying, "[when] you called Black Flag a bunch of suburban rich kids . . . we wanted to tear your ears off" (Grow 2019). After this, Lydon went after Ramone, lambasting his brief tenure in the band and pointing out that Marky was not part of the original lineup—thus implying that Ramone should be discredited from any claim he may have to creating or bettering the genre from its inception, as his "punk credibility" is not as strong as Lydon's. Unsurprisingly, a heated and profanity-laden exchange occurred, one that both entertained and discomforted the audience. Ramone fired back with his involvement in Richard Hell's *Blank Generation* album—a record that predated the Sex Pistols' first and only album, *Never Mind the Bollocks, Here's the Sex Pistols*, by a month—claiming the Sex Pistols took heavily from that record and Hell's aesthetic. After more back and forth, Sparks chimed in among the chaos, celebrating the argument by stating, "[T]his is fucking punk rock . . . unpolished. Unrehearsed. Off the fucking rails," and later admitting of the punk she first discovered, "I am fucking terrified of [Sex Pistols] and I love it" (Grow 2019).

What the audience witnessed at this panel was an aggressive display of colonial hierarchy in punk rock, one which perpetuates the notion that punk rock celebrates acts of violence for the dissonance and "anarchy for anarchy's sake," for no other reason than to craft destruction out of boredom, and to lay claim to its foundation for the spoils of winning a competition over keeping a heritage alive. At one point, Lydon got up from his seat and danced around the stage, loudly refuting Ramone's claim that "Johnny Rotten talked, but couldn't walk," and this action further cemented the idea that white punks have an urgency to prove their worth in a genre they have worked so hard to usurp. His confrontational gesticulation toward Marky Ramone was a physical act of dominance, a show of muscle when wits proved to be too deficient to make a point. Moments prior, Lydon even stated that "punk was . . . proof positive that we can change our lives by music, [by] meaning what we say, [by] attack[ing] the political systems" (Grow 2019), though the only attacking done was to supposed like-minded punks gathered to celebrate the genre as a community.

This exchange, which was largely for show and was widely reported in the mainstream press, both highlights and exacerbates many problematic elements of punk and race. White punks like Lydon and Ramone are able to play with the idea of violence and authenticity, but actual danger is absent from their platform. Over and over again, the spotlight falls on punk's love of violence rather than what necessitates it. The white punk's careless fascination with violence, along with the fantasy that their socioeconomic status as a "suburban rich kid," or "working class Brit," was the marginalization necessary to claim ownership of the genre, all worked to create a caricature that not only undermined punk, but also undermined the POC communities ousted from the genre. The punk panel therefore underlines such omissions within punk history, in exactly the same manner that all previous popular music genres have done before it. This all exemplifies how rock and roll—a musical genre derived from black musicians—is manipulated by white musicians, contorted in a manner to utilize the rhythm and blues developed by black musicians without the attached melancholy—and this is all amplified within punk. As the noted contemporary punk musician Jasmine Nyende of the all-black and all-femme punk band Fuck U Pay Us has said about their own interactions with white punk, "they want the rhythm, but they don't want the blues."

This statement was made tangible at a May 1, 2019, performance at the Hollywood Palladium, when Fuck U Pay Us opened for seminal Riot Grrrl band Bikini Kill. Here, white punk required its fans to watch Fuck U Pay Us play, and then award Bikini Kill with accolades pertaining to progression and transgressing of racial divides. Bikini Kill then received praise for being "brave" enough to trot out a punk band from a subgenre despite its distance from "real" punk—i.e., the music produced by the canonized white punk bands that were known even by the mainstream audience they would subsequently fight against. Here, white punk requires listeners to remember Kathleen Hanna's cry of "girls to the front" in the 1980s and forgive the missing "black" or "queer" or even a simple "nonwhite" in that sentence as time moved forward and the mosh pit evolved. White punk, especially, requires the listener to forgive Kathleen Hanna's silence after Fuck U Pay Us exited the stage, where Nyende was accosted by the Palladium's security for not having the "correct credentials," despite having just played on their stage. Cell phone footage has shown the security guard treating Nyende as a trespasser, insinuating violence against Nyende for being disruptive. Further reports note Nyende's bandmate Uhuru Moor was treated with equal hostility by staff, being forced to move their own equipment despite Bikini Kill having a separate team for such labor, all while misgendering Moor after several attempts to convey their preferred pronouns as they/them. White punk will ask the listener to overlook the fact that Kathleen Hanna—champion of (white) feminist punk—was nowhere to be seen during these altercations and did not publicly decry any of the evening until nearly a week later:

> We called a meeting with Palladium management the following day to express our concern over the allegations, and to ask why a member of their band was not allowed into the building after the show to use the restroom. We never want racism or transphobia to happen at our shows. We are continuing to do what we can to make sure that [Fuck U Pay Us's] concerns about security's actions that night are being addressed by Palladium management, and to make sure that everyone feels welcome and safe at our shows.
>
> (Bikini Kill 2019)

This falls short of placing blame and calling for any immediate action against those who had wronged FUPU. By calling Nyende's situation "allegations" despite hard evidence, there develops a neutral stance on the attack on women and femme bands, thereby siding with the white patriarchal system punk is meant to rally against. It is a way of subtly stating that the tower the band sits atop—one that allows Bikini Kill a fan base wide enough to play sold-out shows at a venue known for selling tickets with capitalistic gain in mind over substantive artistic expression—is a position they will not relinquish for the greater good. All of which is, decidedly, not punk.

What *is* punk, however, is acknowledgment—something often missing in punk circles, especially with white punks. This is not limited to acknowledgment of other punks, but acknowledgment of privilege as well. In literary circles, the writer James Baldwin once addressed what he saw as a need by whites to partake in the marginalized experience. When meditating on writers such as Jack Kerouac—noted for writing *On The Road*, a novel ostensibly romanticizing the rejection of society and local responsibility, as well as dictating the ease and wonder of removing oneself from the "grid"— who claimed that he "wish[ed he] were a negro [or a] Denver Mexican," in order to get a more full grasp on the wonders of life, Baldwin dashed the notion as being an irresponsible look into identity, calling it "objectively... offensive nonsense" (Baldwin 1993, 278). The very act of being a person of color is not one of costume nor of hiding. The *want* for the life of a person of color is that of malaise and fantasy, of believing that a life without hardship accrues boredom rather than safety, of believing that being an outsider by choice holds the same weight as being an outsider by birth. These beliefs create a white person who is concerned with an identity that will not be misconstrued as objectively evil. However, as Baldwin writes, "[a hip white person would feel] compelled to carry [people of color's] mystique further than they had ... to dominate, in fact, the dreaming field; and since this mystique depended on a total rejection of life, and insisted on the fulfillment of an infantile dream of love, the mystique could only be extended into violence. No one is more dangerous than he who imagines himself pure in heart: for his purity, by definition, is unassailable" (277).

The white fetishization of marginalized living more than extends into the punk world, as Kerouac's sentiments are mirrored by Patti Smith's single, "Rock N Roll Nigger," for her 1978 album *Easter*. The song itself was an attempt to unify so-called outcasts. The idea of a "Rock N Roll Nigger" is Smith's understanding that the violence of whiteness has plagued civilization, and she is making a concerted effort to personally detach from that history in order to create a sense of solidarity by the marginalized specifically hurt by said whiteness. However, this is, in itself, a damaging form of othering: stating that a white person who *feels* like an outsider (i.e., someone who does not feel comfortable living up to white standards for normalcy) can be on the same level of othering as a person of color who had done nothing significantly subversive beyond having darker skin. Furthermore, Smith ignores the idea of choice within the song; the chorus signifies that her ousting is self-afflicted and wanted. As with punk, being a social outcast from a white perspective does not need to be permanent. Piercings heal and leather jackets do not have to be worn, but black skin stays no matter the phase of life one is in. By attempting to be inclusive by appropriating a term used to damage the black community, Smith simply created a wider fissure between blacks and "normalized" society.

Another band with a similar lack of qualms about usurping the plight of the marginalized is Minor Threat. In December 1981 they released the single "Guilty of Being White," a song wherein singer Ian MacKaye rejects the label of "racist" and lambasts the notion that he holds inherently racist thoughts simply because he was born a white male. The song acts as a defense against stereotyping and labels, themes that are inherently punk and give visibility to the Other. However, the act of writing against the stereotype of being called a "racist" in this context—MacKaye specifically targets his experience in high school, where black youths were the ones mocking about the possibility that MacKaye's ancestors could have been slave owners—is one that negates the black experience. It labels the black youths as more harmful than the idea of racism, stating that the reason that violence against marginalized communities continues is because these remarks alone (remarks made sometimes out of safety, sometimes as a way to test the waters in saying, "you're *not* one of them, right?") are what perpetuate the notion that racist acts are caused primarily by whites, outright denying the power dynamic in play by whites.

Some might defend the song by arguing that "'Guilty of Being White' is in no way a song about racism, but [is] about being the minority, and being on the short end of the straw," but the context of this song still negates the black critique of historical whiteness when MacKaye sings, "I'm sorry / for something I didn't do / lynched somebody / but I don't know who . . . I'm a convict / of a racist crime / I've only served / nineteen years of my time" (Minor Threat 1981). The apology in the song exudes an obnoxious level of white privilege. Rather than ruminate on the idea that one's history may be rife with unfortunate pasts and lingering guilt inherited by problematic ancestors, the image of lynching is invoked in a manner whereby the speaker passively looks at the act as something he merely "didn't do." MacKaye himself has reflected on the song, stating, "I never thought I'd have to deal with [the repercussions of 'Guilty of Being White']. I never thought I'd be talking about those lyrics with anyone. I wrote these songs for my group of friends and myself. I didn't think I'd be having this conversation . . . about it over twenty years later" (Maider 2010). Regardless, decades have passed and the song still exemplifies the fragility within white punk, and further amplifies FUPU's words revolving around white punks: "wanting the rhythm, but not the blues" (Fuck U Pay Us 2019b).

MacKaye's lack of foresight as to how the song about alienation may *alienate* those who are constantly hurt should not be a surprising revelation. "Guilty of Being White" was always meant to be an anthem for the outcast, for the punk given weight they were not ready to carry. However, this approach in understanding othering through race does not just prove harmful for how racism should be interpreted—even through an "ally's" mouth—it also sets the precedent that the white punk's tangential interactions with racial plight are more than enough for the punk ethos of equality to subsist. This annihilates the need for punks of color to offer their own interpretation, their own experiences, their own anthems pertaining to struggles they have faced from birth. Obviously, MacKaye does not hate black people—it can even be inferred by his current political views that he is quite fond of them—but "Guilty of Being White" is firm evidence that white punks treat (not only black punk, but) the black experience as a phenomenon that is foreign to punk rock, that can only be misunderstood in the hands of punk rock.

It thus comes as no surprise that, for decades after punk was created, punk was white. Punk was violent. Punk was bored and suburban and was fashion first. So in 2003, when James Spooner released the documentary *Afro-Punk*, which focused exclusively on the black experience in contemporary punk scenes, it created a wave of visibility that was not afforded upon punk's genesis. Though it only spotlighted four bands—including the already canonized Bad Brains—the film did manage to convey a message that was always lying dormant in the annals of punk history: punk was inherently black. One section of the film follows a female punk who states that the genre of music conveyed a sense of togetherness with her culture and the music. The aesthetic was akin to that of aboriginal African tribes—striking piercings and other body modifications—and though the modern punk follows a contemporary and Eurocentric adoption of the aesthetic, she states her choice of fashion relates to the "traditionally African aesthetic [and] it was through punk that [she] had those [cultural] senses reawakened" (Spooner 2003). The film follows this current of unity, with contemporary black punks sharing their love of the music, disdain of white appropriation of rock in general, and—most importantly—acknowledging that black existence within punk rock is not only welcomed, but necessary. One black punk speaks for the rest in terms of representation in punk rock when he says, "Having the Bad Brains as like the baddest fucking [punk] group ever . . . that shit just made me feel like, 'yo, I'm supposed to be here, too'" (Spooner 2003). That feeling of "supposed" to be in punk rock is what was missing from punk for so long, but newly reclaimed with the declaration of Afropunk. Blackness will always be punk, but Afropunk is the medicine that keeps black punks breathing in a world suffocated by whiteness.

Since the film's inception, more concentrated attention has been paid to marginalized punk, especially black punk. The Afropunk festival was founded in 2005 shortly after the film by Spooner himself; over time, the festival expanded to represent African culture laterally related to punk. The punk ethos was not just present in the heavy rock music, but elements of alternative music, fashion, and arts have been on full display at the festival, exhibiting the heart of punk rock—the necessity to right the wrongs of injustices and let the individual be the individual without interference from societal (read white) norms. Through this outlet, black punk has managed to regain its name within the punk community: Death and Pure Hell have both been recognized as pioneers in the genre, and more scrutiny has been placed on white punk throughout the years. The black punk band the White Mandingos (founded by original Bad Brains bassist Daryl Jenifer) even recorded a cover of Minor Threat's "Guilty of Being White" in the same mutilated and restructured format as Pure Hell's treatment of Sinatra's "These Boots Are Made For Walkin'." As expected, the white punks were angered by the lack of purity and reverence for the original. For black punks, however, it was a sigh of relief. Restructured in a manner they felt necessary and artistically viable, the cover begins with a reworking of the bridge, adding emphasis on the singer's age. When the lyrics read, "I've *only* served nineteen years of _my_ time," which emphasizes "only" and "my" to sardonically amplify the original's bratty complaint about how much time one has to spend trying to be forgiven, White Mandingos galvanize the objective fact that nineteen years is nothing compared to four hundred years of slavery.

That all being said, the advent of Afropunk came after years of invisibility, years of questioning (often negatively) whether blackness was allowed in a genre that blackness created—questioning if these black lives in punk mattered. While the idea of celebrating Afropunk is still beautiful in its fulfillment of black visibility and acknowledgment, it is still a reminder of how much history was lost in past decades, and that a new foundation for a genre needed to be established—basically, once a home was stolen, a new home had to be built; how does one not resent the loss of that previous home? Even now, whiteness still tries to acclimate and appropriate Afropunk; some consider Dead Kennedys' drummer D. H. Peligro's (deceased 2022) very existence within the band enough to define the *entire* band as Afropunk. Though Dead Kennedys celebrate the destruction of injustices and inequalities in modern society, Jello Biafra at the helm, with his vocal political stances and eccentric personality, leaves no question that they are very much a white-fronted band (Peligro 2013). Peligro's visibility within the punk canon should absolutely be on display, especially considering the ferocity of his drumming and the backbone it creates for many of Dead Kennedys' hits, but to give the white members "black cred" by proxy simply does a disservice to the aims of Afropunk.

However, there is no doubt that Afropunk—the term, the festival, and the driving idea behind it—does intend to take the forgotten black lives and bring life back into their voices, just as the Black Lives Matter movement asks people to consider the voices of the marginalized alongside their own. In that spirit, reader, I would like you to erase Fuck U Pay Us's mistreatment at the Hollywood Palladium for just a few moments—after all, blues needs rhythm in order to be crafted into punk. After all, black punks appreciate fewer questions about their marginalization, and more about when they first learned to play a guitar.

Picture an all-black, all-femme band on a grand Los Angeles stage they were never meant to take. In front of them is a sea of white faces who have paid an absurd amount of money to see punk rock in a capitalism-forward venue. But that's OK, because they are watching an all-black, all-femme punk band, and, for at least thirty minutes, they are the only punk band in the world to this room. Jasmine Nyende wears a wedding gown to a funeral in service for their silence. Their face is painted white, and they croon over Uhuru Moor's spaced out guitar riffs like a child of Jimi Hendrix (Fuck U Pay Us 2019a). Picture the black femmes as they scream on their own terms, in a language crafted by punk—the reparations they take are the reverberations of their guitars, the march of their drums, the notes they *choose* to play. There is no violence in their performance beyond the call to dismantle the obstacles keeping humanity from being humane. They croon to extinguish their pain, to reclaim a humanity that should have never been lost.

There are cheers. Watch the chaos they control, the chaos given to them by ancestors to speak their freedom into the air for everyone to breathe.

They sing.

They sing.

They sing

References

Abdurraqib, Hanif. 2017. "I Wasn't Brought Here, I Was Born: Surviving Punk Rock Long Enough to Find Afropunk." In *They Can't Kill Us Until They Kill Us*. Columbus, OH: Two Dollar Radio.

Baldwin, James. 1993. "The Black Boy Looks at the White Boy." In *Nobody Knows My Name: More Notes of a Native Son*. Reissue ed. New York: Vintage.

Bikini Kill. 2019. Follow up comment to an April, 27, 2019, Instagram Post. https://www.instagram.com/p/BwxCJcigbBn/.

Covino, Mark Christopher, and Jeff Howlett, dirs. 2012. *A Band Called Death*. Documentary. Drafthouse Films.

Evans, Mike. 2005. *Ray Charles: The Birth of Soul*. London: Omnibus Press.

Fong-Torres, Ben. 1973. "The Rolling Stone Interview: Ray Charles." *Rolling Stone*, January 18, 1973.

Fuck U Pay Us. 2019a. "Board Up." Hollywood Palladium, May 3. Available on YouTube: https://www.youtube.com/watch?v=ov9DQ07AxVM.

Fuck U Pay Us. 2019b. We Don't Need the English: Punk and its Afterlives: 1st Annual UCR PunkCon, Riverside, CA, May 4, 2019.

George, Cassidy. 2018. "Interview: The Forgotten Story of Pure Hell, America's First Black Punk Band." *Dazed*, August 8, 2018. https://www.dazeddigital.com/music/article/40942/1/pure-hell-first-black-american-punk-band-history.

Grow, Cory. 2019. "'Punk': Johnny Rotten, Marky Ramone Spar at 'Off the F-king Rails' Documentary Event." *Rolling Stone*, March 7, 2019. https://www.rollingstone.com/music/music-news/johnny-rotten-marky-ramone-spar-epix-punk-804248/.

Hampton, Fred. 1969. "I Am a Revolutionary." YouTube clip of his 1969 Speech. https://www.youtube.com/watch?v=StTK4IHaRa4.

"If Hips Could Kill: Elvis' Lower Half is Censored on 'The Ed Sullivan Show.'" 2017. Television Academy Foundation, January 5, 2017. https://interviews.televisionacademy.com/news/if-hips-could-kill-elvis-lower-half-is-censored-on-the-ed-sullivan-show.

Letts, Don, dir. 2005. *Punk: Attitude*. Documentary. 3DD Productions.

Maider, Ted. 2010. "Icons of Rock: Ian MacKaye" *Consequence*, June 13, 2010. https://consequenceofsound.net/2010/06/icons-of-rock-ian-mackaye/.

Minor Threat. 1981. "Guilty of Being White." On *In My Eyes EP*. Dischord Records.

Peligro, D. H. 2013. *Dreadnaught: King of Afro-Punk*. Los Angeles: Rare Bird Books.

Pure Hell. 1978a. *Noise Addiction*. 12″ album. Welfare Records.

Pure Hell. 1978b. "These Boots Were Made for Walking/No Rules." 7″ single. Golden Sphinx Records.

Ramones. 1977. *Ramones*. 12" album. Sire Records.
Rankine, Claudia. 2014. *Citizen: An American Lyric*. Minneapolis: Graywolf Press.
Smith, Pattie. 1978. "Rock N' Roll Nigger." On *Easter*. 12" album. Arista Records.
Spooner, James, dir. 2003. *Afro-Punk*. Documentary.
Thompson, Stephen. 2010. Death: A '70s Rock Trailblazer, Reborn | WBUR News. WBUR.org. https://www.wbur.org/npr/124710357/story.php.
"20 Wildest Iggy Pop Moments: The Self-Destructive Legacy of the Infamous Stooge." *Rolling Stone*, April 21, 2016. https://www.rollingstone.com/music/music-lists/20-wildest-iggy-pop-moments-72545/iggy-appears-fully-nude-on-the-cover-of-little-caesar-1979-23648/.

CHAPTER 14

PUNK AND AGING

ANDY BENNETT

In certain respects, from its very early days, punk was more disposed to the presence of aging (or at least "older") participants than might be said of popular music genres and associated scenes up to that point. Some of the people who became involved in punk, such as Ian Dury and Stranglers' drummer Jet Black, were well above the then "accepted" age for popular music artists and, in particular, those with a pop chart presence. Part of this, of course, had to do with punk's shunning of the accepted trappings of the popular music industry at that point. While punk had its own image, which in the fullness of time became as rife for commodification (Hebdige 1979) as previous and subsequent "youth" styles, this did not orientate primarily around the physical appearance of the artist.

However, in a UK context at least, punk's emergence coincided with an era of economic downturn and an increasingly disenfranchised and alienated youth (Chambers 1985). As such, whatever the age or status of punk's musical personnel, for many youth, punk became a personal musical soundtrack that resonated with their often bleak experiences of growing up in late 1970s Britain. Similarly, through its demonization in the UK press, punk became the center of a new moral panic (Cohen 1987) concerning the nation's youth and the allegedly corrupting influence of new youth icons such as the Sex Pistols and the Clash. By the end of 1980s, however, it was clear that punk had longevity, a fact evidenced not least by the fact that it had provided inspiration for new genres such as hardcore and grunge—styles that also indicated the increasingly global presence of punk. But more than this, punk also had an impact on the broader cultural fabric, its do-it-yourself (DIY) ethos having been an important source of inspiration for new forms of DIY culture and associated grass-roots protest movements (McKay 1998). This in no small part was due to the aging denizens of punk, people who had not only grown up with punk, but grown older with it, too. Indeed, as research in youth and music has begun to focus on aspects of aging, heritage, and legacy, punk has become a key focus for understanding how conventional readings of youth culture are challenged as the latter becomes less focused on biological age and more on personal investment, aesthetics, and lifestyle.

Music and Aging

The fact that an individual becomes a follower of a style of music as a "young" person may matter far less than what that music continues to mean to them as they grow older.

—Bennett 2013, 20

Since the early 2000s, there has been increasing interest in the relationship between popular music and aging. In large part this interest has been inspired by one salient, and quite visible, observation: age no longer appears to act as a barrier to participation in popular music scenes. In previous decades, newly emerging genres of popular music, from 1950s rock and roll through the beat and psychedelic rock of the 1960s and glam in the early 1970s, had served to create divisions between generations—particularly between youth and the parent generation. There were some clear precedents for this. Unlike their parents, the baby boomer generation had not experienced the horrors of war and the shortages of basic consumer goods—and in some cases other more vital commodities such as food and clothing—that went along with this. By contrast, the baby boomer era was one of rapid technological development and the plentiful provision of consumer products—including many that were specifically targeted at youth (Bocock 1993). With the beat music movement of the early 1960s, the connection between youth and music was made more steadfast by new generational spokespeople such as the Beatles, the Rolling Stones, and the Who, providing powerful voices and a new soundtrack typified in the Who's 1965 hit "My Generation."

Psychedelic rock took this stance further through its association with the counterculture, whose rejection of mainstream society and its governing institutions frequently manifested in organized demonstrations across North America and Europe (Roszak 1969). While glam rock was not overtly political in the same way, it issued a soft political challenge to the hegemonic order of gendered and sexual identities and relationships (Auslander 2006). Through its aforementioned "calling to arms" of a disempowered youth, initially in Britain but then further afield, punk extended the postwar association between youth culture and music, absorbing along the way the musical and stylistic influences of rock and roll, beat, and glam in what Hebdige (1988) has described as an example of postmodern bricolage.

With the turn of the twenty-first century, however, it became clear that the connection between youth and music might not be as exclusive as had previously been thought. In the context of academic scholarship, an early development pointing in this direction was the opposition to terms such as "subculture." Although the resulting "post-subcultural" literature initially focused on the problems it perceived with the class-based and homological focus of subcultural theory evident in the work of various theorists, such as Clarke et al. (1976) and Willis (1978), via the notions of individualism and reflexivity introduced by post-subcultural scholars (see, for example, Muggleton 2000), it became possible to perceive other ways in which music and identity fed off each other in non-youth contexts, or at least in ways that saw youth becoming an aesthetic rather than an exclusively biological category (Bennett 2018b). Initial studies, such as Calcutt's *Arrested Development* (1998) and Ross and Rose's introduction to their edited anthology *Microphone Fiends* (1994), presented a somewhat one-sided picture of music and aging, suggesting that older music fans were somehow locked into a form of nostalgic wish fantasy to be "young" again. However, an innovative study by Andes (1998), one of the first academic analyses of aging punks, suggested a different way of reading the relationship between music and aging. Andes observed how aging brought with it new levels of experience and competence, allowing older punks to move into different roles and assume different responsibilities in local punk scenes, serving, for example, as managers and venue owners. This theme is returned to later in the chapter.

Other developments in academic scholarship, although not directly focusing on punk, or indeed on popular music and stylistic scenes per se, have also provided useful insights into how the analysis of aging music fans can be cast in a more positive and productive light than has been forthcoming from arrested development perspectives. Important here is the work of Katz (2005), and particularly his critical take on the concept of *cultural aging*. The term cultural aging began to appear more frequently in the 1990s, when theorists such as Featherstone and Hepworth (1995) applied it as a means of problematizing essentialist notions of aging as tied merely to a process of physical deterioration. Similarly, Featherstone and Hepworth suggested that specific conventions of aging governing things such as taste, lifestyle, and visual appearance were sociocultural constructs that varied over time and place. As Katz observes, however, while in principle the concept of cultural aging bespeaks a more progressive means through which aging can be perceived and operationalized in society, its co-option by dominant neoliberal ideologies has served to produce associated discourses of "positive" aging, which are tied to inherently conservative views regarding how individuals should "manage" their aging bodies. Thus, to positively "age" in the now widely accepted sense of the term, individuals should work to keep their body as "young" and healthy as possible through choice of diet, regular exercise, activities designed to promote mental stimulation, and so on.

For Katz, however, this is precisely the point where positive aging threatens to undermine the value of a wider discourse of cultural aging, in that it attempts to pull this back into a pre-proscribed doctrine of what aging individuals should be doing with their lives and what is ultimately "good" for them to be doing. According to Katz, the key point of a term such as "positive aging" should be to allow individuals agency in deciding for themselves what aging positively means for them. In that sense, he argues, positive aging can also "[cultivate] an alternative politics of representation and living in time rather than against it" (2005, 19). In a further elaboration of this point, Katz notes how "older people [are increasingly seen to] engage in a variety of socially productive activities not necessarily limited to the measurable individual activities promoted by gerontologists and professionals" (131).

One obvious way in which individuals may envisage positive aging is through an ongoing engagement with music and associated cultural tastes and practices that they acquired during their youth—or perhaps even earlier—and have essentially grown up with. Although a staunch investment in such practices may be a minority pursuit in middle age and beyond, it is also clear that this is a significant and growing minority. Indeed, as research on the topic of music and aging has served to illustrate, not only do aging individuals hold on to their musical tastes, but such tastes continue to evolve in culturally meaningful ways for them as they age. In this sense, it seems clear that, in the fullness of time, terms such as "aging youth cultures" may serve as less than productive tools for studying a cultural phenomenon that is extending further across the life course.

The Aging of Punk

Punk's aging profile became dramatically apparent in the mid-1990s with the reformation of the Sex Pistols—defunct since 1978—for a seventy-eight-date world tour named the Filthy Lucre Tour. During one of those concerts, at London's Finsbury Park in June 1996, lead singer John Lydon (formerly Johnny Rotten) described the Sex Pistols as "forty, fat, and back," a comment that also reflected back on the audience for the show—many of whom were older punk fans who had turned up to see their generational icons perform. Indeed, the worldwide excitement created by the Filthy Lucre Tour graphically illustrated the ongoing popularity of punk, a music and style that had existed in an essentially underground state since punk's initial moment of critical exposure in the late 1970s. It was in that context, as the lifeblood of scattered local scenes across the globe, that punk's longevity was felt among punk communities that had become intergenerational as young newcomers mixed with aging punks who had invested in punk music and style since the early days of the genre.

The study by Andes (1998) briefly referenced earlier in this chapter was among the first pieces of academic scholarship to not only acknowledge punk's aging status, but also to consider how aging members of punk scenes adapted to the fact of aging within the context of a musical genre that had been previously associated in an almost exclusive sense with the voice of angry youth. As Andes observed, by creating new roles for themselves in punk scenes, aging punks also facilitated an important step in punk's cultural transformation—from a reactive musical and political outburst to an evolving platform for a range of DIY practices and embedded discourses that embodied an ongoing critique of society that was also in many cases a locally specific critique. This is illustrated in work on the punk scene in Portugal (see Guerra and Bennett 2015; Bennett and Guerra 2019), where the emergence of punk in the late 1970s and early 1980s is directly linked to the post-revolutionary transition of Portugal from a primarily agrarian nation governed by a dictatorship to a country embracing cultural and ideological pluralism punctuated by an aspiration toward urbanization and associated lifestyle sensibilities. Within this cultural flux, punk served as an important ideological beacon and source of orientation for Portuguese youth, and it continues to be a fundamental aspect of how punk's significance in the Portuguese context is observed and understood by aging members of Portuguese punk scenes.

While aging members of punk scenes in different parts of the world may be informed by particular localized discourses of punk's sociopolitical significance its history and legacy, what all aging punks appear to have in common is a sense of punk's individual value as a defining part of their individual biographical stories. Bennett's (2006, 2013) work on aging punks in the UK and Australia effectively illustrates this by describing how aging punks in the geographically distanced cities of Canterbury, UK, and Adelaide, Australia, each acknowledge how a long-term investment in punk has shaped them individually. In many cases this has led to a personal understanding of punk as something individually inscribed, and therefore not requiring the visual affirmation of punk status that comes through wearing punk styles and associated forms of body modification. Thus, aging punks frequently talk in terms of having adopted over time a punk personality and an ability to view the world through a "punk perspective." Similarly, the aging punks featured in Bennett's work speak in terms of having toned down their previously more extreme views on concepts such as anarchy, a word made popular in punk speak through the Sex Pistols song "Anarchy in the UK" (1976), from where it became more deeply ingrained through punk's subsequent associations with more extreme political movements, particularly in central and southern Europe and South America (Dunn 2016). While not rejecting such terms out of hand, aging punks often suggest a need for a more informed understanding of the reach of such terms and their practical application (or not), in tandem with a need for tolerance and acceptance.

As noted earlier, there is now a growing understanding of punk, and indeed other "youth" cultural styles, as something not restricted by the confines of biological age, but rather connected with issues of personal taste, lifestyle, and aesthetic preferences—things that extend across the life course. That such shifts are apparent can be measured in part by the changing attitudes toward aging across different music- and style-related cultural scenes. If aging punks and metal fans were once a focus for ridicule in the popular media, it is now increasingly taken for granted that such scenes are multigenerational. Indeed, the media itself has diversified, with a number of publications and television shows and documentaries targeted at older audiences for various genres and styles. Although such age-related commoditization has also extended to punk, as seen in the foregoing example of the Sex Pistols' reunion tour, it would also be fair to say that punk manifests its aging profile in other ways, too. Despite the hype that often accompanied punk in its early years, at the other extreme punk was in part responsible for creating new pathways for disenchanted and disenfranchised individuals to engage in cultural and lifestyle practices that often departed from mainstream cultural life in a critical and anti-hegemonic fashion.

If punk could be said to have deconstructed former dominant views about musical value and the importance of musicianship, the same could be said for its emancipation of other forms of cultural production. It is through this lens that many individuals grew to appreciate and understand punk—and also a way by which many have aged with it. Punk suggested to many of its followers alternative ways of being. In this respect, punk shares a similar legacy with the counterculture of the late 1960s (see, for example, Hall [1968] 2016). However, while the counterculture has frequently been criticized for its promotion of a utopian and romanticized view of social change, punk's gritty social realism produced an understanding among devotees that its mission of social change could only be effectively articulated through adopting it as a lifestyle project.

Punk, Aging Lifestyle, and Careers

What has become clear from research on aging punks is that in many cases the inspiration provided by the experience of being a punk surpasses the status of a stylistic and taste affiliation to become a more deep-seated lifestyle project. Similarly, research has illustrated how many aging punks have chosen career pathways, or indeed forged their own DIY careers, based on their punk aesthetics and sensibilities. Lifestyle was originally applied as a sociological concept by Max Weber (2019) in work on the leisure class of the late nineteenth century. For Weber, the conspicuous use of consumer objects was a way in which social groups were able to mark themselves off as bearers of wealth and status in a society that was rapidly being shaped by early forms of consumer capitalism. During the twentieth century, lifestyle was used in marketing and survey research on consumer trends, only emerging as a more critical concept again in the later twentieth century when, in the wake of the cultural turn (Chaney 1994), sociologists and cultural theorists again became interested in the reflexive properties of lifestyle. Chaney's (1996) concept of lifestyle sites and strategies builds on Weber's initial application of lifestyle through its examination of how late modern individuals inscribe meaning in mass-produced objects, images, and texts, thus giving them specific and localized meanings. At a distance of some one hundred years from Weber's original writings, the sociocultural contexts Chaney investigates are far more complex in terms of the plurality of taste orientations and lifestyle preferences. Indeed, the concept of lifestyle also featured heavily in post-subcultural theory, as a number of researchers suggested that youth groupings conventionally referred to as "subcultures" could be recast as forms of reflexive youth lifestyle (see, for example, Bennett 1999 and Miles 2000).

Studies of aging punks have demonstrated the effectiveness of lifestyle by considering how the cultural resources of punk are retained by aging punks across the life course. Indeed, this has been an important aspect of the critical challenge made to previous notions of aging punks (as well as hippies, rockers, etc.) as being cultural misfits. Rather, it has been demonstrated how the maturation of punk into an ongoing lifestyle project offers an opportunity to see how it has influenced a range of lifestyle tastes and preferences. In addition to music and fashion, these may also extend to things such as choice of literature, food and drink, tourism, and so forth. Political and broader worldviews on issues such as the environment and human and animal rights are also frequently seen to be influenced by an ongoing association with punk and a punk-influenced lifestyle.

The theme of punk influence on choice of career is particularly interesting. For a number of years it was suggested that punk's "obsession" with social and political change was a fundamentally youthful obsession, and thus a naïve concept. Indeed, as several "old punks" were seen to become quasi-establishment figures or wrote features for glossy magazines focusing on the punk exploits of their misspent youth, such a perception proliferated. This position, however, failed to take into account the appeal of punk far beyond the media-profiled aging punks who tended to take on the role of generational spokespeople. Indeed, research on punk and aging has frequently mined the depths of the more mundane everyday circumstances where punk's impact was felt. Indeed, it is in these places where the broader impact of punk on lifestyles and career is more resonantly felt. Although it could be said that punk invented the concept of DIY in the sense of cultural production and practice (see Bennett 2018a), what is clear is that it provided a more accessible and vernacular basis for a notion of DIY as a resistant property. As documented elsewhere, in its initial punk manifestation, DIY had originally been practiced in association with the production and recording of music (Dunn 2016), in the creation of punk fashion (Savage 1992), and in associated areas such as the production of fanzines (Teal 2006). During the 1980s and 1990s, however, this punk-inspired concept of DIY become more widespread, informing a range of single-issue political and lifestyle movements in a global context (see, for example, McKay 1998 and Poldervaart 2001).

Research on punk and aging has revealed the extent to which this DIY cultural sphere has extended and developed over the decades since punk first emerged. A critical part of this work has been the uncovering of aging punks engaged in a variety of punk-inspired DIY careers. Thus, for example, in Bennett's (2006, 2013) work on punk and aging in the UK and Australia, it was shown how many aging punks, in their forties and fifties, were engaged in a variety of full- and part-time occupations in fields such as charity work and community services, as well as voluntary part-time activities such as hosting community radio shows. The common connection across all of these activities is a commitment to working for and with the community, providing some kind of service designed to enhance the well-being of communities and improve the quality of life for those in local neighborhoods—particularly those who are excluded through economic hardship. Similarly Bennett illustrates how, through running a talk-based community radio show, two Adelaide punks sought to dissect and challenge dominant political discourses on various issues such as fast food and global warming. Similarly, Guerra's (2018) work on aging punks in Portugal reveals how an internalized punk DIY ethos has been instrumental across a divergent range of career paths in fields of media, journalism, art, fashion, interior design, and cookery. Haenfler's (2018) work on punk, aging, and careers in the United States illustrates how even in cases where aging punks have opted for more mainstream career paths, skills acquired through being a punk have fostered an ongoing DIY ideology. Thus, observes Haenfler,

> Many participants reported that their scene experiences cultivated self-reliance and a strong work ethic that prepared them for their work. They saw that as central to the

DIY ethic. More than resistance to corporate hegemony, participants claimed that DIY entailed getting things done despite obstacles. (2018, 182)

As such insights reveal, over a long period of immersion in punk, individuals often come to regard its underlying principles and general outlook on the world as integral aspects of their own personalities and biographical trajectories. This suggests that aging punks have often collectively imbibed what could be referred to as a "punk perspective"—a way of looking at the world that they feel is shaped by punk and its ongoing influence over their lives. Although the fact of "youth cultural" sensibilities extending in this way across the life course may not be an exclusive feature of punk, the distinctive resistant and anti-hegemonic qualities that were evident in punk from its early years have provided a particularly potent blueprint for alternative and resistant modes of aging.

Punk and Generations

If punk is at one level an "aging" youth culture, then it is simultaneously a scene to which new, younger members are continually been introduced. As noted earlier in this chapter, following its moment in the media entertainment spotlight, and its concomitant condemnation by the mainstream press who made punk an object of moral panic (Laing 1985), punk has led an essentially underground existence. Certainly the influence of punk has registered in a succession of genres since the late 1970s, among them goth (Hodkinson 2002), indie (Bannister 2006), hardcore (Driver 2011), straight edge (Haenfler 2006), and grunge (Strong 2011). Likewise, punk gave rise to its own "subgenres," including anarcho-punk (Gosling 2004) and ska punk (Bennett 2006). Throughout this time, however, punk has remained as a consistent center-point, with new local punk bands regularly forming in scenes across the world and commanding small but loyal audiences at small, local venues and larger, often translocal, punk festivals (Dowd et al. 2004). Each of these developments in punk has attracted a new generation of fans, with the result that, in a contemporary sense, punk is less a youth culture and more a multigenerational cultural scene. Punk today is a highly diverse space in which punks of different ages coexist, with each successive punk generation bringing something new to the scene. Contemporary punk's more robust grasp of single-issue politics, its views on things such as animal rights, environmentalism, and the frequent preference of punks for vegetarian or vegan food and drug- and alcohol-free lifestyles is testament to the multilayered generational nature of punk and how this has nurtured and evolved the capacity of punk as an alternative cultural sphere of existence.

However, the multigenerational punk scenes have also brought with them some challenges. During the early 1990s, when the first baby boomers began reaching middle age, Grossberg (1994) lamented how this appeared to give rise to a "golden age" effect whereby aging individuals who had spent their youth during the 1960s upheld that decade as the era when youth were "properly youth." The upshot of this, claimed

Grossberg, was a dismissal of subsequent youth generations as apolitical and apathetic (see also Bennett 2001). While such a claim cannot be directly applied to punk, the fact remains that the different generations who have successively engaged with punk have brought a deepening complexity to how punk can be considered in any way unified in terms of its system of beliefs and the cultural codes that (re)produce and maintain such beliefs. Indeed, it has frequently been observed (see, for example, Andes 1998; Bennett 2006; and Haenfler 2006) how aging members of punk scenes seek to legitimate their ongoing presence in the scene through a discourse of age-centered authority. This relates not so much to a felt need to impress a physical authority in punk spaces, but rather to express this authority through the knowledge and competence they have gained through a sustained period of investment in punk. Driver and Bennett (2015) have noted how embodied displays of cultural competence are critical to how members of music scenes are able to demonstrate their authority as seasoned participants in particular scenes. For aging punks, particular devices come into play, including occupying specific spaces in a venue or club. This often involves being away from the main stage or mosh pit, which is regarded as a zone for younger punk fans. Fonarow (1997) has described this practice among aging fans of indie music using the concept of *zoning* to describe how the spaces in venues and clubs are often age-demarcated, with the age of audience members increasing relative to how far they position themselves from the stage. In many punk venues, the smallness of the space, sometimes combined with the absence of a stage, means that band and audience are positioned at the same level in close confines. In such a situation, the age-related positioning of punk generations is highly apparent, as is the way that age bestows authority to act in a particular way within the venue.

Similarly, distinctions of age bring with them different understandings of how audience participation at punk gigs is to be conducted. Thus, in Bennett's (2006) work accounts are provided of how some aging punks were ambivalent about the way their younger peers engaged in stage-diving. Alternatively, many older punks preferred to show their appreciation of the band and its music through pogoing (a punk dance style that emerged in the late 1970s) or by simply watching the performance, perhaps sipping from a bottle of beer. Frequently, however, such age-related distinctions are compensated for by a general reverence among young and old for the longevity of punk and through respect for those (typically older) punks who possess a deep knowledge of the genre and its development over the years. At the same time, rather than being dismissive of newer punk bands and their music, older punks frequently acknowledge that the longevity of punk as a musical and cultural scene is due to the generational innovation that regularly takes place and brings new blood into local and translocal punk scenes. In this sense, the ongoing interchanges between young and old provides a telling illustration of how punk in a contemporary context is regarded by those who form a part of its dynamic and ever-evolving field of cultural practice. Common among all of those who invest in punk over a longer period of time, however, is a shared understanding of punk's significance as a cultural space whose critical mission is to engage with and challenge social and political issues. Here again, the regular influx of new ideas and motivations into punk has served to keep it alert to a variety of ever-evolving themes. In recent years punk's increasing presence on Web 2.0 has provided a telling illustration of how the multigenerational legacy of punk is now working to move the counter-hegemonic voice of punk increasingly into the center as punks of various ages discuss contemporary issues such as racism, homophobia, austerity, and the precarious lifestyles this frequently imposes on individuals.

Aging Punks and Cultural Legacy

Unsurprisingly, aging punks have also played a key role in observing and commenting on the cultural legacy of the genre. And there are decidedly mixed views on the part of aging punk's concerning its transition from an abruptly resistant and anti-hegemonic voice to an aspect of "cultural heritage." For example, while many aging punks have welcomed punk exhibitions such as 2016's Punk London (which was timed to celebrate UK punk's fortieth anniversary), others have questioned the place of punk in the museum space. For those who oppose this formalized treatment of punk's past, the notion that it should be preserved in a way analogous to other aspects of British history that punk itself sought to oppose appears paradoxical. On the other hand, punk's legacy of DIY has offered other (in the view of some, more "natural") ways of preserving punk's memory in the form of small DIY tributes to punk and its legacy. Willsteed (2019) highlights the important role that has been played by the DIY collector and archivist in preserving the material artifacts of popular music scenes, focusing on the example of punk in the Australian city of Brisbane. However, Willsteed's description works as well for other locations where the cultural memory of punk is preserved through the work of dedicated amateurs, many of them aging punks. It is often the case that such artifacts will then be used as a basis for occasional, less formalized events such as Willsteed's own "It's Not the Heat, It's the Humidity," a one-man audiovisual commentary on the history of Brisbane punk held over two nights at Brisbane's Powerhouse in October 2015. As Willsteed subsequently noted,

> Having been present in the [Brisbane punk] scene through the late 1970s and 1980s, I began to develop an interest in extending these methods to include my particular skills as a musician and filmmaker in order to tell a more particular story.
>
> (Willsteed 2019, 167)

Aging punks have also contributed to the legacy of punk and the preservation of the punk ethos through the development of extra-musical careers that have allowed them to develop a profile as punk and generational spokespeople. An early example of this was seen in the BBC 2 ten-part popular music history documentary television series *Dancing in the Street* (1996). In the episode dedicated to punk, various artists associated with the genre, including John Lydon, Iggy Pop, Jonathan Richman, Pete Shelley, Siouxsie Sioux, and Ari Up, offer retrospective impressions of punk's impact at a then twenty-year distance from the "punk summer" of 1976. Such media profiling of aging punks continued with niche television programs such as *The Henry Rollins Show*, an American weekly television show broadcast by the Independent Film Channel between 2006 and 2007 and featuring Henry Rollins, lead singer with legendary US anarcho-punk band Black Flag (see Gosling 2004). The show combined sociopolitical commentary from Rollins, guest interviews, and uncensored musical performances. Those interviewed on the show included film director Oliver Stone; rapper, author, and producer Chuck D; and electronic musician and performance artist Peaches.

The presence of aging punks has also registered in the academy, with an increasing array of publications dedicated to punk that include contributions frequently written by older punks. Examples of this range from Roger Sabin's edited collection *Punk Rock, So What? The Cultural Legacy of Punk* (1999) to the establishment of the Punk Scholars Network (PSN). Founded in 2012, the PSN has served as a forum for those with an academic and/or critical interest in the legacy and ongoing significance of punk to collectively discuss it via a regular series of conferences, symposia, exhibitions, and one-off talks. Bennett (2002) has discussed the value of "insider research" in bringing new levels of understanding to particular music scenes and communities through a potential ability to access participants and engage in a level of discussion that might not be readily accessible to researchers without an insider status. Initiatives such as the PSN provide an example of how insider research is being applied in the case of punk, including the presence of aging punks (many of whom continue to be active in local and translocal punk scenes) applying their cultural knowledge and competence of punk as means of investigating its longevity and cultural legacy.

At a more mundane, everyday level, the role of aging punks in preserving the punk legacy is visible in the ongoing visual and aesthetic presentation of a punk identity. Research by various academics has pointed to the way in which older punks will often tone down their visual appearance as they age (see, for example, Holland 2004; Bennett 2006; and Haenfler 2006). This may be the result of a number of factors, including the need for a less radical image in the workplace or physical factors such as (typically in the case of male punks) hair loss in middle age and later life. Or it may be the case that aging punks feel it to be less of a necessity as they age to show their allegiance to punk through visual image. By the same token, however, many aging punks do continue to retain a visual connection (in whole or in part) with punk, providing a further illustration of how punk has impacted everyday fashion and stylistic sensibilities and worked to challenge previous "standards" and stereotypes of aging and how individuals manage their aging bodies.

Conclusion

This chapter has focused on the relationship between punk and aging, offering a variety of perspectives on how this relationship is envisaged and managed by aging individuals who continue to invest in punk music, style, and ethos. The chapter has illustrated how, through such an ongoing investment in punk over a period of time, aging punks have essentially transformed punk from its youth cultural origins into an ongoing lifestyle project of the self. Similarly, through their ongoing presence in local and translocal punk scenes, and through their interactions with younger members of these scenes, aging punks form part of a new era of punk as a multigenerational sphere of alternative and counter-hegemonic cultural practice. Aging punks have also been critical in preserving the legacy of punk, often acting as spokespeople for punk's ongoing and developing voice in connection with a range of sociopolitical, economic, and cultural issues. Through the various ways aging punks continue to engage with punk and articulate its ethos, they provide an avenue for understanding the deeper transformative qualities of punk upon the fabric of society. For many of its aging followers, punk has become a way of life and is integral to a broad sphere of everyday activities, including work, leisure, interpersonal relationships, and worldview.

References

Andes, L. 1998. "Growing Up Punk: Meaning and Commitment Careers in a Contemporary Youth Subculture." In *Youth Culture: Identity in a Postmodern World*, edited by J. S. Epstein, 212–231. Oxford: Blackwell.

Auslander, P. 2006. *Performing Glam Rock: Gender and Theatricality in Popular Music*. Ann Arbor: University of Michigan Press.

Bannister, M. 2006. *White Boys, White Noise: Masculinities and 1980s Indie Guitar Rock*. Aldershot, UK: Ashgate.

Bennett, A. 1999. "Subcultures or Neo-tribes? Rethinking the Relationship between Youth, Style and Musical Taste." *Sociology* 33, no. 3: 599–617.

Bennett, A. 2001. *Cultures of Popular Music*. Buckingham, UK: Open University Press.

Bennett, A. 2002. "Researching Youth Culture and Popular Music: A Methodological Critique." *British Journal of Sociology* 53, no. 3: 451–466.

Bennett, A. 2006. "Punk's Not Dead: The Significance of Punk Rock for an Older Generation of Fans." *Sociology* 40, no. 1: 219–235.

Bennett, A. 2013. *Music, Style, and Aging: Growing Old Disgracefully?* Philadelphia: Temple University Press.

Bennett, A. 2018a. "Conceptualising the Relationship between Youth, Music and DIY Careers: A Critical Overview." *Cultural Sociology* 12, no. 2: 140–155.

Bennett, A. 2018b. "Music Scenes and Ageing Bodies." *Aging Studies* 45: 49–53.

Bennett, A., and P. Guerra. 2019. "Rethinking DIY Culture in a Post-industrial and Global Context." In *DIY Cultures and Underground Music Scenes*, edited by A. Bennett and P. Guerra, 7–18. Abingdon, UK: Routledge.

Bocock, R. 1993. *Consumption*. London: Routledge.

Calcutt, A. 1998. *Arrested Development: Pop Culture and the Erosion of Adulthood*. London: Continuum.

Chambers, I. 1985. *Urban Rhythms: Pop Music and Popular Culture*. London: Macmillan.

Chaney, D. 1994. *The Cultural Turn: Scene Setting Essays on Contemporary Cultural History*. London: Routledge.

Chaney, D. 1996. *Lifestyles*. London: Routledge.
Clarke, J., S. Hall, T. Jefferson, and B. Roberts. 1976. "Subcultures, Cultures and Class: A Theoretical Overview." In *Resistance through Rituals: Youth Subcultures in Post-war Britain*, edited by S. Hall and T. Jefferson, 9–74. London: Hutchinson.
Cohen, S. 1987. *Folk Devils and Moral Panics: The Creation of the Mods and Rockers*. 3rd ed. Oxford: Basil Blackwell.
Dowd, T. J., K. Liddle, and J. Nelson. 2004. "Music Festivals as Scenes: Examples from Serious Music, Womyn's Music and Skatepunk." In *Music Scenes: Local, Translocal, and Virtual*, edited by A. Bennett and R. A. Peterson, 149–167. Nashville, TN: Vanderbilt University Press.
Driver, C. 2011. "Embodying Hardcore: Rethinking Subcultural Authenticities." *Journal of Youth Studies* 14, no. 8: 975–990.
Driver, C., and A. Bennett. 2015. "Music Scenes, Space and the Body." *Cultural Sociology* 9, no. 1: 99–115.
Dunn. K. C. 2016. *Global Punk: Resistance and Rebellion in Everyday Life*. London: Bloomsbury.
Featherstone, M., and M. Hepworth. 1995. "Images of Positive Aging: A Case Study of *Retirement Choice* Magazine." In *Images of Aging: Cultural Representations of Later Life*, edited by M. Featherstone and A. Wernick, 29–47. London: Routledge.
Fonarow, W. 1997. "The Spatial Organization of the Indie-Guitar Music Gig." In *The Subcultures Reader*, edited by K. Gelder and S. Thornton, 360–370. London: Routledge, 360–370.
Gosling, T. 2004. "'Not for Sale': The Underground Network of Anarcho-Punk." In *Music Scenes: Local, Translocal, and Virtual*, edited by A. Bennett and R. A. Peterson, 168–183. Nashville, TN: Vanderbilt University Press, 168–183.
Grossberg, L. 1994. "Is Anybody Listening? Does Anybody Care? On Talking about 'The State of Rock.'" In Ross and Rose 1994, 41–58.
Guerra, P. 2018. "Raw Power: Punk, DIY and Underground Cultures as Spaces of Resistance in Contemporary Portugal." *Cultural Sociology* 12, no. 2: 241–259.
Guerra, P., and A. Bennett. 2015. "Never Mind the Pistols? The Legacy and Authenticity of the Sex Pistols in Portugal." *Popular Music & Society* 38, no. 4: 500–521.
Haenfler, R. 2006. *Straight Edge: Clean-Living Youth, Hardcore Punk, and Social Change*. Piscataway, NJ: Rutgers University Press.
Haenfler, R. 2018. "The Entrepreneurial (Straight) Edge: How Participation in DIY Music Cultures Translates to Work and Careers." *Cultural Sociology* 12, no. 2: 174–192.
Hall, S. (1968) 2016. "The Hippies: An American 'Moment.'" In *Youth Culture*, vol. 1, edited by A. Bennett, 364–379. London: SAGE.
Hebdige, D. 1979. *Subculture: The Meaning of Style*. London: Routledge.
Hebdige, D. 1988. *Hiding in the Light: On Images and Things*. London: Routledge.
Hodkinson, P. 2002. *Goth: Identity, Style and Subculture*. Oxford: Berg.
Holland, S. 2004. *Alternative Femininities: Body, Age and Identity*. Oxford: Berg.
Katz, S. 2005. *Cultural Aging: Life Course, Lifestyle, and Senior Worlds*. Peterborough, ON: Broadview Press.
McKay, G., ed. 1998. *DIY Culture: Party and Protest in Nineties Britain*. London: Verso.
Miles, S. 2000. *Youth Lifestyles in a Changing World*. Buckingham, UK: Open University Press.
Muggleton, D. 2000. *Inside Subculture: The Postmodern Meaning of Style*. Oxford: Berg.
Poldervaart, S. 2001. "Utopian Aspects of Social Movements in Postmodern Times: Some Examples of DIY Politics in the Netherlands." *Utopian Studies* 13, no. 2: 143–165.
Ross, A., and T. Rose, eds. 1994. *Microphone Fiends: Youth Music and Youth Culture*. London: Routledge.

Roszak, T. 1969. *The Making of a Counter Culture: Reflections on the Technocratic Society and Its Youthful Opposition*. London: Faber.
Sabin, R., ed. 1999. *Punk Rock: So What? The Cultural Legacy of Punk*. London: Routledge.
Savage, J. 1992. *England's Dreaming: Sex Pistols and Punk Rock*. London: Faber.
Strong, C. 2011. *Grunge: Music and Memory*. Farnham, UK: Ashgate.
Teal. T. 2006. "Scissors and Glue: Punk Fanzines and the Creation of a DIY Aesthetic." *Journal of Design History* 19, no. 1: 69–83.
Weber, M. 2019. *Economy and Society: A New Translation*. Translated by K. Tribe. Cambridge, MA: Harvard University Press.
Willis, P. 1978. *Profane Culture*. London: Routledge and Kegan Paul.
Willsteed, J. 2019. "'Here Today': The Role of Ephemera in Clarifying Underground Culture." In *DIY Cultures and Underground Music Scenes*, edited by A. Bennett and P. Guerra, 160–170. London: Routledge.

CHAPTER 15

IDENTITY? HOW 1970S PUNK WOMEN LIVE IT NOW

LUCY O'BRIEN

As a punk feminist academic writing this chapter, I have had trouble with the pronoun "we." In some drafts I have taken it out. In other drafts it has stayed in. I realize that that the trouble with "we" is an advantageous troubling of the categories. It is the link to in-between spaces, a creative friction between the identities of punk, feminist, and academic. In the same way that Greg Dimitriadis (2015, 40) found self-reflexivity fundamental to his hip-hop scholarship, so reflection on my part in the scene is essential for a study of how 1970s punk women live the punk ethos now.

With the help of subheadings adapted from lyrics from the 1978 X-Ray Spex song "Identity," this chapter revisits and builds on "The Woman Punk Made Me," a polemical essay I wrote in 1999 (O'Brien 1999). And over twenty years later, I am exploring how punk continues to define us. I am struck by how much punk, for its 1970s participants, has become both an internalized thought process and a source of strength and agency in the world around us. In order to explore this idea further, I need to establish the first principles we are working from. The next section is a stream-of-consciousness reflection on those first principles, a way to access the original mental space that created punk for me.

> *When we made music we tried consciously to make sounds that we hadn't heard before. It had to be new. When we dressed we consciously tried to wear clothes that hadn't been worn that way before. We tried to cut our hair in a way that we hadn't seen before. We tried to dance in a way we had not seen before. Conscious is the key word. Viv Albertine says, "we were very conscious and alert" (Albertine, July 2015).*

> *We took note. Everything we did or said was the result of a choice and a decision. People ask me to define what punk is . . . and it wasn't about what we wore (though sometimes it was), and it wasn't about spikey hair (though sometimes it was), and it wasn't just about music (though that was a key part). Punk is a state of mind and decision-making.*

That doesn't change if you grow older, or if you grow your hair, or if you have children, or if you move to the country. That doesn't change.

What are we deciding? Whether this is a con. Whether we are being sold to. Whether we are being co-opted. And whether our creativity is being taken away from us. There is a set of questions we ask, and it's so automatic, it's like driving: I no longer think "mirror, signal, manoeuvre," I just do it—without looking.

I have an idea for a memoir on punk and feminism—a publisher wonders if my Twitter account is big enough and whether I've been on satirical BBC quiz show Have I Got News for You. *And if the stars I have stories about are big enough. They are buying my access to the stars I write about, but not my story. I meet a potential new agent. She sizes me up, asks when my last original book came out and how much it sold, whether I might like to write about groupies from the 1960s because they were like, empowered women. Empowered? Really?*

I go home. Regroup. I'm in my fifties but I'm still a punk. What do punks do? I decide I will write the book myself, because no one else can tell my story. I will do it in my own way and my own time. That is DIY. Do It Yourself. Those words resonate. It's not a punk cliché, it is a way of life. In the absence of a role model, or a path, or a channel—you make it yourself. If it hasn't been done before in the way you imagine, you do it yourself. "Making" is the key word. Punk was always about construction. It was very physical. I want to make something happen, so I get the tools to do it. I get the guitar, we buy the drums on Hire Purchase, we get the Saturday job to get the drums and guitar. We make the earrings and bake the cakes to sell at school and buy our instruments. We meet every Tuesday and every Thursday after school and we work at creating new sounds on our instruments and record them and put them together into tracks and songs, and then we stop for Marmite sandwiches, and listen back to what we have done, and then listen to PIL or the Slits, or Siouxsie and the Banshees' first album, or Joy Division's drumming, or the keyboard rush of B52s and we deconstruct it. Take it apart and listen.

Punk was about construction and deconstruction. It was like brutalist architecture. The mechanics are on the outside. The logic is on the outside. Punk had a work ethic. In his book Global Punk, *Dunn argues, "If you're trying to rebel you don't volunteer to check out, you step to it" (Dunn 2016, 11). We worked hard, we grafted. Like Henry Rollins with his working out and his stand-up and his spoken word. We had the tools of a physical, analogue culture. We used printed words and makeup and hair dye and guitars and cut-ups and photocopiers and drums and textiles and paint and montage and lipstick and boots and skirts and speakers and amps and we had tools. Everything we had we made a decision about. Everything was a tool for expression.*

Do You See Yourself?

Female participation in subculture is under-researched—yet women shape the future of music scenes in many creative ways. The participation of older women in punk subculture is documented even less. I am grateful to Andy Bennett for his work on fan practices of punk individuals beyond the age of thirty. His study "Punk's Not Dead" posits that self-identified older punk fans tended to be male, while female punks he contacted had either "moved on" from the 1970s scene that spawned them and that they made, or declined to be interviewed (Bennett 2006, 224). To find out whether they had moved on or disappeared from the scene, in July 2017 I put up a Facebook post asking any 1970s female punks to get in touch. The response was immediate: within a day my post had 80 likes, 38 comments, and 58 shares. I then sent out a structured questionnaire and did a set of semi-structured interviews via phone, email, and face-to-face, asking women from the original punk generation how they articulate and manage punk in their lives now (see Acknowledgements for details). Though supportive of the project, many respondents to my Facebook post have busy work and family lives, so not all had time to do interviews or the questionnaire. Those that did were open and fulsome in their answers. It can be argued that they were a self-selecting group, rather than representative of 1970s punk women as a community. However, even women who do not consider themselves to be "living punk" now, when questioned further, realized that values of community and authenticity still resonate with them.1

The results, collated during 2017–2018 from a diverse group of eighteen women in their fifties, show that, far from moving on, older women's punk identity has grown with them, affecting their decision-making in every area of life—from clothes to music, work, and politics. Subculture offers a way to maintain gendered dissidence (Cofield and Robinson 2016, 1072), and older punk women are practiced at negotiating the fault lines and creative frictions of their subcultural and more "normative" identities. The subcultural experience of their youth is woven into their psychology and decision-making in family and workplace environments, often to profound effect. In this chapter I will look first at the social factors influencing the female punk generation in the 1970s, before discussing how those women live punk now.

Identity Is the Crisis You Can't See

I have found that Karl Mannheim's sociology of generations is an enduring method and a useful way to frame 1970s female punk (Pilcher 1994). "Generation" can be defined as a way of understanding differences between age groups and as a means of locating people within historical time. If the study of generations marks social change and continuity, what is pronounced in the 1970s punk story is the relationship between personal and social change. According to Mannheim, formative experiences during youth are the key way in which social generations are formed. A "cohort" is defined as people who experience the same significant event within a given period of time (Pilcher 1994, 483). Male and female punk peers experienced the 1970s era as a cohort, and those still living it now see themselves as defined by the punk cultural battlefield. The 1970s youth culture could be fiercely tribal, for instance, and punks were frequently attacked by other subcultural tribes like skinheads and rockabillies (O'Brien 1999, 193).

Jane Pilcher builds on Mannheim's legacy, exploring how young people are integrated into society via mechanisms of socialization. What is desired and expected by the parent generation is a gradual evolution of the social order. Generations can be drivers of social change, but not every generation develops an original and distinctive consciousness. I am not claiming punk exceptionalism, but there were a number of cultural factors in the 1970s that combined to create a radical new articulation of feminism for young women. Active generation units become agencies of change in times of accelerated social shifts, when normality is disrupted. The fresh contact of new generations means a "novel approach in assimilating and developing the proffered material" (Pilcher 1994, 491). Much of this change is located in the discourse used by political and social thinkers, in the vocabulary they use to express nuances of meaning and value. For many of my female interviewees there is a sense of groping for words to express their experience, a formulation of an emotional language that does not yet exist. "We were trying to find a new vocabulary," said Linder Sterling, the artist who repurposed images of pornography for the Buzzcocks' 1977 "Orgasm Addict" record sleeve, looking back in 1997 (quoted in O'Brien 1999, 186). A further two decades on, punk women are still redefining that vocabulary.

In order to explore the "proffered material" of 1970s female punk, it is useful to identify the social triggers for a new female, and feminist, consciousness. The Equal Pay Act of 1970 and Sex Discrimination Act of 1975 opened up many new career opportunities for women. Widespread use of the contraceptive pill and an active National Abortion Campaign meant greater sexual and reproductive freedom, while second-wave feminism and greater access to higher education through government grants informed women's personal and political choices (Rowbotham 2014, 247). We were aware of how our mothers' lives had been restricted, and how many of them responded to that restriction with depression, anger, or a passive-aggressive acceptance of the status quo.

Feminism, the New Left, and punk all worked together for us in creating a dialectic relationship between individual consciousness and wider social structures. The late 1970s and early 1980s formed a highly politicized environment marked by riots, strikes, recession, and unemployment, and framed by the activist work of Marxist and socialist political groups like the Socialist Workers Party (SWP) and Revolutionary Communist Party (RCP). This combustible cultural mix was very different from the hippie principles of peace and love. Yet though many punks viewed the 1960s counterculture as a failed experiment, they embraced that generation's artistic freedom, antiwar message, and love of experimentation. Early punks were also inspired by anarchism (no hierarchies, self-government from below) and Situationism—what better way was there to disrupt Guy Debord's spectacle of alienated consumerism than wearing a bin liner and safety pins (Worley 2017, 79)?

Mannheim argues that in a period of significant social and cultural change, the youngest social generation that grows to adulthood fully embodies that change. Punk in the 1970s was formative, creating the foundational generation. Members of a foundational generation have a concrete bond through their exposure to and participation in the "social process of dynamic destabilization," such as in time of war (Pilcher 1994, 490). It is significant that punks saw everyday culture as a place of confrontation; to be punk in the 1970s meant being subject to violence—getting beaten up on the street or attacked at gigs and demonstrations was commonplace. As the Clash vocalist Joe

Strummer once advised, "Always wear shoes that are good for running or fighting" (quoted in Alper 2016). That maxim applied to women as well as men; all punks were seen as a provocative affront to mainstream society (O'Brien 1999, 193).

When You Look in the Mirror Do You See Yourself

In her historical study of the Daughters of Charity, Susan O'Brien adapted Mannheim's sociology of generations to talk about the life cycle or "biography of a community" (2017, 14). The same principles of generational units can be applied to the biography of punk feminism, with the movement going through five distinct phases: foundation, expansion, conserving, renewal, and transformation (see Table 15.1). I am not making a case

Table 15.1. A Generational Biography of Punk Feminism

Generation	Characteristics
1. Foundation (establishing)	The (establishing) generation of 1970s/early 1980s punk is the focus of this study. Here female participants laid the groundwork for a DIY and dissenting feminism, particularly in fields of music, fashion and visual art.
2. Expansion (period of growth)	The 1990s generation emerged with the diversity and multiple subject identities of third-wave feminism. This found a focus in the fanzine-led Riot Grrrl network, which started in Washington State and quickly moved through North America to the UK and Europe.
3. Conserving	The 2000s generation entered a more stable, and potentially reactionary, phase, with a postfeminist hybridization of media and consumer culture. With their populist version of "Girlpower" (a former Riot Grrrl term), the Spice Girls were an example of the co-option of punk feminism.
4. Renewal	The 2010s marked a return to and a development of foundational principles, with the arrest of the feminist punk collective Pussy Riot after their anti-Putin protest in a Russian Orthodox church in Moscow in February 2012. Pussy Riot's intervention was a stark reminder that in many countries the idea of postfeminism was purely academic.
5. Transformation generation	From 2017 onward there has been a rise in DIY activist feminism through social media campaigns like Hashtag MeToo and Time's Up. This has been fueled by enthusiasm for second- and third-wave feminist history in young girl punk bands like Trashkit and Skinny Girl Diet.

for a hierarchy of cultural capital, that one generation is better or more knowledgeable than another. Each generation has its own strong characteristics, its own iteration of female punk within a changing political context, its own expression of "the proffered material." What I do hope the table shows is how early punk laid the groundwork for later developments in DIY punk feminism.

In considering the markers of the foundational generation of female punk, it is useful to consider identity salience; that is, how frequently an individual's identity framework is used in diverse situations (Stryker and Burke 2000, 286). My female respondents maintain that their punk identity is used in many different circumstances. It is felt to be a source of strength and used to negotiate difficult life transitions (whether in terms of jobs or relationships or bringing up children). Self-identity significantly predicts behavior, particularly for participants who identified strongly with the group, or cohort. From my research into the 1970s foundational generation, respondents' thoughts cohere around four main categories of identity salience: *hair*, *clothes*, *fear*, and *power*. Respondents sent me "then and now" pictures, and I include some in this chapter to illustrate how they express punk style in a way that is different from, yet consistent with, their younger selves.

Hair

As noted, it was an important part of the female punk project to construct a new visual vocabulary: reversing the male gaze by jamming the "gendered repertoire of allowable looking" through spikes, peroxide, and extreme makeup (Biddle-Perry and Cheang 2008, 228). In disrupting what is considered normative or natural, we were making explicit how the body is socially marked and culturally constructed as a woman's. Our parent generation saw dyed hair as cheap, brassy, and non-intellectual, so we used harsh peroxide dye in a way that felt vivid, dramatic, and beautiful. My respondents have very distinct, powerful memories of their hair: "I had curly hair (very un-punk), so at first I dyed to blue and wore it in tight plaits. Then one day somebody patted me on the head, and I was so irate that I sliced all my hair off with a razor blade and dyed it orange," recalls Helen Reddington (Reddington, August 2017). Karen Amsden (see Figure 15.1) remembers having "a mohican of varying colours and a whole can of Boots extra-hold hairspray was put on it every week to keep it staying rigid. The colours I dyed it ranged from pink, red, blue and green" (Amsden, August 2017.).

Liz Naylor views her transformative haircut as a combination of liberation and self-harm: "Prior to punk my hair was shoulder length and frizzy. Then I saw the Sex Pistols on [the UK television program] *So It Goes* and literally cut my hair off in front of the mirror. I had patches where I went down to the scalp. It was quite violent" (Naylor, October 2018).

FIGURE 15.1. Karen Amsden, London, 1979.

Clothes

High Street clothing available to 1970s women in the UK was restricted to a palette of disco-flared jeans and glittery tops or floaty, feminine Laura Ashley styles. The mass market girls' magazine *Jackie*, with its regimented hair and beauty advice, set the tone. "I read it like it was a manual, like a horror show, with no enthusiasm," remembers Polly Hancock. "It was like someone had cut out a template I had to fit into, or be an outcast" (Hancock, September 2018). All of my respondents recall turning to jumble sales and vintage shops for their clothing. "The punk era was a peak moment, a gilded age for finding things in jumble sales," says Vivien Goldman. "We were getting the postwar stuff, from the 1940s, even the 1930s. I remember getting one black velvet tea dress from Portobello Road that was from the 1920s. Whatever happened to my gorgeous, gorgeous tartan trench coat, with a belt? I'd like to wear it right now" (Goldman, August 2017). For Goldman, whose father was in the London "rag trade," clothes symbolized creative freedom. "There was a cognitive dissonance at the heart of the punk look. We put things together that weren't supposed to go together. That's prevalent now in a way that people take for granted."

Punk women were recycling not just the clothes of the parent generation, but also from their grandparents' era, wearing "old lady dresses" with Dr. Marten boots, or suede kitten heel stilettos with homemade drainpipe jeans. "I was a lesbian and punk gave me permission. I wore a mixture of '50s and '60s men's clothes. Beautiful old collared shirts and winklepickers. We were cross-dressing not just in gender, but also decades," recalls Naylor. In customizing and reworking clothes of previous generations, punk women were critically reconstructing the experience of their parents and grandparents. Consciously or unconsciously, they were making a satirical comment on the gender coding that restricted the choices of their mothers and grandmothers. "There was a massive distance between how old and young people dressed. Older women dressed in a uniform, they had to conform" (Liz Naylor). Another respondent saw freedom in reimagining her mother's clothes. "Being mixed race I loved Poly Styrene and X-Ray Spex. I had a skinhead style with a copper fringe. I discovered my mum had loads of pencil skirts with bolero jacket suits she'd made in '60s. I wore those with slingback stiletto winklepickers and heavy black eyeliner and trotted down the road in Bromley to meet friends, get pissed, and sing in all-girl punk band" (Marion, September 2017).

Dressing punk was a risky activity. Alison Goldie recalls wearing "ripped jeans, an old double-breasted fireman's jacket, earrings made out of pickled onions and varnished, or dangling bullets. Once, early on, in the blue hair phase, when I was wearing a leopard short coat and hefty men's work-boots, a man punched me in the face on the street—I think I was a terrible visual affront to him" (Goldie, September 2017; see Figure 15.2). Women instinctively know that codes around beauty are one of the biggest issues about being a woman. We know how deep it goes, and how much it frames, implicitly or explicitly, our interactions with other women. Punk was a culture jam that deconstructed that culture of looking. As a result, violence, or the threat of violence, was constant. Many respondents talked about being attacked in the streets, at gigs or on demonstrations, but felt that these experiences gave them ways of negotiating fear.

Fear

Women are trained from girlhood to avoid confrontation. A woman should not invite attention and prompt men's libidinous desires. If she makes her body available for looking, she signals that she wants sex. As John Berger writes, "men act, women appear (Berger 1972, 47). Turning the male gaze back on the viewer, according to Viv Albertine, "freaked men out. That mixture of rubber stockings, DMs and fuck off you wanker, what are you staring at?" (quoted in O'Brien 1999, 193). Dealing with fear was a key part of the punk project. Helen Reddington asserts that she felt fear "because of things that happened when I was a child. But what punk did was to teach me that if you accept fear as being part of life, you can take it on and beat it." Amsden says punk gave her courage:

FIGURE 15.2. Alison Goldie, at a party in Hull, 1979.

"I would never have got up onstage and performed in a band without punk. Sometimes I felt scared though, when I was threatened or insulted for the way I looked." In their memories of negotiating fear in everyday situations, many respondents demonstrate an understanding of power relations, particularly gendered power.

Power

A Foucauldian notion of power as distributed through networks and institutions, containing individuals within the rules of an organization, is relevant here. If a woman disrupts the codes of gendered social relations, she is disciplined—either overtly (encountering aggression) or covertly (nuanced advice or suggestions about what she should wear or how she should behave). An individual body "becomes an element that may be placed, moved, articulated on others" (Foucault 1975, 164). Within the distribution of power there is resistance, and punk women became skilled at negotiating this space of resistance. Judith Roche, the bassist in our band the Catholic Girls, recalls how restrictive gender rules at our convent school sparked a spirit of enquiry and rebellion:

In our school we were expected to become a secretary, a nurse, or a wife. It was very hierarchical. The nuns were more interested in defining you than allowing you to define yourself. I thought, I'm not sure I want to be defined by that. By forming a feminist punk band called the Catholic Girls we were intrinsically interested in disrupting the system. That act of saying "No" brought us into conflict with them. We were more threatening and influential than the girls that bunked off or went behind the sheds to have a smoke. We were contesting their power. I remember teachers trying to imply I was a bit mad, or psychologically unbalanced. That's a tool society uses for women who want to step out of the box.

(Roche, April 2018)

Another respondent used the power of punk to deal with racism. "Growing up in a very white environment which was openly National Front made me feel vulnerable, but punk made me feel more comfortable. It led to me to have a strong self-motivated self. It also made me question the status quo and I became politically active, going on marches, in particular anti-racism/nuclear/apartheid" (Marion). My interviewees talked about becoming attuned to the nuances of gendered power relations, and how this sensitivity increases over time. As lead guitarist for indie punk band The Popinjays, Hancock recalled a moment in the early 1990s when they had an "accidental hit" in the US and were invited over to Epic Records in New York.

Before the meeting, just to intimidate us, they put us in this massive board room. All round the walls were pictures of Michael Jackson and Whitney Houston. They left us there for half an hour. Then they came in, "We love you guys, we love everything about you, we love your record. . . . There's just one little thing. There's this guy we know, you should talk to him, he's great!" What it boiled down to was, we all had to lose weight and I had to stop looking like such a dyke. They didn't mention any music, it was all about how we looked. They made us feel immediately that they were more powerful. All we did was come home and feel like giving up, we felt so misunderstood.

After that encounter the band recorded a "silly pastiche Popinjays song with a massive chorus" and another that was more downbeat and honest. When Epic expressed a preference for the pastiche pop song, the band backed out, deciding to operate independently. Hancock believes that it was her 1970s punk background that enabled her to see the situation so clearly. In 2018 she started a popular blog, Punk Girl Diaries, as a way to archive and articulate the female punk experience. "It was a way of finding the vocabulary to talk about ourselves. Even if you can only remember the pair of trousers you liked, let's go from there."

Do It in a Fit Before You Read About It

In their study of identity salience, Sklar and DeLong (2012) suggest that older participants in a subculture tone down the subcultural signifiers in the workplace and "void out" the riskier elements in order to blend in and gain workplace benefits resulting from viewer perceptions. This implies a separation between selves; that the punk self reserves more flamboyant codes (such as display of tattoos, piercings, dramatic makeup) for evenings and weekends, and subculture is predominantly about the visual display of resistance, that in later years becomes a ritual, a hobby, or a privatized self-identity. For my interviewees, their thinking around dress and identity is just as rigorously and politically defined as it was in their youth. Nuances are subtle. The right shade of lipstick, the pair of boots, or a certain jacket act as triggers to a punk consciousness. Suspicious of what it means to tone oneself down, they reject notions of "age appropriate" dress, showing a deep conceptual understanding of clothes and inbuilt interior critique (see Figure 15.3). Karen Amsden says,

> I'm now a working mother in a punk band. Six years ago the band I am in reformed after 25 years and we now play regularly. This return to music came after six years at home looking after my young children and not earning an income. So I have loved

FIGURE 15.3. Karen Amsden, performing at London's Dublin Castle, 2016.

the excuse to become a punk again especially as a middle-aged woman it can feel like a drab time of life, so to spend it clad in leopard spot and travelling around to play gigs is fantastic. I feel like a punk rocker again and it's a mixture of my anger and frustration with the world I am living in and the desire to show that I will not conform to the idea of what a woman in her 50s looks like.

Many interviewees prioritize looking cool over looking smart or pretty. "People say, that shirt would look great on you. I'll think, 'It's not very punk rock.' I can see a sell-out. Something about the cut, color, texture. Blousy. Too conformist," says Hancock. They do not necessarily reject traditionally feminine colors or prints, but feel the need to anchor their look with boots or studs or strong lipstick. Such sartorial anchors work like an affirmation of self, enabling them to get on with the business of living punk in everyday life.

Negotiating and understanding power are key skills that 1970s punk women have developed over time. While their views on hair and beauty and image are still forceful, their resistance is now expressed less in visual terms and more in the strategies they use for agency at home or in the workplace, not just for themselves but also on behalf of others. Punk women in their fifties and sixties are a defiant and committed subcultural community. "People get upset—'punk is the Establishment, punk in the museum.' Why shouldn't we get that respect? It doesn't all grind to a halt. We still behave in a punk manner. Punk isn't dead because it's in a museum. A museum or library nowadays—what could be more frontline than that?" argues Goldman. Though many respondents for this study are confident about expressing agency, they are also honest about when they feel frustrated or powerless. Now a writer and academic based in New York, Goldman remembers pitching a feature idea to the *New York Times* on Poly Styrene, when the artist was about to release her last and (unknown to many) what would be posthumous album in 2011. "I talked to a male editor there who said, 'I'm going to run it past the boys' and he didn't get back to me. Then she died. I'm in anguish about her. I'm kicking myself for waiting for the validation of the patriarchy. I delayed it because I wanted to contact her and say, here's the glittering prize. I'd have done better just to be a punk and say, look I want to talk to you. Why didn't I do that?" Now Goldman honors Styrene in writing about punk, declaring, "I'm messianic about female punk because it absolutely liberated me."

Certain key themes have emerged from my research. All interviewees, like Hancock and Amsden, show strong *self-motivation*. Many are *politically active*. Fiona Watt, for instance, is a Green Party member and a trade union rep for the Public and Commercial Services Union (Watt, September 2017). DJ Wendy May is a member of Hastings Solidarity and the local Labour Party. "Punk allowed me to openly voice my feminist beliefs, and during that time I met some really strong women who were well-read and political. Some of whom I'm still good friends with now, still fighting the cause!" she says (May, August 2017). These 1970s punk women often work in a way that is *collaborative* and *improvisatory* (see Figure 15.4). Alison Goldie says,

FIGURE 15.4. Alison Goldie performing at Bristol Improv Festival, 2016.

I am punk in that I've always been self-employed. I am anti-authoritarian to the last. I have been a performer, theatre director, freelance drama teacher and writer. I am a specialist in improvisation, which is the most punk rock type of performance you can do. Punk gave me a DIY ethic that has never left me. I came from a one-parent, lower middle-class background in the suburbs. I had nothing much going for me but my curiosity. Punk created a climate in which an ordinary person like me could be extraordinary.

Many 1970s punk women are active in *workplace mediation* or *leadership roles*. This stems from a punk analysis of power structures and a refusal to be intimidated by authority. Sandra Baum works with people with disabilities and believes strongly in advocacy for those less fortunate than herself. "I am mindful about their position in society and I like to challenge that, and help people to find their own voice. I always speak up and let my views be heard and never let the establishment silence me. I do this via

FIGURE 15.5. L-R: Donna Sussenbach and Sandra Baum, Forest Hill, London, 1983.

writing and speaking from a senior position in the NHS. I always carry the 'inner punk' with me," she says (Baum, August 2017).

A significant number of respondents see the radical potential in parenting and teaching. Watt started the Girls Rock School Edinburgh in 2013, "to encourage more women and girls to take up instruments and start bands in our city. Girl Rock Schools have now been started in Glasgow, Belfast, London, and Dublin—we are a mighty force!" Donna Sussenbach feels that punk is a state of mind she has passed on to her two sons. "They are very socially and politically aware," she says. In 1994 she set up an organization for young people going through the care system into independence. "It has worked with thousands of young people going through that difficult transition in their lives. That is my punk mindset—young adults are creative and resilient and our future" (Sussenbach, August 2017; see Figures 15.5 and 15.6).

All respondents use a DIY approach, especially if they encounter a challenging situation or if they are starting a new project. Liz Naylor wrote a punk fanzine in the 1970s and worked as a manager of Riot Grrrl band Huggy Bear in the 1990s. She now runs Foundation for Change, a London charity based in Shoreditch that provides education and training for ex-addicts. "I run it like a DIY indie label," she says. "It is the same process. It's extremely radical in terms of public health. We teach people feminism, and psychology—attachment theory, CBT, transactional analysis, basic principles. We allow addicts and former addicts an intellectual framework for what they're doing."

FIGURE 15.6. L-R: Sandra Baum and Donna Sussenbach, Queen Elizabeth Olympic Park, Stratford, London, 2016.

Conclusion

What emerges strongly from the research is that the foundational female punk generation experienced their subculture as a place of nurture and life training. They discovered dissension as a creative practice and a life skill, and are still searching for a new language to describe their experience. "I don't think the language has been developed yet," says Naylor. Perhaps unsurprisingly, those who were active participants at the time as musicians, writers, artists, and so on still consider punk a vital part of their identity. In their search for words to define objects, practices, and processes that felt new,

1970s punk women have become skilled in advocacy. Cohen defines advocacy as a process of identifying problems, gathering facts, articulating competing interests, and then analyzing the information gathered with courses of action. In an increasingly complex environment for public sector areas like health and education, advocacy "is a precious commodity in a diverse society" (Cohen 2004, 16). Aware that power resides in language and communication, a significant number of my female punk interviewees work in teaching or the care system, speaking up for people struggling to articulate their reality. Naylor puts it like this:

> For me, punk is about authenticity and existential philosophy. We work with addicts who don't know who the fuck they are and never have. Lots of people have been abused and subjected to trauma, so they disassociate. That question of authenticity is really present. You can only advocate on behalf of somebody if you're listening and being listened to. It's a dual process. Punk started that by thinking about the artist's relationship with the audience and reciprocity.

A number of historians, like Dominic Sandbrook and Andrew Marr, represent punk as a visually Situationist youth culture that did not trouble the Establishment and that had no lasting effect (see Street et al. 2018, 273). John Street et al. examined documentary evidence (such as parliamentary records and diaries of senior government figures) at the time of early punk and found scant evidence of subverting or overthrowing elites in the 1970s. However, they acknowledge that even if "punk's effects were not felt at the time by those in positions of formal political and administrative power, today ex-punks may now occupy those self-same positions" (287). Many from that generation are in such positions, and this study contributes to the view that affecting political change is a lifetime's work. Punk feminism, for example, has grown and developed through generations, and the influence is felt through former 1970s punks now working at a senior level in the public and private sector.

Dick Hebdige defined punk as a signifying practice, as repeated performative acts of making (1979, 117–127). Because it was a foundational movement, there was an absence of role models, particularly for women, and that gap created room for productive and imaginative DIY activity. Like the male band Scritti Politti, detailing and demystifying the means of production on the back of their record sleeves, we externalized the process of female self-making. We consciously pass this information down; it is present in what we tell ourselves and our daughters about body image, female friendship, and female solidarity and strength. We say that punk is about expressing your creativity and your activism. Endeavoring to do what has not been done before is a political act. Punk provides us with a valuable political framework because it is has been built with the input of many dedicated ideas. It works like feminism. It is continually contested, but withstands that conflict because punk, like feminism, is born out of paradox, conflict, and ambiguity. It allows for difference and multiple identities. And our self-making, our self-identity as a woman, is a lifelong project—not just for ourselves but for our culture and society.

Dedication

In memory of Ari Up (1962–2010), and Poly Styrene (1957–2011).

Acknowledgments

I owe thanks to the female punks who have engaged with and contributed to this project, including the ones quoted in this chapter. Interviews and correspondence quoted in the text took place between 2015 and 2018. On first quotation only from each, name and date are included for reference. Interviewees, respondents, and dates are as follows.

Marion (not her real name), email correspondence with author, September 2017.
Viv Albertine, email correspondence with author, July 2015.
Karen Amsden, email correspondence with author, August 2017.
Sandra Baum, email correspondence with author, August 2017.
Alison Goldie, email correspondence with author, September 2017.
Vivien Goldman, interview with author, August 2017.
Polly Hancock, interview with author, September 2018.
Wendy May, email correspondence with author, August 2017.
Liz Naylor, interview with author, October 2018.
Helen Reddington, interview with author, August 2017.
Judith Roche, interview with author, April 2018.
Donna Sussenbach, email correspondence with author, August 2017.
Fiona Watt, email correspondence with author, September 2017.
Photographs are from my interviewees' private collections, and are used with permission. Figure 15.4 credit: Mr & Mrs Hardcore Photography.

Note

1. I acknowledge that my research is the result of a partial survey from a self-selecting group of respondents. There may be ex-punk women in their fifties and sixties who have not thought much about their teenage years. I did not come across any in my wider research, but welcome responses from ex-punks who feel the era is no longer significant to them.

References

Alper, Eric. 2016. "'Always Wear Shoes That Are Good for Running or Fighting.' Joe Strummer—The Clash." Twitter, May 12. https://twitter.com/thatericalper/status/730752256837099521.
Bennett, Andy. 2006. "Punk's Not Dead: The Continuing Significance of Punk Rock for an Older Generation of Fans." *Sociology* 40, no. 2: 219–235.

Berger, John. 1972. *Ways of Seeing*. London: Penguin.
Biddle-Perry, Geraldine, and Sarah Cheang. 2008. *Hair: Styling, Culture and Fashion*. Oxford: Berg.
Butler, Judith. 1990. *Gender Trouble: Feminism and the Subversion of Identity*. 2nd ed. London: Routledge, 1999.
Cofield, Laura, and Lucy Robinson. 2016. "'The Opposite of the Band:' Fangrrrling, Feminism and Sexual Dissidence." *Textual Practice* 30, no. 6: 1071–1088.
Cohen, Elias S. 2004. "Advocacy and Advocates: Definitions and Ethical Dimensions." *Generations* 28, no. 1: 9–16.
Dimitriadis, Greg. 2015. "Framing Hip Hop: New Methodologies for New Times." *Urban Education* 50, no. 1: 31–51.
Dunn, Kevin. 2016. *Global Punk: Resistance and Rebellion in Everyday Life*. New York: Bloomsbury.
Foucault, Michel. 1975. *Discipline and Punish: The Birth of the Prison*. Translated by Alan Sheridan. London: Penguin, 1991.
Hebdige, Dick. 1979. *Subculture: The Meaning of Style*. London: Methuen.
O'Brien, Lucy. 1999. "The Woman Punk Made Me." In *Punk Rock, So What? The Cultural Legacy of Punk*, edited by Roger Sabin, 186–198. London: Routledge.
O'Brien, Susan. 2017. *Leaving God for God: The Daughters of Charity of St. Vincent de Paul in Britain, 1847–2017*. London: Darton, Longman & Todd.
Pilcher, Jane. 1994. "Mannheim's Sociology of Generations: An Undervalued Legacy." *British Journal of Sociology* 45, no. 3: 481–495.
Punk Girl Diaries. https://punkgirldiaries.com.
Rowbotham, Sheila. 2014. *Women, Resistance and Revolution: A History of Women and Revolution in the Modern World*. Rev. ed. London: Verso, 1974.
Sklar, Monica, and Marilyn DeLong. 2012. "Punk Dress in the Workplace: Aesthetic Expression and Accommodation." *Clothing Textiles Research Journal* 30, no. 4: 285–299.
Street, John, Matthew Worley, and David Wilkinson. 2018. "'Does It Threaten the Status Quo?' Elite Responses to British Punk, 1976–1978." *Popular Music* 37, no. 2: 271–289.
Stryker, Sheldon, and Peter J. Burke. 2000. "The Past, Present, and Future of an Identity Theory." *Social Psychology Quarterly* 63, no. 4: 284–297.
Worley, Matthew. 2017. *No Future: Punk, Politics and British Youth Culture, 1976–1984*. Cambridge: Cambridge University Press.

PART FOUR

SAFE EUROPEAN HOME

From the Provincial to the International

CHAPTER 16

"I DON'T CARE ABOUT LONDON"

Punk in Britain's Provinces, circa 1976–1984

MATTHEW WORLEY

AMONG the flurry of fanzines conceived, cut, and pasted as British punk emerged over the course of 1976–1977, the northern English industrial city of Sheffield's *Gun Rubber* was one of the most engaging (for background on fanzines, or "zines," see Worley 2024; Subcultures Network 2018). Put together by Paul Bower, Adi Newton, and others associated with the Meatwhistle arts project, the seven issues that ran through 1977 embodied punk's spirit in rudimentary form. Scribbled reviews and pithy diatribes were interrupted by cribbed newspaper headlines and images culled from media detritus. Irreverence struggled to disguise enthusiasm, and rants about the local student union gave way to excitable reviews of all things remotely "punk." Crucially, too, *Gun Rubber* chartered and informed the Steel City's own budding new wave. From the outset it asked (and answered) "What's happening in Sheffield?" (*Gun Rubber* no. 1). Alongside features on "name" bands (Ramones, Damned, etc.) and irregular trips down south, attention was given to homegrown groups barely formed. Plans for cassette compilations and showcase gigs were mooted. In issue 5, an image of a graffitied wall revealed the suitably caustic credo "I Don't Care about London," before December's final edition allowed Bower to survey the city and insist, "Never before has there been more bands, more magazines and more independent labels in operation . . . it's a lot better than this time last year." Sheffield was pushing toward "the brand new wave around the corner," Bower accurately forecast, with the likes of Cabaret Voltaire and The Human League in the vanguard. Experimentation, not bondage trousers, would define Sheffield's post-punk landscape (*Gun Rubber* no. 5; *Gun Rubber* no. 7, cited in Lilleker 2005, 44).[1]

The flowering of provincial scenes—coalescing around bands, record shops, fanzines, labels and venues—was arguably the most significant indicator of punk's cultural impetus. Notwithstanding London's claim to Britain's punk origins, along the Kings Road, beneath the Westway, and into the suburbs of the capital's surround, the logic of Johnny Rotten's call to "get off your arse" relied on dissemination into the outer reaches of the country.[2] Much has therefore been made of the Sex Pistols' performances at Manchester's Lesser Free Trade Hall in the summer of 1976 (see Nolan 2006). For Paul Morley, writing in the *NME* (*New Musical Express*), Manchester had "no identity, no common spirit or motive" prior to the fledgling Buzzcocks' inviting the Pistols to the city. Within a year, however, Morley was able to list an array of bands, fanzines, and record labels formed in the aftermath. All that was needed, he concluded, was "an all-girl group" and "a central 'factory' to organise proceedings" (Morley 1977, 6–7). But similar—if less renowned—tales may be told elsewhere, as interest piqued by the music press led young minds hotwired by a gig or a freshly-acquired 7-inch single to seek co-conspirators with whom to make a noise and make a culture. From Leeds and Liverpool to Glasgow, Edinburgh, Belfast, Cardiff, Nottingham, Southampton, and all stops in between, punk triggered an urge to *do it*. And whether perceptions of mid-1970s cultural desolation were accurate or not, it was the formation of local scenes—in provincial backwaters large and small—that ensured punk assumed a legacy beyond the Sex Pistols' initial assault and the "moral panic" (Cohen 1972) that ensued.

This chapter will look at punk's impact across Britain's towns and cities, moving away from the London- and Manchester-centric narratives that tend to dominate most historical accounts. By so doing, it endeavors to offer a provincial view of punk's dissemination, shedding light on the culture's transmission and mutation. Punk culture morphed as it was received away from its initial source; its aesthetics, sounds, and performance were filtered through local contexts to be mis- and reinterpreted in about equal measure. By drawing attention to the infrastructure of punk in the provinces, historically mining the traces left by certain spaces, record labels, and fanzines, the chapter recovers the legacy of punk at the grass roots and reveals the deeply engrained stains left on the cultural fabric.

Punk and the Provinces: Just a Satellite of London?

Though some may try, it is hard to write a history of British punk without leaving the capital. True, the Sex Pistols' early provocations—not to mention the media and music industry that took the bait—were concentrated in and around London. But punk's "shock of the new" soon spread, permeating outward to stimulate or galvanize youth cultures gestating beyond London's confines (see Savage 1991; Cobley 1999; Worley 2017). For a time, between 1977 and 1981, the music press's attention even turned away from the metropole, looking to places such as Manchester, Leeds, Bristol, Sheffield, Coventry, and Glasgow for "post-punk" sounds and styles (see Reynolds 2005). Regional writers were recruited, and round-ups of local scenes sought to capture the sheer breadth of activity motivated by punk's demand for agency (see Gill and Thrills 1978 on Leeds and Sheffield; Parsons and Hamblett 1978 on Leeds; Sweeting 1982 on East Anglia). Normal service was later resumed, of course. Industry attention spans waned and both "New Pop" and "New Romanticism" were seized upon (by music papers and emergent style magazines alike) as better reflecting the aspirational tenets of the 1980s (Rimmer 2011; Wilkinson 2016; Gorman 2017). Nevertheless, the creative processes stimulated by punk's configuration of rock 'n' roll continued in ways not measurable by "official" chart sales or industry opinion. On the ground, beyond the media gaze of TV and the music press, punk continued to provide both a template to form a band and a means to cultivate homegrown scenes from the bottom up.

As this suggests, what punk informed as a style, a practice, and an inspiration continued to mutate through to the 1980s (and beyond). Open up an old *NME*, or flick to the back of *Sounds*, and the "independent chart" therein lists band names and record labels obscured by time but signaling punk's lingering effect. Sub-scenes (then or later codified as industrial, post-punk, Oi!, anarcho, goth, psychobilly, grindcore, or indie) came into being and jostled for position at "alternative" nights or in backstreet pubs. Late evening airplay by John Peel on BBC Radio 1 broadcast nationwide the sound of young Derry or young Perth into British bedrooms and bedsits, while fanzines continued to multiply and pick over the minutiae of punk's contested diffusion (Cavanagh 2015). Indeed, it was in just such a context—the "provincial towns you jog round," to quote a voyeur of Manchester's early punk milieu[3]—that most British people contributed to, consumed, or engaged with punk-related cultures. For this reason, studies that hone in on the regional and provincial are useful, both in terms of an antidote to London-centric accounts of British youth culture and as a way to better understand punk's wider sociocultural influence.

To date there are but a few such studies. Simon Reynolds's recognition that the "long 'aftermath' of punk up to 1984 was musically *way* more interesting than what happened in 1976–7" led him to argue that "revolutionary movements in pop culture have their widest impact after the 'moment' has allegedly passed, when ideas spread from the metropolitan bohemian elites and hipster cliques that originally 'own' them, and reach the suburbs and the regions" (Reynolds 2005, xv–xvi). To this end, his history of post-punk delved into local scenes buoyed by punk but keen to reassemble its components. Russ Bestley has also done much to recover punk's provincial legacy across the UK, tracing the evolving visual codes—via record sleeves, posters, fanzines, clothes—that lent meaning to local scenes as they endeavored to relate punk's critical ire to their respective environments. So, for example, Bestley (2007, 2012) analyzed the imagery, graphics, and language of regional punk bands into the 1980s, noting how the use of indigenous signifiers—be it the cooling towers on the label of Stoke's Clay Records or Skroteez's paean to the punks of Livingston ("Livi Punkz")—helped align cultural and social identities. In the process, Bestley reaffirmed punk's continued relevance in places where the "dole queue rock" mythologized in 1977 became all too resonant in the early 1980s.

Thereafter, glimpses of punk's provincial history are fleeting. True, studies exist of distinct scenes, often revolving around notable record labels (2-Tone, Factory, Good Vibrations, Postcard), clubs (Eric's, Hacienda) and bands (Cabaret Voltaire, Joy Division, The Fall) (Eddington 2004; Fish 2002; Florek and Whelan 2009; Goddard 2014; Hooley and Sullivan 2010; Middles 2002). David Wilkinson's work (2014, 2018) has uncovered the countercultural legacies that infused post-punk in Manchester, while Helen Reddington's (2007) analysis of punk women builds from a Brighton base. Local enthusiasts have also done impressive jobs producing labors of love to their respective locales (e.g., Beesley 2009; Cavanagh 2009; Lilleker 2005; O'Neill and Trelford 2003). More recently, in true DIY spirit, Greg Bull has compiled (with others) compendiums of ephemera and reflections on anarcho-punk, amid which are numerous accounts of lives lived in provincial squats, streets, and gig halls (Bull and Dines 2014, 2016, 2017; Bull and "Penguin" 2015). Alastair Gordon (2005, 2016), in particular, has used ethnographic methods to evoke the sounds, smells, and tensions of punk scenes in Bradford and Nottingham. Peter Webb (2016), too, has shone light into the crustier corners of Bristol's squats.

It is, moreover, in the memoirs of both the well and lesser known that the experiences of provincial punk are most redolently expressed. So, for example, Julian Cope's autobiography (1999, 14–31) recalls the barbed entrances to Liverpool's punk milieu, running the verbal gauntlet in Pete and Lynne Burns's clothes shop, or perusing imported 7-inch singles in Geoff Davies' Probe Records, or determining the local pecking order at gigs in Eric's. Not dissimilarly, Boff Whalley's (2003, 17–51) recollection of his pre-Chumbawamba youth in Burnley centers on clumsy-but-still-thrilling attempts to embrace punk: painted T-shirts turning stiff as a board; taking abuse from "football thickies" defining sexual persuasion by the width of a trouser leg; catching buses to buy records and then "scrutinising sleeves, reading and re-reading the labels"; imagining and forming ramshackle bands enabled by punk's "anyone can do it" mantra. From a fanzine-style history of Norwich punk, we catch Jyl Bailey describing her pre-night-out ritual, sharing makeup with male friends, and staining the bathtubs of bedsits with hair dye, before later returning home with smudged eyes and flattened tresses: the "mark of a great evening" (Worley 2016). And while Alastair Gordon's (2014) reminiscences of punk-infused substance abuse in Nottingham rekindle odors of glue, Polo mints, and residue-stained hands, so Justine Butler's (2014) memories of her Bristol squat combine tense political debate with shared needles and the impending gloom cast by the heightening Cold War of the early 1980s.

We could go on.[4] Such accounts capture the youthful exuberance, sometimes recklessness, that punk—and pop music more generally—excites, or excited. They recall the thrills, but also the violence, petty proclivities, and drab day-to-day of lives lived with or without spiked hair and a burgeoning record collection. They mythologize, refine, and no doubt exaggerate personal pasts in a hue of reverie. But they simultaneously warn against projecting overly deterministic readings onto punk's point and purpose. For the historian, they open portals into local experiences that disrupt the well-rehearsed narratives of punk's London evolution. Likewise, they show how punk did not simply pass as a fad into New Romanticism, indie and, later, rave. Rather, they demonstrate how punk opened up myriad and overlapping possibilities that were understood and responded to in different ways. To frame this, we need to recognize the infrastructures that served as conduits.

Spaces and Places: Record Shops and Clubs

While music papers spread the teenage news across the 1970s, the record shop serviced the hard product (Cartwright 2018). Perhaps it was a review in the *NME*, or a tip-off from an astute friend, but all paths led eventually to the rows of 7-inch and 12-inch vinyl that soundtracked adolescence. Packed into racks or displayed on walls behind the counter (the effect of which could be stunning once punk-informed graphics began to reimagine the possibilities of a record sleeve), single and album covers offered clues to new worlds, new emotions, and new ideas. Pennies carefully spent promised musical thrills and the tools to amass at least a degree of cultural capital.

Initially, for those away from London or distanced from any established gig circuit, punk was as much read about as heard. Michael Bradley, living in Derry and just about to play bass in The Undertones, later recalled the process. The music paper was purchased on its day of publication, then shared among friends who "believed every word" and studied every picture. "I was fourth in line to read [John O'Neill's] copy," Bradley remembered. "For us punk rock fans in Derry, *NME* was the only way we would even see what the Clash or the Damned looked like" (Bradley 2016, 48–49). Later, as punk's canon grew, key records were bought or borrowed from friends, spinning in bedrooms to be discussed and picked over. Cover versions provided links back to punk's formative influences, opening up new channels of pop history. Artwork and imagery served as cultural references, portals to creative and political wellsprings. Names and contact addresses generated further research to be acted upon. This was especially the case once anarchist bands such as Crass and Poison Girls began to present records as communiqués. As Chris Low (2017) remembers, Crass's records—replete with essays, lyrics, posters, and inventories of anarchist bookshops—ushered him into a "secret society." From his bedroom in Stirling, Low followed the leads, perusing the Small Wonder mail order catalogue in *Sounds* for bands "like Crass"; writing to the "seditious contacts" listed on records such as "Bloody Revolutions" b/w "Persons Unknown" (1980) to receive anarchist pamphlets and periodicals; communicating with fanzines that featured related bands, then swapping tapes and his own zine (*Guilty of What*) in return.

As is well known, punk proffered both a challenge to the prevailing pop and rock sounds of the 1970s and stimulated alternative networks of commerce and distribution. London's Rough Trade would prove integral to this as a shop and a distribution center that forged links to equivalent independent record stores across the UK. The cannier of these, alert to punk's nascent appeal and always willing to cater to minority taste, became focal points for those alive to the cultural shift: Probe in Liverpool, Ace (then Backs) in Norwich, Bruce's in Edinburgh and Glasgow, Jumbo in Leeds, Revolver in Bristol, Listen Ear in Newcastle, Good Vibrations in Belfast (Cartwright 2018, 208–219). Some, such as Red Rhino in York (and Rough Trade in fact), opened concurrently with punk's emergence, establishing connections that would tie their identity to the new wave's evolution. Of course, the burgeoning Virgin Records empire also served a useful purpose. But it was the smaller independents that dealt with Rough Trade and, like the London shop, set up their own record labels that fed into the regional distribution system known as the Cartel by 1982 (Hesmondhalgh 1997; Taylor 2010; Young 2006). It was in such shops, too, that friendships were made, knowledge was gained, and, occasionally, careers in the music industry were begun behind the counter in exchange for records on account, holding the fort, and making the tea. Or, as James King remembered in relation to Scotland's fledgling punk scene,

> [From] about January 1977 people started hanging around record shops . . . and that's how you got to form bands. I'd say most of the bands that were formed in Glasgow at that time were actually formed in record stores. And places like Graffiti [a record shop] had copies of *Punk* magazine from New York. . . . These guys knew what was happening . . . and if you had any questions you could ask them and they'd play you stuff. . . . I used to go to the record store six days a week.
>
> (King n.d.)

Records provided a material trace of punk's intervention. Although their product status was a site of tension for a culture born of frustration at mediated pop and aging rock 'n' roll, the 7-inch single and 12-inch album nevertheless served as a marker of creative achievement, not to mention a document of time and place. But if punk helped demystify the means of production and enabled bands to release their own records, then cultures also need spaces to grow and develop. Beyond the record shop, therefore, and beyond the sanctum of the teenage bedroom, wherein identities were (and still are) collated and constructed, clubs and pubs became vital sites for the collective experience of both recorded and live music. In the words of Lee Gibson, remembering his formative years as a "solitary born rebel" in the Durham village of Longnewton, punk provided ways of "seeking out fellow minds . . . seeking justification or mutual support" (2013, 18). This meant traveling to Middlesbrough Rock Garden to catch the first wave of punk bands venturing out of London; forging connections that led to gigs in the Teessider, a pub that provided for the slew of mainly short-lived local bands formed in punk's wake (Bombay Drug Squad, Vermin, The Filth, The Extreme, etc.); hanging around Stockton avoiding rival youth cults and the police; or writing a fanzine. Speak to punks elsewhere and similar tales abound. In Hull, for example, Spiders remained an "alternative" club long into the twenty-first century, having opened in 1979 to provide space for those infected by punk's fallout to gather (Haslam 2015). The 1 in 12 Club in Bradford began a little later, in 1981, galvanizing the cultural and political tendencies pulsing through punk to forge a collectively run community space based on the local Claimants' Union. Still going in 2018, the 1 in 12 served as a hub amid Yorkshire's evolving punk and post-punk culture, offering access to music, poetry, publication, and community activism (Cavanagh 2009, 138–179).

Bigger cities likewise cultivated important centers for punk-related cultures to develop and evolve away from London media scrutiny. In Manchester, the "factory" that Paul Morley wished for in 1977 soon emerged, first as a night held at the Russell Club in Hulme from May 1978, then as a record label dedicated primarily to local bands (including Joy Division/New Order), and finally as The Haçienda. Leeds, too, served as an important incubator of post-punk culture. Initially, bands formed at the university and polytechnic gigged at the F-Club run by John Keenan from various venues in the late 1970s. Therein, the overtly political approach of the Gang of Four, Mekons, and others allowed space for connections to Rock Against Racism (RAR) and other progressive causes to cement, while Keenan further ensured that Leeds hosted three of the five Futurama festivals showcasing punk's mutation between 1979 and 1983. In the city itself, meanwhile, clubs like the Warehouse and Le Phonographique offered testing grounds for a gaggle of Yorkshire bands (Sisters of Mercy, March Violets, Red Lorry Yellow Lorry, etc.) whose brooding take on post-punk forged a template for what eventually became goth (Haslam 2015, 274–275).

Again, we could go on, declaring Birmingham's Rum Runner a substitute site for New Romanticism; or positing the various gay clubs across the country that offered refuge for punks (and Bowie advocates) seeking to live out "alternative" ideas and lifestyles; or looking to Sheffield's The Limit, Liverpool's Eric's, and Sunderland's Bunker as varied exemplars of provincial ingenuity. The point is that punk's impetus created opportunities for venues old and new to provide space for the wealth of bands forming, touring, and playing in the Sex Pistols' wake. Some such spaces came and went; others gained legendary status. A few, such as Birmingham's Barbarellas, even had songs dedicated to them (in this case, "Barbarellas" by The Prefects). But punk's reinvigoration of provincial nightlife helped kindle an important sense of *something happening*.

Nowadays, evidence of punk's provincial flowering is often captured on websites and Facebook pages dedicated to lost youth and cherished memories. Indeed, a range of informal archives—in some way reminiscent of punk's DIY spirit—have been created to preserve punk's heritage, serving to collate histories from below that document cultures passed over by more London-centric accounts. Here, as on the Punk in the East website or the Scottish Post-Punk Facebook page, uploaded images of gig tickets and flyers combine with once-lost grainy photos to offer a rare glimpse inside venues that spark reminiscences of good nights, bad nights, lost friends, and fist fights. The claim of *being there* remains important, be it a gig or the club that housed any local scene. Equally, however, it was the vinyl record, cassette, or press-cutting that served best to document punk's incitement to *do it*, providing both the form and the substance of youth-cultural creativity. All you had to do, as John Peel put it, was get the bass player to sell his bike and knock off a phone box or two (see Tickell 1995). The local independent shop would then stock it. The local fanzine would review it. And Peel might even play it, broadcasting the sounds of the provinces nationwide, transmitting and communicating what no other national media broadcasting outlet deigned to notice.

Local Independent Labels: It Was Easy, It Was Cheap, Go and Do It

Fittingly, punk's first decisive move to wrestle pop music away from the clutches of the established record labels came not from London but from Manchester. True, Stiff and Chiswick served as pre-1977 independents that helped facilitate punk's emergence. And most of the early bands, including the Sex Pistols and the Clash, sought battlegrounds inside the existing industry by signing with major labels. But it was the release of Buzzcocks' *Spiral Scratch* EP on the New Hormones label set up by the band with Richard Boon in early 1977 that marked punk's separation from the industry norm. Self-issued to capture a moment before it had passed, and in lieu of any other labels existing in Manchester, *Spiral Scratch* appeared with no industry backing or experience. Ingenuity and money borrowed from family led to a booked studio, a Polaroid sleeve, a local pressing, and self-distribution. Recording details (number of takes and overdubs) were displayed on the back cover; the songs were four frantic but ingenious ruminations on breakdown and boredom. And the message sent? Anyone could make a record and you don't have to move to London to do so. Or, as Jon Savage stated in *England's Dreaming*, "The implications of *Spiral Scratch* were enormous. There had always been independent record companies, such as Joe Meek's Triumph or Andrew Loog Oldham's Immediate, but they were, in the main, small companies trying to be big." New Hormones and *Spiral Scratch* came from *within* punk's emergent culture: the "aesthetics were perfectly combined with the means of production" (1991, 296–297).

Over time, *Spiral Scratch*'s example was noted and followed. A network of labels, retailers, studios, and manufacturers soon emerged (or were found) to cater for punk-informed scenes evolving beyond the metropolitan monopoly (Ogg 2009). This, in turn, culminated in the publication of a weekly "independent chart" by the British Market Research Bureau from 1980, confirming at least the notion of an alternative to the music industry mainstream. (The criteria for inclusion in the independent chart was that a "record had to be independently manufactured, distributed and marketed without recourse to the machinery of the majors" [Ogg 2009, 369].) The effect on the wider industry was also soon apparent, with an unprecedented drop in production from 250 million to 190 million units between 1978 and 1981, coinciding with a simultaneous rise in the number of registered independent labels, from 231 in 1978 to over 800 in 1980 (falling again thereafter as the industry responded and the "New Pop" challenged post-punk's indie prerogative) (Ogg 2009, 164; Orme 1979, 21; Tyler 1982, 3).

What this meant at the local level varied. Very generally, it encouraged a growing number of individuals and bands to self-release their own records irrespective of music industry input. This was sometimes conceived as a means-to-an-end, a way of generating interest by securing press coverage and airplay via John Peel's late-night radio show. Several well-known punk bands—from Buzzcocks themselves through 999, Stiff Little Fingers, Angelic Upstarts, The Skids, and The Exploited—first recorded on their own imprints before moving to larger or more firmly established labels. Equally, however, the process of starting a label, self-releasing a record, or cultivating a cassette network became a raison d'être in itself, spawning a DIY culture rooted in punk's back-to-basics attitude but willing to experiment within its own limitations.

Ironically, perhaps, these records—in cheap paper sleeves with cut-out inserts and stamped labels—now fetch collectors' prices. In the late 1970s and early 1980s, they proliferated. Their sound may have tended toward the rudimentary but it also served to loosen punk's basic rock 'n' roll framework to a collapsing point. Self-designed covers allowed for creative expression of variable quality, while a disregard for market pressures ensured lyrical freedom that ranged through the abject and the absurd to the political and pertinent. Two examples will illustrate the practice and its development. First, from Leamington Spa, The Shapes released their *Part of the Furniture* EP as 1978 became 1979 on their own Sofa Records. Financed by the selling of a Honda motorbike and wrapped in a minimal black-and-white sleeve, its four tracks (including the absurdist/infantile "Wot's For Lunch Mum? Not Beans Again!") received John Peel's attention and led to regular trips around record shops and distributors dropping off copies piled up in the boot of a car.[5] Second, APF Brigade from Peterborough, whose anti-commercial inclinations led them never actually to release anything as standard product-oriented as a record, but instead invited people to send a stamped self-addressed envelope to receive a one-off cassette recording of a set that comprised songs such as "Anarchist Attack," "Plastic Crap," and "Religious Dictator." As one of the first bands to extend the logic of Crass's emergent anarcho-punk politics, APF Brigade were an integral but unheralded part of punk's DIY advance.

As this suggests, to be independent was recognized by some to represent an opposition to the existent music industry. In their somewhat different but overlapping ways, Rough Trade and Crass Records embodied this position at a more sustained level. But so too did countless local labels forged to provide space for provincial expressions of punk-infused agency. A few of these grew organically from punk's dissemination, forming through the independent record shops that stocked, distributed, and eventually produced records inspired by a DIY ethos. Thus, beyond London's Rough Trade and Small Wonder, the likes of Remember Those Oldies in Cambridge begat Raw Records, while Bruce's helped launch a series of small Scottish labels. Many of the shops listed in the previous section—Backs, Good Vibrations, Probe, and Red Rhino—had their own imprints, while Brighton's Attrix was a label before it transformed into a shop (Ogg 2009, 127–171).

More generally, local labels were formed by a veritable combination of entrepreneurs, mavericks, and creatives, often collapsing the boundaries between business acumen and artistic endeavor in the process. So, for example, if Simon Edwards's Heartbeat Records (Bristol) was among the more market-orientated and diffuse, comprising various sub-labels to account for different genres, then Bob Last's Fast Product (Edinburgh) was perhaps the most creative, paying much attention to packaging the pop oddities that he and Hilary Morrison released in ways that simultaneously celebrated and critiqued the semiotic language of design (Reynolds 2005, 94–96). Where John Robb's Blackpool-based Vinyl Drip and Dave Parsons's Long Eaton–based Ron Johnson became known as disseminators of abstract punk clatter, so Alan Horne's Postcard transmitted the "Sound of Young Scotland" from Glasgow. Indeed, most local labels retained or displayed their provincial credentials, be it via signifiers such as Clay's aforementioned smokestacks and Riot City's reference to Bristol's reputation, or by foregrounding local acts, as was the case with Belfast's Good Vibrations. Famously, Tony Wilson and Alan Erasmus built their Factory Records' identity on Manchester's industrial heritage, with the label name, Peter Saville's early graphics, and Ben Kelly's design for The Haçienda all evoking the city's past. But the late 1970s and the 1980s also saw a series of compilations released to showcase local scenes, all of which combined the short-lived with the soon-to-be renowned, and all of which captured the youthful exuberance and diversity of punk's provincial manifestations.[6] As imaginations pushed against ability and artifacts were made, only the most vulgarly ambitious thought of heading toward London's bright lights.

Punk's Provincial Media: The Fifteen Fame-Filled Minutes of the Fanzine Writer

Fanzines have become synonymous with punk. While their origins stretch back to sci-fi communities swapping stories before the Second World War, their low-cost, cut-and-paste style provided the perfect medium for punk's bricolage culture. As is well known, Mark Perry's *Sniffin' Glue* was the first self-defined punk fanzine to be produced in the UK, beginning in the summer of 1976 as an eight-page screed celebrating a music Perry accused the music press of ignoring. Rudimentary in its style and presentation, *Sniffin' Glue* nevertheless captured British punk in embryo, extending to twelve (plus two supplementary) issues over the course of a year and growing from an initial Xerox-run of "about 50" to several thousand (Perry 2000). Just as importantly, others were quick to follow Perry's example, both in London (*Bondage*, *48 Thrills*, *London's Outrage*, etc.) and across the country. Before the end of 1976, Tony Drayton had started *Ripped & Torn* from Cumbernauld in Scotland, while early innovators such as Steve Burke in Manchester (*Shy Talk*), Tim Williams in Bristol (*Loaded*), and Kevin Anderson in Hebburn (*Deviation Street*) began to detail emergent local scenes amid general punk coverage in 1977. Very soon, all but every town and city (not to mention the odd village) had its own fanzine, often existing for just a handful of issues before new zines emerged to take over and trace punk's diffusion into the 1980s (and beyond).

Fanzines were (and are) important for a number of reasons (Triggs 2010; Worley 2024). From a historical perspective, they offer a vivid snapshot of the interests, concerns, and opinions of a significant milieu of British youth in a particular time and place. Culturally, they reveal the shifting parameters of the musical and stylistic forms that emerged in and around British pop over the 1970–1980s and beyond. In media terms they stand as an important new practice in alternative media, drawing on the potential of new technology (e.g., accessible photocopying machines) to challenge the hierarchy of access (see Atton 2002). Crucially, too, they demonstrate the extent to which (youth) cultures are not simply produced and consumed, but also constructed and utilized. If punk fanzines first emerged in lieu of informed media coverage, then they soon cultivated their own narratives and interpretations of punk's meaning and development distinct from—or at least entwined with—that presented by the music business, media, and music press. Conversely, fanzines facilitated access to the established culture industry, providing a "way in" to journalism or the music business for those who wished to pursue it. Among the numerous punk-generation journalists and writers who served a (provincial) fanzine apprenticeship were Paul Morley (*Out There*, *Girl Trouble*), Cath Carroll (*City Fun*), Johnny Waller (*Kingdom Come*), John Robb (*Rox*), Simon Reynolds (*Monitor*) and Steve Lamacq (*A Pack of Lies*).

Looked at politically, fanzines provided opportunity for opinions to be espoused and ideas explored. By so doing, they offered a sounding board for young people estranged from or denied access to existent political realms. This was taken to a glorious extreme in anarchist zines such as Sunderland's *Acts of Defiance* or Southend's *New Crimes*, wherein notions of pacifism, feminism, and animal liberation were debated and filtered through a punk lens toward cultural creativity and activism. But the leftist and feminist critiques offered by Manchester's *City Fun* and Birmingham's *Brass Lip*, or the anti-Thatcherite diatribes of the poet ranters in Liverpool's *Another Day Another Word*, serve to remind us how volatile the shifting political and socioeconomic terrain of the 1970s and 1980s felt to many. Creatively, meanwhile, zines allowed for collage, illustration, and design to complement punk's cultural politics, doubling as paper Petri dishes in which to experiment and innovate. Linder's *The Secret Public*, for example, produced as a collection of collages with Jon Savage in Manchester in 1978, remains a brilliant dissection of mediated gender constructs (see Hoare et al. 2006). As Teal Triggs (2006) has made clear, the visual language developed through fanzines became an essential part of punk's cultural revolt, informing a recognizably distinct aesthetic that was later absorbed into conventional design.

Of course, provincial fanzines could also be insular and elitist, as well as repetitive and simplistic. But the best may be seen to represent an alternative press, with countercultural and political roots revealed by the print shops and bookshops that sometimes helped produce and sell zines for eager young punks (BBC 1980). Art schools, small copy shops, and workplace Xeroxes provided other means, with limited print runs giving way to wider distribution if the impetus to *do something* extended beyond simply producing a "one-off" or handful of issues. Let us take one example: Coventry was a city that generated a number of fanzines over the late 1970s and 1980s. As well as incubating the two-tone music of multiracial youth, the city spawned a burgeoning punk and post-punk scene from which zines emerged to cover and cohere around such local bands as Squad, God's Toys, Urge, Criminal Class, Attrition, and Stress. The most long-lasting of Coventry's early zines was *Alternative Sounds*, produced by Martin Bowes (and others) from 1979 through to 1981. Featuring local and national groups alongside reviews, band indexes, and pieces on how to "do it yourself," it was very much a *fan*zine: knowledgeable, celebratory, and inclusive.[7] Experiments were attempted as to style and form, but its text and type tended to be ordered beneath the slightly skewed layout. And just as the fanzine's name declared it an alternative to the music press (i.e., the national weekly *Sounds*), so Bowes's growing centrality to the local scene paved the way for his role in the release of the relatively well-known (and well-received) *Sent from Coventry* compilation in 1980.

Far more chaotic and acerbic were Nic Bullen's zines, produced from the age of eleven and running through shifting titles (*Antisocial, Discarded, Out of Vogue, Twisted Morals, Autopsy, Black Cross, Museum Farce, Sine Nomine, Unreason*) as he grappled with punk's emergent politics and the technological possibilities of offset lithography and customized production. Bullen, who journeyed into Coventry from the small village of Meriden, would later form Napalm Death with *Antisocial*'s cofounder Miles Ratledge, pushing punk to one of its extremes. But it was through fanzines that Bullen recalled finding his way into this "brave new world," connecting to bands "on a deeper personal level, speaking to me in a direct manner that was absent from the mainstream music papers and providing communication that forged a relationship—however tenuous—between their producers and myself" (Bullen 2018).

Alan Rider, too, thought hard to overcome the restrictions of the medium. Across a series of zines, the most consistent and well-known of which was *Adventures in Reality*, Rider experimented with size, imagery, and design. "Numbered" from A to L, *Adventures in Reality* moved beyond music to ruminate on architecture and offer a range of "free gifts" (discount vouchers, anti-vivisection leaflets, toffees, tea bags, etc.). Simultaneously, like Bowes and Bullen, Rider made music, set up labels, organized gigs, and fed into wider zine and cassette networks (Rider 2017). By so doing, he served unconsciously and intuitively to both document and galvanize Coventry's post-punk culture, helping to construct its identity and generate activity.

There were other Coventry zines. As in towns and cities across the UK, titles came and went as enthusiasm vacillated and cultures morphed. These, in turn, contained moments of insight alongside snide attacks on bands made good or scenesters who, for whatever reason, were deemed to have gotten too big for their boots. Paradoxically, the very fact that fanzines were not made for posterity, that they commented immediately and often instinctively, means they now retain a special historical value. In their stapled pages we catch sight of cultures being made at the grass roots, almost outside the frame of the media spectacle. By collating opinions and ideas in the midst of formation, they offer a near unrefined archive of youthful ingenuity and occasional stupidity—a testimony to both the temporal, exciting, and confusing *moment* of adolescence and the cultural impetus of punk in the UK's back of beyond.

Conclusion: Hicks from the Sticks

Integral to punk's significance was the urge to *do it* rather than simply—or not just—consume it. Punk worked through participation. If "There are no Spectators," as Bristol's Pop Group insisted, then action had to be taken: "escapism is not freedom."[8] Many, of course, did not set the stakes so high. Punk's rejuvenation of pop arguably enhanced the fetishization of its related product (all that colored vinyl and picture sleeves in "unlimited supply"). The overtly political or confrontational dimension to punk was as much projected *onto* as cultivated *through* practice and rhetoric. Nevertheless, the implicit politics of dressing differently, forming a band that eschewed convention, self-producing a magazine or record, or self-organizing a gig or a club night should be obvious. The sense of event, the anticipation of excitement and doing-it-yourself drove punk's cultural impact. Indeed, the oft-repeated refrain that punk provided tools for young people thinking "I could do that" is enough to justify its continued discussion.

At the provincial level, beyond London's relatively more available and accessible routes to cultural stimuli, punk's call to agency was further amplified. Where once there was nothing, now there was something. Or at least it felt that way to many young people at the time. And while such an observation risks romanticizing the often limited and willfully puerile aspects of punk, it helps explain the culture's pertinence as a historical touchstone. The emphasis on practice, on *doing*, means debate as to the "quality," "effectiveness," or "meaning" of punk can be left to repeat over and over and over. For all the rhetoric of individuality ("I wanna be me"), punk forged cultural communities in which agency and participation were key. More to the point, the activities engendered by punk threw up a cultural diaspora of invention and ingenuity, be it the scattered vinyl oddities produced, or the stylistic invention that stood stark against drab surroundings, or the creative expressions of youthful anxiety, fear, anger, and fascination. If punk was co-opted quickly in the capital over the course of 1977, then it blossomed in the provinces, where the unfolding vistas of post-punk opened wide and a punk identity retained an outsider/oppositional impulse long after it had been dropped by London's self-appointed fashionistas. Punk's provincial manifestations facilitated cultural spaces and bristled with a vibrancy that continues to reverberate into the twenty-first century.

Notes

1. Bower and Newton were active on the music side, too, forming and/or being involved with the bands 2.3 (Bower), the Future, and Clock DVA (both Newton). For similar anti-London rhetoric from 1977, see the cover of Manchester's the Panik, *It Won't Sell*, an EP released on the proudly provincial Rainy City Records.
2. See the Sex Pistols' first TV appearance on Granada's *So It Goes* (August 28, 1976), performing "Anarchy in the UK." After a brief preamble, the song kicks in with Johnny Rotten shouting "get off your arse."

3. The line comes from Morrissey's lyric for the Smiths' "Panic," a single released on Rough Trade in 1986.
4. For a couple of good memoirs with good provincial flavor, see Marc Almond's *Tainted Life* (1999) and Lol Tolhurst's *Cured* (2016). See also books such as *Punks on Scooters: The Bristol Mod Revival, 1979–85* (Salter 2016); *"I Though Solihull Was for Snobs"* (Panic 2015); *The Kids Are All Square: Medway Punk and Beyond, 1977–85* (Collins and Snowball 2014); and *The Palace and the Punks* (Hill 2011).
5. This and myriad other examples have been collated by Hyped2Death Records on their *Messthetics* series.
6. Among the more notable of such compilations were Z-Block's *Is The War Over?* (Cardiff), Attrix's *Vaultage* series (Brighton), Aardvark's *Bouquet of Steel* (Sheffield), Object Music's *A Manchester Collection*, Bluurg's *Wessex '82* EP, Heartbeat's *Avon's Calling* (Bristol), Romans in Britain's *A Fine City* (Norwich), Pink Record's *Voxhall Tracks* EP (Luton), Guardian Records' *Compilation NE1* (North East), Vinyl Drip's *Blackpool Rox* EP, Kathedral Records' *Sent from Coventry*, Rumpo Records's *Rumponia* (Northampton), Brain Boosters' *South Specific* (Portsmouth), and Open Eye's *Street to Street* (Liverpool).
7. For the fanzine's own "do it yourself" guide, see *Alternative Sounds* 17 (1980): 15.
8. The line comes from the Pop Group's "There Are No Spectators," on their 1980 album *For How Much Longer Do We Tolerate Mass Murder?*, released on Y Records.

References

Almond, Marc. 1999. *Tainted Life: The Autobiography*. London: Sidgwick & Jackson.
Atton, Chris. 2002. *Alternative Media*. London: SAGE.
BBC. 1980. *Guttersnipe*. Open Door series. London: BBC Community Programmes Unit.
Beesley, Tony. 2009. *Our Generation: The Punk and Mod Children of Sheffield, Rotherham and Doncaster*. Peterborough, UK: Fastprint.
Bestley, Russ. 2007. *Hitsville UK: Punk Rock and Graphic Design in the Faraway Towns, 1976–84*. PhD diss., University of the Arts London.
Bestley, Russ. 2012. "From 'London's Burning' to 'Sten Guns in Sunderland.'" *Punk & Post-Punk* 1, no. 1: 41–71.
Bovier, Lionel, Philip Hoare Morrissey, and Linder Sterling. 2006. *Linder—Works, 1976–2006*. Zürich: JRP/Ringer.
Bradley, Michael. 2016. *Teenage Kicks: My Life as an Undertone*. London: Omnibus.
Bull, Gregory, and Mike Dines, eds. 2014. *Tales from the Punkside*. Portsmouth, UK: Itchy Monkey.
Bull, Gregory, and Mike Dines, eds. 2016. *Some of Us Scream, Some of Us Shout*. Portsmouth, UK: Itchy Monkey.
Bull, Gregory, and Mike Dines, eds. 2017. *And All Around Was Darkness*. Portsmouth, UK: Itchy Monkey.
Bull, Gregory, and Mickey "Penguin," eds. 2015. *Not Just Bits of Paper*. Charleston, SC: Perdam Babylonis Nomen.
Bullen, Nicholas. 2018. "From Year Zero to 1984: I Was a Pre-teen Fanzine Writer." In Subcultures Network 2018, 214–225.
Butler, Justine. 2014. "Disgustin' Justin." In Bull and Dines 2014, 85–94.
Cartwright, Garth. 2018. *Going for a Song: A Chronicle of the UK Record Shop*. London: Flood Gallery.

Cavanagh, David. 2015. *Good Night and Good Riddance: How Thirty-Five Years of John Peel Helped to Shape Modern Life*. London: Faber.

Cavanagh, Gary. 2009. *Bradford's Noise of the Valleys*. New Romney, UK: Bank House Book.

Cobley, Paul. 1999. "Leave the Capital." In *Punk Rock: So What? The Cultural Legacy of Punk*, edited by Roger Sabin, 170–185. London: Routledge.

Cohen, Stanley. 1972. *Folk Devils and Moral Panics*. London: MacGibbon & Kee.

Collins, Bob, and Ian Snowball. 2014. *The Kids Are All Square: Medway Punk and Beyond, 1977–85*. Hitchin, UK: Countdown.

Cope, Julian. 1999. *Head On: Memories of the Liverpool Punk Scene and the Story of The Teardrop Explodes (1976–82)*. Rev. ed. London: Thorsons.

Eddington, Richard. 2004. *Sent from Coventry: The Chequered Past of Two Tone*. London: Independent Music Press.

Fish, Mick. 2002. *Industrial Evolution: Through the Eighties with Cabaret Voltaire*. London: SAF Publishing.

Florek, Jaki, and Paul Whelan. 2009. *Eric's: All the Best Clubs are Downstairs, Everybody Knows That....* Runcorn, UK: Feedback.

Gibson, Lee. 2013. *A Punk Rock Flashback*. London: Lulu Press.

Gill, Andy, and Adrian Thrills. 1978. "This Week's Leeds—Sheffield, Yorks." *New Musical Express*, September 9, 1978, 6–8.

Goddard, Simon. 2014. *Simply Thrilled Honey: The Preposterous Story of Postcard Records*. London: Ebury Press.

Gordon, Alastair. 2005. *The Authentic Punk: An Ethnography of DIY Music Ethics*. PhD diss., University of Loughborough.

Gordon, Alastair. 2014. "Glue and Bastards." In Bull and Dines 2014, 15–28.

Gordon, Alastair. 2016. "To End Up on Your Table..." In Bull and Dines 2016, 141–147.

Gorman, Paul. 2017. *The Story of "The Face": The Magazine that Changed Culture*. London: Thames & Hudson.

Gun Rubber no. 1. 1977. Cited in http://www.sheffieldvision.com/aboutmis_gunrubber.html.

Gun Rubber no. 5. 1977.

Haslam, Dave. 2015. *Life after Dark: A History of British Nightclubs and Music Venues*. London: Simon & Schuster.

Hesmondhalgh, David. 1997. "Post-Punk's Attempt to Democratise the Music Industry: The Success and Failure of Rough Trade." *Popular Music* 16, no. 3: 255–274.

Hill, Tony. 2011. *The Palace and the Punks*. Mansfield, UK: Northern Lights.

Hooley, Terri, and Richard Sullivan. 2010. *Hoolygan: Music, Mayhem, Good Vibrations*. Belfast: Blackstaff Press.

King, James. n.d. Interview. https://www.youtube.com/watch?v=8_EpzVhDVss. Accessed June 7, 2018.

Lilleker, Martin. 2005. *Beats Working for a Living: Sheffield Popular Music, 1973–1984*. Sheffield, UK: Juma.

Low, Chris. 2017. "Confessions of a Pre-teen Punk." In Bull and Dines 2017, 29–42.

Middles, Mick. 2002. *From Joy Division to New Order: The True Story of Anthony H. Wilson and Factory Records*. London: Virgin.

Morley, Paul. 1977. "They Mean it M-a-a-anchester." *New Musical Express*, July 30, 1977, 6–7.

Nolan, David. 2006. *I Swear I Was There: The Gig That Changed the World*. Shropshire, UK: IMP.

Ogg, Alex. 2009. *Independence Days: The Story of UK Independent Record Labels*. London: Cherry Red.

O'Neill, Sean, and Guy Trelford. 2003. *It Makes You Want to Spit: The Definitive Guide to Punk in Northern Ireland*. Belfast: Reekus.

Orme, John. 1979. "Crisis? This Crisis!" *Melody Maker*, June 30, 1979, 21.

Panic, Paul. 2015. *"I Though Solihull Was for Snobs": The Mell Square Musick Story*. Solihull, UK: No Rip Off.

Parsons, Tony, and John Hamblett. 1978. "Leeds: Mill City UK." *New Musical Express*, August 5, 1978, 7–8.

Perry, Mark. 2000. *Sniffin' Glue: The Essential Punk Accessory*. London: Sanctuary.

Reddington, Helen. 2007. *The Lost Women of Rock Music: Female Musicians of the Punk Era*. Aldershot, UK: Ashgate.

Reynolds, Simon. 2005. *Rip It Up and Start Again: Postpunk 1978–84*. London: Faber.

Rider, Alan. 2017. "Adventuring into Reality, 1979–85." In Bull and Dines 2017, 57–64.

Rimmer, Dave. 2011. *Like Punk Never Happened: Culture Club and the New Pop*. Rev. ed. London: Faber.

Salter, Michael W. 2016. *Punks on Scooters: The Bristol Mod Revival, 1979–85*. Bristol, UK: Tangent Books.

Savage, Jon. 1991. *England's Dreaming: Sex Pistols and Punk Rock*. London: Faber.

Subcultures Network. 2018. *Ripped, Torn and Cut: Pop, Politics and Punk Fanzines from 1976*. Manchester, UK: Manchester University Press.

Sweeting, Adam. 1982. "Union City Blues: Words and Music in East Anglia." *Melody Maker*, March 13, 1982, 25–26.

Taylor, Neil. 2010. *Document and Eyewitness: An Intimate History of Rough Trade*. London: Orion.

Tickell, Paul, dir. 1995. *Punk and the Pistols*. Arena series. London: BBC.

Tolhurst, Lol. 2016. *Cured: The Tale of Two Imaginary Boys*. London: Quercus.

Triggs, Teal. 2006. "Scissors and Glue: Punk Fanzines and the Creation of a DIY Aesthetic." *Journal of Design History* 19, no. 1: 69–83.

Triggs, Teal. 2010. *Fanzines*. London: Thames & Hudson.

Tyler, Andrew. 1982. "Cold Wind Hits Record Industry." *New Musical Express*, May 22, 1982, 3.

Webb, Peter. 2016. "Dirty Squatters, Anarchy, Politics and Smack: A Journey through Bristol's Squat Punk Milieu." In *The Aesthetic of Our Anger: Anarcho-Punk, Politics and Music*, edited by Mike Dines and Matthew Worley, 179–198. Colchester, UK: Minor Compositions.

Whalley, Boff. 2003. *Footnote**. Hebden Bridge, UK: Pomona.

Wilkinson, David. 2014. "Prole Art Threat: The Fall, the Blue Orchids and the Politics of the Post-Punk Working Class Autodidact." *Punk & Post-Punk* 3, no. 1: 67–82.

Wilkinson, David. 2016. *Post-Punk, Politics and Pleasure in Britain*. Basingstoke, UK: Palgrave Macmillan.

Wilkinson, David. 2018. "'Pam Ponders Paul Morley's Cat': *City Fun* and the Politics of Post-Punk." In Subcultures Network 2018, 91–109.

Worley, Matthew. 2016. *Young Offenders: Punk in Norwich, 1976–84*. Norwich, UK: Bestley Press.

Worley, Matthew. 2017. *No Future: Punk, Politics and British Youth Culture, 1976–84*. Cambridge: Cambridge University Press.

Worley, Matthew. 2024. *Xerox Machine: Punk, Post-Punk and Fanzines in Britain, 1976–88*. London: Reaktion.

Young, Rob. 2006. *Rough Trade*. London: Black Dog.

CHAPTER 17

PUNK IN RUSSIA
From the "Declassed Elements" to the Class Struggle

IVAN GOLOLOBOV

INTRODUCTION

PUNK in Russia is a vibrant and highly diverse culture, one that resists "being rendered as [a] neat, linear story" and "fails to conform to the rules of an iconic historically narrative," instead manifesting multiple subjective interpretations and showing conflicting and contradicting understandings of what punk is (Gololobov et al. 2014, 22). As shown elsewhere (Gololobov et al. 2014, 22–48), in Russia punk represents a dialogue that, on the one hand, reflects on the structural transformations of the social, economic, and political contexts of the late Soviet Union and post-Soviet Russia, and, on the other, responds to the internal dynamics of the scene, looking for its own authenticity in the environment of the transnational punk scene and the Russian national cultural, musical, and poetic tradition (see Olson 2004; Steinholt 2003).

With such a complex and diverse nature, punk in Russia defined a particular trajectory of how the meaning of punk was discussed and negotiated in the Soviet and post-Soviet context. This negotiation focused upon specific relations between the social and, in particular, class appeal of punk in Russia and the degree of its political engagement. To unpack these debates, one needs to look back at the cultural identity of early punk in the West, where punk, as much as an aesthetic gesture, was also a form of political expression. It openly addressed urgent social and political issues, and, as Worley and Copsey (2018, 119) note, "[p]olitical symbols, slogans and signifiers of 'crisis' formed a core component of punk's iconography." Indeed, from the very beginning, "the style, sound and aesthetic of punk came loaded with potential meaning that took it beyond the real of 'just' music for fashion. Punk's influence spread around the world and for many *did* become a medium for political expression, providing a *modus operandi* for radical ideas and innovative cultural practice" (Lohman and Worley 2018, 52).

The political engagement of punk went hand in hand with a particular social appeal. In Britain first, and then in other countries, punk made a clear claim of speaking for and on behalf of the marginalized working class. Fryer (1986, 1) writes that "[t]he rhetoric of punk has always insisted that both the music and the style were strictly working-class, the expression of the dispossessed and the economically downtrodden," while Simonelli (2002, 121) has argued that "[t]he punk subculture in Britain was the most outspoken effort to restore working-class values in British rock and roll in the late-1970s." Even in terms of the style of its clothing, in Britain, for example, "[p]unk reproduced the entire sartorial history of post-war working-class youth cultures" (Hebdige 1979, 26). Even though the influence of art circles on the formation of the punk scene is quite obvious, it is also clear that, in comparison to other genres, punk clearly appealed to working-class audiences. Simonelli, for instance, acknowledges that the influence of Malcolm McLaren and Vivienne Westwood on the aesthetics and ideological message of the Sex Pistols was significant, but adds that John "Lydon's working-class background provided an agenda too, as did the backgrounds of the dozens of musicians inspired by the Pistols" (Simonelli 2013, 229). Moreover, it is also clear that "Johnny Rotten [aka John Lydon] meant punk to be the voice of working-class youth, calling on them to have fun and rebel against a society that had ignored their interests for too long" (Simonelli 2013, 221; see also Albiez 2003, 359).

Soviet Punk's Antagonism Toward the Working Class

The danger here, of course, is in overstating the working-class credentials of Western punk; nonetheless, class orientation was indeed an integral part of punk discourse. Obviously, interpretations of punk in the West also vary significantly. Sabin (1999, 2) suggests that punk remains a "notoriously amorphous concept." Not every scene is engaged in discussion of working-classness, and not every scene declares its clear political identity. However, in punk the fusion of political engagement and working-class appeal remains more visible than in many other genres of popular music and music-based subcultures. But in Russia, punk was born in quite different circumstances. While anti-authoritarian feelings and expressions were certainly shared by disillusioned and disenfranchised youth, involvement in "labor struggles" and organic affiliation with working-class communities were something early Russian punk—from the Soviet era—was clearly missing.

The then USSR was a socialist state where "workers" were recognized as the backbone of Soviet society and, at least at the level of ideology and official cultural narratives, treated as a privileged class. The official cultural doctrine of socialist realism promoted principles of collectivism, equality, devotion to the ideas of communism, loyalty to the Communist Party, and aversion of capitalism and everything that came with it, including its cultural environment (Clark 1981). What youth in the West experienced as an existential threat—the atomizing force of the beginnings of neoliberal transformation—in the Soviet Union was only a mythical condition, associated with the problems of the "capitalist West." What punks in the West saw as threatened—working-class culture, equality, collectivism, community coherence, and so on—in the Soviet Union were endemic conditions of life. In the Soviet Union at the end of the 1970s, it was not workers or youth from working-class neighborhoods who felt themselves disenfranchised and marginalized, but rather those who were smothered by these endemic conditions and those who felt threatened by the cultural hegemony of the working class. Institutionalized in the media, education, public spaces, and the leisure industry, the Soviet hegemony of class inclined to exclude and devalue cultural narratives that did not conform to or openly contradicted the official cultural ideology. Such excluded narratives included those promoting individual initiative, creativity, and originality, those expressing an interest in Western "capitalist" culture, or those having a critical attitude to or lack of appreciation for communist ideas, as well as a lack of respect for the opinion of Soviet society in general. Members of the intelligentsia and young people from educated backgrounds leaning toward critical and independent stances found themselves marginalized and excluded, and it is in these sectors of society that the seeds of punk rebellion found their most fertile soil in the late-era Soviet Union. In this situation the working class became not the point of social departure for the emerging punk culture, but rather its "significant other," and, moreover, the working class was an antagonist against which cultural identity of punk was initially articulated.

What has been called the "punk virus" (Aksyutina 1999) came to Russia in the late 1970s. The first punk band in the Soviet Union—Avtomaticheskie Udovletvoriteli (Automatic Satisfiers—a vague reference to Sex Pistols)—was formed in 1979 by Andrey "Svin" Panov. According to Artemy Troitsky (1990, 72), "[l]ike all Soviet 'punks' Svin did not have anything to do with proletariat. His father is a choreographer, his mother is a ballet dancer." Alexei Rybin, in his history of early Russian rock, confirms the point more broadly:

> In Russia [punk] started its triumphal march (way more powerful and interesting than the sluggish crawling of "rock" . . .) from bohemian circles. The first heralds of punk rock were people with university education, graduates of technical departments, departments of journalism, philology: all kind of enlightened "intelligentsia" threw itself on punk rock as a hungry bear throws itself on the raspberry bush looking for vitamins.
>
> (Rybin 2013, n.p.)

Not only was an organic connection alien to punks in the Soviet Union, but so were ideas of working-class unity and a broadly leftist political imaginary. When in 1988 Billy Bragg came to play to Leningrad and met with local rock musicians, his appeal to play for the workers was left completely ununderstood. The Leningrad rockers replied, "Are you crazy? Which kind of music for the working class you are talking about?" (Fanaylova 2012). Indifference toward working-class cultural and political imaginaries in Russian punk, and in rock music in general, reflects a negative attitude toward the working class among certain circles of Soviet intelligentsia more broadly:

> To the intellectual of those times, the representative of a broad section of Soviet society, the worker—contemptuously called by the nickname of "hegemon"—was a poorly educated, lazy slob, an embezzler and a crook, who tyrannized the poor intellectual for seventy-some odd years. In contrast, the Soviet worker understood anyone with a higher education as a useless mama's boy, looking for the easy life; his social-productive existence as a parasite on the proletarian body could not be justified in any way. In this sense, one can understand why there was hardly any after-hours contact between workers and intellectuals during the Soviet era.
>
> (Salnikov 2004)

In this situation of near-open antagonism toward the working class, punk, born in intellectual circles, defined itself not in association but in opposition to working-class culture. This enunciation of "significant difference," inherent in punk's subcultural identity (Hebdige 1979, 102), was expressed in the articulation and celebration of one's non-belonging to the community, in self-marginalization, self-abasement, antisocial hedonistic nihilism, and militant but often self-destructive individualism (see Rybin 2008; Spirin 2004).

In differentiating themselves from the hegemonic working-class culture, punks in the Soviet Union often assumed the identity of—in the lyrics of Kino's 1982 song "Bezdel'nik" (The Idler), an "idler," "redundant like a heap of waste," a "needle in a haystack," "a man with no goal" who hangs about all day and knows nothing (Kino 1982; see also Gololobov et al. 2014, 26). Andrey "Svin" Panov of Avtomaticheskie Udovletvoriteli went even further and despised the very ethic of work as such by avoiding a job (*tuneyadedstvo*):

> Today I am not a worker really / Tomorrow is Lenin's day of community work / But I don't go to work / I am spending my day in *vytsezvitel'* [the drunk tank].
>
> (Avtomaticheskie Udovletvoriteli 1987, 1988)

The dissociation of early Russian punks from working-class culture was taken further by the next waves of local scenes formed in the mid-1980s. There punks not only declared their disengagement from the dominant cultural ideology of the working class, but also expressed their clear opposition to that class frame by assuming the identity of "declassed elements." Such an embrace of "declassed elements" was especially notable in Siberian punk (see Gololobov et al. 2014, 28–32; Steinholt 2012). Yanka Diagileva, a punk singer and songwriter from Novosibirsk, and one of the most popular figures in Russia's underground scene, used this term in the title song of her album *To the Declassed Elements* recorded in 1988 in collaboration with Egor (or Yegor) Letov, the key ideologue and the leading figure of probably the most influential Russian punk band, Grazhdanskaya Oborona. Letov, like many other intellectual youths, experienced his hostility toward the working class in general, and expressed his difference in a spectacular way. His brother Sergei Letov recalls the first visit of Egor to Moscow:

> Once Egor was taking a suburban train somewhere, he got out at the station called Frezer [industrial milling cutter], some young lads came to him and said, "Oh, he is wearing glasses!" and broke his glasses. He then refused to buy new ones and decided to wear the old, with a triangular piece of broken glass in the right eye. This was the meeting of Egor and Moscow in the beginning of the 1980s.
>
> (quoted in Lagina 2014, 58)

The antagonism felt by Letov toward the working class is seen in his lyrics for Grazhdanskaya Oborona, such as on 1988's "Insects":

> Save us away / From an angry effort / Meaty eyes / Watery speeches / From abundant museums / Drunken commentaries / Proletarians whom you cannot escape.
>
> (Grazhdanskaya Oborona 1988)

Antagonism toward the working class and the imagery of the "labor struggle" is evident in other references toward the symbols of the workers' movement made by Grazhdanskaya Oborona. The sleeve of the 1985 release *Disgusting Youth* depicts a group of scared and abused punks surrounded by ordinary Soviet citizens holding red flags and red slogans. In 1987 Letov recorded *Red Album*, which included a song titled "I Hate Red Color" and containing the refrain "I hate red color / Destroy people like me!" In other *Red Album* songs he subverts Soviet imagery by agonizingly screaming and almost spitting out words and phrases referring to the Soviet state and official Soviet ideology—red banner, Communism, the Party, and so on—and articulating them in the context of physiological disgust, illness, murder, suicide, and death.

By the end of the decade, the semiotic assault on working-class culture and the working class itself became more overt. Workers and collective farmers, the "positive heroes of socialist realism" (Clark 1981, 46), were openly humiliated, laughed at, and ridiculed. One of the most explicit examples of such ridicule comes from a Leningrad band Nol'. In the 1990s Nol' released *Severnoe bugi* (Northern boogie) with a title song having the following lines:

> Birds are singing over the town / Blurry sunrise is on its way / With his head toward his own factory / A hungover worker is laying on the ground.
>
> (Nol' 1990)

Other, and probably the most radical, examples of such an attitude can be found in the songs of Sektor Gaza, a band formed in Voronezh in 1987. Sektor Gaza created an entire subgenre of punk called "kolkhoznyi punk" which can be translated as "collective farm punk," or "country" or even "redneck punk" (Gololobov 2015; Tikhonov 2001). Here the songs were supposedly performed for and on behalf of the "working man," to include both the collective farm and industrial worker—but in no way defending, empowering, or even portraying him in a positive light:

> [A]t the collective farm I was the only one into punk / I was wearing leather trousers and was dirty like a swine / My dad is on a tractor doing triple daily shifts / And my mom, ... she is all day pulling cows' tits.
>
> (Sektor Gaza 1991)

Russian Punk and a Politics of Individualism

The attack on the "hardworking" ethos, "working men," and working-classness in the situation where the working class was still, officially, the foundation of Soviet society, inevitably led to the "apolitical" character (in the sense that punk is considered political in the West) of Soviet punk. Soviet punk was visibly indifferent to any kind of formal politics, social commitment, or collective action as a whole. Even the concept of anarchy in Soviet punk was interpreted in a particular way, different not only from the dominant reading of this concept in Western punk, but also from the understanding of this concept by such foundational Russian theorists as Bakunin and Kropotkin. Instead of self-organization and mutual aid, anarchy for many Russian punks was first and foremost a space of individual freedom and independence. As Egor Letov put it, "Anarchy is such an organization of the world which is only for one. Two is already too much, way too much. Anarchy for one and one only" (Letov [1990] 2017).

Celebration of the individual revolt, rejection of collective action, or even collective positioning and a negative stance toward the official political frames of reference remained dominant in Russian punk in the first post-Soviet decade through the 1990s. For Petr Fomenko, the singer of the crustcore band Zverstvo, formed in Krasnodar in 1993, "We don't understand punk from a social point of view but as part of culture and art" (quoted in Gololobov et al. 2014, 2–3). In many other segments of the scene that emerged in the 1990s, the very idea of "politics" became either rejected or subverted. Alexei Fishev, a.k.a. Ugol, the leader of Orgazm Nostradamusa, a band formed in Ulan-Ude in 1995, has reflected on this disengagement:

> [L]et's take anarchists, for example, left radicals, they promote an idea, which is shit, of economic and social equality. Let's take the right-wing, for instance. What are they? Theocracy, bluntly, some kind of monarchism, patriotic and spiritual values—all are also shit. There is a center. The center is a bourgeoisie, which rules our

world. We represent the anti-elite. The anti-elite represents marginals and criminals. The truth is that we don't give a damn about the laws, rules, and ideas of the right-wing. The same goes for the left-wing and the center. What are we? We are morons. Morons—from their point of view, but from the point of our spiritual, sophisticated, spiritual organization—they are all morons.

(Fishev 2010)

The detachment of punk from formal politics in post-Soviet Russia went hand in hand with the continued dissociation of the scene from working-class culture. However, in the 1990s and the 2000s, this dissociation began to take different forms. If the working class was previously rather seen as a threat to the individual freedom of intellectual youth, in the post-Soviet condition it was more like a "sick person" of democratic transition, possessing almost no economic, cultural, or political capital and slowing down the liberalization and opening up of society. Hans, one of the active members of the Krasnodar local scene in the 1990s and 2000s, recalled an episode from his past of violent confrontation with members of the public reacting to his Mohican haircut, commenting, "These [we]re proletarians. . . . This was the 1990s. These were proletarians who no longer got paid. But they had not yet shed their values and they despised everything new" (Gololobov et al. 2014, 135). Other key members of the local scene from the same generation agreed that the very notion of "working class" in post-Soviet Russia was highly problematic to start with; as another Krasnodar punk put it, "Unlike in the West, we have no such notion as 'working-class culture.' It is absent" (quoted in Gololobov et al. 2014, 133). Or as Maksim, a member of the hardcore band Zasrali Solntse, followed on,

> I could not see [the] class belonging. I think it is disappearing in the world generally, and in Russia it has been somewhat erased. Because we all lived, were born in the 1990s, when . . . a lot of people lost their jobs, did not work.
>
> (quoted in Gololobov et al. 2014, 135)

Indeed, in post-Soviet Russia, workers were no longer the hegemonic identity. In a society that was rapidly turning toward the market economy, people "of capital"—entrepreneurs, financiers, gangsters, and other kinds of "new Russians"—rather than the "men [and women] of work" were the central actors in the new discourse. As a result, what in the late Soviet Union was a specific opinion of the marginalized intelligentsia, portraying the worker as "a poorly educated, lazy slob, an embezzler and a crook, who tyrannized the poor intellectual," would by the 1990s become the dominant attitude toward workers in mass culture. Workers, as a social group, were either erased from mainstream cultural narratives or ridiculed.

The ridiculing of and negativity toward workers remained widespread in Russian popular music during the following decade. The band Leningrad, formed in 1997 in Saint Petersburg, and who would go on to be one of Russia's most popular rock bands, presented one extreme form of such derogation:

I am killing myself at work / Then I am drinking / Then I am in vomit.

(Leningrad 2000)

I don't go to work . . . / I will walk around my flat . . . / I will go to the balcony / To spit a bit at the working class.

(Leningrad 2003)

Even though Sergei "Shnur" Shnurov, the leader of Leningrad, often plays the role of a "declassed" worker, as the music critic Artem Rondarev has noted, such an image has nothing to do with an appeal to the working class. In Rondarev's view, Shnur is aiming to appeal to the new Russian middle class, the urban "managers" to whom Shnur is serving a slice of "declassed" life in a safe environment of nightclubs and corporate parties (Rondarev, quoted in Medvedev 2016). And Shnur himself confirms this:

[They say] Leningrad is a group for managers! . . . but who the fuck else there is in the country apart from managers?! There is nobody! Whom are you trying to sing for? Sing for proletarians! Okay, where are those proletarians!
Question: Are you going to discuss working professions in your songs?
No. Because there are very few workers. Because they no longer define anything. And there will be less and less workers because they will be replaced with machines. A worker is an atavism, it is a dying story. "Workers of the world – unite!"—it is the beginning of the past century. There is no one to unite anymore.

(Shnurov 2016)

The success of Leningrad and their take on working-class identity captures the dramatic cultural transformation post-Soviet society went through. By the end of the 2000s, the very figure of a worker was increasingly disappearing from the horizon of popular culture. In the situation where formerly marginal voices dismantling the hegemony of the working class became mainstream, punk had to redefine its attitudes to its social background and political engagement. Remaining antagonistic to the working class and indifferent to any form of collective political action would immediately identify punk in relations of equivalence to the commercial mainstream, which, in addition, regularly showed clear connections to the authorities: something, as already mentioned, punk was always positioned against.

New Class Consciousness and Collaborations

By the end of the decade, Russia punk started to move toward what Moore (2004, 307) calls a "culture of authenticity," or "a quest for authenticity and independence from the culture industry . . . renouncing the prevailing culture of media, image, and hypercommercialism." As a part of this move, initially small but well-organized and well-networked hardcore, Oi!, and anarcho-punk scenes grew in Russia. These scenes were explicitly uninterested in commercial success and less oriented toward musical adventurism, aesthetic shock, or a search for existential freedom. Instead, they focused on social and political commitment (Aksyutina 2008). As Khrust, a bass guitar player from Izhevsk punk/hardcore band Red Card, has reflected:

> Punk/hardcore is not music, not songs' lyrics, not fashion and not even a way of life. Punk/hardcore is first of all people, their actions, it is what they do, their life principles, their ability to defend their beliefs and to fight for their ideals. Generally, I don't give a shit about music and lyrics. This is all secondary. Even though I am fucking around with the bass in two bands from Izhevsk (Red Card and Reasons) I am not a musician and I never gave a toss about this! I am a DIY activist, anarchist, autonomist, antifascist, committed vegetarian and straight edger, AFL [American Fight League] fighter and organiser of FNB [Food Not Bombs], eco-activist, punk-rocker, and hardcore-skinhead, etc. But I never was and will never be a musician.
>
> (Khrust 2016)

Such a strong political commitment was fixed around a clear realization of the "enemy" that Oi! and anarcho-punk scenes were standing against, and this enemy was a possibly new version of an old one: capitalism. In this struggle the notion of "working class" was no longer an "atavism," as it was in the commercially successful punk of Leningrad, which became part of the discourse of new Russian bourgeoisie, but an oppressed social group. The oppressed position of workers became actively discussed in the lyrics of the bands coming from hardcore and anarcho-punk scenes, while the bands started to see themselves as the voices speaking for and to the workers. Bands such as the aforementioned Red Card from Izhevsk, Krasnyi gorizont (Red Horizon) from Kirov, Brigadir (Brigadier), formed in Saint Petersburg in 2007, or The Zavod (The Factory), formed in 2014 in Moscow, fully adopted ethics and aesthetics of the oppressed and seemingly forgotten workers (Brigadir 2009, 2016; Krasnyi gorizont 2009; Red Card 2009; The Zavod 2014a, 2014b, 2015a, 2015b, 2017). In 2009 Brigadir released their first album, a collaboration with Krasnyi gorizont heroically titled *Vmeste k pobede!* (Together to Victory!), which opened with Brigadir's "Krasnye and anarcho skiny" (Red and anarcho skins):

> In the world full of oppression people have nothing to lose / And in the fight against capitalism we are ready to give our lives away / We—the skinheads—will stand for the working class / Till the last drop of our blood! . . . / Honour and pride of the working class! / Red and anarcho skins!
>
> (Brigadir 2009)

Not all would be so aggressively masculine, yet collaboration between bands took place elsewhere. Despite their name, in 2010, Moscow Death Brigade, a "circle pit hiphop" formation composed of members of several hardcore bands, including What We

Feel and Razor Boys, recorded a track called "Geroi" (Heroes), which called on the audience to switch their attention from the televised superheroes promoted by popular culture to the ordinary people around them. Among the real heroes, so the song goes, who routinely "commit exploits without asking for a reward," are "firefighters, rescue workers, doctors, teachers / Who wake up before dawn and work all day long / Who kill themselves in three jobs to raise their families / Who forget about their own life in their own commitment" (Moscow Death Brigade 2010). From 2014 to 2016 The Zavod released several records specifically discussing the oppressed position of working-class people in contemporary Russia. In 2016 Brigadir released "The Song of Anarchist Workers," rearticulating the working-class affinities of the Russian Oi!, punk/hardcore, and anarcho-punk scenes.

These voices were expressed in the first person. The Oi! and street-punk musicians not only discussed working-class themes, they considered themselves as working class and saw their performance as expressing the interests and demands of the working class. This affinity was not a spectacular one. As members of the Moscow Death Brigade and What We Feel, a hardcore band from Moscow, put it in a collaborative statement on social media:

> We were raised in the working class neighborhoods. . . . Just so the reader understands the situation a little better, we'd like to provide a little background on the members of 210 [another Oi! band from Moscow]. Most of these guys come from the working class, work at the factories, and grew up in some of the worst neighborhoods. They are simple people who didn't have the luxury of government-sponsored education or financial aid provided by the state.
>
> (What We Feel and Moscow Death Brigade 2015)

Many of the key figures of that punk/hardcore scene did indeed come from working-class backgrounds. For instance, the leader of Moscow anti-fascist skinheads Ivan "Bonebraker" Khutorskoi, killed by neo-Nazis in November 2009, "grew up in a working-class district of Golyanovo. . . . It seems that young people are mobilized to the 'ground force' of contemporary neofascism exactly from these kind of working-class suburbs" (Cherkasov 2010).

By the end of the 2010s, unity between the punk scene and working-class movements in Russia became a growing trend. More and more musicians took up the task of rehabilitating the figure of the worker, who had been ignored, avoided, disgraced, or ridiculed in Russian punk and rock music previously, and who, more disastrously, was being increasingly marginalized and oppressed by the exploitative "resource capitalism" of the post-Soviet economy. In 2016 Arkady Kotz, a "political punk big-band" named after an early twentieth-century Russian Communist who did one of the first Russian translations of the *Internationale*, recorded an album called *Muzyka dlia rabochego klassa* (Music for the working class), which featured songs such as "Byt' rabochim ne stydno" (Being a Worker is No Shame"), "Kto strelyaet v rabochikh" (Who shoots at workers), and "Stachka" (Strike). Even the British leftist Billy Bragg was finally embraced, as they included a cover of his "Power in the Union." The album is introduced with the following text:

> We dedicate this album to our brothers and sisters—workers and union activists in Russia and around the World... *Music for the Working Class* is a history of class pride, songs of workers' protests, rallies, and strikes. This album is released in camaraderie and is a collaboration with the workers' movement, and is supported by the Confederation of Labour of Russia.
>
> (Arkadiy Kotz 2016)

Conclusion

Tracing the evolution of punk in Russia via its relations with political engagement and working-class identity allows us to understand how punk internationally has been able to construct, negotiate, and transform its ideologies differently. Unlike in the West, the scene started as a radical and often militant denial of any affiliation with the working class or involvement in collective action, and only came to a realization of its working-classness and articulation of clear political demands, including via cultural collaborations, relatively recently. Punk in Russia remains a highly vibrant scene, sensitive not only to the transformation of structural social, economic, and political contexts, but also to the dynamics within Russian popular music in general. And, paradoxically enough, the social and cultural intelligence of politically committed Russian punk achieved what many Russian rock and pop musicians tried and failed to do for decades: cross national borders and get the message about Russian society to a global audience. From the mid-2010s onward, bands like What We Feel, Brigadir, and Moscow Dead Brigade performed regularly at large international punk and rock festivals such as 0161 Festival or Boomtown. In 2018, Moscow Death Brigade played a sold-out Britain and Ireland tour, where one of their gigs was reviewed by local activists as the "most banging gig of the year":

> Their lyrics and words between songs are spot on, eloquently and clearly rejecting nationalism, borders, racism, fascism, misogyny and patriarchy and capitalism. In the face of the evident rush to the right and an upsurge of racist and fascist attacks and organising everywhere, we need strong movements to face them down and fight them back. And we need bands like MDB [Moscow Death Brigade] as they motivate us to carry on the fight, rapping hard about helping each other out, sticking together in the face of it all, recognising that we are everywhere and stronger together.
>
> (Bristol Antifascists 2018)

References

Aksyutina, Olga. 1999. *Pank-virus v Rossii (sbornik interview)*. Moscow: Lean.

Aksyutina, Olga. 2008. *"Esli ya ne mogu tantsevat," eto ne moya revolyutsiya!' DIY pank/khardkor stsena v Rossii*. Moscow: Nota-R.

Albiez, Sean. 2003. "Know History! John Lydon, Cultural Capital and the Prog/Punk Dialectic." *Popular Music* 22, no. 3: 357–374.

Arkady Kotz. 2016. *Muzyka dlya rabochego klassa/Music for the Working Class*. Bandcamp. https://arkadiy.bandcamp.com/album/music-for-the-working-class.

Bristol Antifascists. 2018. "Review of the Moscow Death Brigade Gig." Facebook, November 14, 2018. www.facebook.com/bristolantifascists/posts/2226459037591622.

Cherkasov, Aleksandr. 2010. "Ivan Igorevich Khutorskoi. 17 fevralya 1983–16 noyabrya 2009gg." *Ezhednevnyi zhurnal*, November 18, 2010. http://ej.ru/?a=note&id=10562.

Clark, Katerina. 1981. *The Soviet Novel: History as Ritual*. Chicago: University of Chicago Press.

Fanaylova, Elena. 2012. "Istoriya gruppy 'Arkady Kotz' na fone istorii protestnogo dvizheniya." Svoboda.org, July 22, 2012. https://www.svoboda.org/a/24655402.html.

Fishev, Aleksei. 2010. "Ugol, Filosof podvalov, pomoek." YouTube, April 27, 2010. http://www.youtube.com/watch?v=x4gAllQAq5k.

Fryer, Paul. 1986. "Punk and the New Wave of British Rock: Working Class Heroes and Art School Attitudes." *Popular Music and Society* 10, no. 4: 1–15.

Gololobov, Ivan. 2015. "Russian Punk in the 'Biggest Village on Earth.'" In *Hopeless Youth!*, edited by Francisco Martínez and Pille Runnel, 331–348. Tartu: Estonian National Museum.

Gololobov, Ivan, Hilary Pilkington, and Yngvar Steinholt. 2014. *Punk in Russia: Cultural Mutation from the "Useless" to the "Moronic."* London: Routledge.

Hebdige, Dick. 1979. *Subculture: The Meaning of Style*. London: Methuen.

Khrust. 2016. "Moe mnenie o izhevskoi pank/hardkor stsene." vk.ru, April 6, 2010. https://vk.com/topic-11662160_22429202.

Lagina, Irina. 2014. "Zerkalo dlya Egora." *Rolling Stone Russia* 11, no. 122: 54–59.

Letov, Egor. (1990) 2017. "'Ya tam, a vy—zdes. Schastlivo ostavatsya' Latentnoe avtointervyu Egora Letova i istoriya vypuska 'Sta let odinochestva.'" *Lenta.ru*, December 23, 2017. https://lenta.ru/articles/2017/12/23/letov/.

Lohman, Kirsty, and Matthew Worley. 2018. "Bloody Revolutions, Fascist Dreams, Anarchy and Peace: Crass, Rondos and the Politics of Punk, 1977–1984." *Britain and the World* 11, no. 1: 51–74.

Medvedev, Sergei. 2016. "Protest na labutenakh." Svoboda.org, May 11, 2016. https://www.svoboda.org/a/27730770.html.

Moore, Ryan. 2004. "Postmodernism and Punk Subculture: Cultures of Authenticity and Deconstruction." *Communication Review* 7: 305–327.

Olson, Laura. 2004. *Performing Russia: Folk Revival and Russian Identity*. London: Routledge.

Rybin, Aleksei. 2008. *Anarkhiya v RF: Pervaya polnaya istoriya russkogo panka*. Saint Petersburg: Amfora.

Rybin, Aleksei. 2013. *Tri kita: BG, Mail, Tsoi*. Saint Petersburg: Amfora.

Sabin, Roger, ed. 1999. *Punk Rock: So What? The Cultural Legacy of Punk*. London: Routledge.

Salnikov, Vladimir. 2004. "The Image of the Worker in the Visual Arts." Emancipation of-from Labor, no 3. Helsinki: Museum of Contemporary Art Kiasma. https://chtodelat.org/b8-newspapers/12-72/the-image-of-the-worker-in-the-visual-arts/.

Shnurov, Sergei. 2016. "Nichego bolee russkoko, chem nashi pesni, kinechno zhe, ne naidesh." *Bizness-gazeta. Delovaya gazeta Tatarstana*, July 17, 2016. https://www.business-gazeta.ru/article/317043.
Simonelli, David. 2002. "Anarchy, Pop and Violence: Punk Rock Subculture and the Rhetoric of Class, 1976–78." *Contemporary British History* 16, no. 2: 121–144.
Simonelli, David. 2013. *Working Class Heroes: Rock Music and British Society in the 1960s and 1970s*. Lanham, MD: Lexington Books.
Spirin, Dmitry. 2004. *Tupoi pank-rok dlya intellektualov: Chetyre tarakana i Tarakany!* Moscow: Rok-arsenal.
Steinholt, Yngvar. 2003. "You Can't Rid a Song of Its Words: Notes on the Hegemony of Lyrics in Russian Rock Songs." *Popular Music* 22, no. 1: 89–108.
Steinholt, Yngvar. 2012. "Siberian Punk Shall Emerge Here: Egor Letov and Grazhdanskaia Oborona." *Popular Music* 31, no. 3: 401–415.
Tikhonov, Vladimir. 2001. *"Khoi!" Epitafiya rok-razdolbayu*. Moscow: OOO Antao.
Troitsky, Artemy. 1990 *Rok muzyka v SSSR: Opyt populyarnoi entsiklopedii*. Moscow: Kniga.
What We Feel and Moscow Death Brigade. 2015. Response to the article "Die Bands What We Feel und Moscow Death Brigade als Beispiel eines zu kritisierenden 'Antifaschismus'". Facebook, February 9, 2015. https://www.facebook.com/moscowdeathbrigade/photos/dear-all-on-behalf-of-what-we-feel-and-moscow-death-brigade-we-are-presenting-ou/10153078679669660/.
Worley, Matthew, and Nigel Copsey. 2018. "White Youth: The Far Right, Punk and British Youth Culture, 1977–87." In *Tomorrow Belongs to Us: The British Far Right since 1967*, edited by Nigel Copsey and Matthew Worley, 113–131. London: Routledge.

Discography

Arkady Kotz. 2016. *Muzyka dlia rabochego klassa (Music for the working class)*. Konfederatsiia truda Rossii (Confederation of Labour of Russia).
Avtomaticheskie Udovletvoriteli. 1987. "Subbotnik"/*Subbotnichek (A day of voluntary work)*. DIY.
Avtomaticheskie Udovletvoriteli. 1988. "Tuneyadets"/*Paren' vrednyi (Naughty guy)*. DIY.
Brigadir. 2009. "Krasnye i anarcho skiny (Red and Anarcho Skins)"/Brigadir/Krasnyi Gorizont/*Vmeste k pobede (Together to the victory)*. Street Influence.
Brigadir. 2016. *Power in Unity*. Mad Butcher Records.
Diagileva. 1988. "Deklassirovannym elementam (To the declassed elements)"/Yanka and Krasnye oktiabri. GrOb Records.
Grazhdanskaia Oborona. 1985. *Poganaya molodiozh (Disgusting youth)*. GrOb Records.
Grazhdanskaia Oborona. 1987. *Krasnyi al'bom (Red album)*. GrOb Records.
Grazhdanskaia Oborona. 1988. Nasekomye/*Armageddon-Pops*. GrOb Records.
Krasnyi Gorizont. 2009. Brigadir/Krasnyi Gorizont/*Vmeste k pobede (Together to the victory)*. Street Influence.
Kino. 1982. "Bezdel'nik" (45'). AnTrop Records.
Leningrad. 2000. "Dachniki"/*Dachniki (Dacha people)*. Gala records.
Leningrad. 2003. "Raspizdiai"/*Dlya millionov (For the millions)*. Misteriya zvuka.
Moscow Death Brigade. 2010. "Geroi" (single). DIY.
Nol'. 1990. "Vstavai"/*Severnoe bugi (Northern boogie)*. AnTrop records.

Red Card. 2009. *Geroi spal'nykh raionov (Suburban heroes)*. DIY.
Sektor Gaza. 1991. "Kolkhoznyi pank"/*Kolkhoznyi pank (Redneck punk)*. Gala Records.
The Zavod. 2014a. *My ne budem platit'(We won't pay for)*. DIY.
The Zavod. 2014b. *Tiazholaia rabota—moshchnyi kutiozh (Hard Work—Powerful Spree)*. DIY.
The Zavod. 2015a. *Volya k svobode sil'nee vsekh tyurem/The Will to Freedom Is Stronger Than All Prisons*. DIY.
The Zavod. 2015b. *Solidarnost' i vzaimovyruchka/Solidarity and Mutual Aid*. DIY.
The Zavod. 2017. *Proletariy, ne teryai nadezhdu!/Proletarian, Don't Lose the Hope!*. DIY.

CHAPTER 18

THE "NEW FLOWERS" OF BULGARIAN PUNK

Cultural Translation, Local Subcultural Scenes, and Heritage

ASYA DRAGANOVA

THIS chapter is inspired by an early Bulgarian punk band called Novi Tsvetya, or New Flowers, first formed in the late 1970s in the small southern town of Kyustendil. Embodying aspects of the arrival of punk in the communist Eastern European Bloc, the band is used here to explore how "Western" subcultural music styles—deemed a decadent influence on youth by the authorities at the time—translated into local social and cultural contexts. The symbol of flowers gained currency in Bulgarian subcultural music styles, as it was explored further through key texts such as post-punk band Revu's cult song "Flowers of the Late 80s." This chapter argues that the metaphor of flowers, suggesting naturality, brightness, and fragility, has been conceptually employed to refer to the generations of young people involved with the genealogy of local rock, punk, and post-punk scenes.

Using ethnographic and textual approaches to this qualitative exploration, I suggest that those young people involved in subcultural scenes—"the flowers"—positioned themselves as a contrasting alternative to what was portrayed in artistic outputs as a gray, monotone, and oppressive social reality, toward the collapse of the communist era in Bulgaria and the end of the Cold War, and the challenging beginnings of post-1989 transitions. While the bands and artists that this chapter discusses are mostly musically and aesthetically engaged with punk and post-punk, the symbol of flowers highlights the connectedness of subcultural scenes with the earlier hippie phenomenon, a perceived milestone in globalized histories of popular music and youth cultures. Therefore, the metaphor of flowers suits the breadth, the productive coexistence, of Bulgarian subcultural scenes, united by their involvement with exploring a variety of forms of musical artistic expression: tools for articulating a set of ideological perspectives associated with resistance. This chapter argues that while there is ongoing intergenerational continuity across subcultural scenes, in Bulgaria, the phrase "flowers of the late 80s" has become a conceptual device for promoting the memorialization of subcultural practices and the construction of a distinct DIY heritage discourse around pre-1989 youth cultures.

To contextualize the findings and theoretical interpretations presented in this chapter into the areas of their contribution, this chapter discusses the evolution of punk into a holistic, intergenerational space—or a global language—that enables symbolic resistance through distinct aesthetics and a DIY ethic. Drawing on interviews, observations, and the study of relevant musical, lyrical, and visual texts, this chapter addresses its ethnographic approach to qualitative methodologies.

Punk, Place, and Resistance: Contextualizing Subcultural Scenes

Within popular music culture, punk has acquired the position of an epitome of resistance through symbol, style, and sound. Its subcultural significance has informed a vast body of work around the concepts of subculture, scene, underground, and DIY ethics, evidenced by the punk focus of a number of comprehensive publications, as well as scholarly and wider communities of critical inquiry and writing, including the Punk Scholars Network, the Subcultures Network, the international project/conference KISMIF (Keep It Simple, Make it Fast), and the *Punk and Post-Punk* journal. The continuous explorations of punk suggest its ongoing, intergenerational role for enabling individual, collective, and ideological expressions through creativity (Bennett 2006, 2013); its position as a subject of heritage practices around youth cultures, for example, the *Punk 1976–1978* exhibition at the British Library (2016); and a style enabling aesthetic cosmopolitanism (Regev 2013, 38–40), through its global reach as a voice for protest and resistance (Worley et al. 2014, 1–12).

Beginning its genesis in "Western," particularly British and US, contexts, punk reached its proclaimed "peak" in the 1970s, particularly 1976–1979 (Savage 2005). This moment of incorporation into mainstream culture (Hebdige 1979, 92) can be interpreted as the point of impoverishment of punk from its oppositional, political potential. At the same time, this moment enabled the increased internationalization of punk, or, the processes of "cultural translation" (Maitland 2017, 31, 62) into new political and social contexts. The moment of the punk "peak," like others that have acquired key positions in the study of youth cultures—such as the opposition between mods and rockers (Cohen 2002; Feldman-Barrett 2009), Beatlemania (Millard 2012), and the hippie movement—took place during the Cold War: a historic era, symbolized by the Berlin Wall, which divided Europe into the opposed capitalist West and the communist Eastern Bloc. In the Bulgarian context, which this chapter focuses on, Western styles such as punk were branded as "decadent" influences on young people: an approach replicated widely east of the Wall, with varied degrees of restrictiveness in relation to engagement with Western styles as expression (Draganova 2019, 187–188; Taylor 2006, 53–59). The imposed limitations, it has been suggested, acted as an engine of cultural curiosity and a creative impulse that has led to the formation of distinct scenes (Statelova 1990, 35), associated with punk and post-punk (Pilkington 2012, 253–255), but also the wider context of the rock music constellation. In pre-1989 Bulgaria, the state had full control over official music performances as well as music recording, publishing, and distribution of music.

The earlier local incarnations of resistance through the symbols and rituals of youth cultures from the other side of the Wall were, to an extent, "tamed" through the creation of local versions that corresponded to the cultural politics of the state (Draganova 2019, 101–104). For example, the interest in rock styles preceding punk was controlled through the creation of milder versions, which included some of the softer genre characteristics but excluded the harder sound and darker, more ideologically charged topics and nuances. However, punk, with its raw sound and "threatening" style, was incongruous to the official norms and aesthetics and proposed new, radicalized forms of struggle for rock autonomy (Pilkington et al. 2016, 27–30; Piotrowski 2016, 203–205). The cultural translations of punk took place autonomously, in the underground spaces of youth cultural agency, and through an organic evolution that attained longevity, particularly through diversification into "post-punk" styles. The development of punk and post-punk styles in Bulgaria, and in a wider range of Eastern European contexts, also coincides with a set of technological changes that enabled DIY politics of music recording and distribution. Furthermore, the 1980s were marked by the processes of "perestroika" and "glasnost," articulated through a set of reforms that even included the recognition and initial study of youth cultures through the invention of the term *neformali* (informals) (Draganova and Blackman 2018, 238–240), which highlighted the suggested leisure—rather than ideological—nature of subcultural scenes.

To understand the specificities of punk in pre-1989 and subsequently post-communist Bulgaria, this chapter draws on the concept of cultural translation, derived originally from linguistic studies, intercultural communications, applied linguistics, and anthropology (Asad 1986, 141–143; Bhabha 2000, 304–305; Maitland 2017). It suggests a process that lies beyond the direct translation of meaning, to emphasize the significance and complexities of local contexts for enabling nuance in the relevant application of a concept. Within studies in popular music, elements of it have been explored in relation to K-Pop (Yoon 2017), for example. Punk music had contrasting contexts in the spaces of its origin and in the case of its Bulgarian translations, which led to the formation of locally specific approaches to the style. While early punk is often associated with a critique of capitalism (Worley 2012, 233–235), its Bulgarian versions, in radical contrast with the officially approved local popular culture, suggested a protest against the communist regime. This apparent disparity suggests the flexible, fluid nature of punk as a simultaneously distinctive yet universal repertoire of symbols and styles, providing a global language for resistance that enables the construction of interpretations responsive to diverse social, political, and economic situations.

Recognizing the adaptable and translatable nature of punk allows for addressing key discursive contradictions that influence how punk has been studied. For example, early punk—through its rawness and accessibility—has been framed as a reaction to the complexity, virtuosity, and suggested elitism of 1970s progressive rock (Holm-Hudson 2002; Laing 1985), emerging from the earlier psychedelic sounds associated with the hippie movement. Visibly opposed to the colorful, nature-inspired leitmotifs of hippie countercultural aesthetic, punk developed its own DIY approach to producing styles that challenged perceptions of everyday social appropriateness. Simultaneously, different aspects of punk, particularly anarcho-punk, and the early hippie movement carried inherent similarities, including their pro-peace and social justice ideological stance (Cross 2004). Similarly, this chapter suggests, metaphors such as the "flowers" present in Bulgarian punk can be associated with the symbolism of the hippie/flower power 1960s approach to resistance articulated in key songs such as the folk-derived "Where Have All the Flowers Gone?" (1962), by Pete Seeger and performed by Peter, Paul and Mary, and "If You're Going to San Francisco (Be Sure to Wear Flowers in Your Hair)" (1967), by Scott McKenzie. Seemingly incompatible with punk sensibilities, the metaphor of flowers might acquire new meanings and relevance in the translations of punk in new cultural contexts.

A popular music phenomenon described by contradictions, the diversification of punk into a constellation of styles has contributed to the conflicted relationship punk, holistically, has with its own past: the ways in which punk is memorialized and produces a distinct heritage discourse with both "official" and DIY incarnations (Bennett 2015, 15; Robinson 2017, 309–310). On one hand, the incorporation of punk into the histories of popular culture suggests the loss of its potential to accommodate resistance; on the other hand, punk as heritage is an element of its intergenerational (sub)cultural continuity. These conflicts within the interpretation of punk from the perspective of a historic turn (Feldman-Barrett 2018) and a heritage discourse (Cohen et al. 2015) are also relevant in the context of Bulgarian subcultural scenes. Nearly thirty years after the disintegration of the communist Eastern Bloc, pre-1989 subcultural scenes have acquired—to use Benjamin's ([1936] 1999; [1939] 1999) terminology—an "aura of authenticity," retrospectively celebrating the significance of subcultural creativity, and questioning its contemporary role.

Growing in the Field: Notes on Ethnographic Immersion and Researcher Positionality

The ideas for this chapter's focus and its title are biographically informed and therefore highlight the need to acknowledge and employ, instead of overthrow, a cultural researcher's lived experiences, positionality, and stance (Berger 2015, 219–220; Savin-Baden and Major 2012, 78). Engaging with reflexivity as a realm of research that addresses the personal contexts of research choices, strategies, and interactions, I suggest that researcher reflexivity can inform all stages of a qualitative scholarly exploration—from the inception of a question, through data collection, to immersive analysis and the theoretical interpretation and organization of findings (Blackman and Kempson 2016).

Going to gigs as a fan, and later as part of fieldwork data collection for my research, I encountered a specific sense of collective experience and identification around a song called "Flowers of the Late 80s," performed by the punk/post-punk band Revu, whom I have seen on multiple occasions across a range of venues. For us—my friends and I—the song suggests that *we* are the flowers, as it invites an identification with the uniqueness of our liminal "generation": one that grew up in (post-communist) transition. Many of us were born in 1989, right on the edge of a decade: a year that has acquired a symbolic status through the fall of the Berlin Wall and the beginning of post-communist changes. Yet the song embodies the struggles and inspiration of another generation, one that was already creating music and engaging in punk and post-punk scenes a long time before us, in the 1980s. In this sense, it is they who are the "flowers," I suppose. And what does it really entail to be a "flower," and yet to make and listen to music that is raw, that contains hardness, distorted sound, and metaphors of revolt?

Engaging in my studies in Bulgarian popular music, with a specific interest in subcultural scenes, I attended and took part in a series of events dedicated to subcultures in Bulgaria; it was through them that I came across the band Novi Tsvetya (New Flowers), emerging in the 1970s, and deemed one of the earliest incarnations of punk locally. It made me wonder: How could the tacit connectivity between the different generations, enabled through the metaphor of the flowers, be explored within a critical reflective approach? I integrated the interest in the genealogy of subcultural scenes, their intergenerational nature I feel part of, into the wider scope of my research. Drawing on an immersive, ethnographic approach to qualitative research, this chapter articulates findings based on a series of interviews-as-conversations, taken in person and online, with a range of artists and cultural intermediaries involved with constructing and interpreting the Bulgarian punk and post-punk styles.

The chapter draws particularly on an open-ended group interview with New Flowers, in their current line-up: Ivan Popov—"Johnny" (guitar, vocals), Valyo Osogovsky (bass, vocals), Sasho Bozovaysky (guitar, vocals), Pavel Bozovaysky (drums), and Krassi Barakliysky (backing vocals, percussions). Respecting their preferred interpretation, the responses to questions are not assigned to individuals from the group, but rather to New Flowers as a collective. The chapter also draws on a series of participating observations as well as interviews and conversations with key musicians and figures within the punk and post-punk scenes and heritage practices, including recent exhibitions and popular publications on the contributions of early Bulgarian subcultural scenes.

This chapter seeks to present a holistic mosaic of perspectives by including a varied set of qualitative data, incorporating an awareness of a range of musical, lyrical, and visual texts. My positionality as a researcher and an insider within the field has enabled access to insight and achieving "thick," rather than "thin," description, saturated with lived experience rather than alien literary devices (Geertz 1973).

Early Cultural Translations of Punk

The early "translations" of punk as a collection of musical, aesthetic, and thematic features took place as part of a broader process, which relates to the incorporation of Western popular music styles into the fabric of the youth experiences in communist Bulgaria. Accessed predominantly outside the censorship-controlled state-approved media platforms, music records and performances, rock—as an umbrella category—carried subcultural connotations. Interview insights and visual documentations from performances and gathering places suggest that pre-1989 subcultural scene participants interpreted rock holistically, rather than as a field where opposing cultural tastes and ideologies were performed through a set of styles. Rock styles could be described as a language that enables the expression of individuality, raw energy, and the need for connectivity to a youth turn taking place internationally. Therefore, I argue that the cultural translations of punk in Bulgaria took place

1. through DIY politics of accessing, creating, performing, and consuming music content and related styles,
2. as part of a holistic (rock) music experience that embodied youth agency and expression in symbolic opposition to perceived repressive aspects to the social and political environment, and
3. through the accessibility of punk performance that enabled participation and directness.

The band that became known as Novi Tsvetya first emerged in the small town of Kyustendil in the 1970s. Even though they have been framed as a punk band in interpretations of pre-1989 subcultural scenes and in popular music journalism, their early musical attempts comprised an eclectic mix of DIY interpretations (see Figure 18.1). When asked about their first encounters with punk music, the members of Novi Tsvetya said this:

> The band began spontaneously in the middle of the 1970s. On acoustic guitar, piano, a kid's toy drum, a goblet drum, and whatever else we found, really, and which could produce noise . . . we tried to play songs by Uriah Heep, Mungo Jerry, Gary Glitter, Bijelo Dugme and so on. . . . The sound was truly deafening.

The initial repertoire listed by Novi Tsvetya articulates the fluidity of their early musical influences: from Mungo Jerry's softer, skiffle-derived rock, through Uriah Heep's hard rock with "progressive" elements, to the Yugoslavian Bijelo Dugme, who frequently

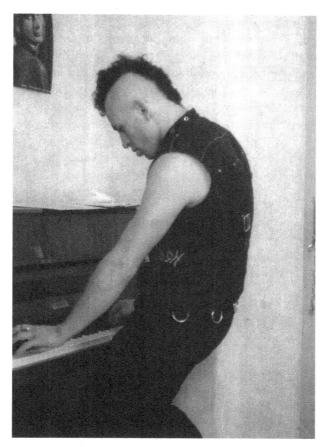

FIGURE 18.1. Contrasts: Ivan Popov (Johnny) playing the piano; New Flowers personal archive.

intertwined a range of styles in rock and pop with Balkan-derived folkloristic influences. With a DIY ethos toward the interpretation of rock music, the band never performed songs with their original lyrics: rather, they created witty and humorous interpretations in Bulgarian, suggesting a pursuit of new meanings. Aligned with perceived principles of accessibility and rawness prevalent in early punk (Guerra 2018), none of the members of Novi Tsvetya consider themselves formally as musicians or have had any systematic musical training.

The repertoire of original songs Novi Tsvetya created and recorded, in terms of globally recognizable artists, resembles most the sound of Dead Kennedys and Black Flag. Yet they openly cite as their early sources of inspiration bands such as The Beatles, Queen, and AC/DC. The perceived strictness of distinctions, or even rivalries, between musical categories, it appears, had little relevance in relation to how cultural translations of rock-related styles operated in a pre-1989 Cold War context. Rather, a flexible approach to drawing on a range of influences (Reynolds 2005, 2–14) enabled a ubiquitous approach to expression through music and style.

The translations of punk were aided particularly by young people's identification with the geographic, linguistic, and cultural proximity of nearby Yugoslavia. Despite the general communist Eastern Bloc label, there were significant variations in the characteristics and development of the political situations across the central, eastern, and southeastern regions of Europe. Yugoslavia demonstrated notable openness to products and cultural outputs derived from the Anglophone Western contexts. For Bulgarians in southwestern regions, the nearness of the Yugoslavian border entailed access to media sources unregulated by the local authority. Precisely those undesignated pathways to access were framed by Novi Tsvetya as a key reason the band emerged in a small town, distant from the prominent cultural influence of the capital Sofia:

> The fact that we emerged in Kyustendil may be seen as sheer coincidence, but we actually think that geographical location had a lot to answer for: we had the access to information from Radio Skopje. Furthermore, family gatherings happened annually at the Bulgarian-Yugoslav border, and through that we sometimes managed to get our hands on a record or a book, although we knew it was likely to get confiscated.

Novi Tsvetya considered the proximity of Yugoslavia to be essential for their first encounters with punk, too. The context of illegality of access to content triggered an impulse of cultural curiosity:

> Punk first came on the waves of Radio Skopje, which had mass popularly in Kyustendil. The first punk song we heard was played in the show *Three Gongs* in 1977 and it was "Peaches" by the Stranglers. To be honest, we were not particularly enthusiastic. We were expecting something more dynamic, louder. Only a few were impressed by the "new" style. However, towards 1980 we heard the Yugoslavian band Pekinska Patka (Peking Duck) and things changed radically. Adam Ant, Devo, and Električni Orgazam (Electric Orgasm) followed and things finally fell into place with understanding punk.

Presenting culturally proximate models of how punk can be interpreted in new environments, Yugoslavian punk-inspired engagement with the style beyond the direct imitation that can precede the creation of original material and the construction of distinct sound in locally conceived scenes (Draganova and Blackman 2018; Webb and Lynch 2010). The rawness and energy of punk music became the set of expressive tools and the canvas for articulating discontent with local circumstances, using the emotional and sonic nuances of the Bulgarian language. Themes in Novi Tsvetya's music include the outdatedness of social norms and issues of unfairness and inequality; confinement to a set of rigid rules of everyday urban life, such as living in identical, gray tower blocks; a sense of a "poisoned" reality where both literal and metaphorical pollution dominate the environment; and conflicts between institutions—particularly the militia at the time—and young people. Yet the band suggests that it does not consider its music directly political:

According to us, punk and ideology are not symbiotic: punk is just a simplified, pure, and honest musical form, which enables free expression and enjoyment for nearly anyone. And in "those" times the only way to escape from the grayness of everyday life, the constant limitations, and prohibitions.

At the same time their pre-1989 songs put forward direct criticisms. To illustrate, the song "Training" explores the taming and standardization of youth through "brainwashing" education stages and military service; "Tower Block" describes the experience of everyday poverty and conflict on the periphery of town; and "Radiation" refers directly to the Chernobyl crisis as a metaphor for the contamination of all aspects of a dystopian, pathologized everyday life. Furthermore, the band drew on their clashes with the representations of the communist state as tokens of authenticity and legitimacy:

> Throughout the whole time, before the end of the regime, we had trouble with the People's Militia: because of the noise from our rehearsal room, an appropriated summer kitchen, because of our hair styles, badges, clothes, anything you can think of.... They constantly threatened us with deportation into camps in the mountains of Strandzha or Sakar. There was slapping, constant checks of document. We have spent endless hours of our lives in militia stations. We'd often have two of their militia cars turn up to our rehearsal room to dig through it; but we got used to it. Recently, we found out that our "criminal" dossiers are still preserved.

The revolt against prescribed models of youth behavior appropriateness, embodied by organizations such as the youth *Komsomol* (Zhuk 2017, 173), took place through visual symbol and style, alongside music (see Figure 18.2). Engaging in innovation through bricolage (Levi-Strauss 1966), Novi Tsvetya appropriated everyday objects not only into musical instruments but also into fashion objects, used to perform deviance and ridicule the perceived sterile nature of everyday realities. In conversation, they described that the customs control under communism was extremely strict, yet they occasionally got access to cut-outs from magazines where diverse punk styles were depicted in a way different from the extremely limited and deliberately negative representations in Bulgarian press. Seeking to avoid the "appropriateness" of mass-produced clothing, the band members used their own handmade templates to print on cotton T-shirts, painted their clothes black, and developed a set of specialized skills to produce their own jewelry of metal and leather.

The journalist Petar Milanov, later involved with the organization of multiple music festivals and exhibitions around contemporary and heritage punk and post-punk acts, described his first encounter with Novi Tsvetya in the 1980s:

> I first saw them at a Serbo-Bulgarian gathering along the border with Yugoslavia. I couldn't believe they were Bulgarian! Until then, such outfits, hair-styles, and stage behavior could only be seen on Serbian TV, if we could ever get to watch that. It was the mid-1980s and Gorbachev's *perestroika* was in motion. Later, I saw similar punk

FIGURE 18.2. 1982: a playful photo shoot in front of Novi Tsvetya's improvised kitchen rehearsal room. The "villain" with the saw is Ivan Popov (Johnny); the "victim" is Lyudmil, brother of Valeri Milovansky of new wave band Tangra; drummer Pavel Bozovaysky wears black eye makeup; and the man posing with the guitar is Yuri, singer in some of the bands' early records; New Flowers personal archive.

bands even in Russia. Revolt against the norm—through mannerisms, language, music, and style—had find its way to the surface.

Indeed, the processes of *perestroika* and *glasnost*—restructuring and opening up—introduced in the mid-1980s by USSR leader Mikhail Gorbachev, addressed a need for a democratic reform enabling the accommodation of a "human factor" (Kimura 1988). While censorship and state control remained in place, opportunities for expression grew (Pilkington et al. 2016, 27). Youth cultural formations, outside the regime-designated ones dedicated to the replication of communist ideologies, became recognized through the formulation of the term *neformali*, or "informals." The concept deliberately stressed the suggested leisure—rather than ideologically potent—core of youth practices.

In conversations taking place in the field with members of rock and punk scenes of the 1980s, it is acknowledged that *perestroika* and *glasnost* increased access to Western-derived styles and, as a result, produced a widespread engagement with the direct replication of material originally produced by bands such as the Sex Pistols and the Clash. Yet the process of culturally translating a musical cultural form extends beyond copying and toward deriving new opportunities for expression. This is evident in Novi Tsvetya's creation of original material in Bulgarian, drawing on locally specific, socially potent references. Furthermore, the language used in their energetic, angry punk music poetry channels a sense of an emerging distinction highlighting a new generation; so, who were those "new flowers"?

Flowers of the (Late) 1980s

Prior the mid-1980s reforms, the punks from the small town of Kyustendil were aware they had no chance of performing on stage or releasing a record. Like many other artists from subcultural scenes at the time, they did not have the chance to publish material until long after it had first been written. Under the constant monitoring of the militia forces, they kept changing names until an opportunity arose:

> The godfather of our band was Oleg Mihaylov-Perry, a legendary local DJ, who got us to take part in a songwriting context. To get us the chance to perform, he had to give us the most bland, harmless name so that the event organizers don't figure out what they're about to hear. At the time punk was totally prohibited! So, we went on stage as New Flowers, which suited nicely with the socialist aesthetic. . . . We played two utterly ruthless punk songs, one of which was called "Life." The venue, the youth club, was packed and the audience went crazy. The band ended up in the militia station, as they suggested there'd been Nazi chanting, which was completely untrue and was used to criminalize subcultures. They basically thought we mocked socialism.

The name New Flowers was invented to channel harmlessness and compliance: to catch by surprise the "gatekeepers" to live performances and audiences. At the same time, intentionally or not, the name established symbolic links with the hippie subcultural phenomena of the late 60s and early 70s, familiar to younger Bulgarian audiences particularly through texts such as the musical-based film *Hair* (1979). According to participants in my research, *Hair* had somehow "slipped through" censorship loopholes, particularly as it was interpreted in terms of its criticism of "Western" politics rather than its glorification of youth individual expression. And while the Bulgarian punks from New Flowers continuously highlight their apathy to the band name, they never renamed themselves. The band name's hippie connotations can be interpreted as a disregard of the common reading of punk as an opposition to "flower power" aesthetics, hedonistic lifestyles, and ideals. This affirms an integrated approach—a sense of connectivity, rather than fragmentation—in the context of subcultural scenes emerging in a restrictive context. From a "bland" name, used to infiltrate the state-controlled musical opportunities, New Flowers—as pioneers of punk—participated in the creation of symbols of rebellion and change. Although New Flowers do not refer to such links, their name can be interpreted as a reference to Western punk, too, particularly the lyric "we're the flowers in the dustbin" from the Sex Pistols' 1977 "God Save the Queen" and *The Flowers of Romance*, Public Image Ltd.'s 1981 LP.

FIGURE 18.3. One of the "flowers": Katya Atanasova (Nova Generatsia) under a communist street sign urging citizens to destroy flies as they are "enemies of humanity."

Photography by Neli Nedeva-Voeva.

The concept of the "flowers" acquired new meanings in relation to 1980s Bulgarian subcultural scenes; framed as "early," it was the 1980s by the time they first became visible and recognized (see Figure 18.3). The flower theme—as a metaphor of a young generation—gained popularity particularly through Revu's 1987 song "Flowers of the Late 80s" written by Vasil Gurov. The song, which aesthetically moves away from some of rawer forms of punk to a sound more akin to new wave and post-punk, poetically describes "for years getting used to tolerating darkness" and the "withering of wings tightly knotted in square shapes." As an antithesis to the portrait of restriction, the lyrics highlight a "thanks for all the flowers," which had "grown their thorns specially for the purposes of fight."

Recent texts commemorating the significance of Bulgarian subcultural scenes from the 1980s and the early years of democratic transitions have drawn heavily on the "catch-all" metaphorical potential of flowers. Examples include the book *Flowers of the Late 80s* (2014), focused on Bulgarian rock history and poetry, compiled by Rumen Yanev and Emil Bratanov, and a series of photography exhibitions under the same title taking place across a number of venues in 2017 and 2018 with the works of Neli Nedeva-Voeva curated by Dorothea Monova. As I was involved with translating the exhibition texts to allow for international audiences to engage, I was particularly interested in the following interpretation:

> They were not standard, cultivated flowers. According to the "botanical specialists" in power, those flowers fell into the category of the weeds. Autonomous. Wild and natural. Bright and provocative. Annoying. Unbearable to anyone who had successfully learned and trained to accept their fate of growing into the strictly designated line.
>
> The seeds of those wild flowers were brought by the wind of change: the one overcame the [Berlin] Wall to bring things from the West. The West that the leading Eastern gardeners found intolerably decadent and dangerous.
>
> But enough of this abstract indulgence, romantic metaphors, and chatter. During the era of Gorbachev, it was not appropriate to speak about "deviants" anymore, or about other derogative figures such as "national betrayers." So, instead, those in power came up with an updated word to stamp us with—"informal youth movements and rock groups," In short, *informals*.
>
> But the alternative, beautiful name "Flowers of the Late 80s" used to address those groups came up spontaneously, like a verse and chorus, from the cult song by *Revu*. With his song lyrics Vasil Gurov—both on purpose, and by chance—became the godfather of his entire generation.
>
> (Dorothea Monova, 2017; translated by, Asya Draganova)

As this passage suggests, the "flowers" as a designation for a new generation of critical and creative young people emerged organically from musical expressions and everyday language. Therefore, it operates in opposition to the artificially conceived terminology around youth *informals* used by the pre-1989 state to acknowledge the existence of youth cultural phenomena, yet preempt their significance by highlighting a focus on informality and "fun." With its presence in the title of one of the earliest Bulgarian punk bands, Novi Tsvetya, and the song lyrics of later bands such as *Revu*, *Klas*, and *Nova Generatsia*, "flower" metaphors gained longevity in the genealogy of intergenerational local scenes. Furthermore, the term performs the connectedness between scenes in Bulgaria and globally recognized historic subcultural phenomena from the 1960s.

The coherence of Bulgarian subcultural resistance across punk, post-punk, heavy rock, and blues is achieved through metaphors of stagnation, repression, and alienation used to formulate a generation that is antithetic to its perceived restrictive realities. For example, New Flowers dedicated their song "Patriot" (1986), which follows a well-recognized, raw punk formula, to the falseness of pride whereby "my cities look like prisons, the streets are tied with chains, proud shores rise from the sea, eternally linked by bridges collapsed." Soon afterward, with the more sophisticated expressive tools of post-punk and cold wave, the band Nova Generatsia (New Generation), who also identified themselves with a sense of newness, described the "Dark Land" (1990) they inhabited: "Wave a black flag, that says with no words it is filthy in my soul . . . it's a dark land with no lights, in a dark sea I seek no kindness." Expressing a similar sentiment of desperation and differentiation from a perceived "mass," hard rock band Ahat sang "People are now mindless herds . . . but I chose myself this fate, to be forever the black sheep" (1989). And while the common themes across pre-1989 and early post-communist music conceived within subcultural scenes appear dominated by turmoil and youth estrangement, the "flowers of the late 80s" have been celebrated for their inspired, inventive, and poetic critique. The perceived peak in subcultural creativity is interpreted through nostalgic lens; blues musician Vasko the Patch said in an interview with me:

> Our generation came up with Milena, Kontrol, Poduene Blues Band, we created songs which will be taught at school one day. We made it *because* it was so hard. This is my wish for these guys [young music artists]—to experience hardship, to be stamped on, so that they find out what it is like to reach for the depths of their souls to write amazing new songs. Because these boys and girls play very well, they are virtuoso musicians, but that is not enough.

The idealization of the creative impulse triggered by the struggle against perceived repressive contexts can also be associated with the growing body of publications, films, exhibitions, and music events dedicated to Bulgarian subcultural heritage. The heritage phenomena, which has now become a global theme (Baker 2015), accommodates for acknowledging cultural contribution, yet reinforces a focus on the past, creating a sense of finished-ness rather than continuity, of exhaustion rather than growing potential. For example, the images and words produced by punk bands like Novi Tsvetya, once considered provocative in their stark contrast to the aesthetic norms imposed through the pre-1989 state cultural politics, have now been incorporated into international exhibitions and collections of "historic" musical artifacts. The punks from Novi Tsvetya summarized this:

> We view the heritage phenomenon positively, though we are also alarmed. The growing interest in the past suggests that in our day boredom, ignorance, and apathy have come to the forefront and we are forced to look back in time to discover something meaningful and authentic there.

When exploring the nuance of subcultural popular music heritage initiatives in Bulgaria, the research suggests that there is a distinctly dominating DIY and lived memory ethos around archiving, commemoration, and curation (Long 2015, 76–90) of "early" subcultures. To illustrate, a key figure in organizing and providing material for photography exhibitions is Neli Nedeva-Voeva, who photographed the everyday youth subcultural practices and performances in multiple contexts of the late 1980s and early 1990s.

Neli is the wife of Dimitar Voev—who passed away in 1992—a poet, songwriter, and lead singer of punk, post-punk, and experimental bands Wozzek & Chugra, Kale, and Nova Generatsia. In the 1980s and early 1990s, Neli toured with bands and presented pop-up exhibitions in venues, using everyday objects as props, particularly washing lines, where photographs were hung. One of her prominent "traveling" exhibitions—Neli recalls—had the title *A Flight Over a Chemical Field*, and included portraits of members of subcultural scenes, where pictures of work play graffiti from Sofia by Kamen Belopitov were used to provide captions for other photographs. In recent years, she has been involved with the exhibitions *Youth Countercultures in Bulgaria in the 1970s and 1980s* at Sofia University; *The Revolution Goes on 2017* at Goethe Institute; and *The Footprints Remain* at the International Photographic Encounters festival, Plovdiv.

Similarly, the recent film *The Revolution Goes On* (2017) was directed by Svetoslav Draganov, with the participation of Georgi Marinov, using his existing footage from an unfinished art film project with Dimitar Voev, alongside new documentary material from subcultural "insiders". In another example, a 600-page book titled *Flowers of the Late 80s*, and consisting of interviews and reports, was compiled by authors and photographers who were originally involved with subcultural scenes as fans as well as intermediaries.

As all these examples indicate, the sense of "ownership" of the heritage and interpretation of original, or early, local subcultural scenes, is not institutionalized or commercially conceived but remains independently led by the "flowers"—by those originally involved with their formulation, pursuing cultural justice (Long et al. 2017, 61).

Grow or Wither? A Summary

Focusing on the band Novi Tsvetya, this chapter has described how punk music culture has "translated" into a new local context, in Bulgaria, under 1970s and 1980s Cold War circumstances. Moving beyond copying and imitation, punk became a potent platform for constructing new meanings and participating in a distinct subcultural discourse that communicated local social experiences, incorporating an internationalized musical language and visual aesthetic. In an environment defined by restriction and censorship, DIY techniques were essential in enabling music and style: from strategies for gaining access to records and pictures, to appropriating existing resources to engage in music-making and the construction of visual markers of punk identity. The rawness, directness, and accessibility of punk formulated an attractive set of new possibilities for channeling emotionally charged forms of discontent; furthermore, the proximity of the linguistic and cultural Yugoslavian punk experience highlighted the relevance and potential of punk in Bulgarian context. At the same time, instead of existing in opposition to other subcultural styles emerging in a local context, Bulgarians participated in a holistic rock music experience that embodied youth agency and expression.

Punk participated in the genealogy of scenes involving styles such as post-punk, heavy metal, and blues that were symbolically united by critical themes such as alienation, repression, and the affirmation of a new and different generation. Referred to by the pre-1989 state as *informals*, the participants in "early" Bulgarian subcultural scenes invented for themselves the alternative term "flowers," a metaphor explored implicitly and explicitly in punk and other styles. On the surface, it suggested harmlessness, which would allow for gatekeepers to surpass the ideological potential of the "flowers"; however, beneath that were the flowers' thorns—bright and resilient, critical to their restrictive realities, positioning themselves in relation to global youth cultural phenomena.

With recent publications and exhibitions referring to the "flowers of the late 80s," a heritage discourse, actively constructed by original insiders in Bulgarian subcultural scenes, has become visible. But does that suggest that memorialization positions the potency of alternativity in retrospect?

The emergent heritage perspectives highlight a perceived need for cultural justice in relation to youth contribution through creativity and innovation in music, style, language, and expression. It succeeds in diversifying and attaining nuance in the image of pre-1989 Bulgarian—and wider Eastern European—cultural identities. By communicating the significance of phenomena that emerged in organic opposition to the reinforced aesthetic norms in popular music, supported through state cultural politics, these heritage perspectives create opportunities for intergenerational continuity. The original "flowers" highlight their claim to the continued relevance of the texts and meanings they produced, referring to issues such as corruption and limited media freedom that define contemporary Bulgarian post-communist realities. And while key "early" bands such as Novi Tsvetya and Revu continue to respond to social issues, particularly environmental concerns and misuse of power, their longevity in local scenes has also enhanced and supported the emergence, artistic confidence, and legitimacy of new flowers of the twenty-first century.

Acknowledgments

Special thanks to Gina Arnold and George McKay for the opportunity to participate in this collection. Thanks to all the "flowers" for the music, the art, and the wonderful conversations that have inspired my research. This chapter would not have been possible without the support of Novi Tsvetya, Neli Nedeva-Voeva, and Petar Milanov.

Bibliography

Ахат (Ahat). (1989) 2003. "Черната овца" [The black sheep]. In *Походът* [The march] (music album). Sofia: Balkantone/Harbour Island Records.

Asad, Talal. 1986. "The Concept of Cultural Translation in British Social Anthropology." In *Writing Culture: The Poetics and Politics of Ethnography*, edited by James Clifford and George E. Marcus, 141–164. Berkeley: University of California Press.

Baker, Sarah, ed. 2015. *Preserving Popular Music Heritage: Do-It-Yourself, Do-It-Together*. London: Routledge.
Benjamin, Walter. (1936) 1999. "The Work of Art in the Age of Mechanical Reproduction." In *Illuminations*, 152–196. London: Pimlico.
Benjamin, Walter. (1939) 1999. "On Some Motifs in Baudelaire." In *Illuminations*, 211–244. London: Pimlico.
Bennett, Andy. 2006. "Punk's Not Dead: The Continuing Significance of Punk Rock for an Older Generation of Fans." *Sociology* 40, no. 2: 219–235. https://doi.org/10.1177/0038038506062030.
Bennett, Andy. 2013. *Music, Style, and Aging: Growing Old Disgracefully?* Philadelphia: Temple University Press.
Bennett, Andy. 2015. "Popular Music and the 'Problem' of Heritage." In *Sites of Popular Music Heritage: Memories, Histories, Places*, edited by Sara Cohen, Robert Knifton, Marion Leonard, and Les Roberts, 15–27. London: Routledge.
Blackman, Shane, and Michelle Kempson, eds. 2016. *The Subcultural Imagination: Theory, Research and Reflexivity in Contemporary Youth Cultures*. London: Routledge.
Berger, Roni. 2015. "Now I See It, Now I Don't: Researcher's Position and Reflexivity in Qualitative Research." *Qualitative Research* 15, no. 2: 219–234.
Bhabha, Homi K. 2000. "How Newness Enters the World: Postmodern Space, Postcolonial Times and Trials of Cultural Translation." In *Writing Black Britain, 1948–1998*, edited by James Procter, 300–307. Manchester, UK: Manchester University Press.
Cohen, Sara, Robert Knifton, Marion Leonard, and Les Roberts, eds. 2015. *Sites of Popular Music Heritage: Memories, Histories, Places*. London: Routledge.
Cohen, Stanley. 2002. *Folk Devils and Moral Panics: The Creation of the Mods and Rockers*. 3rd ed. London: Routledge.
Cross, Richard. 2004. "The Hippies Now Wear Black: Crass and the Anarcho-Punk Movement, 1977–84." *Socialist History* 26: 25–44.
Драганов, С. (Draganov, S.), dir. 2017. *Революцията продължава 2017* [The revolution goes on 2017]. Available at https://www.bnt.bg/bg/a/1987-revolyutsiyata-prodlzhava-17052017.
Draganova, Asya. 2019. *Popular Music in Contemporary Bulgaria: At the Crossroads*. Bingley, UK: Emerald.
Draganova, Asya, and Shane Blackman. 2018. "A Howl of the Estranged: Post-Punk and Contemporary Underground Scenes in Bulgarian Popular Music." In *DIY Cultures and Underground Music Scenes*, edited by Andy Bennett and Paula Guerra, 230–242. London: Routledge.
Feldman-Barrett, Christine. 2009. *"We Are the Mods": A Transnational History of a Youth Subculture*. Oxford: Peter Lang.
Feldman-Barrett, Christine. 2018. "Back to the Future: Mapping a Historic Turn in Youth Studies." *Journal of Youth Studies* 21, no. 6: 733–746.
Forman, Milos, dir. 1979. *Hair*. Los Angeles: United Artists Pictures.
Geertz, C. (1993, originally 1973) *The Interpretation of Cultures: Selected Essays*. London: Fontana Press.
Guerra, Paula. 2018. "Raw Power: Punk, DIY and Underground Cultures as Spaces of Resistance in Contemporary Portugal." *Cultural Sociology* 12, no. 2: 241–259.
Hebdige, Dick. 1979. *Subculture: The Meaning of Style*. London: Routledge.
Holm-Hudson, Kevin. 2002. *Progressive Rock Reconsidered*. London: Routledge.
Kimura, Hiroshi. 1988. *The Gorbachev Regime: Consolidation to Reform*. New York: Routledge.

Laing, Dave. 1985. *One Chord Wonders: Power and Meaning in Punk Rock*. Milton Keynes, UK: Open University Press.

Levi-Strauss, Claude. 1966. *The Savage Mind*. London: Weidenfeld and Nicolson.

Long, Paul. 2015. "'Really Saying Something?' What Do We Talk about When We Talk about Popular Music Heritage, Memory, Archives and the Digital?" In *Preserving Popular Music Heritage*, edited by Sarah Baker, 76–90. London: Routledge.

Long, Paul, Sarah Baker, Lauren Istvandity, and Jez Collins. 2017. "A Labour of Love: The Affective Archives of Popular Music Culture." *Archives and Records* 38, no. 1: 61–79.

Maitland, Sarah. 2017. *What Is Cultural Translation?* London: Bloomsbury.

Millard, André. 2012. *Beatlemania: Technology, Business, and Teen Culture in Cold War America*. Baltimore, MD: The Johns Hopkins University Press.

Monova, D. 2017. Introduction to the exhibition *Flowers of the Late 80s* by Neli Nedeva-Voeva; Translated by Asya Draganova.

Monova, D. 2018. "Следите остават" [The footprints remain]. Introductory text accompanying the exhibition *The Footprints Remain*; Translated from Bulgarian by A. Draganova, 13–22. Plovdiv: International Photographic Encounters, Plovdiv.

Нова Генерация (New Generation). 1991. "Тъмна земя" [Dark land]. In *Forever* (music album). Sofia: DS Music.

Нови Цветя (New Flowers). 2004. *Радиация 1979-1995* [Radiation 1979–1995].Sofia: AON Productions.

Pilkington, Hilary. 2012. "Punk—But Not As We Know It: Punk in Post-Socialist Space." *Punk & Post-Punk* 1, no. 3: 253–266.

Pilkington, Hilary, I. Gololobov, and Y. Steinholt. 2016. "Панк в России: краткая история эволюции" [Punk in Russia: A Short History of Its Evolution]. *Logos* 26, no. 4: 27–61.

Piotrowski, Grzegorz. 2016. "Punk against Communism: The Jarocin Rock Festival and Revolting Youth in 1980s Poland." In: *A European Youth Revolt*, edited by Knud Andresen and Bart van der Steen, 203–216. Palgrave Studies in the History of Social Movements. London: Palgrave Macmillan.

Regev, Motti. 2013. *Pop-Rock Music: Aesthetic Cosmopolitanism in Late Modernity*. Cambridge: Polity Press.

Ревю (Revu). 1989. "Цветя от края на 80-те" [Flowers of the Late 80s]. In *Милена+Ревю*, [*Milena+Revu*] (music album). Sofia: DS Music.

Reynolds, Simon. 2005. *Rip It Up and Start Again: Post-Punk 1978–1984*. London: Faber and Faber.

Robinson, Lucy. 2017. "Exhibition Review Punk's 40th Anniversary—An Itchy Sort of Heritage." *Twentieth Century British History* 29, no. 2: 309–317.

Savage, Jon. 2005. *England's Dreaming: Sex Pistols and Punk Rock*. 2nd ed. London: Faber and Faber.

Savin-Baden, Maggi, and Claire Howell Major. 2012. "Personal Stance, Positionality and Reflexivity." In *Qualitative Research: The Essential Guide to Theory and Practice*. London: Routledge.

Стателова, Р. (Statelova, R.). 1990. "Рок и демокрация: Забраната като креативен импулс" [Rock and democracy: Prohibition as a creative impulse]. In *През годините: Розмари Стателова на 70* [Through the years: Rosemary Statelova at 70], 35–45. Sofia: Institute for Art Studies Press.

Taylor, Karin. 2006. *Let's Twist Again: Youth and Leisure in Socialist Bulgaria*. London: Transaction.

Webb, Peter, and John Lynch. 2010. "'Utopian Punk': The Concept of the Utopian in the Creative Practice of Björk." *Utopian Studies* 21, no. 2: 313–330.

Worley, Matthew. 2012. "Shot by Both Sides: Punk, Politics and the End of 'Consensus.'" *Contemporary British History* 26, no. 3: 333–354. doi:10.1080/13619462.2012.703013.

Worley, Matthew, Keith Gildart, Anna Gough-Yates, Sian Lincoln, Bill Osgerby, Lucy Robinson, John Street, and Peter Webb. 2014. "Introduction: From Protest to Resistance." In *Fight Back: Punk, Politics, and Resistance*, edited by the Subcultures Network, 1–12. Manchester, UK: Manchester University Press.

Янев, Р., and Е. Братанов (Yanev, R., and E. Bratanov). 2014. *Цветя от Края на 80-те: БГ Рок История/Поезия* [Flowers of the Late 80s]. Sofia: Paradox.

Yoon, Kyong. 2017. "Korean Wave: Cultural Translation of K-Pop among Asian Canadian Fans." *International Journal of Communication* 11: 2350–2366.

Zhuk, Sergei I. 2017. "'The Disco Mafia' and 'Komsomol Capitalism' in Soviet Ukraine during Late Socialism." In *Material Culture in Russia and the USSR: Things, Values, Identities*, edited by Graham H. Roberts, 173–196. London: Bloomsbury.

CHAPTER 19

IBERIAN PUNK, CULTURAL METAMORPHOSES, AND ARTISTIC DIFFERENCES IN THE POST-SALAZAR AND POST-FRANCO ERAS

PAULA GUERRA

INTRODUCTION: A NIGHT OF FORTY LONG YEARS

THERE are similarities between the dictatorial regimes of António Salazar in Portugal and Francisco Franco in Spain.[1] Both were established during the era of fascism, at a time when the German and Italian regimes sought to establish a new *European order*. With the defeat of nazi Germany and fascist Italy in World War II, both Iberian dictatorial regimes had to face the reality of political isolation. They went through a process of adaptation marked by economic opening, without this leading to any significant political changes. In the 1960s and 1970s, both regimes lived through contradictory phases marked by a deep (re)politicization of civil society and social conflict. The Portuguese reality was marked mainly by the Portuguese Colonial War, between 1961 and 1974, in which more than 900,000 young men fought. At this time in Spain, there was a consolidation of significant sociocultural changes, but also a resurgence of institutional violence by the regime, particularly between 1968 and 1975 (Loff 2010).

Notwithstanding their proximity, the differences between the regimes were evident—especially with regard to their collapse. In Portugal, on April 25, 1974, a military coup resulted in a democratic regime. This revolution became known as the *Revolução dos Cravos* (Carnation Revolution).[2] In Spain, the dictatorial regime underwent a

Transición. Influenced by what had happened in Portugal, after the death of Franco, the elites of the Spanish regime began a process of reform by pact.

So close—and touching (sharing a 1,200 km border)—but so far apart: the sociohistorical dynamics of the two countries dictated different rhythms regarding the genesis and consolidation of youth cultures, including their creations and their musical consumptions. In Spain, youth cultures appeared in the late 1950s and early 1960s. The 1960s were marked by high rates of industrialization, leading to profound changes that led to a metamorphosis of Spanish society. The regime itself was sympathetic to changing youth expectations (Feixa 2004). The process of mass education in Spain played a central role here, spawning a generation of highly qualified young people with far more options—it was a true generational break. Despite the familiar moral panics referring to all juvenile behavior that broke around imported "juvenile delinquency," Franco's regime was characterized by a significant openness to American culture. There were established plans for cooperation with American tourism companies, as well as with film studios, some of which chose Spain as a filming location. Spain also became a major European tourist destination, and with tourists came new consumption, cultural, and leisure practices. Similarly, the establishment of US military bases in Spain brought rock 'n' roll to the country, and the radio stations on the US bases could be listened to by anyone who had a radio. Overnight, Spanish youth were aware of the most innovative pop-cultural things happening abroad (Wilkins 2018).

Music festivals were held in tourist locations, such as Benidorm, leading to a massive influx of Anglo-American pop music. The first rock festivals in the 1960s were largely supported by official media—especially radio. As would occur in Portugal a decade later, in Spain the radio announcers introduced new sounds and attitudes alike. One of the most emblematic was Ángel Álvarez, who in 1960 started the *Caravana Musical* (Musical Caravan) program with great success. It was rapidly replicated, both on other radio stations and on television. Musical magazines were another prominent means of disseminating music. Magazines such as *Discóbolo* (1962–1971), *Fonorama* (1963–1968), and *Fans* (1965–1967) impacted on a generation of young Spaniards who read them voraciously in search of musical and aesthetic novelties (Gonzalez 2012). The Spanish industrialization process meant that young people enjoyed increased purchasing power, enabling them to acquire records and record players. Attending live gigs also suddenly became possible. Not surprisingly, the Spanish music industry was flourishing, and this change had a profound effect on young people, who experienced a glimpse of modernity and cosmopolitanism that in turn made the modernization of behaviors and mentalities possible (Gonzalez 2012).

The Portuguese reality was quite different. The conservative and autocratic characteristics of the regime, embodied in a paternalistic Salazar, viewed any new ideas from abroad with deep suspicion. Despite the promotion of foreign tourism, the tourist industry never had the predominance it would enjoy in Spain. In the face of the establishment of US military bases in the islands of Santa Maria in 1943 and Lajes, in the Azores Islands, in 1948, the American influence—particularly its economic and cultural power—was never well received, partly because it included the rejection of economic aid in the form of the Marshall Plan, which was regarded as a threat to the stability of the regime and to the "proudly alone"[3] stance regularly iterated in Salazar's speeches (Rosas 2012). If we add to this Portugal's peripheral position in the European geographic space, a weak penetration of the education system,[4] and the small size of the country, we begin to understand why Portugal did not really begin to develop a youth cultural industry until the end of the Salazar regime in 1974.

In a way similar to the Spanish case, however, Portugal underwent a process of massification in the 1960s and 1970s, which altered the social experiences of the majority of the Portuguese population (Loff 2010). Schooling is one example: despite the use of the basic education system for ideological purposes, the compulsory four years of education stimulated the possibility of a greater number of young people entering secondary and higher education. A set of cultural practices accompanied the growth of schooling: there was a strong increase in the number of public libraries, the appearance of several record labels, and an increase in the number of theater and cinema patrons. As Bebiano (2003) points out, these media served as a window to the world, giving rise to a still incipient urban youth culture.

The new winds were already felt in the countless listeners that Anglo-American pop music had attracted among Portuguese youth. Whether it was through (rare) imported records, national press, or listening to foreign pirate radio stations, the truth is that pop made a strong impression in Portugal. It was an alternative to the ubiquitous *fado* and national-songwriting that had monopolized the music industry and radio stations.[5] Portuguese radio began to cater to the new youth tastes. In 1965 the program *Em Órbita* (In Orbit), of *Rádio Clube Português* (Portuguese Radio Club) was dedicated to the divulging and framing of Anglo-American popular music, locally translated as *Ié-Ié* music (after the term "yeah, yeah" in English, popularized by bands like the Beatles) in the early 1960s (Guerra 2010, 2016). Some groups also sought to emulate the few references they had from British and American bands. However, the musical careers of these bands were restricted mainly to performances in student venues or recreational dance halls. They rarely performed concerts or recorded original material. Appearing at around the same time—in 1971—were the first musical festivals: the Vilar de Mouros Festival and the I Jazz Festival. These events would enable the kinds of practice and even celebration of hedonistic behaviors that would challenge the norms and values in force in Portuguese society.

The regime even attempted to capitalize on the new forms of youth culture and attitudes. There were two editions of the *Ié-Ié* Competition, the first in 1965 and the second in 1966, but properly framed by the regime: they were organized by the newspaper *O Século* (The Century) and were publicly in favor of the colonial war. All alternative challenges to the totalitarian cultural perspective of the regime, however, were viewed with suspicion. The feeble state of the discographic world did the rest. It was extremely difficult for a Portuguese pop-rock band to make a record. The few labels[6] that did exist would rather take their chances on "typical" music: *fado*, folklore, and national songwriting. The new Portuguese groups were also devalued by the labels, seen as not good enough (Andrade 2015). Yet, despite the economic and social changes, the

Colonial War, and the tenuous opening to new international record labels, Portuguese society has undergone a transformation in values and behaviors—albeit much more restricted and less intense than happened in Spain. In the beginning, therefore—after the 1974 revolution, we can say—there was *only emptiness and the desire to fill it.*

The Future Is Now and Here: Punk, Post-Punk, Youth (Sub)Cultures and Aesthetic Cosmopolitanism

Franco died in 1975, and Spanish political elites, taking into account what had happened in Portugal a year earlier, decided to undertake a democratic *Transición*. Punk appeared in England the following year. It was a fractured aesthetic and musical movement with an ethos that broke with the decadent hippie movement. *La Movida* appeared in Spain—a new countercultural movement particular intense in Madrid (see Lechado 2005, 2013). In Portugal, the Faíscas (the Sparks; see Figures 19.1 and 19.2) were the country's first punk band in a cultural revolt of a generation of young people who wanted to live the future now—to approach Europe, the world, the universe.[7]

Of course, this cultural revolution of *La Movida* did not emerge from nowhere. It began, according to Fouce (2004a), in Madrid as an underground phenomenon of a small group of young people who shared the same artistic sensibilities and the economic possibility of making contact with the most recent events abroad. For a cultural phenomenon to go from underground to massified, it takes much more than just will and word of mouth. There was a need to develop productive structures (venues, radio and television programs, specialist press and fanzines, and a record industry) and cultural industries. In addition, there was a specific political context that helped to catapult this phenomenon: Spain was a very young democracy in search of international legitimacy, and it was hoped the Francoist ethos could be replaced by a modern and cosmopolitan image. *La Movida* was the Spanish answer (Lechado 2005, 2013).

When did all this start? We can locate its beginnings in 1977 around *El Rastro*, the Madrid flea market. This was where the Cascorro Factory was located—one of the main art collectives of the time. On the other hand, there was also *La líviandad del imperdible* (The Freedom of the Safety Pin), a collective that was involved in discussions and theorizations about punk and other vanguard musical movements, as well as editing fanzines. One of the specificities of the Spanish case is the confluence between several different artistic areas. The members of this collective formed the Kaka de Luxe. As with DIY punk elsewhere, the fact that some of its members did not know how to play did not seem to be a problem. Participating in the newly created Rock Villa Competition in Madrid, they placed second, and consequently recorded an album in 1978, *Kaka de Luxe*. A few years later, the band La Polla Records captured the sense of a new generational subcultural and musical expression in the Spanish scene—even if articulated as

FIGURES 19.1 AND 19.2. Early Portuguese punk: a gig of the Faíscas in the National Society of Fine Arts, Lisbon, 1977.

Source: KISMIF Archive, through Paulo Ramos.

a negative—in their song "No somos nada": "We are the grandchildren of the workers that you could never kill / We are not punk, nor mod, nor heavy, rocker, nor skin, nor techno" (La Polla Records 1987).[8]

The years 1979–1980 marked a key period for the history of *La Movida*, when a cultural industry began to emerge from and around it. Concert halls appeared, international punk and post-punk bands began to visit Spain, and radio stations created programs focused on the new popular music. Radio Nacional opened a new radio station, Radio 3, which was dedicated to pop culture; the band Aviador Dro started their own label, the DRO; new bands swarmed to the new rock music competitions with the aim of recording an EP; several magazines and fanzines appeared; Andy Warhol's *Trash* and *Flesh* movies were shown in the Bellas Artes cinema; and, finally, in 1980, some of the most emblematic films of the period were released: Iván Zulueta's *Arrebato* and Pedro Almodóvar's *Pepi, Luci, Bom and otras chicas del montón* (Fouce 2004a; Lechado 2013).

The impact of *La Movida* exploded in 1982, when an impressive number of independent labels emerged, and commercial labels increasingly began to support (and/or exploit) this new artistic sector. By 1985 this cultural phenomenon was dominant in Madrid and other Spanish cities, and also being reported on by foreign magazines and newspapers (Stapell 2009). Nevertheless, breaches began to appear in this supposed apogee: a person died due to a fight inside the emblematic space Rock Ola, leading to its closure; the television program *La Edad de Oro* (The Golden Age), dedicated to youth culture, was taken off the air; and the main magazine of *La Movida*, *La Luna de Madrid* (The Moon of Madrid) experienced a deep crisis (Fouce 2004a).

What were the characteristics of this scene? According to Imbert (1990), it was a climate of effervescence that affected a small group of individuals from Spain's intellectual and artistic circles—individuals who sought to break with the relational, ethical, aesthetic, and cultural codes inherited from the Francoist regime. It involved the rejection of ideology (both left and right) and an ascetic ethic, which operated to the detriment of a playful and hedonistic ethic. With *La Movida*, a new culture was born—a culture with new reference points. Its new musical canon included the likes of Lou Reed, the Sex Pistols, and Echo & the Bunnymen, among others. It involved a complete change of codes and values, in which the borders between culture and pop became blurred (Valencia-Garcia 2017). There was also a concerted effort to make up for lost time. Spain had not experienced the cultural effervescence of the 1960s and pop art, so it was trying to catch up with the rest of the West (Stapell 2009).

At the musical level, although there was no homogeneity, English punk had a central influence, which then extended to new genres such as *rock siniestro* and *rock radikal vasco*. There was also a determined effort to break with typical Spanish music on several fronts: against the *cantautores*, progressive rock, and the Catalan and Andalusian rock and pop singers. *La Movida* comprised a plurality of musical genres that only approached consensus in their desire for modernity and cosmopolitanism. For example, the reception of punk was crucial, but the term "punk" here is very loose. Members of *La Movida* were influenced by a combination of punk, post-punk, and even the avantgarde bands of the 1960s (Fouce 2004a). One might see this as a reduced musical literacy, but that would be a mistake: the combination of these genres symbolized a desire for everything that was innovative and that broke with tradition.

This hedonistic reality was only representative of a specific time and context: Madrid in the first years of the *Transición*. In the Basque Country, for example, the reality was quite different. There, the *rock radikal vasco* (Basque radical rock) ethos was closest to the British model: controversial and politicized—a response to the Basque sociopolitical context. There was a sense of incredulity in the region about the changes that had occurred during the *Transición*. The Basque Country was suffering from the first impacts of deindustrialization, which provided fertile ground for the message of "No Future" (Balsera and Albizu 2003). It was in this context that *rock radikal vasco* arose. Initially an isolated publisher's marketing strategy, it quickly went beyond that to become a popular music genre. However, it was more than just music: *rock radikal vasco* also involved fanzines, independent labels, pirate radio, and the *gaztetxes* (a Basque term to identify occupied social spaces that are generally self-managed).

When considering the emergence of punk in Portugal, it is important to bear in mind the deep inequalities and contradictions that existed in the country during the mid-1970s. Although Portugal had become a democratic country by this time, it was still deeply defined by a rural, largely uneducated community and by a patriarchal organization of society. However, in the main cities, Lisbon and Porto, the demands for openness, cosmopolitanism, leisure, and opposition to the prevailing conventions, morality, and traditions of the country were beginning to force significant social change.

Although the first Portuguese punk bands emerged in the late 1970s, most disappeared quite quickly, and it was only from the mid-1980s that punk began to show signs of significant development there. The main reasons for this spread include the increasing openness of Portugal to overseas influences, which manifested largely in the form of records, clothes, magazines, and news; the relevance of bands like Crise Total,[9] which embodied what was to be Portuguese punk at the time; the importance of the Rock Rendez Vous club in Lisbon,[10] with its regular schedule of shows by international punk and post-punk bands; the entry of Portugal into the European Economic Community in 1986; the openness of television to programs with live performances by punk bands and the screening of video clips; increasing urbanization; and the emergence of youth recreational spaces in Portugal's major cities (Guerra 2010, 2016).

The fact that most punk bands wrote and performed songs using only Portuguese lyrics was a particularly important aspect of this appropriation. Equally important was the introduction of punk lyrics with themes of protest and revolt against specific personalities, contexts, and events associated with the sociopolitical landscape of Portugal during the late 1970s and early to mid-1980s. This local reappropriation of the punk ethos supports the assertion that punk rock is an example of cultural hybridism, since it is not the same everywhere; instead, it is locally molded and redefined according to the social and political resources of a specific place in a process that mixes characteristics of global punk with local elements (Guerra and Silva 2015).

The Portuguese case seems to have had several elements of hybridism. Pop-rock music contests held at the Rock Rendez Vous in Lisbon provided a significant platform for the promotion and exposure of many local Portuguese punk bands. As well as featuring international bands, the club showcased local Portuguese punk and rock music, evolving a type of urban concert that did not exist in Portugal prior to the emergence and establishment of these genres (Silva and Guerra 2015).

At the time of punk's emergence in Portugal, there were no major publishers or labels interested in signing punk artists, particularly during its formative years. This resulted in the local punk scene being an exclusively DIY affair. The production and availability of punk fashion and style followed a similar route. There was no Portuguese equivalent of, for example, Carnaby Street or the King's Road until the mid-1980s, when the first fashion shops and punk fashion designers appeared in Portugal (Guerra 2015). Likewise, the secondhand clothing market, which writers such as McRobbie (1994) claim was of critical importance for supplying fashion and stylistic resources for punk and new wave in the United Kingdom, did not begin to establish itself in Portugal until the late 1980s or even early 1990s. During the early years of Portuguese punk, its fashion and style dimensions consisted of clothes, footwear, and artifacts from two sources: those imported from the United Kingdom or United States, and those created from clothes and footwear from parents' or grandparents' wardrobes, adapted to punk styles.

There are distinct positions regarding appropriation of the punk lifestyle in Portugal, inspired by the Anglo-American template. These point either toward an acknowledgement and historical understanding of punk grounded in the late 1970s and early 1980s, or toward a lack of knowledge of the movement's past in a narrative of punk built from personal experience of punk in the present (Guerra and Bennett 2015; Guerra and Silva 2015). In this sense, Portuguese punk is described in a rather atomized way, segmented around axes that refer, in the end, to the presence of individuals and bands in particular regions of the country, such as Lisbon, Coimbra, Porto, Braga, Leiria, and Viseu. With more or less cohesion, the movement assumed its presence and took its place according to the will of its more committed followers and devotees. The evolution of the punk scene pivoted on local neighborhood networks and school and peer groups, as well as the interrelationships between these and the micro-circuits of local production—punk bands, record companies, and the music, official and unofficial radio, and music press in particular fanzines.

Not Just Holidays in the Sun: Singularities of Punk outside the Anglo-American Context

> We're here to destroy
> To plant the anarchy to come
> We're here to fuck you.
>
> — Kú de Judas, "Vítimas do sistema" (1996)

> Everything we want / Will go down the drain
> If we don't remove / Killers in power.
>
> — Crise Total, "Assassinos no poder" (1984)

One of the greatest specificities of Portuguese and Spanish punk relates to language. Unlike some countries outside the Anglo-American world, in Portugal at present approximately 70 percent of the bands sing only in Portuguese. The "Portugueseness" of Portuguese punk is notorious in a constant struggle to retain a sense of national identity so many times claimed and threatened by exogenous forces (Guerra 2010, 2016). The same can be said of a "Spanishness" in Spain, but with nuances. While the Madrid punk bands mentioned above all use the Castilian language in their songs, in the Basque Country there are few bands that opt for Castilian rather than Basque. Less frequently, but still significantly, Catalan bands opt for Catalan. These are regional specificities and rivalries; however, they do agree on one thing: not singing in English (Fouce 2004a; Lopez Aguirre 2011).

On the other hand, the importance and uniqueness of Portuguese punk relates to the fact that it was the most visible face of youth culture in Portugal in the late 1970s. Thus, contrary to other countries—notably those in the Anglo-American world—Portuguese society witnessed the emergence of style-based youth cultures during the transition from the 1970s to the 1980s, whereas in other contexts such youth cultural forms emerged following World War II. This is important at two levels: on the one hand, the evolution of the country in the post-revolution context of 1974, with its dynamic opening to modernity, resulted in the legitimacy of youth, their rituals and sociability; on the other hand, and only because of the entering of Portugal into European Community in 1986, the liberalization of national television, and then later the rise of the Internet, there was a sustained increase in youth manifestations connected to punk (Guerra 2015).

Spanish punk also has these specificities, but with additional peculiarities. Although there is no homogeneous Spanish punk movement, in the early years of the *Transición*, punk from Madrid was characterized by a more aesthetic than programmatic take on British punk. For a better understanding of this option, it is necessary to explain the different contexts in which it evolved. The Spanish case was distinguished by the absence of a differentiated youth culture, an immaturity of the political and media structures that emerged during the *Transición*. Despite coming from different socioeconomic backgrounds and with different career perspectives, bands such as Kaka de Luxe and Las Vulpes shared a disenchantment with politics (Fouce 2004b). In this first phase, Spanish punk became a symbol of the modernism that Spain had been seeking. It turned into a rallying cry in those early years of democracy, and was eventually capitalized on by political power, which looked for the image of a New Spain (Fouce 2004a).

On the other hand, the importance of *rock radikal vasco* from 1980 led to a different branch of punk appropriations. At that time, the Spanish punk scene drew its inspiration from Basque radical rock and its demands for the political autonomy of the Basque Country. Spanish punk became a very important means of expression for youth resistance. Eskorbuto,[11] a Basque band from Bilbao, achieved near-mythical status due to the emphasis in their lyrics on themes of institutional corruption, abuses of power by the authorities, and the decline of middle-class values, in a register that was deeply nihilistic. For the Spanish punk scene, the 1980s was a decade of great vitality and affirmation of desire.

The adoption of a more mimetic stance in some periods and a more original and innovative stance in others led to a rather different configuration of Portuguese punk. This configuration, in that same swinging course between both poles—not solely mimetic or original—has produced an energetic local punk scene shaped by various subgenres (anarcho-punk, punk hardcore, punk 77, crust/d-beat, riot grrrl, ska punk, Oi!, pop-punk/melodic hardcore) that coexist in different geographical areas throughout the country. In Spain, by contrast, arguably, the punk scene is in a lethargic state after a very creative, intense period in the 1980s (Guerra 2010; Guerra and Quintela 2016).

Also in Spain, in the initial phase there was an asymmetry with British reality. It is important to understand the social origins of the participants of *Movida*, as well as their cultural and social capital, since through this we are able to better understand how these artists understood their work and the ways in which they related to the music industry. *Movida* members were part of the new middle class (Gouldner 1979), which emerged in the 1960s and 1970s and occupied the new jobs of tertiary capitalism. This is the milieu that formed the basis for the legitimation of rock as an artistic form all over the world (Regev 2013).

Those who became part of the middle class were social actors who, due to their social origins, had an important cultural and academic background. This allowed them to travel abroad—especially to London—and thereby absorb the aesthetics of punk culture. They had subcultural capital, exclusive knowledge of the scene, news about the music universe, and the right haircuts, clothing, and fashion, among other things. If we analyze the biographies of many punk artists, we see a pattern: young people with a high amount of cultural capital that was inherited and/or acquired, and who were fluent in English and able to enjoy regular trips abroad. This allowed them to have access to the discographic innovations that were produced elsewhere. In turn, such capital evolved into subcultural capital (Thornton 1996). In short, they developed a form of (post)modernity—an ability to understand and be familiar with musical and aesthetic novelties. When we talk about *La Movida*'s modernity, we have to talk about the elitism that existed in it. Being modern meant embracing the new and the foreign—especially if it came from the Anglo-American world. In the 1970s and 1980s, few people had sufficient finances to travel to London or New York; therefore, if being modern meant being aware of such novelties, a large part of the Spanish population had no chance of being modern (Val Ripollés 2014).

The evolution of punk in Portugal illustrates the same reality found in Spain. The origins of the Portuguese punk scene can be traced to Lisbon, and specifically to small groups of youngsters belonging to the middle and upper classes whose travels to the United Kingdom and United States brought them into contact with new music and youth cultural scenes, including punk (see the example of the Porcos Sujos [the Dirty Pigs] in Figure 19.3). It is not surprising that the epicenter of the Lisbon punk scene was Alvalade, an area of the city inhabited by urban middle-class families—the aforementioned new middle classes. These young people were able to travel and attend festivals abroad, as well as to import records, magazines, and punk fashion. As in Spain, cultural capital was converted into subcultural capital. In this early period, it was not a class

FIGURE 19.3. Performance of Porcos Sujos (Dirty Pigs) in the mid-1990s, Lisbon.
Source: KISMIF Archive, through Francisco Dias.

claim that was discussed, but rather an affirmation of a transversal changing of social values, which involved an opening up of Portuguese youth to new music, new aesthetics, and new forms of sociability—basically, catching a (post)modernity rhythm (Abreu et al. 2017; Guerra 2010).

The similarities between the two countries were also accompanied by differences, however. There was social homogeneity between the early Portuguese and Spanish punks, but the consequences of punk differed between the nations. If the Madrid punks focused on an uncomplicated and hedonistic style of punk without political connotations, the Portuguese punks came closer to the British idea of "No Future." This is evident in song lyrics: a sub-political perspective on the Spanish side and an overpoliticization on the Portuguese side. A possible answer lies in the different paths followed by the democratic course of both countries: on the Spanish side, a broadly peaceful transition that sought, above all, to forget the differences and resentments that had come from the dictatorship; and on the Portuguese side, a revolution that was fertile in political struggles and that marked (and still marks) the Portuguese imaginary. Despite rejecting the model of partisan political participation, Portuguese punks who emerged shortly after the revolutionary period maintained a political concern. This was a politics of rupture characterized by a disenchantment with the opportunities lost in the post-revolution era, as well as the perpetuation of a very closed and conservative cultural and social order (Silva and Guerra 2015).

This overpoliticization may have been one reason for the invisibility later suffered by Portuguese punk. The violence, sexual threat (as in a song like Kú de Judas's "Rape the President"), and eschatological attacks—the norm in song lyrics—may well have made political and media acceptance of punk very difficult. It was very confrontational for punk to be capitalized on politically, so these Portuguese innovators suffered repudiation and vexation in their attempts to assert their right to be part of the public, social, and artistic sphere. The Spanish case was different. The absence of political connotations, the hedonism, and the fact that they were seen as modern made the political and media capitalization that was the target of *La Movida* possible. There were newspaper reports, television programs, and political support—direct and indirect. This support notably came from the City Council of Madrid, but also from the government, which saw in these young people a way to promote, nationally and internationally, a new image of Spain: cosmopolitan, without complexes, transcending Francoism, and, above all, modern.[12] This had consequences in terms of the path taken by the two manifestations of punk: one remained essentially underground, while, for a short period of time, the other was mainstream.

The preponderant focus given to politics led to another difference between the two countries: there was no reappropriation of Portuguese popular culture by punks. On the contrary, *fado*, bullfights, and national history—especially the period of the Maritime Discoveries—were all politically rejected as reactionary. Nor did an ironic reinterpretation exist—just a rejection, both in the songs themselves and in the pages of fanzines. In the Spanish case, popular culture, such as bullfighting or *toreo*, was reappropriated—in some cases ironically, but in others not. Thus, *torero rock* was a new music subgenre, characterized by a fusion of punk rock and Spanish cultural elements. There was a desire to do something more than imitate London or New York. More than a simple aesthetic concern, it contained political resonance: this reappropriation served to mark a frontier, a break from the previous generation, which saw in these traditions the cultural remnants of Francoism and reactionaryism (Val Ripollés 2014).

The Embedding of a DIY Ethos in Contemporary Iberian Punk

> A real network of friends / That's what we aim to be / Doing it with passion / Revolution and solidarity / You don't belong here!
> It's time to say goodbye / This is not MTV / This is punk, DIY!
>
> New Winds, "The Real Judas Syndrome" (2004)

Contemporary manifestations of the DIY ethos show us the peculiarities of the Portuguese and Spanish punk scenes. DIY culture was always present in the Spanish punk scene. The first punks from Madrid, faced with a lack of structure, had to turn to DIY to fill these gaps: band members simultaneously produced fanzines, organized concerts, and so on. While this scarcity was quickly addressed in Madrid, however, this did not occur in other parts of Spain. For example, Basque punk had its anchoring in a DIY culture and a self-managed ideology. It was allowed effective praxis without any need for musical literacy. This meant that in the 1980s more than 1,500 bands appeared in the Basque Country alone, together with a musical scene to support them: independent publishers, free radio, fanzines, and *gaztetxes*. Squats served as a space for young people to carry out their cultural practices (Balsera and Albizu 2003).

One of the most remarkable features of Spanish DIY culture were the *okupas*. In Spain, this was a movement that began in the mid-1980s, with activities and demands that went beyond the right to the city. The *okupas* were autonomous spaces for an anticapitalist and countercultural political expression—part of a DIY culture (McKay 1998) and a mixture of resistance and celebration (Feixa 1998). In Barcelona, perhaps drawing on the city's proud anarchist heritage, an active group of *okupas* still operates today. They are spaces used to promote sociability, and to produce flyers or fanzines, conferences, workshops, and concerts, among other cultural practices. One peculiarity is that few of these *okupas* are solely punk—that is, their worries go way beyond punk. They can stage punk concerts or have a publisher that essentially records punk bands, but they also join forces with other social issues: the defense and integration of immigrants, feminism, ecology, animal rights, the legalization of some drugs, anti-militarism, and so on. In many cases, an *okupa* serves as a node that feeds and sustains a local scene (O'Connor 2004; Feixa 1998).

With regard to Portuguese punk, in the period between bands forming and beginning to play live, everything took on a DIY aesthetic, in which the whole structure of the local scene was situated and shared by those involved in it. That said, the local context in which a punk scene emerges may serve to nuance the particular ways in which this DIY ethic ultimately is articulated and understood by those involved in it. In Portugal, punk has always been a space of valorization of amateur local resources. Its actors established their own networks of communication, writing fanzines, making records, and organizing events outside the established channels of production, which emphasized the movement's autonomy (Guerra and Quintela, 2014). It remains important to consider that the Portuguese punk universe moves a set of actors who do not have a full-time occupation in punk, but simultaneously play multiple roles within the scene: musicians, promoters, record label managers, fanzine producers, and so on. This characteristic leads to another issue: the informality and non-institutionalization of Portuguese punk, marked by a lack of its own spaces of belonging, as well as by the absence of the formal recording and release of punk songs, favoring instead the DIY production of cassettes and demo tapes. In turn, all the material and tangible components of punk that have manifested themselves over the decades have these same characteristics of volatility and absence (Guerra 2017, 2018).

An important and ongoing example of the strong DIY ethos of the Portuguese scene has been the production of fanzines. The number of fanzines increased with the growing number of participants in the scene, but fanzines continue to be produced manually and their significance as a strong marker of punk's DIY ethos endures even with the emergence of e-zines (Guerra 2015; Guerra and Quintela 2014). This DIY ethos works with intensity in the activation of strong and mutual networks of interknowledge and familiarity among Portuguese punks—something that is perhaps dictated by the small size of the country and the relatively small numbers of people participating. But the perpetuation of DIY is seen in other ways too—for example, in the peer-to-peer supply and lending of musical instruments, transport, the logistics of light and sound for concerts, and the collective organization of halls and other venues for live performance (Guerra 2018). Bands that have an established position in the scene are rare, and they are often the subject of intense criticism. Portuguese punk never really became embroiled in the processes of mass production and marketing; for some four decades it has remained in an "independent" space, from which it protects and preserves its own subjective claim to be fighting the system (Guerra 2015, 2018). In many ways, it is the indelible result of a DIY Portuguese "youth" music industry that is still in a very pioneering phase regarding its stance against mainstream pop-rock—a characteristic that sets it apart from punk in most other Western countries.

Conclusion

This chapter has sought to situate the Iberian punk scene in a broader, more global context, without overlooking the specificities resulting from appropriation of a non–Anglo-American context and a society located in southern Europe—hence the importance of maintaining a global-local perspective. This genealogy shows us that punk's arrival in the Iberian Peninsula is very much a subsidiary of the 1974 April Revolution and the Spanish *Transición*, through which the two countries went from being dictatorships to democratic regimes. These worked as a window, allowing a focus on a variety of social issues in ways not previously permitted. Initially in the capitals, Lisbon and Madrid, and later in other regions, punk emerged with its own bands, gigs, fans, fanzines, and scenes. It was not the product of a blank generation of young people with their own specificities; nor was it so much about a new sonority (as this was influenced by the American and British contexts). Instead, it was a new form of engagement with issues of identity, society, politics, norms, and values in the very Catholic context of southern Europe.

Similarly, this analysis allows us to break with the idea that the Iberian countries were just uncritical receptacles of music originating in London or New York (see Hooper 2006; Wilkins 2018). The history of pop-rock music in these countries is the result of intense cultural hybridity, as we have seen; it is certainly far more than the replacement of one form of imitation by another. Furthermore, the simple inclusion of Portugal and Spain in the same discussion is a way to remove their historicity. These are countries that share similarities; however, as a consequence of profound sociopolitical differences, there are more differences in the paths followed by their various youth cultures. As we have seen, the first Portuguese and Spanish punks came from the new middle classes, but the ways in which they received punk music and the aesthetics of their movements could not have been more different. So how do we explain why Portuguese punk was ignored and *La Movida* was so widely and enthusiastically celebrated? What are the reasons for the Portuguese overpoliticization and Spanish subpoliticization that occurred initially in these movements? This points to inherent specificities in each country, which should not be ignored. To paraphrase the Sex Pistols: Portugal and Spain are much more than just *holidays in the sun*.

Acknowledgments

The publication of this chapter was supported by the Foundation for Science and Technology (FCT) within the scope of UID/SOC/00727/2013.

I am grateful to Manolo Almeida of Crise Total for permission to reproduce lyrics from "Assassinos no poder," to João Andrade of Kú de Judas for permission to reproduce lyrics from "Vítimas do sistema," and to Bruno Piairo Teixeira of New Winds for permission to reproduce lyrics from "The Real Judas Syndrome."

Notes

1. The Portuguese regime, called the *Estado Novo* (New State), endured between the coup d'état of 1926 and the 1974 revolution. *Franquismo* (Francoism) extended between the Civil War of 1936–1939 and the referendum of 1976. The Portuguese regime had two heads of state: António Salazar (1932–1968) and Marcello Caetano (1968–1974); the Spaniards had only one: Francisco Franco (1936–1975).
2. The carnation became the symbol of April 25, 1974, a consequence of the offering of this flower to the soldiers by the population.
3. A famous sentence given by Salazar in a speech in 1965, which defended the Colonial War to maintain the Portuguese empire.
4. In the late 1970s, about 25 percent of the Portuguese population was illiterate (Barreto 1996).
5. *Fado* is a music genre that can be traced to the 1820s, but probably has much earlier origins. In popular belief, *fado* is a form of music characterized by mournful tunes and lyrics, often about the sea or the life of the poor, and infused with a sentiment of resignation, fatefulness, and melancholia. National songwriting was a type of light music born in the 1940s, with authors, composers, and maestros very famous in Portugal; they wrote and composed songs that portrayed traditional Portuguese values, but also the ideals and principles of the *Estado Novo*.
6. The main Portuguese labels were Valentim de Carvalho, Rádio Triunfo, Sassetti, and Arnaldo Trindade. We should note that these were national (and very familiar) labels. None of the major foreign labels had representation in Portugal at this time.
7. The Faíscas formed in Lisbon in 1977. They lived an ephemeral life, ending the band in 1979, with only one live recording broadcast on Rádio Comercial.
8. All translations, including those of song lyrics, are the sole responsibility of the author.

9. This band, formed in 1983 (and still active today), was one of the pioneers of Portuguese hardcore in the 1980s. Their best-known song is perhaps "Assassinos no poder" (Assassins in power), an attack on Portuguese politics and government.
10. Rock Rendez Vous (RRV) was one of the most important Portuguese clubs in the 1980s. At that time, one of the objectives of all Portuguese bands was to perform a gig at the RRV, which illustrates its importance. RRV promoted the first Festival of Portuguese Modern Music, an event that was of great importance to the Portuguese music scene. Although it closed in 1990, for some important years it served as a showcase of the most innovative Portuguese music.
11. A Spanish punk band from Bilbao, one of the most prominent and polemic bands of the 1980s and 1990s on the Spanish music scene.
12. With some years of delay, this also happened in Portugal. In the 1980s a cultural scene emerged in Bairro Alto, around the Bar Frágil (Fragile Bar), very similar to *La Movida* in Madrid, and achieved what the first punks did not get: media and political attention.

References

Abreu, P., A. S. Silva, P. Guerra, T. Moreira, and A. Oliveira. 2017. "The Social Place of the Portuguese Punk Scene: An Itinerary of the Social Profiles of Its Protagonists." *Volume!* 14, no. 1: 103–126.

Andrade, R. 2015. "Mistérios e maravilhas: O rock sinfónico/progressivo em Portugal na década de 1970" [Mysteries and wonders: Symphonic/progressive rock in Portugal in the 1970s]. *Revista Portuguesa de Musicologia* 2, no. 2: 239–270.

Balsera, P. D., and J. A. Albizu. 2003. "Juventud, identidad y cultura: El rock radical Vasco en la década de los 80" [Young people, identity and culture: the Basque radical rock in the 80th]. *Historia de la Educación* 22–23: 213–231.

Barreto, António, ed. 1996. *A situação social em Portugal, 1960–1995* [The social situation in Portugal, 1960–1995]. Lisbon: Instituto de Ciências Sociais.

Bebiano, R. 2003. *O poder da imaginação: Juventude, rebeldia e resistência nos anos 60* [The power of imagination: Youth, rebellion and resistance in the 60s]. Coimbra: Angelus Novus.

Feixa, C. 1998. *De jóvenes, bandas y tribus* [Of young people, bands and tribes]. Barcelona: Ariel.

Feixa, C. 2004. *Culturas juveniles en España (1960–2004)* [Youth cultures in Spain (1960–2004)]. Madrid: Instituto de la Juventud.

Fouce, H. 2004a. *El futuro ya está aquí: Música pop y cambio cultural en España: Madrid, 1978–1985* [The future is here: Pop music and cultural change in Spain: Madrid, 1978–1985]. PhD diss., Universidad Complutense de Madrid.

Fouce, H. 2004b. "El punk en el ojo del huracán: De la nueva ola a la movida" [Punk in the eye of the hurricane: From the new wave to La Movida]. *Estudios de Juventud* 64: 57–65.

Gonzalez, P. O. 2012. "La música pop en la España franquista: Rock, ye-ye y beat en la primera mitad de los años 60" [Pop music in Franco's Spain: Rock, ye-ye and beat in the first half of the 60s]. *ILCEA* 16: 1–15.

Gouldner, A. W. 1979. *The Future of Intellectuals and the Rise of the New Class*. London: Palgrave.

Guerra, P. 2010. "A instável leveza do rock: Génese, dinâmica e consolidação do rock alternativo em Portugal" [The unstable lightness of rock: Genesis, dynamics and the consolidation of alternative rock in Portugal). PhD diss., Universidade do Porto.

Guerra, P., ed. 2015. *More Than Loud: Os Mundos Dentro de Cada Som*. Porto: Afrontamento.
Guerra, P. 2016. "Keep It Rocking: The Social Space of Portuguese Alternative Rock (1980–2010)." *Journal of Sociology* 52, no. 4: 615–630.
Guerra, P. 2017. "'Just Can't Go to Sleep': DIY Cultures and Alternative Economies from the Perspective of Social Theory." *Portuguese Journal of Social Science* 16, no. 3: 283–303.
Guerra, P. 2018. "Raw Power: Punk, DIY and Underground Cultures as Spaces of Resistance in Contemporary Portugal." *Cultural Sociology* 12, no. 2: 241–259.
Guerra, P., and A. Bennett. 2015. "Never Mind the Pistols? The Legacy and Authenticity of the Sex Pistols in Portugal." *Popular Music and Society* 38, no. 4: 500–521.
Guerra, P., and P. Quintela. 2014. "Spreading the Message! Fanzines and the Punk Scene in Portugal." *Punk & Post Punk* 3, no. 3: 203–24.
Guerra, P., and P. Quintela. 2016. "From Coimbra to London: To Live the Punk Dream and 'Meet My Tribe.'" In *Transglobal Sounds: Music, Youth and Migration*, edited by J. Sardinha and R. Campos, 31–50. London: Bloomsbury.
Guerra, P., and A. S. Silva. 2015. "Music and More than Music: The Approach to Difference and Identity in the Portuguese Punk." *European Journal of Cultural Studies* 18, no. 2: 207–23.
Hooper, J. 2006. *The New Spaniards*. London: Penguin.
Imbert, G. 1990. *Los discursos del cambio: Imágenes e imaginarios sociales en la España de la Transición* [Discourses of change: Images and social imaginaries in the Spain of the Transition]. Madrid: Akal.
Lechado, J. M. 2005. *La Movida: Una crónica de los 80* [La Movida: A chronicle of the 80s]. Madrid: Algaba.
Lechado, J. M. 2013. *La Movida y no sólo Madrileña* [La Movida and not only from Madrid]. Madrid: Sílex.
Loff, M. 2010. "Salazarismo e franquismo: Projecto, adaptação e história" [Salazarism and Francoism: Project, adaptation and history]. *Revista de História das Ideias* 31: 449–498.
Lopez Aguirre, E. 2011. *Historia del rock vasco* [History of Basque rock]. Vitoria-Gasteiz: Aianai.
McKay, G., ed. 1998. *DIY Culture: Party and Protest in Nineties Britain*. London: Verso.
McRobbie, A. 1994. *Postmodernism and Popular Culture*. London: Routledge.
O'Connor, A. 2004. "Punk and Globalization: Spain and Mexico." *International Journal of Cultural Studies* 7, no. 2: 175–195.
Regev, M. 2013. *Pop-Rock Music: Aesthetic Cosmopolitanism in Late Modernity*. Cambridge: Polity Press.
Rosas, F. 2012. *Salazar e o poder: A arte de saber durar* [Salazar and the power: The art of knowing how to continue]. Lisbon: Tinta-da-China.
Silva, A. S., and P. Guerra. 2015. *As palavras do punk* [The words of punk]. Lisbon: Alêtheia.
Stapell, H. M. 2009. "Just a Teardrop in the Rain? The *Movida Madrileña* and Democratic Identity Formation in the Capital, 1979–1986." *Bulletin of Spanish Studies* 86, no. 3: 345–369.
Thornton, S. 1996. *Club Cultures: Music, Media and Subcultural Capital*. Hanover, NH: Wesleyan University Press.
Valencia-Garcia, L. D. 2017. *Antiauthoritarian Youth Culture in Francoist Spain: Clashing with Fascism*. New York: Bloomsbury.
Val Ripollés, Fernán del. 2014. *Rockeros insurgentes, modernos complacientes: Juventud, rock y política en España (1975–1985)* [Insurgent rockers, complacent moderns: Youth, rock and politics in Spain (1975–1985)]. PhD diss., Universidad Complutense de Madrid.

Wilkins, R. R. 2018. *El futuro ya está aquí: A Comparative Analysis of Punk in Spain and Mexico*. MA diss., Brigham Young University.

Discography

Crise Total. 1984. "Assassinos no poder" [Assassins in power]. On *Ao Vivo No Rock Rendez Vous Em 1984* (Compilation CD). Lisbon: Dansa Do Som.

Kú de Judas 1996. "Vitimas do sistema" [Victims of the system]. On *The Voices of Anger 03* (Compilation CD). Lisbon: Fast'n'Loud.

La Polla Records. 1987. "No somos nada" [We are nothing]. On *No Somos Nada* (12″ album). Bilbao: Txata.

New Winds. 2004. "The Real Judas Syndrome." On *A Spirit Filled Revolution*. Lisbon: Refuse Records.

CHAPTER 20

PUNK IN BELFAST, NORTHERN IRELAND
Critical Perspectives on the Troubles and Post-conflict "Peace"

JIM DONAGHEY

ULSTER[1] was (and is) a "unique 'stronghold'" for punk (O'Neill and Trelford 2003, v). Belfast had a place of prominence in the early punk era: the Clash posed for photos beside British Army squaddies after their cancelled gig in 1977; Crass, DIRT, and Poison Girls played the "Anarchy Centre" punk club in the early 1980s; and the twenty-nine-year conflict of the Troubles (1969–1998) was lyrical fodder for everyone from the Sex Pistols ("Anarchy in the UK," 1976), to Conflict ("The Ungovernable Force," 1986), to the Au Pairs ("Armagh," 1981), to the Pogues ("Streets of Sorrow/Birmingham Six," 1988). Homegrown bands like Stiff Little Fingers and the Undertones found commercial success and became seminal punk staples, and the Good Vibrations label was part of the decentralizing tide of DIY(ish) punk production—but punk mattered (and still matters) here in ways that it did not elsewhere. In a society divided deeply along national-ethno-religious cleavages, punk has provided an alternative identity and cultural space that is not just *non*sectarian but is actively *anti*-sectarian.

Figure 20.1 shows some "artifacts" from the Ulster Museum's "The Troubles and Beyond" exhibition (National Museums NI 2018). The mannequin in the old garb is perturbing—punk is entombed in a glass display case, condemned to a historic moment, a calcified curio, a spent spectacle (and this process of "nostalgification" is resisted by contemporary punks in Belfast, as discussed below—see also Stewart 2019). But it is striking that punk is *so* prominent in this historic account of the Troubles. Visitors following the suggested path through the museum start at the "The Troubles and Beyond" exhibit, and the punk mannequin is the first thing one encounters in that display. *Punk is front and center in Northern Ireland's own conception of itself.* This recognition of punk

FIGURE 20.1. "The Troubles and Beyond" exhibit at the Ulster Museum, permanent display. Clockwise from left: clothes donated by Greg Cowan of the Outcasts (on loan from the Oh Yeah! Centre); gig poster (c. early 1980s); gig ticket (c. early 1980s); gig ticket 1987. Photos taken November 2018.

carries over into the scholarly literature on the Troubles—which is surprising, because punk is often overlooked altogether in other areas of "serious" academia. Volumes with sober titles such as *Governing Ethnic Conflict: Consociation, Identity and the Price of Peace* (Finlay 2011), *The Troubles in Northern Ireland and Theories of Social Movements* (Bosi and De Fazio 2017), *Northern Ireland after the Troubles: A Society in Transition* (Coulter and Murray 2008), and *The Contested Identities of Ulster Protestants* (Burgess and Mulvenna 2015), as well as articles on the Cultural Traditions Group (Finlayson 1997), sectarianism in the Ardoyne (Shirlow 2003), and even Paisleyism (Gallagher 1981), all at least mention punk, even if it is rarely the focus. This recognition is also reflected in the everyday experience of being a punk in Belfast nowadays—more often than violent abuse or attack, an overt punk aesthetic draws approving nods from people a decade or two older who eagerly inform that they "usta[2] be a punk," and a tale from "back in the day" will likely ensue (and note well that "their day" is always "*the* day" no matter when that was). This recognition is significant, but in each of the museum, academic, and bar-propping contexts, this risks succumbing to dewy-eyed nostalgia. Gary Fahy, of Punkerama Records in Belfast, notes the "growing nostalgia for punk music in Northern Ireland" (quoted in BBC 2015), especially for bands from the late 1970s and early 1980s such as Rudi, the Outcasts, the Defects, Protex, Ruefrex, the Undertones, and Stiff Little Fingers. In September 2018 a blue plaque[3] was unveiled at the Trident Bar in Bangor, County Down, to commemorate it as the "birthplace of the Ulster punk scene 1977." The "nostalgic" scholarly analysis of punk in Northern Ireland from this period views it "as a kind of community relations programme *avant la lettre*" (Finlay 2011, xii), or "an original 'community relations council'" (McLoone 2004, 33), bringing together young people from both sides of the national-ethno-religious divide despite the condition of (near) civil war going on around them.[4] However, some academics have been quick to dismiss this "rose-tinted" view of punk in Northern Ireland (see Bell 1990, 1996; Rolston 2001; McLoone 2004)—Bell even goes as far as to make the absurd suggestion that punk was responsible for reinvigorating loyalism in the 1980s and 1990s (in Finlay 2011, xii). These academics are right to critique the simple narrative of early punk as a forgotten panacea to the Troubles, but in common with most punk nostalgists, their recognition of punk only extends to a narrow historical window in the late 1970s and early 1980s—Campbell and Smyth describe it as "the short-lived subculture of punk" (2008, 239), and McLoone writes that "it did not last of course" (2004, 36). As argued elsewhere (Donaghey 2013), this "early punk" historical calcification correlates with the rise and fall of commercial music industry interest in punk, an approach that is antithetical to the DIY and anti-capitalist ethos that runs through punk, and one which completely neglects the continued significance of punk in Northern Ireland through the 1980s and 1990s, and into the "post-conflict" era of the 2000s and 2010s (Stewart 2014b, 40).

This chapter challenges the historicized, neatly packaged analyses of punk in Northern Ireland, whether of the rose-tinted or dismissive variants, and points to the continued significance of punk as a critical and oppositional culture and identity. Almost all the interviewees and bands mentioned here have an association with the Warzone Collective, an anarchist punk group in Belfast that has been releasing records, running social centers, and organizing gigs (among a wide array of other cultural production and activism) since the early 1980s. This provides a focus in the selection of material, but it also provides the anarchist grounding for the critiques of sectarianism, neoliberalism, conflict, and "peace."

"You say you usta be a punk?"/"Fuck nostalgia"

Iconoclasm was a defining feature of punk's initial emergence into the popular consciousness in the mid-to-late 1970s. In the contemporary punk scene in Belfast, this iconoclastic sensibility is expressed in opposition to punk nostalgia and ridicule of "icons" of the early punk period. This trope is evident as early as 1990 when Pink Turds in Space dedicated their cover of the Undertones' 1978 hit single "Teenage Kicks" to "Feargal Sharkey's chin" (1990d)—the cover is more parody than homage, stripping out the original's bubblegum musicality and saccharine adolescence to be replaced with a screamed, fifty-five-second blast of thrash-crossover punk. In the 2000s, Billy Riot and the Violent Fuckwits skewered punk nostalgists with their choral refrain: "You say you usta be a punk? Just fuck off and die" (2004). More recently, in November 2014, an event called "Fuck Nostalgia Fest" took place at the Warzone Centre on Little Victoria Street in Belfast (see Figure 20.2). The event's Facebook page included, as a condition of entry, "NO GLASS/ NO ASSHOLES/NO POGO"—"pogo" referring to the quintessential dancing style of the early punk period (Fuck Nostalgia Fest 2014). At this event a comical piñata effigy of Terri Hooley, the former proprietor of Good Vibrations record shop and label, and "godfather of punk in Northern Ireland" (BBC 2015), was enthusiastically smashed to bits. The video footage had to be removed from YouTube after a furious backlash to both the violence

FIGURE 20.2. Poster for "Fuck Nostalgia Fest" at the Warzone Centre, Belfast, November 14, 2014.

of the act and the disrespect to a local punk icon, though Hooley himself seemed to see the funny side and attended a gig at the Warzone Centre a few weeks later. To be sure, Hooley's legacy has been vaunted significantly in recent years, with a critically acclaimed feature film entitled *Good Vibrations* in 2012 (Barros D'Sa and Leyburn), and a related stage musical production at the Lyric Theatre in 2018 (Carberry and Patterson 2018).

There is a great deal of tongue-in-cheek humor to this punk anti-nostalgia impulse, but it contains a salient point, and it is a distinct critique from the scholarly dismissal of "punk nostalgia." Punk did not disappear just because the label executives lost interest, and it is certainly not the case that "the punk scene in Belfast collapsed back into sectarianism," as McLoone erroneously asserts (2004, 36). Punks who had been exposed to the anarcho-punk movement by the likes of Crass, DIRT, and Poison Girls at the Anarchy Centre on Long Lane in 1981–1982 (a punk club organized by the Belfast Anarchist Collective—see Hyndman 2010), and who had been hanging out at the café at Just Books anarchist bookshop on Winetavern Street, went on to establish the Warzone Collective as an explicitly anti-sectarian countercultural alternative, first as a practice space above Belfast Unemployed Resource Centre on Donegall Street, before setting up their own venue nearby in 1986 (see Jardine and Chantler 2010). This anarchist-informed scene was more resolutely DIY than their predecessors, which explains why they are overlooked in the commercially focused punk histories, and they tackled their political and social situation far more directly and consciously than the early punks did. As interviewee[5] "Ryan," a founding member of the Warzone Collective, put it:

> People came to Warzone who had come from loyalist backgrounds and republican backgrounds and we had this policy where *you didn't leave your politics at the door*, you brought it in and you discussed them, but in an open and amicable way. And a lot of people changed their viewpoints . . . over time, they seen what was going on and what we were trying to do. They kind of thought "this is special." (emphasis added)

The murderous violence of the Troubles has largely (though not completely) subsided since the 1998 Good Friday Agreement,[6] but the core impetus of the Warzone Collective persists. Against the backdrop of continued segregation and increasingly sectarian social attitudes (most markedly among young people),[7] with a Stormont Assembly (nonfunctioning periodically) explicitly premised on sectarian division and opposition when it *is* in operation,[8] and with the "border question" and the threat of renewed violence more prominent than at any time in the last twenty years as a result of "Brexit" (Beesley 2018; Hayward 2018), the punks living and breathing at the time of writing manifest an alternative culture of creative resistance, and they are explicitly critical of the post-conflict "peace."

Punk Analyses of a Divided Society

As has been noted elsewhere (Rolston 2001; McLoone 2004), the punk bands of the late 1970s in Northern Ireland generally avoided singing about the Troubles, with the exception of Stiff Little Fingers (and their engagement with the conflict is somewhat qualified, since most of their conflict-related lyrics were written by an English journalist, and they anyway moved to London early in their career). This changed, in some respects, in the 1980s. Ruefrex sang about the conflict from their particular background in the loyalist Greater Shankill area—they took an avowedly nonsectarian stance, but criticized American funders of the IRA in "The Wild Colonial Boy" (1985), sang about the IRA murder of eleven Protestants in 1976 in "On Kingsmill Road" (1987), and eulogized the 36th Ulster Division of the British Army, which fought in the First World War, in "The Fightin' 36th" (2005).[9] This direct engagement with the conflict was significant—while it may have carried some kudos elsewhere in the world, talking openly about the Troubles in Northern Ireland was (and remains) contentious, if not outright taboo, and in the case of Ruefrex their political outspokenness actually made them unpopular in some circles—Elvis Costello called them "Orange bastards" (quoted in Burgess and Mulvenna 2015, xi) and they were "subject to sectarian abuse" at gigs at the Harp Bar (Mulvenna 2013).

The anarcho-punk bands of the 1980s made direct reference to the conflict as well—for example, the Toxic Waste/Stalag 17 co-release (1985) focuses exclusively on the Troubles across the songs (titled "Traditionally Yours," "Forgotten Victims," "Burn Your Flags," 'Party Talk, "Song For Britain") and imagery (see Figure 20.3).

The anarchist punk scene of the 1980s and 1990s in Belfast also tackled the (expected) wider "anarcho-topics"[10] of Cold War nuclear annihilation, animal liberation, religion, apartheid, and so on,[11] and the opposition to violence, war, militarism, and paramilitarism chimes with the "peace punk" of Crass and their anarcho-punk ilk, but this anarchist analysis of sectarianism is especially significant in the local context. In contrast to Ruefrex or That Petrol Emotion (1987a, 1987b), who were coming at the issue from one or the other "side," the anarchist punks wove their analysis of the Troubles

FIGURE 20.3. Artwork from Toxic Waste and Stalag 17 (1985), *The Truth Will Be Heard*, Mortarhate Records. Front cover (left) features caricatures of prominent politicians in the crowd scene. Details from the lyric insert (center) show paramilitaries, British troops, RUC officers, and clergymen, with a barbed wire motif. The back cover (right) has an image of an army sniper, a child standing in front of a Saracen armored personnel carrier, and the Warzone Collective logo of a clenched fist with an anarchist circled-A inside a ring of barbed wire.

into a wider (intersectional) critique of the state and oppression, and rejected the "two traditions" society of opposing sectarian identities, cultures, and backgrounds. Toxic Waste typify this anarchist analysis, as they boil the conflict down to a choice between competing oppressive elites, asking the listener, "Which set of leaders do you want? Choose and be damned," in "Tug of War" (1986). Pink Turds in Space make a similar point in "No More Sectarian Shit" (1990c), highlighting the same power relations on either "side": "When will you realise? Fighting the same war. This power and greed. It's time you faced the facts."

Into the "post-Troubles" era, punk bands have continued to address themes of conflict (one mid-2000s band in Belfast even went as far as to name themselves The Troubles ["NI Punk" website]) and the anarchist critique has remained to the fore—for example, Still Birth's 2009 track "Smash Both States" echoes the sentiment of Toxic Waste's "Tug of War" in its rejection of both "sides" as oppressive. In the anthemic "Bollox to the RUC," Mr. Nipples & the Dangleberries (2003)[12] apply the anarchistic (and punk) anti-police trope in the Northern Irish context:

> SSRUC. Bollox to the RUC, sectarian majority...
> ignorance, brutality... you have no authority...
> fuck your policing policy.

The "SSRUC" chant—linking the province's then police force (the Royal Ulster Constabulary) with the Nazis—has long been a staple of street protests and confrontations with the police—Gilligan (2008) points to its use in street protests of the 1960s, while Weitzer (1987), in a bizarre effort to show that the police were becoming somehow less sectarian, highlights Protestant protestors using the SSRUC chant in the 1980s. It has also been deployed frequently in punk songs from Northern Ireland, such as Rudi's "Cops" (1977), the Defect's "Brutality" (1982), Runnin' Riot's "Judge, Jury & Executioner" (1998) and Decoy 47's "Vision from Above" (2001), but Mr. Nipples & the Dangleberries explicitly incorporate it with a critique of the state: "fuck your policing policy." Ridicule of political figures is another repeated trope—this is evident in the caricatures on the Toxic Waste/Stalag 17 co-release *The Truth Will Be Heard* (1985, see Figure 20.3); the caricatures on Pink Turds in Space, *Greatest Shits* (1989, see Figure 20.4); the cover of the Rejected Records compilation (Volume III, 2002), which parodies a Rev. William McCrea record cover (a unionist politician and religious conservative); and on the FTS (Fuck The Scene) records compilation of 2006 (Various Artists) (see Figure 20.5),[13] which in a cut-and-paste fashion superimposes the heads of politicians onto a photograph of the Belfast ska-punk band the Hypocrites. The result is humorous, especially for those personally familiar with the members of the band, but the finger pointing in the image adds (at least a degree of) political critique as well. On a more serious tack, the punk-rooted ska band Aggressors BC tackle the perpetuation of sectarian attitudes in "29 Years" (2013) (the title is a reference to the duration of the Troubles):

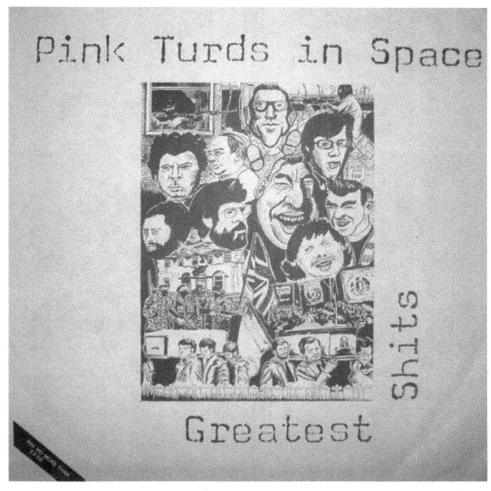

FIGURE 20.4. Pink Turds in Space (1989), *Greatest Shits*, In Your Face Records. The politicians caricatured on the cover include David Trimble (top center), John Hume (top left), Gerry Adams (second from left on the bottom), and Ian Paisley (center), along with images of an army sniper, balaclava-clad paramilitary, and funeral scenes from either "side."

I find some attitudes don't change, no, hate still remains. Brooding beneath the surface, coursing throughout old veins. There's no peace, there's no trust, there's no purpose. The cycle of blame starts again.

Ignorance come inherit our children. And it's a new generation engrained. There goes another doomed generation.

This analysis of sectarianism, from the street-level punk perspective ("For 29 years I have walked these streets"), echoes the pessimistic findings of research by Shirlow (2001), Nolan et al. (2014), the Commission for Victims and Survivors (2016), and

FIGURE 20.5. Various Artists (2006), *Punk in Ireland 2006*, FTS Records. From left to right the superimposed heads belong to George W. Bush (US president), Gerry Adams (Sinn Féin), Ian Paisley (DUP), Tony Blair (British prime minister), and Bertie Ahern (Irish Taoiseach).

Yiasouma (2016). An anarchist-informed analysis of the conflict also appears in the song—Aggressors BC sing "The working man's just a pawn in the game," pointing to a critique of the Troubles as cynical "politicking" by competing sectarian elites ("the game"), combined with a class analysis (though the gendered language of "working *man*" is limiting).

Anti-sectarian Punk

These various punk responses to the Troubles and its aftermath are rooted in anti-sectarianism—this goes beyond " nonsectarianism" to a wider rejection of the conditions and institutions that make sectarianism a persisting reality. As noted earlier, there has been a tendency to romanticize early punk in Northern Ireland in this regard, and in an effort to avoid repeating that narrative, this section will foreground an experience of sectarianism in the punk scene, as articulated by Liam:

> There's always been sectarianism in the scene... A good way to explain I guess is that my best friend was from a Protestant background and I was from a Catholic background and we used to get like snidey ridiculous remarks about us being like "the peace process" or something, y'know like... he'd have to dye his Mohican red and I'd have to dye mine green, really strange sort of like passive aggressive... bullying from the older people.... It wouldn't be really openly sectarian remarks being made... it was veiled in like this "huh huh, jokey jokey" way. The scene certainly wasn't perfect then, and it's certainly not perfect now as far as that. Sectarianism's just like what's happened—within Northern Ireland, even in the punk scene, it's gonna take a lot of getting rid of. Primary socialization of people. We have separate schoolings, separate histories, basically separate educations, and then pushed together into a workforce while living in separate areas. So punk or not, it's something that needs to be taken on.

This is a crucial point, and it goes hand-in-hand with Ryan's point about "not leaving your politics at the door." The process of "taking on" sectarianism within the punk scene should not be viewed as some kind of magic wand—as Liam points out, the punk scene and its participants in Northern Ireland are steeped in a sectarian and deeply divided society, and this needs to be continually renegotiated. But, without wanting to re-don the rose-tinted spectacles, the simple fact of people from either "side" socializing freely was *and is* hugely significant. Two interviewees involved in the punk scene and anarchist movement in the late 1970s and early 1980s point to this significance at the height of the Troubles:

> RYAN: The police would stop a group of punks and ask their names, and they were really surprised to find like a Catholic amongst a group of Protestants, or vice-versa, to the extent that they asked "Have you been kidnapped?"
> ADAM: Nobody cares if you're a prod [Protestant] or a taig [Catholic]...there was definitely an anti-racist, anti-sectarian element to it. Which is something that really can't be underestimated, particularly in Belfast in those days and the years previous to it. Y'know, alright, it's nothing short of amazing really.

Beyond the social mixing of people from both "sides," anti-sectarianism is explicitly expressed in the punk scene in Belfast, not least in the standards of behavior expected within the Warzone Centre itself. The latest incarnation of the Centre, which ran from 2011 to 2018 on Little Victoria Street, had posters on the walls reading: "NO RACISM. NO SEXISM. NO HOMOPHOBIA. NO SECTARIANISM. NO ASSHOLES. NO EXCUSE" (see Donaghey, Woods, and The Warzone Collective 2019). Liam, one of the volunteers who helped run the Warzone Centre, reflected on the Collective's anti-sectarian policy:

> Culturally, y'know, I don't think sectarianism really exists within the scene any more. I think there was like early stumbling blocks . . . I guess the punk scene had a process of its own. . . . As far as like hearing sectarian remarks, nowadays, it just doesn't happen within the scene, and if it does *it's met with the same hostility as a racist remark*. (emphasis added)

Interviewee Terry, another Warzone volunteer, echoed Liam's comments: "Our general consensus on ethics has to kinda shine through, not just anti-sectarianism but y'know just pro-equality." For both Liam and Terry, anti-sectarianism is bound up with opposition to prejudice and oppression in a wider sense. An anonymous interviewee also gave a veiled comment on the likely repercussions of sectarian behavior in the Warzone Centre: "Try bein' sectarian in here. We're all lovely, but everybody has their buttons, like." This non-tolerance of sectarianism was illustrated in 2018 when an Austrian goregrind band called Vaginal Penetration of an Amelus with a Musty Carrot played at the Warzone Centre. As part of their mid-set "banter," the band called out to the crowd: "OK, we want all the Protestants on the left, we want all the Catholics on the right—we wanna see you guys fight!" The entire crowd vacated within a few seconds and the band were left to finish their set to an empty room.[14] Perhaps they were making a clumsy attempt at humor, or perhaps it was a genuine attempt to offend (as is a theme in goregrind generally), but the reaction of the *entire crowd* is telling.

As has already been suggested, this anti-sectarian stance is facilitated by an imagined "other" identity outside of the prescribed "two traditions"—as Francis Stewart puts it, this "rejection of the past . . . then required [the] creation of something new" (2014a, 84). Seminal Belfast Oi! band Runnin' Riot celebrate this "other" punk identity in "Bold as Brass" (2009):

> He defies the lot, walks the streets with pure impunity.
> He's the underclass so you really can't knock him.
> He's between the walls, pissing up no man's land.
> Both sides just don't want him, cos he's got nothing to prove.

The gendered language here is not unproblematic (and this is an prominent aspect of Oi! in general), but the line "both sides just don't want him" is instructive—and this rejection echoes the anarchist rejection of the "two traditions" choice exemplified by the likes of Toxic Waste and Stalag 17 (1985) and Still Birth (2009), above.

An openness to "otherness" has been a defining feature of the Warzone Centre since its first incarnations in the 1980s. Ryan, a Warzone volunteer at that time, recalls that "it wasn't just the Protestant/Catholic thing, but y'know more women coming into what had originally been a male punk scene . . . it also kind of brought the city's, for want of a better word, bohemians and weirdos and anybody who was kind of other or outside, it brought them in." Nathan, a Warzone volunteer until 2017, identified this same openness, especially with regards to people from other places living in Belfast:

For a city that doesn't have a large . . . international community there's an overrepresentation of people from abroad involved in anarchism in Belfast . . . it's providing an alternative kind of way of socially organizing in a city that has really staunch lines of social organization, that are incredibly fucked up . . . If you're from abroad and it's not something that comes naturally to you, it's really fucking scary for a lot of people I think. Whereas you can get involved with us and not need to know those social cues, like it is a real alternative to the way that people organize . . . their social lives and their day-to-day lives in Belfast . . . we provide a choice other than the traditional bifurcated society here.

So, again, this is not just a nonsectarian space where people from either side can mix or "integrate," this is an *anti*-sectarian space populated by people who are rejecting the social norm of being part of one "side" or the other, and are, to at least some extent, performing an identity that is "other" to the "two traditions"—and, crucially, this is distinct to the nostalgic "community relations" reading of punk dismissed by McLoone (2004) and Finlay (2011).

However, this imagined "other" punk/anarchist identity is inevitably affected by the all-pervading "politics" of Irish/nationalism/republicanism versus British/unionism/loyalism, and the rejection of either "side" is qualified in complex ways according to individuals' positions in a deeply divided society. Interviewee Adam, who is from a loyalist background, reflected on this historically:

People could get into punk and go along with . . . [the] idea that socialist republicanism isn't sectarian, it's somehow apart from the sorta sectarian divide in our society . . . The republican thing was still sort of anti-system, y'know, in a very immediate way then [1970s–1980s] . . . whereas [laughs] loyalism most definitely wasn't. It was blatantly reactionary.

Liam (from a nationalist/republican background) concurred with Adam's assessment, reflecting on the late 1990s: "There was still like a weird, not active republican element, but . . . it was a lot more acceptable to be from a republican background. . . . So it was a little strange." However, Liam noted that this situation "changed very quickly" in the early 2000s: "We had . . . this huge turnover of people coming into the scene at that point . . . it grew hugely. . . . It was a strange progression that happened quickly—I think stuff starting getting politicized a lot more."

Loyalist tropes of empire and militarism, and links between loyalist paramilitaries and English fascist groups such as the National Front or Combat 18 are, of course, extremely problematic from a punk/anarchist perspective, while the language of republicanism, and especially its socialist variants, has clear parallels (freedom, liberation, resisting oppression, anticolonialism, etc.). This unevenness of sympathies or potential alignments is seen further in the "Celtic punk" genre of bands such as the Pogues, Blood or Whiskey, Greenland Whalefishers, Flogging Molly, and the Dropkick Murphys, which combines Irish traditional music styles with punk, and features a plethora of Irish "rebel song" covers. There is not really a corollary British/unionist/loyalist "other side" to this combination of punk/anarchism and Irish cultural tradition.[15] Burgess, of Ruefrex, laments that "subversive popular culture . . . remain[s] exclusively the unimpeachable birthright of the dispossessed, the revolutionary and the freedom fighter" (Burgess and Mulvenna 2015, xi). Through 2013 the Warzone Centre hosted a series of Irish culture/intercultural events titled "Craic House," featuring Irish set dancing and traditional music, while the following year it hosted a Féile Unplugged event (in association with the republican-associated Féile An Phobal [Festival of the People]), and "An Gspota," "an event that provides a space for Irish speakers" (Warzone Collective Facebook page), none of which seems to have caused any publicly expressed objection.[16] These Irish music, dance, and language events held at Warzone during 2013 and 2014 are anomalous to the purported rejection of nationalist cultures associated with either "side"—notably, after some changes in the membership of the Warzone Collective, no similar events were held between 2015 and 2018. Because anarchist-informed punk relies on an imagined "other" identity in its rejection of either sectarian "side," the complications of trying to synthesize an ethno-nationalist tradition with punk should be avoidable—but the crucial point is that explicitly Irish cultural events *were* hosted at the Warzone Centre (even if they smack as incongruous and were relatively short-lived), while even the notion of British or Orange cultural events being held in the space seems absurd. To flip the Good Friday Agreement's "parity of esteem" principle on its head, the expected "parity of scorn" toward *both* the Irish and British ethno-national traditions from an anarchist-informed punk perspective does not play out so simply in practice.

While the anti-sectarianism of punk *is* defended here, especially against the dismissive views of those taking a naïve reading of punk in Northern Ireland, it is clearly not a simple or uniform process. Anti-sectarianism is renegotiated at the individual and (counter)cultural level on a day-to-day basis. It needs to be, because while the punk scene is marginal, it is still influenced by the wider sectarian/divided society. This ongoing renegotiation is also essential, because the dynamics of sectarianism are constantly shifting—the anti-sectarianism of the 1980s does not map onto the contemporary context. Because the Warzone Collective takes an anarchist approach, it can remain critical while not being constrained by dogmatism—this is especially evident in contemporary punk analysis of "the peace."

Against the Neoliberal "Peace"

The ways that punk responded to the Troubles and the conflict in Northern Ireland, while diverse and often imperfect, have been shown to go beyond a "nonsectarian" approach, taking a critical "anti-sectarian" stance that is enabled by the ideal of an "other," outsider punk identity, and informed by an anarchist critique. Arguably, punk responses to "the peace" illustrate the most thoroughgoing and interesting anarchist critiques—and this is an aspect that is completely ignored in most scholarly discussions of punk in Northern Ireland.

The fold-out poster insert from 1000 Drunken Nights' *Blank Cheque for Peace?* album (2009) is rich with vernacular conflict-related imagery (see Figure 20.6): the landmarks of Belfast city are shown in flames at the top; in the middle stand the hellish figures of Ian Paisley and Gerry Adams, the clergy with their "lies" and "holy shit," the riot police and the flaming "meat wagons" (armored police vehicles) of the "SSRUC"/"SSPSNI," balaclava-clad paramilitaries of both "sides," "the hoods" emblazoned with the ubiquitous graffiti tags FTP, FTQ, KAT, KAH,[17] a mountain of skulls; and beneath it all, the punks giving a middle-fingered "fuck you" gesture. The overall effect of this imagery resonates strongly with punk's relationship to the conflict—the overarching bigotry, hatred, and corruption is rejected by the subclass punks. However, both the poster and the title of the album (*Blank Cheque for Peace?*) point to a further critique of the conflict, and especially of "the peace." This is evident in the text on the police riot shield: "I PROTECT

FIGURE 20.6. Poster from 1000 Drunken Nights (2009), *Blank Cheque for Peace?*, Carbomb Records.

THE (BUSINESS) COMMUNITY" and in the oversized figures on either side, wearing "City" pin-striped suits and bowler hats with British and US flags on their sleeves, dangling a case of "BLOOD MONEY" above the grasping politicians. This fiercely critical and utterly contemporary critique stands in sharp distinction to assertions by the likes of punk historian Dee Wilson that the early punks of the 1970s "had our own organic peace process before the 'other' peace process even began. . . . The politicians and the negotiators of the Good Friday Agreement *only picked up where we left off*" (quoted in McDonald 2017b; emphasis added). The *Blank Cheque for Peace?* poster demonstrates an anti-sectarianism that is opposed to both the institutionalized sectarianism heralded by the Good Friday Agreement and to the impetus of that "peace" settlement and its underlying capitalist/neoliberal "development" agenda. 1000 Drunken Nights pick up the "blank cheque" theme again in their 2015 track "Glass Tombstones":

> As the curtain falls on our "civil unrest" and American investors begin to infest.
> Take a final look at the streets where yer from, 'cause none of it will matter when the NIO's [Northern Ireland Office] done.
> A blank cheque for peace? Now that's just insanity. Glass and metal tombstones that reach for infinity.
> Pacification of the red brick maze. Gentrification at a covert stage . . .

The observation (or accusation) that "post-conflict" Belfast is now subject to "development" and "gentrification" (Murtagh 2008; McFall 2018) is in some ways prescient, with subsequent waves of eviction on North Street in 2017 as part of the Council's "Belfast Agenda" that seriously disrupted numerous arts organizations (Scott 2017), the campaign in 2015–2016 to save the Sunflower Bar from being demolished to make way for student accommodation as part of the Ulster University Belfast campus development (Williamson 2015; Fitzmaurice 2016; Donaghey 2017a), the 2018 "Sunshine Not Skyscrapers" campaign in the Markets area (Fitzmaurice 2017; Erwin 2018; Human Rights NI 2018; *Irish News* 2018), and the very direct impact on the punk scene with the eviction of the Warzone Centre from Little Victoria Street in September 2018 (see Figure 20.7) and its subsequent demolition to make way for yet more student flats (Donaghey et al. 2019).

Interviewee Franky reflected on this process of gentrification, and Warzone's eviction as a result:

> Local buildings and local landmarks are being "regenerated"—they're being flattened and replaced, and the social history's being replaced as well. So what's going on with Warzone and the building is just part of wider project in Belfast by outside investors to try and erase the social history of the "lower classes" in Belfast and replace it with a shiny new identity.

The Warzone Collective clearly situate themselves as victims of, and in opposition to, this wave of development—usually simply expressed as "Fuck Gentrification"

FIGURE 20.7. "Fuck Landlords. Eat the Cops." Graffiti outside the Little Victoria Street Warzone Centre, September 2018.

(see Figure 20.8). Interviewee Adam saw that this closing down of physical space was accompanied by a closing off of "space" to express dissenting or critical views:

> I actually think what we have now makes being anti-sectarian much more difficult. You're allowed to be nonsectarian, as long as you don't upset anybody, and as long as you don't tread on anybody's culture, because "everybody has the right to their own culture." Even if their culture has the most awful reactionary fuckin' bullshit involved in it, and fundamentally rests on one type of nationalism or the other. I feel now that *it was easier to be anti-sectarian when people were fucking shooting each other and bombs were goin' off*. Not that I want to return to that. But I think a certain amount of space has been closed down. (emphasis added)

"Peace" is mobilized to justify neoliberal development agendas in two ways. First, "underdevelopment" is blamed on the conflict and neoliberal policies are forwarded as a response to resuscitate the economy (not least in the "A Fresh Start" agreement of 2016, which, typifying the attempt to shroud neoliberalism in the language of "peace," purports to "consolidate the peace, secure stability, enable progress and offer hope"; OFMDFM 2016; see also Preston 2018). Second, as Adam suggests, critical perspectives are dismissed as being insufficiently supportive of "the peace"—Adam even has to justify his response by asserting that he doesn't actually want a return to conflict, as if that's not completely obvious. As Tomlinson (2015) points out, the logic of waging a neoliberal

FIGURE 20.8. Detail from "Fuck Gentrification" T-shirt, produced on occasion of the last Warzone Fest at the Little Victoria Street Centre, August 24–26, 2018 (screenprinted by Grimmed Out at the Warzone Centre).

"war on the poor" under the guise of safeguarding "peace" is perverse—1000 Drunken Nights point to this in "Glass Tombstones" (2015), with the lyric: "The bankers are privy to short term memory. It's only yesterday that they called us bomb city!"

Despite the eviction of the Little Victoria Street center, Warzone volunteer Franky was adamant that the punk scene would continue to offer a critical alternative:

> People in the collective almost feel a responsibility at this point in time with what's goin' on in Belfast to try and maintain some sort of indigenous sort of, y'know, whatever you wanna call it, street culture, working-class culture, punk culture, DIY

culture, whatever slant you wanna put on it, I think a lot of us feel the responsibility in the city to keep it goin'.

To bring the chapter full circle, such a statement of resistance, deeply situated in the contemporary, with its assertion of creative, autonomous culture, stands in stark contrast to the co-opted and neutered punk mannequin in the Ulster Museum (Figure 20.1). The efforts to nostalgically historicize punk are as much a threat as the bulldozers, and the Warzone Collective resist both: "FUCK NOSTALGIA," "FUCK GENTRIFICATION."

Conclusion

The current dynamics of the conflict in Northern Ireland have been characterized as a "culture war" (McDaid et al. 2014; Wilson 2016; Meredith 2017; McDonald 2017a; Mitchell 2018)—it is less murderous, for now, but sectarianism is increasingly entrenched and reconciliation seems a distant prospect. The punk scene in Belfast is an alternative counter-voice in that culture war. With its focus on cultural production and creative resistance, it continues to provide an anti-sectarian space that is explicitly critical of the sectarian "peace" of the Good Friday Agreement and the neoliberal "peace" characterized by gentrification. In no way would the Warzone Collective wish to be held up as some kind of policy recommendation to the Stormont Assembly, but there are lessons to be drawn from this persisting countercultural critique, and the scholarship on punk in Northern Ireland is impoverished by its cataracted focus on punk as a distant historical moment and its ignorance of this contemporary manifestation of punk.

Acknowledgments

Many thanks to the Warzone Collective members, past and present, and especially to the interviewees, some of whom were interviewed in 2013 as part of PhD research, others in 2018 as part of The Warzone Dialectogram Project (Donaghey et al. 2019). Thanks also to Robert Porter at Ulster University's Centre for Media Studies for inviting me to speak at a seminar in November 2017 (Donaghey 2017b), research for which formed the basis of this chapter. Thanks to several reviewers for comments on earlier drafts.

Images permissions: Figures 20.1, 20.8—photographs by the author; Figure 20.2—poster by the Warzone Collective, used with permission; Figures 20.3, 20.4, 20.5, 20.6—from the author's archive; Figure 20.7—photograph by Billy Woods, used with permission.

Lyrics permissions. All extended lyric quotations ("Bollox to the RUC," "29 years," "Bold as Brass," 'Glass Tombstones') used with permission of and approval by the bands concerned.

Interview Information

"Ryan"—interview conducted October 8, 2013.
"Liam"—interview conducted October 6, 2013.
"Adam"—interview conducted August 28, 2013.

"Terry"—interview conducted August 10, 2018.
"Anonymous"—interview conducted c. August 2018.
"Nathan"—interview conducted October 6, 2013.
"Franky"—interview conducted June 15, 2018.

Notes

1. Ulster is the northernmost of Ireland's four provinces. Northern Ireland consists of six of Ulster's nine counties—the "micro-state" was created in 1921, remaining part of the United Kingdom after the Partition of Ireland.
2. Belfast vernacular for "used to."
3. The plaque was commissioned by the "Alternative Ulster Historical Society"; the Ulster History Circle, which normally commissions the "official" blue plaques, said that while it commemorates music venues and musicians, "its constitutional remit did not extend to musical genres" (Foster 2018).
4. See also "A Riot of Our Own" symposium (2014).
5. All interviewees are anonymized. Interview details are provided as an addendum.
6. The death toll was almost 3,600 between 1969 and 1998 (McKittrick et al. 2001, 1552), with a further 158 conflict related deaths between April 1998 and April 2018 (Nolan 2018).
7. In 2001, research by Peter Shirlow revealed that sectarian attitudes were more pronounced than at any time during the Troubles, and were most pronounced among young people. Shirlow commented to the *Observer* newspaper at the time: "When the Good Friday Agreement was signed there was no policy agenda to change attitudes on the streets, which begs the question: did the politicians that signed it really want things changed or did they prefer to maintain these divisions?" (quoted in McDonald 2001). In 2016 the picture was no better. A report by the Commission for Victims and Survivors stated, "In Northern Ireland, segregation is part of life. Much of the population lives in communities which are predominantly made up of people perceived to be of one religious or community background" (2016, 15), and a 2014 report on the Flag Protests Dispute found that "[m]any children and teenagers in Northern Ireland have inherited a legacy of conflict that has negative influences upon their personal experiences and their socio-political views. Large scale studies of the attitudes of children and teenagers in Northern Ireland continue to show an awareness and wariness of community divisions" (Nolan et al. 2014, 89). A 2016 paper by the Northern Ireland Commissioner for Children and Young People pointed to "increasing recruitment to paramilitary organisations" among young people (Yiasouma 2016, 4).
8. The consociational mechanisms of the Stormont Assembly, such as appointing a First Minister and Deputy First Minister from either "side" of the national-ethno-religious divide, and especially the "petition of concern" veto (intended to prevent discriminatory legislation being passed by a dominant community at the expense of the other), mean that elected members entering the Assembly designate themselves as "nationalist" or "unionist," institutionalizing sectarian societal divisions. The Green Party (environmentalist), Alliance Party (liberal) and People Before Profit Alliance (Trotskyist) all designate as "other" (a total of 11 Members of the Legislative Assembly out of 90 at the 2017 election). See Wilford 2014 and Schwartz 2015.
9. On the other "side," That Petrol Emotion, not commonly identified as a punk band but formed by members of the Undertones, took up a political position from a republican

background, most notably in "Big Decision" (1987a) criticizing the controversial "Diplock courts," and in "Genius Move" (1987b) which was banned by the BBC because the cover artwork featured a reference to Gerry Adams (though, like Stiff Little Fingers, That Petrol Emotion had by this time relocated to London).

10. For example, nuclear annihilation: Bleeding Rectum, "Scorched Earth" (1993) and "Countdown" (on Various Artists 2002); Pink Turds in Space, "Really Depressing Song" (1989); Toxic Waste, "Fallout Children" (1983). Animal liberation: FUAL's name was originally an acronym for "Fuck Up And Live" but was later reimagined as "Freedom Under Animal Liberation"—they sang about veganism, animal liberation, and anti-vivisection in many of their songs. Religion: Toxic Waste, "Religious Leader" (1987); Pink Turds in Space, "Christians" (1990b); FUAL, "Dead Clergymen" (1988). Apartheid: Pink Turds in Space, "Apartheid Kills" (1990a).

11. It is notable that, while the Belfast anarcho-punk scene featured women prominently, especially as vocalists (Toxic Waste, FUAL, Pink Turds in Space, Jobbykrust), feminism or women's experiences were not a common lyrical focus compared with anarcho-punk bands in Britain (such as Poison Girls or Crass's *Penis Envy* album [1981]).

12. The song, originally written in the late 1990s, was finally released in 2003, two years after the RUC (Royal Ulster Constabulary) had been disbanded and replaced with the PSNI (Police Service of Northern Ireland). However, the "SSRUC" chant is still used in confrontations with the police, as evidenced in a 2013 *Belfast Telegraph* report of someone being arrested for doing so.

13. Fuck The Scene Records (ca. mid-2000s) was based in Letterkenny, County Donegal, which, while being an Ulster county, is in the Republic of Ireland rather than Northern Ireland.

14. See The Warzone Dialectogram Project (Donaghey et al. 2019). On other occasions, bands have tried to take a position on the conflict without much understanding of the situation on the ground—for example, Brian Young from Rudi describes the Clash as talking "absolute shit" (in Sleazegrinder 2003, 103) and they were criticized for producing a T-shirt featuring a photo from their posed session in Belfast in 1977 (McLoone 2004, 37–38; see also Worley 2017, 235); Stza Crack, of New York crack-rocksteady band Leftöver Crack, playing at Auntie Annie's on Dublin Road, Belfast, in 2009, launched into a bumbling speech in support of the "freedom fighters" of the IRA, which was not well received by anyone. Chumbawamba, who were more clued-in than most, were challenged by the Warzone Collective for their expressed support for the IRA at their gigs in England during the late 1980s, which was viewed as naïve. Chumbawamba argued that "they were trying to expose an English audience to what was going on by being confrontational about it" (Interviewee "Ryan").

15. A punk band from the North Coast called Schiehallion (ca. late 2000s) did use bagpipes, nodding to an association with Scottish culture (but the name is Scots Gaelic rather than Ulster-Scots), and the anarchist folk-punk band Gulder (ca. late 2010s) took their name from the Ulster-Scots language word for "shout"—but this is far short of the full-hearted synthesis of "Celtic punk."

16. This unevenness was also evident in the Belfast anarchist movement of the 1970s–1980s. Just Books stocked local publications that were in keeping with their broad political emphases, which meant they had to refuse some loyalist newsletters (but by no means all), while republican papers such *An Phoblacht* (published by Sinn Féin) could be stocked relatively unproblematically. The anarchist publication *Ainrail* (1985–1987) took its name

from the Irish Gaelic translation of "Anarchy," and referred to Northern Ireland as the "Six Counties," suggesting an affinity with republicanism (see Irish Anarchist History website for the cover of issue 1, August 1985).
17. Meaning, respectively, Fuck The Pope, Fuck The Queen, Kill All Taigs (Catholics), Kill All Huns (Protestants).

References

"A Riot of Our Own—a symposium on the Clash," held at Ulster University's Belfast campus and co-organized by the National University of Ireland Maynooth, June 20–21, 2014. https://ariotofourown.wordpress.com/.
Barros D'Sa, L., and G. Leyburn, dirs. 2012. *Good Vibrations*. BBC Films.
BBC. 2015. "Passion for Northern Ireland Punk Remains Undimmed." BBC News, April 29, https://www.bbc.co.uk/news/uk-northern-ireland-32431572.
Beesley, A. 2018. "Violence in Northern Ireland Puts Pressure on Good Friday Pact." *Financial Times*, July 13, 2018. https://www.ft.com/content/c16d1236-86a9-11e8-96dd-fa565ec55929 [paywall].
Belfast Telegraph. 2013. "Man in 'SS RUC' Rant at Officers to be Sentenced." *Belfast Telegraph* September 21, 2013. https://www.belfasttelegraph.co.uk/news/northern-ireland/man-in-ss-ruc-rant-at-officers-to-be-sentenced-29594482.html.
Bell, D. 1990. *Acts of Union: Youth Culture and Sectarianism in Northern Ireland*. Basingstoke, UK: Macmillan.
Bell, D. 1996. "Interview." In *Further Afield: Journeys from a Protestant Past*, edited by M. Hyndman. Belfast: Beyond the Pale Productions.
Bosi, L., and G. DeFazio, eds. 2017. *The Troubles in Northern Ireland and Theories of Social Movements*. Amsterdam: Amsterdam University Press.
Burgess, T. P., and G. Mulvenna, eds. 2015. *The Contested Identities of Ulster Protestants*. London: Palgrave MacMillan.
Campbell, S., and G. Smyth. 2008. "From Shellshock Rock to Ceasefire Sounds: Popular Music." In Coulter and Murray 2008, 232–252.
Carberry, C., and G. Patterson. 2018. *Good Vibrations*. Theater musical production.
Commission for Victims and Survivors and the Victims and Survivors Forum. 2016. *Children and Young People Engagement Project Research Report*. Belfast: CVSNI.
Coulter, C. and M. Murray, eds. 2008. *Northern Ireland after the Troubles: A Society in Transition*. Manchester, UK: Manchester University Press.
Donaghey, J. 2013. "Bakunin Brand Vodka: An Exploration into Anarchist-Punk and Punk-Anarchism." *Anarchist Developments in Cultural Studies* 1: 138–170.
Donaghey, J. 2016. "Punk and Anarchism: UK, Poland, Indonesia." PhD diss., Loughborough University.
Donaghey, J. 2017a. "Soundbite Storymap—Old Belfast: Legacies of Conflict, Conflicting Visions." Creative output as part of the "Sounding Conflict: From Resistance to Reconciliation" research project. http://soundingconflict.org/ResearchFindings/ResearchOutcomes/MWBDerryLondonderry/BelfastStorymap2017.html.
Donaghey, J. 2017b. "The Warzone Collective, Belfast: An Introduction to Punk Perspectives on Conflict and 'Peace' in Northern Ireland." Seminar hosted by the Centre for Media Studies, Ulster University, November 29. https://www.ulster.ac.uk/faculties/arts-humanit

ies-and-social-sciences/events/the-warzone-collective,-belfast-an-introduction-to-punk-perspectives-on-conflict-and-peace-in-northern-ireland.

Donaghey, J., B. Woods, and the Warzone Collective. 2019. *The Future Was (and Is) Punk: The Warzone Dialectogram Project*. PS² Gallery, Belfast, May 25–26. Exhibition. https://www.pssquared.org/projects/short-residencies [Residency 13]. A digital upload of The Warzone Dialectogram is available at https://uploads.knightlab.com/storymapjs/4fe627b7bedf4689de348d77187a36c7/the-warzone-collective-dialectogram/index.html.

Erwin, A. 2018. "£55m Belfast Markets Office Block Approval 'Unlawful,' Judge Rules," *Belfast Telegraph*, May 24, 2018. https://www.belfasttelegraph.co.uk/news/northern-ireland/55m-belfast-markets-office-block-approval-unlawful-judge-rules-36941726.html.

Finlay, A. 2011. *Governing Ethnic Conflict: Consociation, Identity and the Price of Peace*. London: Routledge.

Finlayson, A. 1997. "The Problem of 'Culture' in Northern Ireland: A Critique of the Cultural Traditions Group." *Irish Review* 20 (Winter–Spring): 76–88.

Fitzmaurice, M. 2016. "Belfast's Sunflower Pub Saved from Bulldozer after £300m Development Project Ditched." BelfastLive, April 27. https://www.belfastlive.co.uk/news/belfast-news/belfasts-sunflower-pub-saved-bulldozer-11250125.

Fitzmaurice, M. 2017. "Protesters Block Belfast Road to Rally Support for Continuing Calls for Social Housing." BelfastLive, November 13. https://www.belfastlive.co.uk/news/belfast-news/protesters-block-belfast-road-rally-13893509.

Foster, A.-M. 2018. "Alternative Ulster: Marking Punk's Bangor Birthplace." BBC News, September 10, https://www.bbc.co.uk/news/uk-northern-ireland-45317415.

"Fuck Nostalgia Fest." 2014. Facebook event page, November 14, 2014. https://www.facebook.com/events/395092987309041/.

Gallagher, T. 1981. "Religion, Reaction, and Revolt in Northern Ireland: The Impact of Paisleyism in Ulster." *Journal of Church and State* 23: 423–444.

Gilligan, C. 2008. "Community Responses to Disaster: Northern Ireland 1969 as a Case Study." In *Handbook of Community Movements and Local Organizations*, edited by R. A. Cnaan and C. Milofsky, 311–328. Boston, MA: Springer.

Hayward, K. 2018. "Who Really Cares about Northern Ireland?" Blog post. *LSE Brexit*, April 12, 2018.

Human Rights NI. 2018. "Sunshine not Skyscrapers: The Housing Crisis in Northern Ireland." Human Rights NI, January 19, 2018. https://www.humanrightsni.com/single-post/2018/01/19/Sunshine-not-Skyscrapers-The-Housing-Crisis-in-Northern-Ireland.

Hyndman, D., dir. 2010. *The A Centre or the Lost Tribe of Long Lane*. Northern Visions TV. https://vimeo.com/14859971.

Irish Anarchist History. "Ainrail, Belfast no. 1 (1985)." https://irishanarchisthistory.wordpress.com/2012/12/15/ainriail-belfast-no-1-1985/.

Irish News. 2018. "Market Area Residents Take Legal Challenge to £55 Million Office Development Being Built Beside Their Homes," *Irish News*, January 17, 2018. https://www.irishnews.com/news/2018/01/18/news/market-area-residents-take-legal-challenge-to-a-new-55-million-office-development-being-built-beside-their-homes-1234993/.

Jardine, D., and J. Chantler, dirs. 2010. *Giro's*. Northern Visions TV. https://vimeo.com/10976273.

McDaid, S., A. Mycock, C. McGlynn, J. W. McAuley, and C. Gormley-Heenan. 2014. *The Northern Ireland "Culture Wars" Symposium Report: November 2013*. Research Report. Huddersfield, UK: University of Huddersfield.

McDonald, H. 2001. "Belfast Youths 'More Bigoted' Than the Troubles Generation." *Observer*, September 23, 2001. https://www.theguardian.com/uk/2001/sep/23/northernireland.northernireland.

McDonald, H. 2017a. "'Culture War' Is Sticking Point in Northern Irish Power-Sharing Talks." *Guardian*, June 28, 2017. https://www.theguardian.com/politics/2017/jun/28/culture-war-sticking-point-northern-irish-power-sharing-talks.

McDonald, H. 2017b. "Four Decades On, 'It's Time to Honour' The Punk Dreamers of an Alternative Ulster." *Observer*, February 18, 2017. https://www.theguardian.com/uk-news/2017/feb/18/alternative-ulster-punk-dreamers-trident-bar-bangor-stiff-little-fingers.

McFall, C. 2018. "Gentrification in a Post-Conflict City: The Case of Belfast." *New Socialist*, February 9, 2018. https://newsocialist.org.uk/gentrification-in-a-post-conflict-city/.

McKittrick, D., S. Kelters, B. Feeney, and C. Thornton. 2001. *Lost Lives: The Stories of the Men, Women and Children Who Died as a Result of the Northern Ireland Troubles*. New York: Random House.

McLoone, M. 2004. "Punk Music in Northern Ireland: The Political Power of 'What Might Have Been.'" *Irish Studies Review* 12, no. 1: 29–38.

Meredith, R. 2017. "Culture in NI 'Used as Continuation of Conflict.'" BBC News, November 2, 2017. https://www.bbc.co.uk/news/uk-northern-ireland-41838993.

Mitchell, C. 2018. "I Voted for Peace, and All I Got Was This Lousy Culture War." *Slugger O'Toole*, April 15, 2018. https://sluggerotoole.com/2018/04/15/i-voted-for-peace-and-all-i-got-was-this-lousy-culture-war/.

Mulvenna, G. 2013. "The Protestant Working Class and Popular Culture: The Case of Ruefrex Continued." March 21, 2013. https://gmulvenna.wordpress.com/2013/03/21/the-protestant-working-class-and-popular-culture-the-case-of-ruefrex-continued/.

Murtagh, B. 2008. "New Spaces and Old in 'Post-conflict' Belfast." Divided Cities/Contested States Working Paper.

National Museums NI. 2018. "The Troubles and Beyond." Permanent display, opened March 30, 2018, Ulster Museum, Belfast. https://www.nmni.com/whats-on/the-troubles-and-beyond.

N.I. Punk. "Bands T-Z." http://nipunk.weebly.com/bands-t---z.html. Accessed November 21, 2018.

Nolan, P. 2018. "The Cruel Peace: Killings in Northern Ireland since the Good Friday Agreement." *The Detail*, April 23, 2018. https://www.thedetail.tv/articles/the-cruel-peace-killings-in-northern-ireland-since-the-good-friday-agreement.

Nolan, P., D. Bryan, C. Dwyer, K. Hayward, K. Radford, and P. Shirlow. 2014. *The Flag Dispute: Anatomy of a Protest*. Queen's University Belfast.

O'Neill, S., and G. Trelford. 2003. *It Makes You Want to Spit! The Definitive Guide to Punk in Northern Ireland*, Dublin: Reekus.

OFMDFM (Office of the First Minister and Deputy First Minister). 2016. *A Fresh Start*. Northern Ireland Executive.

Preston, A. 2018. "£417,000 Spent on Stalled Bid to Lower NI Corporation Tax." *Belfast Telegraph*, March 6, 2018. https://www.belfasttelegraph.co.uk/news/northern-ireland/417000-spent-on-stalled-bid-to-lower-ni-corporation-tax-36673236.html.

Rolston, B. 2001. "'This Is Not a Rebel Song': The Irish Conflict and Popular Music." *Race & Class* 42, no. 3: 49–67.

Rudi. 1977. "Cops." https://www.youtube.com/watch?v=X1fICxURSX8. Accessed 5 September 2019.

Schwartz, A. 2015. "The Problem with Petitions of Concern." *QPOL*, May 26, 2015. http://qpol.qub.ac.uk/the-problem-with-petitions-of-concern/.
Scott, S. 2017. "These Are the Modified £400m Plans to Rejuvenate Part of Belfast City Centre." BelfastLive, October 25, 2017. https://www.belfastlive.co.uk/news/belfast-news/modified-400m-plans-rejuvenate-part-13806845.
Shirlow, P. 2001. "Fear and Ethnic Division." *Peace Review* 13, no. 1: 67–74.
Shirlow, P. 2003. "'Who Fears to Speak': Fear, Mobility, and Ethno-Sectarianism in the Two 'Ardoynes.'" *Global Review of Ethnopolitics* 3, no. 1: 76–91.
Sleazegrinder, ed. 2003. *Gigs from Hell: True Stories of Rock and Roll Gone Wrong*. Manchester, UK: Critical Vision.
Stewart, F. 2014a. "'Alternative Ulster': Punk Rock as a Means of Overcoming the Religious Divide in Northern Ireland." In *Irish Religious Conflict in Comparative Perspective*, edited by J. Wolffe, 76–90. London: Palgrave Macmillan.
Stewart, F. 2014b. "The Outcasts: Punk in Northern Ireland during the Troubles." In *Tales From the Punkside*, edited by G. Bull and M. Dines, 33–44. Portsmouth, UK: Itchy Monkey Press.
Stewart, F. 2019. "'No More Heroes Anymore': Marginalized Identities in Punk Memorialisation and Curation." *Punk & Post-Punk* 8, no. 2: 209–226.
Tomlinson, M. 2015. "Risking Peace in the 'War against the Poor'? Social Exclusion and the Legacies of the Northern Ireland Conflict." *Critical Social Policy* 36, no. 1: 104–123.
Warzone Collective Facebook Page. https://www.facebook.com/warzonecollective/. Accessed 24 November 2018.
Weitzer, R. 1987. "Policing Northern Ireland Today." *Political Quarterly* 58, no. 1: 88–96.
Wilford, R. 2014. "Two Cheers for Consociational Democracy? Reforming the Northern Ireland Assembly and Executive." *Parliamentary Affairs* 68, no. 4: 757–774.
Williamson, C. 2015. "Save the Sunflower Bar: Petition Reaches More than 1,500 Signatures in Less Than 24 Hours." *Belfast Telegraph*, December 1, 2015. https://www.belfasttelegraph.co.uk/news/northern-ireland/save-the-sunflower-bar-petition-reaches-more-than-1500-signatures-in-less-than-24-hours-34249255.html.
Wilson, R. 2016. *The Northern Ireland Peace Monitoring Report: Number Four*. Belfast: Community Relations Council.
Worley, M. 2017. *No Future: Punk, Politics and British Youth Culture, 1976–1984*. Cambridge: Cambridge University Press.
Yiasouma, K. 2016. "The Impact of Conflict Legacy Issues on Children and Young People." Presentation given at the Commission for Victims and Survivors Conference, March 9, 2016. https://www.niccy.org/media/2430/cvs-conference-niccy.pdf.

Discography

1000 Drunken Nights. 2009. *Blank Cheque for Peace?* Carbomb Records.
1000 Drunken Nights. 2015. "Glass Tombstones." On *Empyres*. Visions of Warning/Warzone Records/Black North Records.
Aggressors BC. 2013. "29 Years." On *The Tone of the Times*. Warzone Records.
Au Pairs. 1981. "Armagh." On *Playing with a Different Sex*. Human Records.
Billy Riot & the Violent Fuckwits. 2004. "You Say You Usta Be a Punk." On Billy Riot & the Violent Fuckwits and 1000 Drunken Nights, *Drunken Fuckwit Diplomacy*. DIY release.
Bleeding Rectum. 1993. "Scorched Earth." Co-release with Man Is the Bastard. DP Records.
Conflict. 1986. "The Ungovernable Force." On *The Ungovernable Force*. Mortarhate Records.

Crass. 1981. *Penis Envy*. Crass Records.
Decoy 47. 2001. "Vision from Above." On *Anti-RUC* EP. DIY release.
The Defects. 1982. "Brutality." On "Survival/Brutality" single. WXYZ Records.
FUAL. 1988. "Dead Clergymen." On *Veganic Wind*. Warzone Records.
Mr. Nipples & the Dangleberries. 2003. "Bollox to the RUC." On *Nipples Militia*. DIY Records.
Pink Turds in Space. 1989. "Really Depressing Song." On *Greatest Shits*. In Your Face Records.
Pink Turds in Space. 1990a. "Apartheid Kills." On co-release with Sedition. Real to Real Records.
Pink Turds in Space. 1990b. "Christians." On co-release with Sedition. Real to Real Records.
Pink Turds in Space. 1990c. "No More Sectarian Shit." On co-release with Sedition. Real to Real Records.
Pink Turds in Space. 1990d. "Teenage Kicks." On *Wild & Crazy "Noise Merchants"... Invade A City Near You: Worst Of The 1 In 12 Club Vol.9/10*. 1 in 12 Records.
The Pogues. 1988. "Streets of Sorrow"/"Birmingham Six." *On If I Should Fall From Grace With God*. Pogue Mahone Records.
Ruefrex. 1985. "The Wild Colonial Boy." Kasper Records.
Ruefrex. 1987. "On Kingsmill Road." On *Political Wings*. Flicknife Records.
Ruefrex. 2005. "The Fightin' 36th." On *Capital Letters... The Best Of...* Cherry Red Records.
Runnin' Riot. 1998. "Judge, Jury & Executioner." On *Reclaim The Streets*. Rejected Records.
Runnin' Riot. 2009. "Bold as Brass." On *Boots & Ballads*. Dead Lamb Records/Dirty Old Man Records/Record Rebellion.
Sex Pistols. 1976. "Anarchy in the UK"/"I Wanna Be Me." EMI Records.
Still Birth. 2009. "Smash Both States." On *Distorted for Life, Disgusted til Death. A DIY Punk Compilation from Scum Island*. Two Headed Dog zine.
That Petrol Emotion. 1987a. "Big Decision." Polydor Records.
That Petrol Emotion. 1987b. "Genius Move." Virgin Records.
Toxic Waste. 1983. "Fallout Children." *On Unite To Resist*. Warzone Tapes.
Toxic Waste. 1986. "Tug of War." On Toxic Waste, Asylum and Stalag 17, *We Will Be Free*. Warzone Records.
Toxic Waste. 1987. "Religious Leader." On *Belfast*. Belfast Records.
Toxic Waste and Stalag 17. 1985. *The Truth Will Be Heard*. Mortarhate Records.
Various Artists. 2002. *Rev. William McCrea Selects His Rejected Favourites: Rejected Volume III*. Rejected Records.
Various Artists. 2006. *Punk in Ireland 2006*. FTS Records.

PART FIVE

NEAT NEAT NEAT? STYLE, SOUND, MEDIA

CHAPTER 21

FROM PUNK TO POSER

T-Shirts, Authenticity, Postmodernism, and the Fashion Cycle

MONICA SKLAR AND MARY KATE DONAHUE

Introduction

I am quite proud to wear band T-shirts I own, which if they still fit, I occasionally do, though more for casual wearing around home rather than dressing up to go out clubbing.
—Robert, Chicago, 2018

Our clothing communicates lifestyle. The aesthetics of an ensemble give messages to the public, such as inclusion in a social group, financial status, religious background, and hobbies. This is done through the use of the specific visual cues, the wearer's embodiment of the garments, and the physical and social context where it all takes place (DeLong 1998). Punk styles in North America, especially graphic T-shirts, are examples of garments that are coded with cues that are recognized by the wider society and, more specifically, within the insular community they emerged from. Musical genres, fashion, and material culture have long and dynamic life spans, and therefore a T-shirt with a punk slogan or logo on it can span an array of users. Consequently, the intention and impact of a seemingly identical piece of clothing could vary depending on the wearer and context. It is debatable whether the shift between wearers strips a garment of original meaning or creates new symbols per wearer, but an examination of the subject of punk T-shirts allows us to see one of the ways in which punk style has infiltrated and influenced culture at large.

Punk T-shirts are an especially rich area of study because, unlike more mass-manufactured goods (like those displaying the logos of more popular acts, which are more widely distributed at chain stores, for example), people in the punk scene are ideologically inclined to account for the means of production. This research included literature reviews; a survey of open-ended short questions; and interviews with a random sample of individuals from the punk community, retailers that merchandise products to that scene, and others who wear the garments associated with the style.

In punk, specifics of the garment, such as its color, logo, and cut, are part of the whole garment's presentation, as are factors like how it was manufactured, where it was purchased, where it is worn, and how it is eventually disposed of. In punk, the original wearer's use of the shirt is what gives the garment its depth and meaning, as its adoption can imply that the wearer was or knew the person who silkscreened and embellished the details in their garage, spent hours listening to the album represented by the logo, or was someone who traveled cross-country to attend a festival to see the band playing their last show—actualities that go well beyond merely purchasing a garment or "liking" the band pictured on it. Many punks have laughed and argued their way through endless weekends with friends rummaging the bins of resale shops or the sales at athletic and workwear stores to find the perfect fit, the affordable price, or the best level of worn-in texture.

In punk, the T-shirt's intended purpose plays a fundamental role in understanding an object's meaning in a particular context, and subsequently how perspectives of authenticity develop. In the case of punk, and its T-shirts, there may be three simultaneous types of wearers in this postmodern era, and this variety of wearers can result in competing or complementary narratives. Sometimes the parallel usage of differing wearers means the original punk feels the need to pivot away from wearing the shirt, but maybe that is not always needed. At times the new wearers appear as interlopers and mal- or misintentioned; however, they can also be nonthreatening and even at times validate the success of punk ideals—or, in a best case scenario, begin to adapt to the original meaning, or at least mood, of the artifact and its antecedents.

Background Literature: Punk T-Shirt and Related History

Punk fashion can be described as consisting of a combination of garments designed and produced within the indigenous punk community, as well as items purchased through mass markets. These interwoven configurations of items and their meanings have been developed into a subcultural ensemble mostly in how they are embodied when worn altogether.

The Symbolism in Subculture

Elliot and Davies (2006) point out that subculture members have a symbolic connection to many styles. They state, "It is important to recognize that subcultural choices are also consumer choices involving brands of fashion, leisure, and a wealth of accessories, which speak symbolically to members of the group. A key issue amongst these symbolic brand communities is the authentic performance of style" (157). The sense of ownership about a style arises when the garment purchase is not the endpoint of coding, but instead when the symbols are developed along the way through actions—that is, how the style is performed.

Furthering this notion on the intricacy of the symbolic connection, Winge (2012) explains that "The subcultural body is highly time-sensitive and complex in its existence. What was once considered a subcultural body style over time becomes the societal norm instead of the exception" (1). Not only do punk styles evolve over time, but they also become highly defined by a particular era.

"Punk style exists where the person and the form become intertwined. It has transformed many times over, using bricolage and appropriation, to accommodate the counterculture milieu of each era and has maintained certain signifiers linking it back to core ideas and stylistic concepts" (Sklar 2013, 137). Thus, punk styles evolve according to individuals and their era, but, overall, certain tenets about punk will remain the same.

The punk graphic T-shirt is an example of a ubiquitous garment that goes through this process of meaning making. As noted in a study of the Ramones logo's relationship to fashion, "[j]ust as every social group, the rock fans have a series of symbolic elements for identification and construction of identity: various behavior styles, haircuts, color palettes, accessories, clothing, etc. Among those indexes of belonging that are part of the material culture, the T-shirt printed with a band or an idol is an important item, almost mandatory" (Boeschenstein and Pereira 2017, 187). The T-shirt is an item that can be purchased off-the-rack to visually represent a style, but the actions tied to it can imbue it with different codes.

The T-shirt can also be a primary artifact signifying being part of the scene, or a secondary tool to gain access to social or cultural capital. Context plays a role regarding the reach of the market and the content. For example, as noted in the Boeschenstein and Pereira study, the volume and longevity of the Ramones' impact and, relatedly, their iconic logo T-shirt is now so widespread that there is a lesser expectation of its wearer being deeply a part of the punk scene than there would be toward the wearer of a shirt representing a more obscure punk reference like Crass.

The Rips and the Logos Tell a Life Story

Punk style is distinguished by characteristic visual elements and is built on experience. Within the scene, there are internal trends and subgenre variations:

> Punk style has a forty-year history, with a host of influences and a myriad of characteristic pieces that make up the look, as well as flexibility to include new components. Origins of the key aspects of punk style—which include the color black; heavy accessories; boots; clothing that is tattered and manipulated; piercings; tattoos; unnatural hair colors; facial hair; band logos; and jeans, T-shirts, and hooded sweatshirts—have become fragmented and fractured through various subgenres under the punk umbrella.
>
> (Sklar 2013, 26)

Time also plays its part. As the punk graphic T-shirt moves throughout its scene and around the fashion world, these elements are picked up and replicated or reimagined.

The T-shirt is a garment with a rich history. In 1904, the Cooper Underwear Company manufactured just the top half of the union suit and called it the "bachelor undershirt." It was crew-necked and button-free to appeal to those men who had no women to resew buttons back onto their shirts. In 1920, the term "T-shirt" was born and popularized when F. Scott Fitzgerald wrote it into his novel *This Side of Paradise* (Kennedy 2013). Then, during World War II, T-shirts gained esteem, as they were worn by the troops: *Life* magazine drew attention to the garment when it featured a military man in one of these shirts with logos on his chest on its cover in 1942 (Tortora and Marcketti 2015). In 1951, the T-shirt transformed streetwear and the youth market when sex-symbol actors who pushed boundaries appeared in them. Marlon Brando donned a white-ribbed T-shirt in the film *A Streetcar Named Desire*, and not long after this, the actor James Dean wore a white T-shirt in the iconic *Rebel without a Cause*. Because Brando and Dean often played defiant, unconventional characters in their films, America's youth began to associate the look with this type of nonconformity. In the 1960s, the shirt then shifted into the counterculture, particularly among the era's protest movements, which were able to combine its functionality and low cost to manipulate it for new styles such as slogans and tie-dye. Doing so was especially symbolic, since it inverted its association with the military style of the 1950s, transforming its wear into a more rebellious, antiwar statement.

Alongside that development, graphic T-shirts associated with music and various subcultures have been prevalent since the late 1960s. Band T-shirts have been an inexpensive, one-size-fits-all, unisex way to quickly connect with numerous social meanings. According to Boeschenstein and Pereira (2017, 187), "[t]he designs vary: photos of the musicians, album covers, cool designs, logos, and even stylized versions, created by professional designers, that bring elements such as lyrics or cartoons that matches with the band theme." One of the original ideas for band-branded T-shirts was that bands could increase their earning potential through the sale of merchandise (McIntyre 2017), a strategy much in use today. In 1968, the concert promoter Bill Graham on the west coast of the United States produced some of the original rock T-shirts for acts such as the Grateful Dead and Jefferson Airplane, while shortly thereafter in the early 1970s on the east coast merchandiser Irving Sokoloff was making shirts for the Allman Brothers, all of whom were in rock culture. The shirts were produced as a way to embody the music, for fans to take the show home with them and relive it through continued wear, and to link themselves to other like-minded people who would know the (at the time) obscure logo or color palette familiar to scene insiders. Today, over two billion T-shirts are sold (Wallander 2012), in part due to the many uses it can encompass.

This background has led to T-shirts becoming a logical component of punk style. In 1973, Vivienne Westwood and Malcolm McLaren took overstock Vive Le Rock concert T-shirts from their rockabilly store and distressed them to create what would later be referred to by historians as possibly the first punk T-shirts. As their shops transitioned to be called SEX, and later Seditionaries, they included other stylistic elements that would become the hallmarks of British punk style, aspects that became characteristic of how punk is often interpreted internationally, especially from those outside of the knowledge of the subgenre details. They took T-shirts and "began to experiment with basic printing and dyeing techniques on capped sleeve T-shirts, to which they added chains, studs, and crude applique, and although it is very labour-intensive, this fresh approach and custom Do It Yourself (DIY) look to their clothes, with its primitive trial influences, would later become one of their established trademarks" (Burton 2017, 290).

Around the same time, in the early to mid-1970s, Richard Hell of Television, and also of the band the Voidoids, wore distressed T-shirts with holes in them, with safety pins used to close them, a style that would be widely copied. Hell's version, which had points in common with Westwood's, is also sometimes considered the first punk T-shirt style, and illustrates how the US and UK punk movements did in fact mix personalities and aesthetics at times. Meanwhile, Hell's contemporaries the Ramones were also wearing T-shirts, paying homage to 1950s rebel and youth-culture history, which they paired with their leather jackets, jeans, and sneakers. Later, they would work with the designer Arturo Vega to develop a logo that encapsulated their image, and the one they came up with was so successful that, today, Ramones T-shirts widely outsell their music by a factor of millions (Browne 2008).

Over time, as punk continued to diversify, T-shirts have remained a constant element of style among almost every scene. Indeed, whether oversized or undersized, ripped-up or crisply athletic, graphic T-shirts have been a crucial piece of the look, and maintain most of the visual and historic elements, of punk rock (Nedorostek and Pappalardo 2008). Appreciation for them as artifacts has grown, and punk T-shirts are now hotly traded, collected, and even chronicled in books such as *Life.Love.Shirts* (Öner and Kuper 2017) and Instagram feeds such as Band of Shirts.

The Cyclical Nature of Fashion

One element that sets punk T-shirts apart from other types of garments is that the mode of their production and dissemination is often closely observed and valued by their consumers. While T-shirts in the punk style are merchandised today through a variety of avenues, the original and most authentic way to source one is through local punk scenes. Within the community they are frequently designed and produced by in-scene people and sold via merchandise tables at shows, or at stores and via catalogs and/or websites within the scene. The punk T-shirt can be purchased already made, as vintage, or it can be bought as a blank shirt with no printing on it through wholesalers or chain stores and repurposed within the scene, often through the use of DIY methods such as silkscreening and patches. Drew, a punk from California, said, "I taught myself how to silkscreen T-shirts (and record covers and patches and jackets) after seeing others had done it." Sometimes the production of the shirts is outsourced and they are ordered in bulk, usually for a band, and often there is a conscientious goal of quality control that includes making clear who did the shirt design, who the producer is, and what their work methods and costs are.

Punk T-shirts were initially deeply embedded in local punk scenes, but as the market for punk rock grew and changed (throughout the 1990s), some chain stores emerged that sit at a midpoint between the punk community and the wider fashionista who is not associated with the scene. Foremost among these is Hot Topic. According to Ryan, a punk from the greater Los Angeles area, "Hot Topic became a thing in the late 90s, and in their early days you could actually get good band shirts there." In-scene boutiques and "core stores" that are retailers where the proprietor and consumer base are coming from within the punk scene will attempt to source their reproduced lines of T-shirts through in-scene distributors, and at times through more commercial wholesalers, while the larger chains, like Hot Topic, more commonly use the larger wholesalers. This consumer and retailer selection process of merchandising production and consumption is similar for in-person and online options. The broader distribution through chains and the Internet has provided wider access to the styles. However, the increase in sales options and availability of once exclusive items also means that there is now diffusion away from the lifestyle background that originally informed the "aura" of punk T-shirts, thus initiating a discussion of authenticity and appropriation.

"Appropriation" is a highly contentious concept, often reserved for discussions of race, religion, and ethnicity, and it may be questioned whether punk, as an identity marker, has the same politically charged community characteristics to fall within the same kinds of conversation. While the stakes may be lower regarding appropriation and punk, Boeschenstein and Pereira (2017) explain how the idea of appropriation fits into the discussion of subcultures through its ability to legitimate a commodity. When analyzing the appropriations process, including reappropriations and assigning new meanings, Brown (2007, 17) uses the term "culture circuit" to explain this cycle. A "culture circuit" is when "the commercialization made by manufacturers leads to commercialization made by consumers and thus resets and forms the sub-cultural goods, so that it is reaffirmed as such. The reappropriation and recommodification of something produced for and by the mainstream is able to strengthen the significance of its subcultural sense" (188).

Outside of the punk scene and its related chain retailers, there are also fast-fashion, high-fashion, and general mass-market segments through which graphic T-shirts in punk styles are now sold. In 2016, the luxury retailer Barney's carried a line of Madeworn T-shirts costing $175 apiece that featured bands such as the Misfits and Nirvana (Geslani 2016). In 2018, Saks Fifth Avenue sold T-shirts from Dsqaured2 priced in the $200 range with punk-styled graphics paying homage to the lettering style of Jamie Reid, as well as familiar punk aesthetics, including stripes, newsprint/zine cut-and-paste, and the color black with accents of pink neon. In 2012, the fashion designer Nicolas Ghesquière sent heavy metal graphics down the runway with his "Balenciaga" slogan sweatshirts printed in Iron Maiden's graphic red font and with imagery of that genre (Yotka 2016).

Among this stylistic confusion, some high-fashion punk graphic T-shirts may have roots in the community, as with the designer Hedi Slimane's cut and graphics on T-shirts for Celine and the general vibe with all the lines he creates (McCauley Bowstead 2015; Sherman 2018). Slimane has been known throughout his career to blend his creations with established and up-and-coming alt-music acts, using that influence to create new silhouettes in menswear, such as his signature ultra-thin look and flooded hems, while at the same time making T-shirts of punk and post-punk acts such as Joy Division, the Arctic Monkeys, and Razorlight (Rees-Roberts 2013), among many others. Slimane could be positioned as being in the lineage of Westwood and related designers.

Mass-market and fast-fashion chains also sell an array of licensed or bootleg punk graphic T-shirts, and this may act as a way for an individual to dive into scene aesthetics and memories framed within accessible and on-trend merchandising-focused retailers. Examples found at fast-fashion stores may include a Nirvana T-shirt sold at Urban Outfitters for $39 (the Nirvana Unplugged T-Shirt Dress, sold in 2020), an AC/DC graphic T-shirt retailing at Forever 21 for $17.80 (also in 2018) or a Misfits T-Shirt selling for $16 at ASOS (2020). Because these punk-graphic garments have been manufactured and marketed outside of their initial format, however, they initiate a complicated dialogue about symbolic ownership and appropriation. These shirts are missing some key elements to the subculture, yet may well contain new aspects for their revised usage.

T-shirts are a logical piece to go through fashion trends due to their potential affordability, ease-of-use, and familiar symbols. The "fashion cycle" is the movement of items from innovators to wider society over time. Rogers (1995) explains that products move through the culture, starting with innovation and then going up and then down a usage curve, with rise, peak, decline, and obsolescence. Simultaneously, most people have their "comfortable point," at which they start to pick up on a product on that curve. They can be divided into five categories: "innovators—venturesome; early adopters—respect; early majority—deliberate; late majority—skeptical; and laggards—traditional" (Rogers 1995, 279).[1]

In general, the public at large is not interested in adopting all of punk's aesthetic intricacies, and their lack of insight into the genre's ideological underpinnings would make that nearly impossible anyway (Lewin and Williams 2009). However, some aspects of punk authenticity are within reach for consumers without pushing every boundary, such that some members of the public may try out non-natural hair colors, selected tattoos and body modifications, and, simplest of all, the graphic T-shirt. A conflict arises regarding whether the styles of a subculture were intended as the innovation point on the mainstream curve. But regardless of a purposeful intention to start a new mainstream trend, this often happens.

Matching Closets with Mismatched Lifestyles in Postmodernism

Postmodernism is clearly a touchstone for the way that punk style has infiltrated the mainstream. "We could argue that postmodernism defines an ethos, a set of sensibilities, or a politics of cultural experience and production in which style and image predominate. Thus, although postmodernism may not be about style alone, style is one of the chief characteristics of a postmodern ethos. The term postmodern has been used to describe fashions" (Sturken and Cartwright 2009, 313). Also, according to Featherstone (2007, 92), "with postmodernism, traditional distinctions and hierarchies are collapsed, polyculturalism is acknowledged which fits in with the global circumstance; kitsch, the popular, and difference are celebrated. Their cultural innovation proclaiming a beyond is really a within, a new move within the intellectual game which takes into account the new circumstances of production of cultural goods, which will itself turn be greeted as eminently marketable by cultural intermediaries." As these theorists posit, various cultures are established on an equal footing within postmodernism, and punk is one of them.

Within our current complex social structure, individual wearers' design selections can have varied root intentions and, simultaneously, differing viewpoints they perceive as valid. "To understand the aesthetic of postmodern dress, clothing choices must be examined and viewed in detail separately, then placed within the context of the whole" (Henderson and DeLong 2000, 239). Debates over authenticity and appropriation with design ownership generally center on figuring out what the "context of the whole" is, in terms of the entire ensemble; it's embodiment with the person wearing it; the environment it is worn in; and the social environment surrounding it.

Furthermore, on a logistics level, licensing, counterfeits, "inspired-by" designs, and loving imitations can make it difficult to assign ownership pertaining to design. For the punk T-shirt, this is likely an emotional issue tied to memory before it is a legal one. The fashion industry is ripe with duplications and copies that sometimes result in legal complexities attempting to sort out design ownership versus design inspiration. In 2015, Fordham University became the first institution to "offer a degree in fashion law, consisting of a combination of intellectual property, cargo, and contractual law" (Marte 2015). Licensing is one option for punk bands, artists, and companies to take control of these problems, such as the decision by *Thrasher* magazine to allow the use of its signature logo on garments for the mall-chain Zumiez. This was greeted by mixed reviews from the underground punk and skate scenes, who felt that it would lead to further bootlegs and an overall dramatic uptick in the proliferation of the logo's use among non-skaters. In fact, the retailer Eric Zeimbowicz, a punk skater who owns Refuge Skate Shop in the Metro Detroit area, says,

> You see *Thrasher* flame logo T-shirts everywhere. I'll pick up my daughter from school and I can count kids wearing *Thrasher* shirts and she'll go, "Not one of those

kids skates. Not one of those kids know what *Thrasher* magazine, they don't even know it's a real magazine." . . . Most of the people who are buying that shirt aren't going to the skate shops, they're going to the mall stores like Zumiez that pretend to be skate shops and they sell through them. . . . I think if it was back in like the 80s, like the late 80s people would be like "aw man, dude come on"; now it's like, people know why they did it. I think the education on that stuff now is more out there, where people actually process the like, "oh these dudes are doing, because if they don't the magazine isn't going to exist anymore. Thrasher 's not going to exist anymore.

Zeimbowicz further adds that, to his knowledge, the magazine is self-referential and "makes fun of" their T-shirts' replication within mainstream fashion.

Similarly, the frequency of bootlegging, or reproduction of garments without permission, led the famously anti-corporate punk musician and label owner Ian MacKaye to rethink how shirts for his long-defunct band Minor Threat would be sold in the wider market. The decision was to have the company Tsurt, based out of California, produce and oversee sales of official T-shirts that could be sold at chain retailers, including Urban Outfitters, which targets teen and college-age consumers, some of whom are participants in subculture, but most of whom are not, and who merely aim to dress in a way associated with a current zeitgeist. MacKaye "thinks the asking price ($28) is ridiculous, but he's more or less resigned to it" (Schweitzer 2013). There is also a quandary for punks on the production end, who want to satisfy consumer demand that is creating the need for bootlegs, and thus get them in on the profits of their own imagery, and yet possibly not water down their messaging, their preferences about the industry supply chain, or the notion that there is a social cost of entry for shirt-wearing (i.e., being a punk).

As Trevor, a punk from southeast Michigan explained, "Vintage band shirts from the 1990s are very popular now, and that's in line with the 20-year retro cycle that seems to have held steady for quite a while. It's just another manifestation of consumerism within our capitalist society, and it's not surprising or troubling to me anymore, whereas at the time I was active in the scene it would have pissed me off that others were co-opting the culture."

Results

Modern punk-styled T-shirts are worn by three types of people: the Lifestyle Wearer, the Semi-Adopter, and the Design Wearer. In addition to the aesthetics, the production and consumption process, and the merchandising, impacts one's experience with the garment. The incremental movement along the fashion cycle from one group to another of the three types of wearers is also a movement farther away from garment production and purposeful consumption.

The Lifestyle Wearer

The Lifestyle Wearer feels a kinship with fellow wearers and the music or message of the shirt. Therefore, this wearer is perceived as being "authentic" by others donning the same shirt for similar purposes.

The shirt for the Lifestyle Wearer is generally a standard unisex tunic cut, although occasionally a slim fit or women's cut (referred to as a "girlie-t" by some). Often it is black or neutral colors, such as white or gray, or sometimes red or navy, and occasionally it has "punky" splashes of color such as neon pink or green, but rarely other colors, except if the garment is vintage. The print on the shirt is commonly white or black, though sometimes multicolored, but the simplicity can be related to the lower cost or difficulty of one- or two-color screen printing. Also, this color palette represents the aggressive, contrarian, yet functional and unisex nature of the theme.

Graphic design, including font selection, will represent the particulars of the band, scene, or time period, such as soft lowercase hand-printing from the emo world, the strong caps and block print of straight edge, or the scratchy and hard-to-discern lettering of punk metal. Images are associated with the oeuvre of the band or activity, whether romantic, political, satirical, or in homage to popular references, such as a swastika with a strikethrough or a female symbol with a fist enclosed. Often a band shirt will be an image from an album, including sometimes the band themselves, or a logo or pictorial representation they use in repetition, such the Black Flag bars or Crass's inventive logo.

Lifestyle Wearers usually gets a punk T-shirt if they were present at the band's inception, at a show or a festival, performed the activism associated with the band, know the backstory of the image, and/or know those engaged in the making of the garment. Most likely the garment is purchased at the activity or directly from the band members or the producer of the shirt. Sometimes it can be alternatively acquired, with no money exchanged, in an act of camaraderie. Secondarily, it could be bought from a boutique, a catalogue, a website or zine, a reseller such as an online site, or it could even be self-made.

These items are not promoted by a hired marketing firm and created by other designers distant from the wearer; rather, they are often bought at the event or through an in-scene retailer. The garment represents being a part of the community and/or having knowledge of the community. According to Boyd (2016), "Usually wearing a band T-shirt is seen as a badge of honour, a way of telling the world what cool taste in music you have." Thus, he speaks for the community of Lifestyle Wearers when assuming that someone wearing a band T-shirt would and should be an avid listener.

The merchandising process of the garment, including attention to its production and consumption, is frequently part of what has imbued the T-shirt with its punkness. The garments are associated with experiences, socializing, and ideas, and are commonly worn or kept for long periods of time, furthering their validation of a lifestyle that is not disposable. Lifestyle Wearers may not see their usage as innovators or early adopters on the larger fashion cycle, but instead may consider it as insular.

Sarah, a punk from Ottawa and Montreal, reflecting on band T-shirts, said this:

> There is an etiquette and value attached specifically to band tees that I've come to identify with. Band tees should be purchased when seeing that band performed. At the very least you should have seen the band live. You don't wear the tee at the show you are buying it from and usually avoid wearing it to that band's future shows unless you are die-hard fan. The Ramones and Joy Division are two bands who are frequently found on tees in mainstream stores and worn as an "edgy/cool" item frequently by those not in the scene (and usually are assumed to have never seen or really know the music of these bands). It feels like a cultural appropriation but also a way to identify "posers." T-shirts are also a primary revenue source and promotional tool for small local bands who tend to make very little money off cover or CD sales. Big companies taking over that space is frustrating.

The Semi-Adopter

The Semi-Adopter uses the garment on the fashion cycle as a different kind of social vehicle than the Lifestyle Wearer. This wearer has some familiarity with the music and scene related to the punk T-shirt on a surface level, but is not actively engaged with the scene. Often these individuals are aware of the punk content that has crossed from the underground to wider media coverage, yet may not know the details, smaller bands, and related activities or lifestyle choices, and do not self-identify as punk.

Caroline, a fashion student who does not identify as punk, explains:

> I have a few T-shirts from the Ramones, CBGBs, the Doors, the Clash, Led Zeppelin, and Rolling Stones. I chose them based off of the music I listened to growing up and still listen to, and for style reasons because I loved how the band logos and graphics look and remind me of the music and time/style periods I love. I wear them whenever. Recently I have liked wearing them when I go out with my friends and style it up for night time.

As Caroline's words indicate, the motivations of the Semi-Adopter may be a mix of being on trend for mainstream styles and being able to live within conventional boundaries, yet they role play an edgy persona of subculture without the risk of being seen as a social outcast. Wendy Ezrailson, the former owner of the punk- and subculture-oriented boutique Commander Salamander in Washington, DC, described a portion of her customers as "wanna-bes," in a manner that would have some of them fall into the Semi-Adopter category. She said that "they wanted to be a punk. But they didn't have the courage." She explained that some local punks would derive their styles through disparate routes of innovation, while some of her customers were looking to have that previously worked out for them, so that they could come to her store and the styles were laid out for their selection, in line with the rise/peak and majority placements on the fashion cycle. Shopping at her store was certainly not the same as complying with mainstream trends, but she acknowledges that some of her customer base were not the initial wearers of the styles.

For both the purchasers and the makers of the T-shirts aimed at the Semi-Adopter, the production and consumption moves further from their hands than the merchandising methods used for T-shirts aimed at the Lifestyle Wearer. Points of separation are possibly developed through mass production, hired designers, and larger corporate retailers, and less attention or awareness is paid to production methodologies.

Semi-Adopter shirts differ as well. They may have the standard silhouette, but also may be more likely to incorporate design trends that are in fashion at that time, such as a V-neck, boat neck, three-quarter sleeves, fringe, or cropped hem. This playing with aesthetics does reflect a connection to originators, such as Vivienne Westwood's stud, chains, and bones embellishments, but for the most part premade adaptations by designers went out of favor with punks. Where Westwood's or, later perhaps, Slimane's creative license was considered innovation within the community, it also picked up a highly complex embodiment. When a style is replicated by a manufacturer outside of the community, it is a complexity of the private and wider fashion cycles' intersection. Mainstream trends and insular ideals may complement one another, but they may also contrast, and this is epitomized by the Semi-Adopter's mixed intent to wear these styles.

The garments of Semi-Adaptors may be purchased from luxury designers, mall and chain stores, mainstream-oriented boutiques, and fast-fashion retailers. This shift in the merchandising system from that of the Lifestyle Wearer impacts the symbolism in the garment. Commonly, consumers buy their first punk band T-shirt at a chain store or big-brand website. These types of wearers certainly draw a stark contrast with in-scene collectors purchasing a T-shirt off eBay or a sweaty fan buying one immediately after the band plays at their merch table at a small club. Austin, a punk from Texas, explained his reaction to the sight of a T-shirt worn by a Semi-Adaptor: "The Nirvana shirt that was sold on tour in the 90s is now at Forever 21 for $20, but the original holds much greater value and respect because of the story, thought, and history behind it."

The Semi-Adopter buys into the "cool factor" of the lifestyle but presents different goals than the Lifestyle Wearer. This wearer's position on the fashion cycle of the early majority (and also early adopters) phase makes the garments that represent punk feel like a commodity up for purchase rather than a lifestyle choice. Another problem is that the symbols and aesthetics on the shirts are not carefully selected, produced, and merchandised in specific ways to correspond with their initially intended meanings. This wearer changes the design meaning by interlacing punk styles and mainstream trends to role play or climb a social ladder, which inevitably makes other punks, like Austin, feel this is a disingenuous usage.

Whether the T-shirts are part of a fashion designer's seasonal line walking on a runway or on a crowded fast-fashion clearance rack with endless quick-change choices, the result is a merchandising system that lends itself to replaceability. Consequently, these consumers are often considered offenders by the Lifestyle Wearer, as they are knowingly using the punk cachet associated with the T-shirt and disregarding, or reducing, the punk lifestyle to a single garment.

To the Lifestyle Wearer the garment is a symbol of experience; thus, when that experience is removed, it becomes a costume. However, Semi-Adopters may see themselves on the larger fashion cycle as having positioned Lifestyle Wearers as innovators they benefit from.

The Design Wearer

Design Wearers are attracted to the punk T-shirt for its aesthetics—the color, the logo, the font—and the feelings it evokes within them. On a continuum, the Design Wearer is the furthest away from the Lifestyle Wearer, as this new consumer barely knows the background of the garment's graphics. However, unlike the Semi-Adopter, these individuals are not aiming for social gains from association. It could be argued the Lifestyle and Design Wearers share some version of authenticity, because the Design Wearer is likely having a gut reaction to the aesthetics not dissimilar to the Lifestyle Wearer's motivations to select those designs.

Mackenzie, a fashion student who does not identify as punk, says this:

> I am guilty of wearing a band tee when I have no association with that particular band/group whatsoever. I have worn a tee with a band's name or logo on it that I have never even heard of or listened to. For example, I own a Ramones tee and a Pink Floyd tank. But for me, it is not really about the specific band. It is more about the overall aesthetic of the shirt and the mood I want to portray to the public when wearing it. When I put on a band tee, I feel eccentric, edgy, and trendy, but without having to try too hard.

Mackenzie clearly admits that her attraction to the band T-shirt is solely design-based; however, she often chooses to wear a band T-shirt when trying to portray a certain mood. Thus, although she is not a participant of the scene, she still understands the nuances of the band's aesthetics.

The Design Wearer is somewhat similar to the Semi-Adopter in both distance from depth of knowledge and removal from the production and distribution process. The shirt itself is likely a close approximation to the look of the Semi-Adopter. The look may be a new standard silhouette tunic with a highly reproduced image of a popular band, or a stylized version of the garment with decorations, faux aging, and what might be deemed a fashion-forward appearance, like asymmetry or embellishments. It can be purchased through all merchandising channels except within the scene, as this wearer is not present for that.

In terms of design symbolism, color and font can denote certain moods and aesthetics. For example, the color black represents power, mystery, evil in some cases, and rebellion in some cultures (Chapman 2010). Also, fonts play a role in design, as "the emotion generated from font choice is directly tied into the shape of the letters and our psychological response to those shapes" (Harrison 2018). In addition to color and font, other T-shirt aesthetics, such as rips, metal embellishments, and specific necklines, all play a role in appealing to the wearer's personal style. The Design Wearer might be drawn to the grayscale image of an animal, the fraying at the neckline, or the jagged font. "Aesthetics implies interest and involvement in what you sense and feel. Aesthetics also relies significantly on the time and place in which you live, to who you are, and to the social groups to which you belong" (DeLong 1998). Because aesthetics can be personal and vary from person to person, DeLong portrays the experience of connecting with a particular design. Involvement with aesthetics is certainly visual, but also involves the other senses and the overall ambiance of the item, in this case the punk T-shirt.

Prior to purchasing the T-shirt, chances are the Design Wearer never listened to the band or participated in the representative activity, but since the purchase, perhaps has begun to explore the scene associated with the imagery. The punk T-shirt could be the Design Wearer's "gateway" into the subculture or other forms of expression that are built off the same set of emotions drawn from those design choices.

Design Wearers may appear to be placed on both the early majority and late majority positions of the fashion cycle because of the mass-market way the T-shirts are acquired and the fact that these buyers are not associating them with the innovator's intentions. However, they also may not see themselves on the larger fashion cycle positioned after the other two wearers, but instead have their own forms of innovation. Within their social scene, the aesthetics of a punk T-shirt may provide a sense of artistic release or identity expression. Their lack of attachment to the garment frees up a path to go in any direction on the cycle. Design Wearers may perceive themselves as innovators, especially to a close-knit group of friends, yet on a larger scale they fall further along the curve. The Lifestyle Wearer may scoff at this usage, as it remains devoid of the action component within the scene and the merchandising process to make the shirt authentically punk; however, it is possible this user is not on the same fashion cycle.

Discussion

Punk clothing, and this case study of its graphic T-shirts, lies on the fashion cycle, or on a series of co-existing cycles; thus, its embodiment is quite varied. Whether there is a legitimate hierarchy of wearers is nuanced. It may be that the punk shirt a Lifestyle Wearer has developed is almost a different garment than what the other two have purchased.

A genre's style can sometimes work as style innovation for wider society, and sometimes, as with punk, when the symbols are built around experience, the style meaning can remain insular. As Young (2008, 60) states, "to say that a work of art is authentic is to say that it is an expression of the experience of one who has lived as a member of a culture. This sort of authenticity may be termed experience authenticity." In some cases, a certain individual or group can claim ownership of the item, depending on original intention. Such intentions include community protection, status, or inclusion within a scene. The various intentions for wearing clothing can lead to the concept of appropriation. It is possible this can apply to punk graphic T-shirts, but it's not simple.

Punk style includes using objects from other communities and then conscientiously remaking them to give them a new meaning. When this is done in reverse, with other consumers using punk objects, it can be contentious, especially if the new use is more passive than active (Sklar 2013). What it comes down to is design purpose for the wearer. A complication lies in whether punk styles are a closed loop meant for privacy, or if they are intended as innovation for the wider society. If elements of punk style were intended to initiate dialogues about revised beauty standards, expanded musical appreciation, or progressive political choices, and then those things are adopted by others, then it may be perceived as punk having its voice heard. The sincere use of a garment that presents those ideas could boil down to follow-through.

Punk Might Be in the Eye of the Beholder

Authenticity is a term that often comes up in conversations surrounding particular clothing items, such as the punk T-shirt. Widdicombe and Wooffitt (1990, 274) delineate between those who "do" punk and those who "are" punk. Correct grounds are needed for genuine membership, but these grounds are not always "available to everyone." According to Elliot and Davies (2006, 156), "in-authenticity of group membership is defined by failing to truly appreciate the culture, history rituals and traditions of the community." Thus, the assumption that those outside of the subculture are seen as inauthentic can be considered a valid concern.

One possibility is that each of the wearers is moving through the Cultural Historical Activity Theory system to reach the outcome of the shirt having their own desired meaning (Engeström 1999). They are learning the symbols of the artifact, dividing the labor of the garment production and consumption, participating in the rules of the community, and imparting their sense of self into the equation. The Lifestyle Wearer may be embodying their day-to-day behavior and ethos. The Semi-Adopter may be portraying a temporary message, without full involvement. The Design Wearer may be playing with identity and rules within their own community. This apprentice learner may absorb available content and practice before moving further inside a community (Lave and Wenger 1991). All are adding their own experiences and purpose, as well as perspective. As Eric of Refuge says, "I think the core purpose is individuality and expressing yourself through fashion. . . . I think that even the younger generations that maybe aren't as worried about the authenticity of the garment or that, I think that their motivation is still totally the same."

A sentiment on authenticity comes from William Force, who asserted the following:

> Familiarity with applicable cultural forms is of chief importance in maintaining a sense of what is and what isn't genuine or real. To "slip up" in this effort is to leave

oneself open to authenticity challenges, such as being "called on your shit" by others in the punk scene when one is too punk or not punk enough with one's "merch." Authenticity practices not only construct the genuine but regularly point to the nongenuine.

(Force 2009, 305)

This is explained in detail by Elise, a punk from Ottawa and Montreal:

> I didn't like the idea of something I deemed so special, so "underground" and anticonformist to be appearing in the mainstream, which is exactly what I was trying to differentiate myself from. But with age and a better understanding of trends, fashion, society, and popular culture, it just makes me shake my head and cringe a little, all the while not taking it too seriously. Of course, I roll my eyes when I see someone wearing a Nirvana shirt who doesn't even know the names of the band members. Of course. But that's why there are such things as claims to authenticity and subcultural capital, and why performance and knowledge can mean so much within the scene itself. If you can't enact or embody punk (or grunge, or hardcore, or metal), it's clear as day that your "affiliation" with the scene is strictly superficial and style-based, rather than anything else.

Differing types of garment production can be perceived as inauthentic by the initial wearers. According to Young (2008, 46), "as used by an insider, an image may have rich symbolic significance. It may be the insigne of a clan or of a deity. As used by an outsider, the same image is simply a strong graphic design. Since the outsider's work lacks the symbolic or cultural significance of works by insiders, there is a sense in which it is inauthentic." Susan Scafidi (2005, 94), of Fordham University's fashion law program, writes that "cultural appropriation rarely occurs without at least some consideration of the significance of the original product, if only to ensure its marketability." Thus, she believes that designers (though perhaps not consumers) are fully aware of their use of another culture's product. At some point, the tipping point can become appropriation, as the fashion cycle begins to not resume in its normal manner.

Communication or Appropriation

T-shirts are a seemingly low-stakes way to approach issues of appropriation. Yet the shirts are laden with sentiment. The T-shirt can link a wearer to a scene or introduce a wearer to the aesthetics of a scene, and perhaps act as a gateway for membership. There are considerations of whether there exists a hierarchy of garment usage within postmodernism.

Wearing a subcultural graphic T-shirt without strong background can be seen as insincere, callous, or even downright foolish if the shirt's messaging blatantly contradicts other aspects of the wearer's existence. This is generally when the dreaded title "poser" populates conversations and gains power. Within a postmodern society, it is difficult to lay claim to a certain garment. Considering the impact of fast fashion and wide image distribution through social media, items move along the fashion cycle more quickly than items in the modern and premodern eras. However, there does seem to be a tipping point for this sense of ownership and consequent theft, or at least an overstepping. The apparel market is growing faster than the global economy, according to Singh (2017), and nowadays fast fashion relies on streamlined supply chains, globally integrated guidelines, and a quick implementation process.

Conclusions

The punk graphic T-shirt in North America creates three types of wearers as it moves through various fashion cycles. Sometimes it shifts from one to another, and sometimes it is in use among all at the same time. The social communication and general function of the garment are impacted and nuanced by the wearer's intention and the viewer's perception of the T-shirt and its wearer. It is a case study of merchandising, consumption, and aesthetics, and at its core it is about authenticity and sincerity. A distinction must be made between aligning with current fashion trends and changing a shirt to achieve personalization purposes. This is complicated, as many who buy fast fashion or high fashion are choosing the more distinctive manner in an effort to personalize themselves, especially in this Instagram era when everyone wants to feel like an individual. Some of the concepts parallel the Hell or Westwood goals, but they lose the co-alignment with Dean and Brando, and their utilitarian and rebellious use of the T-shirt. Thus, the shirt allows for individuals to draw attention to themselves, so that one gets the "look at me" quality without the "I'm with my own special gang" aspect.

While it has wide appeal, the punk T-shirt remains special and relevant specifically to the punks. Their wide usage does not strip the punk T-shirts of their initial intent or validity. The mass usage is parallel and challenging, but nuanced too. In the end, the garment's meaning lies in the eye of the beholder and his or her community, which makes the action of wearing a punk T-shirt highly multifaceted.

Note

1. Note that an individual may be an innovator for one type of product, yet a member of the late majority for another product category. Also, groups such as subcultures can have their own mini fashion cycles, with products and people placed along their private path, and this happens in coexistence with larger society's trends.

References

Bekhrad, J. 2018. "The T-Shirt: A Rebel with a Cause." *BBC*, February 2, 2018. https://www.bbc.com/culture/article/20180202-t-shirts-the-worlds-most-expressive-garment?referer=https%3A%2F%2Fwww.facebook.com%2F.

Boeschenstein, L. and C. Pereira. 2017. "From CBGB to Forever 21: the Ramones T-Shirt and T's Representations on the Mainstream." In *Keep It Simple, Make It Fast! An Approach to Underground Music Scenes*. Vol. 3, edited by P. Guerra and T. Moreira, 185–192. Porto, Portugal: University of Porto.

Boyd, B. 2016. "I'm with the T-Shirt: How a Punk Band Invented a Design Classic." *Irish Times*, October 13, 2016. https://www.irishtimes.com/culture/art-and-design/i-m-with-the-t-shirt-how-a-punk-band-invented-a-design-classic-1.2822727.

Brown, A. 2007. "Rethinking the Subcultural Commodity: The Case of Heavy Metal T-Shirt Culture(s)." In *Youth Cultures: Scenes, Subcultures and Tribes*, edited by P. Hodkinson and W. Deicke, 63–79. New York: Routledge.

Browne, D. 2008. "Hey! Ho! Let's Shop!" *Spin*, February 8, 2008, 35–36.

Burton, R. K. 2017. *Rebel Threads: Clothing of the Bad, Beautiful, and Misunderstood*. London: Laurence King.

Chapman, C. 2010. "Color Theory for Designers, Part 1: The Meaning of Color." *Smashing Magazine*, January 28, 2010. https://www.smashingmagazine.com/2010/01/color-theory-for-designers-part-1-the-meaning-of-color/.

Cochrane, L. 2017. "Not Heard Nirvana? Nevermind . . . How Fashion Co-opted the Band T-Shirt. *Guardian*, July 26, 2017.

DeLong, M. 1998. *The Way We Look: Dress and Aesthetics*. 2nd ed. New York: Fairchild Books.

Elliott, R., and E. Davies. 2006. "Symbolic Brands and Authenticity of Identity Performance." In *Brand Culture*, edited by J. E. Schroeder and M. Salazar-Mörling, 155–167. New York: Routledge.

Engeström, Y. 1999. *Activity theory and individual and social transformation*. In *Perspectives on Activity Theory: Learning in Doing: Social, Cognitive and Computational Perspectives*, edited by Y. Engestrom, R. Miettinen, and R.-L. Punamaki. Cambridge: Cambridge University Press.

Featherstone, M. 2007. *Consumer Culture and Postmodernism*. Los Angeles: SAGE.

Force, W. 2009. "Consumption Styles and the Fluid Complexity of Punk Authenticity." *Symbolic Interaction* 32, no. 4: 289.

Geslani, M. 2016. "Barneys Is Selling Obscenely Expensive Band T-Shirts." *Consequence of Sound*, August 3, 2016. https://consequenceofsound.net/2016/08/barneys-is-selling-obscenely-expensive-band-t-shirts/.

Hanbury, M. 2018. "Target Is Being Sued by Burberry, and It Reveals One of the Biggest Problems Facing the Clothing Industry." *Business Insider*, May 9, 2018.

Harrison, K. 2018. "What Message Does Your Logo Convey?" *Forbes*, August 14, 2018. https://www.forbes.com/sites/kateharrison/2018/08/14/what-message-does-your-logo-convey/#42072a723741.

Heaney, K. 2017. "Hey Teens, Please Hang onto Your Concert T-Shirts." *Racked*, June 8, 2017. https://www.racked.com/2017/6/8/15676238/fake-vintage-band-concert-tshirt.

Henderson, B., and M. DeLong. 2000. "Dress in a Postmodern Era: An Analysis of Aesthetic Expression and Motivation." *Clothing and Textiles Research Journal* 4: 237–250.

Kennedy, P. 2013. "Who Made That T-Shirt." *New York Times Magazine*, September 20, 2013. https://www.nytimes.com/2013/09/22/magazine/who-made-that-t-shirt.html.

Lave, J., and E. Wenger. 1991. *Situated Learning: Legitimate Peripheral Participation.* Cambridge: Cambridge University Press.

Lewin, Philip, and J. Patrick Williams. 2009. "The Ideology and Practice of Authenticity in Punk Subculture." In *Authenticity in Self, Culture and Society,* edited by Phillip Vannini and J. Patrick Williams, 65–83. Aldershot, UK: Ashgate.

Marte, M. 2015. "Fordham Becomes First Law School Accredited for Fashion." *Fordham Observer,* August 26, 2015.

McCauley Bowstead, Jay. 2015. "Hedi Slimane and the Reinvention of Menswear. *Critical Studies in Men's Fashion* 2, no. 1: 23–42.

McIntyre, H. 2017. "The New Role Merchandise Plays When Creating a Musician's Brand." *Forbes,* April 17, 2017. https://www.forbes.com/sites/hughmcintyre/2017/04/17/the-new-role-merchandise-plays-when-creating-a-musicians-brand/#5a1642a129e6.

Nedorostek, N., and A. Pappalardo. 2008. *Radio Silence: A Selected Visual History of American Hardcore Music.* New York: MTV Press.

Öner, O., and R. Kuper. 2017. *Life.Love.Shirts: A Collection of Hardcore Clothing.* Huntington Beach, CA: Revelation Records Publishing.

Rees-Robert, N. 2013. "Boys Keep Swinging: The Fashion Iconography of Hedi Slimane." *Fashion Theory* 17, no. 1: 7–26.

Rogers, E. 1995. *Diffusion of Innovations.* 4th ed. New York: Free Press.

Scafidi, S. 2005. *Who Owns Culture?: Appropriation and Authenticity in American Law.* New Brunswick, NJ: Rutgers University Press.

Schweitzer, A. 2013. "Ian MacKaye Says Urban Outfitters' Minor Threat T-Shirts Are Legitimate." *Washington City Paper,* July 31, 2013. https://www.washingtoncitypaper.com/article/411229/ian-mackaye-responds-to-urban-outfitters-minor-threat-t-shirts/.

Sherman, L. 2018. "Hedi Slimane and the Art of the 'Drop.'" *Business of Fashion,* November 8, 2018. https://www.businessoffashion.com.

Singh, G. 2017. "Fast Fashion Has Changed the Industry and the Economy." Foundation for Economic Education, July 7. https://fee.org/articles/fast-fashion-has-changed-the-industry-and-the-economy/.

Sklar, M. 2013. *Punk Style.* New York: Bloomsbury.

Sturken, M., and L. Cartwright. 2009. *Practices of Looking: An Introduction to Visual Culture.* New York: Oxford University Press.

Tortora, P. G., and S. B. Marcketti. 2015. *Survey of Historic Costume.* 6th ed. New York: Fairchild Books.

Wallander, M. 2012, July 3). "T-Shirt Blues: The Environmental Impact of a T-Shirt." *Huffington Post,* July 3, 2012.

Widdicombe, S., and R. Wooffitt. 1990. "Being" versus "Doing" Punk: On Achieving Authenticity as a Member. *Journal of Language and Social Psychology* 9, no. 4: 257–277.

Winge, T 2012. *Body Style.* New York: Berg.

Yokta, S. 2016. "How Metallica Went Mainstream: The Rise of Metal Iconography in Fashion." *Vogue,* March 31, 2016. https://www.vogue.com/article/metal-logos-in-fashion-vetements-kanye-west-balenciaga.

Young, J. O. 2008. *Cultural Appropriation and the Arts.* Malden, MA: Blackwell.

Quote Citations: Survey

Austin, survey by author, March 12, 2018.

Drew, survey by author, February 17, 2018.
Elise, survey by author, February 22, 2018.
Lauren, survey by author, February 19, 2018.
Robert, survey by author, January 7, 2018.
Ryan, survey by author, January 19, 2018.
Sarah, survey by author, January 28, 2018.
Trevor, survey by author, March 3, 2018.

Quote Citations: Interviews

Caroline, e-mail interview, November 14, 2018.
Eric, personal interview, July 10, 2018.
Mackenzie, e-mail interview, November 11, 2018.
Wendy, personal interview, October 11, 2018.

CHAPTER 22

KICKS IN STYLE
A Punk Design Aesthetic

RUSS BESTLEY

LIKE the music that accompanied it, punk graphic design cannot be tied down to a single set of approaches, processes, or concepts. Punk's visual style was often aggressive and rhetorical, reflecting and commenting on its surroundings, and with a corresponding focus on individuality, creativity, and personal expression that set itself in opposition to the norm. Punk witnessed an explosion of new sounds and styles, from music to fashion, art, graphic design, film, writing and publishing, and embraced a number of ideological positions, including the notion that expertise is unnecessary (anyone can do it), a call-to-arms for action and independence (do-it-yourself, or DIY), and an implicit critical questioning of authority (see Bestley and Ogg 2012; Kugelberg and Savage 2012).

Punk was a term that could be applied to an eclectic and disparate range of activity. This was clear with regard to the diversity of music that fell under its umbrella as the subculture began to coalesce and define itself in the late 1970s, but was equally apparent in relation to punk's visual and graphic languages. Dick Hebdige (1979) first theorized punk's approach to bricolage as a radical process whereby an assemblage of disparate signs was employed as an act of countercultural aggression, primarily through clothing and dress, and subsequently via the use of collage or other visual strategies on flyers, posters, and record sleeves. Hebdige linked these approaches primarily with Jamie Reid's work for the Sex Pistols, and went on to suggest that the visual and aesthetic codes of early UK punk rock, disseminated through a variety of means, were directly related to the "first wave of self-conscious innovators" (Hebdige 1979, 122), an elite vanguard of cultural style-makers.

This suggests that these original innovators created authentic moments of resistance through the employment of bricolage in the construction of new meanings, though the limitations of Hebdige's theoretical model have more recently been questioned (Cartledge 1999; Muggleton 2000). Michael Bracewell (2005, xiii) reflected on the range of interpretations of punk identity, noting that "the history of punk rock has subsequently raised countless issues of ownership and authorship; and at the heart of this dispute lie further questions relating to authenticity. Which was punk rock's real identity? Which version was closest to the founding spirit of the idea?" This notion of "punk authenticity" might be better understood as a reflection of motive and intent, a personal reinvention by participants from a range of backgrounds rather than a stereotypical (and often mythological) voice of "the street." Hebdige went on to argue that once these stylistic innovations were publicized, the subsequent marketing of a style to a wider audience created a distinction "between originals and hangers-on" (1979, 122). However, dress codes also provided punk followers with a collective identity (see Figure 22.1)—as Frank Cartledge later noted, generic styles were widely adopted, creating a common bond among punk fans: "For the 'average' punk a more likely scenario would be that clothing was regarded as an expression of style, a cultural language that formed a community" (Cartledge 1999, 150).

Punk's musical and visual identity was at least in part about group solidarity, although it was often expressed in a language that proclaimed individuality and autonomy. Graphic design styles relating to the punk movement follow similar patterns—the need to be recognized as a part of the new style is counterbalanced by the desire to stand out as an individual or to display an originality of intent. (For a further discussion of subcultural participation and notions of agency and subcultural capital, see Thornton 1995.) Punk's graphic language needed to be recognizable to potential audiences—to be effective, record sleeves generally had to communicate that they contained punk material—but at the same time designers often strove for an individual identity for the band or label within the developing field of punk iconography. While record sleeves could be said to be at the less formal end of the graphic design profession, it is important to note that they are closely related to branding, packaging, and identity design, and that the recognition of visual codes by an intended audience is extremely important to a record's success. Record sleeves, in the most basic sense, are a form of packaging: they protect a fragile plastic disc, while at the same time offering graphic information to a potential buyer.

The provocative, deliberately awkward and amateur image of the early punk explosion—in the UK in particular—also obscures a number of contradictions that merit closer scrutiny. The first of these is the complex relationship between the new generation of punk musicians, artists, and designers and the established music industry, media, fashion, photography, and graphic design professions. While a notion of punk's "Year Zero" has prevailed within the mainstream media, much academic research has questioned this by placing punk on a continuum of subcultural activity dating back to at least the late 1960s and evolving up to the present day in a variety of local and global incarnations (see, for example, Bestley and Ogg 2012; Bestley et al. 2019; McKay 1996). The rhetoric of autonomous youthful rebellion and anti-commercial individuality (a myth in large part derived from the previous two decades of rock 'n' roll history) was to become more closely associated with independent production as the punk subculture evolved.

Graphic design as a practice stemmed largely from the discipline of commercial art in the early 20th century. The role of the designer, particularly in relation to the preparation of artwork for print production, changed radically between the mid-1950s and

FIGURE 22.1. Music press advertisement for punk style clothing, at "dirt cheap prices," *New Musical Express*, November 1977 (author's collection).

late 1970s. A shift towards photolithography in the UK and Europe after World War II led to the widespread adoption of photographic techniques in engraving and platemaking. The professional graphic designer's activities centered on a process of specification, whereby a team of skilled practitioners in what was termed the "art production department" (phototypesetters, type compositors, illustrators, plate-makers, printers, and print finishers)—at least within larger studios—would be given a series of instructions in order to achieve the desired end results. (For further reading on the history of graphic design and links to technological change, see Cherry 1976; Hollis 1994.) The designer's role was to plan, predict, and specify required outcomes, rather than to originate them in their entirety at the drawing board stage. Even with smaller studios and freelance designers, the complexity of the printing process and the cost of machinery placed tight restrictions on the range of activities that could be undertaken without access to larger commercial print operations. The power of the print unions at the time should also not be underestimated, with closed shop agreements across the industry severely curtailing access for nonprofessional designers. Any design material sent to print production had to be stamped by a senior designer affiliated to the print unions before the job could be run. Do-it-yourself punk designers could often fall foul of such rulings, unless alternative production methods could be sourced outside of the print profession (such as photocopying, stamping, screen-printing, and other hands-on techniques), as Malicious Damage designer Mike Coles later recalled:

> A lot of artwork in those days had to have a union stamp on the back, but I had a very accommodating studio manager at one of the studios who'd stamp the back of my jobs so that they went to print OK. . . . I remember the suited and booted union reps coming round to one studio for a meeting with all the freelancers, threatening all sorts of doom and destruction if we didn't all sign up. It was like a visit from the Krays [notorious London gangsters]. (quoted in Bestley 2016)

To an extent, the techniques adopted by Jamie Reid for the Sex Pistols were already widely accepted as the established graphic languages of anger and protest. The *samizdat* tradition of lo-tech graphic material disseminated through personal networks, originally a feature of the postwar Eastern European underground, where the term denoted the clandestine copying and distribution of government-suppressed literature or other media, led to the evolution of a particular visual style associated with subversion and revolution. The natural limitations of simple tools and materials, as well as the quick production of graphic work by untrained designers, led to a repetition of certain graphic conventions: simple black-and-white or two-color artwork, hand folding and binding techniques, and hand-rendered, simple letterpress or typewritten text. It is also important to make a distinction between the origination of artwork for print reproduction and the final artifacts that resulted from the printing and manufacturing process. Reid's original collage and paste-up artwork has been collected by major cultural institutions, including the V&A Museum in London, but the designed objects themselves—mass produced record covers or printed posters, for instance—are often treated as ephemeral and lacking cultural significance. Confusion between the origination and reproduction of graphic material has also led to common misunderstandings, with early punk record sleeves sometimes described as "DIY" purely on their aesthetic qualities, ignoring their commercial mass production.

The long-standing relationship between rock and pop music production and art school training has been investigated by a number of writers, including Simon Frith and Howard Horne (1987). Connections have also been made between punk and earlier art movements, notably to the Situationist International (SI) during the 1960s, in part reflecting interviews with Malcolm McLaren and Jamie Reid, both of whom had a strong interest in the SI, along with the wider late-1960s counterculture in general (Reid and Savage 1987; Savage 1991), but it would be erroneous to extrapolate this personal interest as being reflected by other punk designers. Similarly, connections between the early work of Peter Saville or Malcolm Garrett and modernism have been well established (King 2003; Poynor 2003), but again a direct relationship between the work of later designers within the post-punk subculture and, for instance, Russian Constructivism, is harder to pinpoint. The impact of Herbert Spencer's classic book *Pioneers of Modern Typography* (1969) upon graphic design and typography students in the 1970s should, however, not be underestimated.

A number of thematic design methods can be associated with the punk movement, though they should not be seen in isolation. While precursors to a particular visual approach may be apparent to the art historian, it should not be automatically inferred that the designers knew of those connections when they created the work. New punk graphic styles were often developed by untrained designers, and it would be erroneous to assume an art-historical context, rather than seeking parallels elsewhere within popular visual culture or considering the expediency of designing with available techniques and materials—or indeed simply picking up on the contemporary zeitgeist and their peers in the same scene. The use of parody and pastiche, for instance, has been a common design strategy in political satire for hundreds of years, while visual codes denoting or reflecting a sense of immediacy and the quick dissemination of ideas had been a feature of political propaganda throughout the 20th century. Jamie Reid's awareness of the work of the US and European counterculture may have led him toward more informed interpretations of agitprop graphic material, but many subsequent amateur and do-it-yourself punk designers made no such historical allusions. The look was simple, dirty, and aggressive, and it meant "punk."

Surprisingly, little attention has been paid to the commercial and professional relationship between antecedents in popular culture and punk, particularly the role of the music industry and the business that operates behind the creation and development of new styles and markets. This includes not only investors, managers, marketing teams, promoters, manufacturers, distributors, and other commercial sponsors, but also designers and branding and identity consultants. Punk brought a sense of urgency and energy to a music industry then in a period of stagnation and complacency, and many established professionals took the opportunity to contribute positively to the new movement.[1] While the evolution of a new form of punk-inspired visual communication enabled a generation of young, innovative designers in the UK—from those with art school experience (Jamie Reid, Malcolm Garrett, Linder Sterling, Gee Vaucher, Peter Saville, Neville Brody) to the punk-inspired amateurs who struggled against the odds without any clear historical or aesthetic reference points (Mark Perry, Tony Moon)—it also owed an obvious debt to a generation of graphic designers who could utilize their skills in the marketing and branding of the new style. These included experienced design industry figures such as Barney Bubbles, George "God" Snow, Bill Smith, Jo Mirowski, Paul Henry, Nicholas de Ville, and David Jeffery, along with up-and-coming professionals such as Chris Morton, Russell Mills, Rob O'Connor, Alex McDowell, and Jill Mumford.

A number of professional photographers also moved into music graphics alongside their photographic practice, including Michael Beal, Jill Furmanovsky, and Phil Smee. At the same time, smaller independent operations were obviously much less likely to incorporate a design team, and graphics were usually either produced by the punk groups or labels themselves, or through freelance contracts and commercial pre-press studios. As a result, a do-it-yourself ideology that initially focused on the relationship between authorship and control of an artist's music was extended to their visual identity and the artifacts that were marketed under their name—notably record sleeves and other graphic material.

In some ways, early punk's diversity was its core strength. Creative responses to punk's call-to-arms were often witty and engaging; sometimes radical, challenging, innovative, and experimental; and sometimes simplistic, superficial, or downright inane. There was no inherent punk "style," at least beyond the restrictions imposed by amateur production and a lack of skills or technique—early punk fanzines, for instance, shared aesthetic similarities that were largely a product of the process of design and print manufacture, rather than a set of coordinated intentions. Mark Perry has said that he set out to create a "proper magazine" with *Sniffin' Glue* but admitted that he lacked the skills to create a professional product (Perry, in conversation with the author, Logan Hall, London, November 10, 2016). The result was something of a happy accident—a graphic style that embodied the urgency, energy, and attitude of the new punk DIY generation. Other punk fanzine producers followed suit, though again the visual aesthetic and graphic style reflected as much the tools and techniques employed as it did a desire to emulate successful punk fanzines already in existence. In fact, the opposite is closer to the truth—punk fanzine producers wanted their own work to stand out from the crowd, to retain a sense of individuality and autonomy, in the same way that many bands were looking for their own unique stylistic or rhetorical point of difference.

A New Wave: The New Punk Designers

By the end of 1975, British punk scene-leaders the Sex Pistols were developing their own punk visual style. During the early part of 1976, Helen Wellington-Lloyd designed the first Sex Pistols logo and created a number of early gig flyers for the band, frequently using type cut out from tabloid newspapers, felt pens, and Letraset (a dry transfer, rub-down lettering system used by designers to set small amounts of type) to create a hard-hitting visual aesthetic (see Bestley and Burgess 2018). Jamie Reid began working directly with manager Malcolm McLaren and the band in the summer of 1976, and developed the aesthetic further over the following year. The "ransom note" typographic style was to become synonymous with the Sex Pistols, and to an extent with the wider punk movement itself, though its origins are contested. Various accounts have attributed the origins of the visual style to Wellington-Lloyd and photographer Nils Stevenson, as the latter recalled: "The punk aesthetic was simple. Me and Helen Wellington-Lloyd were doing the handouts for the Pistols, and we ran out of Letraset so we cut up a newspaper and pasted it. If we hadn't run out of the Letraset there wouldn't have been the blackmail lettering. We made things from what was available" (quoted in Robb 2006, 207).

This version of events contradicts earlier statements, including those of Reid himself, who attributes the first use of the ransom-note style to a flyer he produced for a gig at the 100 Club in August 1976 (Reid and Savage 1987). Paul Stolper and Andrew Wilson also note that the design of flyers changed radically that autumn, when Jamie Reid took over full design direction for the group (Stolper and Wilson 2004, 30–32). Elements of the style had certainly been in evidence within Reid's work for SI-influenced Suburban Press in the early 1970s, for which he later recalled, "[W]e had to produce cheap (no money), fast, and effective visuals, so collage was the dominant look; things cut out from papers and magazines—photos and lettering—which [became] the so-called 'blackmail punk' look, which looked great" (quoted in Stafford 2015).

The success—and notoriety—of the Sex Pistols as the figureheads of the new movement was reflected in the wider public acknowledgement of a set of visual stereotypes that sat alongside media clichés and commonly held assumptions about punk music, fashion, and behavior. In terms of graphic design, this was a double-edged sword: on the one hand, punk was beginning to develop a recognizable set of visual styles, largely centered on Reid's work for the Sex Pistols (the "Anarchy in the UK" promotional poster and press ads, and gig flyers, as well as the iconic record sleeve and posters for the group's most notorious single, "God Save the Queen"). However, the sheer power and dominance of that aesthetic coupled with the subculture's self-professed focus on individuality, autonomy, and authenticity meant that other up-and-coming punk bands were conscious of the need to avoid being seen as copying the Sex Pistols and stand out on their own from the pack. Largely due to its powerful visual impact, ransom-note typography—along with safety pins, razor blades, and, more problematically, swastikas—quickly became symbolic of early UK punk in the mainstream media, and therefore a cliché to be best avoided unless the designer's intention was parodic.[2]

When asked to create a visual identity for Buzzcocks, Malcolm Garrett later noted, "I'd already resolved to develop a graphic style for Buzzcocks that was as distinct from what was the visual norm in the rest of music and pop world, as it was from the rough and ready, cut and paste vernacular of the Sex Pistols. I wanted to set Buzzcocks apart from this Punk look, which merely exploited a style that was already proving clichéd and consequently locked in time" (quoted in Brook and Shaughnessy 2016, 9). Garrett attempted to reflect the ironic obtuseness of Buzzcocks' music and lyrics in his approach to their record sleeves and posters, to capture something of their sardonic wit in visual form: "I felt that this approach reflected the group's lyrics, which were on the one hand quite 'domestic,' but also bittersweet, slightly dehumanized (there is no 'he' or 'she' in a Buzzcocks lyric), and somewhat aggressive all at the same time" (quoted in Bestley and Ogg 2012). Other strategies adopted by Garrett included playfully highlighting the production process itself and labeling specially designed bags for the debut album with the word "Product." For the 1978 single "I Don't Mind"/"Autonomy," the United Artists logo and catalogue number were massively enlarged to dominate the sleeve instead of the usual band name and song titles (see Figure 22.2). Garrett had visited the pressing plant at United Artists and noted how records were known throughout the entire process simply by their catalogue number, with no reference to artist, songs, or musical style, and he chose to focus on this mechanical production concept for the design approach. Both songs on the single were taken from the debut album (contradicting punk's widespread value-for-money ideology), a label strategy that Buzzcocks themselves and Garrett disagreed with: the deliberately obtuse promotional poster boldly stated "marketing ploy: the single from the album . . . this single out now, new single out soon."

FIGURE 22.2. Malcom Garrett's design for the rear cover of Buzzcocks' "I Don't Mind"/"Autonomy" single playfully highlights the production process itself (Designer Malcolm Garrett, used with permission).

A number of other designers gained their punk graphic design reputations through close collaboration with up-and-coming groups and labels, including Barney Bubbles (Stiff Records and Radar Records), Gee Vaucher (Crass/Crass Records) and Mike Coles (Killing Joke/Malicious Damage Records). A loan from Dr. Feelgood singer Lee Brilleaux helped to set up the new, independent Stiff Records (founded by Brinsley Schwarz manager Dave Robinson and former Dr. Feelgood manager Jake Riviera), which was to become closely associated with punk after signing the Damned and issuing their debut single, "New Rose," in October 1976, and the album *Damned Damned Damned* in February 1977. Stiff employed graphic designer (and former Hawkwind lighting man) Barney Bubbles to lead their visual identity, along with Chris Morton (aka C-More-Tone), in the process helping to establish a fresh, contemporary, and witty brand image that was to prove influential across the wider punk and new wave subculture (see Balls 2014; Gorman 2008). Details such as these illustrate some of the continuities across the industry as punk apparently exploded, as well as the degree of movement between the old and the new within creative teams behind the scenes.

When Riviera left Stiff to form Radar Records with former United Artists A&R manager Andrew Lauder in late 1977, Bubbles worked across both labels, creating a strong visual identity for Ian Dury and the Blockheads at Stiff while also continuing to work with former Stiff charges Elvis Costello and the Attractions, Nick Lowe, and the Yachts at Radar. Although Bubbles was more experienced within the graphic design profession, having worked as a senior designer for the Conran Group in the 1960s, and subsequently designed album sleeves for Hawkwind, the Sutherland Brothers, Kevin Coyne, the Edgar Broughton Band, and many others, his connection to the music and his attitude toward the corporate music industry helped set him apart. Malcolm Garrett saw himself and the new generation of punk-specific graphic designers as fundamentally distinct from the professional design studios that dominated the music industry, and included Bubbles in his summary of that perceived divide—as part of the "new": "I definitely felt at odds with, if not exactly at war with, the in-house designers and felt that their attempts to produce work for the Stranglers or 999 or whomever was simply not 'authentic' in the way that mine or Barney's or Jamie's was. It isn't really to do with age or generation, just about attitude and 'involvement'" (Garrett, personal correspondence via e-mail, November 6, 2018).

Gee Vaucher was an experienced commercial illustrator, having studied art and design at South-East Essex Technical College and School of Art between 1961 and 1965 (see Vaucher 1999; as well as Binns 2018 and Shukaitis 2016). In 1967 she set up an open house in Epping Forest, Essex, with fellow art graduate Penny Rimbaud (Jeremy Ratter), and both were involved in the late 1960s counterculture. Vaucher traveled to New York in 1977, where she worked as a freelance illustrator for mainstream magazines, including *New York Magazine* and the *New York Times*, before returning to the UK to rejoin Rimbaud, who by this time had established a radically outspoken punk group, Crass. Vaucher's visual work for Crass and for the label that they established, Crass Records, was highly charged and strongly political, reflecting the aesthetic and ideology of the group themselves. In turn, Crass would become hugely influential on a new punk subgenre, retrospectively known as anarcho-punk, and Vaucher's design aesthetic, employing a collage/photomontage sensibility, though in practice largely hand-drawn by the artist herself, helped to establish a visual style for the movement. Virtually all the new designers who attempted to follow in Vaucher's footsteps lacked the technical skill and subtle appreciation of art history and philosophy that was embedded in her work, but at least some rudimentary graphic principles did translate—including stark, black-and-white designs featuring stencil typography and images depicting senior politicians, antiwar themes, animal exploitation, or gender relations.

Mike Coles, by contrast, had only briefly studied art and design prior to becoming involved in the industry. Coles attended art school in northeastern England in the late 1960s but found the atmosphere stifling and left within his first year, spending some time drifting and working in various low-key occupations before relocating to London in 1976. He managed to secure a job as a freelance paste-up artist at a studio that, in his words, was "one of the last of the old-fashioned, traditional art studios left in London—hot metal type, Cow Gum, Letraset, and a tea lady" (personal correspondence vial e-mail, August 22, 2016). A chance meeting with a group of musicians looking to set up a new record label gave Coles the opportunity to apply his design vision to a collective identity, Malicious Damage Records. The commercial success of the main band on the label, Killing Joke, afforded the designer a creative outlet, though he still had to work on commercial briefs for other clients in order to pay the bills. Coles's early work for Killing Joke combined collage with drawing and his own photography, and was as much a product of the mechanical processes he employed as his handiwork. He made extensive use of the photocopier, recopying repeatedly to increase the grain and tone of the image, along with the PMT camera (a large machine used in pre-press studios for scaling monochrome images and producing film copies ready to print) (see Figure 22.3).

FIGURE 22.3. Artwork by Mike Coles for the gatefold cover of Killing Joke's 1980 eponymous debut album (Designer Mike Coles, used with permission).

Like Vaucher and other successful punk and post-punk graphic designers, the level of autonomy that the scene provided was key to Coles's approach: "In my early studio days I wasn't allowed within a typographical mile of a creative brief as I had no training or qualifications, but the artist in me was all the time struggling to get out. Hence the eagerness to get involved with the Malicious Damage set-up" (personal correspondence vial e-mail, August 22, 2016).

Manufacturing Dissent: Design Professionals and DIY Producers

Within the graphic design groups at the major record labels, the need to tap into an evolving market while at the same time offering a sense of uniqueness and originality to artists on the roster was also very familiar. George "God" Snow's identity for the punk group 999 at United Artists was direct, colorful, and hard-hitting, with the group's signature "logo" based on a simple cloakroom ticket. At Polydor, meanwhile, Bill Smith was tasked with the creation of a graphic style for the Jam. Smith chose to tile a wall in the photography studio, break the tiles and spray the name of the band over them—photographed in high contrast monochrome, the raw aesthetic communicated urgency, rebellion, and urban decay, in much the same way that Roberta Bayley's group portrait on the cover of the eponymous debut album by US punk pioneers the Ramones had done the previous year. Such strategies were far from new—while an evolving "punk visual aesthetic" was developing through 1976 and 1977, a number of influential images and identities were the product of professional graphic design studios and designers who had experience of marketing youthful rebellion through rock music going back nearly twenty years. The Rolling Stones, the Who, Led Zeppelin, Black Sabbath, Slade, Alice Cooper, and countless others had been branded as authentic representatives of rock music's dark mission, and the punk brief was not entirely unfamiliar in this respect.

Some of these professional designers had a distinctly un-punk background. Bill Smith created identities for the Jam and the Cure, as well as dozens of other artists from disparate musical fields such as the Fatback Band, the Count Basie Big Band, Peggy Lee, the Hollies, and Hank Williams, while Jo Mirowski created record sleeves for Sham 69 alongside designs for Bing Crosby, the Dubliners, Slade, and James Last at the same label. George Snow designed sleeves for 999, while also creating work for the Groundhogs, Rick Wakeman, and others, and Paul Henry's work for the Stranglers sat beside his sleeve designs for Jan and Dean, Bing Crosby and Shirley Bassey. Prior to working with the Adverts, Nicholas de Ville had enjoyed a successful design career producing record covers for Roxy Music, Sparks, and King Crimson. Jill Mumford, meanwhile, worked within the Polydor and Virgin design teams, creating graphics for punk and new wave groups including XTC, the Depressions, Siouxsie and the Banshees, the Skids, and Sham 69 alongside an eclectic selection of artists, including rockabilly performer Charlie

Feathers, reggae artists the Gladiators, Sly Dunbar, and Prince Far I, and more traditional family fare such as Bert Kaempfert and His Orchestra, Captain Beaky and His Band, and the Band of Her Majesty's Royal Naval Home Command, Portsmouth.

Much like the muddy history of punk's musical evolution, the visual languages that came to be associated with punk had many antecedents and parallels. In some instances, the two came together—the rock photographer Michael Beal's June 1976 sleeve for the second single by the Canvey Island rhythm and blues outfit Eddie and the Hot Rods (a cover of Sam the Sham and the Pharaohs' 1965 hit "Wooly Bully") featured a striking graphic image that he would rework in colorized form for the group's debut album as slightly reinvented punks, *Teenage Depression*, later the same year. Eddie and the Hot Rods were at that time part of a wider pub rock scene that embraced hard-hitting rock music and a down-to-earth approach to live performance that was highly influential on the nascent UK punk scene.[3]

Not only did the music of some of the harder-edged pub rock groups (including Dr. Feelgood, Brinsley Schwarz, and Ian Dury's first band Kilburn and the High Roads) cross over to punk, a number of approaches to visual communication followed suit. Pub rock scene-leaders Dr. Feelgood released their debut album, *Down by the Jetty*, in January 1975, and the sleeve by A.D. Design featured a raw, black-and-white photograph of the band with the windswept, industrialized Thames Estuary behind them. In some ways the design harked back to the era of Chicago blues, from which the band sourced much of their musical inspiration, but at the same time it looked ahead to the urban grit of a punk aesthetic. Dr. Feelgood subsequently topped the charts in the summer of 1976 with the album *Stupidity*, an album that captured the band at the height of their power in live performance. The cover designer for that album, Paul Henry, would be heavily involved in marketing new United Artists signings from the punk scene, the Stranglers, the following year. The similarities did not stop there—plans for the Stranglers' debut initially centered on a live album titled *Dead on Arrival*, recorded at the Nashville Rooms, London, at the end of 1976. The album was intended to follow in the footsteps of Dr. Feelgood while at the same time capturing the spirit of the new wave, but plans were scrapped in favor of a studio recording of the same material, released under the title *Rattus Norvegicus* in April 1977.

Another important factor was the evolution of a do-it-yourself independent punk and post-punk subgenre, whereby groups took control of the whole process of recording and production of their records, usually along with the design and reproduction of sleeve artwork (see Dale 2012). Independence thus became an overtly ideological position as well as an example of self-initiated cottage industry for production and manufacture. As Kevin Lycett of the Mekons reflected on the sleeve design of the group's debut single, "Never Been in a Riot" (Fast Product, 1978), "the DIY letrasetting and collage came from a strongly held stance—no way were you going to let a designer near your artwork. You knew what you wanted to say and you were going to say it. No designer was going to come and pretty it all up and mess with what you were saying, making it just a pose" (quoted in Bestley 2007) (see Figure 22.4). This touches on a key issue in regard to rock music graphics more widely, and particularly to punk graphic design—the notion of

FIGURE 22.4. The Mekons, "Never Been in a Riot" single cover: "no way were you going to let a designer near your artwork."

authenticity and the difficulties faced by writers and critics when attempting a dispassionate and rational analysis of the visual form without relating this directly to the (sub) cultural capital of the artist. Divorcing claims to authenticity—and thus credibility—of a group or artist from the visual communication of their brand identity (through record sleeves and promotional images for instance) is problematic. Adding a critique of the level of direct engagement and authorship further complicates matters for the academic researcher, especially when the punk subculture prides itself on notions of DIY and the avoidance of being seen as a "poseur" through artifice or calculated marketing.

Authenticity came from the ways in which the apparently "natural" and uncorrupted style of punks such as Johnny Rotten struck a chord with audiences. However, this conceit of an apparent absence of staged performance—whether intentional or simply a product of naiveté—only added to a number of paradoxical dilemmas within the subculture, as outlined by Hugh Barker and Yuval Taylor:

> It was widely believed that punk's message was one of being authentic, of cutting through the bollocks and simply telling it how you saw it. But the reality was far more

confused. Punk was riddled with a series of paradoxes: it hymned authenticity but relied heavily on simulation in its performance; it aspired to success on its own terms but glamorized failure; its do-it-yourself aspect raised the issue of how to take and keep control in a genre that glorified the individual against the corporate machine; and it presented itself both as simple negation and as something far more knowing. (Barker and Taylor 2007, 265)

Of course, do-it-yourself ideals and practices predate the punk explosion of the 1970s, from traditional folk music through to the bottleneck rural blues players of the 1930s and 1940s, the 1950s UK skiffle boom, and early 1960s US garage bands. As Louis Barfe (2005) and Travis Elborough (2008) have each noted, popular music traditionally centered on performance, and songwriting and publishing remain at the heart of the industry. Thus, ownership of the *creation* of original music was essentially always central to the medium, with the additional layers of recording and reproduction (records and other physical formats) a secondary, though lucrative, consideration. The punks turned their own do-it-yourself vision into a mantra associated with authenticity, but they were inheriting a tradition that was established many years earlier and would expand much more widely through the following four decades, particularly with the advent of new technologies and the shift toward digital recording and distribution.

While an early independent punk band such as Buzzcocks communicated DIY principles through the context of their debut release (*Spiral Scratch* EP) and associated media commentary, others, such as the Desperate Bicycles, went one stage further, specifically encouraging others to action via the content and the medium itself, through song lyrics and graphic design strategies. Five hundred copies of the Desperate Bicycles debut, "Smokescreen"/"Handlebars," were released on the group's own Refill label in April 1977, with both songs pressed on each side of the record due to the proscriptive cost of cutting a master for two separate sides. The end of the second song features a sole shouted voice—"it was easy, it was cheap, go and do it!" The first pressing sold out within four months, resulting in a profit of £210. Using this money, a second pressing of one thousand records was made, which sold out in a fortnight. The profit from that was used to finance their second release, "The Medium Was Tedium"/"Don't Back the Front" in July 1977, again with both tracks pressed on each side of the record. "The Medium Was Tedium" repeats the lyrical theme and cultural instruction—the words "it was easy, it was cheap, go and do it!" form the chorus. As if to graphically reaffirm the point, the sleeve notes on the back sleeve of the single read, "The Desperate Bicycles [would] really like to know why you haven't made your single yet. . . . So if you can understand, go and join a band. Now it's your turn." (The Desperate Bicycles 1977) (see Figure 22.5).

However, even at this level of punk do-it-yourself activity, the notion of authorship and control of the full means of production is problematic. While the Desperate Bicycles had some autonomy in the creation of their own music, they were at the mercy of commercial facilities for recording, cutting, pressing, and distribution of their records, as well as the printing, folding, and gluing of sleeves and labels. Songs were recorded at a small studio in Dalston, East London, and the records were pressed at Lyntone, an

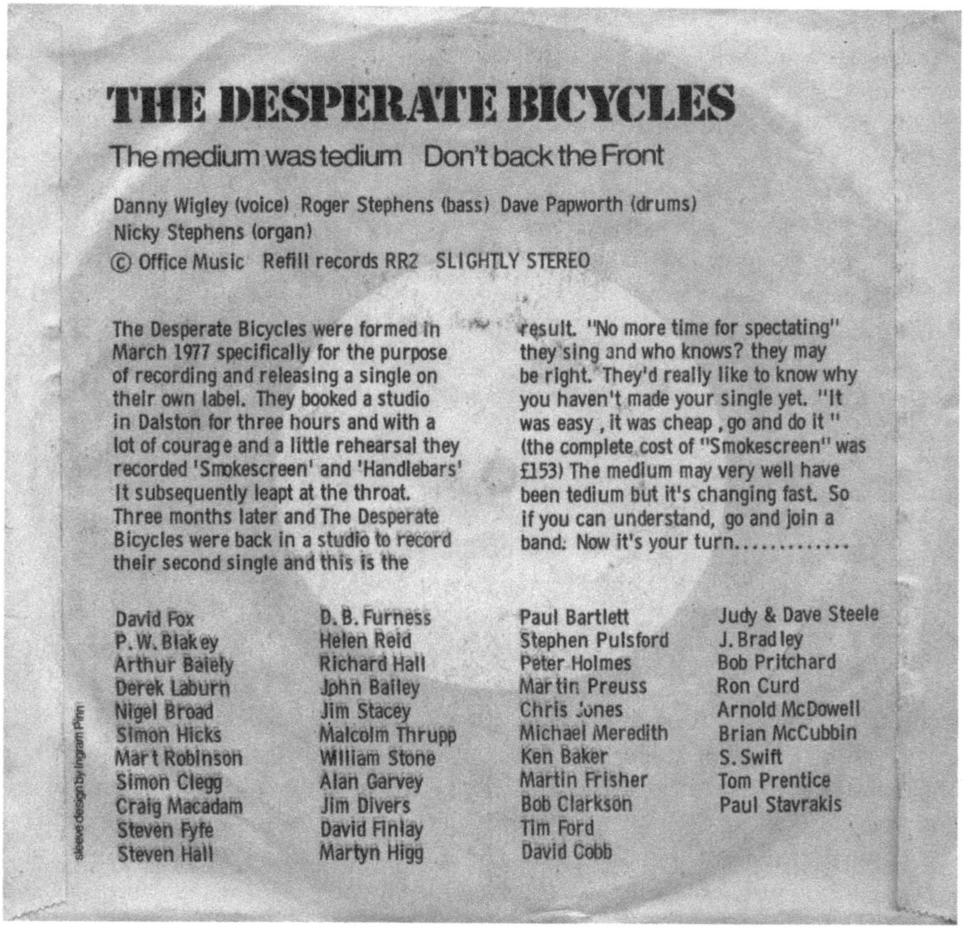

THE DESPERATE BICYCLES
The medium was tedium   Don't back the Front

Danny Wigley (voice) Roger Stephens (bass) Dave Papworth (drums)
Nicky Stephens (organ)
© Office Music Refill records RR2 SLIGHTLY STEREO

The Desperate Bicycles were formed in March 1977 specifically for the purpose of recording and releasing a single on their own label. They booked a studio in Dalston for three hours and with a lot of courage and a little rehearsal they recorded 'Smokescreen' and 'Handlebars' It subsequently leapt at the throat. Three months later and The Desperate Bicycles were back in a studio to record their second single and this is the result. "No more time for spectating" they sing and who knows? they may be right. They'd really like to know why you haven't made your single yet. "It was easy, it was cheap, go and do it" (the complete cost of "Smokescreen" was £153) The medium may very well have been tedium but it's changing fast. So if you can understand, go and join a band. Now it's your turn..............

David Fox
P. W. Blakey
Arthur Baiely
Derek Laburn
Nigel Broad
Simon Hicks
Mart Robinson
Simon Clegg
Craig Macadam
Steven Fyfe
Steven Hall

D. B. Furness
Helen Reid
Richard Hall
John Bailey
Jim Stacey
Malcolm Thrupp
William Stone
Alan Garvey
Jim Divers
David Finlay
Martyn Higg

Paul Bartlett
Stephen Pulsford
Peter Holmes
Martin Preuss
Chris Jones
Michael Meredith
Ken Baker
Martin Frisher
Bob Clarkson
Tim Ford
David Cobb

Judy & Dave Steele
J. Bradley
Bob Pritchard
Ron Curd
Arnold McDowell
Brian McCubbin
S. Swift
Tom Prentice
Paul Stavrakis

sleeve design by Ingram Pinn

FIGURE 22.5. On "The Medium Was Tedium" single cover, the Desperate Bicycles graphically reaffirm and encourage punk's DIY practice: "Now it's your turn..."

established commercial pressing plant in Holloway. Sleeve artwork was designed by Diana Fawcett, who worked as a junior designer with Barney Bubbles, and the sleeves were commercially reproduced—a single color print (red) for the first release and in two colors (blue and black) for the second. In many ways, perhaps, this level of scrutiny regarding the full process of design and reproduction is unnecessary—the Desperate Bicycles were, like most other punk DIY ambassadors, true to the spirit of independence and had their hands tied by the very nature of the physical processes involved in record reproduction. In short, they took control of as much of the process as they could within the means available to them at the time.

Even so, an analysis of such nuances and detail can help to unpack the notion of punk "independence." Barry Lazell's working definition on the establishment of an Indie Chart within the trade journal *Record Business* in January 1980 suggests that in order to be classed as independent, records had to be "independently distributed: produced, manufactured, marketed and put into the shops without recourse to the major record companies" (Lazell 1997, ii; see also Ogg 2009 for a detailed history of independent record labels in the United Kingdom). Part of the problem here lies in the complexity and machinery involved in the manufacture of physical music formats—at least in the late 1970s and early 1980s, prior to the evolution of digital formats and streaming technologies. The major record companies were deeply enmeshed in recording studios, record cutting and pressing plants, and especially commercial distribution at the time—even pioneering independent labels such as Chiswick and Stiff Records established production and distribution deals with major labels, and the success of punk and post-punk artists created a situation where a much greater volume of records needed to be manufactured, distributed, and sold in order to meet demand.

Conclusion: A Punk Graphic Design Legacy

The anarcho-punk and hardcore scenes from the early 1980s onward helped to establish an ideology of punk DIY that has to an extent been internalized by participants and retrospectively applied to the entire history of the subculture as a benchmark for authentic participation. In practice, do-it-yourself activity during the early period of punk was often limited to live performance and fanzine production, along with the rhetorical notion that "anyone can do it," while the music industry still maintained a tight grip on the production and distribution of recorded music (see Bestley 2018). Internal debates within punk communities have also at times failed to recognize the much broader, and longer, history of do-it-yourself cultural activity involving myriad participants unrelated in the slightest to "punk" (see McKay 1998). It is true, however, that the legacy of those earlier punk DIY ideals can still be seen in networks of underground punk activity, notably in the field of live gigs and music distribution. To a degree, contemporary punk's marginalized position in relation to the commercial music industry helps participants to retain a level of autonomy and agency, at least on a relatively small scale of activities, and many punk and hardcore scenes operate largely on a system of mutual support and social networking.

But an accurate history of punk visual aesthetics, and particularly the graphic design styles and methods embraced by the subculture, requires a greater degree of flexibility and nuance. Punk was a continuation of long-standing countercultural themes, and at the same time it was a musical trend that both drew upon and reacted against its immediate context and history. The scope of punk graphic design ranged from the raw and untrained outpourings of teenage rebels to the construction of sophisticated new visual approaches at the hands of active punk participants with a degree of technical training or skill. At the same time it encompassed the branding of successful punk and new wave artists through traditional music industry conventions. Punk's initial commercial success led to the adoption of methods of mass production and distribution, which fitted neatly with the practices and traditions of the industry. At the same time, new styles arose from the contribution of lesser-known artists and designers who could target niche audiences and embrace complex and labor-intensive methods in the production of short batch runs of records and other ephemera. This resonated with punk's rhetoric of independence, autonomy, and authenticity and enabled it to grow into an international subculture that continues to evade recuperation by the industry that (perhaps inadvertently) helped bring it to life.

Notes

1. Of course, the music industry has long held a reputation for maverick approaches to business and commercial operations, and an implicit recognition of the "rebellious" nature of creative artists was certainly not something that suddenly arrived with punk.
2. Parodies include, for example, Television Personalities (1978), *Where's Bill Grundy Now?* EP, London: Kings Road; the Monks (1979), "Johnny B Rotten," London: EMI Records.
3. The group headlined the Mont de Marsan Punk Festival in the south of France in August 1976, with the Damned in support, and returned a year later to headline again, alongside the Clash, the Damned, the Police, and another successful British rhythm and blues group that also overlapped with the early punk scene, Dr. Feelgood.

References

Balls, Richard. 2014. *Be Stiff: The Stiff Records Story*. London: Soundcheck Books.
Barker, Hugh, and Yuval Taylor. 2007. *Faking It: The Quest for Authenticity in Popular Music*. London: Faber.
Barfe, Louis. 2005. *Where Have All The Good Times Gone? The Rise and Fall of the Record Industry*. London: Atlantic Books.
Bestley, Russ. 2007. "Hitsville UK: Punk and Graphic Design in the Faraway Towns, 1976–84." PhD diss., University of the Arts, London.
Bestley, Russ. 2016. "'I Wonder Who Chose the Colour Scheme, It's Very Nice...': Mike Coles, Malicious Damage and *Forty Years in the Wilderness*." *Punk & Post-Punk* 5, no. 3: 311–328.
Bestley, Russ. 2018. "Design It Yourself? Punk's Division of Labour." *Punk & Post-Punk* 7, no. 1: 7–24.
Bestley, Russ, and Paul Burgess. 2018. "Fan Artefacts and Doing It Themselves: The Home-Made Graphics of Punk Devotees." *Punk & Post-Punk* 7, no. 3: 317–340.
Bestley, Russ, Mike Dines, Alastair Gordon, and Paula Guerra, eds. 2019. *The Punk Reader: Research Transmissions from the Local and the Global*. Bristol. UK: Intellect.
Bestley, Russ, and Alex Ogg. 2012. *The Art of Punk: Posters + Flyers + Fanzines + Record Sleeves*. London: Omnibus.
Binns, Rebecca. 2018. "There Is No Authority but Yourself: Political Autonomy, Collective Art Practice, Crass and Anarcho-Punk Visual Conventions in the Work of Gee Vaucher." PhD diss., University of the Arts, London.

Bracewell, Michael. 2005. "Foreword." In *Punk Rock: An Oral History*, edited by John Robb, xi–xiii. London: Ebury Press.
Brook, Tony, and Adrian Shaughnessy, eds. 2016. *Action Time Vision: Punk and Post-Punk 7" Record Sleeves*. London: Unit Editions.
Cartledge, Frank. 1999. "Distress to Impress: Local Punk Fashion and Commodity Exchange." In *Punk Rock: So What? The Cultural Legacy of Punk*, edited by Roger Sabin, 143–153. London: Routledge.
Cherry, David. 1976. *Preparing Artwork for Reproduction*. London: BT Batsford.
Dale, Pete. 2012. *Anyone Can Do It: Empowerment, Tradition and the Punk Underground*. Aldershot, UK: Ashgate.
The Desperate Bicycles. 1977. "The Medium Was Tedium"/"Don't Back the Front." 7″ single. London: Refill Records.
Elborough, Travis. 2008. *The Long-Player Goodbye: The Album from Vinyl to iPod and Back Again*. London: Sceptre.
Frith, Simon, and Howard Horne. 1987. *Art into Pop*. London: Methuen.
Gorman, Paul. 2008. *Reasons to be Cheerful: The Life and Work of Barney Bubbles*. London: Adelita.
Hebdige, Dick. 1979. *Subculture: The Meaning of Style*. London: Routledge.
Hollis, Richard. 1994. *Graphic Design: A Concise History*. London: Thames & Hudson.
King, Emily, ed. 2003. *Designed by Peter Saville*. London: Frieze.
Kugelberg, Johan, and Jon Savage, eds. 2012. *Punk: An Aesthetic*. New York: Rizzoli.
Lazell, Barry. 1997. *Indie Hits: The Complete UK Independent Charts 1980–1989*. London: Cherry Red Books.
McKay, George. 1996. *Senseless Acts of Beauty: Cultures of Resistance since the Sixties*. London: Verso.
McKay, George, ed. 1998. *DIY Culture: Party and Protest in Nineties Britain*. London: Verso.
Muggleton, David. 2000. *Inside Subculture: The Postmodern Meaning of Style*. Oxford: Berg.
Ogg, Alex. 2009. *Independence Days*. London: Cherry Red Books.
Poynor, Rick. 2003. *No More Rules: Graphic Design and Postmodernism*. London: Laurence King.
Reid, Jamie, and Jon Savage. 1987. *Up They Rise: The Incomplete Works of Jamie Reid*. London: Faber.
Robb, John. 2006. *Punk Rock: An Oral History*. London: Ebury Press.
Savage, Jon. 1991. *England's Dreaming: Sex Pistols and Punk Rock*. London: Faber.
Shukaitis, Stevphen, ed. 2016. *Gee Vaucher: Introspective*. Colchester, UK: First Site.
Spencer, Herbert. 1969. *Pioneers of Modern Typography*. London: Ben Uri Gallery and Museum.
Stafford, James. 2015. "Cover Stories: Never Mind the Bollocks, Here's the Sex Pistols." *Diffuser FM*, June 19, 2015. http://diffuser.fm/cover-stories-never-mind-the-bollocks-heres-the-sex-pistols/.
Stolper, Paul, and Andrew Wilson. 2004. *No Future: Sex, Seditionaries and the Sex Pistols*, London: The Hospital Group.
Thornton, Sarah. 1995. *Club Cultures: Music, Media and Subcultural Capital*. Cambridge: Polity Press.
Vaucher, Gee. 1999. *Crass Art and Other Pre-postmodernist Monsters*. London: AK Press.

CHAPTER 23

THE ART OF SLOUCHING
Posture in Punk

MARY FOGARTY

VISCERAL CUES: THE HUNCHED POSTURE IN PUNK

Johnny Rotten's hunched posture set the stage for the semiotics of punk performance. When people think of punk rock, they often visualize a hunched-over performer, and the most notorious figure, when it comes to defining punk's early days and performance aesthetics, was Johnny Rotten (Johnny Lydon). Rotten's "hunched" posture was championed and imitated by his fans, who related his theatrical body to a punk aesthetic. His reception thus exemplifies what is at stake in thinking about corporeality and embodiment in the understanding of musical performance.

In her memoir, Viv Albertine (2014) recalls how she was moved by Rotten's posture during his early performances with the Sex Pistols. She identified kinesthetically with Rotten's performance, and felt that he represented an everydayness and ordinariness that she could relate to in exciting ways, unlike the glamour and fantasy of rock and pop performances that had come before. Suddenly music was something she could make too. Similarly, in *Shakin' All Over: Popular Music and Disability*, George McKay (2013) describes his first impressions of Rotten, and how his hunched posture proved a source of information and identification for the author—a meaningful symbol of attack against an able-bodied discourse. In other words, in both accounts there was an ordinariness to Rotten that felt familiar, yet was also outside the gamut of what representations of popular music had on offer before punk aesthetics.

Every musical genre seems to have its own semiotic posture. Hard rock musicians arc backwards, jazz chanteuses thrust their chests upward, and punk has challenged the pop and rock performance sensibilities that came before it through its embodied ethos. McKay (2013, 11) suggests that "music-centered subcultures have opened up new cultural spaces and corporeal expectations—so punk and post-punk enfreakment were embodied in the seminal example of the staring, sneering, spiky-haired, hunched, pierced, swearing and spit-covered figure of Johnny Rotten." Rotten's hunched posture was exaggerated and extreme, but other punk artists also cut a pose to distinguish themselves from rock musicians. Joey Ramone and Patti Smith both had anterior head tilts that brought their faces to the microphone in a way that performed a sort of reluctance—a posture refusing proper mic technique to signal their broader cultural refusal. This was further exemplified by punk performers who refused to even sing into the microphone (see Spheeris 1981). This anterior tilt with eyes projected downward would be further explored in shoegaze and ska dancing.

In this chapter, I suggest that punk corporeality harkens back to earlier corporeal expectations rooted in the figure of the hunchback in the arts. I also examine pre-punk, classic punk, and post-punk theatrical renderings of posture through the examples of Iggy Pop, Johnny Rotten, and Kurt Cobain, respectively, and demonstrate how posturing relates to and shifts genre conventions and their affective meanings. Historical conditions inform a variety of contemporary understandings of punk posture, and, in this chapter, I question how the measures made of posture impact musical performances. To do so, I will address the recent restatements of older models of posture, taken up in online magazine articles and popular self-help books, that have arguably revitalized pop performances by Justin Bieber and Taylor Swift. I argue that the championing of Rotten's punk posture by his (former) fans offers an alternative to the propriety of posture that emerges in everyday discourses about the body, including Rotten's own take on his persona.

Although not a disability, "bad" posture (i.e., the labeling of nonconforming bodies) does share with disabilities an ongoing stigmatization.[1] I problematize a history of posture education, which has had consequences on the (self-)regulation of bodies, to identify what is at stake for political agendas, including those that center on body surveillance and regulation, even if that regulation is positioned as health advice.

According to Lisa Blackman (2012), bodies can be seen as a process of ongoing entanglement with the world. In other words, posture in a living body is never static. In modern times, the self and identity are increasingly and intimately tied to the body (Giddens 1991). Corporeality is constantly regulated in society, from the learning of social etiquettes, through formal techniques of work, dance, and sport, to expectations about gendered performances in everyday life (Foster 1997; Wolff 1997). Corporeality takes on special significance in the British educational system, where students were taught, post–World War II, to "sit up straight." In fact, as Sander Gilman (2018, 63) notes in his recent survey, *Stand Up Straight! A History of Posture*, the military meaning of posture (related to holding a weapon) appears as early as 1611. If the British educational system, based on military techniques and practices, demanded that students "sit up straight," then punk's semiotic rejection of this model is both symbolic and familial. To choose not to sit or stand up straight—regardless of the reason—was to challenge an educational system bent on organizing the body properly to be an "upright citizen." This syncs with the larger "civilizing" process of the middle class, described by the sociologist

Norbert Elias (1982) and historian John F. Kasson (1990), who both demonstrate that the regulation of manners in societies is about distinguishing oneself and one's class from others. This education inevitably takes place in the home. Notably, punk's parent culture also involved fathers that did military service and often asserted military expectations about upright posture and its regiment on their children. Posture was also explicitly connected with the disciplining of students in schools, whether seated or standing, and used pedagogically to create judgments about what sort of a body a superior, moral person would have. This connection between posture and pedagogy appears in John Locke's (1712) *Some Thoughts concerning Education*, through a phrase from the Latin poet Juvenal: "mens sana in corpora sano," which translates as "a healthy mind in a healthy body," cementing the idea that mind and body should be educated as one.

Hunchbacked: The Rotten Rise to Power

Attention has been paid in the press to Johnny Rotten's childhood meningitis as the cause of issues with his eye and spine (McKay 2013; Semenza 2010). Rotten himself discusses his posture and spine in his memoir, *Rotten: No Irish, No Blacks, No Dogs*: "They [the nurses] would draw fluid out of my spine, which was bloody painful. I'll always remember that because it's curved my spine. I developed a bit of a hunchback" (Lydon 1994, 17). Although this is medically improbable, Rotten's account explicitly links pain with his curve. Similarly, in an interview for *GQ* (Marino 2016), Rotten was asked what the experience of having his spinal fluid drained, as part of the treatment of his meningitis, felt like:

> Severe pain. Severe, unreal pain starting at the tip of the anus where your tailbone is, going all the way up into your brain. I can feel the spine curling with it, the lung punctures.... I was, you know, just born to be tortured, really.

And when asked if this affects his posture:

> Yeah, so much so. Yeah, it curves my spine permanently, which is why I have a slight stoop figure. I was supposed to put a broom handle between my arms to straighten my back, but I just found that did nothing but cause more pain.
>
> (Marino 2016)

There isn't any scientific evidence of the links between spinal taps and the curving of the spine. But what is made clear is that this assignment that Rotten was tasked with, to "fix" his posture in a violent way with a broom, has undertones of cruel discipline or maybe even corporal punishment. Rotten's recollections encompass the body as a site of self-construction, and speak to a longer trajectory of body posture education, with its roots in military drills, sports training in the image of the statuary of ancient Greece, and beliefs that the body can be trained into a "natural" or perfected alignment.

Whereas most of the contemporary media coverage about the posture of performers suggests that fixing one's posture will also fix pain (the organizing rationale of so-called posture experts), it is clear from Rotten's account (and contemporary scientific studies) that one can do more harm than good if trying violently to modify one's body into what is considered a "proper" or superior posture.

These attitudes, however, need to be placed against a different set of realities. Although slouching was described by punk fans at the time as distinct from the conventions of popular music, representations of the figure of the hunchback in art practices date back further. Rotten described how the persona of Richard III and the Hunchback of Notre Dame resonated with, and potentially informed, his onstage performances (Temple 2000). The persona of a man who overcomes his physical deformities to gain power and success is the aspect that resonated with Rotten the most (Semenza 2010).

This more celebratory or hopeful reading departs starkly from art representations of the hunchback in the Hellenistic and Roman times, which have most often been of marginalized men, and in most cases are accompanied by "grotesque, facial features and an emotive expression (Trentin 2015, 15). Yet they are treated as subaltern beings. With punk rock, the subaltern is personified but the effect differs. The semiotic of punk etched by subcultural theories that explained punk, notably early accounts by Dick Hebdige (1979) and Dave Laing (1985), originate in sociological theories of social stigma. The move, it would appear, seems to have been from the hunchback as deformed social outcast or "other" to a deliberate, even defiant, art of slouching, a kinesthetic operation to refuse dominant conventions of mainstream entertainment. The move from subaltern and subservient hunchback to abject refusal of the parent culture in punk rock is the abject refusal of straight society in a manner nonetheless distinct from rock's earlier refusals. Further to that, theatrical representations offer up an understanding beyond semiotic readings (forever etched into the fabric of punk studies). Much of the historical coverage I offer later in the chapter predates vaccines for polio and other diseases, and so helps in understanding the emergence of punk's semiotic understandings when posture became less linked to disease and more readily perceived as an aesthetic area. In other words, punk performances embodied the undoing of Western models of civilization through techniques of the body that caved in on themselves.[2]

It's perhaps not surprising, then, that uber-erect posture figures in alt-right patriarchy, such as the work of Jordan Peterson (2018, 1). Unlike Rotten, whose mantras included "I Am Anarchy" and "Cash from Chaos," Peterson sees posture as an "antidote to chaos," as the subtitle of his self-help book tells us. In the chapter titled "Stand Up Straight with Your Shoulders Back," he visits some of the scholarship around the posture of lobsters, to speculate that having a confident posture is central to the good life.[3] Wildly criticized for cherry-picking the scientific claims, what is more striking is the location of evolutionary theory in this work about human bodies.

Posture has been seen as a biological signifier of domination in animals (birds), but its link to masculinity is tenuous, and generally touted by discredited defenders of the patriarchy, like Peterson. Peterson[4] describes the songs of songbirds as being about domination and warding off competitors. Similarly, he argues that chickens also have dominance hierarchies. In the first chapter of his book, he explains how "serotonin helps regulate postural flexion," and how lobsters that win a contest over territory have different brain chemistry than losing lobsters, which is reflected in their postures. In his model, the males assert dominance and the female lobsters are attracted to the winners. He complicates this argument briefly, but the general point is that acting and being aggressive (in touch with the "monster" inside yourself) is a good power move.[5]

Although Peterson's understanding of the centrality of posture to exhibitions of male dominance is rooted in biological rhetoric, the impetus is taken up in a similar fashion to how popular music video directors treat posture in performance. For example, Director X (2017) described in an interview at Toronto's TIFF Bell Lightbox how he taught Justin Bieber to have an "S" posture, to show his confidence and authority as an alpha male:

> I taught him this thing called the "S," is what I called it at the time. So well if so. . . . If you push the small of your back, forward, it puts you into proper posture. So really it's an alpha male thing. . . . I could say hit the "s" . . . and [he'd] stand up a little straighter.

The "S" posture isn't Director X's idea but rather the contemporary popular understanding of the "correct" shape of the spine's curves. Yet the consideration of posture as a survival tactic, and one that indicates having power over others, is not insignificant to this discussion. Punk posture does the opposite—or at least that's what another popular self-help book suggests. In Jen Sincero's bestselling self-help book, *You Are a Badass: How to Stop Doubting Your Greatness and Start Living an Awesome Life* (2013), she reminisces that she was once in a punk band, but then sorted herself out, improved her posture and appearance, and joined the world of making money and having commercial success. Each of these accounts, by Peterson, Director X, and Sincero, associates organization of the body with success in society, and success in society with competitive domination over others. Although these seem in direct opposition to punk's questioning of the values of society and its measures of success, Rotten's performance similarly presents the overcoming of hunchback "deformity" to gather power as the symbolic exercise his performance is infused with.

In 1968 an illustration emerged demonstrating the evolution from ape to man. "The Road to Homo Sapiens," largely discredited now, suggests to viewers that the modern civilized man is the result of progress related to uprightness. This image shares with the etiquette manuals at the turn of the century a visual cueing of how the body should look in an ideal state.[6] Self-help books abound with somatic suggestions on how to correct "alignment." These somatic practices are also cited in media accounts analyzing the posture of politicians and performers by the consultants who weigh in on what is wrong with the posture of various people. This sort of regulation and surveillance of performers often identifies "good" posture with the moral character of the person. Keith

Wailoo (2014) argues that the way in which different political parties in the United States address body pain harkens back to when American soldiers returned from World War II, and decisions needed to be made about how to trust whether or not someone was actually in pain. The Republican policies, concerned that ex-military would take advantage of the system, required more readily the intervention of body experts to determine whether or not someone was indeed in the pain that they purported to be in.

Ideas about training posture did not only come from the military but also from related and problematic agendas such as eugenics, which found its way into both the academy and government practices. The American social historians David Yosifon and Peter N. Stearns (1998, 1061) suggest that American scientists were applying posture to racial analysis, distinguishing Europeans with their "erect spines" from other "less civilized races of men." The 1930s marked a curious shift in some of the medical and health books about posture, which turned to indigenous people for insights into good posture. Some of the books I found suggested that, as opposed to the declining posture of "modern" man organized by technology and increasingly sedentary lifestyles, indigenous peoples had superior posture from a healthier lifestyle. For example, one such book, published in 1930, has chapters such as "How Indians Acquire Pose," with various illustrations showing such postures (Williams 1930). With a similarly exotic lens, Ettie Hornibrook (1931) recommended that married women start the day with belly dancing, and suggested that native dances of the pelvis will help with constipation.

What Rotten offered so clearly was a rejection of what society asked him to be, and his lack of postural correctness, articulated through interviews and persona, is punk. Given that Rotten inspired many people with differently abled bodies, it is no surprise that punk became associated with a hunched-over posture, or that posture was a critical signifier of the rejection of particular ideals cultivated in the society at that time. This would later become explicit in song lyrics and band names, such as Bad Posture, the name of a hardcore band from San Francisco.

The lack of postural correctness may be why Viv Albertine felt empowered by the fact that that Rotten looked like her, and this made her believe that she too could be a musician, yet her account of punk has a stronger root in the DIY aesthetics' rejection of aspirations of power performed through rock's pompous. Here the staging of posture acts as a means of empowerment and inclusion through recognition rather than instruction. There is a social mobility afforded by punk music. In Dave Laing's *One Chord Wonders: Power and Meaning in Punk Rock*, he describes how "[p]unk rock began as a kind of outlawed shadow of that industry and its fate depended equally on the response to it of the industry" (Laing 2015, 4). This is just as true for Rotten's posture, in the shadow of a societal history of an upright posture deemed to be superior or proper. The same can be said for singing styles, with certain techniques, related to the posture of the performer, deemed to be superior (see Gilman 2019). Yet, punk is an outgrowth (tumor!) of rock. As Laing (2015) argues, women in punk provided more explicit disruptions to the images that had come before, while punk rock men retained more of a position on a rock continuum. Support for this idea can be found in the performance postures of Iggy Pop. While he often thrust his chest out as he dominated the crowd like a rock star,[7] his contorted writhing on the ground of the stage, often in broken glass, suggests instead a model that is the antithesis of rock pomp, and thus a crucial precursor to punk rock.

The Labor of Flexion: Pre-Punk Spines, Iggy Pop as Art

Creating music can be seen as an act of labor, and one that shapes the spine of the musician. Iggy Pop himself describes how his posture was transformed through all the plane rides he took, when he couldn't afford first-class tickets, and the toll those hours in cramped seating took on his body.[8] Part of Pop's account of the effect of those plane rides on his posture has to do not only with pain, but also with class. By suggesting that he couldn't afford better seats on planes while traveling as a working artist, he is describing the classed body in constant flexion, and the impact this had on his mobility. Pop suggests that the pain of performance is also to be found in the labor of being a touring artist.[9] Similar to Johnny Rotten, when interviewed and asked questions about his body, Pop uses the opportunity to make the body symbolic and stand in for social critique. For Iggy Pop, the labor of the working class is synced with the working performer.[10]

The wear and tear on his body is as likely from the intensity of his showmanship, which has been an inspiration for visual artists as well as choreographers. Like road crews who never stretch or condition for the labor of the road, many musicians and artists ignore the needs of bodies in motions. (Many successful artists now bring massage therapists on the road and stretch appropriately to care for the body.[11]) In other words, Pop's performances are about spectacle and grand gestures.

Musicians, as a larger group, have previously been identified with both slouching and "hunched-back" posture. Take two health books as examples. First, according to Cleveland Pendleton Hickman (1946, 61), "The most common defect of the standing posture is that of the 'hunched' position. In this, the weight of the body is shifted largely to one leg; the other leg is used chiefly for stability." And, more specifically, "Musicians, watchmakers, and shoemakers often have poor curvature of the spine acquired from the nature of the work" (62). The effects of work, or a profession, on bodies was also discussed in a book from 1906, describing, for example, countrymen as distinct from city folk: "The rustic's gait is heavy, and his walk is slouching. You can see that his natural habitat is a ploughed field" (Spurgeon 1875, 99); or, alternatively, "Drill brings a man's shoulders down, keeps his arms from excessive swinging, expands the chest, shows him what to do with his hands, and, in a word, teaches a man how to walk uprightly." These sorts of consideration of the human body in relation to tools and types of work have been present not only in self-help books about posture, but also in current accounts of posture by (often so-called) posture experts.

Pain is one of the dominant discourses today in the discussion of posture. Whereas in the past, etiquette manuals associated posture with civility, class, and composure, suggesting that ordinary people should improve their posture to reduce or prevent pain. This can also be seen in the surge of articles about Hollywood actresses and female pop stars with "bad posture" in contemporary press coverage. Many articles warn parents that actresses and pop stars are to blame for their children's bad posture, as they are not fulfilling their duties as role models. In other words, it's as much about success as about resemblance—a sort of mobility that celebrity affords.

Visceral performances and facial gestures represent societies in conflict with audience members (Pilkington 2012). This is evident in Hilary Pilkington's research on the Russian punk scene in Vorkuta. She argues that the poses and facial gestures that a band take up, that are contorted and visceral, resonate with an audience of seemingly ordinary citizens living through extraordinary times. Pain also appears in its most exaggerated form, as in the case of performances by the punk band Bikini Kill. Sara Marcus (2010, 13) describes Kathleen Hanna singing in a hunched-forward posture, "holding her left hand to her crotch, a gesture that twists the Madonna-esque virility pose into an act of pained protection." Here the posture is abject. Marcus continues, "Kathleen is instantly back in motion, leaning over as if she might vomit and roaring *I'll resist you with every inch and every breath I'll resist this psychic death.*"

How people hold themselves, and how they move (whether dancing or simply walking down the street) can be interpreted as good or bad, familiar or alien; there is, as described above, a semiotic of posture. For audiences, how artists hold themselves matters, not only for how they identify with (or idolize) particular performers, but also for what they map onto those performances, and how they read meaning onto the body. In the theater of the abject that punk personas provided, punk performers were performing both onstage and off, and developing personas for visceral effects. In other words, they were honing their "techniques of the body" (Mauss 1973) through habits and practices intended to make audiences react.

Why do histories of postural practices matter to punk analysis? For popular music, especially post–World War II, visualization matters, and relates to musicality. Performers such as Johnny Rotten, Iggy Pop, and Kurt Cobain have addressed, in many interviews, how important their bodies have been to the meaning of their performance. Iggy Pop chose to move out in front without his instrument (drums), to demonstrate not only the visual but also the kinesthetic energy of his lyrical meanings. His contortions often involved rolling around on the ground, or, if upright, stretching his arms out as if on a crucifix with microphone in hand (see Figure 23.1).

In other words, the shape of the body and its movements not only frame musical meanings, but also embody them. It's about experiences of pleasure and displeasure that are located in the body, and that inform the identifications with audiences through powerful kinesthetic routes.

Scholars have argued that active concern with posture faded out by the 1960s (Yosifon and Stearns 1998). Yet punk demonstrates how posture was still a source of fascination and meaning for audiences of musical performances. With the rise of music videos in the 1980s (Kaplan 1987), visualization became a hot topic of consideration in popular music scholarship, mostly from the field of film studies. While postmodern

FIGURE 23.1. Iggy Pop in Montreal. Photographer Susan Moss.

interpretations of music videos were subsequently rejected in favor of considerations of the music industry (Goodwin 1992), the kinesthetic sphere of popular music reception remained unacknowledged. And yet, as noted above, claims by artists such as Iggy Pop spoke to his kinesthetic through their choices. PJ Harvey offers an interesting comparison here. Both artists had an interest in sculpture early on, and both decisively moved away from their instruments because they understood the power of their body movement to portray the meanings of their performance, which happened at the kinesthetic level for audiences watching live performances.

Iggy Pop's posture and posing have been the fuel for much attention, and have been positioned as the ideal image of the rock body. In this discourse, impressions of Pop's posture have been likened to the object of the "male gaze."[12] However, as McKay (2013) has pointed out, the (differently abled) male has often been the object of the gaze, and performing onstage offers a public platform for this way of looking. What is interesting is the juxtaposition of punk representations being read as "everyday," and thus unique in the history of musical performance, and also "larger than life," as in the spectacle of bodies on display. The "to-be-looked-at-ness" of rock and punk even extends to the performances of Henry Rollins, known for his bodybuilding, and Ian MacKaye, the lead singer of Fugazi, who promoted straight-edge culture, involving making explicit choices about what not to put in your body (alcohol). The straight-edge movement choice is expressed externally, with Xs on hands, and signifies a moral stance as well (Haenfler 2004, 2006). What is apparent from various examples of shifts in the choices of performers regarding their posture is that they are specific to context. The same is true of audiences. For example, to dance in a very stiff, upright way might be a response to an environment where everyone looks relaxed, and is made interesting through its distinction.

The Morality of Slouching: Kurt Cobain's Grunge Gait

The human body, and choices about its comportment, have long been linked to claims of civility and moral judgments, and this study finds value in staking out some claims about "upright" posture and its aesthetic counterpoint, slouching, as related to punk ethos and political posturing. If punk has been linked to the decline of Western civilization, this transition speaks to white culture's trajectory from colonialism to the postcolonial moment of reparations.[13]

With artists such as Kurt Cobain, the macho rock persona gets explicitly unpacked through his performances, from kissing his bass player and wearing dresses to song lyrics, his networks of feminist performers and influences such as Bikini Kill and the Raincoats, and his slouching persona. Curiously, Kurt Cobain identified his scoliosis as a source of pain (an X-ray apparently of his spine has made its rounds on the Internet). He also suggested that the pain was worsened when he played his guitar. He credits the guitar with making the condition worse, and although this seems to not be consolidated by current understandings as a causal force, it certainly could increase perceived pain. This section will look at the longer history of posture, and where musicians' "bad" posture, especially those holding instruments, fits into this punk and post-punk narrative.

Kurt Cobain identifies Iggy Pop as an early influence among many. Although there are some similarities in their appearances—both white guys with blond bobs of hair—their performance strategies are often in direct opposition. Iggy Pop went without a shirt, actively contorting his muscular, powerful body through spectacular twists and twerks, which demonstrated physical dexterity and control. Kurt Cobain was typically in an oversized long-sleeved shirt or cardigan, and when playing guitar his posture was relaxed unless deconstructing the performance through throwing himself into the drum kit. What the two performers share is a political commentary at the site of the body. Both courted success yet attempted to redefine the terms of the agreement. Kurt Cobain personifies the art of slouching in post-punk performance.

Slouching has been a source of moral indignation for the past century. In the 1919 poem "The Second Coming," the Irish poet W. B. Yeats (1924) described an unknowable "rough beast" that "slouches towards Bethlehem to be born." At the time of the original publication of the poem, etiquette manuals that prescribed how to improve one's posture were hugely popular. Take this account from the book *How to Live: Rules for Healthful Living Based on Modern Science*, published in the same year as the poem: "A slouching attitude is often the result of disease or lack of vitality; but it is also a cause" (Fisher and Fisk 1919, 71). This statement encapsulates the scientific claims of the time that centered a body's health on "proper" posture. Yeats clearly points, in his poem, to a moral dimension, where bad posture reflects on the very humanness of the slouching body, its animal regression evident in its gait and aspect. Semiotically speaking, in this reading, slouching gives an impression that conflates the social and the moral with the biological.

In 1914, only a few years before Yeats's slouching poem was published, one handbook for teaching school children cited the evidence provided by the development of X-ray technology to prove the medical importance of posture:

> Round shoulders and sunken chests are matters of concern to many a parent, and the development of X-ray photography has confirmed the far-reaching harm that may come to both children and adults through failure to achieve and hold the erect position. We now realize that many functional disturbances, both acute and chronic, are traceable to the sag and displacement of organs due to poor posture, so that the carriage of one's head and shoulders may have as much influence upon digestion as the attitude of the chest upon the lungs.
>
> (Bancroft 1914, vii)

These analyses present physical harm as the main consequence of the slouch. By the 1950s and 1960s, X-rays had moved into the world of beauty pageants, where up until 1969 contestants in some contests were judged not only on their exterior beauty, but also on X-rays of their spines and the quality of their postures.

Theories of posture can be found in most of the major philosophers, especially older philosophical claims about what it means to be human. Immanuel Kant believed that improving your posture was an important part of a larger project of self-improvement, although illustrations indicate that this was more of a theoretical and abstract statement for him (Gilman 2018). Friedrich Engels suggested that bipedalism was central to what made humans distinct from other animals because it freed their hands (Yosifon and Stearns 1998). For Charles Darwin, the distinction of humans can be attributed to cognitive abilities, and yet his understanding of capitalist society and its effects on the worker demonstrate how machines began to shape humanity. This emphasis on labor and the body is juxtaposed with a time when languid slouching was an aristocratic norm. Yosifon and Stearns (1998, 1059) write:

> The origins of modern posture standards were part of the redefinition of middle-class etiquette that took shape from the 1750s onward. Previous aristocratic norms had emphasized languid slouching, at least in social settings, and colonial American gentry followed these models in their valuing of ease. Europeans began to reassess their posture habits as part of new military codes and dance styles, beginning in the seventeenth century.

In other words, a slouching posture is culturally contingent in its meanings.[14] For children born in the 1950s, to parents who had most likely experienced the postural regimentation of military service in the Second World War, the decade was an important time for cultural shifts in the United States related to body posture and rigidity. Yosifon and Stearns (1998) have argued that the end of the American "posture wars" occurred by the 1960s, when slouching (or relaxed postures) began to win out over more "uptight" postures of the past. However, Beth Linker (2012) describes an American history of surgical interventions in scoliosis that clearly tie posture to a discourse of disease and disability that is unfounded, and which persisted into the 2000s.

In everyday discourses, slouching is not so much about an aesthetic choice but rather about being shaped by technologies. This is not unlike discourses about cell phones and laptops and how they shape the spine and posture of users. Alexis Pauline Gumbs (2018, 160) writes, "and then there was the posture-breaking impact of the handheld digital device, training everyone's gaze downward and yes stretching the neck." Interestingly, the early etiquette manuals on posture never mention the gaze. This comes later. In punk performances, and later exaggerated in shoegaze as a genre, where the performer is looking contributes greatly to the meaning of any individual performance. From this perspective, jazz is the precursor: with Miles Davis's back turned to the audience, he set the stage.[15] The suggestion that the performance is for the audience, or in spite of them, is a typical interpretation, as is the professional training of the performer that can be inferred by their "projection" to the crowd, often encapsulated in where exactly they seem to look.

There has been a resurgence of interest in the historical impulse to medicalize "proper" posture from self-help books, as well as a resurgence in the popularity of posture consultants within a range of professional disciplines, from somatic training such as the Feldenkrais technique, through osteopathy and physiotherapy, to Pilates, tai chi, and what MiRi Park recently referred to as the "white industrial yoga complex."[16] I argue that this interest, often couched in a scientific discourse about "alignment" and the relief of pain, rather than the moral posture projects of the past, not only reflects contemporary political concerns about shifting populations and their contaminating influences, but is also shaped by them at the level of the body.

To put the scope of this topic in a contemporary perspective, it's useful to think about gait, which is typically defined as how we move when we walk, like Yeats's slouching beast. Gait is one of the easiest ways to recognize another human from a distance. Gait recognition software is even being developed that, although in its early phases of development, has been said to be more accurate than facial recognition software, as people can recognize another individual with more authority at an even further distance (Zhang, Hu, and Wang 2011). Thus, at international border-crossings, people's posture and gait are used as ways of identifying those who do not "belong." Similarly, Beth Linker's research linked the concerns over posture as a "non-contagious epidemic" to current concerns about depression (see Baillie 2018).

Backstage Pass: Pop Posturing versus She-Punks' Posing

Beliefs in superior postural alignment are often informed by various somatic practices, such as the Feldenkrais or Alexander techniques, that are often used in musical training, especially around injuries. These techniques are presented as being in keeping with the latest scientific developments about improving "alignment" and "mobility." Yet clickbait news stories about celebrities, accompanied by paparazzi photos, have devoted a great deal of content to the everyday postures of pop stars, and are often supported by quotes by somatic experts or consultants who weigh in on the matter for exposure.

It would seem from the amount of attention that Taylor Swift's posture has received that she has struggled to abide by such pressures on how to be a "proper" lady. This is reminiscent of how posture has taken on specifically gendered instructions, from the early French courts, when a posture expert was brought in to fix the slouching of the women of the court, to the corsets that demanded a particular way of standing and being shaped to the correct proportions (Gilman 2018). In the Netflix documentary *Taylor Swift: Miss Americana* (Wilson 2020), Swift can be seen barely able to breathe (and commenting on this) while wearing a tight dress for an award ceremony. Around her, we hear her team cooing in surprise at how good she looks.

In contrast, As Vivien Goldman (2019, 4) has suggested in *Revenge of the She-Punks*, when she "first heard Poly Styrene of X-Ray Spex shout, 'Oh Bondage, Up Yours!,'" she "knew at once that with all its saucy frisson, the bondage she sang about was not S&M; rather, it was the patriarchy." Goldman further suggests that, "pre-punk, the more closely a female artist physically resembled Joni Mitchell—tall, thin, and Aryan—the better" (5). Nowhere is this more evident in contemporary times than in the case of Taylor Swift, who was labeled an "Aryan Goddess" by neo-Nazis (Sunderland 2016), a group who also discredited her for hiring Black back-up dancers for her music videos. And yet her posture tells a different story. Taylor Swift's "bad" posture offstage was repeatedly treated as newsworthy by the press, alongside many mostly female celebrities.

In 2015 there was a flurry of online articles about Taylor Swift's posture, critiquing the shape of her spine. Consultants weighed in on how she could fix her posture, sometimes arguing that they were concerned about the pain she may experience. News stories bore titles such as "Could Taylor Swift Be Heading for Back Surgery?" (Wolf 2015) and "Taylor Swift Needs Lessons on Posture" (Twiddlesmith 2015). One journalist even went so far as to report that Taylor Swift's "hunched" posture was related to heartbreak in a relationship (Fredette 2017). By the end of that year, her "statuesque" posture in interviews was described as "nearly inhuman" (Lindner 2015) by MTV News, as if she was the figure of perfection in the media. Swift's interviews (Wilson 2020) reveal that her ambitions were indeed to be as perfect as possible (the opposite of punk ethos), and that she had come around to challenging some of these expectations. It is clear from the accounts of Rotten, Pop, and Cobain that the press and audience are fascinated to discuss nonconforming bodies for males. So although the bodies of women and racialized bodies have always been judged in the press (no explanation required), punk men have been asked to account for their bodies in interviews. In other words, the posture project is as evident in punk as it is in pop.

Another avenue where performers are discredited, often related to their gender, is through the label of poser. "Poser" comes to the English language from the French word *poseur*, but it takes on new meanings. A poser is someone who is pretending to be something they aren't. So, for example, in Viv Albertine's account of a woman in a subculture, she wanted to prove she could play her instrument and thus not be accused of being a poser. Significantly, one of the first uses of the term poseur in the English language was in an obituary of Oscar Wilde, where the author suggests that he put on effeminate airs (so the queer/transphobic origins are there). Likewise, "posing" and "posturing" are derogatory labels for the most part, suggesting someone is not being authentic. (Posing has another meaning: someone who poses for artists, usually nude. Iggy Pop would partake in the art of posing in this capacity as well later in his life.)

Political Posturing

As we have seen, posture is often framed as natural, and thus not often seen as an intentional aesthetic choice, whereas "posturing" is seen as unnatural, or, as in the case of Oscar Wilde, who was called a poseur, is related to an "effeminate" gender performance (Ellis 1918).

Much attention has been paid to where performers of punk are from, encompassing arguments about social class and educational background (see Bestley 2015). I am interested in particular artists and performers who had social mobility, and the relationship between that mobility and representations of class, disability, ethnicity, and gender through bodily comportment, gait, and posture. Regardless of musical genre, my examples have been of artists who had success that situated them in a different economic status from that in which they first began, albeit with careers that had highs and lows (as in the case of Iggy Pop). Entertainers having some degree of success will experience a degree of social mobility, and this has been a part of the lives of musicians throughout history, although exclusions curtailed the careers of women and nonwhite artists, musicians, and dancers. As Friedman (2014, 2–3) suggests,

> a high rate of relative social mobility *is* generally considered one of the strongest indicators of an open, fluid and meritocratic society. However, what I aim to tackle here is rather what may be lost, intellectually, amid the political posturing that dominates thinking on mobility. In particular, simplistic political rhetoric may be threatening to reduce mobility to an increasingly narrow concept, one which collapses "achievement" into measures of economic resource or occupational status and ignores the multi-faceted axes through which most people actually judge personal success and wellbeing.

As we have seen, posture is often framed as natural, and thus not often seen as an intentional aesthetic choice, whereas "posturing" is seen as unnatural, or, as in the case of Oscar Wilde, is related to an "effeminate" gender performance.

And yet, at the same time, posture has long been weaponized and subject to surveillance. Posture is a source of pain and also the solution to various pains, because, if done "right," posture is said to be an extension of the mind and the emotional health of the person. But slouching does become an aesthetic statement that is fulfilled through daily habits. According to Simon Reynolds (1986), physical fitness often gets rejected in alternative cultures. All of this got turned on its head when Maura Jasper and Hilken Mancini published *Punk Rock Aerobics* (2004). Providing a discography of punk tracks, the authors also advise readers to get their "minor sweat" on.

In some theorizations, posture is even directly equated to social mobility. According to Friedman's reading of Bourdieu's (1987, 1993) concept of habitus, class is forever tied to body:

> [Habitus] explains how, even when the mobile person's conscious presentation of self may align with the subjectivities of those that mobility has brought them into contact with, elements of their bodily "hexis"—accent, pronunciation, vocabulary, posture, taste—may always bear the trace of their class origins (Bourdieu 1977, 93–94).
>
> (Friedman 2014)

If posture is tied to social mobility, it holds an especially interesting place in popular music, and especially punk, which posits itself as class-less music. And posture is symbolically significant to musical performance because it is filled with choices on how to stand, how to hold an instrument or microphone, and whether to crowd surf or turn a back on the audience. The choices many punk rockers have made are in direct contrast to the discourses of health, nature, power, and beauty that more ordinarily circulate the topic. We have all been subjected, each generation, to various reminders that test the permeability of the body, from military service to disease to aging. Across generations of punk rock performers, each set to a different medical backdrop, the human body has been shaped by discourse.

Conclusion: Body Techniques Updated

I have considered here the aesthetics of punk performances against the backdrop of a larger history of social constraints and assumptions about posture. This longer historical framing of punk posturing and performance within cultural paradigms also situates the everyday, common-sense thinking about the meaning of posture. The analysis offered by historians lays some of the foundation for my current focus on how performances are experienced socially, but a sociological challenge to normal explanations of the relationship of posture to pain has been explained, in psychological and self-help accounts, is long overdue. Punk performers address a relationship between pain held in the body and public exposure, and through a consideration of this longer narrative about posture, I have analyzed punk's embodied and kinesthetic meanings, and how they compare to considerations of other performances in pop and rock.

Current discourses about posture, healthy bodies and minds, and the spine have been shaped by a longer social history that maps an obsession with posture. Textbooks about women's health demonstrate this, alongside the aesthetic play with posture that accompanied the birth of punk. I suggest that much of our present thinking about posture can be traced to these histories, even as new scientific models of visualization emerge. This ultimately has consequences for our somatic understandings of bodies and alignment, and for our ability to experience new forms of radical art that challenge regulating discourses that propose a one-size-fits-all method for best postural practice.

The history of posture is the history of what it is to be human, and what it means to do work. From etiquette manuals, to self-help books, to schoolteacher's reprimands, posture has been seen as a sign of the civilizing process of how to be an upright citizen. Thus, it makes sense that at the level of the body, punk performances have challenged these assumptions and, at times, provided alternative modalities. Johnny Rotten presented onstage a different way of being in the world that resonated with his audiences, whereas Taylor Swift's posture in paparazzi photos did not allow for the same affordances. Iggy Pop exuded body awareness and bravado, Kurt Cobain the art of slouching. The issue is not how we hold ourselves, but rather how we organize the meanings we make around posture. This necessitates a move beyond a discourse of pain and the body, where "good posture" is seen as the necessary self-improvement measure that all should be willing to take to have success in society. Cripping popular music studies is necessary (McKay 2015), as is moving away from models of human exceptionalism found underpinning conversations about creativity and the arts in the recording and live music industries. Cripping popular music studies involves punk's questioning of the measures of success that are laid out in bodily signage as inevitable.

How can we move beyond scientific discourses about pain, prevalent in accounts by somatic "body experts"? The overvaluing of posture as something that should be transformed or reconfigured needs to be questioned. Onstage performances of spectacular postures, and the everyday, larger-than-life confidence of creative reimagining, are essential to this. Music is a crucial locus for such reimaginings, since music is not just about aesthetic choices, but also about labor, expectations, and disavowal. Through sonic and visual representations, punk offered up a different way of being in the world. It responded to the social and political circumstances encountered by specific bodies with alternative modes of posturing that challenge our regulation of bodies.

This chapter has taken an unusual angle in the analysis of punk rock. I have suggested that various societies have been captivated with how we organize our bodies, rendering our self-presentation as telling in terms of class, ethnicity, sex, sexuality, and able-bodiedness. I did this through an overview of historical ideas about posture—both the word and its activations. My hope is that, like stage performers, people can choose how they want to organize themselves, beyond surveillance, self-surveillance, and ambitions, to fit in. Nowhere is this more apparent than in the person of country star turned pop star Taylor Swift, whose self-presentation morphed from the model of "bad posture," in the press, to a celebration of her "inhuman" and "ideal" posture in interviews. As Gilman (2018, 66) suggests, "art presents a model for perfect posture with all its implications, not a reflection of actual practice." My point here is that we can reorganize our bodies to fit in, but why should we want to?

Notes

1. For McKay (2013), it was harder to find examples of female performers' cripping musical performances. Lucy O'Brien (2002) argues that women with a disability have difficulty in the music business, as women are on display in ways that are far more rigid and purposeful.
2. See Hollis Taylor (2018) for an excellent posthumanist critique of scholarship in the arts that claims dance and music aesthetics to be solely human activities.
3. See Nassim (2018) for a layperson's introduction to a neuroscientist's work in this area.
4. Like Reiman, Peterson is one of the "posture experts" interviewed by Lindner (2015). He deconstructs Taylor Swift's body online and describes her body language as primal and preverbal for humans in her corporate talks on her website.
5. This fits with his larger trajectory of wistfully remembering better days for scholarship before gender and race politics and social constructionism entered the fray—a position that parallels the idea that punk, with its lack of "good" (i.e., dominating) posture, and its reliance on a pose of effeminacy and "gender bending" x, is part of the ruination of the social order.
6. Philosophically, part of the argument about human exceptionality in relation to other species has to do with our uprightness, whether that meant freeing up our hands to work or civilizing projects rooted in sport and oratory. Sandar Gilman (2018) argues that most of our ideas about posture come from the Enlightenment. The thinkers of the Enlightenment shifted the conversation about human posture from a theological basis to incorporate the "language of medicine and science" (62). Harold Cook (2007) identifies how important commerce was to the development of science, and that exchange routes as early as the sixteenth and seventeenth centuries shaped the development of medical advancements as traders exchanged information and sources of treatments. In *Postures: Body Language in Art*, Desmond Morris (2019) argues that in the history of art, those members of higher status were depicted as more upright, and it wasn't until after the French Revolution that more compassionate representations of lower-status members were given in art. He identifies the exhibition of *The Gleaners*, an 1857 painting by Jean François Millet, as one of the most significant moments in art for challenging the content of such representations by depicting in a more sympathetic light three peasant women with bent-over bodies working in a field. (In Flemish art this tradition went back to the sixteenth century, where people are often portrayed bent over and working). However, this portrait still depicted class distinctions in the postures portrayed.
7. See photo on the cover of Steve Waksman's (2009) book *This Ain't the Summer of Love: Conflict and Crossover in Heavy Metal and Punk*.
8. Historians have presented arguments about how furniture forever transformed American culture as the style of living room furniture altered, so this isn't a far stretch.
9. See Singer 2017. Here Iggy Pop is presented as the quintessential *rock* body.
10. Rudolf Laban's (1947) early theories of the body were inspired by his consulting work in factories, where production lines had recently emerged, and the repetitive movements required were causing difficulties for workers. This mirrors the work of Frederick Winslow Taylor in his "time and motion studies" in trying to find the most efficient set of body movements for a given task. Here, a scientific discourse has replaced older models infused with morality judgments. In fact, many dance scholars will now assert that posture is no

longer considered in dance studies (especially posture rooted in morality judgments about class), and that in its place is the scientific study of alignment.
11. I know this from speaking to the massage therapist on the road with Tool in 2019, pre-COVID 19 pandemic and the cancellation of international stadium and arena tours since March 2020.
12. See Iggy Pop's interview in Montreal for an example of this sort of analysis, as the interviewer clearly references ideas about the male gaze from film studies and tries to apply this to Iggy Pop's "to-be-looked-at-ness," and Pop's humorous response to such a query: "Iggy Pop talks about his COLOSSAL career | Red Bull Music Academy," YouTube, October 7, 2016, https://www.youtube.com/watch?v=YoC6FkGrsWw.
13. Robin D. G. Kelley (2020) notably suggested on Episode 2 on *Errol Garner Uncovered* featuring Chick Corea that "the metaphor of Miles Davis single-handedly bringing down Western Civilization is just too precious to ignore."
14. Gait recognition software is even being developed that, although in its early phases of development, has been said to be more accurate than facial recognition software, as people can recognize another individual with more authority at an even further distance (Zhang, Hu, and Wang 2011). Thus, at international border-crossings, people's posture and gait are used as ways of identifying those who do not "belong." Similarly, Beth Linker's research linked the concerns over posture as a "non-contagious epidemic" to current concerns about depression and obesity (see Baillie 2018). In other words, posture set the model for reform programs to come.
15. Alana Gerecke and I discuss the possible meanings of front-facing backs in performance further in Gerecke and Fogarty Woehrel 2019.
16. Interview with MiRi Park on her involvement with digital activism related to Black Lives Matters as part of my presentation for KISMIF 2020 Keep It Simple, Make It Fast! DIY Cultures and Global Challenges. July 11, 2020. https://vimeo.com/464209643 (accessed December 24, 2020).

References

Albertine, Viv. 2014. *Clothes, Clothes, Clothes. Music, Music, Music. Boys, Boys, Boys: A Memoir*. London: Faber and Faber.
Baillie, Katherine Unger. 2018. "Examining 20th-Century America's Obsession with Posture, a Forgotten 'Epidemic.'" An interview with Beth Linker. *Penn Today*, June 7, 2018. https://penntoday.upenn.edu/news/examining-20th-century-americas-obsession-poor-posture-forgotten-epidemic.
Bancroft, Jessie H. 1914. *The Posture of School Children*. New York: Macmillan.
Bestley, Russ. 2015. "(I Want Some) Demystification: Deconstructing Punk." *Punk & Post Punk* 4, no. 2–3: 117–127.
Blackman, Lisa. 2012. *Immaterial Bodies: Affect, Embodiment, Mediation*. London: SAGE.
Bourdieu, Pierre. 1977. *Outline of a Theory of Practice*. London: Cambridge University Press.
Bourdieu, Pierre. 1987. *Distinction: A Social Critique of the Judgement of Taste*. Translated by Richard Nice. Cambridge, MA: Harvard University Press.
Bourdieu, Pierre. 1993. *The Field of Cultural Production: Essays on Art and Literature*. New York: Columbia University Press.

Charmaz, Kathy. 1994. "Identity Dilemmas of Chronically Ill Men." *Sociological Quarterly* 35, no. 2: 269–288.

Cook, Harold. 2007. *Matters of Exchange: Commerce, Medicine, and Science in the Dutch Golden Age*. New Haven, CT: Yale University Press.

Director X. 2017. "DIRECTOR X – In Conversation With . . . | Canada's Top Ten Film Festival | TIFF." 2017. YouTube, February 9, 2017. https://www.youtube.com/watch?v=cTevKSiPbJo.

Elias, Norbert. 1982. *The Civilizing Process*. Vol. 2. New York: Pantheon Books.

Ellis, Havelock. 1918. "A Note on Oscar Wilde." *Lotus Magazine* 9, no. 4: 191–194.

Fisher, Irving, and Eugene Lyman Fisk. 1919. *How to Live: Rules for Healthful Living Based on Modern Science*. New York: Funk & Wagnalls.

Foster, Susan Leigh. 1997. "Dancing Bodies." In *Meaning in Motion: New Cultural Studies of Dance*, edited by Jane Desmond, 235-258. Durham, NC: Duke University Press.

Fredette, Meagan. 2017. "Taylor Swift's Body Language Changed When She Met Joe Alwyn." Refinery29, December 15, 2017. https://www.refinery29.com/en-us/2017/12/185397/taylor-swift-hunchback-ex-songs.

Friedman, S., 2014. "The Price of the Ticket: Rethinking the Experience of Social Mobility." *Sociology* 48, no. 2: 352–368.

Gerecke, Alana, and Mary Fogarty Woehrel. 2019. "Backspace: A Special Issue on Dance Studies." *Performance Matters* 5, no. 1: 1–6.

Giddens, Anthony. 1991. *Modernity and Self-Identity: Self and Society in the Late Modern Age*. Cambridge: Polity.

Gilman, Marina. 2019. "The Science of Voice and the Body." In *The Oxford Handbook of Music and the Body*, edited by Youn Kim and Sander L. Gilman, 62–78. Oxford: Oxford University Press.

Gilman, Sander. 2018. *Stand Up Straight! A History of Posture*. London: Reaktion Books.

Goldman, Vivien. 2019. *Revenge of the She-Punks: A Feminist Music History from Poly Styrene to Pussy Riot*. Austin: University of Austin Press.

Goodwin, Andrew. 1992. *Dancing in the Distraction Factory: Music Television and Popular Culture*. Minneapolis: University of Minnesota Press.

Guerra, Paula. 2014. "Punk, Expectations, Breaches, and Metamorphoses: Portugal, 1977–2012." *Critical Arts* 28, no. 1: 111–122.

Gumbs, Alexis Pauline. 2018. *M Archive: After the End of the World*. Durham, NC: Duke University Press.

Haenfler, Ross. 2004. "Rethinking Subcultural Resistance: Core Values of the Straight Edge Movement." *Journal of Contemporary Ethnography* 33, no. 4: 406–436.

Haenfler, Ross. 2006. *Straight Edge: Clean-Living Youth, Hardcore Punk, and Social Change*. New Brunswick, NJ: Rutgers University Press.

Hebdige, Dick. 1979. *Subculture: The Meaning of Style*. London: Routledge.

Hickman, Cleveland Pendleton. 1946. *Physiological Hygiene*. New York: Prentice-Hall.

Hornibrook, Ettie A. 1931. *Restoration Exercises for Women*. London: William Heinemann Medical Books.

Jasper, Maura, and Hilken Mancini. 2004. *Punk Rock Aerobics*. Cambridge, MA: Da Capo Press.

Kaplan, E. Ann. 1987. *Rocking Around the Clock: Music Television, Postmodernism, and Consumer Culture*. New York & London: Methuen.

Kasson, John F. 1990. *Rudeness and Civility: Manners in Nineteenth-Century Urban America*. New York: Hill and Wang.

Kelley, Robin D. G. 2020. *Erroll Garner Uncovered*. Episode 2, *Chick Corea / Closeup in Swing*. ErrollGarner.com, podcast, August 28, 2020. https://www.errollgarner.com/podcast.
Laban, Rudolf. 1947. *Effort*. London: Macdonald & Evans.
Laing, Dave. 1985. *One Chord Wonders: Power and Meaning in Punk Rock*. Oakland: PM Press.
Laing, Dave. 2015. *One Chord Wonders: Power and Meaning in Punk Rock*. Oakland: PM Press.
Lindner, Emilee. 2015. "16 Times Taylor Swift's Posture was Nearly Inhuman." MTV News, December 29, 2015. http://www.mtv.com/news/2719033/taylor-swift-posture/.
Linker, Beth. 2012. "A Dangerous Curve: The Role of History in America's Scoliosis Screening Programs." *American Journal of Public Health* 102, no. 4: 606–616.
Locke, John. 1712. *Some Thoughts concerning Education*. London: A. & J. Churchill.
Lydon, John. 1994. *Rotten: No Irish, No Blacks, No Dogs*. London: Plexus.
Marcus, Sara. 2010. *Girls to the Front: The True Story of the Riot Grrrl Revolution*. New York: HarperCollins.
Marino, Nick. 2016 "Johnny Rotten: Still a Punk at 60." *GQ* (online), January 31, 2016. https://www.gq.com/story/sex-pistols-johnny-rotten-ravaged-body.
Mauss, Marcel. 1973. "Techniques of the Body." *Economy and Society* 2, no. 1: 70–88.
McKay, George. 2013. *Shakin' All Over: Popular Music and Disability*. Ann Arbor: University of Michigan Press.
McKay, George. 2015. "Punk Rock and Disability: Cripping Subculture." In *The Oxford Handbook of Music and Disability Studies*, edited by B. Howe, S. Jensen-Moutlon, N. Lemer, and J. Straus, 226–245. Oxford: Oxford University Press.
Morris, Desmond. 2019. *Postures: Body Language in Art*. London: Thames & Hudson.
Nassim, Charlotte. 2018. *Lessons from the Lobster: Eve Marder's Work in Neuroscience*. Cambridge, MA: MIT Press.
O'Brien, Lucy. 2002. *She Bop II: The Definitive History of Women in Rock, Pop and Soul*. London: Continuum.
Peterson, Jordan B. 2018. *12 Rules for Life: An Antidote to Chaos*. Toronto: Random House Canada.
Pilkington, Hilary. 2012. "Mutants of the 67th Parallel North": Punk Performance and the Transformation of Everyday Life." *Punk & Post-Punk* 1, no. 3: 323–344.
Reynolds, Simon. 1986. "Against Heath and Efficiency: Independent Music in the 1980s." In *Zoot Suits and Second-Hand Dresses*, edited by Angela McRobbie, 245–255. London: Palgrave Macmillan.
Semenza, Greg Colón. 2010. "God Save the Queene: Sex Pistols, Shakespeare, and Punk [Anti-] History." In *The English Renaissance in Popular Culture: An Age for All Time*, edited by Greg Colón Semenza, 143–164. Reproducing Shakespeare: New Studies in Adaptation and Appropriation. New York: Palgrave Macmillan.
Sincero, Jen. 2013. *You Are a Badass: How to Stop Doubting Your Greatness and Start Living an Awesome Life*. Philadelphia: Running Press.
Singer, Matthew. 2017. "An Annotated History of Iggy Pop's Body." *Williamette Week*, August 15, 2017. https://www.wweek.com/music/2017/08/15/an-annotated-history-of-iggy-pops-body/.
Spheeris, Penelope, dir. 1981. *The Decline of Western Civilization*. Nu-Image Film.
Spurgeon, Charles Haddon. 1875. *Second Series of Lectures to My Students: Being Addresses Delivered to the Students of the Pastors' College, Metropolitan Tabernacle*. London: Passmore and Alabaster, 1875.

Sunderland, Mitchell. 2016. "Can't Shake It Off: How Taylor Swift Became a Nazi Idol." *Vice*, March 23, 2016. https://www.vice.com/en_us/article/ae5x8a/cant-shake-it-off-how-taylor-swift-became-a-nazi-idol.

Taylor, Hollis. 2018. "Can George Dance? Biosemiotics and Human Exceptionalism with a Lyrebird in the Viewfinder." *Social Semiotics* 28, no. 1: 60–76.

Temple, Julien, dir. 2000. *The Filth and the Fury*. London: Film4 Productions.

Trentin, Lisa. 2015. *The Hunchback in Hellenistic and Roman Art*. London: Bloomsbury.

Twiddlesmith, William. 2015. "Taylor Swift Needs Lessons on Posture." *The Blemish*, February 4, 2015. https://theblemish.com/2015/02/taylor-swift-needs-lessons-posture/.

Wailoo, Keith. 2014. *Pain: A Political History*. Baltimore, MD: Johns Hopkins University Press.

Waksman, Steve. 2009. *This Ain't the Summer of Love: Conflict and Crossover in Heavy Metal and Punk*. Berkeley: University of California Press.

Williams, Maud Smith. 1930. *Growing Straight: The Fitness Secret of the American Indian*. New York: A.S. Barnes.

Wilson, Lana, dir. 2020. *Taylor Swift: Miss Americana*. Tremolo Productions.

Wolf, Joanne. 2015. "Could Taylor Swift Be Heading for Back Surgery?" popdust.com. https://www.popdust.com/could-taylor-swift-be-heading-for-back-surgery-1891236125.html.

Wolff, Janet. 1997. "Reinstating Corporeality: Feminism and Body Politics." In *Meaning in Motion: New Cultural Studies of Dance*, edited by Jane Desmond, 81–100. Durham, NC: Duke University Press.

Yeats, William Butler. 1924. "The Second Coming." In *Yeats, Volume I: The Poems, Revised*. New York: Macmillan.

Yosifon, David, and Peter N. Stearns. 1998. "The Rise and Fall of American Posture." *American Historical Review* 103, no. 4: 1057–1095.

Zhang, Zhaoxiang, Maodi Hu, and Yunhong Wang. 2011. "A Survey of Advances in Biometric Gait Recognition." In *Chinese Conference on Biometric Recognition*, 150–158. Berlin: Springer.

CHAPTER 24

WORLD'S END

Punk Films from London and New York, 1977–1984

BENJAMIN HALLIGAN

The film *Saturday Night Fever* (Badham 1977) concludes with the protagonist, seemingly weary of the company of his friends (given over to gang violence and gang rape, and in the wake of the needless death of the youngest and most disorientated), finding a moment of peace in the apartment of his previously unenthused girlfriend. They have reconciled, a future together has begun, and "How Deep Is Your Love" by the Bee Gees—a major international chart hit of 1977—plays over the closing credits. The couple's connection was initially based on shared disco-dancing abilities, and their get-togethers on the dance floor and in the dance studio have offered the opportunity of an escape for each. For Tony Manero (John Travolta), the escape is from his underpaid blue-collar job and suffocating family tensions—where his life at home, as a second-generation Italian immigrant, seems like stepping back into the old country for family meals, in sharp contrast to the grooming he devotes to his appearance, upstairs in his bedroom. Once outside, the very streets of New York seem to have been recast as a dance floor—via mobile shots of Travolta's feet, pacing with a cocksure swagger to the beat of the Bee Gees soundtrack. For Stephanie Mangano (Karen Lynn Gorney), the escape is from more obscure forms of patriarchal exploitation, enacted via her aspirations to a glamourous and independent life, which can be read as calibrated to an imagining of the nightclub Studio 54 (which opened in 1977), not least in her celebrity name-dropping and initial distaste for her uncultured suitor. The final shot of *Saturday Night Fever* frames the couple in her apartment: polished wooden floors, exposed brick walls, a healthy rubber plant, an acoustic guitar resting against a sofa, and a window ledge looking out across Manhattan—a much more desirable locale than the film's initial setting of Tony's Brooklyn (see Figure 24.1). In short, to return to "How Deep Is Your Love," the couple have realized that they were "living in a world of fools / breaking us down when they all should let us be / [since] we belong to you and me," and enshrine this shared sentiment

FIGURE 24.1. From disco ubiquity to urban domesticity: the slum spaces of New York City are reappointed as snug apartments for the upwardly mobile, anticipating the inner-city regeneration of the 1980s, and the communalism of *Friends*, in *Saturday Night Fever* (1977).

in domestication. The New York of 1977 has tested them, and their success in meeting this test has allowed them to take a synchronized step forward, establishing themselves on an upwardly mobile trajectory.

An argument early in the film between Tony and his hardware store manager is telling in this respect. Tony's request for a pay advance to buy a new shirt he has spotted is declined, in part on the paternal grounds that he would spend his money before he had earned it. This prompts Tony to declare "fuck the future!," to which the manager counters, "No, Tony—you can't fuck the future: the future fucks you. It catches up with you and it fucks you if you ain't planned for it." But disco culture (and its competitions and glamour) has allowed Tony to dodge that which is suggested as his preordained fate—to step into this manager's shoes—and so the shirt would have been deemed an enabling factor in this exit strategy.[1] And the imminent existential crisis of uncritically following paternal plans, or believing that a vocation is for life, is illustrated in the film's subplot concerning Tony's older brother. He suddenly returns home and, to the horror of his parents, announces that he has abandoned the priesthood. He is uncertain of his next move, is painfully uncomfortable when he visits a disco with Tony and, talking of a house shared with others also going through this transition, drives off in a battered station wagon (reminiscent of hippies setting out on trips of discovery in the late 1960s—the preferred solution of the generation prior to the disco generation), and then seems to vanish altogether. In choosing disco over hardware retail, Tony's transition to a smarter part of town has begun. This is in stark contrast to the generally bleak position on working class aspirations in American cinema of the 1970s, across almost all New Hollywood (with Jack Nicholson in particular specializing in young characters more gifted than their allotted roles in life), and then into more populist films such as *Slap Shot* (Hill 1977) and *Stripes* (Reitman 1981). Such opportunity now seems a possibility, in *Saturday Night Fever*, for all such Tonys. And, crucially, this matter also seems to be New York's opportunity too. That is, the interior decoration of Stephanie's apartment is redolent of the domestication of New York—the semi-derelict lofts of the Lower East Side now remade into the kind of cramped but cozy city apartments that laid the foundations for the return to the inner cities of young professionals, and the reclamation and remaking of those formerly dangerous and squalid locations. And, with this repopulation, new patterns of life and work and socialization emerge. But this shift is one that is seen to be afforded to a white heterosexuality: the vibrancy of the multiculturalism and queerness of early disco scenes, as recalled by Edmund White (1981) of these years, is erased in the film. From this vantage point, the television series *Friends* (1994–2004, set in Lower Manhattan) and *Gossip Girl* (2007–2012, set across Brooklyn and Manhattan) could be said to pick up where *Saturday Night Fever* ends, one generation beyond.

Saturday Night Fever was made in parallel with the rise of another music-focused youth culture of the late 1970s: punk rock. Indeed, *Saturday Night Fever* can be glimpsed on a cinema marquee in *Blank Generation* (Lommel 1980) as the punk protagonist (played by Richard Hell) leaves plusher uptown environs to travel to the punk club CBGB. *Times Square* (Moyle 1980) opens with a similarly direct contrast: a young female punk playing guitar (riffs and feedback) outside a disco club. But *Saturday Night Fever*'s optimism could not be more different from the types of lifestyle, and modes of living, that the films that looked to punk, rather than disco (and, indeed, the roller disco subgenre), explored. Whereas Tony travels into the metropolis and finds the allure and promise of disco, the waifs, runaways, and dreamers of punk cinema seem to find little there other than dense urban ruins. There is no immediate sign of a postindustrial remaking of the city: the wreckage of buildings—home (or squat) to the distressed, the drug-addled and their dealers, criminals, pimps and prostitutes, and the forgotten elderly, and with an ethnic diversity not evident "uptown"—suggests end times rather than exit. Domestication seems an impossible or entirely irrelevant condition for these transitory figures, who are mostly downwardly mobile, with only a favor or two keeping them from street homelessness, and with a penchant for occasional low-level criminal activities when deemed necessary. Yet punk culture of this time is recalled as redeeming this unenviable situation with moments of collective freedom, arising from the gatherings of those outside any domestic trajectory, and their giddy embrace this marginalized status. Lydia Lunch recalls the Bowery, Times Square, and the cultural scene around CBGB:

> Yes, we were angry, ugly, snotty, and loud . . . [yet b]eneath the scowls of derision, the antagonism and acrimony, and the nearly unbearable shrillness that was our soundtrack, we were howling with delight, laughing like lunatics in the madhouse that was New York City, thrilled to be rubbing up against the freaks and other outcasts, who

somehow, for some unknowable reason, had all decided to run to land's end and all at once scream their bloody heads off.

(Quoted in Moore and Coley 2008, 4)

The "we" and "all" indicates the punk packs that formed around such cultures, as coming together for gigs—that which Dick Hebdige referred to (almost religiously) as punk's "communion of spittle and mutual abuse" ([1979] 1981, 110)—and so constituting a wider scene. And the wreckage of the inner cities is layered into the subcultures presented. That is, unlike the derelict, waiting-for-demolition New York tower blocks that make such distinctive backdrops to films such as *Bye Bye Monkey* (Ferreri 1978) or *Wolfen* (Wadleigh 1981), punk cinema seems to place this wreckage as central to the punk scene. The protagonists live on and in the wreckage, in a precarious and unsettled, liminal state, from which new lifestyles are seen to grow. In the case of *Downtown 81* (Bertoglio 2000), which follows the young black artist Jean (also called Jean-Michel, and played by Jean-Michel Basquiat, then part of the graffiti group with the tag SAMO©), this wreckage makes for a condition of "the studio of the street" (as per Basquiat et al. 2007).[2] For the documentary *D.O.A.: A Rite of Passage* (Kowalski 1981), the setting of grim, wind- and rain-swept London council estates seems to prompt the filmmaker to locate and dissect a control group of hopeless wannabes, in following the formation of the punk group Terry and the Idiots. In both cities, the working-class and sub-working-class districts evidence governmental fiscal crises and the resultant civic paralysis, and so the failure to arrest or turn around postindustrial decline—leaving the inhabitants to endure deteriorating conditions. In the case of New York City, this was the bankruptcy of 1975. In the case of London, this was the "Winter of Discontent" of 1978–1979. And the solutions to these crises were to be found in the coming to power of the New Right: Ronald Reagan in 1981 and Margaret Thatcher in 1979, respectively.

Punk and Alienation

In this context, *Saturday Night Fever*'s "fuck the future" seems a positively proactive choice—one could select this hedonistic option or alternatively remain financially prudent. The Sex Pistols' famous outro to "God Save the Queen" bluntly restated, three times, the operative and alternative assumption of punks of 1977: that there is "no future / no future / no future for you." And the post-apocalyptic feel of so many punk films at times suggested that the world had indeed ended and the future has been cancelled. The protagonist of *Smithereens* (Seidelman 1982) relates a dream along such lines, while struggling to keep warm under a blanket in a friend's van, surrounded by prostitutes and nursing a bloodied nose—and a dream that lends the film its title: "The whole world had been blown up five years ago, and right to smithereens—and everyone is just floating around on parts [unintelligible] and they haven't even realized what had happened yet."

Jean, in *Downtown 81*, says much the same thing, in voice-over, in introducing the setting of the film: "The Lower East Side looks like a war zone—like we dropped a bomb on ourselves." Likewise, *Born in Flames* (Borden 1983) is set in a near-future dystopia, with militant feminist gangs waging a counterinsurgency. And the very title of Penelope Spheeris's documentary on the LA punk scene at the turn of the decade, *The Decline of Western Civilization* (1981), satirically suggests an Edward Gibbons–like *History of the Decline and Fall of the Roman Empire*. This is more than a conceit for Spheeris; her documentary evidences as much, with a club owner's concerns about audience moshing, pogoing, stage-invading, and flailing violence, and characters in states of extreme anxiety (particularly Darby Crash of the Germs): an exploration of the terminal nature of a doomed youth culture or cult, fatally living up to its own mythology. For Bifo Berardi, this "no future" declaration was quite literal: 1977 is seen as "a turning point," where "the *utopian imagination* was slowly overturned, and has been replaced by the *dystopian imagination*" (Berardi 2011, 17; his italics), resulting in, as "[b]orn with punk, the slow cancellation of the future" (18). Critical theorists tend to characterize the onset of institutionalized neoliberalism, aligned to the ascendancy of the New Right, as the ending of a sense of future in the breaking with the postwar consensus of a meritocratic society offering opportunity for all—and they place popular culture, with punk as the year zero (where 0 = 1977), as the most sensitive barometer to this new era (see, for example, Fisher 2014, 2–29).

Punk film, then, could be said to be the attempted dramatization of the shift in imagination that Berardi identifies. Or, equally arrestingly, punk film can illustrate the failure or unwillingness to dramatize it.[3] Punk's do-it-yourself ethos, with no bars to the musically or artistically limited, combined with the way in which unregulated squats and lofts seem to have been remade as multimedia environments along the lines of Andy Warhol's Factory, suggest that any one of the figures on the make, drifting through these environments, could suddenly become the next big thing. In this way, a utopian aspiration or strain seems to take root in the dystopian imagination; a new future, in the beginnings of a cultural renaissance, is offered against the prospect of the world ending. So, for example, a film like *Blank Generation*, despite the artsy pretensions and presence of preeminent punk icon Richard Hell throughout, is tiresomely clichéd: a troubled romance between a diffident, zeitgeist-channeling musician at the heart of the New York punk scene and a model-like French television journalist enticed by his vulgar, proletarian vitality. The debris of the punk mise-en-scène—scuzzy backstage areas, messy crash-pad apartments—is rendered alluringly, via pristine cinematography (see Figure 24.2). Similarly, *Times Square*, which follows two teenage girl runaways who form a punk band and amass a substantial following, could almost be a Disney film from the time (that is, from Disney's most disorientated period in terms of youth filmmaking), with its cross-class bonding, adventures in the big city, comedy parental confusion, and coming-of-age narrative.

Outward trappings of punk only carry an identification of "punk film" so far; many films have punk group performances in them, or actual or fictional punk figures in situ, or punk music featured on their soundtracks, but it would be limiting to uncritically

FIGURE 24.2. The punk aesthetic as invigorated via osmosis: downtown environments for edgy performers, as with Richard Hell in the inferno of New York: Open City, in *Blank Generation* (1980).

assemble a canon of self-identifying punk cinema exclusively along these lines. A more satisfactory framing is via a stronger or deeper shared sensibility (or ethos or philosophy) between film and punk and post-punk music. Nicholas Rombes (2005, 3), in considering the influence of punk film on subsequent filmmaking, acknowledges such looseness of identification by opting for the term "tendency" in relation to a common aesthetic sensibility, rather than "movement." And "punk," at any rate, was a widely applied term: Tony and his friends are even referred to as "punks" (in the sense of disrespectful or disreputable youngsters) in *Saturday Night Fever*, and, more generally, the idea of the punk can be said to coalesce with the idea of the teenager in postwar American popular cinema. In its postmodern pastiche, *Rumble Fish* (Coppola 1983) seems to usher in rebel punks from a number of decades—with the Motorcycle Boy (Mickey Rourke), a detached, softly-spoken drifter given over to reading, seemingly the late 1970s representative, in contrast to the 1950s-style youth gangs given over to "rumbles" (fighting)—and so posits just such a continuum.

A characteristic element of that shared sensibility, between punk and punk film, is found in a pervasive sense of alienation. The restless and outspoken proto-punk protagonists of postwar teen cinema, and then of early New Hollywood films, almost invariably seemed to kick back against parental or societal expectations of them, so that these rebel figures can be read as ciphers for a progressive critique of that society. Their fight is against the danger of alienation that they see as repressed or sedated by the slightly ridiculous utopian imagination that underwrites these expectations—as dramatized in the glum, noncommunicative young protagonist as first encountered in Mike Nichols's *The Graduate* (1968). This moment of active critique seems to have passed at the point of punk cinema: the protagonists are presented as victims—the critique has been ignored, the battle has been lost, and psychological and physical damage has resulted. Now alienation is the condition that seems endemic to urban life, from which there is no clear way out. The punk is one who seems terminally engulfed by alienation rather than spurred on to exorcise it or take flight from it. This results in turns to violence, as in *Taxi Driver* (Martin Scorsese 1976), or hard drug use, as in *Out of the Blue* (Dennis Hopper 1980) and *Christiane F.* (Edel 1981), or an escape into the hedonism of new sexual subcultures, as in *Querelle* (Rainer Werner Fassbinder 1982) and *Cruising* (Friedkin 1980, but also in the scenes documented by the photographers Robert Mapplethorpe (1978) and Nan Goldin (1985), or seemingly lost in psychosis, as in *Eraserhead* (Lynch 1977), *Breaking Glass* (Gibson 1980) or *Pink Floyd: The Wall* (Parker 1982).[4] Or, in an amalgamation of many of these ills, the hysteria of John Waters's films of the 1970s.

A film noted as important to the inception of the London punk culture, *The Man Who Fell to Earth* (Roeg 1976) was one in which alienation reached such a pitch that the world was partially presented through the cat-like eyes of a literal alien, played by David Bowie. This film screened at a cinema on the King's Road in summer 1976 (see du Noyer 1996; Savage 2001, xvi), and then regularly at the Scala Cinema (sometimes programmed with punk and post-punk screenings and live performances; Giles 2018, 65). The alien even belatedly swerves through a pop music phase, recording and releasing an album while in an alcoholic daze. Bowie's otherworldly presence at this time, particularly in respect to the glacial and dissonant albums of his Berlin period, and his appearance as a performer in *Christiane F* or a subject in the documentary *Cracked Actor* (Yentob 1975), seem built on the sense of the individual alienated to a deranged extent—and with the resultant music understood as resonant with or a *cri de cœur* of that alienation. This was music, then, that spoke of the modern and impossible condition: a contemporary "outsider art," paranoid and hopeless, locked in its moment, lacking in causes, and presented as if it is the only honest response to the times. The alien's androgyny, anorexic body, pallor, and unnatural hair color, not to mention cognitive and physical abilities seen to be degraded by alcohol use, anticipate the punk template of figures such as Richard Hell, Johnny Rotten, and, in particular, Sid Vicious, as well as, a couple of years later, John Foxx and the young Robert Smith, of the Cure.

Punk Spaces

A sense of new modes of existence arises from the ways in which the use and repurposing of vacant spaces, particularly inner-city spaces abandoned after deindustrialization, occurred. Such found spaces were not constructed or organized around a separation of the activities of living and working, creating and resting. The consequent state of "in-betweenness," for that strata given over to rejecting societal norms, radically undermines givens of social organization: of family units and divisions of labor, of the allocations of hours in the day, of what is living and what is working. Consequently, and evidencing punk's gender balance, female protagonists and female filmmakers have not been difficult to locate in terms of scoping this period of film history. Sheila Whiteley, in her history of women and popular music, speculates that a space for women was opened up by and for punk's "'do-it-yourself' spontaneity and established individualism, discovery, change and outrage [since these were] crucial ingredients in style and image" (Whiteley 2000, 97). To this observation one could add that women also later centrally determined the ways in which this cultural moment has been remembered and tapped—a crucial mitigation in terms of the rockist and male impulses behind canon-forming in popular music history.[5] This resultant liminal existence (in the sense of being between thresholds) nudges forward the crossing of further boundaries, between classes and ethnic groups, music genres and their particular cultures, and even sexual "norms." In this respect, alienation seems to be, paradoxically, a liberating force: protagonists cannot be expected to be themselves, since their sense of self has been eroded, and so are prone to act out of character, becoming different people.

Cruising fills such freed spaces (semi-communal apartment blocks, nightclubs, public parks after dark) with a teeming sexual subculture, features punk music and leathers, and seems to suggest the social price of unpoliced liminal states, with serial killings apparently enabled in such "free for all" cultures and seemingly arising from the resultant promiscuous sexual practices. In *Jubilee* (Jarman 1978), the formation of new groups of militant and sexually unusual cells occurs in such liminal spaces. *Liquid Sky* (Tsukerman 1982) seems entirely preoccupied with exploring gender ambiguities and free sexual experimentation in those parts of New York (lofts, roofs, clubs) that seem invisible to that other teeming mass, the grey flows of commuters and businessmen (seen in sporadic cutaway shots): "Homosexual, heterosexual, bisexual . . ." observes one character, "whether or not I like someone doesn't depend on what kind of genitals they have." With such expanded horizons of possibility, and the precarity of existence in liminal zones, the punk film was not one geared up to happy (as with *Saturday Night Fever*) or even particularly neat endings, or even an ending per se. Outcomes cover the entire spectrum: the victims' corpses in *Cruising*, the fame and stardom and its downsides in *Breaking Glass* and *Desperate Teenage Lovedolls* (Markey 1984), the protagonist of *Smithereens* seemingly winding up walking the streets as a prostitute, and Jean in *Downtown 81* finding his fortune. And while *D.O.A.* follows the most commented-upon group of that moment, the Sex Pistols, a "compare and contrast" element is added via no-hope prenascent punk group Terry and the Idiots, setting those who will tour North America and initiate a cultural watershed against those who will never leave their council estates. In just such liminal terms, there seems to be a fine balance between a dead-end existence with drifters in squatted lofts, as in *Permanent Vacation* (Jarmusch 1981), *Suburbia* (Spheeris 1984) or *Downtown 81*, and edgy loft parties overrun with models, generating the next wave of fashion, as in *Liquid Sky*, *Times Square*, or *Blank Generation*. This chapter will now turn to examples that struck such balances, examining the kinds of films that resulted, along with their differing readings and imaginings of the New York and London punk and post-punk scenes and cultures.

New York Punk Films

The narrative of *Smithereens* (Seidelman 1982) is founded on liminality. The punky/New Wave protagonist Wren (Susan Berman) seems to know with certainty what she does not want from life—which is glimpsed in the scenes in which she visits her older sister (hair in curlers, husband demanding food). But the alternative of a New York bohemian life, once she has positioned herself according to this aspiration, seems perilously close to homelessness. And her plans of becoming a scenester and angling for a groupie role by hanging out at the Peppermint Lounge come to nothing. Wren is locked out of her shared apartment, with months of back rent owing, and so is ejected into the city at night. She conspires to sleep in Eric's (Richard Hell) squatted commune/studio, in which unannounced interlopers suggest that these bare rooms might also function as a drug den. But mostly Wren walks the streets at night, lugging shopping bags of her clothes, or sleeps on the subway, or in the back of the van of a young man she has encountered, whose road trip (or fleeing from home) seems to have stalled. She engages in petty crime and, evidencing a growing mastery of the city and its spaces (and egged on by Eric), pretends to pick up an eager "client" in a bar only to successfully shake him down in a taxi journey afterward. But this mastery, by the end of the film, also seals her fate—as she seems to street-walk for actual clients. In this way, no one location seems able to function as a home for Wren, and plans that determine her actions come unstuck, or hopes fade, and are replaced by her working to mitigate unwelcome contingencies.

The dream that fails in *Smithereens* is that of Warhol's fifteen minutes of fame, supposedly allotted to everyone in the media age. For Wren, these fifteen minutes simply do not arrive, despite a vigorous self-mounted media campaign around the dissemination of her image: self-shot Polaroids, graffiti, photocopies of photos of herself with the slogan "who is this?," coupled with being seen in the right clubs and at the right concerts, and constantly striking a pose (accessorized with stolen sunglasses), as if she is the next Edie Sedgwick, only waiting to be talent-spotted and contracted into a life of hip glamour (see Figure 24.3). It is as if, in freely throwing images of herself around the city, some will eventually stick—as strategically mixed into, and so validated by, semi-official punk media (for example, a gig by Gina Harlow and the Cutthroats, at Max's Kansas City, is seen as advertised with straight graffiti). A similar campaign proves entirely successful for the sixteen-year-old girls of *Times Square*. One is middle class, and the daughter of the mayor's crusading commissioner to "clean up Times Square," and the other a punk, described as "angry" and a "delinquent," and seemingly from a dysfunctional background. They meet in the hospital to which they have been sent for observation, form an unlikely friendship, and abscond together. But feminism, rather than a stand-offish individualism, here seems to be the fillip to fame and notoriety—along with the help of

FIGURE 24.3. D.I.Y. Warhol: the crash pad as factory for image generation—but self-promotion via proto-selfies, for a runaway Edie Sedgwick wannabe, only results in the hard lessons of "no future" rather than any mythical fifteen minutes of fame, in *Smithereens* (1982).

a Svengali-like (and, tellingly, English) New York disc jockey. The girls crash in a disused warehouse, describe their adventures as "our own renaissance" (working in a seedy strip club notwithstanding), initiate their media campaign (of throwing television sets off buildings), and form the Sleez Sisters for a live performance broadcast of polemical punk—effectively hijacking the airwaves.

An upbeat ending consists of impending fame for punk Nicky (Robin Johnson) after a crowded guerrilla gig atop a Times Square building, and Pam (Trini Alvarado) warming to the idea of returning to her respectable former life, allaying her parent's fear of a Patty Hearst-like transformation of their "kidnapped" daughter. The critique of patriarchy and the opportunistic media has occurred; a new youth culture of inclusivity (and cross-class friendship), channeling the authentic experience of the New York streets, has been formed; and perhaps Times Square has been unwittingly regenerated in this.

An attempted cultural intervention into New York urban life also determines *Downtown 81*, via the need to leave an impression on the world. Jean says, in voice-over, "I could see the handwriting on the wall, and it was mine; I've made my mark on the world, and it's made its mark on me." The graffiti extends to societal critique (rather than self-promotion):

> Which institutions have the most political [...]
>   a television
>   b the church
>   c ~~SAMO~~©
>   d McDonalds.

Jean surveys his handiwork once he has also been ejected from his slum-like apartment for nonpayment of rent, whereupon he embarks on a homeless odyssey—a nightclub, groups rehearsing, a strip club, a fashion show—with music (diegetic and extra-diegetic) shifting from jazz to rap to post-punk. But Jean, with spray can rather than easel, produces art constantly, with the streets serving as blank canvases. He is a walking reflector of, and offers continuous commentary on, the alienated urban condition. Jean assumes that the fifteen minutes are effectively already in operation, and the equivocation is merely whether his audience comprises hobos or hedge fund managers. So the fairytale fantasy that concludes the film does not seem, in the context of Basquiat's actual life at least, so far-fetched. Debbie Harry, of Blondie, is transformed from a homeless woman to the wand-wielded "Bag Lady Princess" once Jean has graciously kissed her, and leaves a suitcase of bank notes, with which Jean, exclaiming his catchphrase ("boom for real!") then absconds into the night, leaving these downtown environments. "Was I dreaming?" he asks. "No. Maybe I was just waking up—waking up to my own luck. Luck is where you find it." So a mise-en-scène of garbage and destitution is transmogrified into sudden wealth and escape—and, for Basquiat himself, street art into the most collectible of art pieces. This was to occur at the point of a boom in the international art market, for which a fresh credibility, or even "realness," was needed—as found in figures who seemed to channel authentic street art to uptown galleries, such as Basquiat and Keith Haring.

But Jean's company, and thus his positioning for finding luck, is cannier than Wren's. The punks of *Smithereens* listlessly note that the New York punk scene is over at the point of Wren's arrival, with Los Angeles as the new center—leaving the aspirant scenester without a scene, and hopelessly chasing after something that may not exist. In *Downtown 81*, figures such as Debbie Harry, Kid Creole, Fab 5 Freddy, and Kool Kyle indicate the emergence of a multicultural, multimedia pop art scene for the 1980s. And Jean, in their locale, is therefore positioned at the point of something that is about to exist. The resultant cultural and urban regeneration is so strange and rich, and future-oriented, that *Liquid Sky* places an unnoticed visiting UFO in the midst of the post-punk melee. Here aliens are able to crash New York loft parties to "score" their equivalent of heroin, which is an orgasm-induced neurological chemical reaction—and with only a stiff academic interloper aware of this visitation ("aliens appearing in specific subcultures—punk circles").

Even once the term "downtown" had been fully recovered, for the purposes of real estate vocabulary, some ghosts of punk seemed to remain, haunting the upwardly mobiles classes who then moved in on punk's old stomping grounds. In *Copkiller* (Faenza 1983), John Lydon plays a character who occupies a spacious Central Park apartment owned by a violent renegade police officer, wages psychological warfare against him, and finally seems to drive him to suicide—as if a return of the repressed punk sensibility.[6] In *Desperately Seeking Susan* (1985), Seidelman's next film after *Smithereens*, a bored suburban housewife is sucked into a street life picaresque once she encounters and follows the freer spirits who make New York's public spaces their own, engendering an existential crisis that destabilizes her comfortable middle-class existence. And punks were often cast as class-boundary-crossing home invaders in innumerable exploitation and vigilante films from the time, as for *The House on the Edge of the Park* (Deodato 1980), or the Dirty Harry or *Death Wish* cycles of films: violent, dispossessed, and returned to their former role as savage delinquents.

London Punk Films

Hebdige ([1979] 1991) is precise in his dating of the emergence of punk as "a recognisable style," with the "critical attention" (142) afforded to the Sex Pistols in part through their "sensational debut in the music press" (25). This was during the "strange apocalyptic summer" (25) of 1976, with the resultant "moral panic" around this rebarbative new culture following in September 1976 (142). But other voices from the time, perhaps more familiar with the rougher parts of King's Road—such as the World's End council estate (a Victorian slum transformed by Brutalist architecture, awash with hard drugs across the 1970s, and in close proximity to Malcolm McLaren and Vivienne Westwood's fetish boutique shop, SEX)—are less certain in terms of punk as the emergence of a style and a sound.[7] Musician Jah Wobble's (2009) recollections of the time are mostly given over to punks as a minor faction in internecine and bloody street warfare, caught between existing mobs of Teddy Boys, football hooligans, and the National Front. Lucy Toothpaste's ([1979] 1982, 296) recollection of the emergence of punk was, as part of the Rock Against Racism organization, functioning as a bulwark against the sexism and misogyny of the music industry (especially of the 1960s), as well as racial violence. And violence determines many London films of this time: some suggest a society on the brink of civil war (e.g., *Pressure* [Ové 1976], *Babylon* [Rosso 1980], *Made in Britain* [Clarke 1982], or *Breaking Glass*), or a postwar wasteland (e.g., *Jubilee*), or an authoritarian central government keen to exert ever great control over revolts in the abandoned slums (e.g., *D.O.A.*, *Pink Floyd: The Wall*). Council estates are presented as battlegrounds, and state institutions are seen to be in terminal decline, as in *Britannia Hospital* (Anderson 1982). All of this is bluntly counterpointed with the heritage and pomp of the Silver Jubilee celebrations for Queen Elizabeth II: two diametrically opposed visions—a United Kingdom versus a dis-United Fiefdom.

Political groupings in this mix are seen to be merely interested in gaining power—an anarchist reading that seems to have informed *Jubilee* in particular. Jarman had initially envisaged a film that radically broke with the social realism he read as synonymous with politically engaged cinema (see Walker 2002, 191) for a film called *HAGH FATHION*, to be dedicated to "all those who secretly work against the tyranny of Marxists fascists trade unionists maoists capitalists socialists [sic] etc . . . who have conspired together to destroy the diversity and holiness of each life in the name of materialism" (quoted in Peake 1999, 246–247). Such an anarchistic reading would have been apparent too in the unfinished Sex Pistols film *Who Killed Bambi?*, scripted by McLaren and Roger Ebert, with initial shooting begun under the direction of Russ Meyer in 1977.[8] Even a relatively commercially conventional film such as *Breaking Glass* follows the struggles of a poppy "new wave" group in the face of such tyranny: fascist punks, police aggression, music industry indifference to anything other than the escapist disco sent blaring across housing estates, record companies staffed by aging and predatory hippies, and a threadbare civil infrastructure immobilized by industrial action. Such embraces of a total critique seem in keeping with the entire orientation of the early years of punk: a fight against one unified establishment, mounted via visceral shock, which could be said to represent both a radical rejection of the establishment order (and its plans for the best of its youth), and a revealing of the actual degeneracy of these establishment-best youths, as evidenced in the rebarbative nature of the punk culture in which they participate.

Thus *The Punk Rock Movie* (Letts 1978) documented, on Super 8mm film, the new youth culture of punk performances and punk audiences at the Roxy Club in 1977—often from the middle of the action (shot from the audience's vantage point, along with shots of the audience)—and the results present a scene that challenges the viewer to find affinity. But the film does present the punk culture aligned to such a total critique. Nazi insignia decorates bondage gear, and intravenous heroin use and self-harm are seen at length—compared to which a performance by the minor punk band Eater, in which a severed pig's head is hacked with meat cleavers on the stage and the remains lobbed into the audience ("you ain't got no brains"), seems little more than shock-tactic theatricality. In the context of the ascendancy of right-wing militancy, and compared to the engagements with state oppression found in the reggae work of Linton Kwesi Johnson or Misty in Roots, or activism such as the Black People's Day of Action organized by Darcus Howe in 1981, or even the film *Nighthawks* (Peck 1978), concerning London's underground gay culture, punk, as documented by Letts, seemed little more than an inward-looking phase of (white) petit bourgeois nihilism. Indeed, the only police intervention seen in *The Punk Rock Movie* is around complaints about the "offensive" window display in SEX. This punk-as-shock, or punk as given over to rebarbative excess as an end in itself, may seem to be, for *The Punk Rock Movie*, a reading founded on an encounter of the white quarter of punk, in the Roxy Club and its environs. Letts himself was a figure working at the wider intersections of punk and reggae during these years (see Letts and Nobakht 2008), where these seemingly disparate genres of music, and their followers, found elements of common, progressive ground. Julien Temple's *The Great Rock 'n' Roll Swindle* (1980) could be said to deal entirely with shock tactics too, as a canny strategy of cashing-in on the bewilderment of record companies in the late 1970s, and punk is considered entirely in this respect by the manager of the Sex Pistols throughout the film. Temple extends the shock-tactics approach to the film itself, by staging both softcore pornography (with glamour actress Mary Millington simulating public sex at length) and pedophilic pornography (a nude and seemingly underaged girl filmed, and positioned, in a sexually objectifying way—for Sex Pistol Steve Jones, who acted in the film, "that noncey scene"; Jones and Thompson 2017, 209).

For *Rude Boy* (Hazan and Mingay 1980), ideological battle lines are established through the graffiti and posters that cover the public spaces of the young protagonist's Brixton council estate (seemingly from the National Front, skinheads, the Anti-Nazi

League, and a number of campaigning socialist parties), as well as the protests, marches, lines of riot police, hurled bricks, and burning cars he sees as he travels to his job. But Ray's (Ray Gange) job—minding the cash register, in a desultory way, of an unheated late-night Soho sex shop—does not suggest the need to radicalize and rally the everyman at such a divisive time. Ray is presented as politically confused: idolizing the Clash (which, when seen for the first time, includes Joe Strummer in a Red Army Faction T-shirt), sporting a Bob Marley T-shirt himself, on the receiving end of police hassle, and yet agreeing with his skinhead friend's rants against "left-wing wankers" and reveling in an anti-intellectual bent. The politics of punk (and reggae) culture seem not to be understood. Ray's proletarian odyssey, which comes across like the vicarious plot of a Richard Allen skinhead novel for the New English Library (a night in prison after giving a policeman some lip, snooker in a youth club, dealing with requests for "harder" pornography in Soho, sweaty punk gigs, popping pills and stealing booze, being fellated in the toilets of a nightclub, hitching lifts from lorry drivers by the side of motorways, and fellow roadies roaming around in their underwear in cheap hotels), suggests no quarter for a developing political consciousness.[9] The concerts by the Clash seem to work as a crucible of social tensions, with the band channeling the alienation of their fans into their energetic screeds against the establishment, which form the basis of a collective experience for those in the venue. But the audience members are beaten by the bouncers, and the band members repeatedly arrested by the police, and seem unable to connect with Ray (and, by extension, those he represents). Freedoms, as associated with liminal spaces, seem in very short supply: all the characters seem propelled from one dire environment to another, constantly searching for food and cadging drinks, washing their clothes in makeshift ways, dodging the police or lugging their belongings with them. Despite their commitment and raw power, then, the Clash gain no ideological traction, and all the while the Conservative Party moves closer to power—from the glimpsed Saatchi and Saatchi election poster "Labour isn't working" to, in the closing seconds of the film, Thatcher entering office as prime minister in May 1979.

Babylon (Rosso 1980), which, with reggae rather than punk, Brixton rather than Soho, and Jah Shaka rather than the Clash, can be read as a Rastafarian *Rude Boy*, and is more exacting in respect to the overwhelming challenges to forming proletarian consciousness. National Front and police violence (and constant aggressive racism from white working-class Londoners) against the "immigrants" seems to drive some in the Jamaican community to conservative religious groupings, some to retreat into newly formed family units (as with Ové's *Pressure*), and others to random violence. The key figure in respect to the nascent multiculturalism of *Babylon* (a cultural inclusivity that capitalizes on liminal spaces)—the porkpie-hat-wearing former skinhead Ronnie (Karl Howman), who hangs out with his Jamaican friends in their lock-up, and shares their recreational drugs and sound systems—is eventually tagged as an unwelcome emissary of the white world, despite his impassioned protestations, and assaulted accordingly (see Figure 24.4). Thus, resistance is assembled along ethnic rather than class lines, indicating a successful dividing and conquering of members of those strata who may

FIGURE 24.4. Ghetto of the city: the foundations of a fledgling multicultural front, uniting Rastafarians and a former skinhead through a love of dub vibrations, cannot withstand the violence of the political vibrations emanating from the London of the New Right, in *Babylon* (1980).

otherwise have helped mount a collective cultural front—even "Punky Reggae Party" of opposition, to recall Bob Marley's 1977 single.

Conclusion

An essential difference that emerges between the New York and London punk films is one of the reading of the punk lifestyle. At its most optimistic then, in New York, this reading anticipates new forms of bohemianism and creativity, and a culture (and cultural industry) reborn from the wreckage. Even though there are many losers, the films tend to prefer the winners (the Jeans over the Wrens)—the new cultural scene requires, and so generates, individuals' success stories. In London, however, this existence is swept into an ideological battle between more extreme political formations: the coming Tory neoliberalism of Margaret Thatcher, and right-wing militants (particularly the National Front) versus—and in a literal sense, in the rioting on the streets—various socialist formations. In this respect, the cameo of Warhol in *Blank Generation* (talking about the films of Jean-Luc Godard) can be appropriately contrasted with, in *Rude Boy*, the "cameo" of Thatcher herself (at a party conference, vowing to eradicate the youth crime endangering wealth creation). Both these figures are correctly identified by the filmmakers as pointing to emergent cultures of the 1980s.

For New York punks on screen, alienation is an access to a liminal picaresque, freeing the individual from the pull of parental and societal expectations—for better (as in

Downtown 81) or for worse (as in *Smithereens*). For London punks on screen, alienation immobilizes and disorients those who once could have been expected to form a cultural opposition, and in grimy liminal spaces more reminiscent of the flophouses of Orwell's *Down and Out in Paris and London* (1933) than the sweep and adventure of Kerouac's *On the Road* (1957). In both of these social contexts, disco seems to offer a tempting circumnavigation of all these issues: seduction over sedition, hedonism over alienation, domestication over squatting, and, with disco's entry into the mainstream, new uptown fashion hot spots over the dangers awaiting downtown.

If the year 1977 can be taken as Berardi's "turning point," then the years of punk across this can be read as a riotous interregnum: a culture after the failing of the old order but before the re-establishment of law and order on the cusp of the new decade. Around this interregnum, New York punk film seems to chart the ending of one world and the beginnings of another (with elements of post-punk, new wave, and hip-hop already surfacing). London punk film, which seems to chart the end of the world altogether, necessarily lacks such optimism.

Notes

1. In this respect, the film reads disco as much more than a fad or evening pastime; disco represents a new lifestyle altogether, presenting opportunities for romance and betterment for its initial enthusiasts. Recent scholarship on disco has argued for the genre as a radical continuum of utopian dissent, extending the countercultures of the 1960s through queer and gay cultures and communities of the 1970s (and on into AIDS activism in the 1980s; see Crimp 2016), and emergent drag cultures and non-heteronormative performance (see Hilderbrand 2014), and also anticipating, in the idea of massed dancing bodies communing with the machine music of synthesizers and drum machines, radical currents in electronic dance music (see Halligan 2016). Disco is no longer, then, "a five letter word that can't be uttered in polite company; no longer the guilty pleasure hidden in the closet," as Peter Shapiro (2007, 276) puts it. But all such readings note the degeneration of disco, from its early years as associated with gay nightclub scenes to its commercial zenith, with a disco floor in every mid-range hotel. See also Lawrence 2004, 2016.
2. The film, originally called *New York Beat Movie*, was shot in 1980–1981, and edited and first released in 2000, with the lost dialogue soundtrack recreated. On the setting of *Wolfen* in respect to its particular moment, see Toscano and Kinkle 2015, 108–136.
3. Despite some overlaps with the films under examination, this chapter will not consider the loose No Wave film movement, which was associated with No Wave music—that quarter of purist punk that was antagonistic to their sold-out punk contemporaries (in the sense of having signed with major record companies, as was the case with the Sex Pistols; on this position, see Moore and Coley 2008, 116). On No Wave filmmaking, see Goddard (2013, 115–130). While many of the No Wave films were taken as artifacts of the punk sensibility of the time or communiqués from the punk underground, my concerns is more with films that sought to reflect rather than extend this scene, from the moment of this scene.
4. Cultural connections between leathersex subcultures and punk—which shared close sartorial concerns, and the coming together of a number of men in semi-public spaces

for collective physical exertions—remain unexplored. Strains of gay pornography from North America in the 1970s could therefore be read as punk cinema—including the work of Fred Halsted, such as *Nighthawk in Leather* (1982), and the blending of the enacted threat of violence from leathermen with the promise of rough sex (see Halligan and Wilson 2015).

5. This has occurred through, for example, Nirvana working with and reviving the Raincoats—which seems to have been a crucial element to Kurt Cobain's feminism (on this, see Raphael 1996, 98–113)—or Raincoat Gina Birch's importation of punk aesthetics and sensibility into the music videos she subsequently directed, particularly for the Libertines, and the same with Vivienne Westwood's fashion designs, to the present, and those exemplifying her influence, such as Alexander McQueen. Or through autobiographical writing reclaiming the era from a female perspective, as with Lydia Lunch ([1997] 2007), Alice Bag (2011) and Viv Albertine (2014), who writes about her time with the Slits with a sense of sisterly mentorship and support, and a sexual liberation that was not beholden to desire (164, 113–116, for example, respectively). If I bring these specific and indicative examples to attention here, it is in part from a feeling that some of the women discussed in terms of punk films still teeter on the edge of uncritically assuming old roles: for the food preparation seen in *The Decline of Western Civilization*, in the romantic fickleness of *Breaking Glass*, in the sexualized models of *Liquid Sky*, and as a vision of beauty and salvation in *Downtown 81* and *Rumble Fish*—and to which could also be added Richard Hell's posses of female followers in two of the films discussed in this chapter.

6. The film is also known as *Corrupt* and *Order of Death*. On its reworking of the seminal 1960s countercultural film *Performance* (Roeg and Cammell 1970), with Lydon in the Mick Jagger role, see Prothero (1999, 62) who also considers the way in which *Copkiller* uses Lydon's Johnny Rotten persona for its dramatic conceits: Is Lydon's presence "really" that of "the homicidal anarchist he claims, or merely a whining, over-indulged poseur? In other words, much the same question that hung over Lydon's head through the Sex Pistols period and beyond."

7. In one of its several redesigns, SEX would later reopen under the name World's End.

8. For the script, see Ebert 2010.

9. Allen's actual novel on punk, *Punk Rock* (1977), in part centered on "aggro" on the King's Road, conspiratorially cast the entire culture as a sophisticated attempt by the media establishment to fleece the young.

References

Albertine, Viv. 2014. *Clothes, Clothes, Clothes. Music, Music, Music. Boys, Boys, Boys: A Memoir*. New York: Thomas Dunne Books.

Allen, Richard. 1977. *Punk Rock*. London: New English Library.

Bag, Alice. 2011. *Violence Girl: East LA Rage to Hollywood Stage, a Chicano Punk Story*. Port Townsend, WA: Feral House.

Basquiat, Jean-Michel, Glenn O'Brien, Diego Cortez, and Deitch Projects. 2007. *Jean-Michel Basquiat 1981: The Studio of the Street*. New York: Deitch Projects.

Berardi, Franco ("Bifo"). 2011. *After the Future*. Translated by Arianna Bove, Melinda Cooper, et al. Oakland, CA, and Edinburgh, Scotland: AK Press.

Crimp, Douglas. 2016. *Disss-co (A Fragment)*. New York: MoMA PS1.

Du Noyer, Paul. 1996. "One King's Road Summer." *Independent*, August 18, 1996. https://www.independent.co.uk/life-style/one-kings-road-summer-1310190.html.

Ebert, Roger. 2010. "*Who Killed Bambi?*—A Screenplay." http://blogs.suntimes.com/ebert/2010/04/who_killed_bambi_-_a_screenpla.html.

Fassbinder, Rainer Werner, dir. 1982. *Querelle*. Gaumont S.A. Paris; Scotia, Gaumont.

Fisher, Mark. 2014. *Ghosts of My Life: Writings on Depression, Hauntology and Lost Futures*. Hampshire, UK: Zero Books.

Giles, Jane. 2018. *The Scala Cinema, 1978–1993*. Surrey: FAB Press.

Goddard, Michael. 2013. "No Wave Film and Music Documentary: From No Wave Cinema 'Documents' to Retrospective Documentaries." In *The Music Documentary: Acid Rock to Electropop*, edited by Robert Edgar, Kirsty Fairclough-Isaacs, and Benjamin Halligan, 115–130. London: Routledge.

Goldin, Nan. 1985. *The Ballad of Sexual Dependency*. New York: Aperture.

Halligan, Benjamin. 2016. "Mind Usurps Program: Virtuality and the 'New Machine Aesthetic' of Electronic Dance Music." In *The Oxford Handbook of Music and Virtuality*, edited by Sheila Whiteley and Shara Rambarran, 529–550. Oxford: Oxford University Press.

Halligan, Benjamin, and Laura Wilson. 2015. "'Use/Abuse/Everyone/Everything': A Dialogue on *LA Plays Itself*." *Framework: The Journal of Cinema and Media*. 56, no. 2: 299–322.

Hebdige, Dick. (1979) 1991. *Subculture: The Meaning of Style*. London: Routledge.

Hilderbrand, Lucas. 2014. *"Paris Is Burning": A Queer Film Classic*. Vancouver: Arsenal Pulp Press.

Hopper, Dennis, dir. 1980. *Out of the Blue*. Discovery Productions, Robson Street; Les Productions Karim.

Jones, Steve, with Ben Thompson. 2017. *Lonely Boy: Tales from a Sex Pistol*. London: Windmill Books.

Kerouac, Jack. 1957. *On the Road*. New York: Viking Press.

Lawrence, Tim. 2004. *Love Saves the Day: A History of American Dance Music Culture, 1970–1979*. Durham, NC: Duke University Press.

Lawrence, Tim. 2016. *Life and Death on the New York Dance Floor, 1980–1983*. Durham, NC: Duke University Press.

Letts, Don, and David Nobakht. 2008. *Culture Clash: Dread Meets Punk Rockers*. London: SAF.

Lunch, Lydia. (1997) 2007. *Paradoxia: A Predator's Diary*. New York: Akashic Books.

Mapplethorpe, Robert. 1978. *X Portfolio*. Washington, DC: Harry Lunn.

Moore, Thurston, and Byron Coley. 2008. *No Wave. Post-Punk. Underground. New York. 1976–1980*. New York: Harry N. Abrams.

Orwell, George. 1933. *Down and Out in Paris and London*. London: Victor Gollancz.

Peake, Tony. 1999. *Derek Jarman*. London: Little, Brown.

Prothero, David. 1999. "Copkiller." In *Harvey Keitel: Movie Top Ten*, edited by Jack Hunter, 57–66. London: Creation Books.

Raphael, Amy. 1996. *Never Mind the Bollocks: Women Rewrite Rock*. London: Virago.

Rombes, Nicholas, ed. 2005. *New Punk Cinema*. Edinburgh: Edinburgh University Press.

Savage, Jon. 2001. *England's Dreaming: Anarchy, Sex Pistols, Punk Rock, and Beyond*. Updated and expanded edition. New York: St. Martin's Griffin.

Scorsese, Martin, dir. 1976. *Taxi Driver*. Bill/Phillips Productions, Italo/Judeo Productions; Columbia Pictures.

Shapiro, Peter. 2007. *Turn the Beat Around: The Secret History of Disco*. London: Faber and Faber.

Toothpaste, Lucy. (1979) 1982. "Love Music/Hate Sexism." In *Spare Rib Reader*, edited by Marsha Rowe, 295–297. Middlesex, UK: Penguin.

Toscano, Alberto, and Jeff Kinkle. 2015. *Cartographies of the Absolute*. Winchester, UK: Zero Books.

Walker, John A. 2002. *Left Shift: Radical Art in 1970s Britain*. London: I.B. Tauris.

White, Edmund. 1981. *States of Desire: Travels in Gay America*. Toronto: Bantam.

Whiteley, Sheila. 2000. *Women and Popular Music: Sexuality, Identity and Subjectivity*. London: Routledge.

Wobble, Jah. 2009. *Memoirs of a Geezer*. London: Serpent's Tail.

Filmography

(Most list both production company/companies and distribution company.)

Anderson, Lindsay, dir. 1982. *Britannia Hospital*. British Lion Film Corporation, EMI Films, Film and General Productions, National Film Finance Corporation; Columbia-EMI-Warner.

Badham, John, dir. 1977. *Saturday Night Fever*. Robert Stigwood Organization; Paramount Pictures.

Bertoglio, Edo, dir. 2000. *Downtown 81* (shot 1980–1981 as *New York Beat Movie*). Rizzoli; Kinetique, Music Box Films, Saggittaire Films, Zeitgeist Films.

Borden, Lizzie, dir. 1983. *Born in Flames*. Jerome Foundations, C.A.P.S, Young Filmmakers Ltd.; First Run Features.

Clarke, Alan, dir. 1982. *Made in Britain*. Central Independent Television.

Coppola, Francis Ford, dir. 1983. *Rumble Fish*. American Zoetrope; Universal Pictures.

Deodato, Ruggero, dir. 1980. *The House on the Edge of the Park / La casa sperduta nel parco*. F. D. Cinematografica; Adige Film 76.

Edel, Uli, dir. 1981. *Christiane F.* Solaris Film, Maran Film, Popular Filmproduktion, CLV-Filmproduktions, Süddeutscher Runkfunk; various distributors.

Faenza, Roberto, dir. 1983. *Copkiller* (also known as *Corrupt* and *Order of Death*). Cooperativa Jean Vigo, RAI Radiotelevisione Italiana, Aura Films, New Line Cinema, Virgin Films; various distributors.

Ferreri, Marco, dir., 1978. *Bye Bye Monkey/Ciao maschio*. 18 Dicembre, Prospectacle, Action Films; various distributors.

Friedkin, William, dir. 1980. *Cruising*. CiP-Europaische Treuhand, Lorimar Film Entertainment; United Artists.

Friends (US television series). 1994–2004. Bright/Kauffman/Crane Productions; Warner Bros. Television.

Gibson, Brian, dir. 1980. *Breaking Glass*. Allied Stars Ltd., Film and General Productions, Sprint N.V.; Paramount Pictures.

Gossip Girl (US television series). 2007–2012. Warner Bros. Television, Alloy Entertainment; CBS Television Distribution, Warner Bros. Domestic Television Distribution.

Halsted, Fred, dir. 1982. *Nighthawk in Leather*. Cosco Studio; HIS Video.

Hazan, Jack, and David Mingay, dirs. 1980. *Rude Boy*. Buzzy Enterprises, Michael White Productions; Tigon Film Distributors.

Hill, George Roy, dir. 1977. *Slap Shot*. Pan Arts and King's Road Entertainment; Universal Pictures.

Jarman, Derek, dir. 1978. *Jubilee*. Whaley-Malin Productions, Megalovision; Cinegate.

Jarmusch, Jim, dir. 1981. *Permanent Vacation*. Cinesthesia Productions; various distributors.
Kowalski, Lech, dir. 1981. *D.O.A.: A Rite of Passage*. Lightning Video.
Letts, Don, dir. 1978. *The Punk Rock Movie* (also known as *The Punk Rock Movie from England*). Notting Hill, Punk Rock Films; Cinematic Releasing Corporation, Danton Films.
Lommel, Ulli, dir. 1980. *Blank Generation*. International Harmony.
Lynch, David, dir. 1977; *Eraserhead*. American Film Institute; Libra Films International.
Markey, David, dir. 1984. *Desperate Teenage Lovedolls*. We Got Power Films; independent distribution, then various distributors.
Meyer, Russ, dir. 1977. *Who Killed Bambi?* (initially known as *Anarchy in the U.K.*, and incomplete). Warner Bros, 20th Century Fox.
Moyle, Allan, dir. 1980. *Times Square*. EMI Films, Robert Stigwood Organization; Associated Film Distribution.
Ové, Horace, dir. 1976. *Pressure*. BFI Production Board; Crawford Films.
Parker, Alan, dir. 1982. *Pink Floyd: The Wall*. MGM; MGM, UA Entertainment Company.
Peck, Ron, dir. 1978. *Nighthawks*. Universal Pictures, Martin Poll Productions, The Production Company, Herb Nanas Productions, Layton Productions; Universal Pictures.
Reitman, Ivan, dir. 1981. *Stripes*. Columbia Pictures.
Roeg, Nicholas, dir. 1976. *The Man Who Fell to Earth*. British Lion Film Corporation, Cinema 5; various distributors.
Roeg, Nicholas, and Donald Cammell, dirs. 1970. *Performance*. Goodtimes Enterprises; Warner Bros.
Rosso, Franco, dir. 1980. *Babylon*. Diversity Music; Pan-Canadian Film Distributors.
Seidelman, Susan, dir. 1982. *Smithereens*. Domestic Productions; New Line Cinema.
Seidelman, Susan, dir. 1985. *Desperately Seeking Susan*. Orion Pictures; Orion Pictures.
Siegel, Don, dir. 1971. *Dirty Harry*. The Malpaso Company; Warner Bros.
Slava, Tsukerman, dir. 1982. *Liquid Sky*. Z. Films Inc.; various distributors.
Spheeris, Penelope, dir. 1981. *The Decline of Western Civilization*. Spheeris Film Inc.; Nu-Image.
Spheeris, Penelope, dir. 1984. *Suburbia*. Suburbia Productions; New World Pictures.
Temple, Julien, dir. 1980. *The Great Rock 'n' Roll Swindle*. Boyd's Company, Kendon Films, Matrixbest, Virgin Films; Virgin Films.
Wadleigh, Michael, dir. 1981. *Wolfen*. Orion Pictures; Warner Bros.
Winner, Michael, dir. 1974 *Death Wish*. Dino de Laurentiis Cinematografica; Paramount Pictures.
Yentob, Alan, dir. 1975. *Cracked Actor*. BBC documentary.

CHAPTER 25

SOUND RECORDISTS, WORKPLACES, TECHNOLOGIES, AND THE AESTHETICS OF PUNK

SAMANTHA BENNETT

INTRODUCTION

IN 2004 the renowned alternative music recordist Steve Albini gave a lecture at the Middle Tennessee State University Student Union in which he "lamented" the age of "overproduction" in the 1980s and 1990s (Young 2004). Albini heavily critiqued the state of rock music production of the era, focusing on the role of producers and engineers as superior to musicians and songwriters; the resulting, skewed hierarchies formed in recording studio sessions; the foregrounding of recordists' technological and processual interventions; and the subsequent "overproduced" sound of records of the era. Albini's recognition of this production aesthetic is one shared by scholars (Zak 2001; Bennett 2018), who have argued that, at the turn of the 1980s, the digital technological shift in commercial music record production resulted in a "fork in the road" (Bennett 2018), with traditional, "performance-capture" approaches to recording and production retained by some recordists, and more constructionist, technology-led approaches embraced by others. The effects of technological change on both the commercial music and sound recording industries are well documented (Cunningham 1998; Théberge 1997; Katz 2004), as are histories of sound recording and production (Schmidt Horning 2013; Milner 2009; Doyle 2005). Among these discourses, however, is a tendency to focus on commercial, often canonized recordings. In popular music and sound studies, parallel workplace, technology, and recordist canons have emerged where the appetite for detail around canonized recordings is apparently insatiable. The problematic result of this largely pop and *rockist*-leaning discourse is that musical works written, produced, and disseminated outside the commercial mainstream are overlooked. This is certainly the case with punk, despite plenty of works focused on canonized punk artists (Savage 1991; Rombes 2005), as well as oral history collections of leading punk genre musicians (McNeil and McCain 1996; Robb 2006).

In the scholarly domain, punk is almost always discussed socially or sociologically, in terms of subculture (Laing 1978; Hebdige 1979), audiences, and reception (Bennett 2006), as well as in local and global culture (McKay 1996; Dunn 2008). Relatively rarely are the musical and/or production elements of punk examined in detail. Despite the origins of punk in late 1960s US garage rock—and the ongoing close relationship of punk to broader rock music—works focused on the specificities of punk music, its structures, arrangements, melodic and harmonic content, and orchestration are few and far between. This chapter is predicated on the sonic aesthetics of punk as originating in the United States during the late 1960s and developing through the 1970s, particularly in the UK and beyond.

In *Understanding Rock*, Covach and Boone are dismissive of punk, playing down its musical relevance as "personal expression" and stating the genre tends to "celebrate musical amateurism" (1997, 5). By its omission, the suggestion is that punk does not belong in the same discourse as rock music, nor even in rock musicological studies. Allan Moore takes a different tack in *Rock: The Primary Text*, with a focus on what he calls the punk aesthetic. While suggesting that the historical importance of punk may "prove to be very limited" (2001, 129), Moore nevertheless recognizes the analytical value in tracks such as the Sex Pistols' "Holidays in the Sun" (1977) and the Damned's "New Rose" (1976), as well as the integration of reggae musicality in the Slits' *Cut* (1979). Moore also identifies musical friction as a punk differentiator in the wider context of rock music, which is a useful point when considering production values in the punk genre. In a detailed analysis of Patti Smith's *Horses* (1975) and Siouxsie and the Banshees' *The Scream* (1978), Sheila Whiteley comes much closer to unpacking the musicality of punk as an "identification of eccentricity" (2000, 98). With a particular focus on vocals, lyrics, and performativity, Whiteley recognized the potential space punk carved out for its relatively few female performers. These studies go a small way in unraveling the musical ramifications of recorded punk music. However, missing from the discourse is an acknowledgement of the *site* of punk recording and production—specifically, the ways in which the genre is brought to bear on record; the workplaces, recordists, and technologies involved; the intentions of musicians and recordists toward the recording process; and the aesthetic reflections present in the final recordings.

In his 1978 article "Interpreting Punk Rock," Laing suggested that, as a genre defined by its hostility to the status quo, UK punk recordings "initially marked a sharp break with this whole [excessive production] trend. They [punk recordings] were made quickly and cheaply in a small recording studio, often in the group's home city rather than in London" (1978, 125). Indeed, where scholarly discourse does briefly acknowledge the recording and production aspects of punk, it tends to do so in the broader context of the DIY aesthetic. For example, Triggs (2006), Moran (2010), O'Connell (2012) and Dunn (2012) have explored DIY practices in punk fanzines, subculture, DIY production, and record labels, respectively. While Dunn recognizes that DIY recording "represents an attempt to realize Benjamin's challenge to produce culture progressively and collaboratively" (2012, p. 218), the site of punk production is glossed. We know little about the specificities of the technological means used to produce punk, the agency of punk recordists, and key sites of punk recording and production. Writing on punk aesthetics, Angela Rodel suggests that recording quality is "another important aspect of badness in punk and hardcore. 'Slick' or overly-produced sounds immediately raise suspicions of having commercial pretensions" (2004, 239). Yet the further we move away from its 1970s inception, the greater the attention and relevance punk appears to attract, and the more the commercial mainstream appears to adopt punk aesthetics. British punk, for example, was initially perceived as a threat, with the *Daily Mirror*'s "The Filth and the Fury" newspaper headline from 1976 encapsulating the outrage and moral panic incited by the advent of punk (Greig et al. 1976). Yet in 2016 the British Library hosted a punk exhibition; forty years later, punk is viewed through this establishment lens as being worthy of commemoration and celebration among a mainstream audience. Another dichotomy lies in the gradual adoption of punk into the established rock canon. Since the turn of the 1990s, the ways in which punk has been adopted into the long-established rock pantheon (Moore 2001; von Appen and Doehring 2006) apparently undermine its DIY aesthetics and blur previously differentiated stylistic distinctions. For example, that the Sex Pistols often appear in the same canonical realm as the Beatles and Pink Floyd, both in scholarly discourse (Moore 2001) and in music criticism (Dolan et al. 2016), points to a blurry historicizing of punk; if the aesthetic intention of punk was anti-establishment and, as Laing pointed out in 1978, a disruption to the status quo, then its legacy is one of treasured cultural phenomena by the very establishment it intended to disrupt.

This chapter aims to build upon previous work that exclusively addresses punk recording and production (Bennett 2015, 2017). With a focus on well-known recorded punk texts from the 1970s through to the 1990s and their concomitant sites of production, the intention is to address the omission of punk recording and production aesthetics from both sound recording and production history, as well as punk historiography in general. Here, I am more concerned with how recording and production is overlooked in recognizable UK and US punk recordings as opposed to localized punk (Gordon 2012). In doing so, the chapter will reframe punk recording as a site of tension and contradiction. The relationship of early punk to established classical and rock hierarchies is closer than perhaps its discourse acknowledges, and its embodied recorded aesthetics suggest more in the way of technological and processual intervention than broader DIY discourses suggest.

Recordists

The relationship between early punk music and art music, the avant-garde, and experimental music is well documented (Henry 1984; Gendron 2002). Early punk does, however, have further strong links to classical music via a number of recordists involved in the production of its early recorded texts. One recordist featuring prominently in the recording of early US punk is Craig Leon, well-known for his classical works with the London Symphony Orchestra, the Berlin Music Ensemble, and modern classical artist Izzy, who worked from Plaza Sound Studios located on the eighth floor of New York's Radio City Music Hall. Credited as producer on the Ramones' *Ramones* (1976), Suicide's *Suicide* (1977), and Blondie's *Blondie* (1977), Leon is a central figure in documenting an emergent US punk; his processual application bound numerous artists into a sonically identifiable genre. He stated, "My style of production is very much arranging and song-orientated. I got a technical lesson by the seat of my pants. The kind of things I wanted to record, nobody else wanted to record" (quoted in Jopson 2014). Leon was at the forefront of punk recording during arguably its most significant era, yet his practice resembled established rock production techniques. Plaza Sound was a large facility with a separate control room, studio floor, and drum booth, and it featured multitrack recording capability. He stated of recording *Ramones*, "Quite honestly, it wasn't a live recording. It was quite layered. What we wanted people to *perceive* was *cinéma vérité*" (quoted in Jopson 2014). Here Leon reveals his intention to present the recording as an illusion of a live performance; the meticulous multitracking and postproduction inherent to *Ramones* was concealed.

The late Bill Price is another recordist who worked across punk and classical recording. As engineer for both the Sex Pistols' *Never Mind the Bollocks . . .* (1977) and the Clash's *London Calling* (1979), as well as multiple recordings for the London Symphony Orchestra, Price recognized the performance-led values inherent to punk, and even drew similarities between punk and classical musicians. Yet, almost mirroring Leon's US punk production aesthetic, Price, along with producer Chris Thomas, recorded *Never Mind the Bollocks . . .* using a 24-track rock production template. Regarding the tensions between the Sex Pistols and the elite recording facility they recorded at, he said this: "They treated the studio like the BBC Home Service and looked at me as if I was wearing a white lab coat. . . . It was as if they had walked into the arms of the Establishment, and there was also a general reluctance to comply" (quoted in Buskin 2004). Price recognized the Sex Pistols, Wessex Studios, and himself as an incompatible, awkward fit. Yet in producing *Never Mind the Bollocks. . . .* which underwent further mixing at George Martin's AIR studios, to a rock aesthetic arguably resulted in the acceptance of British punk among the rock establishment.

San Francisco recordist and studio owner Oliver DiCicco was heavily influenced by the avant-garde, citing composer Harry Partch as a key inspiration. DiCicco initially built Mobius Studios in 1976, having built up connections with local musicians and artists across a range of genres. DiCicco suggests that his work on Dead Kennedys' *Fresh Fruit for Rotting Vegetables* (1980) was spontaneous and fresh—"I didn't really know what I was doing" (quoted in Johnson 2005), he stated in an interview with *Mix* magazine. DiCicco's emergent Mobius Studios in the Noe Valley region was a modest facility. Featuring a "a 16-input Quantum console, a pair of early EPI speakers and a 'limited' mic collection that included U47 and U87s, a couple of 421s and a pair of KM84s" (quoted in Johnson 2005), this was by no means an elite setup, yet it was also far more technologically realized than many home studio setups of the era. A key area in record production discourse generally concerns the "producer as auteur." While scholars such as Gillett (1977) and Eisenberg (2005) have espoused auteurism in their discussions of record producers, others (e.g., Zak 2001; Bennett 2018) have critiqued the idea as limited, since record production is a collaborative process. DiCicco positioned himself as auteur in his record production: "The producer in the music world is a film director" (quoted in Raggett 2016), he stated, yet he went on to say his role was closer to what Mike Howlett has termed "the producer as nexus": "The producer is the liaison between the musicians and the music and the technology. So if he has a vision—hopefully!—of what they want to accomplish, he's there to be an objective ear for the musicians. He's got to be able to communicate with me the kind of sound they want to get." This communicative connection between recordist and musician(s) is most often cited as the most important factor in the collaborative production process. The stakes are, however, much higher for punk bands, particularly where the musical content features subversive themes and/or political sentiments that fall far outside the commercial mainstream and even beyond the independent music industry. Indeed, Craig Leon's remark about wanting to record artists that "nobody else wanted to record" is a recurrent theme. Consider Dead Kennedys' lead vocalist and songwriter Jello Biafra's comments on finding the right recordist at the time: "It was hard to find an engineer who was friendly to this kind of music because a whole generation of recording engineers had been trained to make mellow, clean, Eagles-sounding recordings" (quoted in Johnson 2005). This demonstrates a demand for a different kind of recordist at the turn of the 1980s, one that possessed the technological and processual competence necessary for the practical aspects of record production, but that also recognized the need for musical understanding. Biafra attributes this need *not* to the sharing of political views, lyrical understanding, or even a shared value system, but rather to the need for the recordist to imbue the record with a particular set of sonic qualities not commensurate with the sound of rock records. In 1980, US punk was (arguably) more than ten years old, but many recordists were affiliated with classical and rock genres, and punk music featuring political and/or subversive themes may have been perceived by some recordists as a risk.

A similar sentiment is expressed by Steve Ignorant of the UK anarcho-punk band Crass and the recordist John Loder in reference to the band's 1983 album, *Yes Sir, I Will*: "I mean, what record producer or studio owner in their right mind endorses something like that?" (Ignorant 2016). This highlights the significance of the recordist in punk recording and production, the risks the recordist took in working with subversive artists, and the importance of shared understanding of the mechanisms inherent in the fast-developing genre. By the turn of the 1980s, recordists affiliated with classical or rock music were no longer a good fit for the evolving genre, which was taking on a new sonic identity in both the UK and US. In "Songs about Fucking" (2017), I argued that, starting with Crass in the late 1970s, John Loder pioneered a subversive sonic aesthetics befitting of the subcultural artists he worked with. Poison Girls, Rudimentary Peni, Big Black, and Babes in Toyland were just a few of hundreds of acts Loder recorded, and while all featured social, cultural, and/or politically subversive music, it is the sound of Loder's studio and production that binds them together most compellingly. I defined Loder's subversive production aesthetic as featuring the following key characteristics:

- "Undermixed" vocals comparative to adjacent instruments
- "Enveloping" of the "undermixed" vocals with spatially off-centered distorted guitars
- Lack of low-end frequencies in the overall mix
- Little to no audible time-based processing (reverb, echo, or delay) present
- An "upfront," direct, and sonically confronting aesthetic
- Instruments "fixed" in their stereo field position throughout; no audible manual panning
- No apparent volume automations; instrument position "fixed" throughout
- drums positioned louder than other instruments in the mix
- "Percussive" vocal treatment featuring either distortion, lack of time-based signal processing, absence of bass frequencies, presence of high frequencies, and/or band-pass filtering

Of course, these sonic components are far removed from Leon's and Price's meticulously crafted 1970s canonized punk recordings, and as such they demonstrate a marked sonic shift. I also argued that, via the US acts Loder worked with—in particular the pioneering alternative music recordist Steve Albini and his hardcore band Big Black—these production aesthetics transcended Southern Studios and its concomitant independent UK punk genre and can be heard in much US alternative music of the 1980s, and later on in the commercial music industry via the mainstream acceptance of grunge. The work of Albini in driving an underground recording aesthetic through the heart of the commercial mainstream is well documented (O'Hare 2007; Shepherd 2011; Bennett 2017). However, other recordists were perhaps more influential in shaping the stateside version of Loder's sonic aesthetic. Almost simultaneously to Loder's work at Southern, US recordist Glenn Lockett (Spot) was pioneering an almost identical sound. As the former bassist in Black Flag, Lockett became the in-house recording engineer at the Long Beach, California–based SST Records. This basement facility was initially called "Media Art Studios" before the investor Wyn Davis bought it out in 1980 and changed its name to "Total Access Recording."

At the turn of the 1980s, Lockett worked closely with the independent label's founder Greg Ginn on a raw, stripped back version of confrontational punk that would come to be known as hardcore. Along with Ginn, whose focus was the dissemination of punk via his SST record label, Lockett worked on bringing the much harder—and, arguably, less accessible—emergent punk style to the fore, stating, "I was just a guy with a hammer, glue and not near enough duct tape" (quoted in Seymour 2015). Even though he had a background in jazz, experimental, and progressive music, Lockett viewed his role as a craftsman as opposed to an auteur. Rather than seeking to stamp his own sonic signature on the records he made, he instead allowed the bands to direct most of the sessions.

Additionally, Lockett saw an opportunity to realize the harder, more aggressive sound of hardcore via Media Art Studios, and, like DiCicco and Loder, he was willing to take the risks associated with such artists. As he put it, "I like listening to really out-there jazz, and all of that progressive stuff where people really took chances. Suddenly, the chances were happening in a different way, but they were *big* chances that people were taking" (quoted in Backer 2018). Again, like both DiCicco and Loder, Lockett's technique focused on capturing the band's live aesthetic on record. In part because he was hampered by time and budget constraints, Lockett's sessions were fast-moving; even after Davis's investment in 1980, Lockett continued with a fast-and-furious methodology that captured a true-to-life picture of a band's live performance: "Everything was based on the idea of playing the music right when you were playing it live, and then recording that" (quoted in Backer 2018). Here, Lockett distinguishes his method from the constructionist rock mode so prevalent in the era.

What is notable about these early punk recordists is their emphasis on representing a strong performative aesthetic in the recorded text. This is consistent with what I have previously termed a "music first" approach evident among sound recordist attitudes toward their tech-processual practice between the 1970s and 1990s (Bennett 2010, 2018). Interestingly, at the core of this recording aesthetic lies a traditionalist approach to recording and production, including a strong inclination to work to a "performance capture" method as presented by the performer; to refrain from excessive, or even sonically discernible, technological, and processual intervention beyond the cohesion necessary for realizing a recorded text; and to place the wants and needs of musicians and their works first. This sort of recording approach is commensurate with approaches taken by classical and jazz recordists; the intention is to present the recording as close to a "live" concert experience as possible. Yet the records of DiCicco, Loder, and Lockett all share a frenetic sense of urgency, a spontaneous, heat-of-the-moment, and upfront text featuring a confrontational sonic aesthetic.

Workplaces and Technologies

In scholarly discourse and cultural commentary, the depiction of the site of punk recording as a small, DIY, dingy, perhaps basement studio with barely operational equipment is, at best, a flawed representation and, at worst, mythology. As Alan Williams has pointed out of popular music more broadly, the site of recording and production is one that is historically concealed (Williams 2010). To that end, since punk is a genre predating the so-called "democratization of technology" (Théberge 1997) in the 1980s—and the concomitant "revealing" of studio technologies and techniques—much historical recording practice is undocumented. Furthermore, oral histories, recordist interviews, and biographies are some of the only sources available when researching this topic, and such materials feature obvious flaws. Many are written in hindsight and do not rely on documented information of the time in question, and most recordists considered notable are the ones affiliated with canonized albums (Bennett 2018). As such, representations of punk recording and production are skewed.

One punk recording example where its cutting-edge workplace is downplayed lies in the Sex Pistols' *Never Mind the Bollocks*... The album was recorded at London's Wessex Studios, an elite recording studio situated in a converted church in Highbury and synonymous with progressive rock recordings by the likes of Queen and King Crimson. At the time of the Sex Pistols' recording, Wessex was equipped with world-leading recording technologies, to include two custom Cadac mixing consoles, including the 32-channel model used for the Sex Pistols; the UK's first 3-M M79 24-track tape machine; and a range of cutting-edge processors, including the then-latest Neve, Urei, and DBX compressors and Eventide's then-brand new digital processors, including the Harmonizer (Massey 2015). The presence of technological intervention on *Never Mind the Bollocks*... is significant and is a strong example of punk music having undergone rock production (Bennett 2015). The depiction of the recording process of *Never Mind the Bollocks*... in the *Classic Albums* documentary of the same title contains an interesting point of tension (see Longfellow 2002). While Wessex recordists Chris Thomas and Bill Price feature throughout, the band are depicted recording in Gooseberry Studios—a basement studio in Shepherd's Bush, operated by Dave Goodman. Goodman was responsible for recording Sex Pistols' demos prior to their album recording at Wessex (see Bennett 2015). Even at this early stage of preproduction, Goodman's session log evidence (Gilbert 2012) showing 16-track recordings with plenty of overdubs demonstrates the Sex Pistols working to an established "constructionist" rock music recording aesthetic, as opposed to a live, "performance capture" approach, which is often thought of as the dominant punk method (Bartel 2017). In the *Classic Albums* documentary, footage of the recording sessions, including a particularly notable scene of John Lydon recording vocals to "God Save the Queen," is, however, deceptive, because the master recording of the track is overdubbed onto the footage. Since the master recording is a result of the sessions at Wessex Studios, the overdubbing of the resulting audio onto the Gooseberry Studios footage erases the elitist technological and processual means by which the record was constructed; no footage of the Wessex Studios recording sessions is presented in the documentary. As such, the presentation of the Sex Pistols in the *Classic Albums* documentary is one that fits established notions of DIY aesthetics commensurate with the punk genre. However, the record's sonic aesthetics—its constructivist, technology-driven method coupled with foregrounded technological and processual intervention (Bennett 2015)—remain. On the one hand, the *Classic Albums* documentary succeeds in the *visual* portrayal of the Sex Pistols comfortably within the realm of punk ideology; on the other, it disassociates the Sex Pistols from the elite recording situation, thus denying the affiliation of the resulting recorded text to the rock establishment.

By the late 1970s, Wessex Studios was one of the UK's leading recording facilities. Following the Sex Pistols, a host of punk recordings were made there, including the Clash's *London Calling* (1979) and the Specials' *More Specials* (1980). While these records are certainly considered as at the mainstream end of the punk genre, their ties to the elite recording industry allow the texts to retain punk aesthetics while the studio situ and tech-processual construction validates them as rock. We can also consider these recordings as laying bare a certain aspirational aesthetic within punk, since the raw, live, performance capture approach to recording so inherent to punk is eschewed in favor of rock's technology-driven, constructionist approach.

Of course, there are multiple examples of independent recording workplaces that, through their trajectory of recorded music output, have slowly shifted away from their subcultural roots and toward the mainstream industry. Returning to John Loder, his Southern enterprise, which began in the mid-1970s as a recording studio venture for the creation of radio jingles, is a good example. Soon after the studio's inception, Loder began recording demos for the anarcho-punk band Crass. Between 1978 and its closure in 2012, the output of Southern Studios was largely independent, which had much to do with Loder's auteurism; by the early 1980s, Southern Studios had both distribution and record label arms. To that end, Loder could avoid any affiliation with even the independent music industry, and thus retain control over the entire production and dissemination process. Yet even Southern attracted major-label artists, and by the mid-1980s it was making recordings for numerous high-profile acts, including the WEA-signed Jesus and Mary Chain.

From its inception in the late 1960s until today, punk has traversed the most transformative age in sound recording. Yet, in doing so, it has retained a strong analog aesthetic, with its recordists and workplaces not ascribing to digital workflows until the late 1990s. The retention of analog recording technologies by exponents of punk production is certainly commensurate with a commitment to a "music first" aesthetic, as recognized earlier. When considering the trajectories of both punk recordists and workplaces, two clear aesthetics are evident among the technological complements applied to punk recordings. First, there is a clear "upgrade" aesthetic present whereby workplace income is ploughed back into technologies—four-track recorders are upgraded to eight tracks, 24-channel consoles upgraded to 32, and the complement of outboard effects processors expanded. While this could be simply ascribed to technological change, it does not comfortably align with the ways in which larger-format, elite, and commercial facilities upgraded as a matter of course and to keep up with cutting-edge technology. Second, and seemingly antithetically, there is a clear "hand-me-down" aesthetic in the acquisition of technologies by punk recordists and workplaces.

One major difference between technological ownership by commercial mainstream recordists and facilities and that of punk surrounds the acquisition of secondhand equipment. A further aspect of this "hand-me-down" aesthetic pertains to the nature of the technologies, which are often precursors and almost never the most advanced technologies available. These aesthetics play out across punk recording and production, and a good example is found in the work of recordists Butch Vig and Steve Marker and their Madison, Wisconsin–based Smart Studios. In the early 1980s, the studio featured very little equipment, with an SM57 microphone being "the most expensive mic we had" (Vig, quoted in Vanderslice 1998), and only one compressor. The recordists worked with local, emerging punk bands for the remainder of the decade before the clientele—and, along with it, the technological complement of the recording facility—became stronger. As Vig put it:

Everything that we started making we put back into the studio. It was like, "We need to get a better monitor system, we need to get more reverbs, we need to get more compressors, we need to get better mikes," and the list, of course, if you own a studio never stops. Everything we made we pretty much plowed back in. Over a period of time, we went to a more sophisticated eight-track to a sixteen-track to a 24 to a 48, to now a full-on Pro Tools System. It was a slow evolution.

(quoted in Vanderslice 1998)

Not only did Smart Studios grow into one of the foremost alternative music recording sites, but it also coincided with the rise of grunge music and its crossover into the commercial mainstream. Artists such as Nirvana, Smashing Pumpkins, and, later into the 1990s, Vig's own band Garbage transcended the outsider, anti-establishment status of punk and, with significant major label backing, were instead absorbed into the mainstream music industry.

While there is a good deal of work on the punk DIY aesthetic—even an international scholarly punk forum such as KISMIF asserts a celebratory position, its name an acronym for "Keep It Simple, Make It Fast" (see KISMIF website)—the idea that punk production emphasizes demo-quality recordings made in emergent workplaces is flawed. Historically, punk recording workplaces—and the concomitant tech-processual aesthetics inherent to them—are quite often sites of aspiration. Some of the most significant punk recordings were made at prominent workplaces with strong ties to the rock canon. Not only that, much subcultural music is often recorded in facilities associated with mainstream pop and rock record production, and the acoustic qualities of the recording space, technologies, and recordists thus imbue similar sonic aesthetics. To a large extent, this explains how punk musical and stylistic characteristics, as delineated from rock by Moore and Whiteley, are, paradoxically, bound to the same sonic canvas: via workplace, recordists, processes, and technologies. To that end, the reason why Nirvana's *Nevermind* (1991) appears in the same rock canon lists as Fleetwood Mac's *Rumours* (1977), or that Sex Pistols' *Never Mind the Bollocks . . .* (1977) rubs canonical shoulders with Queen's *News of the World* (1977), is perhaps more easily understood.

Where the smaller, independent workplace garners a strong reputation for punk and other alternative and/or subcultural genres, the workplace often evolves to absorb the work of major-label artists, thus instilling punk recording aesthetics into the commercial music industry. In parallel to the continuum of the punk genre, the independent recording facility has undoubtedly been at the nexus of the subcultural/commercial boundary.

Conclusion

In summary, matters of workplace, recordist agency, and sound recording technologies have greatly impacted the inception, development, and evolution of punk. Where punk ideology champions DIY, cheap and quick modes of production, and working-class labor, its most renowned texts from the 1970s through the 1990s embody complex and, therefore, contentious sonic attributes. Much renowned 1970s punk was recorded by established classical, jazz, experimental, and rock recordists in elite recording studios. Records including the Ramones' *Ramones* and Sex Pistols' *Never Mind the Bollocks*... were made with significant technological and processual intervention and are representative of "constructionist" rock recording modes. As such, these recordings embody an aspirational aesthetic: while the musical and stylistic components mark a move away from traditional rock modes, the production elements aspire to established rock values. The DIY aesthetic so central to punk discourse may apply most clearly to localized, emergent punk recording modes. But even the anarcho-punk and hardcore of the early 1980s relied upon midsized recording workplaces with multitracking capabilities. Nevertheless, the "live" "performance capture" approach is embodied in these recordings, and as such we could consider the texts representative of such (sub) genres closer to punk ideology than perhaps their 1970s forbearers.

Another key punk recording and production aesthetic lies in the notion of risk. Many scholars and cultural commentators have noted the initial reception of punk as threatening, shocking, and even dangerous. To professionally affiliate oneself with the genre—particularly where the music featured subversive politics, swearing, or presented a sonic challenge to mainstream musics—could be a substantial risk. By the turn of the 1980s, most recordists were freelance. Commercial recording studios employed few in-house technicians. Association with the "wrong kind of music" was a risk to a freelance recordist's career. In the cases of Loder, Albini, DiCicco, and Lockett, they took great risks in affiliating themselves with subversive artists. Sometimes, of course, cultural risk pays off: as the genre evolved, such recordists—and others—eventually became sought after due to their accumulated (sub)cultural capital.

The "live" aesthetic is a point of contention in punk recording and production. Many canonized punk recordings of the 1970s did *not* ascribe to such a recording method and instead were made using a long-established "constructionist" rock mode. Featuring plenty of sonically discernible multitracking, overdubs, spatial and timbral manipulations, and effects processing, 1970s punk mirrors the technological and processual intervention so obvious in rock. The "live" aesthetic does survive, however, as punk develops in subgenres like anarcho-punk and hardcore. Nevertheless, while the processual aspect of "performance capture" is embodied in such texts, the recordings were still produced in midsized workplaces with modest but professional technological complements. To that end, it is problematic to attribute a "DIY" aesthetic to the recording of such subgenres. Having said that, punk recordists rarely buy into "cutting edge" or even "new" technologies, preferring secondhand and/or technological precursors. The retention of analog workflows, particularly in punk and other alternative musics, continued long after the digital revolution. Punk retained a strong analog aesthetic, which continued to resonate via the work of Steve Albini and his Chicago-based Electrical Audio.

Punk recordists and their backgrounds are, however, varied. Via the work of recordists, there is a relationship between early punk and classical music and the concomitant "performance capture" and "live" recording aesthetics common to both. While numerous punk recordings have long been assimilated into the rock canon, tensions between punk and rock music are still present in the twenty-first century. On the one hand, punk is now accepted as a mainstream genre. Artists such as the US pop punk act Green Day, for example, carry a commercialized punk aesthetic via heavily constructionist rock production values. One the other hand, "DIY" values remain inherent to broader punk culture and are visible in the return of hard-copy fanzines, cassettes (perhaps as anti-digital statements as well as pro-DIY signifiers), and its enduring presence in global, underground scenes. This chapter has focused on just a few evident punk recording and production aesthetics in renowned recordings. This is a rich site for further exploration, and with the rise in punk studies it promises to be a point of focus for scholars long into the future.

References

Backer, S. 2018. "Behind the Sound of American Punk." *Red Bull Music Academy Daily*. http://daily.redbullmusicacademy.com/2018/11/behind-the-sound-of-american-punk.

Bartel, C. 2017. "Rock as a Three-Value Tradition." *Journal of Aesthetics and Art Criticism* 75, no. 2: 143–154.

Bennett, A. 2006. "Punk's Not Dead: The Continuing Significance of Punk Rock for an Older Generation of Fans." *Sociology* 40, no. 2: 219–235.

Bennett, S. 2010. "Examining the Emergence and Subsequent Proliferation of Anti Production amongst the Popular Music Producing Elite." PhD diss., University of Surrey.

Bennett, S. 2015. "*Never Mind the Bollocks*: A Tech-Processual Analysis." *Popular Music and Society* 38, no. 4: 466–486.

Bennett, S. 2017. "Songs about Fucking: John Loder's Southern Studios and the Construction of a Subversive Sonic Signature." *Journal of Popular Music Studies* 29, no. 2. doi:10.1111/jpms.12209.

Bennett, S. 2018. *Modern Records, Maverick Methods: Technology and Process in Popular Music Record Production 1978–2000*. London and New York: Bloomsbury Academic.

Buskin, R. 2004. "Classic Tracks: The Sex Pistols' 'Anarchy in the UK.'" *Sound on Sound*. https://www.soundonsound.com/techniques/classic-tracks-sex-pistols-anarchy-uk.

Covach, J., and G. Boone. 1997. *Understanding Rock*. Oxford: Oxford University Press.

Cunningham, M. 1998. *Good Vibrations*. London: Sanctuary Music.

Dolan, J., J. Fine, D. Fricke, E. Garber-Paul, A. Greene, W. Hermes, R. Sheffield, and D. Wolk. 2016. "40 Greatest Punk Albums of All Time." *Rolling Stone*, April 6, 2016. https://www.rollingstone.com/music/music-lists/40-greatest-punk-albums-of-all-time-75659/.

Doyle, P. 2005. *Echo and Reverb: Fabricating Space in Popular Music Recording 1900–1960*. Middletown, CT: Wesleyan University Press.

Dunn, K. 2008. "Never Mind the Bollocks: The Punk Rock Politics of Global Communication." *Review of International Studies* 34, no. S1: 193–210.

Dunn, K. 2012. "'If It Ain't Cheap, It Ain't Punk': Walter Benjamin's Progressive Cultural Production and DIY Punk Record Labels." *Journal of Popular Music Studies* 24, no. 2: 217–237.

Eisenberg, E. 2005. *The Recording Angel*. New Haven, CT: Yale University Press.

Gendron, B. 2002. *Between Montmartre and the Mudd Club: Popular Music and the Avant-Garde*. Chicago: Chicago University Press.

Gilbert, P. 2012. *1977—The Bollocks Diaries*. iBook. United States: Universal.

Gillett, C. 1977. "The Producer as Artist." In *The Phonograph and Our Musical Life*, edited by H. Hitchcock, 51–56. ISAM Monograph No. 14. New York: City University.

Gordon, A. 2012. "Building Recording Studios whilst Bradford Burned: DIY Punk Ethics in a Field of Force." In *Punkademics: The Basement Show in the Ivory Tower*, edited by Z. Furness. New York: Minor Compositions.

Greig, S., M. McCarthy, and J. Peacock. 1976. "The Filth and the Fury!" *Daily Mirror*, December 2, 1976.

Hebdige, D. 1979. *Subculture: The Meaning of Style*. London: Routledge.

Henry, T. 1984. "Punk and Avant-Garde Art." *Journal of Popular Culture* 17, no. 4: 30–36.

Ignorant, S. 2016. Interview with the Author.

Johnson, H. 2005. "Dead Kennedys' 'California Uber Alles'" *Mix Online*. https://www.mixonline.com/recording/dead-kennedys-california-uber-alles-365557.

Jopson, N. 2014. "Craig Leon: Record Producer Feature at Abbey Road Studios." http://recordproduction.com/record-producer-features/craig-leon-interview.html.

Katz, Mark. 2004. *Capturing Sound: How Technology Has Changed Music*. Berkeley: University of California Press.

KISMIF (Keep It Simple, Make It Fast). https://www.kismifconference.com/en/.

Laing, D. 1978. "Interpreting Punk Rock." *Marxism Today*, April 1978, 123–128.

Longfellow. M., dir. 2002. Classic Albums: *Sex Pistols—Never Mind the Bollocks, Here's the Sex Pistols*. DVD. Eagle Rock Entertainment.

Massey, H. 2015. *The Great British Recording Studios*. Milwaukee, WI: Hal Leonard.

McKay, G. 1996. *Senseless Acts of Beauty: Cultures of Resistance since the Sixties*. London: Verso.

McNeil, L., and G. McCain. 1996. *Please Kill Me: The Uncensored Oral History of Punk*. London: Penguin.

Milner, G. 2009. *Perfecting Sound Forever: The Story of Recorded Music*. London: Granta.

Moore, A. 2001. *Rock: The Primary Text*. 2nd ed. Aldershot, UK: Ashgate.

Moran, I. 2010. "Punk: The Do-It-Yourself Subculture." *Social Sciences Journal* 10, no. 1: 58–65.

O'Connell, H. 2012. "(Re)turning Money into Rebellion: Reification and Utopianism in Early Punk Production." *Journal of Popular Culture* 47, no. 3: 591–612.

O'Hare, P. 2007. Steve Albini "In Utero's" Ultra-Sound Guy. Paper presented at the Art of Record Production Conference. https://www.artofrecordproduction.com/aorpjoom/symposiums/19-arp-2007/126-ohare-2007.

Raggett, N. 2016. "Oliver DiCicco on Nearly Three Decades with Mobius Music Recording." *KQED Arts—Into The Mix*. https://www.kqed.org/arts/12286750/oliver-dicicco-on-nearly-three-decades-with-mobius-music-recording.

Robb, J. 2006. *Punk Rock: An Oral History*. Edited by O. Craske. London: Ebury Press.

Rodel, A. 2004. "Extreme Noise Terror: Punk Rock and the Aesthetics of Badness." In *Bad Music: The Music We Love to Hate*, edited by C. Washburne and M. Derno, 235–256. New York and London: Routledge.

Rombes, N. 2005. *Ramones*. New York: Continuum.

Savage, J. 1991. *England's Dreaming: Sex Pistols and Punk Rock*. London: Faber & Faber.

Schmidt Horning, S. 2013. *Chasing Sound: Technology, Culture and the Art of Studio Recording from Edison to the LP*. Baltimore: Johns Hopkins University Press.

Seymour, P. 2015. "An Interview with Spot and Joe Carducci of SST Records." Chirp 107.1 FM. https://chirpradio.org/blog/an-interview-with-spot-and-joe-carducci-of-sst-records.

Shepherd, R. 2011. "The Collaborative Recordist." *Musicology Australia* 33, no. 2: 255–264.

Théberge, P. 1997. *Any Sound You Can Imagine: Making Music/Consuming Technology*. Hanover, NH: Wesleyan University Press.

Triggs, T. 2006. "Scissors and Glue: Punk Fanzines and the Creation of a DIY Aesthetic." *Journal of Design History* 19, no. 1: 69–83.

Vanderslice, J. 1998. "Butch Vig: Garbage and Smart Studios." *Tape Op*. https://tapeop.com/interviews/11/butch-vig/.

Von Appen, R., and A. Doehring. 2006. "Nevermind the Beatles, Here's Exile 61 and Nico: 'The Top 100 Records of All Time'—A Canon of Pop and Rock Albums from a Sociological and an Aesthetic Perspective." *Popular Music* 25, no. 1: 21–39.

Whiteley, S. 2000. *Women and Popular Music: Sexuality, Identity and Subjectivity*. London: Routledge.

Williams, A. 2010. "Pay Some Attention to the Man Behind the Curtain—Unsung Heroes and the Canonization of Process in the *Classic Albums* Documentary Series." *Journal of Popular Music Studies* 22, no. 2: 166–175.

Young, A. 2004. "Albini Laments Age of Over Production." *Sidelines—Student Newspaper of Middle Tennessee State University*, March 15, 2004. http://inmyroom.org/writing/albini.html.

Zak, A. J., III. 2001. *The Poetics of Rock: Cutting Tracks, Making Records*. Berkeley: University of California Press.

CHAPTER 26

FANZINE SCENES

KEVIN C. DUNN

ZINES have been an integral part of punk culture since its inception. This entry will provide a brief history of zines, discuss the evolution of zines, and reflect on the implications for punk zines on local scenes and the global punk community. But first, what is a zine?

The term *zine* (pronounced "zeen") usually refers to any self-published work reproduced via a photocopier or small printing press, often with a highly specialized focus to appeal to a particular audience. They are noncommercial, nonprofessional publications that the creators usually produce, publish, and distribute themselves, typically in small numbers. The press run varies greatly, with some scholars suggesting that the circulation must be 5,000 or less, though this seems to be an arbitrary definition. In reality, most zines are printed in much lower numbers, often just a few dozen or a few hundred. Zines can be written in a variety of formats, from computer-printed text to comics to handwritten prose, and can take many different forms, from the single folded sheet to bounded (stapled or otherwise) photocopied paper. Some zines are produced by just one person, while others are collaborative affairs. Part of their appeal is that zines can be produced by anyone and everyone. While topics, formats, means of production, print runs, distribution, and circulations vary greatly, what makes a zine a zine is largely the creator's do-it-yourself (DIY) ethos and the understanding that profit is not the primary intent of publication.

For zine-makers, there is an explicit desire to avoid established commercial networks and practices. Zines are typically traded freely or sold at minimum cost to cover expenses. Profit is usually not the primary concern, and most zines are produced and distributed at a financial loss. Zines are often treated by their producers more as gifts than commodities. This point is underscored by the fact that zine is not short for "magazine." As Larry-bob, publisher of the *Holy Titclamps* zine has stated, "A magazine is a product, a commercial commodity. A zine is a labor of love, producing no profit. . . . Information is the reason a zine exists" (quoted in Wright 1997). Many zine producers create their zines as part of a conscious rejection of consumerist culture, while promoting a DIY ethos and the desire to create one's own culture. Within zine culture, there is a common refrain passed on to readers: make your own zine. Don't just be a passive consumer, but an active producer.

This mentality has meant that zines cover a wide breadth of topics, from John Marr's infamous *Murder Can Be Fun*, which documents various murders in painstaking historical detail, to Dishwasher Pete's popular stories about his experiences washing dishes in every state in the US, to the autobiographical musings of a mother in New York City, as found in Ayun Halliday's *The East Village Inky*. Indeed, the range of topics is unlimited, from politics and art to ephemera, autobiographic confessionals, fan fiction, sexual fantasies, and single topic obsessions. But it was its convergence with punk via the shared commitment to DIY cultural production that revitalized zine culture in the late 20th century and helped turn it into a global phenomenon. After a brief history of the zine, this entry will discuss the development of punk zines from the early scenes in New York City and London to the emergence of punk and punk zines as global phenomena.

A Short History of Zines

It is common for some zine historians to claim that zines first emerged in the 20th century among fans of science fiction (Wright 1997; Spencer 2005: 79; Moore, n.d.). Others have argued that the roots of zine-making can be traced much further back by appreciating the long history of self-publishing as an alternative form of expression. Even before the development of commercial publishing, Thomas Paine self-published his *Common Sense* pamphlet, while Benjamin Franklin created a publication for a psychiatric hospital that he distributed to patients and staff, thus embodying the key elements of modern zine-making. Eighteenth-century political pamphlets exemplified the practice of offering personal interpretations of the news. With the rise of major commercial publishing ventures in the eighteenth and nineteenth centuries came the related development of amateur small presses and self-publishing. Using toy presses and scavenged printing equipment, hundreds of amateur publishers emerged in the nineteenth century, with over five hundred writers and editors and almost as many publications active by 1875 (Duncombe 2008, 54). Literary modernism, which began at the end of the 19th century, was deeply shaped by the development of so-called "little magazines" akin to zines: independently published periodicals featuring short stories, poetry, essays, reviews, and literary criticism, which served as an alternative to larger, more commercially oriented literary magazines (Bulson 2012).

In the 1920s, science fiction magazines like Hugo Gernsback's *Amazing Stories* began being distributed in newsstands across the United States. The editors of *Amazing Stories* made an important and innovative decision to reprint letters from readers, listing not only their names but also their addresses (Spencer 2005, 79–80). This enabled readers to begin connecting with each other, leading to correspondence clubs that began sharing opinions and their own stories via the mail. Soon these readers were creating their own handmade and hand-printed zines, filled with their own stories and writings. It is worth noting that, as an underground vehicle, sci-fi fanzines provided opportunities for females to participate in ways they could not in the traditional, masculine world of professional publishing.

The self-published zine medium soon moved beyond the domain of science fiction. By the 1940s, American beat writers like Jack Kerouac and Allen Ginsberg began self-publishing their work in zines. This was often by necessity, since established magazines and literary publishers were inhospitable to their submissions. Turning to outsider independent presses and embracing self-publishing, beat writers were able to achieve a level of success denied them by the established commercial literary outlets. The beat writers then helped engender a further generation of self-publishing that bridged the earlier "little magazines" and modern zines. In the art world, the Dadaists were producing a wide collection of art zines, such as *Cabaret Voltaire*, *Dada*, *291*, *391*, and *New York Dada*, in many ways creating the template for the modern zine with their use of collage, *détournement*, and appropriation (Spencer 2005, 101–102). Avant-garde political groups such as the Situationist International embraced the form in their attempts to get their ideas and agenda circulated. The Situationist International adopted the novel approach of distribution by mailing their self-published zines to people chosen at random from the phone book. In Russia, political dissidents produced political zines called *samizdat*, literally "self-publishers" (Wright 1997; Spencer 2005,147).

The evolution of zines was partly driven by changing material conditions, which across the 20th century altered dramatically and facilitated the rise of self-publishing. First was the development of offset printing, a relatively cheap and accessible way of printing with cold ink and a rubber "blanket" that provided an alternative to the bulky, expensive, and labor-intensive method of using hot lead and linoleum. This technological development helped contribute to the growth of independent presses in the US and Europe around the middle of the century. But it was the invention of the photocopying machine by Xerox in the 1960s that revolutionized the zine form, making self-publishing inexpensive and accessible to most in the industrialized world.

The 1960s also witnessed the development of rock music and its supporting cultures, including a nascent zine culture. Many of the people who had been producing sci-fi zines began creating rock music-themed zines, such as Paul Williams's *Crawdaddy* and Greg Shaw's *Mojo Navigator Rock & Roll News*. Both creators had been active in the sci-fi fanzine scene (Spencer 2005, 154). While the 1960s had been an active time for self-publishing and underground presses, by the early 1970s, zine-making was experiencing a slump. The political fervor that had fueled the 1960s self-publishing activism had largely dissipated. The two major sources of fanzine interests, music and science fiction, had become increasingly corporatized, with slick professionalism championed over fan accessibility. Enter punk.

THE RISE OF PUNK ZINES

Punks were quick to embrace the zine as part of punk culture, given the convergence of a shared DIY ethos, and punk zines perfectly embodied the ideal of do-it-yourself self-expression. Photocopied fanzines, such as *Sniffin' Glue*, *Punk*, *Search and Destroy*,

Flipside, and *Maximumrocknroll*, became major aspects of punk scenes. Those early punk zines provided readers with invaluable information from emerging punk scenes, but also counteracted the hostile coverage punks were then receiving in the mainstream media. Dick Hebdige has noted that with regards to the early punk zines, "The overwhelming impression was one of urgency and immediacy, of a paper produced in indecent haste, of memos from the front line" (Hebdige 1979, 111). For many readers, this effect of immediacy seemed to provide punk zines with a higher degree of authenticity than glossy mainstream publications.

There is some debate about which was the first punk zine. In 1976, John Holmstrom, Ged Dunn, and Eddie "Legs" McNeil began producing the seminal punk zine, *Punk*, to chronicle the emerging New York punk scene, largely situated around CBGB. *Punk*'s first issue included a feature on the Ramones, Lou Reed, several comic strips, and a fictitious interview with Sluggo from the *Nancy* comic strip. The zine proved to be immediately successful, selling 3,000 copies locally and over 25,000 worldwide. But the previous year, in February 1975, Fred "Phast Phreddie" Patterson published the first issue of the fanzine *Back Door Man* from his bedroom in Torrance, California, featuring Iggy Pop on the cover. *Back Door Man* was arguably the first punk fanzine, with an emphasis on the growing underground musical scene in Los Angeles. As one of the contributors, Don Waller (aka Doc Savage), recalled later, "We wanted to throw a metaphorical brick through the plate-glass window of a pop-cultural world that didn't want to know about anything but an increasingly pointless worship of musical technique or 'going up the country, gonna get my head together' platitudes that stifled any other type of expression. And had absolutely nuthin' to do with the all-too-real lives that we were living" (Waller n.d.). Fifteen issues were put out over the next three-and-a-half years, with a focus on what the writers considered "hard core rock 'n' roll," including the blues, metal, and punk, but not limited to one specific musical genre.

Around the time *Punk* was being distributed in New York City, Mark Perry's *Sniffin' Glue* emerged from the nascent London punk scene. Copies of *Punk* were actually in circulation in London, and Perry has acknowledged that he was inspired by that zine, as well as the New York punk scene, particularly the Ramones, naming the zine after their song "Now I Wanna Sniff Some Glue." The Soho music shop Rock On had encouraged Perry, a bank clerk, to produce a zine, which he finally did in the summer of 1976 after reading a review of the Ramones' first album by Nick Kent and deciding he could do it differently and better. Rock On quickly sold out of the first issue, and Perry discovered there was a substantial market for the zine. Speaking about the first issue, Perry was later to state, "The whole first issue was what I could do at the time with what I had in my bedroom. I had a children's typewriter plus a felt-tip pen, so that's why the first issue is how it is. I just thought it would be a one-off. I knew when I took it to the shop there was a good chance they'd laugh at me, but instead they said, How many you got? I think my girlfriend had done 20 on the photocopier at her work and they bought the lot off me. Then they advanced me some money to get more printed" (Perry 2002). Handmade and hand-photocopied, the zine initially featured Perry's take on such bands as the Ramones and Blue Oyster Cult, as well as reviews of record releases and up-and-coming bands.

Eventually featuring photographs and interviews, *Sniffin' Glue* was intentionally basic in its layout and design. As Perry states, "In a way, we were making a statement—You don't need to be flash. Anyone can have a go" (Perry 2002).

This adherence to punk's DIY ethos helped inspire countless other zines throughout the UK punk scene, including *Ripped & Torn* out of Glasgow, *London's Burning*, *London's Outrage*, *Anarchy in the UK*, *Bondage*, *Sideburns*, *Fishnet Stockings*, and *48 Thrills*. Many of these zines were passed along by hand via the growing social networks of the punk community, both within the UK and beyond. Indeed, there is evidence of early zine exchanges between the UK punk scenes and those across continental Europe. For example, two French zines, *I Wanna Be Your Dog* and *Matheuresusement*, could easily be found within the London punk scene, reflecting interconnections within the growing global punk community (Parsons 1977, 12).

Back in the United States, several punk zines flourished, including what is arguably the most well-known punk zine, *Maximumrocknroll* (aka *MRR*). Initially begun as a radio show in the San Francisco Bay area in 1977, *MRR* began its print life in 1982 and soon became one of the most important punk zines in the world, with a reach that is international in its focus and distribution. Other punk zines emerged across the US, concurrent with emerging local scenes. Inspired by *Punk*, *New York Rocker* was published from 1976 until 1982, first under Alan Betrock and then Andy Schwartz, and had a circulation of around 20,000. In LA, the zine *Slash* was a key component of the development of the local punk zine. Started in May 1977 by Steve Samiof and Melanie Nissen, the zine ran until 1980, and spawned the eponymous Slash Records label. In San Francisco, V. Vale published the influential *Search and Destroy* from 1977 to 1979. As Vale states, "Our approach was really minimalist, we felt that that was the new philosophy. It wasn't just going to be a documentation, it was going to be a catalyst. . . . I soon realized that Punk was total cultural revolt. It was a hardcore confrontation with the black side of history and culture, right-wing imagery, sexual taboos, a delving into it that had never been done before by any generation in such a thorough way" (quoted in Savage 2002, 439).

In the wake of these early punk zines, self-publishing in the US and Europe dramatically increased during the late 1970s and into the 1980s. These zines were not merely catalogs of adulation for the authors' favorite bands. The zines became active parts of the culture, building networks, facilitating the growth of local scenes, spreading news and ideas to others, and providing a forum for the authors' opinions on social and political issues. For example, Johan Van Leeuwen, editor of the Dutch punk zine *Nieuwe Koekrand*, states, "Originally, doing a fanzine was a way to be part of a scene, and as far as I'm concerned, it also was a necessity to stay active and become an accepted member of the punk community. Over the years, it's more and more become a way to have 'my humble opinion' known to others" (Van Leeuwen 1990, 10). Zine writers became instrumental—and equal—members of the punk scenes. In many ways, this reflected the egalitarian nature of punk: tearing down the boundaries between audience and artists. Just as punk bands preached the philosophy that anyone could (and should) pick up an instrument and play, so too did the punk zinesters preaching the DIY ethos of self-publishing. As John Holmstrom wrote in an editorial in issue #3 of *Punk*, "The key word—to me anyway—in the punk definition was 'a beginner, an inexperienced hand.' Punk rock: any kid can pick up a guitar and become a rock 'n' roll star, despite or because of his lack of ability, talent, intelligence, limitations and/or potential" (Holmstrom 1976). As Perry proclaimed in the pages of *Sniffin' Glue*, "All you kids out there who read *Sniffin' Glue*, don't be satisfied with what we write. Go out and start your own fanzines" (Perry 1976).

The punk zine experienced a further resurgence in the late 1980s and early 1990s with the emergence of Riot Grrrl, a movement of female empowerment aimed at reclaiming the multigendered spaces of the initial punk movement. The movement was largely fueled by zine culture. Allison Wolfe and Molly Neuman (members of the band Bratmobile) worked with fanzine editor Jen Smith to establish a collectively authored feminist zine called *Riot Grrrl*. At the same time, Kathleen Hanna was co-producing the zine *Bikini Kill* and began organizing weekly "Riot Grrrl" meetings with about twenty other women. Within a few months, a movement has emerged that spread across North America and beyond. Among Riot Grrrl's main contributions to feminist change were its persistent opposition to the mainstream media and its call for women and girls to publicly express themselves. Zine-making as an alternative feminist form of mass communication was central to the Riot Grrrl movement from the very beginning, with Riot Grrrl growing as much out of zine culture as it did punk. The very name was taken from an established zine, and Bikini Kill was a zine-making collective before it was a band. With its roots in zine culture, Riot Grrrl helped inspire a virtual "revolution" in self-published girl zines. Writing at the time, Joanne Gottlieb and Gayle Wald observed that "zines provide a forum, outside (though not detached from) the music, in which the members of riot grrrl subculture can engage in their own self-naming, self-definition and self-critique—can comment, in other words, upon the very shape and representation of the subculture itself" (Gottlieb and Wald 1994, 265). While networking was clearly an important facet of the zine culture, perhaps a more important aspect was spreading the message of personal empowerment. This was a message that had always been at the forefront of zine culture. Riot Grrrl zines, like most punk zines, encouraged readers to produce their own zines; to be not just consumers of culture, but also producers of their own media.

Over the decades, there have been numerous other influential punk zines, most of which have focused on local scenes. One of the earliest to emerge was *Flipside*, which was first published in August 1977 by a group of teenagers at Whittier High School outside of Los Angeles, California. After exposure to live punk bands at the Whisky in Hollywood, the group decided to start a fanzine to chronicle the nascent Los Angeles punk scene. The first issue was a stapled quarter-page photocopied fanzine that they hand-distributed to local clubs, but they eventually established a distribution deal that took the zine nationwide. At the same time, the zine evolved into a major semi-professional glossy-covered publication, with a related record label. It eventually was sold in major chain outlets like Tower Records and Border Books, with a global distribution reaching as far as Japan. Though maintaining a focus on the LA punk scene, *Flipside* also sought to reflect the globality of the punk community. At the same time, it was one of the textual forces that gave shape and coherence to the movement. *Flipside* eventually went out of business in 2000, largely because of financial difficulties related to problems with Rotz, the distribution company for *Flipside*'s related record label. *Flipside* successively sued the distribution company for lack of payments, only to see the company declare bankruptcy immediately after the verdict. The demise of Rotz had repercussions throughout the indie media world, with one of the casualties being *Flipside* itself. Unable to recover from the financial straits it found itself in, *Flipside* folded.

The death of *Flipside* is not dissimilar to that of *Punk Planet*, another influential American punk zine. But where *Flipside* was brought down when the distributor of their record label declared bankruptcy, *Punk Planet* was the victim of a much bigger distribution catastrophe. Based in Chicago, *Punk Planet* published its first issue in May 1994, reportedly as a response to the view that *MRR* had become too elitist and aggressive in policing the boundaries of punk. Founded by nineteen-year-old Dan Sinker, the zine was originally printed on newsprint (as was *MRR*) but it soon shifted to a format similar to *Flipside* (full-color cover with offset printing). The bimonthly zine's print run eventually reached 16,000, with a global distribution network. Purposefully attempting to be more inclusive than *MRR*, *Punk Planet* reviewed almost all material sent to it, as long as it wasn't on a major record label. Thus, the coverage of the zine included alternative musical genres beyond a strictly delineated understanding of punk. This broader focus generated some criticism, as did its relatively high production values, including a full-color cover, perfect binding as opposed to staples, and professional-looking design and layout. The cost of *Punk Planet*—the list price for the final issues was $4.95—was also notably higher than *MRR* and *Flipside*.

As *Punk Planet* grew in size, so did its distribution needs. *Punk Planet* began distributing through the Independent Press Association (IPA), which was founded in 1996 as a nonprofit that provided its members with technical assistance, access to loans, and other services aimed at supporting independent publishers. But in 2000, IPA made the decision to begin distributing for its members, buying the troubled BigTop Newsstand Services, and relaunching it as Indy Press Newsstand Services. Within a few years, the IPA nonprofit was operating as a multimillion-dollar distribution venture for over five hundred members, including *Mother Jones* and *The Nation*. In 2003 the IPA went through a change in directors that affected its business practices, resulting in a tightly regulated, top-down management approach coupled with high executive salaries (Davis 2007). At the same time, a number of the IPA's members were concerned that they were not receiving the revenue that was owed to them. The collapse of IPA occurred in 2006, with profound repercussions, as it wiped out numerous independent publications. *Punk Planet* continued publishing for a few months, but called it quits in the summer of 2007, publicly placing the blame on the IPA debacle.

In early 2019, *MRR* announced that it was shutting down its print zine, while continuing its original radio program as well as its online presence. It was decided that the financial challenges of producing and distributing the zine made it unfeasible to continue. This left *Razorcake* as the last remaining long-running influential punk zine in America. Started by Todd Taylor, a former editor at *Flipside*, and Sean Carswell,

Razorcake's declared focus is narrowly on DIY culture first and foremost. With a print run of roughly 6,000, *Razorcake* is a small operation with only two full-time employees, a production team of five to six part-timers, and a vast network of over a hundred regular contributing writers, illustrators, photographers, editors, and proofers. Around the time of *Punk Planet*'s collapse, *Razorcake* changed its legal designation to a 501(c)(3) charitable organization that can accept tax-deductible donations. Because of its nonprofit status, it does not have to pay federal taxes, can accept donations, is available for grants, and gets some discounts with the post office. Also, in place of working with a national distributor, *Razorcake* has put together a patchwork array of regional distributors and direct-to-stores networks. But most significantly, it has become its own biggest distributor through subscriptions. While large-scale independent zines such as *Flipside*, *Punk Planet*, and *MRR* failed, *Razorcake* offers an interesting story of survival due to its official nonprofit legal designation and an adherence to the traditional DIY ethos of punk.

While *Razorcake* continues to thrive as an internationally recognized publication, most punk zines have much smaller print runs and tend to be far more locally focused. Moreover, punk zines have become a global form. Over the years, punk and punk-inspired zines have appeared all over the world, but under a variety of guises as local conditions, interests, tastes, and material conditions have shaped their appearance and content. Zines do not belong to a single nation, continent, or hemisphere. In 2019, punk zines can be found on almost every continent, from the Americas to Europe, from Africa and the Middle East to Asia. In addition to their lengthy presence across North America and Europe, zines are notable parts of vibrant contemporary punk scenes in such disparate places as Mexico, Colombia, South Africa, Malaysia, Indonesia, and Japan. With the advent of the internet, social media, and blogging, some punk zines maintain some form of online presence, while others remain solely rooted in print culture.

While no authoritative estimation about the number or location of zines exists, it is still safe to assume that the majority of zines are produced in the Western world, and it would be naive to suggest that the transnational circuits of exchange and circulation are equitable. The divisions between the global core and periphery in terms of the flow of information and products are just as real in DIY punk and other alternative networks as they are in the larger global economic system. The production and circulation of zines face substantial material challenges that limit their mobility, including postal costs, customs, shipping timetables, printing and distribution networks, and so on. One is far more likely to find a copy of *MRR*, *Razorcake*, or *Profane Existence* in Jakarta than an Indonesian punk zine in NYC, London, or Los Angeles.

While the global circulation of zines is important, perhaps more important is that the *zine as form* has become a global medium. Employing a global form like zines, writers may have drawn from Western models, but zine production, circulation, and consumption are not dependent on the West. They are local products, connected to a decentered global universe. And while there are substantial obstacles to their movement, they *do* move, particularly because they operate at the margins of established systems of commercial exchange. Indeed, the zine's global-local interchange is a significant aspect of punk zine culture. For example, the early punk zine *Damage* (1979–1981) was based in

San Francisco but adopted an explicitly global scope, covering punk scenes in London, Paris, Tokyo, and elsewhere. This approach was carried on by *Maximumrocknroll*. Started in 1982 by Tim Yohannan to reflect the Bay Area punk scene, *MRR* quickly evolved to explicitly situate itself within an international punk community. Before its 2019 demise, its self-defined goal was to "keep the worldwide scene connected." It did this by offering reports from punk scenes around the world, actively reviewing non-US musical releases, and maintaining a letters section that regularly features submissions from outside the US.

In an attempt to strengthen global communication across punk scenes, many punk zines, such as *MRR* and *Profane Existence*, featured scene reports from around the world, or at least useful contact information for bands planning tours. Before the advent of the internet, a regular resource for touring was the *Book Your Own Fucking Life* zine, which listed contact information for everything from venues that would book bands to zines that would review your music, stores that would sell your records, and locals who would give bands a place to sleep. Thus, zines have played an important role in connecting local punk scenes to a larger, decentered global punk community.

The Importance of Punk Zines

Punk zines, like both punk and zines more broadly, are a critical response to the status quo. They seek to not just critique the consumerist culture of modern society, but also to also provide alternative ways of being. What is happening in these pages is often an explicit attempt of the zine writers to destroy the seductive pablum fed to consumers in modern capitalism to help keep them passive. At one level, the critical potential of the zine is less about the content, and more about the form itself. Rejection of the status quo begets cultural production itself. Punk zinesters actively challenged the passive relationships inscribed within consumer culture by producing a participatory model of culture. Dan Werle, editor of the zine *Manumission*, put it this way: "Doing something like a zine, as small as it may be, is very much a refutation.... It's refuting the whole pathetic, sit down and be entertained type of environment.... This is saying: No, I'm taking things into my own hands, I'm not gonna allow someone else to bombard me. I'm going to be the entertainer of myself" (quoted in Duncombe 2008, 111). Today's capitalist consumer culture constructs relationships between consumer and product that are devoid of any sort of reciprocal creativity. Products are there to be consumed, passively. Punk zines reinscribe the individual as a cultural producer instead of a passive consumer.

Punk zines are part of networks and cultures that privilege alternative practices that are neither profit-driven nor centralized. Punk zines are distributed for free or at prices that barely cover production costs. There is also a reformulation and, at times, outright rejection of the understanding of "intellectual property" and copyright ownership. The simple fact that the zine exists largely independent of (and in opposition to) established corporate media and commercial culture should be recognized as a subversive act, with political potential. Punk zine makers reforge the links between themselves and the consumerist world we all inhabit. They do so in part by insisting on interacting with commodities—books, music, clothes, TV shows, anything really—in ways that go well beyond what is expected. As Stephen Duncombe observed, "By writing record reviews, interviewing their favorite bands, and commenting on their local music scene, the people who put out music zines are taking a product that is bought and sold as a commodity in the marketplace and forcing it into an intimate relationship. Instead of relying upon sanctioned mediators like *Rolling Stone* or *Spin*, they assert their own right to speak authoritatively about the music they love—making the culture theirs" (Duncombe 2008, 114–115). Thus, they are engaging the dominant culture and recreating their own relationship to it, often in ways that challenge the logic of consumer capitalism.

Note: For additional details, including interviews and analysis, see Dunn 2016.

References

Bulson, Eric. 2012. "Little Magazine, World Form." In *Oxford Handbook of Global Modernisms*, edited by Mark Wollaeger and Matt Eatough, 267–287. Oxford: Oxford University Press.

Davis, Paul M. 2007. "Personality Crisis: When the Independent Press Association Went Under." *Punk Planet* 80: 74–78.

Duncombe, Stephen. 2008. *Notes from Underground: Zines and the Politics of Alternative Culture*. Bloomington, IN: Microcosm.

Dunn, Kevin C. 2016. *Global Punk: Resistance and Rebellion in Everyday Life*. New York: Bloomsbury.

Gottlieb, Joanne, and Gayle Wald. 1994. "Smells Like Teen Spirit: Riot Grrrls, Revolution and Women in Independent Rock." In *Microphone Fiends: Youth Music and Youth Culture*, edited by Andrew Ross and Tricia Rose. 250–273. New York and London: Routledge.

Hebdige, Dick. 1979. *Subculture: The Meaning of Style*. London: Routledge.

Holmstrom, John. 1976. "Editorial." *Punk* 3 (March).

Moore, Anne Elizabeth. n.d. "Be A Zinester: How and Why to Publish your own Periodical." Available at http://www.anneelizabethmoore.com. Accessed June 12, 2009.

Parsons, Tony. 1977. "Glue Scribe Speaks Out." *NME*, February 12, 1977, 12 (reprinted in *NME Originals*, April 2002, 110).

Perry, Mark. 1976. "Editorial." *Sniffin' Glue* 5 (November).

Perry, Mark. 2002. "We Heart UHU" (interview). Q, April 2002, 104–105.

Savage, Jon. 2002. *England's Dreaming: Anarchy, Sex Pistols, Punk Rock and Beyond*. New York: St. Martin's Press.

Spencer, Amy. 2005. *DIY: The Rise of Lo-Fi Culture*. London and New York: Marion Boyars.

Van Leeuwen, Johan. 1990. "Johan Van Leeuwen." in *Threat by Example*, edited by Martin Sprouse. San Francisco, CA: Pressure Drop Press.

Waller, Don. n.d. "About *Back Door Man* Magazine." Available at http://www.myspace.com/backdoormanmagazine. Accessed June 13, 2011.

Wright, Fred. 1997. "The History and Characteristics of Zines." In *The Zine and E-Zine Resource Guide*. http://www.zinebook.com/resource/wrights1.html.

PART SIX

NEVERMIND
The Shifting Politics of Punk

CHAPTER 27

"CAUGHT IN A CULTURE CROSSOVER!" ROCK AGAINST RACISM AND ALIEN KULTURE

JOE O'CONNELL

INTRODUCTION

ROCK Against Racism (RAR) was a grass-roots musical protest movement established in 1976 that opposed fascist political groups such as the National Front (NF) in late-1970s Britain. It has been estimated that 800 RAR events took place in Britain between 1976 and 1979, the largest of which were two 1978 carnivals that drew crowds of up to 100,000 in Manchester and London (Kalra et al. 1996, 138).[1] Events continued to take place under the RAR banner into the early 1980s, culminating in the release of a compilation LP, *RAR's Greatest Hits*, in 1981 (Widgery 1986, 110), and a final large-scale carnival in Leeds the same year (Street 2012, 81).

While the two 1978 carnivals were organized by a central committee, most concerts that took place under the RAR banner were organized by local promoters and fans who, after advice from the movement's nominal leaders, had established regional branches. According to David Widgery (1986, 101), one of RAR's central figures and chroniclers, these existed in over fifty towns and were run in an informal and "anarchic" fashion by coalitions of left-wing activists, punks, and Rastas. He claims that, via their local activities, RAR played a key role in nurturing punk as a genre in regions outside of London by providing performance opportunities for new bands who supported the anti-racist cause (72). RAR could, therefore, be considered an important factor in the development of the popular understanding of UK punk as a regional DIY movement. While RAR reached its zenith after punk's apparent "death"—cited by Reynolds (2006, 5) as coinciding with, or a result of, the release of the Sex Pistols's *Never Mind the Bollocks* in October 1977—it can be said to have played an important role in establishing a nationwide performance network for punk rock acts.

One of the key stipulations of RAR concerts was that the lineup should be multiracial. Despite the breadth of musical styles implied by the word "rock," RAR events were generically dominated by punk, which was taken as representative of white youth, and reggae acts, taken as a representative of young black communities. RAR has been widely recognized as an attempt to harness the political potential of punk rock and direct the nihilistic energy associated with its music and subculture toward purposeful left-wing outlet (Frith and Street 1992; Goodyer 2009; Street 2012). The political meaning of punk performers' involvement with RAR and its goals varied: while groups such as the Tom Robinson Band made anti-discrimination and socialist discourse an explicit focus in their songs and performances (Savage 2001, 396), Sham 69 were encouraged by RAR to perform under their banner to counter a growing support for the NF among their fan base (Widgery 1986, 79–80). White and black communities were certainly represented on stage at RAR events; however, the focus of the NF's activism in this period was firmly on Asian communities. One of the more problematic aspects addressed by scholarly histories of RAR is its engagement with Asian communities: Did it attempt to represent Asian communities onstage as a means of promoting multicultural cohesion? Did Asian audiences engage with its events?

This chapter addresses these questions within a wider analysis of the RAR movement, supported by existing scholarly arguments and utilizing contemporary material published in the *New Musical Express* (*NME*), a useful gauge of youth opinion during the period and a dedicated chronicle of the punk era. Following an examination of the political and cultural landscape in which RAR was established, it then analyzes the involvement of three punk groups that played RAR events: the Tom Robinson Band; Sham 69; and the little-known "Asian punks," Alien Kulture. This third, larger-scale case study is based upon a wide-ranging interview with two members of the group. It serves to demonstrate that, contrary to existing scholarly narratives of RAR, an Asian group did perform on its stages and, moreover, came to be directly involved in its central committee.

Contextualizing Rock Against Racism

The British political landscape in the mid- to late 1970s was in part defined by the vocal and physical presence of the far-right NF, whose growing influence prompted the initial establishment of RAR and its associated political pressure group the Anti-Nazi League (Gilroy 1995; Renton 2006). The NF is the widest-reaching fascist movement in British history, with a policy centered on the "repatriation" of nonwhite British nationals regardless of their place of birth. They have achieved electoral success at a local level in specific constituencies, usually targeted with the intention of exacerbating tensions between "immigrant" and white working-class communities. While at its peak in the late 1970s the NF had become the fourth-largest political party in the UK, it has failed to replicate its local successes on a national level. Despite a determined campaign in advance of the 1979 general election, they failed to gain a seat in the House of Commons and subsequently splintered and diminished in size.

Their poor showing at the 1979 election has been explained as a consequence of the Conservative Party's absorption of the NF vote. The party's recognition and acceptance of immigration-related tensions as valid was exemplified in Granada TV's *World in Action* broadcast of January 30, 1978. In an interview to mark the third anniversary of Margaret Thatcher's election as leader of the party, the then Leader of the Opposition explained her position to Gordon Burns:

> [I]f we went on as we are then by the end of the century there would be four million people of the new Commonwealth or Pakistan here. Now, that is an awful lot and I think it means that people are really rather afraid that this country might be rather swamped by people with a different culture and, you know, the British character has done so much for democracy, for law and done so much throughout the world that if there is any fear that it might be swamped people are going to react and be rather hostile to those coming in. So, if you want good race relations, you have got to allay peoples' fears on numbers.
>
> (Thatcher 1978)

This interview has been interpreted as an important factor in the Conservatives' 1979 success, with Thatcher taking an unprecedented step for the party by speaking on behalf of the white working class and drawing voters targeted by the relatively marginal NF into the mainstream Conservative fold (Widgery 1986, 13; Sabin 1999, 203). While this obviously impacted upon the electoral hopes of the NF, by targeting the "white working class," the Tories were also staking a claim for voters who were traditionally represented by the Labour Party. By appealing to this demographic on a current contentious issue, coupled with wide discontent with the incumbent Labour government, the Conservatives were able to amass a large electorate, which secured their victory in the 1979 general election. While it has been argued that the efforts of campaigns such as RAR diminished the power of the NF (Widgery 1986; Rachel 2016), the mainstreaming and dilution of the single issue on which the party fought would also have been a contributing factor.

The activities of the NF had a wide impact on British society, and diminishing its influence was the focus of RAR's activities. However, RAR was primarily established in response to casual uses of fascist imagery and rhetoric in popular music culture, and the actions of two major rock figures—David Bowie and Eric Clapton—exemplified a perceived complacency toward the threat of far-right attitudes in 1976. Bowie, while touring his album *Station to Station*, gave an interview to Swedish journalists in which he claimed "Britain could benefit from a fascist leader" (Stewart 1976), and upon his return to the UK, this controversy was further stoked when a photograph appearing to show him giving a Nazi salute while in a car at London's Victoria Station—an action Bowie claims was a misinterpreted wave to fans—was published in the British press (Stewart 1976; Rachel 2016, 14–16). John Street (1986, 55) points out that Bowie was also notable as one of the NF's "approved" performers, in whose music the party identified fascist associations in his supposed drawing from "white European culture," rejection of "black American music," and use of "the Futurist imagery of the 1930s": an identification that, most likely deliberately, ignores his 1975 soul-influenced record *Young Americans*.

Clapton, meanwhile, achieved notoriety in the punk era for repeatedly claiming support for the views of former Conservative Party MP Enoch Powell while performing at the Birmingham Odeon in August 1976. Powell is widely remembered for his "Rivers of Blood" speech of April 1968, in which, speaking to a meeting of the Conservative Political Centre in Birmingham, he widely appalled the British establishment by denouncing immigration in strongly racist terms. Multiple sources cite recollections of audience members to construct an oral history of the concert, quoting Clapton's assertions that "Enoch's right—I think we should send them all back" (Denselow 1989, 139) and "England was a white country" (Rachel 2016, 5). It was Clapton's outburst that prompted the photographer Red Saunders to compose a letter that was cosigned by other founding members, including Syd Shelton and Roger Huddle, and sent to the three key weekly rock publications—*NME*, *Melody Maker*, and *Sounds*—calling for the beginning of a Rock Against Racism movement:

> When we read about Eric Clapton's Birmingham concert when he urged support for Enoch Powell we nearly puked. What's going on, Eric? You've got a touch of brain damage? [. . .] Own up, half your music is black. You are rock music's biggest colonist. You're a good musician but where would you be without the blues and R&B? You've got to fight the racist position, otherwise you degenerate into the sewer with the rats and all the money men who ripped off rock culture with their cheque books and plastic crap. Rock was and still can be a real progressive culture. [. . .] We want to organize a rank and file movement against the racist position in music—we urge support—all those interested please write to: ROCK AGAINST RACISM. [. . .] P.S. Who shot the Sheriff, Eric? It sure as hell wasn't you! (Saunders et al. 1976)

The main concern of the letter, the establishment of RAR aside, was to portray Clapton as "inauthentic" and diminish the potential influence of his statements on rock fans. By comparing him with the "money men" of the music industry, who dwell in "the sewer" of any hierarchical interpretation of authenticity, the signatories aimed to devalue his "racist position." The postscript served as a telling parting shot: he did not "Shoot the Sheriff"—Bob Marley did—and by covering the song he was falsely assuming the identity of a "black rebel." They recognized the irony that a person with such strong views on immigration should achieve commercial success with a song composed by a black man that sustains the racial stereotyping of Afro-Caribbeans as delinquent.

The response to the letter is well documented (Denselow 1989; Rachel 2016), and it led to the staging of two RAR events before 1976 was out. While RAR ultimately came to be defined as a "punk" movement, these early gigs took place before the genre had gained enough traction to appear on the organizers' cultural radars. Initial RAR concerts saw the prolonged involvement of Carol Grimes, a singer-songwriter whose style was closer to the rhythm and blues–tinged country rock of the Band than the obnoxious rock 'n' roll of the Sex Pistols. Widgery (1986, 42) recalls booking Grimes to play the first RAR event in November 1976 after Huddle described her style as "RAR's kind of music." She also performed for RAR at a Royal College of Art event later that year (Miles 1976), as well as at London's Roundhouse in May 1977—an occasion that prompted *NME* journalist Phil McNeill to observe that while it had seemed "tentative, even slightly silly, at first, RAR has now progressed to the point where it can put £700 on the line to hire" the venue (McNeill, 1977a).

While this is evidence that RAR was more eclectic in its concert programming than the established narrative suggests, at least in its earliest incarnation, the familiar recipe of punk and reggae became routine as punk's cultural influence grew, especially after the Sex Pistols' (in)famous appearance on *Tonight with Bill Grundy* in December 1976. However, the seemingly disparate musical styles of Grimes's rhythm and blues, punk, and reggae were linked by a belief among concert organizers that they represented an authentic cultural expression suited to the advancement of a political movement. While RAR arguably captured the youth zeitgeist when they began programming punk and reggae groups, Frith and Street (1992, 69) note that other working-class genres popular at the time, such as heavy metal, funk, and disco, were conspicuous by their absence from concert lineups. However, while opposition to funk and disco can be bound up in issues of racism and homophobia, particularly in the US context, Frith and Street suggest that their exclusion from RAR was reasoned on the lines of opposition to mainstream, commercial pop music, whose use value is determined by its danceability.

While RAR took a quantitative rather than qualitative approach to their concert booking policy—filling the stage with performers opposed to racism took precedence over their musical quality (Frith and Street 1992, 69)—the perceived authenticity of the performer's expression was a vital criterion. They eschewed the bureaucratic, top-down approach of traditional political enterprises, but at the same time promoted strict ideologies of musical categorization. Its leaders were keen to establish a community of involvement that accepted definitions of the politics of specific genres located within a conception of authenticity (Frith and Street 1992, 79). As punk increasingly became the dominant force in "authentic" youth expression, its presence on RAR bills was inevitable. In fact, punk's profile and status led to it being viewed as a genre that could be utilized by both the Left and the Right to pursue their opposing political aims. Punk emerged in the midst of a public discourse steeped in the rhetoric of "crisis" (Laing 1985, 30), an atmosphere that explains both the rise of a far-right movement like the NF and the appeal of punk, which, for Hebdige (1979, 87), dramatized this rhetoric. For Widgery (1986, 61), punk was another product of the social crisis that led to the NF's rise, and as such could have gone in any political direction.

Concern about fascism in punk persisted into 1977. The left-wing editorial stance of the *NME* led to its publication of several articles opposed to punks' "ironic" use of fascist iconography, with particular focus upon the display of the swastika (Burchill 1977; Farren 1977). Hebdige (1979, 116) explains its appropriation by young punks as an oppositional tactic void of fascist sympathies; rather, the iconography of Nazi Germany appealed to punks through its signification of evil and "the enemy" to older generations. The appeal of the swastika lay in nihilism: the wearer derived pleasure from the inevitable negative reaction its display was to elicit. This analysis is problematic. While Hebdige reads the swastika as an empty effect, the wearer cannot determine how it will be received by an observer. The symbol continues to signify fascist beliefs, and therefore an observer can assume the wearer to be supportive of far-right ideology (Laing 1985, 96).

While Hebdige claims that punk was an antithetical response to racism, Sabin (1999, 199) argues that it should not be presumed that all uses of fascist imagery were ironic and that their overt display allowed punk's music and subculture to be used by far-right groups for their own ends. This view has been supported by Street (1986, 52), who notes that the NF viewed punk in much the same way as RAR: an opportunity to propagate a (far-right) political message. The reading of punk usage of fascist iconography as ironic is further clouded by examples of youths wearing RAR and NF badges simultaneously (Frith and Street 1992, 70). These accounts serve to prove that, no matter its users' intentions, a symbol can never be "blank."

As Goodyer (2009, 31–32) notes, RAR was separated from the countercultural struggles of 1968 by a mere eight years, and the growing problem posed by racism presented an opportunity for its founders—some of whom were veterans of these struggles—to put into practice what they had learned from the previous decade. As such, their 1960s-inspired approach to musical protest characterized RAR activities, which in turn fed back into the definitions of the increasingly popular punk sphere. Additionally, Frith and Street (1992, 70) claim that the involvement of RAR's organizers with the Trotskyist Socialist Workers Party (SWP) led to its representation of party-political ideologies, and as such the movement has received criticism, mainly from the right-wing groups they fought against, that it attempted to use popular music to encourage socialist revolution. The Far Right were so threatened by such a prospect that a rival Rock Against Communism was established by NF activists in 1979 (Sabin 1999, 208), a name that circumnavigated their racist activism and framed their activities as a McCarthyite opposition to left-wing ideology. Criticism of the SWP's influence also came from left-wing circles. The Maoist composer Cornelius Cardew accused the SWP of being "parasitic" upon the punk scene via RAR to further their own cause and divert "young people's revolutionary sentiments." For Cardew, the youthful discontent of punk did not portray a definite enough cultural goal to maintain a progressive agenda (McNeill, 1977b).

What is clear from arguments about RAR is that, whatever the merits of its approach, it helped punk to attain a reputation as a vehicle for, particularly left-wing, political activism, and those who ran RAR events privileged music that suggested political "authenticity." This is not to say that there was an archetypal "RAR band"; punk bands that performed at RAR concerts varied in their styles of political commitment. This can be observed in a brief examination of two white groups that became associated with the movement.

THE TOM ROBINSON BAND AND SHAM 69

The Tom Robinson Band (TRB) are characteristic of the "second wave" of punk bands to which RAR provided ample opportunities. The political subject matter of most of their songs, combined with their engagement with causes such as RAR, situates TRB within a lineage of bands from this era whose actions are taken as evidence that punk was a political movement (Burchill and Parsons 1978, 95). Their eponymous lead singer occupied a unique position as an openly gay rock performer in the late 1970s. His sexuality was cited as a key factor in his politicization in press coverage of the group (McNeill 1978), and it was a key theme in his songwriting—specifically his most well-known song, "(Sing If You're) Glad to Be Gay"—and political activism—which extended to the printing of the phone number for the Gay Switchboard (alongside the RAR logo and contact details) on the rear sleeve of their debut album, *Power in the Darkness*.

TRB were signed to EMI in August 1977, a deal that was of popular interest: they were the first punk group to be signed to EMI since the termination of the Sex Pistols' contract in January 1977. Following the Pistols controversy, such a signing—of a group fronted by a homosexual man singing vehemently political songs—suggested that EMI saw marketing potential in a group that challenged right-wing morality (Savage 2001, 287). Songs such as "Up Against the Wall," the opening track to *Power in the Darkness*, featured Robinson's passionate and declamatory vocal style singing lyrics that explained society's woes as a result of governmental incompetence at a local level and tyrannical policies set in Westminster. "Better Decide Which Side You're On" is a leftist critique of political apathy in the face of the threat posed by the NF, in which Robinson makes a series of bitter accusations of apathy within working-class communities and iterates that their political future is very much in their own hands.

These songs were written with a specific performance context in mind: RAR concerts. The band became involved with RAR from its very beginnings, which must have influenced Robinson's songwriting (Vulliamy 2007). However, the context in which recordings are heard differs from that of live performances, allowing for multiple interpretations. The atmosphere of a RAR gig, where everybody involved—performers, staff, audience—is assumed to be anti-racist, provides a perfect setting for communal fist-raising, a context that gives the musical text its meaning (Street 1986, 60). Despite the overarching political subject matter of Robinson's lyrics, it cannot be assumed that those who attended TRB concerts were doing so because they identified with his activism, as reflected in an *NME* live review from March 1978:

> Sometimes [Robinson is] guilty of misjudgement, and perhaps only to emphasise his daring commitment snarls at the capacity audience that they shouldn't just sing along with 'the latest hip' NF song [. . .] but do something active, like going to a local Anti-Nazi League meeting, the date and time of which he announces. A faction of the audience freeze, reluctant to join him on the canvas.
>
> (Stewart 1978)

This audience reaction problematizes TRB's political force. While undoubtedly the group's audience understood, and perhaps agreed with, Robinson's message, such apathy toward overt activism suggests that an appreciation for the group's music occasionally took precedence over a deepening of political consciousness. By attending the concert and singing along, they had given their support. RAR had established terms whereby "rocking" against racism was a viable form of action. There was no need to attend further political engagements.

Sham 69's experience of RAR's politics was markedly different from that of TRB. Where Robinson engaged with RAR as a highly engaged participant, Sham 69 were approached by the movement in an attempt to disseminate the anti-racist message to their fanatical white working-class audience, many of whom were vocal supporters of the NF. Sham 69's popularity lay in the perceived "realness" of their frontman, Jimmy Pursey, who displayed what Moore (2002) would term an "authenticity of experience": he spoke to, and for, those who felt that nobody within mainstream culture could represent them. As such, he was reluctant to denounce the fascist political movement that constructed a culture of belonging for members of his audience, even if he did not hold such beliefs himself.

As exponents of the Oi!, or street punk, subgenre, Sham 69 attracted a large number of skinhead fans whose reputation for racist violence preceded them wherever they went. This reputation is thought by Laing to have been cultivated by Oi's "founder"—*Sounds* editor Garry Bushell—after he put out a compilation, *Strength Through Oi!* whose title referenced the Nazi leisure enterprise, Strength Through Joy (Laing 1985, 112). In a feature on Sham 69's RAR gig in the *NME*, a fan tells the writer that "I agree wiv some of [what the NF says], but I'd vote Conservative. Stop more coming in, but those that're 'ere—it's just as much their country," before going on to demonstrate the level of devotion many fans gave to Pursey:

> Sham 69 are for the people. They make sure everybody has a good time, not like the punks. Johnny Rotten don't care, 'ee loves violence. Jimmy Pursey tries to stop it.
>
> (Case 1978, 32)

It was fans such as these that RAR wished to reach. While the band were not engaging in violent and racist activities themselves, RAR recognized that Pursey was allowing it to take place because of the discomfort he suffered in dictating to his fans how they should behave and what they should believe. While bands such as TRB approached RAR as willing participants, Sham 69 were approached by RAR as an opportunity. Pursey was to continue to engage with the movement, however, extending to him taking to the stage at the Victoria Park "Carnival Against the Nazis" to duet with the Clash in a performance of "White Riot" (Widgery 1986, 93).

Pursey's appreciation and understanding of his audience was integral to his accumulation of political capital, and, in RAR's view, this capital was going to waste. By approaching Sham 69 they demonstrated an acute desire to diminish the influence of the NF on Britain's youth, since using the band would allow their message to reach people who may otherwise have been "lost." By putting the band on one of their bills, RAR were also boosting their own publicity by courting controversy. Sham 69 were notorious thanks to the reputation of their fans, and this must have led some supporters of RAR to question the movement's reasoning behind asking them to play. However, the unlikely combination led to plenty of attention for RAR from the *NME*, allowing the event to be viewed as a success in terms of promoting anti-racism.

In TRB and Sham 69, two white RAR groups have been presented. The next, larger, case study examines the experience of one of the very few nonwhite punk bands to have graced the RAR stage.

Alien Kulture

Little has been said or written about the punk band Alien Kulture for one simple reason: they achieved little commercial or critical success beyond the locality of their South London homes. They are, however, an important group to discuss in the context of RAR for several reasons, least of all their racial makeup: alongside white guitarist Huw Jones were three children of Pakistani immigrants—singer Pervez Bilgrami, bassist Ausaf Abbas, and drummer Azhar Rana. Alien Kulture identified with RAR and felt that music was the best way to make their politics and views, largely expressing the experiences of the band's British-Pakistani members, heard. Their involvement with RAR came after participation in protests against the NF. In a personal interview with Abbas and Bilgrami, the singer remembered that, leading up to the 1979 general election, he and his bandmates

> were demonstrating everywhere we could against the National Front, it was as simple as that. We'd go to Islington Town Hall, Battersea Town Hall: we went all over the place. We'd protest against the National Front then go on to a gig somewhere maybe—Tom Robinson or maybe the Ruts [. . .] that sort of thing. We got involved in Rock Against Racism, it was Battersea Town Hall wasn't it that we met some activists, left-wing activists, who, basically, were trying to get a gig off.

As well as demonstrating Bilgrami's political activism, this statement also emphasizes his taste in music—"punk rock" with a political angle—and the fluidity and amateurism with which RAR gig organizers operated. It also dates the band's "coming of age" in late 1978–early 1979: while obviously their involvement with protests was taking place ahead of the general election, this was the period during which TRB and the Ruts were at their most active. Abbas and Bilgrami's involvement with RAR even extended to their being elected to RAR's national committee in the movement's later years, at which point, Abbas recalls, RAR "were obviously trying to broaden their appeal" following the general election, including events under the banner of Rock Against Thatcher (Rachel 2016, 215).

RAR and Alien Kulture's anti-Thatcherism stemmed in part from their belief that she had won the election thanks to her views on immigration. The band assert that they were named after her *World in Action* interview, in which she stated that "people are really rather afraid that this country might be rather swamped by people with a different culture" (Thatcher 1978), but has frequently been misquoted in terms of Thatcher speaking of people being "swamped by people with an *alien* culture" (Spencer 1998, 80). For Bilgrami, RAR's change in focus was inevitable given the circumstances: "[W]hereas you could fight against the National Front [. . .] on the streets, eventually it progressed onto, basically, mainstream politics."

As active participants in the running of RAR events, as well as performers on their stages, Alien Kulture contradict the criticisms of Kalra et al. (1996, 139) that no Asian bands were involved in RAR, and Sabin (1999, 203), who asserts that punk failed politically by neglecting the experience of British Asians. Such criticisms can be appreciated on the terms that at RAR's peak, none of its high-profile acts were Asian. While RAR gave a platform to lesser-known reggae and ska bands, it was white acts who arguably drew in the crowds, such as the Clash at the Victoria Park "Carnival Against the Nazis" in 1978. However, Sabin's critique is highly problematic: while RAR was explicit in promoting multicultural cohesion, punk was not a political movement with stated aims. If those involved in the staging of punk events did "neglect" British Asians, how did Alien Kulture come to be part of the RAR milieu? When asked if he felt that Asian communities were represented by RAR, Bilgrami was clear that

> they weren't [. . .] you can't be represented when there is nothing there because, you know, fine you can have people appear on a RAR stage and they're Asians but there weren't Asian bands there, there weren't Asian performers [. . .]. There was, literally: us; Tara Arts group; Hanif Kureishi; Paul [Bhattacharjee]—who was a member of Tara Arts—and one other arts group in Slough and that was literally it. So, you know, there was nowhere we could have representation, whereas black communities did. You had Steel Pulse, or Misty, or Aswad, or any number of bands or performers—we just didn't have the numbers.[2]

While there were large numbers within Asian communities who were opposed to racism, those who engaged with white-led cultural movements were limited (Kalra et al. 1996). Reggae acts were booked for RAR events, as they "represented" the black communities in London and Birmingham, but Asian communities did not have a popular musical genre that was taken to represent them. Kalra et al. (1996, 139) dispute this, stating that, at this time, Bhangra bands were performing in contexts ignored by organizers of RAR leaders. Abbas, however, believed that at that time Bhangra was not a form that spoke to young Asians and would not have been an appropriate style with which to *rock* against racism:

> I think if Bhangra had existed back then, then there would have been a clear Asian string. That didn't exist back then [. . .] Bhangra was basically, you know, what

peasant farmers in the Punjab used to sing, it wasn't what sort of hard Asian kids on the streets of London were doing. But [. . .] that desire to have music and to identify with music is very strong, and somewhere along the way the Asian community worked out that Bhangra was going to be their equivalent of punk and reggae, and which it clearly was.

It is important to note that while Bhangra music in Britain emerged in the late 1960s, it was only in the mid-1980s that it began to receive attention from mainstream media (Dudrah 2007, 44). Punk established its place on RAR bills only after its breakthrough into the mainstream consciousness, and reggae, rather than being sought out by organizers as a representative of black communities, had established a firm foothold in the consciousness of rock audiences (thanks in no small part to the success of Bob Marley). It should therefore come as little surprise that Bhangra was not considered by RAR organizers. The rhetoric of Kalra et al. suggests a belief that the white-led RAR should have sought Asian representation to address the NF's targeting of such communities. Given that punk and reggae acts were receiving a lot of coverage in the music press and beyond in the late 1970s, it is perhaps naïve to expect that this investigation would have taken place. Moreover, the movement stated an oppositional objective, rather than a message of inclusivity: it Rocked Against Racism; it did not Rock for a Broader Understanding of Multicultural Expression (even if its events did promote an emphasis on communities' similarities). However, the lack of "Asian" music on its stages does raise the issue of RAR's commitment to the promotion of multicultural understanding. A commitment to involving representatives from a broader range of communities from its beginnings may have helped to address this question of balance.

Alien Kulture's interactions with RAR demonstrate as false any assertion that Asian bands were not involved with the movement. However, while their lyrics relayed their experience as "Asian Youth" caught in a "Culture Crossover," the music they were set to was clearly inspired by the reggae-influenced, yet largely white, punk bands they followed. There is no musical language that suggests a desire to incorporate elements of traditional Pakistani music into their songs. As the lyrics of "Culture Crossover" affirm, their interests lay primarily in British popular culture. They tell the listener that they "don't wanna" partake in the traditional activities prescribed by their family and community elders; instead, they "wanna go to [the] Nashville" to watch bands, "hear their records," and read their "*N-M-E!*"

The song deals with the frustrations the band felt in trying to strike a balance between home lives with their families and the youthful rebellion that could be indulged outside. This set up a dichotomy between the traditional Pakistani Muslim culture of their elders, who taught them "how to pray five times a day" and stopped them from enjoying youthful exploits that they saw as essentially British—they "want[ed] to [. . .] run and dance and sing and shout," and had enough "pressure all around" them "without having to fight [their] elders." Abbas recalled his father learning of the song's lyrical content:

That was sort of like, "oh shit"; that was a pretty serious moment. And what I explained to him, I said "look, I'm not—we're not saying that that's our view, we're talking about Asian kids," and I said "you know what *you* need to understand is that Asian kids in many places are leading dual existences: the way that they live at home—the way that they behave in front of their parents—and what they do when they leave the home are complete and total contradictions." And I said that "I am honest and open with you: I am going to a National Front demonstration; I am going here; I am going to a party. You know, they will lie about what they're doing," and managed to sort of fudge it enough to be able to get away with it.

It is clear that the lyrics of the two songs that make up Alien Kulture's only commercially released material are representative of their opinions and desires of the time. Abbas and Bilgrami both recalled avoiding mullahs who would call on their houses on Saturday afternoons to instruct them to go to mosque, and admitted that their "parents were walking a very difficult line" in being relaxed about their socializing with their white peers given that "it was frowned upon by other members of the community. On the B-side of their 7″ single, "Asian Youth," the lyrics emphasize the sense of alienation the band felt by being "torn between two cultures." Young British Asians did not feel entirely accepted by mainstream culture because, as the chorus states, they were not represented by it:

Asian youth, oh where you been?
Asian youth, you wanna be seen.
Asian youth, you dunno who to turn to, Asian youth.

Despite some cultural differences, their lives were not dissimilar from those of their white and black peers:

[You] go to college, you read your books, buy your white pegs and structureless jackets.
Weekends you're on maximum pose down at the disco.

The fact that there is acrimony between white and Asian youth, in spite of their common desires, is a cause for sadness, prompting sentiments that intentionally echo those of Sham 69's "If the Kids Are United"—a song that sought to encourage Jimmy Pursey's peers and followers to unite against an establishment they mistrusted:

[You] come from different countries, you belong to different religions.
Hate each other, you swear and fight but you don't realise that you're the same.
Nothing's achieved by being divided why can't we be united? (Alien Kulture, n.d., "Asian Youth")

The band's commitment to anti-racism is further represented on the record's sleeve, the reverse of which bears black-and-white photographs of each band member alongside unattributed quotes:

Who had struck the killer blow? At the in-quest eleven witnesses swore they saw the teacher hit by police. Not one of the 39 SPG witnesses said they saw anyone hit on the head.
When did you last see a pogoing Punjabi, a mod moslem or a bop-ping Bengali?

The first of these refers to the murder of Blair Peach at the Southall riot of April 1979—an event that is also commemorated with an etching on the record, which states "Remember Southall and Newham"—while Bilgrami attributed the final quote to *Bulldog*, the magazine of the NF, and cites it as one of their reasons for starting the band: to those young British Asians looking for a rock role model, they said, "[N]ow you've got us. And that was our method of fighting back, and hopefully the audience would take notice and then you'd carry on and give your message, whatever your message is." However, while they started the band to give voice to their feelings and hoped to represent a British Asian audience, they found that demand from the community for a punk band was not so high:

> I think at the time, when we were going to punk gigs and this and that, most Asian kids were going to discos. [. . .] Although some disco music was political most of it wasn't. You know, I personally liked it, nothing against it. But [. . .] to me it's an easy way out: you don't have to really think about the music. You can go out on a Saturday night, you can have a good time, you can dance like Michael Jackson, you come back at three in the morning and it's finished [. . .] I went to my fair share of disco nights [. . .] I really enjoyed it but that—that was one side of it—but the proper side of it was [. . .] what we were doing.

For Bilgrami, music has a higher purpose than solely "entertainment." His musical enlightenment was tied to the punk era, and his philosophy on the purposes of music will have been shaped by firsthand experience of the work of RAR and its inherent musical value system, which prized authenticity: to be "proper" music should respond to social situations. While Bilgrami and Abbas identified with the politics and music of the punk era, few of their British Asian peers were interested. For Abbas, the band's musical taste set them apart from the community they sought to represent. Aside from "a core group of Asian followers who were really a lot of [. . .] extended friends" of the band, he felt that they did not significantly broaden the appeal of punk within the community. Bilgrami agreed, saying that while they mainly started the band to try to encourage more Asians to attend demonstrations and gigs, young Asians would "be at the disco on a Saturday night [. . .] they weren't out really where it mattered." Nonetheless, Bilgrami believed that the band did play a small role in bringing Asian communities together to protest racism, citing playing at the front of a march through the West End to protest the British Nationality Act of 1981 as a key example, at which he could see "for miles and miles just Asian faces and it was good to see once in a while that it wasn't white-led."

While their British Asian peers did not always identify with their means of expression, Abbas believed that Alien Kulture's message was understood by them, if only for being "partly rebellious, partly standing up and being counted and not being [...] beaten down." By asserting a self-identity couched in the terms of rock sincerity, which was, in itself, culturally "alien" to the people they hoped to represent, they conformed to a model that they had come to understand as an appropriate means of political expression. It was RAR that had played a key role in coding punk in this way, and, being members of the movement's audience prior to commencing the band, the way in which they and their RAR peers of all skin colors had come to understand punk was determined in large part by the intentions of the movement's founders.

Conclusion

RAR was founded on the belief that certain forms of popular culture were viable conduits through which to put forth political ideals. It invoked punk specifically in its activism as a consequence of its impact as a cultural form. For the mainstream, punk was a manifestation of society's ills, an interpretation that only increased its "power" to those it engaged; for "punks," it was a positive way to identify oneself in opposition to the "crisis" rhetoric of the mainstream. RAR and punk, therefore, were an obvious combination: if punk was born from a society in which the NF was encouraging physical opposition to nonwhite citizens and the Conservatives were validating racial tensions with their rhetoric, then its use to oppose the widely racist values of that society would help to stem the tide of discrimination. Consequently, its reach was limited: it could not affect the mainstream through outright opposition. Its reliance on specific musical styles implicitly excluded some from involvement.[3]

For those performers involved with RAR, the oppositional qualities of punk were important for their songwriting intentions. For Tom Robinson, punk and RAR offered opportunities to pursue a range of left-wing issues. Jimmy Pursey of Sham 69 could speak to the feelings and anxieties of London's white working-class youth, which made him a key figure in RAR's aim to decrease the influence of the NF on such a demographic. The members of Alien Kulture similarly found in punk a way to express their anxieties as the children of Pakistani immigrants. It was they who bore the brunt of the racism perpetrated by the NF, and as such they could engage with RAR not only as opponents of racism, but also to give voice to the frustrations of "Asian Youth" caught in a "Culture Crossover." Alien Kulture prove that, contrary to the common historical narratives of RAR, British Asians did engage with the movement. However, they were a minority at RAR events: as they mediated their anxieties to RAR's largely white audiences, their peers danced their discrimination away, to singer Pervez Bilgrami's consternation, "down at the disco."

Criticism of RAR's approach to concert programming and lack of engagement with British Asian cultural forms is, to an extent, justified. However, it is reasonable to suggest that it was representative of historical structural issues. It did succeed in attracting large audiences to demonstrate an opposition to racial discrimination, which was a result of its approach to programming: by booking punk and reggae bands, they appealed to the zeitgeist. While it did not speak widely to British Asian communities, they were not the ones the movement sought to reach to halt racist violence; ultimately it was the white working class, the NF's target demographic. Multicultural cohesion was an end for RAR's organizers. The means were what they achieved: Rocking Against Racism, an act that in itself could not create the conditions for the structural change required to promote such an end. This would require action on the part of the state, and, given Margaret Thatcher's campaigning rhetoric, this was not a likely course.

Notes

1. Estimates of the exact numbers in attendance at these carnivals vary from source to source. The lack of definitive documentation of much of RAR's operations serves to underline the improvisational approach taken by those involved.
2. Bilgrami went on to say that as a group of Asian artists they "sort of meshed: Hanif Kureishi came to one of our gigs; Tara Arts—Paul we knew through going to protests, we went to a Tara Arts play and saw him there acting, you know, so, it sort of *did* come together, we did loosely know each other, there was this community. We had the same, same notions, the same beliefs really."
3. This was one of the key rationales behind the formation of the Anti-Nazi League: to promote anti-fascism via a more traditional, and less culturally divisive, political channel.

References

Alien Kulture. n.d. "Asian Youth"/"Culture Crossover." 7″ single. RARecords.
Burchill, Julie. 1977. "New Wave Neat Say Nazis." *New Musical Express*, July 23, 1977, 11.
Burchill, Julie, and Tony Parsons. 1978. *"The Boy Looked at Johnny": The Obituary of Rock and Roll*. London: Pluto Press.
Case, Brian. 1978. "Angels with Dirty Faces." *New Musical Express*, March 11, 1978, 32–33.
Denselow, Robin. 1989. *When the Music's Over: The Story of Political Pop*. London: Faber.
Dudrah, Rajinder. 2007. *Bhangra: Birmingham and Beyond*. Birmingham, UK: Punch.
Farren, Mick. 1977. "Fascism in the U.K. '77!" *New Musical Express*, January 22, 1977, 20–21.
Frith, Simon, and John Street. 1992. "Rock Against Racism and Red Wedge: From Music to Politics, From Politics to Music." In *Rockin' the Boat: Mass Music and Mass Movements*, edited by Reebee Garofalo, 67–80. Boston: South End Press.
Gilroy, Paul. 1995. *"There Ain't No Black in the Union Jack": The Cultural Politics of Race and Nation*. London: Routledge.
Goodyer, Ian. 2009. *Crisis Music: The Cultural Politics of Rock Against Racism*. Manchester, UK: Manchester University Press.
Hebdige, Dick. 1979. *Subculture: The Meaning of Style*. London: Methuen.
Kalra, Virinder S., John Hutnyk, and Sanjay Sharma. 1996. "Re-Sounding (Anti) Racism, or Concordant Politics? Revolutionary Antecedents." In *Dis-Orienting Rhythms: The Politics of the New Asian Dance Music*, edited by Sanjay Sharma, John Hutnyk, and Ashwani Sharma, 127–155. London: Zed Books.

Laing, Dave. 1985. *One Chord Wonders: Power and Meaning in Punk Rock*. Milton Keynes, UK: Open University Press.
McNeill, Phil. 1977a. "R.A.R. Collection for 'Islington 18.'" *New Musical Express*, May 14, 1977, 12.
McNeill, Phil. 1977b. "Who Is Cornelius Cardew?" *New Musical Express*, September 10, 1977, 11–12.
McNeill, Phil. 1978. "Tom Robinson." *New Musical Express*, February 11, 1978, 25–30.
Miles. 1976. "Get Down With It and Get Closer: Rock Against Racism, Royal College of Art." *New Musical Express*, December 25, 1976, 31.
Moore, Allan F. 2002. "Authenticity as Authentication." *Popular Music*, 21, no 1: 209–223.
Rachel, Daniel. 2016. *Walls Come Tumbling Down: The Music and Politics of Rock Against Racism, 2 Tone and Red Wedge*. London: Picador.
Renton, Dave. 2006. *When We Touched the Sky: The Anti-Nazi League, 1977–1981*. Cheltenham, UK: New Clarion Press.
Reynolds, Simon. 2006. *Rip It Up and Start Again*. London: Faber and Faber.
Sabin, Roger. 1999. "'I Won't Let That Dago By': Rethinking Punk and Racism." In *Punk Rock: So What?*, edited by Roger Sabin, 199–218. London and New York: Routledge.
Saunders, Red, et al. 1976. "When We Read about Eric Clapton's Birmingham Concert . . ." *New Musical Express*, September 11, 1976, 50.
Savage, Jon. 2001. *England's Dreaming: Sex Pistols and Punk Rock*. London: Faber and Faber.
Spencer, Sarah. 1998. "The Impact of Immigration Policy on Race Relations." In *Race Relations in Britain: A Developing Agenda*, edited by Tessa Blackstone, Bhikhu Parekh, and Peter Sanders, 74–95. London and New York: Routledge.
Stewart, Tony. 1976. "Heil and Farewell." *New Musical Express*, May 8, 1976, 9.
Stewart, Tony. 1978. "Will the Real Tom Robinson Audience Please Stand Up?" *New Musical Express*, March 25, 1978, 42.
Street, John. 1986. *Rebel Rock*. New York: Basil Blackwell.
Street, John. 2012. *Music and Politics*. Cambridge: Polity Press.
Thatcher, Margaret. 1978. "TV Interview for Granada *World in Action* ('rather swamped')." Interview by Gordon Burns. *World in Action*, January 27, 1978. Transcript at http://www.margaretthatcher.org/document/103485.
Vulliamy, Ed. 2007. "Blood and Glory." *Guardian*, March 4, 2007. http://www.guardian.co.uk/world/2007/mar/04/race.otherparties.
Widgery, David. 1986. *Beating Time: Riot 'n' Race 'n' Rock 'n' Roll*. London: Chatto & Windus.

CHAPTER 28

RETHINKING THE CULTURAL POLITICS OF PUNK

Antinuclear and Antiwar (Post-)Punk Popular Music in 1980s Britain

GEORGE McKAY

THIS chapter focuses on the neglected pop end of punk rock in Britain, on a specific point of crossover: its high-profile, commercially successful political songs and performances about antiwar and antinuclear issues. While the Clash could sing accusatorily relatively early on in the punk scene that "The new groups are not concerned—With what there is to be learned" (1978), I want to revisit the extent to which the new groups, either formed or at their most successful in the wake of punk's origins in the late 1970s, *were* concerned with what there was to be learned, and taught. The chapter seeks to identify and address an imbalance in our conceptualization of punk politics, and it has three key points.

First, it seeks to retheorize the relation between punk, peace, and war. In small and large ways alike, punk and post-punk bands mobilized, with musical, media, and activist interventions. For instance, the most influential of the national music weeklies of the punk period, *New Musical Express*, introduced a regular column in 1981 called "Plutonium Blondes," which contained news about nuclear issues and antinuclear protests (Reynolds 2005, xxv; Worley 2017, 240). Mark Stewart, a post-punk singer with the Pop Group, worked at the national office of the Campaign for Nuclear Disarmament (CND); the star singer Paul Weller in late-period the Jam issued "communiqués" to the music press about the dangers of nuclear weapons (Worley 2017, 243); the hit punk-era singer Ian Dury released the single "Ban the Bomb," which reintroduced a key antinuclear slogan from the 1950s, heard musically in John Brunner's classic 1958 protest folk song, "The H-Bomb's Thunder," to a new generation of CND activists (Dury and the Music Students 1984) (see Figure 28.1). But while peace was everywhere in punk, punk also had an ambivalent or complicit relation with militarism. This is one key aspect of the retheorization.

FIGURE 28.1. Ian Dury 1984 single cover, "Ban the Bomb," with CND symbol shaved on head (Polydor POSP 673, 1984).

The chapter's second aim is to reframe punk's use-value in pop culture, especially when considered as protest. At its height and for a few years afterward, punk entered and refreshed the mainstream and did not always simply "sell out" for commercial success (the common accusation of the time) or depoliticize. In fact, punk was a key way in which pop culture "brought nuclear dread into the Top 20" (Reynolds 2005, xxv), and arguably even if/when it *did* sell out, this was not necessarily associated with a conscious act of depoliticization—quite the reverse. In Britain alone, millions of records were made and sold by punk, new wave, post-punk, and anarcho-punk acts that had a core antiwar or antinuclear message, as a significant cultural response to what was widely perceived as the escalating nuclear and military threats of the times. There was an extraordinary number of hit and some chart-topping singles that, as punk's recorded music broadcast on radio and television chart shows demonstrates, constituted a sustained political message. Although rather less studied or acknowledged, punk's mainstream music and its political activities were at least as important as the more obviously radical, DIY, and underground ones that have been more celebrated and historicized. When we consider them in the context of a core marker of their own industry—the vital contemporary pop metrics of records sales, related chart positions, and broadcast media profiles—they are vastly *more* important. Approaching punk as pop music does not mean jettisoning its social criticality, and this is the second key aspect of the chapter's retheorization: it both uncovers a neglected history of punk's peace politics *and* uses that history as a challenge to a dominant reading of punk's radicalism.

Third, and last but not least, the chapter more broadly aims to contribute to our understanding of musical cultures of peace during a critical period of recent British history: the Troubles in Northern Ireland, military mobilization overseas with Argentina during the Falklands War of 1982, and late Cold War international policy developments (US-controlled nuclear missiles being located on UK and other Western European territories), as well as activism against these (including in relation to the revived and highly active CND). In response to the kind of question raised by Elise Boulding—"If every society is a blend of the themes of violence and peaceableness, why is the peaceableness so hard to see?" (Boulding 2000, 4)—I discuss one cultural aspect of "peaceableness" that has truly been hiding in plain sight. In a clear and important cultural connection, there were numerous antiwar and antinuclear singles in the British pop charts during these years, and, as I will show, most of them were connected to punk.

Some of the bands and artists I discuss here can be thought of as "post-punk," a term that, as Guy Mankowski (2014, 160) notes, "clearly resists a tidy musical definition." Chronologically, I am nearer to Simon Reynolds' position (though I hyphenate): post-punk referring simply to the bands that formed swiftly or found success in punk's immediate wake, from around 1978 to 1984. But stylistically and in terms of commercial success and profile, I veer away from the avant-garde and artistically informed and experimental to a keen embrace of and interest in pop. Unlike Reynolds, it is not essential that my bands explore "new sonic possibilities through their embrace of electronics, noise, reggae's dub techniques, disco production, jazz and the classical avant-garde"— already quite a wide-ranging definitional scope, but one which kind of holds together (Reynolds 2005, xvii). What *is* essential is that they have an identifiable link with punk (e.g., sonic, stylistic, attitudinal, corporeal, scene-focused, historical), and that, in the context of this chapter, they made a musical intervention around political campaigning against nuclear weapons specifically, or against war in general. The punk and post-punk work I am discussing here is about the artists, bands, and songs that figured in the pop charts, often on major record labels, singing songs about war and nuclear Armageddon, or playing live fundraising concerts and consciousness-raising festivals in branded support of peace and CND.

Theorizing Punk, (the) War, and the Bomb

Early British punk's largely leftist public politics centered around a small number of key issues, which included, most prominently in the late 1970s, antiracism (notably the influential Rock Against Racism [RAR] campaign), and in the 1980s, peace and antinuclearism.[1] The former, structured around a new socio-musical campaign organization established from within the scene (RAR), has been relatively widely, and even increasingly, researched (see, for example, Goodyer 2013; Rachel 2016; Renton 2019). The latter, formed in partial relation to an already existing campaign organization (CND), and contributing sometimes messily or tensely to CND's revival, rather less so. Each of these was characterized in significant part by a repertoire of what we can think of as a street-facing focus on involvement in and organization of political demonstrations—public marches and gatherings—and live music events, whether benefit gigs and campaign tours, or festivals and urban open-air carnivals. These could and did frequently merge or blur: the public march through the streets, say, culminating in a free open-air concert in a public square or park, whereby the event became "a cross between a political rally and a pop concert" (Cloonan and Street 1997, 228), or perhaps even became a glimpse of a "protestival" (St John 2015). A remarkable number of new protest songs were written and recorded, released as singles and on albums, and these punk and post-punk records constitute another key part of the socio-musical repertoire around antiracism, and around peace and antinuclearism.

A wonderful 1977 song by English punk group Alternative TV, "How Much Longer," offers a way to think about punk's alignment with CND and the peace movement. Released as a single—though never, alas, a pop hit—"How Much Longer" captures the contrasting semiotics of classic British subcultures in the late 1970s, as expressed around music, fashion, and discourse. The lyrics describe first punk rock and then the hippie counterculture:

> How much longer will people wear Nazi armbands and dye their hair . . . talk about anarchy, fascism and boredom? . . .
> How much longer will joss sticks rule . . . Afghan coats, yeah, making peace signs, man, talk about Moorcock, Floyd down the Reading Festival?
> (Alternative TV 1977)

In the song's opposition, while the new young punks of the (then) present talk of anarchy and being bored, the old hippies are discussing science fiction (novelist Michael Moorcock) and psychedelic rock, or "head music," as it was often called (Pink Floyd). But it is the hippies not the punks who are "making peace signs" too. That is to say, the peace movement (arguably, primarily the international antiwar movement around Vietnam) is subculturally fixed—as part of the 1960s and beyond counterculture, which punk claimed to be a rejection of. NEVER TRUST A HIPPIE was one punk slogan; Johnny Rotten famously wore a Pink Floyd T-shirt with the words I HATE scrawled above the band's name; while love and peace were the archetypal sloganized values of the 1960s, "Hate and War" was an early classic punk song by the Clash in the 1970s. And, fundamentally, while the song asks "How much longer," it also asks, indirectly, how informed one's critique of fascism is while wearing a swastika (on this choice, see Stratton 2008, chap. 9; Croland 2016, 31–35)? Yet punk was fashioned in the shade of the nuclear sublime, and CND became a punk cause, indeed a (punk-tinged or -singed) popular music cause. It was of its time: the new soundtrack to military destruction and the apocalyptic imaginary, *and* the new soundtrack to public critiques of these.

In the British consciousness of the time, had (the) war ever really gone away?[2] (I think this is a question for the present tense, also.) Recall here Jon Savage's passing but powerful observation that, when punk happened, in the late 1970s, "the Second World War was in some ways still not over" (Savage 1991, 354). Thinking historically from today, at the time of writing (2020), punk was nearer to World War II (30 years) than we are to punk (40 years). In the context of his early song "Bombsite Boys," TV Smith of the Adverts has talked of the significance of (the) war for his—which is also my—generation growing up in Britain in the 1960s and 1970s:

> The way [our parents and grandparents] behaved was moulded by their experience of war, but to their children—later to become the punk generation—it was a kind of a fairy story ... infused in the culture; an undercurrent of violence and horror that we could never understand, even though in our free time we were playing in the remains of bombed-out houses where almost certainly deaths had occurred and families had been torn apart.
>
> (Smith, quoted in Ogg 2013, 282)

John Lydon was another "bombsite boy," as he tells of his childhood in 1960s London in his second autobiography, *Anger Is an Energy*: "There were bombsites from the war, and thousands of kids running rampant in them. They were absolutely like adventure playgrounds, thrilling. Amazing, a wonderful thing, a bombsite, to a kid" (Lydon 2014, 18–19). For other punks the war was a darker source of material or action. So, Siouxsie Sioux, singer with the Banshees, could explain of her wearing a swastika: "We hated older people ... always harping on about Hitler, 'We showed him,' and that smug pride. It was a way of saying, 'Well I think Hitler was very good, actually': a way of watching someone like that go completed red-faced" (quoted in Savage 1991, 241).[3] The very fact that one of the leading new punk-era antiracism organizations was called the Anti-*Nazi* League signals its own wartime gaze.

Whether or not we then follow Victor Bockris's argument that "[p]unk was the last great reaction to the Second World War" (quoted in True 2002, 59), we should acknowledge further that punk itself was part of Britain's military culture and discourse. This is the case even at its most underground or radical end. Cyrus Shahan (2011, 372) has written of punk rock's "aesthetic violence, what Dick Hebdige has called punk's 'semiotic guerrilla warfare,'" while Savage (1991, 195) describes the original impact of English punk as "an explosion of negatives." Even if I am uncertain that a bomb can be benign, elsewhere George Berger has described anarcho-punk as operating "in the enormous free speech crater that *the punk bomb* benignly left in its explosive wake" (Berger 2008, 127; emphasis added). So, from the critics, punk culture is framed around war, violence, warfare, explosion, bomb. In punk *and* post-punk, what is to be expected when the scene produces or is produced by bands called names like (in Britain) the Clash, the Stranglers, or the Pistols, or—a swift A-Z—Anthrax, Blitz, Blitzkrieg, Blitzkrieg Bop,

Conflict, Demob, GBH, Guns For Hire, Joy Division, London SS, Napalm Death (earlier name: Civil Defence), No Swastikas, the Partisans, Raped, Slaughter and the Dogs, the Spitfire Boys, UXB, Warsaw Pakt? (See also Laing 2015, 60–63.) For all its apparent anti-authoritarianism, punk was mired in militarism; for all its initial energy and driving shock, it seems it could only confirm an embedded social and cultural orthodoxy of violence. Even a holiday in the sun in those days could mean a trip to the Berlin Wall, or worse: "I'm looking over the wall, *and they're looking at me!*" screamed Johnny Rotten in one of the Sex Pistols's 1977 hits, a song that opened with the sound of jackboots. In that least rational of Pistols songs, "Holidays in the Sun," in which the word "REASON" is chanted to a military beat, the apocalypse is just another half-expected away-day kind of (mushroom) cloudy weather: "I didn't ask for sunshine and I got World War Three" (Sex Pistols 1977). Bummer.

Much of the academic research on punk and its war, violence, peace, and nuclear politics to date has tended to concentrate on the hardcore, autonomous, or underground end of the spectrum (see, for example, McKay 1996, 2019; Ogg 2013; Worley 2012, 2017, 239–246), including during the very years under discussion here.[4] There is a wider point here about the critical perspective in contemporary what we might call punk studies, evidenced by a brief survey of two recent influential research activities: the UK-based academic journal *Punk and Post-Punk* (established 2011) and the Porto-led annual, and then biennial, set of conferences called KISMIF (first held in 2014). What follows are generalizations, of course, but I think they have legitimacy. A survey of abstracts of all articles up to 2018 in *Punk and Post-Punk* reveals scholarship much more interested in independent and DIY formations, with a preference for alternative, hardcore, anarcho-oriented music—its aim seemingly to uncover, understand, and value lost and marginal(ized) local scenes and spaces.

KISMIF ("Keep It Simple, Make It Fast") has impressively facilitated a new and engaged intellectual community around punk in historic and contemporary settings alike. KISMIF claims both a punk music critical focus—as its name suggests—but also a wider countercultural terrain around DIY practice, not restricted to punk. The latter is less convincing; for example, its key star speakers have been largely from the UK classic punk era, from Don Letts to the Raincoats, Billy Bragg to Steve Ignorant. While these are high points in punk studies, neither *Punk and Post-Punk* nor KISMIF as research communities have been that much interested in the commercially successful pop end of punk and new wave, which is also to say that, from these important examples, contemporary scholarship may be defining punk in a restricted way.

Elsewhere, in an important contemporary study such as *No Future: Punk, Politics and British Youth Culture, 1976–1984*, Matt Worley includes a list of over 200 British fanzines as well as 85 pages of notes admirably detailing the minutiae of aspects of the scene across the UK, with a clear preference for the grass roots and marginal, which is for him also the regional and often un- or non-commercial. (Almost all the record sleeves included as illustrations in the book are from bands on independent labels.) Although Worley's book has an end date of 1984—thus approaching a decade of punk's active music-making—he largely eschews the commercially successful pop end of punk, as when, for example, presenting the narrative that punk-influenced "new pop" was basically "new romanticism" in which "[p]rotest gave way to pleasure," or in his book's concluding sentence that "the politics of punk resided in its refusal" (Worley 2017, 130, 254). Worley's introduction mentions "[p]unk's transition from subculture to pop culture" (7), but his critical positionality is broadly to maintain, construct, or desire a narrative of punk's subcultural purity: his focus is on how "punk continued to provide a provocative cultural form that existed *beyond the realms of the pop charts*" (7; emphasis added).

Sometimes the versions of punk privileged in these academic fora (journal, conference, monograph) constitute hugely interesting marginal culture—avant-garde or populist—but they are not always popular, and they have never or rarely been mainstream chart-topping. Yet a version of punk, of a punk-influenced music, identifiable attitude, subcultural style, voicing, or corporeality, *did* become popular, and even chart-topping. As punk diluted, its shock or purity or puritanism or novelty attenuating, it became more commercially successful as well as more creative and musically interesting. The dilution was not a diminution but a diffusion. I feel I should elaborate here, for this is a reading to shake the new punk scholarship. Perhaps here the music scholars can learn from the music journalists. In his classic post-punk study *Rip It Up and Start Again*, Simon Reynolds (2005, xv) notes just how *mainstream* punk and post-punk could be in the UK, "where you could hear The Fall and Joy Division on national radio, and where groups as extreme as PiL had Top 20 hits which, via [BBC television's] *Top of the Pops*, were beamed into ten million households." Russ Bestley has traced the inclusion of punk hits on the series of low-budget compilation albums of cover versions regularly released at the time (Bestley 2019).[5] More broadly, what has been largely overlooked is the sheer achievement of popularity of some bands and artists, who used their new visibility to make political interventions. My position is that such overlooking by the academics and historians distorts the wider punk narrative, in particular by under-representing punk's commercial success and spread of appeal—even when that success and appeal was being used for political communication—and understating its social reach and political effort.

Punk and Post-Punk Hit Singles of Peace: 1980, 1984

In *Music and Politics*, John Street undertakes a simple exercise in order to provide one clear measure of the impact on the public consciousness of popular music's political and social campaigns. In a section entitled "Mapping Political Songs," he scans the no. 1 singles in the UK charts from their beginning in 1952 to 2001, to identify the songs of protest and social comment that achieved the top position. While there are limitations to such a methodology, here I am also going to critically employ it, for it offers us an important means of rethinking the scope and popularity of punk's politics. Soberingly for those of us who might feel we are invested in music's social imperative, Street (2012, 47) concludes his exercise with the view that "it is striking to see how few" no. 1 political singles there are. Perhaps unsurprisingly, in that half-century of popular music history, 1969 is Street's most "exceptional" year—"the year of Woodstock," he explains, "echoed to the sound of several explicitly political hits," three of which topped the British charts: "The Ballad of John and Yoko" by the Beatles, Thunderclap Newman's "Something in the Air," and Creedence Clearwater Revival's "Bad Moon Rising." Jon Stewart has undertaken a similar hit singles analysis, though focused on the American charts, entries in the Top 40 rather simply no. 1s, and looking at songs of war and peace, not all political pop. Stewart examines the Billboard pop, R&B, and country charts from 1965 to 1975 for anti- and pro-war hits during the Vietnam War and the counterculture. He finds peak political pop from the years 1969 to 1971: in 1969 there were 11 antiwar Top 40 hit singles, in 1970, 14, and in 1971, 10 (Stewart 2012, 74). Another way that punk can be used to shake up popular music scholarship is in how it allows us to rethink pop metrics as a measure of success.

During punk's high years the singles charts remained a central industry and public marker of popularity; indeed, they constituted the weekly pulse of pop music and its associated broadcast and print media. The charts "provide a convenient aggregation of individual consumer choices[,] . . . imply the tacit endorsement" by purchasers of any song's message, and are "a crude but effective means by which researchers can measure the cultural impact of a song among the record-buying public" (Stewart 2012, 68). But of course charts have drawbacks as a quantitative indicator, including the potential for homogenization of musical styles (Laing 2015, 94), the possibility of manipulation (from payola to playlist), and their exclusionary structure (which means record sales made outside the audit frame would not figure—important for something like punk's DIY scene). Also, for an apparently revolutionary form like punk, the charts could be awkward for its positionality, or at least attitudinality. If punk was going to offer "a different way of listening" (Laing 2015, 141), how could this happen within, say, the established weekly BBC pop radio and television order? When the Sex Pistols finally did appear on *Top of the Pops* in 1977, "how far was it a victory for 'punk', . . . or for the dominant discursive formation" (Laing 2015, 94)? Yet within a few years the pop charts were replete with punk and post-punk protest and pessimism in songs of nuclear, technological, or military apocalypse.

The year 1980 was a remarkable one for British political pop of a punk and post-punk variety. I undertook an audit of the Top 75 singles charts through the year, via the weekly archive of the Official Charts website, cross-referenced to various online lists and fans' fora of political or protest songs. My aim was to identify all chart singles that were concerned with issues of peace or contained antiwar or antinuclear sentiments in lyrics and music, visual images (such as promotional videos), or product (like picture sleeves). That year, there were 22 such Top 75 hits, by 18 different artists (see Table 28.1). For almost the entire year of 1980 (47 weeks), the UK singles charts contained at least one hit song that spoke of antiwar or antinuclear concerns, and usually more than one. From the new chart on November 30 until the end of the year, for instance, each week there were between five and seven antiwar or antinuclear singles in the charts (by Boomtown Rats, UB40, OMD, Clash, Jona Lewie, or John Lennon). For the youth that constituted a large part of the single-buying public, this was an unavoidable sociocultural discourse, an insistent nudging in the direction of a current social movement, and an articulation of a political positionality via cultural consumption, while for everyone else it was impossible not to hear some pop message of peace via the everyday music of Britain at this time.

Within that list of 18 bands and artists, we can see that not many pop acts outside punk actually engaged with the theme: Kate Bush (twice) and Peter Gabriel sang affective protest songs, while John Lennon dominated the end of the year, with two peace-oriented singles re-released to mark his sudden, violent death. Apart from those, the other 77 percent of hits were in some way punk-related (see Table 28.1 for a brief explanation). It is true that some of these were minor hits at best: while 8 of the 17 punk-related singles did in fact make the Top 10, those by the Angelic Upstarts, UK Subs, and Dead Kennedys each charted for just three or four weeks. But then all of the 17 apart from UK Subs and Dead Kennedys broke into the Top 40. These acts and their hits from 1980 illustrate some of the range of musics punk opened up and made popular in its first three or four years, but then there were many punk and post-punk songs in the pop charts. It is more significant that these hit songs were all concerned with the dangers of the nuclear world, of war and destruction, of military violence, of making a statement and taking a stance. A number came from what we can think of as the most readily identifiable angry punk bands, such as the Clash, Dead Kennedys (the sole US representative), UK Subs, Angelic Upstarts, or Stiff Little Fingers—"canonic punk," in Travis A. Jackson's phrase (2013, 165). "Warhead" by UK Subs is notable both for its cover and its lyric (see Figure 28.2). The picture sleeve shows a comics-style image of a physical and heroic uniformed soldier with a machine gun, whose head has, collage-style, been replaced by the tip of a missile: public discourse and internal thought alike are dominated by military threat. For the UK Subs, we are all warheads now, military discourse and culture are normalized and routinized in the everyday, and our thinking is shaped (like a missile) by a process of internalization of orthodoxy. (Perhaps this is the message of the Ian Dury CND hairstyle, too: another warhead.) The lyric references the recently begun Soviet-Afghan War, repeatedly telling us that we are all "getting ready," whether we are "soldiers of Islam" or Russians, or, more globally, "Yankees," or "children in Africa with Tommy guns." The final warning is that the Cold War military logic expressed in the song will result not in a national or regional victory but in total annihilation: "bye bye planet let alone your nation" (UK Subs 1980).

Other 1980 hit antiwar and antinuclear singles were from the arguably more pop-oriented punk of bands like the Jam, Skids, or Boomtown Rats. Paul Weller is particularly interesting: he would write his most directly (and, arguably, obvious) political songs *after* the Jam, in the early years of the Style Council (from 1983), and use live performances and records alike with that band to support antinuclearism. Yet increasingly successful chart singles with the Jam had already clearly drawn a critical view on Britain's macro- and micro-violence, its military elites, and the dangers of nuclear

Table 28.1. 1980 Top 75 UK Chart Singles about Peace/Antiwar/Antinuclear Issues

Artist/Band	Song Title	Highest Position (weeks at no.1)	Weeks on Charts	How Punk-Related?
The Skids	"Working for the Yankee Dollar"	20	11	punk band
The Clash	"London Calling"	11	10	punk band
The Jam	"Eton Rifles"	3	12	punk/new wave band
Peter Gabriel	"Games without Frontiers"	4	11	-
UK Subs	"Warhead"	30	4	punk band
The Jam	"Going Underground"	1 (3)	9	punk/new wave band
Kate Bush	"Breathing"	16	7	-
Stiff Little Fingers	"Nobody's Hero"/"Tin Soldiers"	36	5	punk band
Angelic Upstarts	"Last Night Another Soldier"	51	4	punk band
Piranhas	"Tom Hark"	6	12	punk/ska band
Hazel O'Connor	"Eighth Day"	5	11	new wave, song from punk film
The Beat	"Best Friend"/"Stand Down Margaret Dub"	22	9	ska/new wave, independent label (Go Feet)
XTC	"Generals and Majors"	32	8	new wave
Orchestral Manoeuvres in the Dark	"Enola Gay"	8	15	electronic post-punk, (semi-)independent label (Dindisc)
Kate Bush	"Army Dreamers"	16	9	-
UB40	"The Earth Dies Screaming"	10	12	reggae, formed in punk scene, independent label (Graduate)
Dead Kennedys	"Kill the Poor"	49	3	punk band
Jona Lewie	"Stop the Cavalry"	3	23	independent label (Stiff)
The Clash	"The Call-Up"	40	6	punk band
Boomtown Rats	"Banana Republic"	3	11	new wave band
John Lennon	"Happy Xmas (War Is Over)"	2	9	-
John Lennon	"Imagine"	1 (4)	13	-

Source: officialcharts.com.

FIGURE 28.2. UK Subs, "Warhead" single cover (1980): "we are all warheads now" (GEM/RCA, GEMS 23/PB 9512, 1980).

technology: 1978's "A-Bomb in Wardour Street," 1979's "The Eton Rifles," and 1980's "Going Underground" stand as an extraordinary thematized trio of incisive and socially critical punk-pop singles. Note that as the band became more popular (highest chart positions for these three singles were #25, #3, and #1, respectively) the message did not weaken. Weller has also spoken directly of how later antinuclearism helped further sharpen his social conscience: "We'd been down to Greenham [Common Women's Peace Camp] to deliver some food and clothes to the women [activists who lived there]; a fucking scary place to be. *I went through a period of political awakening*, a realization of how the system worked" (quoted in Rachel 2016, 348; emphasis added).

Others again were new wave: XTC, Hazel O'Connor, or Orchestral Manoeuvres in the Dark (OMD). O'Connor's three-minute epic Top 10 single "Eighth Day" was promoted via an extraordinary robotic live concert scene from the film *Breaking Glass* (1980), in which she starred as a punk-era singer trying to make it in the corrupt music industry (Figure 28.3). The song depicts a dystopian vision of the end of the world. OMD actually chose their name to show that they were precisely *not* a punk band (Wilson 2004, 58), and yet they were formed in 1978, played their first gig at Eric's punk club in Liverpool, supported Joy Division on their second (OMD Live, n.d.), released an early single on

FIGURE 28.3. Hazel O'Connor, performing "Eighth Day," from the film *Breaking Glass* (1980): "On the eighth day, machines just got upset" (film still).

Manchester's Factory Records, then signed to another independent label—as a band they are a punk product. This kind of contextualization is important (as with UB40 and Frankie Goes to Hollywood, below) for it helps us recognize and understand the impact of punk at its widest, even involving those who would go to produce music that might seem relatively removed from it.

British reggae and ska bands provided the remaining antinuclear hits. The multiracial reggae band UB40 in fact had quite a punk name—after the card one carried and had to produce weekly when "signing on" at the job center in order to claim unemployment benefit (hence UB). Like a classic punk band would claim, they were formed when the young men had no work, on the "dole queue." Saxophonist Brian Travers contextualizes UB40's origins in terms of music (punk) and society (unemployment):

> We probably wouldn't have had the "gumption" if that punk thing wasn't going on.... Anybody could start a band.... You didn't have to be that good to get an audience. We left school at 16 and couldn't get jobs.
>
> (quoted in Booth 1999)

In their antinuclear hit single "The Earth Dies Screaming" there is no angry screaming; the song is instead a minor key lament, sparse and repetitive, depicting the landscape and domestic environment in the immediate wake of a nuclear bomb. It finishes with a windy blast through emptiness. It is a reggae song not to dance to (UB40 1980). Both UB40 and the Beat released records on independent labels, and the Beat's is notable because it was a benefit single for the movement. "Stand Down Margaret (Dub)" was a version of their protest song against the right-wing government of Margaret Thatcher, which also touched on the dread possibilities of World War III, as underlined by the blood-red mushroom cloud depicted on the rear of the picture sleeve (Beat 1980). Singer Dave Wakelin explains his thinking behind the song, its local resonance, and the operation of popular music as social protest:

There'd been a novel . . . [that] postulated that the first nuclear bomb would go off above [Birmingham]. . . . It was not only right above the hospital I was born in, but also right above the pub where we started the Beat. We weren't very optimistic and were very much of the mind that it was apocalypso and the world was going to end. . . . It seemed to me that when I danced my mind was freer somehow and I could understand lyrics better. . . . I thought if you could get people dancing they'd perhaps feel a bit stronger to ruminate on some of the lyrics. So I sang about our worst fears. You saw the audience moving as one creature and you got this emotional connection between them, the band and the song.

(quoted in Rachel 2016, 280–281)

The Beat's "Stand Down Margaret (Dub)" is an antinuclear benefit record, thus it stands as one of the hits where there is a direct link to a social movement organization: while the picture sleeve of the Clash's 1980 combined antimilitarist and antinuclear 7" single "The Call Up"/"Stop the World" contains CND's contact information, that of the Beat's includes on the front cover the logos and addresses for the *two* campaign groups it was fundraising for: CND and the Anti-Nuclear Campaign (Beat 1980).

As an outlier, even veteran popster and blues musician Jona Lewie was out of the punk milieu, sort of: his sentimental-sounding Top 10 hit Christmas single "Stop the Cavalry" stayed in the charts for six months—it was released on the classic punk independent label Stiff Records, after all. The contemporary political resonance of "Stop the Cavalry" is enhanced and its historical frame broken by a lyrical reference to the girl who "waits at home—In the nuclear fallout zone" (Lewie 1980). It is not *simply* "novelty pop" (Grant 2017, 78.) Overall then, as Table 28.1 shows, all of these artists, and all of these punk-related hit singles from that one year of 1980, collectively show that the waves of cultural energy and social critique from punk *in its widest definition*, often least tied to its anarchistic or spectacular elements, made an extraordinary and sustained public musical statement about war and nuclear destruction.

Let us turn now to 1984, with its own splash of no. 1 singles from post-punk acts that addressed peace issues. In Street's "Mapping Political Songs" exercise, 1984 (Street actually writes 1983, but it was definitely the following year) is noteworthy for two "hits [that] voiced antiwar sentiment: Frankie Goes to Hollywood's 'Two Tribes' and Nena's '99 Red Balloons.'" There was technically a third antiwar no. 1 that year in fact, Paul McCartney's "Pipes of Peace," a 1983 Christmas single that peaked late, which opens with a surprisingly avant-garde dissonant orchestra playing sounds of war (McCartney 1983). If, following Street's suggestion, "charity records (such as Band Aid's 'Do They Know It's Christmas?') [were] to be included as political songs," that song would constitute a fourth political chart-topper from 1984, albeit not an antiwar one (Street 2012, 47). On that reasonable count, it really is quite extraordinary to note that one-third of the year 1984 (17 weeks) had some kind of political pop song at the top of the British charts. Viewed from that lofty perspective, 1984 must be seen as a peak protest music time in Britain, most of it in the context of antiwar and antinuclear sentiment.

Notwithstanding the presence of John Lennon and Paul McCartney in hits from both 1969 and the early 1980s, the key argument is that this widespread political pop music culture of the early 1980s, of which these chart-topping 1984 singles are a high-profile manifestation, largely originated in the punk rock and new wave scenes from the late 1970s on, scenes from which both Nena and Frankie Goes to Hollywood emerged. Before discussing each of these songs, I want to pursue this argument a little further, for it speaks to punk's politics in popular music: could we say that 1984's Band Aid (and then Live Aid the following year), even though designed as cross-genre and cross-generational formations, originate in punk energy, attitudinality, and practice? These are evident not only in Bob Geldof saying "Fuck" on live television during the Live Aid concert broadcast in 1985 as he pleaded for more money from viewers at home, but also in the key contribution of characteristics such as punk's DIY self-organization and entrepreneurship to establish Band Aid and Live Aid in the first place. After all, its key musical agitators and organizers were Geldof from punk-pop band the Boomtown Rats, his then partner, music journalist and presenter Paula Yates, and Midge Ure from (admittedly, among others) post-experimental era electro-pop Ultravox. Geldof has acknowledged this debt: "I came along in 1976 and we were part of the punk thing. I love disruption. And when it's politically focused, it's very powerful" (quoted in Singh 2014). There was also recent punk practice to draw on: thus, Live Aid "owed something to Rock Against Racism" (Cloonan and Street 1997, 228), reggae and punk's multiracial live music alliance. In different and remarkable ways, then, punk made most of 1984's highest-profile political pop possible; punk, and the cluster of post-punk spin-offs in new wave and punk-pop music changed and popularized the sound of politics around campaigns against war and nuclear weapons during the period.

To turn to the first of 1984's chart-topping antiwar and antinuclear singles, Nena's "99 Luftballons"/ "99 Red Balloons," in more detail. First, how punk was Nena? Or, what features can we identify in the music and performance of Nena in her high-pop success moment that are identifiably punk-influenced? That her single was a German language one originally is significant—it marks her work as part of the post-punk *Neue Deutsche Welle* movement. According to Sabine von Dirke, "[p]unk had a tremendous impact on the West German rock scene, and it fulfilled a specific function in its use of German lyrics," rather than the English lyrics of many of the early German countercultural bands (von Dirke 1989, 69). Von Dirke describes the punk elements of "99 Luftballoons" as including

> the danceable new wave sound—fast synthesizer sequences and eighth measures characteristic of punk rock together with some Reggae or hardrock riffs.... The vocals exhibited more or less an affinity to their origins in punk rock: the predominantly German lyrics were spoken or shouted.
>
> (von Dirke 1989, 72)

In English translation, a year later, one can see a more overt (if somewhat polite) visual punkiness in the band's mode of mediated performance. For example, on a February 1984 BBC TV *Top of the Pops* appearance, band members wear tight leather trousers, big boots, oversized T-shirts with bold monochromatic images, and studded belts; they have big backcombed or cropped hair, sometimes with hairbands, and dance energetically or move awkwardly, while Nena's image is both sexy *and* androgynous (Nena 1984b)—all features that would be readily recognized as new wave by the show's expert popular culture audience. In both languages the lyrics imagine a nuclear attack by error, and criticize the masculine military and government for their enthusiasm, desire, even compulsion to destroy. In English:

> This is what we've waited for
> This is it, boys, this is war.
>
> (Nena 1984a)

In public commercial terms alone, the most remarkable (probably anti)nuclear song in Britain during this late peak of Cold War was undoubtedly the post-punk Frankie Goes to Hollywood's 1984 single "Two Tribes," which reached number one in the pop charts and stayed there for nine weeks, aided by being released in numerous versions in different formats (including the "Annihilation" and "Carnage" 12" mixes) as well as a notorious video showing "President Reagan" of the United States and "President Chernenko" of the USSR fighting hand-to-hand in the ring (Figure 28.4). The band

FIGURE 28.4. Frankie Goes to Hollywood, "Two Tribes" video (1984): Cold War struggle embodied in presidential ring-fighting (video still).

came out of the thriving Liverpool punk scene: lead singer Holly Johnson had previously been in the locally legendary band Big In Japan, and backing singer and dancer Paul Rutherford in the Spitfire Boys, who had released the earliest Liverpool punk single. Rutherford has recalled how "being gay and punk" were "a sort of ticket to ride really... [they] gave me wings.... The punk thing... made me feel like I had arrived" (quoted in Waller 2013). The publicity team for Frankie Goes to Hollywood (primarily *New Music Express* punk-era journalist Paul Morley) emphasized their radical art history understanding through the band's short stellar career—Soviet-style graphics, Situ-inspired slogans on T-shirts ("FRANKIE SAY WAR! HIDE YOURSELF," or "FRANKIE SAY BOMB IS A FOUR-LETTER WORD")—which carried over into sonic aspects of this song too. Arguably it was the music's sound, the video, and the extra-musical aspects surrounding "Two Tribes" that carried the key political articulations: Reynolds (2005, 508) points out that lyrically "as antiwar polemic goes, the chorus... is pretty darn trite. But [Trevor] Horn's supercharged production makes 'Two Tribes' sound almost as momentous as its theme: nuclear doomsday." One memorable sonic description, by a radio DJ in full pop hyperbolic mode, somehow captured the feeling: the bass line sounded "like the end of the world" (quoted in Lester 2014). The contrast of the music with the calm and measured male voice-over extracting from a notorious UK government advice booklet about what do in the event of a nuclear attack seems to magnify the inadequacy of the official advice, and echoes the similar voice-over on pop singer Kate Bush's own antinuclear single from 1980, "Breathing."

Conclusion

Although the material presented here clearly takes issue with the position stated by Jackson (2013, 166), that "[p]unk was not a music whose adherents were allied in any long-term fashion with any political or social causes," that is not in fact my primary purpose. But do let us keep in mind a consistent and near-constant "peaceableness" in this music's protest. Through and for all its energizing contradictoriness (distilled thus: *Aggression, Peace*), across the spectrum from post-punk pop hits to the DIY of anarcho-punk—let us be bold—punk was a plea for peace. My core argument is that the recorded music from primarily the more popular and commercially successful end of the punk and new wave movements evidences that an important and sustained music and social movement dialogue was in process, funded, via record sales, by the public: "Enola Gay" has claimed international sales totaling over 5 million ("Enola Gay," *Wikipedia*); U2's *War* (1983) is a double Platinum album in the UK (meaning over 600,000 sales) (BPI). On this album "U2 turned pacifism itself into a crusade.... Bono described himself as an 'aggressive pacifist' and marched about on stage clasping a white flag" (Reynolds 2005, 450); "Two Tribes" sold 1.58 million copies in the UK alone (Official Charts Company 2012); "99 Red Balloons" was a Gold Record (in German or English language versions) in the US (meaning 1 million+ sales), UK (500,000+), Germany (250,000+), and elsewhere ("99 Luftballons," *Wikipedia*); the Jam's UK certified sales figures for their two biggest antiwar singles ("Going Underground" and "Eton Rifles") total 700,000+ (BPI). These are all impressive record sales figures, confirming that "[e]xplicitly political music is not the preserve of the fringes of musical culture" (Street 2012, 43). John Street's "crude generalization" that "the more explicitly political the song, the lower the chart placing" (47), is challenged in the punk and post-punk context of the nuclear threat of the late Cold War.

It was not only—or even, in fact, not as much—in the context of punk's angry, DIY, independent, autonomous, or experimental music that a large part of its most high-profile political communication was made, but also in the new pop of a number of commercially highly successful punk and post-punk bands and artists, who did not lose their politics in the scramble to the top. The antinuclear and antiwar politics of punk, during a period in Britain of late Cold War nuclear proliferation and even paranoia, international military mobilization in the Falklands War, and paramilitary and military action at home in the Troubles, were a consistent and significant popular cultural expression of discontent. A 1982 fundraising compilation album *Life in the European Theatre* featured songs and hits by many of the most successful British punk and post-punk acts, including the Clash, Jam, Beat, Specials, Stranglers, Ian Dury, and even comic ska band Bad Manners. The sleeve notes explain that royalties from sales were to be distributed to important UK and European antinuclear groups, including CND. In a rich conjunction, the sleeve notes also contain a short piece by the radical English historian E. P. Thompson. Thompson directly addressed for listeners/readers the relationship between popular music and politics, as he saw it:

> This is something bigger than "politics." It is about life going on, about a clean nuclear-free space between West and East. Music can do that better than programmes and speeches. If we want to live . . . we have to get a sound going right across the whole continent.
>
> (quoted on Various Artists 1982)

On this fundraising compilation album—as with the many singles identified here—that musical "sound going . . . across the whole continent" of Europe was a punk and post-punk one.

Thus, for a significant number of pop fans in the early 1980s—some or many of whom also were or had been punks—antinuclear and antiwar protest were not the preserve of the Clash, or the heavier and more angry and accusatory anarcho-punks of Crass or Discharge, say, but U2, Orchestral Manouevres in the Dark, Frankie Goes to Hollywood, the Style Council, Madness, Elvis Costello, Ian Dury, Nena, UB40, Hazel O'Connor, and so on. This is not to present a history of the victors, so to speak (see also Reynolds 2005, xxix), nor an inverted binary of chart-topping winners versus righteous losers (especially when an underground band like Crass, with multimillion record sales achieved outside formal industry structures, problematize that distinction; see McKay 2019, 4). It is, though, to offer a more nuanced history of popular music in a period of political crisis, and a more inclusive understanding of the spread, influence, and social importance of something like punk in its first few years, not even a decade. As a focus on the charts of the years 1980 and 1984 illustrates, in rethinking the cultural politics of punk, one places it centrally in pop: punk and post-punk's most far-reaching social statements against war, militarism, and the entwined nuclear culture of weaponry and power are to be found in its many hit and even its no. 1 singles, in seven-inch vinyl record sales, or mimed on peak-time television and played on national radio in the family home and workplace alike. In the repertoire of protest, popular songs were not just played alongside political "programmes and speeches," they were, in Thompson's view, *ahead* of them, "better" than them. That most of the many high-profile political utterances of punk during these years were from its poppiest incarnation is quite remarkable. We can legitimately say that the peace of punk was a pop phenomenon—but also that the peace of pop was a punk phenomenon. In the pop charts of the times, punk politics were inescapable, and they made a consistent, spectacular, loud, powerful, creative, danceable, and *popular* articulation of antiwar and antinuclear sentiments. This is not evident enough in much of the current scholarship: punk studies needs to rethink its relation to pop, *particularly* in the political context. If we as scholars want to understand the politics of punk better, we need to look in the pop charts, where they were highly visible and audible at the time, week in week out, through the entire year, including at no. 1.

Acknowledgments

I owe thanks to Dr. Gina Arnold and Prof. Matt Worley for generous discussions about the issues explored here, as well as to Drs. Russ Bestley and Mike Dines, and Profs. Andy Bennett and Paula Guerra, for taking time to respond to specific queries. Errors of fact, judgment, or criticality are mine alone. Figures 28.1–28.4, fair use.

Notes

1. This is not a comprehensive list of political pop movements from punk and post-punk, of course. As the music's very existence may validate, these were years of social crisis across the board. For instance, in class terms the Miners' Strike of 1984–1985 is vital, and Jeremy Tranmer (2012, 79) has traced the contribution of "high-profile" post-punk groups publicly supporting the striking mineworkers: "The Style Council, the Clash . . ., UB40, Madness, Bronski Beat, New Order, Orange Juice, . . . Gary Kemp of Spandau Ballet and Elvis Costello all performed at least one concert," even if that level of engagement ("at least one concert") sets the bar quite low.
2. The Antigua-born writer and gardener Jamaica Kincaid has commented on how the British use the term "the war." On a British writer's use of the phrase "before the war," Kincaid noted that the author "did not say which war, the British have been involved in many wars, but it is a small country, so everyone must know which one 'the war' is" (quoted in McKay 2011, 105).

3. An anti-Semitic lyric on an early version of the Siouxsie and the Banshees song "Love in a Void" made the style gesture even more problematic (see Sabin 1999, 208).
4. It should be acknowledged that of the newer musics of the time, punk was not alone in its sonic fascination with war. Heavy metal music had its own interest here—a heavy metal concert was "the sensory equivalent of war," Jeffrey Arnett has argued in *Metalheads* (1996, chapter 1). But punk was particularly important in its articulation of *antiwar* sentiments. The sole heavy rock hit single from 1980 that *could* have been included in Table 28.1, Motörhead's "Bomber" (7 weeks on the charts, highest position 34), may encapsulate the difficulty of pinning down a *message*: does the song make any antiwar statement, or is it about an extreme human, technological and sonic experience, that of war, or is it even some kind of celebration of technological destruction?
5. Of the punk and new wave bands whose hits were covered on the Hallmark Records *Top of the Pops* compilations albums, most popular were the Boomtown Rats, Blondie, the Jam, and the Police (Bestley 2019, 411). But punk hits also covered by the in-house band and singers and released were the Sex Pistols' "Pretty Vacant," the Stranglers' "No More Heroes," the Adverts' "Gary Gilmore's Eyes," and even Public Image Limited's "Death Disco" (see Bestley 2019, 418–421 for a comprehensive list).

References

Arnett, Jeffrey. 1996. *Metalheads: Heavy Metal Music and Adolescent Alienation*. Reprinted 2018. Abingdon, UK: Routledge.
Berger, George. 2008. *The Story of Crass*. London: Omnibus.
Bestley, Russ. 2019. "The Top of the Poppers Sing and Play Punk." *Punk and Post-Punk* 8, no. 3: 399–421.
Booth, Philip. 1999. "Reggae Engine Drives Pop Power of UB40." *Orlando Weekly*, June 16, 1999. https://www.orlandoweekly.com/orlando/reggae-engine-drives-pop-power-of-ub40/Content?oid=2259309.
Boulding, Elise. 2000. *Cultures of Peace: The Hidden Side of History*. Syracuse, NY: Syracuse University Press.
BPI (British Phonographic Industry). n.d. Database of all Silver/Gold/Platinum certified UK record sales. https://www.bpi.co.uk/brit-certified/.
Cloonan, Martin, and John Street. 1997. "Politics and Popular Music: From Policing to Packaging." *Parliamentary Affairs* 50, no. 2: 223–235.
Croland, Michael. 2016. *Oy Oy Oy Gevalt! Jews and Punk*. Santa Barbara, CA: Praeger.
"Enola Gay (song)." *Wikipedia*. https://en.wikipedia.org/wiki/Enola_Gay_(song)#Certifications_and_sales.
Goodyer, Ian. 2013. *Crisis Music: The Cultural Politics of Rock Against Racism*. Manchester, UK: Manchester University Press.
Grant, Peter. 2017. *National Myth and the First World War in Modern Popular Music*. London: Palgrave Macmillan.
Jackson, Travis A. 2013. "Falling into Fancy Fragments: Punk, Protest, and Politics." In *The Routledge History of Social Protest in Popular Music*, edited by Jonathan C. Friedman, 157–170. New York: Routledge.
Laing, Dave. 2015. *One Chord Wonders: Power and Meaning in Punk Rock*. 2nd edition. Oakland, CA: PM Press.

Lester, Paul. 2014. "Frankie Goes to Hollywood: 'No-One Could Touch Us—People Were Scared.'" *Guardian*, August 28, 2014. https://www.theguardian.com/music/2014/aug/28/frankie-goes-to-hollywood-30-years-welcome-to-the-pleasuredome.

Lydon, John. 2014. *Anger Is an Energy: My Life Uncensored*. London: Simon & Schuster.

Mankowski, Guy. 2014. "Pop Manifestos and Nosebleed Art Rock: What Have Post-Punk Bands Achieved?" *Punk and Post-Punk* 3, no. 2: 159–170.

McKay, George. 1996. *Senseless Acts of Beauty: Cultures of Resistance since the Sixties*. London: Verso. See chapter 3.

McKay, George. 2011. *Radical Gardening: Politics, Idealism and Rebellion in the Garden*. London: Frances Lincoln.

McKay, George. 2019. "'They've Got a Bomb': Sounding Anti-nuclearism in the Anarcho-Punk Movement in Britain, 1978-84." *Rock Music Studies* 6, no. 3: 217–236.

"99 Luftballons." *Wikipedia*. https://en.wikipedia.org/wiki/99_Luftballons#Certifications_and_sales_2.

Official Charts Company. 2012. "UK's Million-Selling Singles: The Full List." *Guardian*, November 4, 2012. https://www.theguardian.com/news/datablog/2012/nov/04/uk-million-selling-singles-full-list#data.

Ogg, Alex. 2013. "For You, Tommy, The War Is Never Over." *Punk and Post-Punk* 2, no. 3: 281–304.

OMD Live. n.d. Online Discography for Orchestral Manouevres in the Dark. https://www.omd-live.com/1978-79.html.

Rachel, Daniel. 2016. *Walls Come Tumbling Down: The Music and Politics of Rock Against Racism, 2 Tone and Red Wedge, 1976–92*. London: Picador.

Renton, David. 2019. *Never Again: Rock Against Racism and the Anti-Nazi League, 1976–1982*. London: Routledge.

Reynolds, Simon. 2005. *Rip It Up and Start Again: Postpunk 1978–1984*. London: Faber.

Sabin, Roger. 1999. "'I Won't Let That Dago By': Rethinking Punk and Racism." In *Punk Rock: So What? The Cultural Legacy of Punk*, edited by Roger Sabin, 199–218. London: Routledge.

Savage, Jon. 1991. *England's Dreaming: Sex Pistols and Punk Rock*. London: Faber.

Shahan, Cyrus. 2011. "The Sounds of Terror: Punk, Post-Punk and the RAF after 1977." *Popular Music and Society* 34, no. 3: 369–386.

Singh, Anita. 2014. "Bob Geldof: Don't Like the Band Aid Lyrics? Then F--- Off." *Daily Telegraph*, December 9, 2014. https://www.telegraph.co.uk/news/celebritynews/11281894/Bob-Geldof-Dont-like-the-Band-Aid-lyrics-Then-f-off.html.

Stewart, Jon. 2012. "What's Going On: Anti-War and Pro-War Hits on the Billboard Singles Charts during the Vietnam War Era (1965–1975) and the 'War on Terror' (2001–2010)." In *Representations of Peace and Conflict*, edited by Stephen Gibson and Simon Mollan, 67–85. London: Palgrave Macmillan.

St John, Graham. 2015. "Protestival: Global Days of Action and Carnivalized Politics at the Turn of the Millennium." In *The Pop Festival: History, Music, Media, Culture*, edited by George McKay, 129–147. London: Bloomsbury.

Stratton, Jon. 2008. *Jewish Identity in Western Pop Culture: The Holocaust and Trauma Through Modernity*. New York: Palgrave Macmillan.

Street, John. 2012. *Music and Politics*. Cambridge: Polity.

Tranmer, Jeremy. 2012. "Charity, Politics, and Publicity: Musicians and the Strike." In *Digging the Seam: Popular Cultures of the 1984/5 Miners' Strike*, edited by Simon Popple and Ian W. Macdonald, 76–86. Newcastle, UK: Cambridge Scholars Press.

True, Everett. 2002. *Hey Ho Let's Go: The Story of the Ramones*. London: Omnibus.
Von Dirke, Sabine. 1989. "New German Wave: An Analysis of the Development of German Rock Music." *German Politics and Society* 18: 64–81.
Waller, Paul. 2013. "Interview with Paul Rutherford." *Penny Black Music*, March 24, 2013. http://www.pennyblackmusic.co.uk/MagSitePages/Article/6915/Frankie-Goes-to-Hollywood-Interview-with-Paul-Rutherford.
Wilson, Dave. 2004. *Rock Formations: Categorical Answers to How Band Names Were Formed*. No place: Cidermill Books.
Worley, Matthew. 2012. "Shot by Both Sides: Punk, Politics and the End of 'Consensus.'" *Contemporary British History* 26, no. 3: 333–354.
Worley, Matthew. 2017. *No Future: Punk, Politics and British Youth Culture, 1976–1984*. Cambridge: Cambridge University Press.

Discography/Filmography

Alternative TV. 1977. "How Much Longer"/"You Bastard." 7" single. Deptford Fun City Records.
Beat. 1980. "Best Friend"/"Stand Down Margaret (Dub)." 7" single. Go Feet Records.
Breaking Glass. 1980. Dir. Brian Gibson. Allied Stars Studios. Film.
Clash. 1978. "(White Man) in Hammersmith Palais"/ "The Prisoner." 7" single. CBS Records.
Clash. 1980. "The Call Up"/"Stop the World." 7" single. CBS Records.
Dury, Ian, and the Music Students. 1984. "Ban the Bomb"/"Very Personal." 7" single. Polydor Records.
Frankie Goes to Hollywood. 1984. "Two Tribes"/"One February Friday." 7" single. ZTT Records.
Lewie, Jona. 1980. "Stop the Cavalry." Music video.
McCartney, Paul. 1983. "Pipes of Peace"/"So Bad." 7" single. Parlophone Records.
Nena. 1984a. "99 Red Balloons"/ "99 Luftballons." 7" single. Epic Records.
Nena. 1984b. "99 Red Balloons." Performance on *Top of the Pops*. BBC TV.
Orchestral Manoeuvres in the Dark. 1980. "Enola Gay"/"Annex." 7" single. Dindisc Records.
Sex Pistols. 1977. "Holidays in the Sun"/"Satellite." 7" single. Virgin Records.
UB40. 1980. "The Earth Dies Screaming"/"Dream a Lie." 7" single. Graduate Records.
UK Subs. 1980. "Warhead"/"The Harper"/"I'm Waiting for the Man." 7" single. GEM/RCA Records.
Various Artists. 1982. *Life in the European Theatre*. 12" album. WEA/Elektra Records.

CHAPTER 29

PUSSY RIOT
Punk on Trial

JUDITH A. PERAINO

> For me punk . . . it's a way of life, but not like a music direction. I should say I'm not a musician. I don't know how to play any musical instrument. . . . I'm the last one who can say something relevant about music. . . . But punk for me, it is a way to express yourself, because you can shout as loud as you can, you can be totally abnormal because I kind of hate norms.
> —Pussy Riot's Masha Alyokhina, interviewed by Judith Peraino and Tom McEnaney, Cornell University, November 2, 2016

> Donald Trump may favor stodgy blue suits and boring red ties and wear his hair in a strange double combover, but don't be fooled. That's how he looks, not who he is. Who he is is a guy with a safety pin through his nose and a purple mohawk. He just pulled off the most punk act in American history.
> —Kyle Smith, *New York Post*, November 9, 2016

Two statements in a fateful week of November 2016: the first by an anti-Putin Russian activist, the second by a pro-Trump columnist, both invoking punk to mean self-authorizing action and expression, free from any deference to norms, institutions, experience, or skill. In hindsight, this surface convergence of the United States and Russia under the sign of punk presaged the Trump-Putin bromance, and their shared "autocrat's language," to quote Masha Gessen (2017), where words mean their opposites. Fraudulent elections in Russia are called "the free expression of citizen will," while in the United States fair elections are called fraudulent, fake news no longer means Russian disinformation but verifiable reporting, and facts come in two varieties: actual and alternative.[1] The meaning of punk and DIY is also in doubt, claimed by the left and the right on the political spectrum to describe different visions of populism, one leading to an egalitarian society, the other to white nationalism.

Here's another headline, from October 23, 2018, published in the centrist magazine *Foreign Policy*: "Trump's Punk Rock Nuclear Policy: The only reason to pull out of the INF Treaty is to give a middle finger to the world" (Lewis 2018). The Intermediate-Range Nuclear Forces Treaty was an arms reduction agreement signed by Ronald Reagan and Mikhail Gorbachev in 1987. Yet again, punk is reduced to meaningless insolence and a nihilistic undoing of history, here describing Trump's erasure of the Cold War peacework of a once beloved Republican president and the controversial Soviet-era reformer (then the General Secretary). Gorbachev's policies of *glasnost* (openness) and *perestroika* (restructuring) attempted to westernize the Soviet Union but arguably hastened its collapse and Russia's slide back into totalitarianism. The members of Pussy Riot were born into *glasnost* in the mid-1980s, but came of age within *skrytnost*—the renewed secretiveness of Putin's Russia (Guirard 1987).

How should I write about Pussy Riot in a book about punk rock—especially now in 2021, in this extended era of Trump and his mainstreaming of alt-right conspiracy theories? Isn't it disinformation to call them a punk rock band? Pussy Riot was a fake band operating within a regime of fake news and *skrytnost*. How do I avoid slipping into an autocrat's language? Or an activist's language?

> JP: Do you feel punk is still a word that describes what you are doing now, in your theater work and perhaps also in your work with [the independent media outlet] MediaZona?
>
> MA: You are talking about genres. Like Human Rights or Music or Theater is genres, but punk is way of life for me. I'm not like [going to] pretend to be something.

No, Masha Alyokhina was not going to pretend to be a punk rocker for my 2016 interview. But pretending to be a punk rocker in 2012 is exactly what landed her in a Russian prison.

Punk rock is indeed on trial.

Here's what Pussy Riot was in 2011 and 2012: an anonymous political activist art collective that impersonated a punk rock band in their staging of protests in Russia *against* the totalitarian regime of Vladimir Putin and corruption of the Russian Orthodox Church; and *for* ecology, prisoner and LGBT rights, and feminism. Their protests took the form of sudden unauthorized public actions—pantomime music performances—filmed and edited with a dubbed soundtrack into roughly produced music videos uploaded to YouTube and the Russian blog site *LiveJournal*. The site also included interviews and photos of the group's actions, as well as "in the recording studio," and more stylized publicity photos of the women masked in their trademark bright-colored balaclavas—some ironically recalling the playful poses of the Beatles (see Figure 29.1, and McMichael 2013).

One particular and fateful action at the Cathedral of Christ the Savior in Moscow on February 21, 2012, ended with the arrest and public trial of three of its members—Maria (Masha) Alyokhina, Nadezdha (Nadya) Tolokonnikova and Yekaterina (Katya)

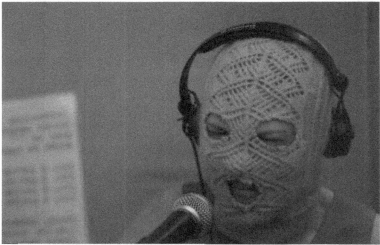

FIGURE 29.1. Screenshot of *LiveJournal* web page for January 24, 2012. The caption reads "The recording of the song "Riot in Russia—Putin Zassal" at the rehearsal base Pussy Riot. Meet the soloists Balaklava, Chowder, Hat, Tyur, Garadzhu, Puck, Schumacher, Seraphim and Kota!"

Samutsevich, and the long-term imprisonment of two (Masha and Nadya). During the imprisonment of Masha and Nadya, the Russian concert promoter Alexander Cheparukhin called on musicians such as Madonna, Björk, and Paul McCartney to join a worldwide call for the release of Pussy Riot, thus associating them with megastar pop musicians. As Masha Gessen (2014, 18) notes: "Never had the worldwide music industry mobilized on this scale and at this speed to support a colleague—especially colleagues who were not, in fact, musicians in any traditional sense."

At the time of this writing in 2021, Pussy Riot is harder to define. Like many a regular punk band, the collective has splintered: anonymous activists in Russia continue to mount unauthorized public actions to call out corruption and oppression, such as disrupting the 2018 World Cup final held in Moscow. Nadya and Masha have mostly gone solo, writing books and creating activist art, sometimes under the name Pussy Riot, in the form of theater pieces, songs, and videos (now with high profile artists and high-end production).[2] Predictable disputes over the rightful claim of the name come and go: should members be cast out once their identities are revealed? Has Pussy Riot become a brand name to help sell music, books, and tickets—as well as ideas of resistance to a totalitarian state?

In many ways Pussy Riot, in all its guises and disguises, embodies the same paradoxes of punk rock: the dance between socialism and capitalism, obscurity and fame, politics and style, authenticity and performance, insurrection and art genre. But Pussy Riot also acts as a mirror of the state apparatus of disinformation, precisely through the increasingly slippery meaning of the word "punk" and its modes of production and dissemination. In his study of the 1980s Peruvian punk band Narcosis, Shane Greene (2016, 288) argues that "punk proposes a means of underproduction, a concerted attempt to intervene crudely but creatively in the problem of capitalist over-production." Further, "one of punk's theoretical dilemmas then is essentially dialogical in nature, an on-going conversation about how something that risks being 'under' in one moment (or according to one voice or as part of one context) is subject to the risk of surfacing into the 'over' in another" (289). The tension between underproduction and overproduction is embedded in the tension between the activist's and the autocrat's language—Pussy Riot and Putin, punk and Trump. After all, Pussy Riot's activism depended on late capitalism's global network, which turns underproduction into viral overproduction. These are, of course, the same technological routes through which Russia attempted to sow social discord to the advantage of Donald Trump in the 2016 and 2020 elections. Shane Greene again: "[W]e might consider that one of punk's overarching discursive intentions—what one *means* to do by engaging in a punk *means* of underproduction—is to disregard: to negate regard; to refuse to respect, to repudiate rather hold in esteem. Punk starts with refusal and then you find a way from there" (Greene 2016, 289). So let's start with a (respectful) refusal:

Punk is not a way of life; it is a genre—of music, theater, and human rights.

Pussy Riot's Punk Music

What does "genre" mean? On the broadest level, the word simply means type, kind, or category; in reference to literature, music, and art, the word designates a shared set of characteristics (form, style, content, idioms) that identify a type. All disclaimers aside, Pussy Riot made their greatest mark utilizing the musical genre of punk rock—specifically the idioms of British Oi! and US Riot Grrrl. Kot, a participant in the Cathedral action who escaped arrest, remarked in a March 2012 interview: "Some of us draw inspiration from classic Oi!-punk bands of the early 1980s; The Angelic Upstarts,

Cockney Rejects, Sham 69, and the other acts in that bunch—all those folks had incredible musical and social energy, their sound ripped through the atmosphere of their decade, stirred trouble around itself. Their vibe does really capture the essence of punk, which is aggressive protest" (Langston 2012). In the same interview, another member of the collective, Garadzha, added: "A lot of credit certainly goes to Bikini Kill and the bands in the Riot Grrrl act—we somehow developed what they did in the 1990s, although in an absolutely different context and with an exaggerated political stance, which leads to all of our performances being illegal—we'll never give a gig in a club or in any special musical space. That's an important principle for us."

Let's pause to consider how odd this pairing is: Oi! was a staunchly masculinist mid-1980s British second-wave punk genre, complicatedly linked to football-fan hooliganism and the rise of white nationalist skinheads in the realignment of working-class identities with right-wing populism.

Matthew Worley (2013, 628) describes Oi!'s narrow political claims as "a class identity that was rooted in the politics of everyday life: in work, the weekend, the community, street, and home." For a band such as Cock Sparrer, "riot" meant a dust-up with the lads cheering for the other team, just to relieve boredom ("Running Riot"); and for The Business, punk's first wave was full of fake leftist revolutionaries and "trendy wankers" who "wave a hammer and sickle, never Union Jacks" ("Suburban Rebels"). Riot Grrrl, in stark contrast, was a staunchly feminist 1990s reaction to mid-1980s masculinist punk, foregrounding gendered aspects of everyday life for women: sexual abuse and systematic oppression by a patriarchal society. Bikini Kill's direct, confrontational lyrics in songs such as "Suck My Left One" gave punk a new feminist hardcore language, and their album *Pussy Whipped*, combined with the zine-derived moniker Riot Grrrl, gave Pussy Riot its name (Wiedlack 2016, 411).

In September 2011 the activist collective conducted their first punk act, which was to include a recording of their song "Kill the Sexist" ("Ubey Seksista") at the conclusion of Nadya's presentation to a small conference of Russian opposition groups (Gessen 2014, 61–67). As Nadya explains:

> We decided to pick the topic of political punk feminism; we were sure something like that must exist in Russia. So we already scheduled our talk with the time and the place. So as usual we do everything at the last moment and about twelve hours before the talk we start researching and discover that there is no such thing in Russia. And so in those twelve hours we suddenly found ourselves with this task, of historic and epic importance, which was to create Russian feminist punk and so we recorded a song, which opened with "you're sick and tired of rotten socks."
>
> (Remnick 2014)

"Kill the Sexist" is the only song that does not have an accompanying video, so we have no action but the recording itself, which was released for download in 2012 during the trial as part of a six-song digital album.[3] Hence, the song has been overlooked by most scholarship on Pussy Riot, inevitably lured by the genre of the music videos into meta questions: Is Pussy Riot authentically punk if they don't perform live (McMichael 2013; Amico 2016)? Are they punk if other Russian underground musicians (gigging Russian punks) did not support them (Rogatchevski and Steinholt 2016)? Are their mediated forms of punk and feminism directed primarily to Western audiences (Amico 2016; Wiedlack 2016)? My recourse to a formalist approach below attempts to keep a focus on the granular level—the generic effects of their underproduction, and how those effects compound to become the Russian feminist punk statement Pussy Riot intended it to be.

"Kill the Sexist" is a punk masterpiece of underproduction, roughly constructed from samples and loops of the choppy four-bar guitar hook from the Cockney Rejects' "I'm Not a Fool" (1979).[4] That song narrates the plight of a young bloke who commits a crime out of boredom, is double-crossed by his friend, and winds up in jail:

> Gotta break out find something else to do,
> I can't stand being stuck in here with you.
> Gonna have a laugh,
> Gonna break into a store,
> I'm so bored that I don't care anymore.
> Told our mate to keep dog eye,
> But he went and told a lie.
> They took us down the station,
> They done us for theft.
> Now my life's in ruins,
> I ain't got nothing left.

Contrary to the facts of the story, the chorus proclaims:

> I'm not so ignorant, I'm not a fool.
> So keep your intelligence, I am not a fool.
> Not a fool, there's nothing left, I'm not a fool, there's nothing left.

Fools are key and somewhat ambivalent figures in Russian literature, art, and Orthodox legend; the "holy fool" (*yurodivy*) being a type of sanctified soothsayer reflecting the foolishness of society in his own disruptive language, behavior, and asceticism. In her closing statement to the Russian court, Nadya declared: "We were seeking true sincerity and simplicity and we found them in the holy-fool aesthetic of punk performance" (quoted in Gessen 2014, 196). In other words, we should understand Pussy Riot's punk action precisely as a specifically Russian genre of social critique.[5]

The punk fool of Oi! is a foil to the punk feminist of "Kill the Sexist"—who is, indeed, no fool. I do not know if the lyrics of Pussy Riot's "Kill the Sexist" were composed with "I'm No Fool" in mind, but it sure seems so: the boredom of a British man shifts to the boredom of Russian women, who don't just blow off steam with a petty crime but rather mount a full-scale bloody rebellion. The musical reconstruction warrants a closer look for the ways in which the means of underproduction can add to a meaning of refusal. Two musical samples repeat inconsistently: sample 1 comprises the first eight bars of the song (or two times through the four-bar riff), and ends just as the bass guitar enters to thicken the texture; sample 2 restarts the song but continues through twelve bars, catching the drum entrance, and cutting off just before the riff breaks into power chords.[6] Although sample 2 occurs only once, its early appearance as the second repetition announces the haphazard underproduction of the track, and heightens the sense of uncertainty.

	[sample 1 begins: 4-bar intro][7]
Tebe nadoeli protukhshie noski,	You are sick and tired of stinky socks,
Papki tvoego protukhshie noski	Your daddy's stinky socks. **[sample 1 ends]**
	[sample 2 begins]
Muzh tvoy budet v protukhshikh noskakh,	Your husband will be in stinky socks,
Zhizn' budet v protukhshikh noskakh.	Your entire life will be stinky socks.
Mat' tvoya v gryaznoy posude,	Your mother is all in dirty dishes,
S protukhshey zhrachkoy v gryaznoy posude	Stinky food remains in dirty dishes.
Perezharennoy kuritsey moet poly.	Using refried chicken to wash the floor,
Mat' tvoya zhivet v tyur'me.	Your mother lives in prison. **[sample 2 ends]**
	[sample 1 begins]
V tyur'me gorshki otmyvaet otstoyno,	In prison she's washing pots like a sucker.
V tyur'me nikogda ne byvaet svobody	In prison, there is no freedom.
Adskaya zhizn', gospodstvo muzhchin,	Hellish life, the rule of men,
Vyydi na ulitsu, osvobodi zhenshchin!	Come out in the street and free the women!
	[sample 1 ends]
	[sample 1 begins]
Nyukhayte sami svoi noski,	Suck on your own stinky socks,
Zhopu svoyu ne zabyvayte chesat'	Don't forget to scratch your ass while you're at it,
Rygayte, plyuyte, bukhayte, srite,	Burp, spit, drink, shit,
A my s radost'yu pobudem lesbiyankami!	While we happily become lesbians!
	[sample 1 ends]
	[sample 1 begins]
Sami, lokhi, zaviduyte penisu,	Idiots, envy your own penis,
Dlinnomu penisu druga po pivu,	Or your drinking buddy's huge dick,
Dlinnomu penisu iz zomboyashchika,	Or the huge dick on the zombie box [TV].
Poka uroven' govna ne doydet do potolka!	While shit piles up and rises to the ceiling!
	[sample 1 ends]
	[sample 1 begins]
Stan' feministkoy, feministkoy stan',	Become a feminist, become a feminist,
Miru—mir, muzhchinam—konets!	Peace to the world, death to men.
Stan' feministkoy, unichtozh' seksista,	Become a feminist, destroy the sexist,
Ubey seksista, smoy ego krov'!	Kill the sexist, wash off his blood!
	[sample 1 ends]
	[4-bar break: sample 1 begins]
Stan' feministkoy, unichtozh' seksista,	Become a feminist, kill the sexist,
Ubey seksista, smoy ego krov'!	Kill the sexist, wash off his blood!
	[sample 1 ends]

None of the looping is seamless: abrupt cuts and micro delays create an off-balance feel. The song conditions us to tolerate the background noise of inconsistencies, of repetitions that are both tedious and teasing, the promises of crescendos that ultimately lead nowhere. The underproduction of the music track creates a grand sonic metaphor for living under an oppressive authoritarian and patriarchal regime. As Masha described in her closing statement during the trial: "What looks orderly and restrictive is in fact disorganized and inefficient . . . people feel acutely lost, in time and space" (quoted in Gessen 2014, 213).

While the backing track is dismantled Oi!, the vocals are pure Riot Grrrl: different women trade stanzas and lines of blunt refusal and rebellion, joining together to shout gleefully, "Go outside, free the women," and "Kill the sexist, wash off his blood!"[8] Bikini Kill's "Rebel Girl" readily comes to mind, but also these lines from their song "Blood One": "I don't fit into your dumb words / Language is memory pushing through my skin." It is a lyric straight out of 1990s feminist theories that considered language as itself a patriarchal system. Bikini Kill's "dumb words" are Pussy Riot's "stinky socks"—a gender system that keeps women imprisoned, and while men's language devolves into burp and spit, women escape into what many Russians believed to be the decadent language and identity world of the West: *my s radost'yu pobudem lesbiyankami!* (We happily become lesbians!). Such words were criminalized as "gay propaganda" in some regions of Russia at that time, and prohibited nationwide in 2013—a key element in Putin's self-promotion as the defender of Russian (Orthodox) values against the advancement of the godless and decadent West (Chan 2017).

Pussy Riot's Punk Theater

Although not part of an action, "Kill the Sexist" set up the dramatic parameters of the actions to follow: a fictional punk rock group transforms public spaces into stages, and creates fleeting live political theater and viral music videos. For their first video release, "Free the Cobblestones," the group engaged a new member ("N"), who brought computer and musical skills to produce the video's soundtrack drawn from samples of the Angelic Upstarts' song "Police Oppression" (1980) (See Gessen 2014, 67–72). Unlike the Cockney Rejects' refusal of politics, the Angelic Upstarts explicitly embraced anti-fascist, anti-racist, and pro-socialist political positions, and so Pussy Riot's choice of "Police Oppression" provides an earnest rather than ironic musical reference. The punk song's lyrics, especially the motif of walking in the street under the constant threat of state-sponsored oppression, provide an appropriate intertext to "Free the Cobblestones," which refers to a famous slogan of the Paris 1968 riots: *sous les pavés, la plage* (under the cobblestones, the beach). The beach refers to the sand bed below the cobblestones that rioters had dug up to throw at the police (Willems 2014, 404).

"Police Oppression" excerpts from verses 1 and 2	"Free the Cobblestones" Verses 3 and 4[9]
I just can't take much more of this oppression. [...] They're asking me how, and they're asking me why, Have you ever seen grown men cry?	It's never too late to take charge. Nightsticks are loaded, the shouts get louder. Stretch your arms and leg muscles And the policeman will lick you between your legs.
Police police police oppression! Police police police oppression!	Free the cobblestones! Free the cobblestones! Free the cobblestones! Free the cobblestones!
Really find it hard even walking round the streets. Hey I know you son, I'll knock you off your feet. [...]	Egyptian air is good for the lungs, Turn Red Square into Tahrir, Spend a full day among strong women, Find an ice pick on your balcony and free the cobblestones.
Police police police oppression! Police police police oppression!	Tahrir! Tahrir! Tahrir! Benghazi Tahrir! Tahrir! Tahrir! Tripoli! The feminist whip is good for Russia[10]

In the Oi! song, a grown man cries in the face of police oppression, whereas in Pussy Riot's song, feminists call to protest—even violent protest—as authorized by historical and contemporaneous global events. Spliced music samples of a few different eight-bar phrases from "Police Oppression" flow seamlessly to provide a steady guitar riff, drum groove, and two options for drum fills. If "Kill the Sexist" sounded the off-kilter reality of the Putin regime, "Free the Cobblestones" sounded a new confident deployment of their sonic weaponry—the cobblestones and the sand base—for their music video art action.

Pussy Riot released the video for "Free the Cobblestones" on November 7, 2011, the anniversary date of the armed insurrection of the Bolsheviks led by Vladimir Lenin (often referred to as the "October Revolution" or "Red October"). According to the *LiveJournal* blog entry for that date, Pussy Riot described themselves as an "Oi! punk band" (ой-панк-группа) who had conducted a series of "illegal partisan speeches" (н елегальных партизанских выступлений) in public locations over the course of the previous month, calling these performances "a tour in support of the upcoming debut album called *Kill the Sexist*" (Тур в поддержку готовящегося к выпуску дебютного альбома под названием "Убей сексиста"). The video, photo essay, blog post, and Q&A published on November 7 served to document the live performances, and, of course, deliver its art piece—promotional material for an imagined album—all rhetorically working together to cement the nascent identity of the collective and its particular theater of punk rock.

The video calls attention to staging—the site, the platform, the space—wherein their bodies enact a punk pantomime, and interpellate viewers into their show. We see the group climbing and performing on construction scaffolding in a Moscow metro station spliced with shots of performances on top of an electric trolley car, and in a small lit alcove in a second metro station. The blog stresses the illegality of the performance, not only in its speech content, but perhaps most importantly in the locations:

> PUSSY RIOT has always performed and will be performing illegally. We are not interested in official sites. The idea of concerts in clubs and corporate parties of oil companies is hopelessly outdated. Our group strongly disagrees with the closure of the musician in the ghetto of the clubs, on the contrary, we believe that the musician should actively work with the urban space, each time discovering a new and sudden audience. You can see the PUSSY RIOT concert, following in a crowded transport after the next working day. Isn't that great?[11]

Leaving aside for now their admonishment of musicians, I want to focus on this creation of a "sudden audience." In the video for "Free the Cobblestones" we see shots of astonished commuters, many smiling and taking videos on their phones (see Figures 29.2 and 29.3). This sudden audience that gathered below the various stages enacted the same gestures as they would attending a rock concert, with smart phones ready to capture the performance. They not only documented a curious event on the way to work, but also a political moment that they unwittingly participated in—an unsanctioned protest event.

If we think in terms of genre—of punk genre—then this disruption of the everyday triggered repeated gestures of DIY underproduction: these phone videos do not match the Pussy Riot version, with its multiple sites and angles and jump cuts; rather, they capture an orientation that is wholly subjective and particularized, like the numbered seat in a theater, or a standing position in a club. And they ironically create a distinction between unofficial and official videos, casting Pussy Riot in the role of (capitalist) overproduction—the sleek technological repackaging of a makeshift musical concert. What we bear witness to in the video, however, are the new "cobblestones" in action: as a member of Pussy Riot rains feathers and confetti down from their stage, the people dig out their smart phones. These micro gestures of action, perhaps little more than a reflex, nonetheless threw the first stones. As the blog entry relates: "A number of separate videos and photos made during the performance on mobile phones by shocked witnesses of our illegal concerts have already appeared on the internet."[12] The blog goes on to answer questions from the stream of comments they read about themselves: Who are Pussy Riot? What are their political beliefs? Why do they perform illegally? These are curated questions designed to elicit political statements. What remains a mystery now, in the digitally edited afterlife of these performances, are the live sounds and live actions the viewers actually witness. But does this matter?

Yes, in the eyes and ears of the state, what actually happened on site is not a trivial question. The charge of "hooliganism" (behavior associated with Oi! bands and their fans, in fact) depended on it. As Polly McMichael summarizes: "The question of whether Pussy Riot's actions in the Cathedral of Christ the Savior had or had not constituted a

FIGURES 29.2 AND 29.3. Screen shots from the video "Free the Cobblestones."

performance of their song became central to debate during the run-up to the trial of Alekhina [sic], Samutsevich and Tolokonnikova. The forty-second performance was taken apart, analysed and retold in a variety of ways" (McMichael 2013, 108–109). Was there sound? Was there amplification? Was there equipment? Was there singing? What could be heard? As Masha tells in *Riot Days*, security guards grabbed Katya as she took her electric guitar out of its case: "She managed to distract them all, and this bought us 40 seconds to do our performance. 40 seconds of crime" (Alyokhina 2017, 24). Many pages deep into the YouTube archive, one can find a 90-second video of the event: what we hear is barely audible: the women's muffled chanting dissolves into the reverb of the cavernous cathedral—their only means of amplification.[13] Masha recalls: "The sound dies away. There is only the echo of our uncoordinated screaming and shouting" (Alyokhina 2017, 26).

"Mother of God, Chase Putin Out" (which they called a "Punk Prayer") is such an effective song and video that it is easy to forget that it bears little resemblance to the shambolic action in the cathedral, which the members of Pussy Riot considered a flop. "I feel that the action in the Cathedral of Christ the Savior was horrible on the whole," Nadya laments, "[w]e didn't accomplish most of what we intended—we didn't even get to the refrain of the song" (Tolokonnikova 2018, 87). "The quality of the performance did not inspire confidence," Masha reflects on the video editing process, "after all, we'd only managed to sing a single verse" (Alyokhina 2017, 29). Gessen (2014, 121) writes: "They had to use the same sequences several times over and resort to including bits where the guards were stopping them or church employees were waving their hands at the camera. They all agreed it was the worst video they had ever published." But these details of underproduction are exactly what makes the video so compelling.

As the music cuts between melodious sounds of a Vespers prayer setting, lifted from Sergei Rachmaninoff's *All-Night Vigil*, and the distorted sounds of punk, viewers witness a repeating cycle of surveillance, menace, and physical confrontation as the Pussy Riot members attempt their choreographed movements of defiant air-punches and high kicks mixed with mock-devotional kneeling and bowing (see Figure 29.4).

As McMichael describes, we hear "the melodically delivered 'prayer' . . . invaded by the electric bass and then guitars, a gradual encroachment of the punk sound familiar from the group's previous tracks, presaging a transition from supplication to critique

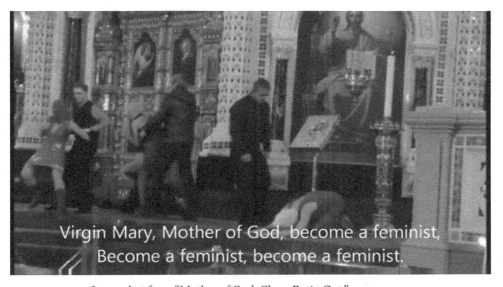

FIGURE 29.4. Screenshot from "Mother of God, Chase Putin Out."

FIGURE 29.5. Screenshot from "Mother of God, Chase Putin Out."

and to the anger-laden tonalities of the sequential solo voices which enter" (McMichael 2013, 108). But we see encroachments of an entirely different sort—the security guards in drab black and blue grabbing and tussling with the brightly dressed bodies of the women. This violent encroachment of the church-state authoritarian complex interrupts critique with domination. We the viewers become part of the melee, too, confronted directly by shots of cathedral caretakers attempting to bat away the (our) camera (see Figure 29.5).

Rachmaninoff's melody is a counterfeit Orthodox chant; and this video is also something of a counterfeit, in its expansion of a fleeting forty seconds into nearly two minutes. Uploaded on February 21, and banned as extremist in Russia on November 29, 2012 (Bryanski 2012; see Figure 29.6), the ten-month residency of the video on Russian websites in turn produced the counterfeit and muddled memories of eyewitnesses who claimed to be victims of the action. The prosecution's first witness was Lyubov Sokologorskaya, the caretaker prominently featured in the video, who claimed lasting moral suffering and damage from bearing witness to Pussy Riot dancing on the altar (where women were not allowed). When asked by the defense about specific words she heard during the performance, she testified: "It's all mixed up with the video clip now. You know, I don't remember" (quoted in Gessen 2014, 177). "If the performance caused you such moral suffering, why did you decide to poison your soul again?" the defense lawyer asked her (Ioffe 2012). The judge struck the question, but we can well imagine the answer: curiosity to see herself on a viral video, as a warrior for the church, representative of moral and political authority, and participant in an event whose historical importance was growing by the day. Perhaps she also experienced a morbid fascination in the violation of the altar by other women.

FIGURE 29.6. Screenshot from *LiveJournal* entry for February 21, 2012.

Using the altar to dance and shout "holy shit," and entreat the Virgin Mary to become a feminist, momentarily converted a platform for religious theater into a stage for Riot Grrrl theater, which then led to a courtroom drama that interpolated state witnesses and state power into the plot. Julia Ioffe, reporting on the trial in August 2012 for the *New Republic*, wrote that "the trial became an inadvertent continuation of their performance piece, one that grew far past the boundaries they had envisioned for it and ended up becoming a monumental, historical work. The kangaroo court, the prison sentence, the martyr status—Pussy Riot didn't expect any of it, but they had clearly hit a nerve and the state's overblown, medieval response had became [*sic*] part of the show.... It was a prime example of a classic Russian genre: a bitter dark comedy depicting the absurdity of oppression" (Ioffe 2012). And Gessen later concurred: "[I]t would be a Soviet political trial repeated as farce. About a dozen trials of groups of Soviet dissidents took place from the early 1960s until the mid-1980s; the transcripts of these trials formed an important part of the dissident literary canon" (Gessen 2014, 168).

Pussy Riot could not escape genre, and in fact used genre to amplify and extend their actions into the Russian dissident canon. In this way, Pussy Riot's version of punk transformed into a genre of human rights.

Pussy Riot's Punk Human Rights

An act of underproduction in the cathedral led to an overproduction of punitive state power, which in turn generated another genre of Pussy Riot punk—the prisoner. In the homosocial world of male prison slang and sexuality, punks took the role of women—that is, they were on the receiving end of a physical and sexual power dynamic. In her memoir, Masha recalls the systematic punking of all prisoners: "Half a year went by before I realized I could say no when the guards said 'Bend Over.' A whole year passed before I could justify my 'no' by citing Russian law and forcing a gasp from each person at a search who told me to take off my underwear or to squat naked" (Alyokhina 2017, 49). This, too, is an account of a punk action, or rather the account of one punk action leading to the other as cause and effect: the bending over, and the moment of refusal.

For nearly two years, Masha and Nadya endured brutal labor camps; solitary confinement; constant surveillance by minders; shunning or harassment by other prisoners who, disenfranchised, became agents of the prison system. High-profile musicians—precisely those they once admonished for being ghettoized in official spaces and clubs—helped publicize their cause to a global audience and a national audience, which also affected the conditions of their imprisonment, for better and for worse. "Nothing will happen to me," Masha writes, "I'm a political. Madonna lifts up her shirt for me on TV. But cellmates, they'll be punished" (Alyokhina 2017, 109). Yet when and where they could, Masha and Nadya made good use of their celebrity to advocate for better conditions in their prisons through letter writing campaigns, legal briefs, and hunger strikes.

Let's consider these actions and their venue, the prison system, within the terms of Pussy Riot's pre-trial blog post: "PUSSY RIOT has always performed and will be performing illegally. We are not interested in official sites. The idea of concerts in clubs and corporate parties of oil companies is hopelessly outdated." In the post-trial story of Pussy Riot, their ideological binaries of legal/illegal performances and official/unofficial spaces blur in significant ways. While incarcerated, both Masha and Nadya enacted punk performances that, ironically, required a full knowledge and investment in the law in order to demand legality from the prison system. "I studied the law that regulates a prisoner's life. I learned labor law too," Nadya recounts (Tolokonnikova 201, 159); Masha writes: "While people outside are decorating their Christmas trees, I'm getting ready to take the guards to court" (Alyokhina 2017, 140). In other words, their principle of illegality outside prison walls became a principle of legality within those walls; illegal venues such as metro stations and Red Square became the legal venues of courtrooms.

This conceptual shift from illegality to legality has ramifications for punk as political practice, and for its principal aims. In this prison context, the aim is not to destroy laws and institutions but to shore them up. As Nadya argues, political activism means "*protecting these institutions* from being eroded by corruption, lobbyists, monopolies, corporate and government control over our personal data" (Tolokonnikova 2018, 2). The Clash once sang "I fought the law and the law won." Pussy Riot's post-trial message is: Use the Law! This is not a vision of anarchy; rather, it is a vision of a functioning legal system and government institutions that protect human rights. Both Nadya and Masha came out of prison with a dedicated focus on prison reform—punk human rights—founding the advocacy group Zona Prava (Zone of Rights) in December 2013 to shine a light on the wretched conditions in Russian prisons by working within the European Court of Human Rights. They also founded the independent media outlet MediaZona in 2014, to counteract Russian disinformation and censorship, and to report on and archive court cases within Russia (Tolokonnikova 2018, 196–203).

How can we reconcile this commitment to the law, institutions, and transparency with the more traditional punk stance of being anti-state and jamming the system with loud noise and mischievous fakery? What is left to punk in the aftermath of Russia's interference in the US election of Donald Trump in 2016, his refusal to accept the election results of 2020, and his incitement of a violent attack on The Capitol on January 6, 2021? Shocking confrontation and disregard may no longer be viable as a punk strategy of underproduction, now that, through Trump, they have become an overproduced political norm, and a means of bludgeoning facts and institutions. In the face of lawless autocracy, punk may take the form of a methodical and rigorous response that thoroughly invests in the rule of law and restores faith in the democratic system. This is how punk becomes a way of life that is not punk—or rather, a way of life that should not have to be punk, but just good citizenship. However, when social institutions fail and the social fabric rips apart, we all must think of ourselves as a punk activist collective.

In my interview with Masha days before Trump's election, I asked, "What advice do you have for those of us anticipating the need for political action?" She gave me a very punk answer:

> I should say that I'm totally not something unique or special. I'm like everybody, and everybody has a story, and everybody in different situations in their lives has to make a choice, and the choice is really to act or to stay at the side. Don't stay at the side because otherwise your history will be written by somebody else.

Notes

1. "Alternative facts" was a phrase used by Kellyanne Conway to defend the White House Press Secretary's exaggerated number of attendees at Trumps inauguration in January 2017.

2. For example, in 2016 Nadya, who now goes by a shortened last name of Tolokno, released an EP under the name Pussy Riot, entitled *xxx (!)*. The EP was produced by TV on the Radio's Dave Sitek on the Atlantic Records imprint Nice Life.
3. The first mention of an album appears in the *LiveJournal* post for November 7, 2011. https://pussy-riot.livejournal.com/2011/11/07/.
4. "I'm Not a Fool," written by Stinky Turner, Michael Geggus, Vince Riordan, and Andrew Scott. Lyric reproduced courtesy of Maxwood Music Limited.
5. For a detailed study of Pussy Riot in relation to the figure of the holy fool, see Woodyard (2014).
6. I have used the transliterated lyrics transcribed on http://russmus.net/song/12002 (Accessed 17 January 2019) to facilitate the listening experience for non-Russian readers. The translation is drawn from Gessen (2014, 66). Used by permission of Riverhead, an imprint of Penguin Publishing Group, a division of Penguin Random House LLC. All rights reserved. I thank Ekaterina for a few modifications to this translation, and for correcting all translations from Russian to English for this essay.
7. Excerpts from *Words Will Break Cement: The Passion of Pussy Riot* by Masha Gessen, copyright © 2014 by Masha Gessen. Used by permission of Riverhead, an imprint of Penguin Publishing Group, a division of Penguin Random House LLC. All rights reserved.
8. Gessen (2014, 66) notes that the vocals were recorded using a handheld Dictaphone.
9. Excerpt from *Words Will Break Cement: The Passion of Pussy Riot* by Masha Gessen, copyright © 2014 by Masha Gessen. Used by permission of Riverhead, an imprint of Penguin Publishing Group, a division of Penguin Random House LLC. All rights reserved.
10. Translation from Gessen 2014, 73. Used by permission of Riverhead, an imprint of Penguin Publishing Group, a division of Penguin Random House LLC. All rights reserved.
11. Pussy Riot. всегда выступали и будут выступать нелегально. Нам неинтересны официальные площадки. Идея концертов в клубах и на корпоративах нефтяных компаний безнадежно устарела. Наша группа категорически несогласна с замыканием музыканта в гетто клубов, напротив, мы полагаем, что музыкант должен активно работать с городским пространством, каждый раз открывая для себя новую и внезапную аудиторию. Концерт Pussy Riot вы сможете увидеть, следуя в переполненном транспорте после очередного рабочего дня. Разве это не замечательно? Accessed 28 February 2019. https://pussy-riot.livejournal.com/2011/11/07/ . This webpage displays a banner that reads "Pussy Riot is Dead," which has nothing to do with the original post, but is an artifact of an internal dispute within the collective that emerged in 2015. For more on dispute that see https://pussy-riot.livejournal.com/.
12. За время выступлений в интернете уже появилось некоторое количество отдельных видео и фото, сделанных на мобильные телефоны шокированными свидетелями наших нелегальных концертов.
13. Published by Radio Liberty (Радио Свобода), titled "Оригинальное видео Pussy Riots из ХХС" (The original video of Pussy Riots from HHS). Accessed 1 March 2019. https://www.youtube.com/watch?v=e6n-jqOZ_to.

References

Alyokhina, Maria *Riot Days*. 2017. Kindle ed. New York: Metropolitan Books, 2017.

Amico, Stephen. 2016. "Digital Voices, Other Rooms: Pussy Riot's Recalcitrant (In) Corporeality." *Popular Music and Society* 39, no. 4: 423–447.

Bryanski, Gleb. 2012. "Russian Court Bans "Extremist" Pussy Riot Video." Reuters, November 29, 2012. https://www.reuters.com/article/entertainment-us-russia-pussyriot/russian-court-bans-extremist-pussy-riot-video-idUSBRE8AM0EP20121129.

Chan, Sewell. 2017. "Russia's 'Gay Propaganda' Laws are Illegal, European Court Rules." *New York Times*, June 20, 2017. https://www.nytimes.com/2017/06/20/world/europe/russia-gay-propaganda.html.

Gessen, Masha. 2014. *Words Will Break Cement: The Passion of Pussy Riot*. New York: Riverhead Books.

Gessen, Masha. 2017. "The Autocrat's Language." *New York Review of Books*, May 13, 2017. https://www.nybooks.com/daily/2017/05/13/the-autocrats-language/.

Greene, Shane. 2016. "Peruvian Punk as a Global Means of Underground Production." *Popular Music and Society* 39, no. 3: 286–300.

Guirard, Jim. 1987. "'Glasnost' vs. 'Skrytnost.'" *Washington Post*, April 27, 1987 https://www.washingtonpost.com/archive/opinions/1987/04/27/glasnost-vs-skrytnost/becd1973-b503-4930-bea2-b5de88ad7fe7/?utm_term=.ea2193afdae8.

Ioffe, Julia. 2012. "Pussy Riot v. Putin: A Front Row Seat at a Russian Dark Comedy." *New Republic*, August 6, 2012. https://newrepublic.com/article/105846/how-punk-rock-show-trial-became-russias-greatest-gonzo-artwork.

Langston, Henry. 2012. "Meeting Pussy Riot." *Vice*, March 12, 2012. https://www.vice.com/en_us/article/kwnzgy/A-Russian-Pussy-Riot.

Lewis, Jeffrey. 2018. "Trump's Punk Rock Nuclear Policy." *Foreign Policy*, October 23, 2018. https://foreignpolicy.com/2018/10/23/trumps-punk-rock-nuclear-policy/.

McMichael, Polly. 2013. "Defining Pussy Riot Musically: Performance and Authenticity in New Media." *Digital Icons: Studies in Russian, Eurasian and Central European New Media* 9: 99–113. http://www.digitalicons.org/issue09/polly-mcmichael.

Rogatchevski, Andrei, and Yngvar B. Steinholt. 2016. "Pussy Riot's Musical Precursors? The National Bolshevik Party Bands, 1994–2007." *Popular Music and Society* 39, no. 9: 448–464.

Smith, Kyle. 2016. "Donald Trump is the Punk Rock President American Deserves." *New York Post*, November 9, 2016.

Tolokonnikova, Nadya. 2018. *Read and Riot: A Pussy Riot Guide to Activism*. Kindle ed. New York: HarperOne.

Wiedlack, Katharina. 2016. "Pussy Riot and the Western Gaze: Punk Music, Solidarity and the Production of Similarity and Difference." *Popular Music and Society* 39, no. 4: 410–422.

Willems, Joachim. 2014. "Why 'Punk'? Religion, Anarchism and Feminism in Pussy Riot's Punk Prayer." *Religion, State & Society* 42, no. 4: 403–419.

Woodyard, Kerith M. 2014. "Pussy Riot and the Holy Foolishness of Punk." *Rock Music Studies* 1, no. 3: 268–286.

Worley, Matthew. 2013. "Oi! Oi! Oi!: Class, Locality, and British Punk." *Twentieth Century British History* 24, no. 4: 606–636.

Interviews

Peraino, Judith and Tom McEnaney. 2016. "Punkfest Cornell Panel with Masha Alyokhina (Pussy Riot), Sasha Bogina (MediaZona) and Alexander Cheparukhin." Ithaca, NY: Cornell

University, November 2, 2016. http://rmc.library.cornell.edu/punkfest/events.html#modalClosed.

Remnick, David. 2014. "Pussy Riot in Conversation with David Remnick." Frieze Talks 2014. *New Yorker*, July 22, 2014. https://www.newyorker.com/video/watch/david-remnick-interviews-pussy-riot.

CHAPTER 30

YOU AIN'T NO PUNK, YOU PUNK

On Semiotic Doxa, Postmodern Authenticity, Ontological Agency, and the Goddamn Alt-Right

DANIEL S. TRABER

It is a question amounting to a philosophical statement. It is a question I am certain every punk rock fan has heard at some point. It is a question I was recently reminded of in perhaps the oddest way possible: a panel from a 2016 special edition *Archies* comic posted in a Facebook punk-themed group. It is special because the title is *The Archies Meet the Ramones*, telling the story of how the Riverdale gang is magically transported to New York City in 1976, landing outside Max's Kansas City, where they happen upon one of the seminal punk bands. Jughead remarks to Tommy Ramone that his red-haired pal is "really into punk," to which Tommy retorts, "He doesn't look like a punk," at which point Betty steps in to defend Archie by delivering the killer counterargument: "Well, what's more punk than *that*?" And that simple question is what got me thinking, once again, about punk identity.

My punk-focused research has always been interested in punk's own points of contention, moments of contradiction, heresies, and self-inflicted wounds. "Well, what's more punk than *that*?" The question forces punk to turn against itself in a way other musical cultures, and any extraneous subcultures associated with them, never experience. This through-the-looking-glass reversal is a favored device of conservative pundits—antifeminist women become the *true* feminists, whites are the *real* victims of racism—but is utterly alien to any self-labeled cultural group, be they marginal or mainstream, that comes to my mind, other than punk. To look, behave, or speak like a hippie, mod, metalhead, preppy, goth, hip-hop aficionado, or whatever, means that you in some way portray, display, occupy, or emulate—which is to say, you *constitute*—that identity. Only punk possesses the curious uniqueness of being a cultural form in which the absence of signifiers of the style and mindset can be twisted into actually representing the style and mindset.

This cannot simply be chalked up to punk promoting itself as a style rooted in rebellion—a form of refusal to a form of authority—since many subcultures do that. Rather, the explanatory value has to be freedom, as Nirvana's Kurt Cobain (2006) famously declared: "Punk rock should mean freedom, liking and accepting anything that you like, playing whatever you want. As sloppy as you want. As long as it's good and has passion." Cobain's vision of punk is based upon an individual's unfettered liberty to act, think, dress, perform, or feel as one wishes. And why not, as freedom has been the center point of most every attempt to posit a punk attitude or spirit? Yet the second part of Cobain's proclamation unwittingly points us toward a problem. He adds a caveat to his punk-as-freedom thesis: "as long as it's good and has passion." In that instant he lays down a law, a rule, a parameter which actually limits how that freedom can be enacted, what it can look and sound like—in essence, what punk can *mean*.

People adopt signifiers associated with a group all the time, and others use those details to try fitting the person into a codified system of meaning. But what happens if we see all signifiers as "floating"? Well before poststructuralism and postmodernism, that notion was central to Ferdinand de Saussure's semiotics, in which the link between signifier and signified is arbitrary; thus, the idea that a sign or symbol can convey must be artificially frozen into a singular, absolute meaning. It is fair to say punk's signifiers tend to be more airborne than those of other cultures, because the principal is built into its philosophical foundation and very act of self-creation. Many of punk's symbols and stylistic cues come from previous cultural expressions, sub- and otherwise, appropriated via quite postmodern gestures of bricolage that rip items out of their original contexts and give them new symbolic duties that necessitate new ways of reading them, and thereby open a space for new meanings to become available. Dick Hebdige argued this point in 1979, and I still heartily agree with him. Punk was built upon privileging openness—like a free-floating signifier—so reducing its possible iterations undermines that value. A curious example of this is a breed of Trumpian conservative described as the "new punk rock." I'll enter the fray to consider how accurate that label may be, how well it "floats," in conjunction with how a closed definition of punk operates against itself—all with an eye toward what this might reveal about authenticity and ontology in relation to identity as a whole, not just a punk subjectivity.

Alt-Right I: A License to Ruin Everything

"Conservatism is the new punk rock." James Parker was one of the earliest to proffer this thesis, in the October 2016 issue of the *Atlantic*: Trump has "co-created a space in American politics that is uniquely transgressive, volatile, carnivalesque, and (from a certain angle) punk rock." But the idea really gained traction in early 2017 when young conservatives started enthusiastically using the line. Michelle Goldberg (2017) quoted James O'Malia, an alt-right college student attending the Conservative Political Action Conference (CPAC), expressing this sentiment, which she translated as his saying that today's right is "edgy and subversive." There were YouTube videos, tweets, and memes (conspiracy-mogul Alex Jones's former protégé Paul Joseph Watson was prominent among them). Scott Galupo (2017) used it to draw comparisons between Trump and punk on matters of amateurism, challenging orthodoxies (like punk did musically), and general taboo smashing. The ultra-right British National Party (BNP) had tried to apply the label to themselves back in 2010 when spokesman Simon Darby announced, "The BNP are like the political Sex Pistols." They later updated their self-promotion pitch in line with the mood of 2017: "Nationalism is the answer . . . and it can't get cooler than the BNP—true rebels WITH a very worthy Cause!" (Watts 2017). (Are you convinced? No, me neither.) Plenty of people opposed this besmirching of punk with the alt-right stain, but it was too late. Then a smug sense of validation arose after former Sex Pistols singer John Lydon (aka Johnny Rotten) spoke positively of Donald Trump on *Good Morning Britain*—where he accused the Left of falsely labeling Trump a racist—and on America's National Public Radio: "I think he's absolutely magnificent. He's a total cat amongst the pigeons" (del Barco 2017).

The alt-*light* defines itself as conservative ideologues without the alt-right's racism. This sounds less noxious because they learned to disguise their fascist identitarian leanings with smoother edges, becoming white nationalists instead of white supremacists, while still ranting about the loss of white influence: political, social, economic, cultural, all of it.[1] Although less overt in style, they still rely on alt-right talking points by first luring you in with the pro–free speech siren's song to then dash your brains out on the rocks with their arguments about how multiculturalism is "white genocide," feminism sparked the death of Western culture, there are only two genders, and blacks typically score lower than whites on IQ tests due to genetic certainty rather than contingent social and historical factors. Such people may find a kinship with punk on the racial level: plenty of critics have noted the subculture's overwhelming whiteness in its participant demographics and musical stylings (myself included, see Traber 2001). Jon Savage (1992, 398) explains the negative optics of this tendency in the context of 1970s England: "Any fascist ambiguity in Punk was fueled by the way that the style had bled Rock dry of all black influences: one way to overcome any taint of white supremacy was to affirm visible links with Reggae." Nonetheless, my opinion is NO. These people poised against establishment conservatives and everyone on the left are not the new punk; rather, it is merely the most recent attempt at engaging in cultural transgression in order to brand their ideology. A large part of punk's appeal is its status as rebel rock, so the alt-right/light used a playbook written by England's anti-immigrant National Front to parasitically feed off a transgressive counterculture in the name of resuscitating the status quo with a politics rooted in tradition, patriarchy, racism, and xenophobia. One can find all these elements given expression throughout punk's history—it's a diverse lot who have claimed allegiance to the subculture—but they have never constituted a spoken or unspoken "official" punk philosophy and politics.

Rebellion itself is typically associated with left-of-center values because the very word *conservative* speaks to defending tradition, authority, and hierarchy. That definitional baseline traps punk subjectivity in a paradoxical bind: the punk rock ethos is antithetical to conservatism; however, it unwittingly replicates its perspective whenever "punk" shifts into "Punk" by erecting identitarian barricades for adjudicating ontological purity; thus, becoming an authority by monitoring a hierarchy through codified traditions. Such a duality was always present on the right. Corey Robin has studied the complexity of conservative political identity. Since its creation, born from Edmund Burke's response to the French Revolution, conservative movements are initiated as a reaction to loss, be it of power, income, property, status, a moral system, or a sense of privilege. To resist a revolution, or reform, that aims to emancipate a group, thereby redistributing power, necessitates co-opting the language of the Left to create a conservative counterrevolution, often, ironically, using radical means to transform the old regime in order to save it (Robin 2017, 56, 47, 193, 197). Robin's portrait of conservatives elucidates the alt-right's underlying motivations—the perceived loss of power and status due to progressive politics, rejecting their establishment elders—which situates their co-optation of punk rock within a long history of desperate reactionaries and revanchists.

So a conservative can disagree with the Left, but can he be a rebel? Yes, but only by framing his enemies as the dominant force controlling politics and culture in the society, and even then only to the extent those ideas are coming from an actual "ruling" class. This is certainly the viewpoint of these predominantly young(ish) white males who send out angry, callous memes as a way to respond to people they disagree with politically or feel are passing judgment on them (for they read even the mildest accusation of racism and/or misogyny as the work of a collectivist tyranny opposed to free-thinking individualists). Elsewhere, I have argued that rebellion is contextual. What is considered transgressive in one social space and among a certain group is only a shadow of rebellion, a useless amusement, to another group (Traber 2017, 204). Such is the case with the Internet subcultures wherein the alt-right/light can imagine themselves as anti-establishment rebels fighting the ideological hegemony of liberal/left "social justice warriors," whose overly sensitive politics and new cultural norms turn every ill-considered word into an intentional hate crime against marginalized people (read: anyone but heterosexual white males). They see themselves as an oppressed political class, as the true victims of intolerance, with suppressed rights and silenced voices. So they lash out with "shitposting" and "trolling" to upset their enemies—"triggering the libs"—and compete among themselves to be the most merciless, outrageous, obscene online "edgelord," all the while portraying their attacks as courageous thought crimes.

Angela Nagle (2017, 29, 67, 95, 115) shows that alt-right similarities to punk certainly exist. They both share a need to be in on the jokes, slang, and secret handshakes of an underground society, but the more significant parallel is found in their investment in shock effect. Nagle implicates countercultures as a whole in a long history of reveling in transgression to attack the rigid strictures of morality and good taste, as well as using it to construct bohemian subjectivities based on individual freedom. It must be noted, however, that while this history includes punk, it well precedes it, so there is nothing inherently "punk" about the new conservatives in this regard. They all dropped their buckets in the same well, so their tones can sound similar even when motivated by dissimilar political goals or using different cultural tactics. For example, Milo Yiannopoulos, the once infamous face of the alt-light's "cultural libertarians," was portrayed as a punkish provocateur in his heyday. His persona and politics are hardly a match with the average punk's, but his blithe willingness to court outrage and behave naughtily in public, while perhaps less organic, is not so different really from what was considered the scandalous behavior exhibited during the Sex Pistols' December 1976 appearance on *Today*, Bill Grundy's early evening live talk show. Johnny Rotten let "shit" slip out under his breath, then Steve Jones answered Grundy's goading to "say something outrageous" with a barrage of curse word–laden insults. The next day they were a national headline, concerts were banned, and the rest is glorious rock history.

And so to examples of punk's "edgy" methods of transgressive cultural warfare—their version of trolling—the spirit of which the alt-right has tried laying claim to forty years later. The British sartorial origins of punk include T-shirts decorated with words meant to anger and images meant to disturb—including one with a twelve-year-old nude male—as well as bondage-wear pieces derived from the "deviant" sadomasochism sex culture hidden away from mainstream society. However, it remains the act of displaying the swastika on shirts and armbands, or self-applied as needed, that registers as the primary example of avant-garde shock and taboo busting, rather than all those bricolaged safety pins. Hebdige (1979, 116–117) theorizes the swastika was used ironically in punk—yes, turned into a floating signifier—to challenge how *all* signs are given a closed meaning restricting the freedom of interpretive flexibility, which parallels ideological enforcement and constraint. That is the academic's reading, to which I earnestly concur, but what most people saw were nasty kids displaying a nasty symbol, perhaps with more dangerous intentions than just scaring the squares.[2] We face a similar quandary today in assessing online memes whose creators claim they use supposedly ironic Holocaust imagery just to rile PC liberals.

Band names could also be designed to shock, as Sex Pistols and Circle Jerks were, but it is Dead Kennedys that wins this contest. Its combination of wry meanness while making a po-faced statement about the failed idealism of the political and social age in which the band was born makes it the best punk band name *ever*. Likewise, punk album covers could be flat out gross or use the disgust mechanism to be provocative, such as the first EP by the Butthole Surfers (another shocking name), with a serial image of a naked starving child with distended belly. You are supposed to be repulsed and outraged, and to associate the band with those feelings.

The next act at the carnival is Fear's 1980 performance in Penelope Spheeris's documentary *The Decline of Western Civilization*. The band openly courts hatred by taunting the audience into a lather: "How many queers are here tonight? How many homosexuals?" The crowd counters by gleefully spitting on the band, and a woman shouts, "Faggot!" Their antics are especially effective on one woman who climbs on stage to attack the singer, Lee Ving, resulting in her being punched and kicked by him. It is a hell of a spectacle, one where the usual rules of behavior delineating the relationship between entertainer and audience vanish. Curiously, the crowd appears familiar with this sort of interactive set-up and plays along until that woman crosses the borderline onto the stage, at which point the old rules of conduct are reinstated by security entering the skirmish. All is forgiven, however, once Fear starts playing and the kids can release their tension upon each other by slam-dancing.

And for your final consideration: the early 1980s American band The Meatmen. Their expressions of "freedom" are made via vulgar humor that intimates something akin to a cultural politics, since Reagan's America was often billed as returning to the clean and moral 1950s. Their songs simultaneously offend archconservatives and bleeding-heart liberals alike. Their attempts at shock are executed mostly through declarations of antisocial deviancy, alongside misogyny and a general cruelty so unsettling you tell yourself it has to be a joke intended to inflict mental pain on overly sensitive souls. The Meatmen are always pushing against the limits of decency, often past the line of transgression. The song titles alone make this clear: "Crippled Children Suck," "I'm Glad I'm Not a Girl," "Tooling for Anus," "One Down Three to Go" (their reaction to John Lennon's murder). Similar tactics of offensiveness were deployed by England's Anti-Nowhere League during the same period, in songs celebrating aberrant behavior ("So What") and misogyny ("Woman," "'Reck-a-Nowhere"), with a possibly tongue-in-cheek homophobic rant in 2006 titled "The Day the World Turned Gay," all as a way to brand themselves as existing outside the system of good taste and politically correct morality.

Nagle emphasizes how the 4chan, 8chan, and Reddit Internet trolls and the altlight types hide behind the cover of cynicism, self-aware irony, and a cold nihilistic pose to shield themselves from criticism that their images and words are threatening and dehumanizing. Saying their hatred and cruelty is just for fun—jokes the "normie" outsiders don't get—distinguishes it from the sincere kind issued by full-bore fascists and white supremacists. This defensive stance definitely links them to the heritage of subversive dark humor found in punk. And if one combs through the subculture's entire history, one will find moments where some punks surely parallel the new conservatives, at least on the level of publicity management through cultural intervention, if less typically their politics. But how does any of this instruct us in the knotty art of representation?

Never Mind the Doxa

The alt-right situation offers a two-sided lesson. We have to be wary of too easily essentializing punk as an art, identity, and concept without overcorrecting by reducing it to a formless nothingness. Punk wants to be seen. Its gesture to evade the mainstream was instigated through an alternate system of encoded signs proclaiming outsiderness to those occupying the center and insiderness to inhabitants of the margins. This gives punk a distinguishable shape, yet the process cannot help but contain punk within ontological borderlines that regulate and restrain. It is hardly original to criticize punk for uniformity through a detectable sameness, a stinging hypocrisy for any art or person with pretensions of iconoclasm (e.g., Dead Kennedys' "Chickenshit Conformist"). Moreover, Nathaniel Weiner (2018) documents the ignored widespread ordinariness of UK punk fans before 1980, further complicating matters by making the ordinary the new rebel in relation to scholarly and journalistic accounts overemphasizing the "spectacular" punk style.

This monitoring of the details of a style can have a sense of innocent fun about it, such as picking apart the accuracy of punk depictions in narrative film. However, the surveillance of style can also have darker undertones of social control. Doxa is generally defined as any commonly held belief or opinion in a society or community. Pierre Bourdieu (1977, 165) adds to this idea the quality of customs and ideas that are "taken for granted," operating as unquestioned Truths which survive as "unnoticed" social knowledge. Unlike orthodox or heterodox beliefs, doxa is what "goes without saying." In its extreme form, such knowledge can function like "political instruments which contribute to the reproduction of the social world by producing immediate adherence to the world, seen as self-evident and undisputed" (164). Signifiers can function as doxa, and can become ideological. Those signifiers can touch all facets of what define punk: music, clothing, attitude, dancing, and bodily posture, culminating in who is classified as belonging. Nonetheless, according to Gary Clarke (1997, 122), "the elements of youth culture . . . are not enjoyed *only* by the fully paid-up members of subcultures. . . . Any empirical analysis would reveal that subcultures are diffuse, diluted, and mongrelized in form." My study of the punk preppy examines people who freely adopt an established punk habitus (a disposition or attitude, a "way of being" that influences actual practices) while not completely dressing or adhering to the ways of that habitus and the unspoken, assumed, naturalized rules informing the subculture's semiotic doxa (Traber 2008; see also Bourdieu, 1977, 214n1). Weiner (2018, 185) also chides critics for their own doxa by arguing, "Yet even the more nuanced understandings of punk style remain focused on the limited set of signifiers that have become codified as punk." Unfortunately, I'm going to continue that tradition by focusing on the early period in London with only a handful of people.

Some argue the New York scene was more eclectic than London in its musical and clothing signifiers, with bands as diverse as Blondie and the Ramones or Talking Heads and the Dead Boys. Richard Hell usually gets the credit for being the first to wear a safety-pinned shirt with spiky hair, but punk as a whole lacked a user's manual, with each band developing its own aesthetic with regard to their appearance and sound. London punk was an equally diverse scene in 1976. All the people on the ground floor of this sociocultural movement were inventing their own ways of being "punk" before it even had the name. Siouxsie Sioux, Jordan, and Soo Catwoman served as early photogenic It Girls, but there are many others in the photographs and news footage who were engaged in trying to figure it all out before the tabloids began publishing "How to Dress Like a Punk" articles. The early Clash sported an aesthetic informed by a postmodern mixing of fragments: slogans painted or stenciled on their shirts, slim straight-leg trousers borrowed from 1960s mods and skinheads, and 1950s Teddy Boy brothel creeper shoes. It is an evocative style; however, I find the Sex Pistols provide a curiously spectral snapshot of punk fashion as it was being born.

On the less spectacular end, Steve Jones and Paul Cook rarely come across as stereotypically punk, with their normal haircuts, jeans, sneakers, and nondescript shirts, other than occasionally sporting pieces from the Westwood/McLaren SEX and Seditionaries store inventory (which were actually expensive "fashion" items) or a leather motorcycle jacket in the odd photograph. The first bassist, Glen Matlock, was willing to model the store's stock as well, but he too occupied a middle space between punk spectacle and regular street attire. The second bassist, Sid Vicious, however, quite willingly became the poster child for the punk costume: raunchy T-shirts (swastika, naked cowboys), tight black jeans, leather motorcycle jacket (a 1950s US motorcycle gang/1960s UK rocker quotation à la the Ramones), spiky hair, and spiky bracelets taken from that deviant BDSM culture.

But it was always the singer, Johnny Rotten, who constituted a one-man punk fashion runway: the Westwood-designed tartan bondage suit worn on the 1978 US tour; the bratty street urchin in torn clothing look; leather pants and boots with the confrontational muslin Westwood/McLaren DESTROY shirt (displaying an upside down crucifix with a nude Christ superimposed over a large swastika) seen in the "God Save the Queen" video. Last, his postmodern suturing of contexts is fully displayed on September 4, 1976, the band's television debut on *So It Goes*, when he combined spiked bracelets, a ripped and stained pink blazer (hint of an upper-crust school or club) defaced with writing—"God save our gracious queen, God save our noble queen"—and attached objects (e.g., a military cross medal, safety pins), mated with pleated, striped pants that are baggy on top and tapering to the bottom—alluding to the early 1940s zoot suit popular with Chicano *pachucos*.

Just these five people from the same band represent the stylistic variance of the early days. But things become more homogeneous after punk transforms from a more or less organic cultural movement into a tabloid-fueled fad in late 1977 and early 1978. It then turns strident during the American and British hardcore periods in the early 1980s, when painted leather jackets, combat boots, and more extreme haircuts ossify into a standardized punk image. While the takeover is never total—confirmed by the cultural and ideological challenges made by the later queercore and Riot Grrrl movements—it does operate as a hostile tool to banish poseurs and tourists who lack tribal loyalty.

The idea of the signifier is obviously applicable to a person's external appearance, but it also works with music in that there are qualities, aesthetic markers, that signal a musical type to a listener, to which they can then associate the sounds with a musical identity. Because of qualities A and B, a song may sound like "punk rock," and doing differently may be an affront to the musical doxa of a true believer. Like the clothing, the music had its own postmodern elements. The music actually isn't as uniform as it may first sound to a tyro, with different variations to be heard arising from the shared practice of melding splintered forms. NYC eclecticism is prominent, with more bands experimenting with more peculiar ideas, negating consensus and the monolithic by consciously rejecting sameness. Even those bands rooted in a more familiar rock vernacular concoct their sound by mangling the blues-based 1950s rock-and-roll structure via increasing the volume and speed, while variously incorporating the amateur rawness of sixties garage bands or perhaps a bit of surf guitar or a rockabilly lick, while others rely on bubblegum pop's aesthetic of simple, short songs with great guitar hooks to help pull it all off (e.g., "Sugar, Sugar," *yes* by The Archies). The lyrical content also ranges widely, from standard teenager concerns, to the corny silliness of old novelty records akin to "Monster Mash," or emulating the seriousness of folkie and hippie protest music. All of these elements mix together in differing variations to define what comes to be associated with a "punk" style. This aesthetic strategy undermines Fredric Jameson's negative assessment of postmodern art being mere pastiche—a blank, uncritical copy—for it is actually bricolage, the self-conscious taking of what is at hand to make something else, and combining it with other seemingly contradictory elements. Punk begins as postmodern alchemy, a sensibility Monica Sklar (2013, 75) credits in *Punk Style* with "provid[ing] the flexibility not to overly commit to only one part of life, and instead acknowledge life's complexities."

Then hardcore takes an almost avant-garde turn by producing what amounts to atonal anti-music in its flattened drumbeat, nearly single-note guitar, turbo-charged ultra-simplicity. That's why the herky-jerky ska-punk and melodic pop-punk, the latter ruling the 1990s, challenged what counts as legitimate signifiers of punk musical authenticity, thereby helping to tear down the wall hardcore punks had built to separate themselves from other genres, other cultures. The composition of new audiences also broke the law when the scene's insular enclave mentality was confronted by an invasion of "jocks" and "frat boys" during the alternative rock nineties—what I have heard berated as the "corporate" punk moment following the success of Nirvana, Green Day, and Rancid. To benefit from that contact—in the role of either band or fan—requires no longer being obsessed with someone else's identity rules. The performers from this later period are still linked to the genre in degrees that vary with each band—be it musical form, inhabiting a DIY spirit, or having a contrarian attitude about appeasing the musical mainstream—and growing out of it allows each band and fan to take their own idiosyncratic path toward freer expression, away from the rigid music and fashion codes that are monolithically Punk.

Postmodernism Redux

First-wave punk's postmodern predisposition is relevant to the new conservative issue because the alt-right hates postmodernism. They are correct to fear its mission to challenge all they hold dear, but not for the reasons they give, such as falsely attributing to it an inherent identity politics advocacy, as well as linking it to a boogeyman they call neo-Marxism by eliding the way most Marxists denounce postmodern theory for its more open, non-macro conceptualization of power and resistance. So, depending on the ideological lens, postmodernism's enemies cast it as too conservative or too leftist.

Punk shares this problem in that its inclination to privilege an individualist, anti-government perspective—one typically bellowed from within a *community* structure—can be ascribed left or right ideological underpinnings. Sometimes it is only a matter of gradations along the spectrum of political values, at other times the shadings hint at unlikely bedfellows. Consider how the DIY ethos motivated performers and fans to shoulder the burden of the product (organizing shows, selling records) by creating an outsider's network of local scenes in an underground economy. They preferred being invisible to the larger public, a choice offering aesthetic freedom but also allowing these young boot-strapping entrepreneurs to operate outside the music industry's system of conformist bureaucracy.

It isn't difficult to twist the anti-corporatism of punk and post-punk independent record labels into actually affirming the capitalism-is-freedom ideology of libertarians who, despite neoliberalism's global influence, boast of their fringe status and opposition to the mainstream. Ross Haenfler finds this ambiguity in his study of former straight-edge punks whose past DIY values influence how they operate as *homo oeconomicus*:

> [DIY] skills and dispositions . . . contribute to a meritocratic vision of success and failure that masks structural inequalities and privileges. . . . DIY music scenes can reinforce neoliberal individualism, leaving dominant market assumptions unchallenged—anyone can make it, they just need some entrepreneurial spirit and drive to succeed.
>
> (Haenfler 2018, 188, 189)

The recurrence of paradox within the subculture's gestures, even a propensity for it, does not make the yoking of punk and the new conservatism inevitable, yet it does account for how the latter could persuade itself that the linkage makes sense.

Such topsy-turvy conditions exist because punk always danced with contradiction, as represented in its aesthetic mixture of historical styles, but also in its complex relationship to capitalism. Performers and fans were ironically implicated in capitalism as manufacturers and consumers who simultaneously critiqued its effects on society, individuals, and art—pushed to become living products shouting against the complicity of their own desires. There can be no total resolution from within capitalism if you are selling or buying, yet an unresolved contradiction does not mean you have succumbed to endorsing market-based politics. Some punks dealt with it by changing how they conducted business under capitalism, seen in the model of the indie music label that doesn't let the profit motive interfere with the kind of bands they sign, paying the artists more fairly, or pricing their wares lower than the corporate labels.

As a method, postmodernism allows for a critique of patriarchy, racism, homophobia, and other discriminatory "-isms" favored by the alt-right, as these positions are all buttressed by tradition, hierarchy, reason, etc., and depend upon a regulatory binary structure to maintain power by controlling what is accepted as a universal Truth. That's how being Punk gets it wrong when it moves to lock down its subjectivity like an alt-right identitarian. As the previous section shows, punk can be read as born from a postmodern sensibility that allowed for individual flexibility, a style of music and dress that weaved together fragments drawn from multiple sources to invent new forms. This enabled new ways of thinking and being, all under the banner of a few shared characteristics given the *pliable* categorical name "punk." But some people elide that history of diversity by promoting a singular authenticity to reduce the permissible strands of difference that might threaten the sameness of their idealized Punk Identity. A similar flexibility should inform one's understanding of postmodernism as a named sensibility and/or theoretical perspective. For the postmodernist, authenticity is reduced from the genuine to performance, to self-consciously meeting the expectations, the *laws*, used to define any group's particular understanding of the authentic. You may not have the official documents proving your *bona fides* with regard to the privileged (and typically essentialized) category—be it a racial or class or subcultural "bloodline" demanding purity—but you can *act* like you do until called out, caught in a lie based on their framework, their discourse, their doxa. Indeed, Linda Hutcheon (1989, 29) celebrates postmodernism's ability, often via irony and parody, to attack a doxa's reliance on the taken-for-granted by making the "invisible visible."

That's why an *authentic* postmodern self is not an oxymoron, but rather is best understood as a singular authenticity in the sense that it is *yours*, one designed and constructed by yourself, to define yourself away from any group identity operating through absolutes. The multiple self speaks to this, a subjectivity unified via culling fragments from sometimes contradictory sources; a self-made cohesive only in that it makes sense to you. I have called this other being the "culture of one":

> Identity is an externally-derived ideal that can be manipulated so as to reclaim, appropriate, poach, cut and mix, all to make the self strange, unknowable, unfamiliar, unrecognizable.... [I]f we don't totally make our own identities neither do we have to simply replicate what is handed to us—there is agency within the system.
>
> (Traber 2017, xx, xxi)

My theory is influenced by Gilles Deleuze and Félix Guattari's guiding principle of a nonrestrictive identity to unleash your ontology: "This subject itself is not at the center ... but on the periphery, with no fixed identity, forever decentered, *defined* by the states through which it passes.... [I]t is a whole *of* these particular parts but does not totalize them; it is a unity *of* all of these particular parts but does not unify them" (Deleuze and Guattari 1983, 20, 42). You begin from a point within a system,

> experiment with the opportunities it offers... find potential movements of deterritorialization, possible lines of flight, experience them, produce flow conjunctions here and there, try out continuums of intensities segment by segment, have a small plot of new land at all times.
>
> (Deleuze and Guattari 1987, 161)

The alt-right followers, on the other hand, are not inspired to frolic along the boundaries of identity. They only want the transgressive energy attached to the Punk Identity—an uninspired sense of "coolness"—but without it infecting their ideology. However, simply bestowing upon yourself the well-worn name of a well-known counterculture amounts to nothing. It is just another act of incorporation that defangs what is still subversive about punk by enlisting it in the cause of reactionary politics. Nonetheless, those "real" punks who try to shout down the discussion in order to salvage what remains uncritically coherent about their group are no more open to deterritorialization. Instead, they blockade rhizomatic pathways to prevent their own potential slide away from the Punk center as well as the movement of those Others who may want to cross the borderline and cursorily explore their segregated neighborhood.

ALT-RIGHT II: THE TRUMP FACTOR

> A word war will set off the keg. . . . Should words serve the truth? . . .
> I speak for truth
> —Minutemen, "Do You Want New Wave or Do You Want the Truth?"

With all the handwringing over the state of truth and facts after Donald Trump entered office—Kellyanne Conway's "alternative facts," Trump's constant propagandistic charges of "fake news"—some have miscast this so-named "post-truth" phenomena as postmodern philosophy taken to its extreme in real life. Postmodernism, however, pursues questioning Truth as a metaphysical notion motivated by universalizing aspirations—calling out how both truth and facts can be exploited as a tactic of power with potentially repressive intentions—rather than to deliver an obvious moral proscription against telling lies, nor instigate conspiratorial suspicion of provable scientific facts like gravity or how planes stay in the air. Postmodernists understand truth as multiple—there is a galaxy of viewpoints—and flexible—touched by the exigencies and vicissitudes to which people react to ensure their own power over and/or within a nation, culture, or society. In other words, truth *floats*. However, that isn't an argument for sacrificing critical practice; indeed, the postmodern rationale for tracing the lineage of any truth indicates a lingering devotion to the notion itself.

The Minutemen epigraph shows that truth is also valued by punks. From the personal to the political, they aim to expose those behind the curtain working the levers of government, society, and culture. Truth's potential for *manipulation* in the interaction between discourse and power is what postmodernists and punks were warning us about, taking their lead from the critique of ideology borrowed from Marxian thinkers, only now all beliefs are treated as operating ideologically and thus to be held to account, especially if posited as ahistorical, natural, and therefore above criticism. Moreover, postmodernism should not be mistaken for offering a clean break with a safe escape route, since the "postmodernist critique must acknowledge its own position as an ideological one" (Hutcheon 1989, 13).

Before taking up the issue of truth with Trump, if we are honest then we *do* find that he has exhibited characteristics easily coded as punk, but without its more typical leftward politics. He would brashly speak off the cuff, which his enemies saw as directionless ignorance and his fans equated with nonpolitician qualities, like being natural and less willing to please the populace or status quo—even in his own party—to win votes. He generally disregarded tradition in attaining his goals and exhibited a negative, nay destructive, attitude toward institutions. Trump has brazenly undermined previous assumptions about how Washington's institutions should operate, especially the White House, and how politicians should conduct themselves in the public sphere, especially the president. But was Trump's presidency what it looks like to "disrupt" the system? Disruption can take many forms, and can be achieved in multiple ways, so his is just one possible result.

Early on, the Trump administration's web of corruption, its fortress wall of lies and misdirection, all seemed like politics as usual through a cynical eye, then as terrifyingly out of control and dangerous to the nation, indeed the whole planet, when viewed though less hazy pupils. Trump is lambasted by one side and praised by the other for overriding the unwritten mores of establishment Beltway government culture through a hundred offenses large and small. The average citizen didn't even know these borderlines existed until the new president crossed them and it made the headlines. At those moments, after the rebel's burn-it-all-down tough talk of doing away with the state and laws ceased to be theoretical, people discovered how much structure they really needed, the actual limits of transgressive chaos they could actually bear, when it was no longer just a song title, T-shirt slogan, or a troll's Facebook meme.

Is this the anarchy promoted in punk? Is this how a punk and/or postmodern politician would behave? Isn't questioning assumptions and traditions—be they musical and sartorial or at the level of state institutional doxa—a foundational tenant of both punk and postmodernism? Does Trump, therefore, operate as a tangential punk/postmodernist? No, because he has proven himself perfectly comfortable with hierarchy and the system as long as they benefit him. He has also displayed authoritarian proclivities, which is neither punk nor postmodern according to their general definitions. Deconstructing institutions doesn't require their actual disassembly, certainly not their utter destruction. As theorized by William Connolly (2005) and Nicholas Tampio (2015), a decentered government aims to be more democratic, not less—it isn't following the model of a stripped-down corporation—because it is designed to allow for input from more voices, not fewer.[3] That's why Trump's relationship with truth is a vital point of difference. Truth is such a major point of contention in the Trump presidency that it is imperative to not mistakenly link him to postmodernism by saying, "Well, what did you expect would happen after the postmodernists made truth impossible?"

As a self-designed billionaire populist, Trump certainly promoted himself as a mixed bag politically, which could be framed, very loosely, as a postmodern*esque* break with a monolithic political identity. For example, he pushed through a massive trillion-dollar tax cut benefitting the rich and corporations, which increased the deficit and conveniently cleared the way to justify a future call for "reasonable" austerity measures that butcher social welfare spending to repair that deficit (typically Republican), but also initiated a protectionist anti-free-trade tariff war with China (atypically Republican). However, Trump definitely did *not* operate from a postmodern belief in the plurality of truth, nor the heterogeneity of social realities shaped by a diversity of backgrounds and experiences. He instead besmirched any questioning of his vision as the work of dangerous ideological Others, so as to perpetually stoke the anger of grievance politics: during the 2016 campaign, pluralism and multiculturalism were liberal plots to inflict unfair social advantage and oppressive political correctness upon white people, in conjunction with the threat of a teeming horde "invading" the country's southern border; in 2020, it was more about a lurking radical socialism. The demagogic politics of Trump and the conservatives, old and new alike, were not informed by treating worldviews, ideologies, and meanings as being affected by different ways of seeing and understanding that are influenced by the contingencies of culture, history, and place. Moreover, postmodernism preaches (yes, it too is a belief system with traceable origins) that despite the weight of such circumstances, we are capable of rethinking our inherited presuppositions and context-specific knowledge. In other words, we can change our minds. That means postmodernism is still legitimately capable of accusing someone of lying or dishonestly manipulating data. What else is the deconstruction of doxa and ideology but exposing a *truth* about a Truth? The assumption fueling the denaturalization and contextualization of beliefs is that people should make an honest accounting of their ideologies' origins and how they benefit from believing in them, in an attempt to answer Derrida's "question of knowing where it comes from and how it functions" (Macksey and Donato 1970, 271).

Trump understood how to deploy signifiers in order to incite his red-state voting bloc, especially by rationalizing their fears. Ideally, someone informed by a punk ethos would disdain engaging in that kind of politics. Individual punks might, but punk as a defined subjectivity, an aesthetic philosophy, a functioning value system, would reject pandering to the crowd. In fact, when they slide over to your side, you should deliver another shock to unsettle the balance. Such an opinion, of course, carries the taint of a personal doxa, which results in the kind of postmodern paradox Linda Hutcheon calls "complicit critique." For example, to be a subversive punk you have to hobble any unified, transcendent conception of Punk, but in so behaving you have relied upon, and further entrenched, a unified conception of what it means to be Punk; thus, acting punk gives power to Punk. The same paradox haunts disagreeing with the "conservatives are punk" position, for it requires a universalized definition of punk as rebellious, but restricts the parameters of rebellion. Thus, punks whose hackles are raised by being linked to conservatives mutate into reactionary guardians of an ossified law; in other words, they act like a stereotypical conservative. In the spirit of deconstruction, however, any anxiety experienced over this state of affairs should disappear with a shrug and sneer from the postmodern punk who realizes he has discovered his own limit, a lingering moral core—a center—fueled by a binary-based metanarrative from which he couldn't detach himself. Trump is neither a punk nor a postmodernist, but sometimes he inadvertently acts like both. That makes him a catalyst for self-directed critique in the same way he should have shocked so many other people—especially Never Trump Republicans—into a fresh awareness of the transparent ideals they have come to take for granted. In short, their doxa.

The Inoperative Subculture

The point to be taken from considering punk through the lens of Trumpian conservatism is to reimagine the limits and possibilities of this subcultural identity, and hence all identities. If punk is really about freedom, then it needs to revive its original postmodern impulse to oppose semiotic doxa intent on enforcing a true Punk Identity. Punk was never supposed to survive this long anyway, certainly not with any expectation of it looking and sounding as it did in 1977 or 1981 or 1994. Over the decades, the bands committing acts of treason against the punk hierarchy—such as Refused's 1998 album *The Shape of Punk to Come*—warn us that frozen culture is dead culture. Claiming punk as a source should function as another act of bricolage, rather than pastiche; it is instead best treated as a point from which to shoot off in a rhizomatic unrestricted pattern, to resist regressing into what Deleuze and Guattari call the arboreal: a rooted form that resists change. We need to avoid imprisoning the spirit of punk—as music, as dress, as a way of thinking, and of moving through the world—in a transcendent realm, while still being able to point at something that can legitimately be called by that name, yet as a flexible form. Wanting ontological closure, to conduct yourself as a Punk, is the fatal flaw.

Jean-Luc Nancy's theory of the "inoperative community" is a model meant to counteract the tendency to Otherize in society, so that a "We" is first and foremost a conglomeration of others. Community is reconfigured as being "formed by an articulation of 'particularities,' and not founded in any autonomous essence that would subsist by itself and that would reabsorb or assume singular beings into itself" (Nancy 1991, 175). Unity and community are redefined through the prism of multiple singularities to emphasize that we are all others. The inoperative community seeks to weaken the rise of a "communion of singularities in a totality superior to them and immanent to their common being," to create a community defined by its "resistance to the communion of everyone or to the exclusive passion of one or several: to all the forms and all the violences of subjectivity" (28, 35). The dissolution of a unified culture based on "we" and "ours" liberates subjectivity via an inherent diversity and uncertainty, which comes to be understood as the only thing "natural" about any person's identity.

This is why an organized subculture, even one with an alternative ethos, risks operating like a traditional social group. The subculture tries to administer the values, beliefs, and codes of meaning associated with its style; therefore, if a member rejects the group's strategies of totalization while still claiming membership, the subculture is rendered *inoperative*, even if only for that individual. A subjectivity that surges over the structural barriers meant to contain it within knowable forms demonstrates agency, for once the limits are recognized it becomes possible to map out their subversion.

And what, I ask you, is more punk than *that*?

Notes

1. Joseph Bernstein (2017) traces the links between the alt-right and alt-light, with the latter normalizing the former.
2. On negative reactions, see Savage (1992, 189, 241–243) and Laing ([1985] 2015, 120–121).
3. For a collection of responses from academics to the proposition Trump is postmodern, see Edsall (2018).

References

The Archies Meet the Ramones. 2016. Archie Comic Publications, October 5.
Bernstein, Joseph. 2017. "Here's How *Breitbart* and Milo Smuggled White Nationalism into the Mainstream." *BuzzFeed News*, October 5, 2017. https://www.buzzfeednews.com/article/josephbernstein/heres-how-breitbart-and-milo-smuggled-white-nationalism.
Bourdieu, Pierre. 1977. *Outline of a Theory of Practice*. Translated by Richard Nice. New York: Cambridge University Press.
Clarke, Gary. 1997. "Defending Ski-Jumpers: A Critique of Theories of Youth Subcultures." In *The Subcultures Reader*, edited by Ken Gelder and Sarah Thornton, 175–180. New York: Routledge.
Cobain, Kurt. 2006. *Live! Tonight! Sold Out!* DVD. Geffen Records.
Connolly, William E. 2005. *Pluralism*. Durham, NC: Duke University Press.
del Barco, Mandalit. 2017. "John Lydon on Anarchy, Politics and 'Mr. Rotten's Songbook.'" National Public Radio, March 31. https://www.npr.org/2017/03/31/521816347/punk-singer-john-lydon-on-his-songbook.
Deleuze, Gilles, and Félix Guattari. 1983. *Anti-Oedipus*. Translated by Robert Hurley, Mark Seem, and Helen R. Lane. Minneapolis: University of Minnesota Press.
Deleuze, Gilles, and Félix Guattari. 1987. *A Thousand Plateaus*. Translated by Brian Massumi. Minneapolis: University of Minnesota Press.
Edsall, Thomas B. 2018. "Is President Trump a Stealth Postmodernist or Just a Liar?" *New York Times*, January 25, 2018. https://www.nytimes.com/2018/01/25/opinion/trump-postmodernism-lies.html.
Galupo, Scott. 2017. "Is Trumpism the New Punk Rock?" *The Week*, March 2, 2017. http://theweek.com/articles/682416/trumpism-new-punk-rock.
Goldberg, Michelle. 2017. "Alt-Right Facts." *Slate*, February 23, 2017. http://www.slate.com/articles/news_and_politics/politics/2017/02/cpac_invented_an_alternate_history_of_the_alt_right.html.
Haenfler, Ross. 2018. "The Entrepreneurial (Straight) Edge: How Participation in DIY Music Cultures Translates to Work and Careers." *Cultural Sociology* 12, no. 2: 174–192.
Hebdige, Dick. 1979. *Subculture: The Meaning of Style*. London: Methuen.
Hutcheon, Linda. 1989. *A Poetics of Postmodernism*. New York: Routledge.

Laing, David. (1985) 2015. *One Chord Wonders: Power and Meaning in Punk Rock*. Oakland, CA: PM Press.
Macksey, Richard, and Eugenio Donato. 1970. *The Structuralist Controversy: The Languages of Criticism and the Sciences of Man*. Baltimore: Johns Hopkins University Press.
Nagle, Angela. 2017. *Kill All Normies: Online Culture Wars from 4Chan and Tumblr to Trump and the Alt-Right*. Alresford, UK: Zero Books.
Nancy, Jean-Luc. 1991. *The Inoperative Community*. Translated by Peter Conner, Lisa Garbus, Michael Holland, and Simona Sawhney. Minneapolis: University of Minnesota Press, 1991.
Parker, James. 2016. "Donald Trump, Sex Pistol." *Atlantic*, October 2016. https://www.theatlantic.com/magazine/archive/2016/10/donald-trump-sex-pistol/497528/.
Robin, Corey. 2017. *The Reactionary Mind: Conservatism from Edmund Burke to Donald Trump*. New York: Oxford University Press.
Savage, Jon. 1992. *England's Dreaming: Anarchy, Sex Pistols, Punk Rock, and Beyond*. New York: St. Martin's.
Sklar, Monica. 2013. *Punk Style*. New York: Bloomsbury Academic.
Tampio, Nicholas. 2015. *Deleuze's Political Vision*. Lanham, MD: Rowman & Littlefield.
Traber, Daniel S. 2001. "L.A.'s 'White Minority': Punk and the Contradictions of Self-Marginalization." *Cultural Critique* 48: 30–64.
Traber, Daniel S. 2008. "Locating the Punk Preppy (A Speculative Theory)." *Journal of Popular Culture* 41, no. 3: 488–508.
Traber, Daniel S. 2017. *Culturcide and Non-Identity across American Culture*. Lanham, MD: Lexington Books.
Watts, Henry. 2017. "BNP are the New Sex Pistols." Wigton, UK: British National Party (BNP).https://bnp.org.uk/bnp-are-the-new-sex-pistols/.
Weiner, Nathaniel. 2018. "'Put on Your Boots and Harrington!': The Ordinariness of 1970s UK Punk Dress." *Punk & Post-Punk* 7, no. 2: 181–202.

CHAPTER 31

TOUCH ME I'M RICH
From Grunge to Alternative Nation

RYAN MOORE

The sound and style that came to be known as grunge developed in Seattle and the Pacific Northwest during the late 1980s and, to the surprise of nearly everyone, infiltrated popular music and mainstream culture in the early 1990s. As a form of music and style, grunge was a hybrid subculture that mixed elements of punk and hardcore with hard rock and heavy metal. "Grunge" aptly described the sludgy tempos and fuzzy distortion of pioneering bands like the Melvins, Soundgarden, and Mudhoney, and it also captured a look and style that superimposed a punk and metal attitude on the flannel-and-jeans look of the Pacific Northwest proletariat. The nucleus of the scene was Sub Pop, an independent record label founded in 1986 that released the music of a great number of bands in the region while also representing a mythology of the Seattle scene for the world to consume. Like the original punk subcultures in the United States and the United Kingdom, grunge germinated among a cohort of disaffected young people facing uncertain futures in a time of economic and social disintegration. But whereas in the UK punk immediately became a popular sensation and point of national controversy, in the US it mostly subsisted on the margins of popular culture through the 1970s and 1980s. Punk's breakthrough in the US was not complete until the 1990s, and grunge led the way: 1991—in the title of a documentary featuring Nirvana, Sonic Youth, Dinosaur Jr., and Babes in Toyland—was "the year punk broke."

The definitive sound of grunge began to take shape with the 1986 release of *Deep Six*, a compilation of regional bands, followed by the first records from Soundgarden on Sub Pop in 1987, and the debut singles by Mudhoney and Nirvana the following year. Sub Pop then began to construct its brand identity with distinctive methods of packaging and marketing that used ironic hyperbole to promote the label, their bands, and the Seattle scene at large. Grunge's breakthrough into popular culture came with the astonishing success of Nirvana's *Nevermind*, which shot up to the number one position on Billboard's album charts in January 1992. With multiplatinum albums by Pearl Jam,

Soundgarden, and Alice in Chains released on the heels of *Nevermind*, grunge and alternative rock significantly reshaped the field of popular music and were incorporated into mainstream culture through Hollywood film, advertising, and even fashion. However, these forms of commercialization provoked a backlash from young people, recently christened "Generation X," who were the target demographic for opportunistic marketing ploys—the term "grunge" was soon scorned by those who had originally created the scene. Following the suicide of Nirvana frontman Kurt Cobain in April 1994, along with Pearl Jam's conscious retreat from the media, the attention surrounding grunge and the Seattle scene quickly dissipated. The music industry was on the verge of major restructuring that led it away from grunge and paved the way for a new cohort of pop stars and boy bands to emerge in the late 1990s.

Grunge thus presents a stark example of how subcultures are appropriated and transformed by the forces of commodification that thrust them into the spotlights of mass media and popular culture. Many scholars have previously examined the impact of media, commerce, and mass culture on subcultures like jazz, punk, goth, and dance club cultures (Becker 1963; Bennett and Kahn-Harris 2004; Hebdige 1979; Hodkinson 2002; Muggleton 2002; Muggleton and Weinzierl 2003; Redhead, Wynne, and O'Connor 1997; Thornton 1996). Hebdige has presented the most well-known analysis of commodification and the forms of incorporation and recuperation that appropriate and convert subcultural signs of music and style into mass-produced, homogenous objects. He argued that "as soon as the original innovations which signify 'subculture' are translated into commodities and made generally available, they become 'frozen'" (Hebdige 1979, 96). However, since then a number of scholars have challenged the notion of co-optation and the discourses of authenticity and originality that underlie Hebdige's argument, and that are often expressed within subcultures themselves (Clarke 1981; Muggleton 2002; Thornton 1996). These critics assert that the boundaries between subculture and mass culture are more fluid than rigid, and are increasingly so in a global political economy of postmodernity. They also question the notions of authenticity that inform the distinction between original innovators and passive consumers in the narrative of co-optation. More explicitly, Thornton's concept of subcultural capital draws from Bourdieu (1984, 1993) to describe how members of subcultures defend their "hip" insider status by distinguishing themselves in opposition to those who are supposedly just consuming the latest trend. Likewise, Muggleton (2002, 144) criticizes the opposition between creators and consumers, asking why adaptation of subcultural styles by mass consumers should be considered "less subversive" in comparison with the "original innovators."

The case of grunge sheds new light on these issues of commodification and co-optation, of subculture and mass culture. The commercial success and sudden popularity of Nirvana and other Seattle-based bands, followed by the fad for flannel shirts and other signifiers of grunge style, clearly did have a decisive and ultimately destructive impact on the original subculture—at the very least, the sudden fame seems to have been a contributing factor in Cobain's suicide. However, the commodification of "grunge"—the forms of marketing that packaged the music with a distinct style and a mythologized notion of the Seattle scene—had begun years earlier, with Sub Pop's various promotional schemes and self-aggrandizing hype. Sub Pop's role in the commodification of grunge confounds the usual oppositions between subculture and mass culture and between underground and mainstream, redirecting our focus toward the social relations of capitalism that predominate within both independent and corporate major labels.

The absorption of grunge into popular culture during the early 1990s must be contextualized within a larger transformation of capitalism that has enabled a more immediate incorporation of various subcultures and styles once regarded as "alternative" or "underground." In *The New Spirit of Capitalism* (2005), Boltanski and Chiapello track the shifts in management literature in France during the 1990s to show how the discourse of authenticity and autonomy expressed in the May 1968 revolts was later appropriated and absorbed into new forms of "flexible" capitalist accumulation. While claiming to dismantle hierarchy and authority in the name of freedom and creativity, this form of capitalism has eliminated all vestiges of security, stability, and public support, subjecting workers to never-ending anxiety and precariousness. Similarly, Thomas Frank and his colleagues at the *Baffler* mocked the forms of management and marketing that extolled countercultural themes of freedom, authenticity, and individual expression in the ideological legitimation of neoliberal capitalism during the 1990s. Capital has effectively recuperated the critique of hierarchy, authority, and conformity expressed by artistic and bohemian subcultures that developed in opposition to Fordism and mass society. Ironically enough, the ideals of authenticity and DIY creativity embodied within subcultures like grunge have turned out to be valuable commodities within this "new spirit of capitalism."

The Origins of Grunge

During the 1980s there was an intense rivalry in many regions of the United States between subcultures based on allegiances with punk or metal, often resulting in violence, especially at shows. The grunge scene was able to develop in the Pacific Northwest at this time, however, because there were stronger social ties between the members of these subcultures, allowing for a sonic and stylistic hybrid that drew from both punk and metal. In the words of Nils Bernstein, a publicist for Sub Pop, "It seems like everywhere else punk and metal were such diametric opposites, and there were fights between metal heads and punk rockers. But in Seattle they kind of coexisted all peacefully. There were a lot of punk rockers and metal heads and hippies, and there were a lot of punk rock hippies and metal punk rockers. Everyone lived together, everyone jammed together, everyone hung out and went to the same shows and had the same record collections" (quoted in Arnold 1993, 158). At a time when hardcore, thrash, and glam metal were locked into standardized conventions of sound, image, and performance, grunge was evolving into a unique subculture where these different styles could intermingle.

The geographic isolation of the Pacific Northwest also played a role in fostering a distinct grunge subculture, particularly in those years before Seattle became a hub of the technology sector. Grunge originated among young people who lacked access to the live music scenes that existed in other parts of the country. According to Mark Arm of Mudhoney, "A lot of touring bands totally skipped Portland and Seattle because it was 14 hours north of San Francisco and 32 hours west of Minneapolis. People in the Northwest had to make up their own entertainment" (quoted in Yarm 2011, 13). By the 1980s, the timber industry that had once supported the Pacific Northwest's regional economy was in a state of steady decline, with especially devastating effects on smaller cities like Montesano and Aberdeen, where the Melvins and Nirvana formed. The dreary sound and distressed style associated with grunge was developed by a cohort of young people who found themselves on the losing end of a transitioning economy, inheriting bleak futures with seemingly nowhere to escape.

Deep Six, released by C/Z Records in 1986, was the first recording to capture the developing hybrid sound of the early grunge scene. The compilation album featured six Seattle-based bands representing a range of musical styles. On the one hand, it included the Melvins, who had followed Black Flag and some other hardcore bands in slowing down their sound with a sludgy guitar sound set to a drop D tuning. *Deep Six* also featured the U-Men, a Seattle-based punk group who were mainly influenced by noise bands like the Butthole Surfers. On the other hand, it also included Soundgarden, who were drawing more of their sound from 1970s hard rock and metal, as well as Malfunkshun, a band that featured the flamboyant frontman Andrew Wood, who later formed the glam rock group Mother Love Bone. The mix of punk and metal styles and sensibilities was especially evident in Green River, which featured the founding members of Mudhoney, Mark Arm and Steve Turner, alongside Jeff Ament and Stone Gossard, who moved on to play with Mother Love Bone and then formed Pearl Jam after Wood's death. The compilation also featured Skin Yard, whose guitarist, Jack Endino, would soon become instrumental in shaping grunge's signature sound as a producer for numerous bands in the Seattle scene. A review of *Deep Six* in Seattle's alternative weekly paper, *The Rocket*, highlighted the unique sound that was emerging from the mixture of punk and metal influences: "The fact that none of these bands could open for Metallica or the Exploited without suffering abuse merely proves how thoroughly the underground's absorbed certain influences, resulting in music that isn't punk-metal but a third sound distinct from either" (quoted in Yarm 2011, 81).

Sub Pop quickly emerged as the central medium in developing and defining Seattle's grunge scene. The label initially evolved from a fanzine called *Subterranean Pop* created by Bruce Pavitt, then a student at the Evergreen State College who was working at the college's staunchly independent radio station, KAOS. In the early 1980s, Pavitt shortened the name of his zine and began releasing compilation tapes of underground bands from across the US, with the *Sub Pop #5* cassette selling as many as two thousand copies (Azerrad 2001, 413). The label's first LP, *Sub Pop 100*, was also a compilation, featuring Sonic Youth, Scratch Acid, and Naked Raygun alongside regionally based bands like the Wipers and the U-Men. Sub Pop turned its focus toward bands from Seattle with the release of Green River's EP *Dry as a Bone*, which was recorded in 1986 but not released until the following year due to a lack of financing. Pavitt then partnered with Jonathan Poneman, who would handle the label's business and legal issues while also providing $20,000 in funding to release Soundgarden's debut single ("Hunted Down"/"Nothing to Say") and EP (*Screaming Life*) in 1987. The following year, Sub Pop released Mudhoney's "Touch Me I'm Sick," perhaps the most definitive expression of the emerging grunge sound, as well as the debut single from Nirvana, "Love Buzz"/"Big Cheese."

Although Sub Pop had evolved from the DIY culture of punk, it employed a shrewd business strategy that distinguished it from other independent labels. Instead of promoting the bands or their music directly, Sub Pop constructed its own brand identity by linking itself with the Seattle scene at large. In Pavitt's words, "We were extremely conscious about trying to piece it together so there was some kind of unity in marketing and presentation. It helped unify the scene and made it seem larger than it actually was" (quoted in Azerrad 2001, 421). Toward this end, Poneman and Pavitt created the Sub Pop Singles Club, whose subscribers were sent a new record every month—a gimmick that guaranteed sales in an unstable market but created a sense of scarcity and mystique for hip consumers. Nirvana's "Love Buzz"/"Big Cheese" was the first single sent to these subscribers. Sub Pop also cultivated a distinctive grunge sound by consistently employing the services of producer Jack Endino, who recorded seventy-five singles, EPs, and albums for the label between 1987 and 1989 (Azerrad 2001, 436). The strategy was to create a sound, style, and sensibility that could be identified with the city of Seattle by way of Sub Pop.

Alongside the music, Sub Pop effectively promoted an image of the Seattle scene and the sense of participatory community that seemed to be flourishing there. Their key asset was the photography of Charles Peterson, who often captured the band and the audience in the same frame to convey a sense of the social dynamics of the scene. As Pavitt explained, "That's why our photos always, from the very start, showed the fans as well as the bands: so people could see the real intimacy between the two, so that they could feel, 'Yes! I could be a part of it!' In our world, the fans were celebrated as much as the bands" (quoted in Arnold 1993, 161). Although Peterson mainly used black-and-white film because it was cheaper to reproduce, his photos conveyed an image of authenticity and the sense that the Seattle scene was something different from the glossy, over-hyped mainstream. Pavitt has said that Sub Pop wanted to "[advertise] the fact that there's a community here—it's not just this industry that's manufacturing bands, it's a happening scene where people are feeding off each other" (Azerrad 2001, 421).

Sub Pop's ambitions set it apart from other indie labels like Dischord or K Records, who were more minimalist and resolutely independent of corporate interests. Sub Pop engaged in a sort of ironic capitalism that used humor and hyperbole to seemingly distance it from these ambitions. The label's motto became "World Domination," and its records were printed with messages like "We're ripping you off big time." Ironic distance enabled Pavitt and Poneman to be capitalists while seeming to lampoon the greed and exploitation that characterized the Reagan era. Indeed, the label's first compilation LP, *Sub Pop 100*, had come with an impossibly grandiose statement printed on its sleeve:

"The new thing: the big thing: the God thing: a mighty multinational entertainment conglomerate based in the Pacific Northwest."

Sub Pop played an active role in constructing and representing an image of the Seattle music scene that would eventually be consumed around the world. A pivotal moment came in 1989, when Sub Pop flew the British music journalist Everett True, from *Melody Maker*, to Seattle and gave him a guided tour of the scene. True returned to England and raved about Mudhoney and other Seattle bands in ways that played on well-worn stereotypes about working-class American "rednecks." Pavitt and Poneman shaped the mythology that True dutifully reported to *Melody Maker*'s readers, constructing an aura of working-class authenticity and crystallizing the idea of "grunge" for an international audience. The incongruity between image and reality was particularly evident in TAD, whose burly frontman Tad Doyle was touted as "the butcher from Idaho" when in reality he was a music student at Boise State University. As True later explained, "Bruce Pavitt and Jonathan Poneman were some of the most charming, eloquent liars that I ever met. . . . If they wanted to portray Tad Doyle as some kind of chain saw-toting, dope-smoking, backwoods redneck who didn't wash and used to be a butcher—I met him, and he was clearly an incredibly intelligent, witty fellow—that was cool by me, because why the hell not?" (quoted in Yarm 2011: 190). Sub Pop's fabrication of backwoods authenticity also applied to their marketing of Nirvana, whom Pavitt saw as "the whole real genuine working class—I hate to use the phrase 'white trash'—something not contrived that had a more grassroots or populist feel" (Azerrad 1994, 71).

Sub Pop's construction of a sound, style, and sensibility that would define "grunge" drew from the class experiences of young people who were downwardly mobile and socially marginalized. The label began selling T-shirts with "Loser" printed on them, creating an ironic badge of pride for young people who often endured low status in their peer cultures as teenagers and then found themselves on the losing end of the labor market as twentysomethings. Pavitt himself identified with this experience of downward mobility and service sector employment, recalling that "throughout the eighties when I was working at all these shitty jobs, I was really, really angry. I was, like, 'I have a college degree, and the guy next to me, he's incredibly talented, and he has a college degree too, and we're both chopping carrots!" (quoted in Arnold 1993, 160). Adopting the identity of a "loser" inverted the social hierarchies of winners and losers created by peer relationships and the labor market. Sub Pop was beginning to construct an image of economic marginality and social disaffection that would become cliché in the early 1990s, once it became associated with Generation X, alternative rock, and "slackers."

GRUNGE GOES MAINSTREAM

At the dawn of the 1990s, a number of bands based in or around Seattle were poised for mainstream success. Soundgarden had signed with A&M Records and released *Louder Than Love* in late 1989. Mother Love Bone, a glam band formed by Andrew Wood, Stone

Gossard, and Jeff Ament after the breakups of Malfunkshun and Green River, had also signed to a major label, Polygram. Mother Love Bone was anticipating the release of their debut LP in the days before Wood died of a heroin overdose on March 19, 1990. By the end of the year, Gossard and Ament had recruited Eddie Vedder to become the singer of their new band, which they initially called Mookie Blaylock, the name of an NBA basketball player, but soon changed to Pearl Jam. After the death of Andrew Wood, Soundgarden's Chris Cornell collaborated with members of Pearl Jam to record the self-titled album of a band called Temple of the Dog. Meanwhile, Alice in Chains had signed with Columbia Records and released their debut album, and in 1991 their video for "Man in the Box" entered MTV's heavy rotation. The Screaming Trees had also signed with a major label and released *Uncle Anesthesia* in 1991, after putting out their three previous albums on SST Records.

During these years, Sub Pop had begun to extend its reach by releasing music from bands outside the Pacific Northwest, like the Afghan Whigs, from Ohio, and the Fluid, from Colorado. The label signed L7, an especially rowdy group composed of four women from Los Angeles, and released their album *Smell the Magic* in 1990. Sub Pop issued records from many bands who would lead the alternative rock movement over the course of the decade, including Dinosaur Jr., Smashing Pumpkins, Babes in Toyland, and the Rollins Band, and it continued to support bands with growing regional followings, like TAD, Dickless, the Walkabouts, and Seaweed. However, it suffered a major setback that year when Nirvana followed their tour mates Sonic Youth in signing with DGC Records, a Geffen subsidiary. Although Sub Pop had enjoyed some modest success with albums like Mudhoney's *Every Good Boy Deserves Fudge*, it was teetering on the brink of bankruptcy in the days before Nirvana's breakthrough. An exponential increase in the sales of Nirvana's first LP, *Bleach*, would eventually allow it to recover.

Nirvana's *Nevermind* came out in September 1991, with modest expectations that it might become a certified gold record (500,000 copies) within a year. Instead, the album rocketed to the top of the Billboard charts as the single "Smells Like Teen Spirit" received heavy airplay on rock radio and MTV, propelling Nirvana past Michael Jackson to the number one spot in January 1992.[1] With the astonishing popularity of *Nevermind* and "Smells Like Teen Spirit," many commentators perceived that a significant shift in music and popular culture was underway. Nirvana's music, along with the general persona of Kurt Cobain, seemed to resonate with large numbers of young people. "Smells Like Teen Spirit," with its opaque lyrics about apathy and angst, was quickly hailed as the anthem for a youthful demographic that was about to be named Generation X.

"Smells Like Teen Spirit" originated in Kurt Cobain's relations with the members of Bikini Kill, the leading punk of the "Riot Grrrl" scene in Olympia, Washington, that mixed punk music and feminist activism. Cobain and Bikini Kill singer Kathleen Hanna had gone on a graffiti spree, spray-painting revolutionary, feminist, and pro-gay slogans in the streets of Olympia, and when they returned to Cobain's apartment Hanna wrote the words, "Kurt smells like teen spirit." Cobain had been dating Bikini Kill's drummer, Tobi Vail, and Hanna was apparently suggesting that he smelled like the deodorant she wore. But Cobain wasn't aware that Teen Spirit was a brand name, and instead believed those words had something to do with the ideas about teen revolution he and Hanna had been discussing. "Smells Like Teen Spirit" was thus written as a response to the ideals circulating in the Olympia scene about anti-corporate DIY punk, feminist and queer politics, and straight-edge and vegan lifestyles. Cobain found those ideals seductive but ultimately naïve, and so the song was fueled by the conflicted nature of his response. "The entire song is made up of contradictory ideas," he once explained, "It's just making fun of the thought of having a revolution. But it's a nice thought" (quoted in Azerrad 1994, 213).

Beginning with *Nevermind*'s ascent, 1992 was the year that grunge infiltrated popular music, mainstream culture, and fashion and style. Soundgarden and Pearl Jam both played prominent roles on the Lollapalooza festival lineup that summer. Pearl Jam's debut album, *Ten*, had broken through into Billboard's top ten by mid-1992, following an appearance on *Saturday Night Live*, and with the music video for "Jeremy" in heavy rotation on MTV. Meanwhile, Nirvana headlined the Reading Festival in England, which featured "Grunge Day" performances by Mudhoney, L7, the Screaming Trees, and the Melvins. Days later, Nirvana and Pearl Jam both delivered intense, iconic performances on the MTV Video Music Awards. By that time, Cobain's marriage to Courtney Love had thrust them into the media spotlight as a celebrity couple, particularly after a *Vanity Fair* story suggested that Love had used heroin during her pregnancy. The fall of 1992 also saw the release of Cameron Crowe's film *Singles*, a romantic comedy about people in their twenties set in Seattle, with the grunge music scene figuring prominently in the story. The film included cameos from Chris Cornell and Pearl Jam, a live performance by Alice in Chains, and a soundtrack full of local bands, including a Mudhoney song mocking the commercialization of Seattle grunge, "Overblown."

The success of Nirvana and grunge seemed to signal a sea change, not only in music but also in popular culture at large. Throughout the 1980s, alternative music, indie labels, and local scenes had remained culturally and commercially marginalized, and bands like Hüsker Dü and the Replacements failed to achieve mainstream success after signing major label deals. However, in the early 1990s "alternative" became the new mainstream, with the Seattle-based grunge and the Lollapalooza festival leading the change. With its disheveled look, unpolished sound, and ethos of authenticity, this form of music and style was seen as a repudiation of the superficiality and shameless materialism of the Reagan era. The ascendance of Nirvana and other bands that personified sincerity ended the cultural relevance of the glam metal scene based in Hollywood. Many observers associated the aesthetic of grunge with a generation that had grown up in the shadow of the baby boomers, who would be the first generation to experience a lower standard of living than their parents, and who had developed an ironic style of consuming popular culture as a consequence of prolonged exposure to media and advertising.

The sudden popularity of grunge music instigated a shift in fashion and style. Department stores and fashion magazines began to appropriate and repackage the subculture's regional style, particularly flannel shirts, long johns, wool sweaters, ski caps, and Doc Martens boots. Most notoriously, the fashion designer Marc Jacobs made grunge style into the basis for Perry Ellis's 1993 Spring collection, describing it as a "hippied romantic version of punk." Jacobs's runway show featured the supermodels Naomi Campbell and Kristen McMenamy in silk shirts that were made to look like flannel, upscaling the rough garments of the grunge scene into fine fabrics for the world of high fashion (Marin 1992). The show was poorly received and widely mocked, causing Jacobs to be fired from Perry Ellis. Nevertheless, grunge did have a significant impact in shifting popular style during this time, with flannel shirts becoming especially omnipresent. The messy, low-budget look of grunge was widely perceived as a rejection of the glamour and excess that had characterized the 1980s. Embodied by downwardly mobile youth expressing collective feelings of alienation and rebellion, grunge style signified the zeitgeist of the early 1990s in its opposition to the greed and excess of the previous years.

In November 1992 the *New York Times* published "Grunge: A Success Story," examining the subculture's sudden and extraordinary impact on both music and fashion. The article was a disaster from its opening line, which mistakenly referred to grunge as a five-letter word (it has six): "How did a five letter word meaning dirt, filth, trash become synonymous with a musical genre, a fashion statement, a pop phenomenon?" The reporter also fell victim to a now legendary prank when he sought to decode the local slang that was supposedly circulating within Seattle's grunge scene. Megan Jasper, then a sales representative at Caroline Records and onetime Sub Pop employee, provided the reporter with a fake list of phrases she said people in the scene used to describe clothing, activities, types of people, and so forth.[2] Jasper invented ridiculously cumbersome terms like "swingin' on the flippity-flop" to describe hanging out and "bloated, big bag of blotation" as code for being drunk. The *Times* printed the list verbatim, titled "Lexicon of Grunge: Breaking the Code" on the front page of its Style section. The hoax was quickly identified and publicized by Thomas Frank, editor of the *Baffler*, and then picked up by the *New Republic*, much to the embarrassment of the nation's most prestigious newspaper. Frank wrote, "We at *The Baffler* really don't care about the legitimacy of this or that fad, but when The Newspaper of Record goes searching for the Next Big Thing and the Next Big Thing piddles on its leg, we think that's funny" (Frank and Weiland 1997, 206).

While grunge was reaching and reshaping the mainstream, corporate forces of marketing and entertainment were desperately in search of new methods of selling to young people. Some advertisers were beginning to suspect that a new generation of youth were too savvy to be seduced by the standard methods of marketing. At a 1992 meeting of the Magazine Publishers Association, Karen Ritchie, executive vice president and director of media relations at McCann-Erickson, warned her audience that they would need new methods for marketing to an up-and-coming demographic they knew little about. "Face it: boomers are getting old," she told the magazine publishers, cautioning that the 18–29-year-olds of "Generation X" were turning away from traditional media like magazines and television. She confessed that those youths, whom she referred to as "the purple-haired people," were largely a mystery to her, and she admonished her audience of media executives that they didn't know anything about them, either. The only thing that was obvious to Ritchie was the skepticism and cynicism with which Generation X viewed conventional media and advertising, which she believed spelled doom for her industry. In short, advertisers were in a mess of their own making, and so they would have to find a new way to represent their products as honest and organic, or else fess up to their own dishonesty and artificiality with a knowing smirk. Ritchie later wrote, "One thing is clear: the more advertising clings to the 'newest, biggest, baddest' model that dominates today, the less successful we will be in convincing Generation X that advertising is an honest and reliable source of information" (Ritchie 1995, 159).

The ideas about Generation X initially developed in the early 1990s with Richard Linklater's film *Slacker* and Douglas Coupland's novel *Generation X*, both of which commented on the fragmentation of consciousness and sense of irony among young people saturated with media and popular culture. They both featured rootless characters who are unable to find meaning or narrate their stories in a world where there is an overload of information and yet nothing seems to happen. *Slacker* and *Generation X* also included highly educated young people stuck in what Coupland dubbed the "McJobs" of the service industry. Meanwhile, the news media had also begun to investigate and speculate about a new generation of youth, with a *Time* cover story about "twentysomethings" in July 1990, followed by articles in *Business Week*, the *Atlantic Monthly*, and the *New Republic*. Like Karen Ritchie, the *Time* article depicted twentysomethings as anti-materialists on a quest for authenticity: "They would rather hike in the Himalayas than climb a corporate ladder," the opening lines of the story read. When grunge suddenly infiltrated popular culture and seemed to speak for a new generation, the media framed its significance within these developing discourses about twentysomethings, Generation X, and slackers. For advertisers, the authenticity and rebelliousness of this "alternative" culture were understood to be valuable commodities that could connect them with a target market of young consumers.

FM rock radio stations and MTV quickly reformatted in the early 1990s to make alternative rock a central part of their programming. In 1992 MTV launched a weeknight show of music videos called *Alternative Nation*, hosted by the bespectacled VJ Kennedy. In popular culture at large, movies and television shows began to include characters based on variations of Generation X clichés, most notably in MTV's *The Real World* and *Friends*' portrayal of post-collegiate lifestyles in gentrified New York City. Some advertisers were more direct in marketing to young people by linking their products with grunge and "alternative." For example, the short-lived Bud Dry advertised itself as "the alternative beer," with pictures of sweaty stage-divers and shirtless singers in a style derivative of Charles Peterson's photography. There was also the infamous television commercial for the 1993 Subaru Impreza that featured a scruffy young man who compared the car to punk rock. The commercial claimed that the Impreza was challenging the conventional thinking about cars in the same way that punk challenged rock 'n' roll when it was "boring and corporate."

In the wake of grunge's startling success, the major labels began scouring other local music scenes in search of the "next Seattle." These scenes had developed during the 1980s with a DIY approach that fostered connections between local bands, indie labels, fanzines, college radio, and small live venues. The majors had previously seen this sort of underground music as commercially unprofitable, but after Nirvana's breakthrough it seemed that all bets were off about what would sell and what would not. The search for the next Seattle thus led record companies to the local scenes in Washington, DC, Chicago, Portland, and San Diego, as well as college towns like Athens, Georgia, and Chapel Hill, North Carolina. Many bands in these scenes came away with major label deals, but the feeding frenzy would have divisive and ultimately destructive effects on these scenes, particularly as bands found themselves in debt to the labels for their recording and promotional costs (Albini 1997).

Commodification and the Devaluation of Subcultural Capital

In considering the relationship between subcultures and mass media, Sarah Thornton's concept of "subcultural capital" describes how "hip" insiders maintain social status through claims of authenticity and distance from "mainstream" culture. Whereas Bourdieu's notion of "cultural capital" examines how the upper classes reproduce their power through their supposedly superior tastes, "subcultural capital" accumulates and circulates among young people who feel like outcasts in society and identify with cultural forms of bohemian rebellion. Subcultural capital is compensatory, offering a sense of social status for those who feel like outsiders or losers in other aspects of society. However, the value of subcultural capital fluctuates in relation to attention from the mass media and consumption by mainstream audiences. When forms of music and style that insiders see as "underground" are made available to a mass market, they experience a sense of alienation from the culture they once felt was their own, which is now being consumed by the very "mainstream" audiences they define themselves against. For example, it was quite common to hear complaints about "jocks" and "frat boys" listening to Nirvana and coming to their shows as the band skyrocketed in popularity. By definition, subcultural capital is a scarce commodity that can only belong to a hip minority, and the threat posed by the media, pop music, and fashion industries is that they will turn music and style into mass-produced commodities for mainstream consumers.

The commodification of culture, style, and symbolic difference is an essential feature of contemporary capitalism. Yet when corporations and media conglomerates put their stamp on underground culture and music, they lose their value as subcultural capital. In the end, capitalism exploits, destroys, and makes waste of subcultural capital in the same way it does with so many other people and resources. The faddish appeal of the subculture expires quickly, as grunge would in the mid-1990s. Innovators feel an immediate need to move on to something else, as the music and style they helped create is quickly liquidated of its value, ultimately finding its resting place in a museum of historical fads. Rebellious subcultures seem to lose their vitality once they become packaged commodities available to the masses, as corporate capitalism destroys their hip and edgy styles in the process of trying to profit from them. Thus, the attempt to transform grunge from subculture to mass culture failed in the long term, provoking a backlash and loss of credibility among the demographic of young people it targeted. The forces of commerce turned a subculture that had developed over a number of years in the Pacific Northwest into a passing fad, a relic of early 1990s popular culture.

The absorption of grunge into popular culture and the music and fashion industries coincided with a broader transformation of capitalism during the 1990s. The most significant development was the growing value of culture, whereby anything "hip" or "cool" came to be coveted in commercial leisure experiences, communications technologies, and various forms of branding (Klein 2000). Through gentrification, the economic significance of the city shifted from a center of manufacturing to a site for the production and consumption of culture and style, as "neo-bohemian" subcultures took root in the derelict industrial districts that had once been centers of manufacturing, warehousing, and transportation (Lloyd 2006). In advertising and consumer culture, new strategies shifted the focus from mass markets to niche markets, highlighting differences in style and taste in distinction from the conformity of mass culture. Meanwhile, the reorganization of the workplace with strategies like "flexible accumulation" incorporated an artistic critique of work into new forms of management discourse that celebrate creativity and individuality but subject workers to conditions of insecurity and immediate disposability (Boltanski and Chiapello 2005). All of these structural shifts within capitalism were prompted by the crisis of Fordism, which combined techniques of mass production and mass consumption in a system that stabilized the relation between capital and labor after World War II but finally stagnated and broke down in the 1970s (Harvey 1989). Whereas Reaganomics thrived on hedonism and avarice, in the 1990s capital discovered new ways to profit from authenticity and rebellion.

Grunge and various alternative subcultures were thrust into the vortex of these transformations within capitalism during the 1990s. Local scenes scattered across the American landscape had originally arisen with a DIY ethic that opposed the corporate music industry in the name of creative autonomy. After subsisting on the margins of popular culture throughout the 1980s, these subcultures suddenly became essential for developing forms of "creative capitalism" that celebrated sincerity of expression and idiosyncrasy of style, particularly in marketing to the newly discovered "Generation X." But this process of commodification provoked a backlash of its own, at least among the insiders within these subcultures, who grumbled about bands who "sold out," major labels that exploited their local scenes, and poseurs who imitated their style. The ideal of authenticity—rooted in a bohemian opposition to conformity, mass culture, and bureaucracy—became increasingly difficult to maintain in the face of this new form of capitalism that could easily commodify dissent. As Boltanski and Chiapello (2005, 447) put it, "In the case of authenticity, what we have is a restoration of control by capitalism, in the sense that it disappoints the expectations which it earlier offered to satisfy. Commodification thus creates new forms of anxiety about the authenticity of things or persons; one no longer knows if they are 'authentic' or 'inauthentic,' spontaneous or re-engineered for commercial ends."

"All the Rage": From the Cover of *Time* to the SeaTac Airport

Having broken through to the mainstream in 1992, Seattle's leading grunge bands were in the glare of the media spotlight in 1993. Upon its release that October, Pearl Jam's sophomore effort, *Vs.*, would set a new record for the most copies of an album sold in its first week, and it held that distinction for the next five years. In conjunction with the release of *Vs.*, Pearl Jam's Eddie Vedder appeared on the cover of *Time* magazine for a story about the popularity and social significance of grunge, titled "All the Rage." Meanwhile, Nirvana's highly anticipated follow-up, *In Utero*, had been released the previous month and also shot straight to the top position on the Billboard charts. Alice in Chains also had a multi-platinum breakthrough with their second album, *Dirt*, along with a prominent position on that summer's Lollapalooza festival. Soundgarden also had their first number one album when they released *Superunknown* in March 1994.

Kurt Cobain's suicide in April 1994 garnered international attention. At that moment, when several bands from the Seattle scene were standing at the summit of the pop music world, the word "grunge" had become anathema within the original subculture because of its association with mass marketing and media trend-watching. There was a new crop of bands, like Stone Temple Pilots, Bush, and Candlebox, who were enjoying multi-platinum album sales with a more heavily produced sound and masculine image that standardized the conventional hard rock (and less punk) side of the original grunge bands. The music industry had moved on to plunder different underground subcultures, especially the California punk scenes following the breakthrough success of Green Day's *Dookie* and The Offspring's *Smash* in 1994. As a subculture, grunge was already "dead," and then Cobain's actual death seemed to put an exclamation point on the matter. Pearl Jam had already chosen to retreat from the media spotlight at the height of their success and begun its ultimately losing battle against the Ticketmaster monopoly. Courtney Love's band Hole released *Live through This* a week after Cobain's suicide and then suffered the tragic loss of their former bassist Kristen Pfaff from a heroin overdose two months later, encapsulating an especially macabre moment in popular culture.

The visibility of grunge within the music industry and popular culture would vanish rapidly during the second half of the 1990s. Alice in Chains's self-titled third album went immediately to the top of the Billboard charts when it was released in late 1995, but soon thereafter the band basically went into hiatus as a result of Layne Staley's worsening drug problem. After releasing *Down on the Upside*, Soundgarden broke up in 1997, citing creative and personal conflicts within the band. While refusing to do interviews or make music videos, Pearl Jam's *No Code* (1996) and *Yield* (1998) still managed to go platinum, but neither came close to matching the phenomenal sales of their previous albums. A host of second-tier bands who had ridden the wave of success within grunge and alternative rock suddenly found themselves back on the sidelines of the music industry in the late 1990s. The Melvins, the Screaming Trees, and L7 were among the many bands from around the country who were either dropped by major labels or broke up after 1997. The music industry was undertaking a process of global concentration and conglomeration—what would ultimately be the last hurrah of the CD era—and grunge wasn't part of the plan.

While grunge's moment in the media spotlight seemed to pass as suddenly as it arrived, its long-term impact on music and culture has been considerable. For instance, Dave Grohl moved on from Nirvana to front one of the most world's most successful rock bands, Foo Fighters, who have since captured four Grammy Awards for Best Rock Album and sold more than 12 million albums in the US. Likewise, Pearl Jam weathered the storm of early success and maintained an enduring career with a devoted fan base, releasing many more studio albums and countless live recordings over the course of more than a quarter-century. After Sub Pop entered a corporate partnership with the Warner Music Group and undertook ultimately failed attempts at further expansion, prompting Bruce Pavitt's departure in 1996, it reclaimed cultural relevance in the indie rock scene of the 2000s with critically acclaimed and modestly successful releases from groups like Band of Horses, Fleet Foxes, the Postal Service, the Shins, and Sleater-Kinney. The label's symbolic association with the city of Seattle has been further enshrined—unashamedly in pure commodity form—with the opening of a gift shop selling music, apparel, and other assorted merchandise at the Seattle-Tacoma International Airport.

Yet, in the long run, the cohort who created grunge will perhaps have their most significant impact in roughly the same place they started: on the margins of mainstream culture and music. The DIY spirit of creativity and community at the heart of the original subculture has survived and taken new shape, perhaps best personified by the longevity of Mudhoney, who returned to Sub Pop in the early 2000s and have continued to release albums that represent their surprising dexterity in shifting between a variety of musical styles over three decades. In 2018 Sub Pop held its 30th Anniversary Party at Alki Beach in Seattle, a free three-day festival attended by some fifty thousand people, and featuring a lineup that was headlined by Mudhoney and included the label's current acts (Shabazz Palaces, Wolf Parade, Metz), along with regional stalwarts like the Fastbacks. In Gina Arnold's words, "Weirdly, since Sub Pop is the opposite of hippy dip, it was a literal love festival, with people simply shouting their love and appreciation at each other, hugging and kissing and moshing in the pit" (Arnold 2018.) The irony is that while grunge may be commonly associated around the world with suicide or selling out, the less sensational but perhaps more significant legacy of this subculture may be the survival and further development of a creative community of people labeled as "losers" by society yet bonded together through music, style, and swingin' on the flippity-flop.

Notes

1. As of 2016, the album had sold 9.4 million copies in the US alone (see https://www.billboard.com/articles/columns/chart-beat/7518783/nirvana-nevermind-nine-chart-facts-anniversary).
2. Jasper is now Sup Pop's CEO.

References

Albini, Steve. 1997. "The Problem with Music." In *Commodify Your Dissent: Salvos from "The Baffler,"* edited by Thomas Frank and Matt Weiland. New York: W. W. Norton.
Arnold, Gina. 1993. *Route 666: On the Road to Nirvana*. New York: St. Martin's Press.
Arnold, Gina. 2018. "Love Buzz." *Fools Rush In* (blog), August 13, 2018. http://foolsrushinredux.blogspot.com/2018/08/love-buzz.html.
Azerrad, Michael. 1994. *Come as You Are: The Story of Nirvana*. New York: Doubleday.
Azerrad, Michael. 2001. *Our Band Could Be Your Life*. New York: Little, Brown.
Becker, Howard. 1963. "The Culture of the Deviant Group: The Dance Musician." In *Outsiders: Studies in the Sociology of Deviance*, 79–100. New York: Free Press.
Bennett, Andy, and Keith Kahn-Harris, eds. 2004. *After Subculture: Critical Studies in Contemporary Youth Culture*. New York: Palgrave McMillan.
Boltanski, Luc, and Eve Chiapello. 2005. *The New Spirit of Capitalism*. New York: Verso.
Bourdieu, Pierre. 1984. *Distinction: A Social Critique of the Judgment of Taste*. Cambridge, MA: Harvard University Press.
Bourdieu, Pierre. 1993. *The Field of Cultural Production: Essays on Art and Literature*. New York: Columbia University Press.
Clarke, Gary. 1981. "Defending Ski-Jumpers: A Critique of Theories of Youth Subcultures." In *The Subcultures Reader*, edited by by Ken Gelder and Sarah Thornton, 175–180. New York: Routledge.
Frank, Thomas, and Matt Weiland, eds. 1997. *Commodify Your Dissent: Salvos from "The Baffler."* New York: W.W. Norton & Company.
Harvey, David. 1989. *The Condition of Postmodernity: An Enquiry into the Origins of Cultural Change*. Cambridge, MA: Blackwell.
Hebdige, Dick. 1979. *Subculture: The Meaning of Style*. New York: Routledge.
Hodkinson, Paul. 2002. *Goth: Identity, Style, and Subculture*. New York: Berg.
Klein, Naomi. 2000. *No Logo: Taking Aim at the Brand Bullies*. New York: Picador.
Lloyd, Richard. 2006. *Neo-Bohemia: Art and Commerce in the Postindustrial City*. New York: Routledge.
Marin, Rick. 1992. "Grunge: A Success Story." *New York Times*, November 15, 1992.
Muggleton, David. 2002. *Inside Subculture: The Postmodern Meaning of Style*. New York: Berg.
Muggleton, David, and Rupert Weinzierl, eds. 2003. *The Post-Subcultures Reader*. New York: Berg, 2004.
Redhead, Steve, Derek Wynne, and Justin O'Connor, eds. 1997. *The Clubcultures Reader: Readings in Popular Cultural Studies*. Malden, MA: Blackwell.
Ritchie, Karen. 1995. *Marketing to Generation X*. New York: Lexington Books.
Thornton, Sarah. 1996. *Club Cultures: Music, Media, and Subcultural Capital*. Hanover, NH: Wesleyan University Press.
Yarm, Mark. 2011. *Everybody Loves Our Town: An Oral History of Grunge*. New York: Crown.

CHAPTER 32

DEATH IN VEGAS

GINA ARNOLD

THERE are few better places to watch the sunset in Las Vegas than the roof of the parking lot of the Hard Rock Cafe. Up there on that high flat surface, under an enormous and gaudy American sky, you can get a spectacular view of a glowing golden desert panorama dotted about with abandoned skyscrapers and enormous holes in the ground where other buildings have recently been imploded. But when you descend the steps and enter the casino, it's a different story. There, an upscale restaurant called Culinary Dropout serves Kobe beef and interesting flatbreads, barely clad trapeze artists dangle above the poker tables, and the walls are enshrined with actual relics, including guitars and costumes. Here, the detritus of Jimi Hendrix and the Jackson Five hang, unjudgmentally, alongside the less hallowed togs of acts like Nickelback, Godsmack, and the Killers. And across one of the main entranceway is a message picked out in gold and bejeweled letters that mimic a ransom note. It says:

"The Only Notes That Matter Come In Wads."

—The Sex Pistols[1]

Since the text overhangs a room full of leathery old men and women who are gambling their pensions away under the shadow of a tiny purple suit that once belonged to Prince, it seems possible that the Hard Rock Cafe has misunderstood its import. The slogan is actually a misreading of a lyric from a song and movie titled *The Great Rock 'n' Roll Swindle*, which purports to tell the story, mockumentary style, of the Sex Pistols' creation by Malcolm McLaren as a cynical cash cow. Directed by Julian Temple in 1980, the film is open to many interpretations, but one of its underlying points is that punk rock was a movement built on puncturing the pretensions of the music industry and the people who wanted to capitalize on it. Hence, seeing that particular lyric capitalized upon the walls of the Hard Rock Cafe is puzzling, as well as disappointing and hilarious, and perhaps entirely apropos

Perhaps, of course, it is all these things and more, as were the 40th anniversary of punk festivities that took place in 2016. Grouped under the title "Punk London" and sponsored by the Mayor of London's Office, the London Tourist Board, and a variety of other organizations, it was paid for out of a 99,000-pound grant from the Heritage Lottery Fund (part of the receipts from the National Lottery). In the words of the press release sent out by the organizers, "Punk is as iconic to the UK's heritage story as Stonehenge and the British Museum, and we're delighted to support the Punk London cultural programme and want to encourage people across the country to celebrate their own punk heritage in 2016" (Babey 2015). As the historian Paul Carter (1988, xvi) has noted, the primary object of imperialist history is not to "understand or interpret, but to legitimate."

By contrast, punk history, almost by definition, does the opposite; that is, it delegitimizes. David Atkinson (2008, 394) has suggested that the rise in electronic media has resulted in what he calls "a democratization of memory," one that, he adds, "allows citizens to identify, produce and consumer articulations of heritage themselves... shifting the gaze from the great stories of traditional historiography toward more commonplace, social, industrial and cultural histories." Such a shift, if it has occurred, would be very punk in a way, or at least DIY (do it yourself). Thus, as Andy Bennett (2009, 487) has noted, rather than being located in imperialist history, cultural heritage is now often located in sites of popular culture and artifacts of the recent past. "The very concept of 'heritage" (and culture)," he says, "has shifted in the recent past as media institutions have become more central to how the world understands, and consecrates, events." That shift can be seen very clearly in attitudes toward rock music, as it is a space that occupies a significant portion of the brain of every baby boomer.

This explains how punk and the punk rock movement could be reassessed as heritage, despite its stated goal to deliberately outrage the government, the monarchy, and the status quo. Whatever Malcolm McLaren later said about it all just being a savvy marketing tactic, its aim was true. In 1977, the year of the Queen's Silver Jubilee, the band released the song "God Save the Queen," which savagely assessed the monarchy as "obscene" and a "fascist regime." In other words, the song intentionally set out to disrupt the concept of the royal family as being a sacred element of British heritage, and it was certainly received that way: "As a sound," Greil Marcus (1989, 12) wrote, " 'God Save the Queen' suggested demands no art of government could ever satisfy." That the song, which was immediately banned from BBC radio, did what it set out to do is clear, because forty years on, the heritage event being celebrated by the Museum of London is not, as one might expect, the Silver Jubilee itself, with its link to hundreds of years of English monarchs and the monarchy, but this (relatively) brief moment of critique. It seems evident that punk has usurped monarchy as being nostalgic, celebratory, and, frankly, salable, to tourists and to Britons, who might be more likely to go to exhibits such as this than to, say, an exhibit of Jubilee paraphernalia. As Bennett (2009, 477) has noted, "the heritage rock discourse is very much part of the aging rock audience's reassessment of rock, not merely as something particular to their youth, but rather as a key element in their collective cultural awareness and a major contributor to their generational identity."

Even so, in this essay, I will try and account for some of the disjunctions that a punk anniversary and retrospective suggests, with especial reference to the preservation of punk rock relics, the paradox inherent in fetishizing punk memorabilia, and the anomalous experience of seeing live punk performances in a festival setting made by a bunch of elderly punk rock acts in, of all places, Las Vegas, a city known for exhibiting the worst excesses of capitalism.

These disjunctions all call into question both punk's original goals and whether they were successful. Additionally, they beg the question as to whether punk is now a historical period that is over with, or (as I think it would posit itself), ahistorical, generative, and still relevant to today's undoubtedly sinister global-political problems. In other words, is punk dead? Another way to frame the problem of punk, if you will, is as a pop culture restatement of the famous debate between Jean-François Lyotard and Jürgen Habermas. Is the Enlightenment—by which one may substitute the once-revolutionary restatement of culture that rock music once represented (briefly: "sex and drugs and rock 'n' roll") and that punk rock sought to overturn with a newer *doxa*, DIY—over and done with? Or are the metanarratives of punk rock worth revising and preserving?

These questions are worth asking, because, despite its promise to be short-lived, punk, as a genre, has not only spanned forty years, but it has never really gone away. Sigmund Freud once posited that all memories in our unconscious will inevitably reemerge in a distorted form. As he put it in his theory about the return of the repressed, all of our impressions are "virtually immortal: after the passage of decades, they behave as if they have just occurred" (Freud 1933, 74), and surely this is one reason why punk rock has had such a hard time giving up the ghost. As Andy Bennett, in his anthology on aging and punk, states, "Nostalgia is not a matter of conscious choice, but a response to emotional needs, offering refuge in what David Lowenthal has called 'a time when folk did not feel fragmented... when life was whole hearted... a past that was unified and comprehensible, unlike the incoherent, divided present'" (Bennett and Hodkinson 2012). It seems odd that punk, which was intended to be so disruptive, could in any way now represent a cohesive past—a kind of democratic unfreedom that is, in the words of Herbert Marcuse (1974, 1), "comfortable, smooth, reasonable"—but such is surely the case.

Punk Rock Bowling (PRB), the festival in Las Vegas where I went to make my investigation, exemplifies this issue. The writer K Punk (Mark Fisher) once made a distinction between being a curator or a portal. A curator, he says, draws people's attention to the good stuff, while a portal provides "a mutual process of libidinization," and it "functions most powerfully when (it is a) transversal connector between cultural domains" (Fisher 2009). It is my contention that punk rock is a portal, and at a festival celebrating its history occurring in Las Vegas, the world's undisputed capital of the human libido, it can be seen busily at work, shuffling people in between the two extremes of commodification and liberation.

Fetishization

Punk was a youth movement grounded in the rejection of mainstream conservative values, and one of the things it most explicitly abhorred was the veneration of the past. The Sex Pistols' song "God Save the Queen" clarified this stance, declaring that there was "no future" for the monarchy, or for England in general, and hammering that idea home with the still definitive image of themselves as a bouquet of flowers rotting in the dustbin of history. Hence, after major cultural institutions like the Museum of London and the British Library allied with the London Tourist Board to declare 2016 the 40th anniversary of punk, Malcolm McLaren and Vivienne Westwood's son Joe Corré announced he was going to burn five million pounds worth of valuable punk memorabilia on a barge outside of Parliament in order to protest the way that the movement has been commodified and repackaged. Much was said about this decision before it happened, but on the 24th of November, Corré set a trunk full of memorabilia as well as effigies of David Cameron and Theresa May alight, stating, "Punk was never, never meant to be nostalgic—and you can't learn how to be one at a Museum of London workshop." "Punk," he added, "has become another marketing tool to sell you something you don't need. The illusion of an alternative choice. Conformity in another uniform" (*The Guardian* 2016).

The barge incident was arranged to recall an event in 1977, when the Sex Pistols performed "God Save the Queen" on one as a protest to the Silver Jubilee. That event, like this one, drew a similar brand of criticism from media commentators who saw it as a cynical form of opportunism. Certainly the 1977 event was very much a self-described "take the piss out of society" publicity move. But it's open to question whether Corré's relic-burning event was quite as cynical, even though Corré, a multimillionaire businessman and fashion entrepreneur who founded the underwear company presciently called Agent Provocateur, had previously sold many items of his mother's collection for a reported sixty million pounds in order to found that business. He reportedly had to buy some of it back in order to burn it, a gesture that earned him the contempt of those who felt that the money could have been better spent (Edwards 2016).

Be that as it may, surely Corré's gesture was ideologically justified. As he himself stated, punk rock was never supposed to be about capitalizing on commodities, and its best ones—the ripped T-shirts, the safety pin earrings, the sounds and projects that turned mundane objects into fetishes—were deliberately cheap, homemade, uncommodifiable. This is what makes the deification of particular objects (like those on display at the Hard Rock Cafe) so difficult to justify from a punk perspective. The Hard Rock Cafe has built its entire empire on the back of rock nostalgia, realized in the form of actual artifacts, and the wrongheadedness of this approach is apparent in Las Vegas in ways that it isn't when it's done in much the same manner by the British Museum. Indeed, from a punk perspective, the burning of such objects—however, acquired—makes perfect sense, as does the inclusion of the ritual burning on the website of the "Punk London" organization.

As previously stated, "Punk London" was the outgrowth of a £99,000 grant from the Heritage Lottery Fund and the Office of the Mayor of London to create a yearlong festival of sorts, in which punk-related talks, lectures, films, and events were curated across venues, and the fact that it was funded under the term "heritage" is worth thinking about. The historian David Lowenthal (1989, 28) has pointed out the way that "[h]eritage aims to convert historical residues into witnesses that attest to our ancestral virtues." With the announcement of its 40th anniversary, punk became *residue*, both elevated far above its initial status and, at the same time, reduced. Many—especially those who read about it in-flight magazines and *TimeOut*—saw Punk London as the ultimate PR stunt. Corré, however, said he saw in that gesture "an opportunity: Destroying something—people had no idea of its value, actually—is an exercise in showing people how manipulated they are, and the sort of reactions they have to things. These are emotional triggers and people get triggered every day" (quoted in MacInnes 2018).

Punk London did indeed trigger people, especially when its cataloging ended up recreating inequities that are more pronounced in mainstream culture than the subject itself: in July 2016, for example, at a punk-related talk at the British Film Institute, the former punk guitarist Viv Albertine defaced a poster that had left out any of the many significant contributions made to punk by women, crossing out the word "Pistols" and replacing it with the name of her own band "Slits," adding Siouxsie and the Banshees and X-Ray Spex to a list of all-male bands, and scrawling, *What about the women*? alongside the text (Guy-Ryan 2016).

Albertine's intervention was inevitably dubbed "punk" by the press, thus managing to both co-opt and delegitimize it simultaneously—much like Corré's barge gesture. But her intervention also called attention to the lack of legitimacy that is inherent in all attempts to recount history. Museums in particular are subject to the taint of bias and its twin specter, absence, perhaps some with more self-knowledge than others. At the Museum of Jurassic Technology in Los Angeles, for example, semi-fraudulent exhibits that are a nonetheless fascinating blend of fact and fiction mimicking natural history allow visitors insight into the process of historicization. This kind of subversion is exactly what's in play with any attempt to taxonomize or display punk in a historical or educational setting. Unlike Punk London, however, the Museum of Jurassic Technology does this knowingly, taking its mission from a quote by the American painter and initiator of the first American museum Charles Willson Peale, in which he enjoins that learners be "led always from familiar objects to the unfamiliar—guided along, as it were, a chain of flowers into the mysteries of life" (Weschler 1996, 29).Obviously, these are the flowers of romance—the same ones that wound up in the dustbin, according to the lyrics of the song "God Save the Queen."

The Museum of Jurassic Technology creates displays that call into question the very nature of knowledge, truth, and our relationship to them. The Hard Rock Cafe—as well as the Motown Cafe, the Rock & Roll Hall of Fame, and the entire Punk London project—does the same thing, but accidentally rather than deliberately. In their eagerness to freeze the memory of a moment, an era, and a feeling, the organizations behind Punk London were clearly attempting to legitimate it, but the project fails in part because punk doesn't need to be legitimated: indeed, it resists legitimation, over and over again. In 2018, a year after Punk London, Corré created an art installation titled *Ash from Chaos*, which documented the barge event. Shown in the Lazinc Gallery in Mayfair, it featured a coffin carrying the ashes from the barge event, a death mask of Corré's father, and slogans like "Apathy in the UK" and "Know Future," and was backed by a film in which the detritus of punk dissolves into a montage of actual shift. Corré said the exhibition's intention was to question the values placed on artifacts, but be that as it may, the *Guardian* said that it also "radiated intense personal feeling" (MacInnes 2018). The Museum of Jurassic Technology, says its biographer Lawrence Weschler (1996, 40), is "a museum, a critique of museums and a celebration of museums, all rolled into one." Corré's burning, and then memorializing, the artifacts of punk was a similarly positioned gesture, emblematic not of punk's sanctity, but of its resistance to sanctification. And the fact that punk lends itself to these confusions is also its strength: the same could not be said about any other music genre, such as psychedelic rock, metal, folk, or rap, which are highly subject to the rigors of nostalgia. Punk defies the strictures of nostalgia for the very reason that it was invented, expressly to banish that affliction from the annals of music.

Svetlana Boym (2001, xiii) has written that nostalgia is "a sentiment of loss and displacement, but it is also a romance with one's own fantasy." Corré's gesture, burning punk artifacts, undoubtedly toys with this notion. At first, the gesture refuses to buy into the sentimentality that fuels the (commodity) fetishizing of the past, disallowing collectors to pander to what Boym calls "the private and collective mythology" of punk (xv). At the same time, the gesture itself—essentially burning money—is the epitome of punk, and therefore a mythologizing gesture in and of itself. If nostalgia is, in Boym's words, either restorative or reflective, punk's most defiant and radical act may be that it is simultaneously both. Which might be its greatest achievement.

THE LOGIC OF LATE CAPITALISM

If, as the Corré incident hints, punk rock is able to successfully fuse capitalism with resistance, there is an argument to be made that punk is the very distillation of late capitalism. The way I was first introduced to the concept in graduate school, "late capitalism" referred to postindustrial society. It meant a second-order commodification since Marx's day—the commodification of brands, ideas, and knowledge, rather than the commodification of things and objects that you can touch. But Annie Lowrey of the *Atlantic* recently wrote an article discussing the resurgence of the phrase "late Capitalism" (*spatkapitalismus*) as a catchall term for incidents that "capture the tragicomic inanity and inequity of contemporary capitalism. Nordstrom selling jeans with fake mud on them for $425. Prisoners' phone calls cost $14 a minute. Starbucks forcing baristas to write 'Come Together' on cups due to the fiscal-cliff showdown" (Lowrey 2017). In short, the *Atlantic* article detected a sea change in its meaning, such that the phrase now describes the way that everything can be commodified, consumed, and collapsed into a superficial, self-referential, and irredeemable kitsch. The logic of late capitalism is, as Frederic Jameson himself told the *Atlantic*, is "symptomatic of people's feelings about the world. About society itself" (Lowrey 2017).

Jameson sees "late capitalism" as kicking into gear in the Thatcher and Reagan years, which would place it directly in line with the invention of punk. But this is probably not a claim he himself would make. In his great work *Postmodernism, or, The Cultural Logic Of Late Capitalism*, the word "punk" only appears once, lassoed to another word, "porn." "Like punk and porn," Jameson writes, attributing to both a similar hegemonic position in the postmodern condition. In another lecture at Stanford, in 1998, he elaborated that both punk and porn are outgrowths of the "unique temporalities of late capitalism," a space that (he claims) valorizes the thrill(s) of the present instant (O'Toole 1999). But here I believe he is wrong: punk and porn have little in common, even if you grant them (a) the shared use of the word "hardcore," and (b) the libidinal bodily pleasure of instantaneity. In *Postmodernism*, Jameson (1993, 196) posits both things as "offensive," but as no longer oppositional to mainstream culture: he says that they are now "dominant aesthetics." And while it is true in the short-run (by migrating to the internet, porn became mainstream, and punk hasn't been oppositional since the release of Green Day's first record, or earlier), this is both an oversimplification and a misunderstanding, for it is to believe that punk, as a category, is a form of third-order simulacrum in the same way that porn is. Rather, while pornographic performances and texts may reify more natural occurrences of sexuality, to participate in punk, as performer or consumer, is not to widen, but to lessen the distance between the two. Punk intensifies, rather than distances, one's relationship to music. As one punk practitioner, part of a tightknit punk scene in Oklahoma City, told the ethnographer Alican Koc in 2015, what they seek to achieve within their punk rock community is, "a place where... cultural hierarchy is negated, and it's just a pure horizontal space. I want it to be like a church, I guess" (Koc 2022).

Intimate punk rock scenes like the one described in Koc's article aren't confined to Oklahoma, either. They exist in cities across the globe, from Rijeka to Berkeley and beyond. The Oklahoma City one stands out because of its description, and its recent-ness: it was not, as the author originally supposed, "a bizarre place in the center of America in which a suffocating climate of religious conservatism in the heat of the prairie gave way to an aesthetic form of pure American hatred—an artistic condensation of the country's legacy of violence"—but rather, his research confirmed, an oasis, a blessing, a breath of fresh air and a place of acceptance (Koc 2022).

Koc's article confirms that contemporary punk rock is not a manifestation of late capitalism, at least not if affect wanes when consumers can no longer trace the original life world of its reference points. According to Jameson (1993, 196), the hallmark of a postmodern art object is its depthlessness. It lacks an anchor in "the real." Famously, he uses An Andy Warhol painting to illustrate this. But punk rock's anchors bite deep. Unlike Warhol's "Diamond Dust Shoes"—incidentally, a work painted during punk's heyday—punk music, with its simple chords and rhythmic structures and its fairly rigid rules ("loud fast," and "DIY"), has cleaved to its roots while simultaneously shooting up hardy new branches.

This becomes clearer when one attends a modern-day punk rock performance, which often span generations both on stage and in the audience. For example, at a 2018 gig by the Descendants, a legendary punk band that began in 1977, the opener was a band called Radkey. The Descendants are white Angelinos well into their fifties; Radkey hails from a small town in Missouri, and consists of three teenaged brothers, Isaiah, Solomon, and Dee Radke. Their father is their manager, and although he's not a musician himself, he claims that their great aunt, great uncle, and grandmother all played in punk bands before them. This kind of actual legacy gives the words "heritage" new meaning, as perhaps does the fact that the members of the Descendants are white while the Radkes are black. Though you might find a similar scenario in the world of jazz—a world that's evaded the epithet "postmodern" and that, in most people's estimate, is the epitome of anticapitalism—I dare you to find a similar concert in country, metal, or rock. Only punk rock can scrape that kind of a genome. Only punk is quite that real.

The Return of the Repressed

Radkey aside, it's easy to see why people think that punk rock sold out. In order to really escape the trap of late capitalism, punk rock would have needed to declare itself good and dead, perhaps even taken a line from the famous World War I poem "For the Fallen" by Laurence Binyon (1914): "They shall grow not old as we that are left grow old / age shall not weary them, nor the years condemn." Undoubtedly, however, punk's practitioners and fans have as much of a right to continue living as anyone, and given that they do, it is perhaps unsurprising that they foregather at festivals the world over. Every summer, in towns like Blackpool, the site of the Rebellion Festival, at RiotFest, Punk in Drublic, and yes, Las Vegas, reunited older punk bands perform to throngs of fans who range across all ages. Some might scoff at the notion, but by so doing, old punk rockers reiterate the generative nature, at least, of its music and its message. As Deena Weinstein (2009, 111) once eloquently phrased it, older heavy metal fans are "wistful emigrants, living a continent away in another world than their own." (The same clearly applies to older punks; a visit to PRB is a voyage to their home country.)

Yet of all the punk rock festivals in existence, PRB, a three-day festival established in 1999, may seem the most unnatural. After all, the setting, Las Vegas, and punk rock seem antithetical, since the first is about exploiting working-class people's false consciousness through skanky capitalist endeavors, and the other is about liberating yourself from that mindset. Somehow, however, in the guise of punk rock, both those mindsets can coexist, and thanks to the digital turn that has killed brick and mortar record stores, radio stations, music magazines, and nightclubs, commitment to music can now be expressed in ways that transcend style and fashion. One of the most tangible of these would be at a festival where the punk diaspora can foregather in the flesh. Older punks may not be likely to go to the local shows, but they have the wherewithal to travel, plus, perhaps, a need to occasionally make their fandom known. According to Bennett (2006, 231), punks have had very little trouble reframing the concept of a festival, with its original negative connotations, into a punk event. His study also suggests that another benefit of festivals is that, today, older fans are able to get that rare sense of what was missing in earlier years, as younger punk fans at festivals respect the "skills and competencies" that older fans exhibit, thus "providing a platform for the celebration of punk as a 'collective identity' whose survival is essentially a product of shared commitment to punk on the part of a disparate but united body of punk fans" (232).

PRB and other festivals like it could easily be called, in the words of Svetlana Boym, "a theme park of lost illusions," as could the city of Las Vegas. Initially I thought PRB might be a mere rendering of the real thing, the way that the hotel/casino New York–New York renders Manhattan and the Luxor recreates ancient Egypt. But that turned out not to be the case. During PRB, a significant part of Vegas fills up with punk rockers of all ages, all clad in black Misfits T-shirts and sporting arm sleeves and leg tattoos. The majority of them are well into middle age, but that doesn't stop them from having Manic Panic hair color and mohawks. The women wear combat boots and fishnet tights and sailor hats and Bettie Page haircuts; the men have shaved heads, beer guts, big arms, and creased red faces. Neither set gives a damn about Vegas's ersatz, tacky version of sexy ladies and hot men: here, as nowhere else, the punk style has circumvented some of the traps of aging.

The lineups at each iteration—Crass, Angelic Upstarts, Turbonegro, L7, Boston's Mighty Mighty Bosstones, NOFX, the Svetlanas, the Briefs, Slaves, X, and Against Me!, to name just a few—are a motley bunch of old and new, but there is a spirit that ignites all of them that it's hard not to feel quite tender about: there is something so innately beautiful about punk ideology when shoved up against the hard cold capitalist wall. *Do it yourself. Take over the means of production. Small is beautiful. Respect is due.* These are mottos that are well worth repeating, and at PRB, they are right up in your face. The merchandise area is stocked only with independent vendors, selling anarchist books and homemade dresses, and hand-screened T-shirts. The food trucks are locally sourced. The bands on stage are all on independent labels. Finally, the music itself is not particularly radio-friendly, and is also essentially nondigitized: although electric and amplified, in some ways these bands bear the same relationship to today's popular music that folk music did in the late 1950s and early 1960s, when it reared itself out of Boston and the Village to mess with the host of identically dressed girl groups and handsome white crooners who were filling the airwaves with nonsensical romantic pop.

Also, for a festival, the atmosphere is mellow. The beer is flowing readily and the audience has kicked up a tiny flurry of dust in front of the stage, but no one seems out of their heads drunk or on speed, and the mosh pit is a kindly one. Aggression is at a bare minimum, and it's not clear if this is because people are too old or too stoned to fight. It is odd. During one of the days I spent there, I made my way to the front during Turbonegro and was able to stop several feet from the stage. This isn't the norm at most concerts these days, and one thing it illustrates is that PRB is, in its way, radical. When punk began, back in the day, it was radical, and explosive, and seriously necessary, but honestly? It still is. Certainly there are some retrograde nostalgic notions mixed up with the music fandom at these shows—for example, someone was moshing in a giant dinosaur outfit during the L7 set, which is funny in a rueful sort of way. But judging by the multi-aged audience, that's not the whole story, not by a long shot.

One of the problems with revisiting punk rock music is that so much of it depended on context for its urgency and brilliance. Sonically, what Andy Medhurst (1999, 220) called the songs' "discordancy and disrespect, the seditious fury of their unforgiving confrontationalism" doesn't necessarily translate down the ages. New music needs to sound contemporary, but the sound of contemporaneity is partially technological: when sound technologies change, older versions sound old, which is why we can't listen to contemporary music on Victrolas, or even make music that sounds good on them either.

Today's streaming and digital technologies have changed not only how music made for them sound, but also how that music changes consumption patterns and identity formation for young music fans, as well as how older fans are able to feel about themselves continuing with their punk fandom. In short, not only has the digital turn had enormous consequences in the live sphere, but it also leaves a whole set of music fans, boomers, with their old identities intact. Bennett, quoting Savage, once argued that every generation in the westernized world born during or after the 1940s has been "effectively trained in the age of consumerism, their lifestyles and identities based around a series of consumption practices of which music fandom is a key element" (Bennett 2006, 221), but thanks to social media, this idea of "youth music" no longer makes sense. Not only is music not the only or even the main type of fandom around which youth foregather—video game forums, Instagram and Tumblr pages, and food blogs now supersede it—but thanks to digital platforms, music fandom and identity formation are now delinked from chronology. You don't need to be a college professor to recognize that young people listen to rock and pop music from across a fifty-year time span: in addition to hyping their own generation of bands, they wear the T-shirts of Nirvana and the Doors and Led Zeppelin and help sell out stadiums for the Rolling Stones.

This differs from the 1970s and 1980s, when punks not only disavowed their parent's musical tastes, but even disavowed the generation just behind them. Thanks to this seismic change in listening practices, today, older fans are able to (re)access their memories in ways that don't seem forced or medieval, and with young people appreciating the bands of their youth, they can feel contemporary for having been there at the start. As Bennett showed in his study on older punk rock fans, fan practices and scenes have changed radically, in part because of the internet and social media. "Older fans may never meet in face-to-face contexts," Bennett says, "but continue to involve themselves in music through participation in virtual scenes perpetuated through the internet and/or print media publications" (2006, 222).

The term *nostalgia*, coined in the seventeenth century, initially referred to an emotion associated only with soldiers far from home. After the French Revolution, the concept became a term used by people who missed not only places but also less explicit things like lost communities and ancient regimes. Today people like to wallow in their memories, which can be poked and disturbed by official memory-makers like museums and monuments. But nowhere does the memory reassert itself more forcefully—more purely, I like to think—than it does in music. Only through music we can reactivate the most fragile of our feelings: melody alone has a direct line into our heart.

And this, I think, explains why punk and everything it stands for is an everlasting phenomenon, why it resists its own impulse to implode, why again and again it forces its fans and practitioners to come to Las Vegas and immediately turn themselves into pillars of salt. Because outside the gates of this concert, the Trump era is raging in all its horror. You can't look up at the buildings without thinking about how a sharpshooter killed 400 people from one of those windows earlier in the year. You can't hear the singer from NOFX mock that event without shuddering. You can't feel the almost synthetically hot breeze that wafts out of the air-conditioned edifices here without thinking about global warming.

How did K Punk put it? "A portal is itself intensifying, there is a mutual process of libidinization between the portal and what it opens onto.... Also—portals function most powerfully when they are transversal connectors between different cultural domains, e.g. fiction and music" (Fisher 2009). Well, the portal has now yawned open, stretching between cultural domains of Las Vegas (fiction) and PRB (music), and all us humans are flowing in and out of it. Outside the gates of PRB, vast numbers of Vegas visitors are having a very rigidly defined kind of fun, the kind based on numbing yourself stupid a la *Brave New World*, *The Matrix*, and the current opioid epidemic. This is because, though the tourist board would argue otherwise, in actuality, fun in Vegas seems to be just flat-out binge drinking. Everything else is just dross—entertainment that's sole intention is to make you want to get blotto. Nightly showcases by artists like Celine Dion, Britney Spears, and Boyz 2 Men, nearly naked trapeze artists placed above every gaming table, the sad-sack solo guitar player who hollers dirge versions of Buddy Holly songs throughout lunch at a local pizza joint—all these things only serve to make people nervous, such that the only way to soothe one's jangled nerves is by downing a cold one. To that end, every place you go provides 36-ounce or even 64-ounce glasses for margaritas and Bloody Marys. There is even a place called Vince Neil's Tatuado, which will sell you a miniature toilet bowl that you can hang around your neck, to barf into. It's at Circus Circus, the kid-friendly casino.

Elsewhere in Vegas, there are other nerve-wracking things that grasp desperately at the concept (and at your wallet). You can go shoot a machine gun, or ride a roller coaster or the giant Ferris wheel, or get yourself lap-danced on. Or you can go on SlotZilla, the zip line that you can take down the middle of the mall. It costs $25 if you do it sitting and $45 if you do it "Superman" style, with your arms out like you're flying. The line for it is tremendously long. While waiting for your turn, you can drink and watch the mall fill up. All along Fremont Street, shapely women with beautiful breasts smashed into teeny tiny bras teeter-totter by on high heels, while shlumpy men in cargo shorts and baseball caps lurch around touching the women's fish-netted butts "on accident."

Other kinds of hordes are there as well, families with small children, couples with strollers, loud brassy hen parties with one girl anointed the bride, and gangs and gangs and GANGS of guys, all swinging invisible dicks. Many of them seem to have some kind of weird side hustle—caricaturists, palm readers, comedians, and people dressed in crazy costumes who stand there for tips. Yeah, you see that in London and Barcelona and Budapest as well, but the ones in Vegas are more naked. The concept of sex here is neither carnal nor erotic, but just based on some incredibly basic, repressive, and socially constructed set of values. All of them—*all*—celebrate women with big boobs who wear servile costumes (nurse, maid, tart).

Gathered here tonight, then, as it is every night, is the raw material of Vegas's famous slogan, "What happens in Vegas, stays in Vegas," and it is against this background that those who have come to go PRB really stand out. Whatever their drinking or drug preferences may be or have been in the past, they pale in comparison to the stag boys and the low/high rollers and the big-bellied men with dead eyes and crazy T-shirt slogans ("Fiscally Republican/Socially Democrat/Sexually Liberal") who haunt this area. In Vegas, the sexual politics of punk rock (such as it is) seems positively equitable: punk rock women are allowed to bear their own stories on their own natural bodies, to dress in ways that please themselves, to act out fantasies that don't seem bounded by those of the men they are with. Also, their tattoos no longer stand out in a world that has proudly inked its own ass with its foibles: compared to the tramp stamps and Disney characters laid across the skin of practically all of Christendom, all punk rockers are righteous, and authentic, and sincere and unafraid.

But the keywords here are "in Vegas." What about outside, in the real world? Over the past fifty years, punk rock has positioned itself by turns as anarchic, apathetic, apocalyptic, apolitical, and even, at PRB and elsewhere in the past, antifascist. On the Sunday evening of PRB, Shawn Stern, one of the festival's founders and a member of the punk band Youth Brigade, made a short but extremely eloquent speech asking participants to put aside any indifference they might feel toward the mainstream, to help defeat the fascist regime Americans live currently under. "Participating in society is a political act," he said. "We are currently facing a fascist propaganda machine. Punk rock has always been about questioning authority, and now more than ever, we have to step up and fight" (Arnold 2018). Stern's plea is understandable, given the time and place he made it, but it doesn't acknowledge that, although punk today is often equated with antifascism, Rock Against Racism, and other liberal and progressive causes, it also has a long history of racial exclusivity and gender inequity that needs to be acknowledged if not embraced. The basic conundrum of punk is that its foremost ability has always been not to legitimate, but to destabilize. When poised as cultural heritage—as at PRB, as throughout the Punk London exhibits, and perhaps even as the subject of an *Oxford Handbook*—it starts to lose that ability. In the words of Greil Marcus (1989, 308), writing about the effect of the Sex Pistols' music, "Unfulfilled desires transmit themselves across the years in unfathomable ways, and all that remains on the surface are bits of symbolic discourse, deaf to their sources and blind to their objects." These, he continues, "are a last link to notions that have gone under the ground, into a cultural unconscious." At these heritage events, these desires rise to the surface, where we are forced to grapple with them over and over again, for better or worse.

Note

1. The actual line is "The only notes that count/are the ones that come in wads."

References

Arnold, Gina. 2018. "Apocalypse, Now." *Fools Rush In*, May 29, 2018. http://foolsrushinredux.blogspot.com/2018/05/apocalypse-now.html.

Atkinson, David. 2008. "The Heritage of Mundane Places." In *The Ashgate Research Companion to Heritage and Identity*, edited by Brian J. Graham and Peter Howard, 381–396. Farnham, UK: Ashgate.

Babey, Ged. 2015. "Punk. London. 40 Years.... 2016 Year Long Festival Is 'Supported by the Mayor of London' and Funded by Lottery Grant." *Louder than War*, December 20, 2015. louderthanwar.com/punk-london-40-years-2016-year-long-festival-is-supported-by-the-mayor-of-london-and-funded-by-lottery-grant/.

Bennett, Andy. 2006. "Punk's Not Dead: The Continuing Significance of Punk Rock for an Older Generation of Fans." *Sociology* 40, no. 2: 219–235. doi:10.1177/0038038506062030.

Bennett, Andy. 2009. "'Heritage Rock': Rock Music, Representation and Heritage Discourse." *Poetics* 37, no. 5-6: 474–489.

Bennett, Andy, and Paul Hodkinson, eds. 2012. *Ageing and Youth Cultures: Music, Style and Identity*. Oxford: Berg. https://doi.org/10.4324/9781003084426

Binyon, Laurence. 1914. "For the Fallen." Poetry Foundation. https://www.poetryfoundation.org/poems/57322/for-the-fallen.

Boym, Svetlana. 2001. *The Future of Nostalgia*. New York: Basic Books.

Carter, Paul. 1988. *The Road to Botany Bay*. New York: Knopf.

Edwards, Jim. 2016. "Joe Corré's Plan to Burn His Massive Collection of Sex Pistols Memorabilia Is Reprehensible." *Business Insider*, November 25, 2016. www.businessinsider.com/joe-corre-burn-punk-sex-pistols-collection-reprehensible-2016-11.

Fisher, Mark. 2009. "My Mind, It Ain't So Open." *K-punk*, May 9, 2009. http://k-punk.abstractdynamics.org/archives/011107.html.

Freud, Sigmund. 1933. "The Dissection of the Psychical Personality." In *New Introductory Lectures on Psychoanalysis*, 57–80. New York: W. W. Norton.

"God Save The Queen." The Sex Pistols. EMI, 1977.

The Guardian. 2016. "Punk Funeral: Joe Corré Burns £5m of Memorabilia on Thames." *The Guardian*, November 26, 2016. https://www.theguardian.com/music/2016/nov/26/punx-not-dead-joe-corre-burns-memorabilia-worth-5m-on-thames.

Guy-Ryan, Jessie. 2016. "Iconic Punk Rocker Defaces the British Library's Punk Rock Exhibit." *Atlas Obscura*, July 17, 2016. https://www.atlasobscura.com/articles/a-punk-icon-defaced-the-british-librarys-punk-rock-exhibit.

Jameson, Frederic. 1993. *Postmodernism, or, the cultural logic of late capitalism*. London: Verso.

Jones, Steve, and Paul Cook, dirs. 1980. *The Great Rock 'n' Roll Swindle*. London: Virgin Films.

Koc, Alican. 2022. "'Trapped in Oklahoma': Bible Belt Affect and DIY Punk." In *Musical Spaces*, edited by James Williams and Samuel Horlor, 23–40. Singapore: Jenny Stanford Publishing.

Lowenthal, David. 1989. "Nostalgia Tells It Like It Wasn't." In *The Imagined Past: History and Nostalgia*, edited by Malcolm Chase and Christopher Shaw, 18–32. Manchester, UK: Manchester University Press.

Lowrey, Annie. 2017. "Why the Phrase 'Late Capitalism' Is Suddenly Everywhere." *The Atlantic*, August 3, 2017. https://www.theatlantic.com/business/archive/2017/05/late-capitalism/524943/.

MacInnes, Paul. 2018. "Joe Corré on His £5m Punk Ashes—and Malcolm McLaren's Death Mask." *The Guardian*, April 20, 2018. https://www.theguardian.com/artanddesign/2018/apr/20/punk-bonfire-artist-joe-Corré-ash-from-chaos-lazinc-gallery.

Marcus, Greil. *Lipstick Traces: A Secret History of the 20th Century*. Cambridge, MA: Harvard University Press, 1989.

Marcuse, H. 1974. *One Dimensional Man*. London: Abacus.

Medhurst, Andy. 1999. "What Did I Get? Punk Memory and Nostalgia." In *Punk Rock: So What?: The Cultural Legacy of Punk*, edited by Roger Sabin, 219–231. New York: Routledge.

O'Toole, Kathleen. 1999. "Literary Historian Jameson Examines 'Myths of the Modern.'" *Stanford Report*, January 27, 1999. https://news.stanford.edu/news/1999/january27/jameson127.html.

Weinstein, Deena. 2009. *Heavy Metal: The Music and Its Culture*. New York: Da Capo Press.

Weschler, Lawrence. 1996. *Mr. Wilson's Cabinet of Wonder*. New York: Vintage Books.

Index

Tables and figures are indicated by an italic *t* and *f* following the page number.

Abbas, Ausaf, 473–478
Abdurraqib, Hanif, 217
"A-Bomb in Wardour Street," 489, 491
Accelerators, 36
AC/DC, 365
Acts of Defiance, 275
ACT-UP, 202, 213
A.D. Design, 390
Adventures in Reality, 276
Adverts, 32, 122–123, 485
Afghan Whigs, 544
Afropunk, 6, 217–218, 227–228
Afro-Punk, 227
Against Me!, 204, 208, 211
Aggressors BC, 340
aging, 231–242, 554–555, 560–561
Ahat, 308
AIDS pandemic, 202, 204, 211, 433n1
AIR studios, 441
Albee, Becca, 59
Albertine, Viv, 90, 118, 129, 245, 252, 397, 402, 409–410, 434n5, 557
Albini, Steve, 438, 443, 448
Aldridge, Roger, 152
Alexander, Dave, 220
Alice in Chains, 538–539, 544–545, 550
alienation, 8, 10, 421–424
Alien Kulture, 466, 473–478
Allen, Richard, 431
Allman Brothers, 362
All The Pretty Horses, 206–207
Almodóvar, Pedro, 319
Alternative Nation, 547
Alternative Sounds, 276
Alternative TV, 110, 484
alt-right movement, 522–526, 529–535

Álvarez, Ángel, 315
Alyokhina, Masha, 502–505, 512–513, 516–517
Ambrose, Joe, 196
Ament, Jeff, 541, 543–544
Amos, Tori, 128
A&M Records, 543–544
Amsden, Karen, 250, 251*f*, 252–253, 255–256, 255*f*
anarchism, 3, 77–78, 82, 286, 344, 351n16
"Anarchist Attack," 273
anarcho-punk, 4, 167, 171, 179, 289–290, 298, 394, 485
  Crass and, 3, 78, 104–107, 273, 337, 387–388, 497
  in Northern Ireland, 336–338, 340
Anarchy Centre, 332, 336
"Anarchy in the UK," 3, 78, 82, 102, 190–191, 234, 332, 385
Andersen, Mark, 87
Anderson, Kevin, 274
Anderson, Mark, 63
Andes, L., 233–234
Angelic Upstarts, 489, 505–506, 509
"Angry Inch," 210
Another Day Another Word, 275
Another State of Mind, 189, 197
Anti-Nazi League, 466, 471, 485
Anti-Nowhere League, 526
antinuclear and antiwar songs and activism, 481–485, 482*f*, 487–489, 490*t*, 491–498
anti-sectarian punk, in Northern Ireland, 340–344, 347
APF Brigade, 273
appropriation, 364, 374–375
Arca, 213–214
Archies Meet the Ramones, The, 521

Arctic Monkeys, 365
"Are You a Boy or Are You a Girl?," 205
"Are You Man Enough to Be a Woman?," 206
Arkady Kotz, 290–291
Arm, Mark, 541
"Armagideon Time," 92
Armstrong, Billie Joe, 160
Arnett, Jeffrey, 499n4
Arnold, Gina, 551
Arrebato, 319
Asheton, Ron, 220
Ash from Chaos, 558
Asian communities, 466, 474–478
"Asian Youth," 475–476, 478
"Assassinos no poder," 321
Atanasova, Katya, 306*f*
Atkinson, David, 554
Attali, Jacques, 130
Au Pairs, 116–117, 120, 129, 332
authenticity, 373–374, 379–380, 390–392, 472, 531–532, 540, 547, 549
Aviador Dro, 319
Avtomaticheskie Udovletvoriteli, 283–284
Azerrad, Michael, 136

Babes in Toyland, 538, 544
Babylon, 429, 431–432, 432*f*
Back Door Man, 455
Backlash (Faludi), 45, 48, 50
Bad Brains, 143–145, 221–222, 227
Badiou, Alain, 73
"Bad Moon Rising," 488
Bag, Alice, 187–188, 191–192, 196–197, 434n5
Bags, 187, 191–192
Bailey, Jyl, 268
Baker, Brian, 133, 136, 139, 143
Baldwin, James, 225
Balfe, Dave, 31
"Ballad of John and Yoko, The," 488
Bancroft, Jessie H., 407
Band Aid, 493–494
"Bankrobber," 96
"Ban the Bomb," 481, 482*f*
Barbarellas, 271
Barfe, Louis, 392
Barker, Hugh, 391–392

Barrett, Wayne, 34
Basque rock and punk, 319–320, 322, 326
Basquiat, Jean-Michel, 421, 428
Baum, Sandra, 257–258, 258*f*, 259*f*
Bayley, Roberta, 389
Bazooka Joe, 121
BDSM, 203–204
Beal, Michael, 390
Beat, 492–493
Beatles, 108, 191, 193, 232, 440, 488
Beatty, Christine, 206–207
Bebiano, R., 316
Becker, H., 29
Bee Gees, 418
Beethoven, Ludwig van, 161
Bennett, Andy, 4–5, 7, 12, 14, 232, 234, 237, 239, 241, 246–247, 554–555, 561–562
Bent Fest, 176
Berardi, Bifo, 422, 433
Berger, George, 105, 485
Berger, John, 252
Berlant, Lauren, 212
Bernstein, Nils, 540
Bestley, Russ, 267, 487
Betrock, Alan, 456
"Better Decide Which Side You're On," 471
"Bezdel'nik," 284
Bhangra, 474–475
Biafra, Jello, 160, 196–197, 228, 442
Bieber, Justin, 398, 401
Big Black, 442–443
Big in Japan, 35–36, 495–496
Big Joanie, 176
Bikceem, Ramdasha, 61
Bikini Kill, 12, 66n16, 130n1, 169, 190
    Cobain and, 406, 544
    FUPU and, 224–225
    posture of, 404
    Pussy Riot and, 506, 509
    Riot Grrrl and, 45–46, 49–50, 57, 59, 62–64, 224
Bikini Kill (zine), 50, 457
Bilgrami, Pervez, 473–474, 476–478
Billy Riot and the Violent Fuckwits, 335
Binyon, Laurence, 560
biopower, 212
Birch, Gina, 115, 126–127, 434n5

Birmingham Centre for Contemporary Cultural Studies, 116
BitchMedia, 213
Black, Gaye, 32, 122–123
Black, Jet, 231
black feminists, 171
Black Flag, 3, 196, 223, 368, 443, 541
Black Lives Matter, 217–218, 228
Blackman, Lisa, 398
blackness, 218, 222, 227–228
black proto-punk bands, 220–222
black punk, 6, 217–218, 220–222, 226–228
black rock and roll artists, 219, 224
Blank Cheque for Peace?, 345–346, 345f
Blank Generation, 420, 422, 423f, 425, 432
Blasey Ford, Christine, 66n25
Bleach, 544
"Blitzkrieg Bop," 1
Blondie, 441, 527
"Blood One," 509
Blue Oyster Cult, 455–456
BNP. *See* British National Party
Bobby Fuller Four, 92
Bockris, Victor, 485
Bodysnatchers, 129
Boeschenstein and Pereira, 361–362, 364
"Boiler, The," 129
"Bold as Brass," 342
Boleyn, Ann, 155–156, 156f
"Bollox to the RUC," 338
Boltanski, Luc, 540, 549
"Bombsite Boys," 485
Bono, 92, 496
Book Your Own Fucking Life, 460
Boomtown Rats, 489, 494
Boon, Richard, 32, 34, 272
Boone, G., 439
Born in Flames, 422
"Bottled Violence," 136–137
Boulding, Elise, 483
Bourdieu, Pierre, 139–140, 411, 527, 539, 548
Bower, Paul, 265
Bowes, Martin, 276
Bowie, David, 424, 467–468
Boyd, B., 368
Boyes, Georgina, 76
Boym, Svetlana, 46, 558, 561

Bracewell, Michael, 379–380
Bradley, Michael, 269
Bradley, Shanne, 117, 119
Bragg, Billy, 76, 78–80, 283–284, 291, 486
Bramah, Martin, 33
"Brand New Cadillac," 92
Brando, Marlon, 362, 375
Brass Lip, 275
Bratmobile, 45, 49–50, 57, 63, 457
Breaking Glass, 424–425, 429–430, 434n5, 491, 492f
"Breathing," 496
Brecht, George, 104–105
Breedlove, Lynne, 206–208
bricolage, 379
Brigadir, 289–290
Brilleaux, Lee, 387
Britannia Hospital, 429
British National Party (BNP), 523
Britpop, 170
Britten, Benjamin, 106–107
Bronfen, Elisabeth, 158
Brown, A., 364
Brunner, John, 481
Brunström, Conrad, 91
Bubbles, Barney, 387, 393
Bulgarian punk and post-punk, 295–310
Bullen, Nic, 276
Burchill, Julie, 116
Burke, Edmund, 524
Burke, Steve, 274
Burns, Gordon, 467
Burns, Pete and Lynne, 268
Burroughs, William, 108
Bush, Kate, 489, 496
Business, 506
Butler, Judith, 202, 206
Butler, Justine, 268
Butthole Surfers, 525, 541
"Buy Me, Sell Me," 72
Buzzcocks, 27, 29, 34, 37, 248, 266, 272–273, 385–386, 386f, 392
Bye Bye Monkey, 421

Cabut, Richard, 103
Cage, John, 104–105, 108
Calcutt, A., 233

Californian Guardians of Morality, 120
"Call Up, The"/ "Stop the World," 493
camp, 123
Campaign for Nuclear Disarmament (CND), 75, 481, 482f, 483–485, 489, 493, 497
Campbell, S., 334
Capistrano, Daniela, 61
capitalism, 79, 289–290, 460–461, 505, 511, 530, 540, 542, 548–549, 555, 558–561
"Capital Radio One," 92
Caravana Musical, 315
Cardew, Cornelius, 104, 470
Carland, Tammy Rae, 61–62
Carlin, George, 160
Carnival Against the Nazis, 472, 474
Carroll, Cath, 116, 275
Carswell, Sean, 458–459
Carter, Paul, 554
Cartledge, Frank, 380
Castrators, 117
Casulana, Maddalena, 155
Catholic Girls, 119, 253–254
Catwoman, Soo, 110, 527
CBGB, 12, 215n10
Cecil Sharp House, 72
Celtic punk, 343
censorship, 153, 157–161
Cervenka, Exene, 194
Chakrabarty, Dipesh, 154
Chaney, D., 236
Charles, Ray, 219, 221
Chefs, 129
Cheparukhin, Alexander, 504
Chiapello, Eve, 540, 549
"Chickenshit Conformist," 526–527
Chinn, Sarah, 206
Chiswick, 272, 394
Christiane F., 424
Church, David, 6–7
City Fun, 122, 275
Clapton, Eric, 467–468
Clarke, Gary, 527
Clarke, J., 232–233
Clash, 13, 35–36, 78, 80, 95f, 117, 481, 489
  in Belfast, 332
  black musics and, 86–87, 92–93
  "The Call Up"/ "Stop the World" by, 493

at Carnival Against the Nazis, 472, 474
  "Hate and War" by, 484
  London Calling by, 91, 93, 441, 445–446
  punk communication and, 88–95
  Pussy Riot and, 517
  in *Rude Boy,* 431
  "selling out," 86, 97nn3–4
  Sex Pistols and, 90–91, 96–97, 231, 272, 304
  style aesthetic of, 527–528
  "This Is Radio Clash" by, 93–94, 97
  "White Riot" by, 89–90, 94, 190, 472
Clash on Broadway, 95f
class, 51–52, 57, 60–62, 64, 139–143, 198, 282–291, 411–412
classical music, 104–107, 154–155, 440–441, 448–449
"Clockwork Hot Spoiled Acid Test," 108
Clockwork Orange County, 197
CND. *See* Campaign for Nuclear Disarmament
Cobain, Kurt, 398, 404, 406–407, 409, 412, 434n5, 522, 539, 544–545, 550
Cockney Rejects, 505–507, 509
Cock Sparrer, 506
Cohen, Stanley, 260
Cold War, 296–297, 483, 489, 495, 495f, 497, 503
Coleman, J., 31
Coles, Mike, 382, 387–389, 388f
colonialism, 154
Columbia Records, 544
Combat 18, 343
Combat Rock, 92–93
"Come Again," 129
Commander Salamander, 369–370
commodification, 539–540, 546–550, 555–556, 558
Common Sense, 453
communication media, 87–97
"Complete Control," 92, 97
Compositions 1960, 105
Conflict, 332
Connolly, William, 533
conservatism, 522–526, 529–535
Conservative Political Action Conference (CPAC), 523
Convertible, Jennifer, 206–207
Conway, Kellyanne, 532

Cook, Harold, 413n6
Cook, Paul, 90, 121, 528
Coon, Caroline, 29, 35, 116, 167
Cope, Julian, 36, 41, 268
Copkiller, 428, 434n6
Copsey, Nigel, 281
Cornell, Chris, 544–545
corporealities, posture and, 397–412
Corré, Joe, 556–558
Costello, Elvis, 337, 387
"Couming of Youth," 108
COUM Transmissions, 101, 108–110
County, Jayne, 204–207, 215n10
Coupland, Douglas, 547
Covach, J., 439
Cowan, Greg, 333*f*
Cowley Club, 179
Cox, Alex, 190
Cox, Laverne, 211
CPAC. *See* Conservative Political Action Conference
Cracked Actor, 424
Crash, Darby, 422
Crass, 14–15, 74–75, 82, 97n3, 101, 108, 110–111, 111n1, 269
  anarcho-punk and, 3, 78, 104–107, 273, 337, 387–388, 497
  design aesthetic of, 387–388
  logo of, 368
  recording, 442, 446
  T-shirts, 361
Crass Records, 273, 387
Crawdaddy, 454
"Cream in My Jeans," 205
Creedence Clearwater Revival, 488
Crise Total, 320–321
cross-dressing, 7
Crossley, N., 14
Crowe, Cameron, 545
Crucial Three, 36
Cruising, 424–425
Cuckoo's Nest, 197
cultural heritage and cultural legacy, 240–241, 557
Cultural Historical Activity Theory, 373
cultural memory, 188–189
cultural translation, 296, 298, 300–305

"Culture Crossover," 475, 478
Cure, 389, 424
Cut, 125–126, 439
Cyrus, Miley, 211
C/Z Records, 541

Dada, 454
Daily Show with Jon Stewart, The, 198
Dale, Pete, 4–5, 14
Damage, 459–460
Damned, 1, 76, 117, 439
Dancing in the Street, 240
Darby, Simon, 523
"Dark Land," 307–308
Darms, Lisa, 59, 61
Darwin, Charles, 407
Da Silva, Ana, 126
Daughters of Charity study, 249
Davidson, T. J., 31, 41–42
Davies, E., 361, 373
Davies, Geoff, 268
Davis, Joanna R., 7
Davis, Miles, 408
Davis, Vaginal, 206
Davis, Wyn, 443–444
Day, Aiden, 92
"Day in the Life, A," 108
DC hardcore, 133–134, 142–144
Dead Boys, 527
Dead Kennedys, 3, 151, 196–197, 228, 441–442, 489, 525–527
Dead on Arrival, 390
Deaf School, 35
Dean, James, 362, 375
Death, 220–222, 227
Debies-Carl, Jeffrey S., 12
Debord, Guy, 128–129, 248
Decline of Western Civilization, The, 194, 196, 422, 434n5, 525
Decolonise Fest, 174, 176
Deep Six, 538, 541
Deleuze, Gilles, 531, 535
DeLong, M., 254–255, 372
Demolición, 193
Denom, Sue, 122–123
Denton, Sandy, 161–162
Derrida, Jacques, 76, 82, 534

Descendants, 560
Desperate Bicycles, 392–393, 393f
Desperately Seeking Susan, 428
Desperate Teenage Lovedolls, 425
Devo, 109
Devoto, Howard, 37
DGC Records, 544
Diagileva, Yanka, 284–285
DiCicco, Oliver, 441–442, 444, 448
Dictators, 215n10
Dimitriadis, Greg, 245
Dinosaur Jr., 538, 544
Director X, 401
Dirt, 550
disability, 6–7
Dischord Records, 49, 139–140, 142–143, 542
disco, 195–196, 418–419, 419f, 429–430, 433n1
"Discoteca Ofreon A Go-Go," 192
Disgusting Youth, 285
Dishwasher Pete, 453
DIY, 3, 7–9, 11, 14, 34, 80–81, 240
    aesthetics, 439–440, 445, 447–448
    Albertine and, 402
    Band Aid, Live Aid and, 494
    in Bulgarian punk, 296–298, 300–301, 308–309
    careers, 236–238
    Dischord Records and, 142–143
    economics, 530
    graphic design and visual style and, 382, 384, 389–394, 393f
    grassroots protest movements and, 231
    in hardcore and anarcho-punk, 179, 394
    independent record labels and, 273, 332
    KISMIF and, 486
    1970s punk women on, 257–258, 260
    in Northern Irish punk, 336
    in Portuguese punk, 321, 325–327
    in punk and hip-hop, 149, 151
    punk feminism, 250
    in queer and feminist punk scenes in UK, 166, 170, 175–177, 179–180
    RAR and, 465
    recording and production, 439–440, 445, 447–448
    Riot Grrrl and, 45, 63, 168–170
    spaces, 173
    in Spanish punk, 325–326
    Throbbing Gristle on, 109–110
    T-shirts and, 363–364
    women in punk and, 425
    zines and, 276, 452–453, 456, 458–459
DIY Diaspora Punx, 174
D.O.A.: A Rite of Passage, 421, 425, 429
Dr. Feelgood, 390
Domino, Fats, 221
"Don't Be Cruel," 219
"Don't Dictate," 129
Don't Look Back, 79
Dookie, 550
"Do They Know It's Christmas?," 493
Douglas, Susan, 54–55
Down by the Jetty, 390
Downes, Julia, 166, 170
Down on the Upside, 550
Downtown 81, 421–422, 425, 427–428, 432–433, 434n5
doxa, 526–529, 534–535, 555
Doyle, Tad, 543
drag, 206
Draganov, Svetoslav, 309
Drake, Jennifer, 52
Drayton, Tony, 274
Dresch, Donna, 62
"Drinking with the Jocks," 211
Drip Music (Drip Event), 105
Driver, C., 239
DRO, 319
Drummond, Bill, 31
Dry as a Bone, 541–542
Duggan, Lisa, 214n8
Dulcinea, 195
Duncombe, S., 7
Duncombe, Stephen, 461
Dunn, Ged, 455
Dunn, Kevin, 4, 12, 83n3, 439–440
Du Noyer, Paul, 119
Dury, Ian, 6–7, 35, 231, 387, 481, 482f, 489
Dylan, Bob, 79

Eagle, Roger, 31, 41–42
"Earth Dies Screaming, The," 492
Easter, 225
East Village Inky, The, 453
Eater, 430

Ebert, Roger, 429
Echols, Alice, 48
Echo & the Bunnymen, 319
Eddie and the Hot Rods, 32, 390
Edwards, Simon, 273–274
EFDSS. *See* English Folk Dance and Song Society
Eichorn, Kate, 68n52
"Eighth Day," 491, 492*f*
Eisenberg, E., 442
Elborough, Travis, 392
Electrical Audio, 448
Electric Circus, 34–35, 37, 41–42
"Electricity," 42
Elias, Norbert, 398–399
Elliot, R., 361, 373
Ellis, Perry, 545–546
EMI, 471
"EMI," 97
Em Órbita, 316
EMP. *See* Experience Music Project
Encarnacao, John, 74–75, 81, 109
Endino, Jack, 541–542
Engels, Friedrich, 407
English Folk Dance and Song Society (EFDSS), 72, 76
"Enola Gay," 496
Epic Records, 254
Epitaph Records, 212–213
Equal Pay Act of 1970, 248
Eraserhead, 424
Erasmus, Alan, 41–42, 274
Eric's, 35–36, 41–42, 268, 491–492
Eskorbuto, 322
Estrada, Blanca, 192
Estrada, Francisco "Frankie," 192
"Eton Rifles, The," 489, 491, 496–497
Ettes, 129
Euse, Erica, 47
Every Good Boy Deserves Fudge, 544
Excuse 17, 45, 63
Exit, 101, 104–106, 108
Experience Music Project (EMP), 52
experimental noise, 107–110
Ezrailson, Wendy, 369

"FAB," 155–156, 156*f*, 157*f*

Fab 5 Freddy, 428
Factory, 41–42
Factory Records, 274, 491–492
fado, 316, 328n5
Fahey, John, 74
Fahy, Gary, 334
Fairbairn, Nicholas, 109
Faíscas, 318*f*
Falklands War, 483, 497
Fall, 33–34, 41, 487
Faludi, Susan, 45, 48, 50
fanzines. *See* zines
fascism, 3–4, 314, 343, 429–430, 465–467, 469–470, 472, 523, 526, 564
Fast Product, 273–274
Fawcett, Diana, 393
FCC. *See* Federal Communications Commission
"FCC," 158–160, 158*f*
F-Club, 271
Fear, 525–526
Featherstone, M., 233
Federal Communications Commission (FCC), 153, 158–161
Feeding the Five Thousand, The, 107
Feld, S., 32
female rap collectives, 148–150, 160–164
femininities, 134–136, 139, 177–178, 190, 213, 256
feminism, 6, 16n8, 150, 155, 157–158, 161–162
  black, 171
  Cobain and, 406, 434n5, 545
  in contemporary UK punk scenes, 171
  intersectional, 54, 64, 173
  1970s female punk and, 248–250, 249*t*, 256, 260
  punk, generational biography of, 249–250, 249*t*
  Pussy Riot and, 506–507, 513*f*, 515
  queer and feminist punk scenes, UK, 166–180
  Riot Grrrl and, 45–46, 48–58, 62–64, 173, 179, 506, 544
  second-wave, 48, 50, 54–55, 171
  third-wave, 46, 48, 50, 54–55, 58
  Times Square and, 426–427
FemRock Fest, 174
fetishization, 556–558

Fifth Column, 169, 204
"Fightin' 36th, The," 337
"Filler," 136–138, 140
Finlay, A., 343
First Timers, 170–171, 176
first-wave punk, 1, 3–6, 8, 13, 27, 100–101, 190, 231, 240–241
Fisher, Mark, 555, 563
Fishev, Alexei, 286–287
Fitzgerald, F. Scott, 362
Fitzgerald, Patrik, 72, 78
Flannigan, Tracy, 207–208
Fleetwood Mac, 447
Flesh, 319
Flipside, 454–455, 457–459
Flores, Erwin, 193
Flowers of Romance, The, 305
"Flowers of the Late 80s," 295, 299, 306
Fluid, 544
Flux of Pink Indians, 3
Fluxus, 101, 104–106, 108, 110
folk, punk and, 72–83
Fomenko, Petr, 286
Fonarow, W., 239
Foo Fighters, 551
Force, William, 373–374
Foucault, Michel, 212
Fouce, H., 317
Foxx, John, 424
France, Kim, 52
Franco, Francisco, 314–315, 317, 319, 325
Frank, Thomas, 540, 546
Frankie Goes to Hollywood, 492–496, 495f
Franklin, Benjamin, 453
Frantic Elevators, 31, 42
"Frat Pig," 208
Freeman, Lance, 193
"Free the Cobblestones," 509–513, 512f
Free Trade Hall, 33–35
Fresh Fruit for Rotting Vegetables, 441
Freud, Sigmund, 149, 152, 154, 158, 161, 164n6, 555
Friedman, S., 410–411
Friends, 419f, 420
Frith, Simon, 4, 11, 125, 383, 469–470
From the Westway to the World, 89
Fryer, Paul, 281
FTS, 338, 340f

Fuck Nostalgia Fest, 335, 335f
Fuck U Pay Us (FUPU), 224–226, 228
Fugazi, 49, 63, 78, 188
Fuller, Matthew, 87
Fun House, 220
FUPU. *See* Fuck U Pay Us
Futurism, 109, 124, 467–468

Gabriel, Peter, 489
Gallix, Andrew, 103
Galupo, Scott, 523
Gang of Four, 271
gangsta rap, 150–151
garage rock, 439
Garbage, 447
Garber, Jenny, 121
GARBiTCH, 199
Garnett, Robert, 9, 12, 14
Garrett, Malcolm, 27, 383, 385–387, 386f
Gaughan, Dick, 75
Gelbart, Matthew, 13, 15
Geldof, Bob, 494
gender, 6, 115–117, 123–125, 167
    drag and, 206
    in first generation queercore, 204–207
    in hardcore punk and gangsta rap, 151
    in indie-pop, 170
    male gaze and, 250, 252
    Minor Threat and, 134–139
    nonconformity, 207
    posing and, 409–410
    power and, 253–254
    punk clothes and, 252
    in queer and feminist UK punk scenes, 171–172, 178
    sexuality and, 171–172, 178
Generation X, 539, 543–544, 546–547, 549
Generation X (Coupland), 547
gentrification, 193–195, 197, 346–349
Germs, 422
Gernsback, Hugo, 453
"Geroi," 289–290
Gessen, Masha, 502, 504, 513, 515
Ghesquière, Nicolas, 365
Gibson, Lee, 270
Gilbert, Pat, 87–90
Gillett, C., 442
Gilligan, C., 338

Gilman, Sander, 398, 412, 413n6
Gina Harlow and the Cutthroats, 426
Ginn, Greg, 443
Ginsberg, Allen, 454
Girls Rock schools, 258
"Give Violence a Chance," 213
"(Sing If You're) Glad to Be Gay," 471
Glamazon, 206–207
glam rock, 232, 545
"Glass Tombstones," 346–348
Glenn, Joshua, 191
G.L.O.S.S., 204, 208, 212–213
"Goddess of Wet Dreams," 206
"God Save the Queen," 305, 385, 421, 528, 554, 556–557
Gogan, Barbara, 124
"Going Underground," 489, 491, 496–497
Goldberg, Michelle, 523
Goldie, Alison, 252, 253f, 256–257, 257f
Goldin, Nan, 424
Goldman, Vivien, 116–117, 251–252, 256, 409
Good Friday Agreement, 336, 344, 346, 349, 350n7
Goodman, Dave, 445
Good Vibrations, 332, 335
Good Vibrations, 336
Goodyer, Ian, 470
Gooseberry Studios, 445
Goose Lake International Music Festival, 220
Gorbachev, Mikhail, 304, 503
Gordon, Alastair, 268
Gordon, Kenny, 222
Gordon, Kim, 52–53
Gore, Tipper, 160
Gosling, Tim, 3–4
Gossard, Stone, 541, 543–544
Gossip Girl, 420
Gottlieb, Joanne, 52, 457
Grace, Laura Jane, 208, 211
Graduate, The, 423–424
Graham, Bill, 362
Grateful Dead, 362
Gray, Marcus, 88–89
Grazhdanskaya Oborona, 4, 284–285
Greatest Shits, 339f
Great Rock 'n' Roll Swindle, The, 96, 190, 430, 553

Green Day, 160, 209, 449, 529, 550, 559
Greene, Shane, 505
Green River, 541–544
Grimes, Carol, 468–469
Grohl, Dave, 551
Grossberg, L., 238
Grundy, Bill, 29, 34–35, 96, 469, 525
grunge, 13, 538–551
Guattari, Félix, 87, 531, 535
Gucci, 202–203, 213
Guerra, Paula, 5, 237
"Guilty of Being White," 226–228
Guilty of What, 269
Gumbs, Alexis Pauline, 408
Gunk, 61
Gun Rubber, 265
Guttersnipe, 121
Gysin, Brian, 108

Habermas, Jürgen, 555
Haçienda, 271, 274
Hackney, Bobby, 221
Haenfler, Ross, 237–238, 530
Hair, 305
Halberstam, Jack, 207–208
Hall, S., 116
Halliday, Ayun, 453
Hammersmith Palais, 93
Hampton, Fred, 218
Hancock, Polly, 251, 254, 256
Hanna, Kathleen, 49, 57, 59–61, 66n16, 68n64, 130n1, 224, 404, 457, 544–545
Hanna, Lynne, 127
Hannerz, Erik, 4, 11
hardcore, 13, 136–137, 145, 529
 Bad Brains and, 222
 DC, 133–134, 142–144
 DIY in, 179, 394
 gender in, 151
 LA, 197
 mosh pit, 194
 Riot Grrrl, queercore and, 175
 Russian, 289–290
 slam dancing in, 196
 SST and, 443–444
 women in, 167
Hard Day's Night, A, 191
Hard Rock Cafe, 553, 556–557

Haring, Keith, 428
Harry, Debbie, 427
Harvey, PJ, 405
"Hate and War," 484
"Having a Coke With You" (O'Hara), 58
Hawk, Tony, 191
Hawkwind, 108
"H-Bomb's Thunder, The," 481
Heartbeat Records, 273–274
Heavens to Betsy, 45, 49
heavy metal, 499n4, 538
Hebdige, Dick, 1–2, 8, 11, 28, 97, 124, 203, 207, 232, 260, 379–380, 400, 421, 429, 455, 469–470, 485, 522, 525, 539
Hedwig and the Angry Inch, 204, 208–211
Hegarty, Paul, 96
Heibutzki, Ralph, 87
Hell, Richard, 122, 223, 363, 375, 420, 422, 424, 426, 434n5, 527
Hell's Angels, 119–120
Helms, Jesse, 160
Hemmings, Clare, 48
Hendrix, Jimi, 228
Henry Rollins Show, The, 241
Henry the VIII (king), 155–156
Hepworth, M., 233
Herder, J. G., 76
Hesmondhalgh, David, 74
heteropatriarchy, 149–151, 154
Heti, Sheila, 61
Heylin, Clinton, 6–7, 10, 97n4
Heywood, Leslie, 52
H♄GH FA卍ION, 429
Hickman, Cleveland Pendleton, 403
Higgins, Dick, 104
Hildegard of Bingen, 154
Hill, Anita, 50
Hill, Joe, 79
Himonides, E., 136–137
hip-hop/rap, 148–153, 157–164, 221
hippies, 2, 297–298, 305, 419, 429–430, 484
Hitler, Adolf, 485
HIV and AIDS, 163, 202
Hobsbawm, Eric, 76
Hoerburger, Rob, 162
"Holidays in the Sun," 96, 439, 486
Hollywood Palladium, 224–225, 228

Holmstrom, John, 455–457
Holstm, Gustav, 105
Holy Titclamps, 452
Home, Stewart, 100, 102, 110–111
Homo-A-Go-Go, 209
homocore, 171, 202. *See also* queercore
Homocore, 168, 172
homophobia and homophobic violence, 167–168, 202, 204–205, 211, 214n2, 215n10, 469, 525–526
Hook, Peter, 33–34
Hooley, Terri, 335–336
Hooligans, Los, 191
Horne, Alan, 274
Horne, Howard, 383
Horses, 439
Hot Topic, 364
House on the Edge of the Park, The, 428–429
Howard, Silas, 206–208
"How Deep Is Your Love," 418–419
Howe, Darcus, 430
Howlett, Mike, 442
"How Much Longer," 484
Hucknall, Mick, 31, 42
Huggy Bear, 169, 258
Human Rights Campaign, 212
hunched posture, 397–404
"Hunted Down"/ "Nothing to Say," 542
Hüsker Dü, 545
Hynde, Chrissie, 117
Hypocrites, 338
hysteria, 158

ICES. *See* International Carnival of Experimental Sounds
Ice-T, 160
"Identity," 245
identity politics, boundaries, and multiplicity, 170–175
Idol, Billy, 12
"I Don't Mind"/ "Autonomy," 386, 386f
"I Don't Wanna Hear It," 136–138, 140
IFMC. *See* International Folk Music Council
"I Fought the Law," 92
"If the Kids Are United," 476
"If You're Going to San Francisco (Be Sure to Wear Flowers in Your Hair)," 298

Ignorant, Steve, 106–107, 442, 486
"I Hate Red Color," 285
imagined violence, 208, 213
Immediate, 272
"I'm Not a Fool," 507
imperialism, 554
"I'm So Bored with the USA," 91
Independent Press Association (IPA), 458
independent record labels, 271–274, 332, 542, 545, 547–548
indie-pop, 169–170, 175
individuality and individualism, 5, 232–233, 286–288, 380, 524, 530
industrial music, 109
"Insects," 285
International Carnival of Experimental Sounds (ICES), 105–106
International Folk Music Council (IFMC), 76, 80
International Pop Underground Convention, 1991, 49
intersectional feminism, 54, 64, 173
In Utero, 550
Ioffe, Julia, 515
IPA. *See* Independent Press Association
Iron Maiden, 365
"I Shot the Sheriff," 468
"It's Not the Heat, It's the Humidity," 240
"It Takes a Man Like Me to Find a Woman Like Me," 206
I Wanna Be Your Dog, 456

Jackie, 251
Jackson, Travis A., 489, 496
Jacobs, Marc, 545–546
Jagger, Mick, 89
Jam, 93, 389, 489, 491, 496–497
James, Cheryl, 161–162
James, Tony, 35
Jameson, Fredric, 529, 559
Jasper, Maura, 411
Jasper, Megan, 546
jazz, 105
J.D.s, 168, 202, 204–205, 208–209
Jefferson, T., 116
Jefferson Airplane, 362
Jenifer, Daryl, 227

Jenner, Caitlyn, 211
"Jeremy," 545
jerk, 192
Jesus and Mary Chain, 446
"Jigsaw Feeling," 80
Joe Strummer: The Future Is Unwritten, 92
Johnson, Holly, 495–496
Johnson, Imani, 195
Johnson, Linton Kwesi, 430
John the Postman, 41
Join Hands, 126
Jones, Alex, 523
Jones, G. B., 168, 202–205, 208–209
Jones, Huw, 473
Jones, Jordy, 210–211
Jones, Mick, 35, 89–91
Jones, Steve, 90, 430, 525, 528
Joplin, Janis, 128
Joy Division, 31, 34, 37, 271, 365, 369, 487, 491–492
Jubilee, 425, 429
Julie Ruin, 59
Juvenal, 399

Kaka de Luxe, 317, 322
Kalra, Virinder S., 474–475
Kant, Immanuel, 407
KAOS, 541
Karpf, Anne, 128
Kasson, John F., 398–399
Katz, S., 233
Kavanaugh, Brett, 66n25
Kearney, Mary Celeste, 52
Keenan, John, 271
Kelleher, Marta, 211
Kelly, Ben, 274
Kennedy, Anthony, 150
Kent, Nick, 455
Kerouac, Jack, 225, 433, 454
Keyes, Cheryl, 162–163
Khrust, 289
Khutorskoi, Ivan "Bonebraker," 290
Kid Creole, 428
Kid Rock, 197–198
Kilburn and the High Roads, 35
Killing Joke, 388, 388*f*
"Kill the Sexist," 506–510

Kincaid, Jamaica, 498n2
King, James, 270
King, Rodney, 49
Kino, 284
KISMIF, 447, 486
"Know Your Rights," 93
Koc, Alican, 559
kolkhoznyi punk, 285–286
Kool Kyle, 428
"Krasnye and anarcho skiny," 289
K Records, 49, 542
Kruse, Holly, 125
Kú de Judas, 321, 325

L 7, 50, 544–545, 551, 562
Laban, Rudolf, 413n10
LaBruce, Bruce, 168, 202–205, 208–209, 214
Lady Bits, 149, 153–156, 156f, 157f, 161
Ladyfest, 170
Laennec, René, 149, 156
Laing, Dave, 8, 14, 16n15, 17n19, 96, 127–128, 400, 402, 439–440, 472
Lamacq, Steve, 275
LA punk scene, 189–190, 195–197
Larry-bob, 452
Last, Bob, 273–274
late capitalism, 558–560
Latina and Chicana punks, 187–189, 199
Lauder, Andrew, 387
LA Weekly, 51
Lazell, Barry, 393–394
Lead Belly, 221
LeBlanc, 167
leftism and leftists, 78, 82, 471, 483–484, 524, 529
Lenin, Vladimir, 510
Leningrad, 287–289
Lennon, John, 108, 489, 493–494
Leon, Craig, 441–442
Leonard, Marion, 52
Lesser Free Trade Hall, 266
Letov, Egor, 284–286
Letov, Yegor, 4
"Let's Talk about Prams," 129
"Let's Talk about Sex," 162–163
Letts, Don, 15, 89, 95f, 97, 190, 430, 486
Levene, Keith, 90–91

Lewie, Jona, 493
libertarianism, 5, 525, 530
Libertine, Eve, 106
Libertines, 434n5
Life in the European Theatre, 497
Limbaugh, Rush, 50
Limp Bizkit, 197–198
Linker, Beth, 408
Linklater, Richard, 547
Liquid Sky, 425, 428, 434n5
Little Richard, 221
Live Aid, 494
LiveJournal, 503, 504f, 510, 515f
Liverpool, punk world of, 28, 30–31, 35–41, 38f
Live through This, 550
Living Tradition, The, 75
Lloyd, A. L., 76
Lock, Graham, 125–126
Locke, John, 399
Lockett, Glenn, 443–444, 448
Loder, John, 442–444, 446, 448
Logic, Lora, 127–128
Lollapalooza, 545
London Calling, 91, 93, 441, 445–446
"London Calling," 91, 93
London punk films, 429–433
"London's Burning," 91
London SS, 35, 90
Lookout Records, 157
"Lost in the Supermarket," 91
Lott, Tim, 127–128
Louder Than Love, 543
Loud Women, 180
Loud Women, 130
Love, Courtney, 52, 545, 550
"Love Buzz"/"Big Cheese," 542
Low, Chris, 269
Lowenthal, David, 555, 557
Lowrey, Annie, 558
Lunch, Lydia, 420–421, 434n5
"Lupe, Es," 192–193
Lycett, Kevin, 390
Lydon, John, 6–7, 191, 234, 266, 391, 424, 445
  on bombsites, 485
  in *Copkiller*, 428, 434n6
  fashion of, 528
  on fights and violence, 120–121

hunched posture of, 397–404, 409, 412
on Pink Floyd, 484
in Public Image Limited, 96
Ramone, M., and, 223
Rhodes and, 90
on *Today*, 525
on Trump, 523
working class and, 282
Lyotard, Jean-François, 555

MacColl, Ewan, 76
Maciunas, George, 104, 110
MacKaye, Ian, 133, 135, 137–139, 141–145, 226–227, 367, 405
Made in Britain, 429
male gaze, 250, 252, 405
Malfunkshun, 541, 543–544
Malicious Damage Records, 388–389
Manchester, 27–28, 30–41, 38f, 40f, 266, 271–272, 274
Manchester Arts Festival, 108
Mancini, Hilken, 411
"Man in the Box," 544
Manitoba, Dick, 215n10
Mannheim, Karl, 247–249
Manumission, 460
Man Who Fell to Earth, The, 424
Mapplethorpe, Robert, 424
Marcus, Greil, 2, 12, 14, 96, 100, 102, 127, 554, 564
Marcus, Sara, 54–58, 404
Marinov, Georgi, 309
Marker, Steve, 446
Marley, Bob, 431–432, 468, 475
Marr, Andrew, 260
Marr, John, 453
Martin, George, 441
Marxism, 77–78, 248, 529, 532
masculinities, 134–139, 150–151, 171, 189, 196, 211
Matheuresusement, 456
Matlock, Glen, 528
Maximumrocknroll (MRR), 454–456, 458–460
Mbembe, Achille, 212
McCartney, Paul, 493–494
McClary, S., 30
McCulloch, Ian, 36, 41

McDougal, Dennis, 160
McKagan, Duff, 223
McKay, George, 6–7, 11, 75, 107, 397–398, 405
McKenzie, Scott, 298
McLaren, Malcolm, 9, 102, 104, 282, 363, 383, 429, 528, 554
  Sex Pistols and, 3, 10, 32–33, 90–91, 96, 101, 110–111, 384–385, 553
McLeod, Kembrew, 124
McLoone, M., 334, 336, 343
McLuhan, Marshall, 87
McMichael, Polly, 511–514
McNeil, Legs, 193, 455
McNeill, Phil, 469
McNeish, Peter, 32–35
McRobbie, Angela, 121, 321
Meatmen, 526
Meatwhistle, 265
Medhurst, Andy, 14, 562
media ecology, 87–96
MediaZona, 517
"Medium Was Tedium, The"/ "Don't Back the Front," 392, 393f
Meek, Joe, 272
Mekons, 271, 390, 391f
Melody Maker, 29, 110, 468, 543
Meltzer, Marisa, 53–56, 58
Melvins, 538, 541, 545, 551
Meredino, James, 194
Merman, Ethel, 128
metal, 538, 540–541
Meyer, Russ, 429
Michelle T., 187–188
Middlesbrough Rock Garden, 270
Middleton, Richard, 76
Mihaylov-Perry, Oleg, 305
Milanov, Petar, 303–304
Miles-Kingston, June, 119
militarism, 485–486, 499n4
Millar, Robbi, 123–124
Millington, Mary, 430
"Ministry of Anti-Social Insecurity," 108
Minor Disturbance, 142
Minor Threat, 133–145, 197, 226–228, 367
Minor Threat, 134–143, 145
"Minor Threat," 134–137, 140
Minutemen, 532

Misfits, 364–365
misogyny, 124, 167, 198, 204–205, 208, 429
Mistakes, 125
Misty in Roots, 430
Mitchell, John Cameron, 209
Mobius Studios, 441–442
modernism, 76–77, 82, 105, 383
Modern Lovers, 10
Mo-Dettes, 119–120
Mojo Navigator Rock & Roll News, 454
Monova, Dorothea, 307
Moor, Uhuru, 224, 228
Moorcock, Michael, 484
Moore, Allan, 439, 447, 472
Moore, Ryan, 288–289
Moors Murderers, 117
Moran, I., 439–440
More Specials, 445–446
Morley, Paul, 33, 41, 126, 266, 271, 275, 496
Morris, Desmond, 413n6
Morris, Kenny, 122
Morrison, Hilary, 273–274
Morrissey, Stephen, 33
Morton, Chris, 387
Moscow Death Brigade, 289–291
mosh pit, 187, 189–191, 194–195, 196–200, 204
Mother Love Bone, 541, 543–544
"Mother of God, Chase Putin Out," 513–515, 513f, 514f
Movida, La, 317, 319, 323, 325, 328
Mr. Nipples & the Dangleberries, 338
MRR. *See* Maximumrocknroll
Ms., 48
MTV, 162, 164, 195–196, 198, 409, 544–545, 547
Mudhoney, 538, 541–545, 551
Muggleton, David, 539
Mumford, Jill, 389–390
Muñoz, Jose Esteban, 58, 206
Munro, Will, 209
Murder Can Be Fun, 453
Murray, Charles Shaar, 125
Murray, Pauline, 126–127
Museum of Jurassic Technology, 557–558
musicking, 30
Muzyka dlia rabochego klassa, 290–291
"My Generation," 232

Mystic Trumpeter, The, 104–105

Nagle, Angela, 524, 526
Naked Raygun, 541
Nancy, Jean-Luc, 535
Napalm Death, 276
Narcosis, 505
National Abortion Campaign, 248
National Front (NF), 116–118, 254, 343, 429–432, 465–468, 470–474, 476–477, 479, 523
National Parent Teachers Organization, 160
Nation of Ulysses, 63
Naylor, Liz, 116, 250, 252, 258–260
Nazi punks, 197, 305, 430–431
"Nazi Punks Fuck Off," 196–197
Nazi symbols and imagery, 117, 220, 430, 467–470, 472, 484–485
 swastikas, 4, 117–118, 194, 469–470, 485, 525, 528
necropolitics, 203, 211–213
Nedeva-Voeva, Neli, 308–309
Nehring, Neil, 52
Nelson, Jeff, 133, 136, 139, 142–144
Nena, 493–497
neoliberalism, 344–349, 422, 432, 530, 540
Neue Deutsche Welle movement, 494
Neuman, Molly, 57, 59, 61, 457
"Never Been in a Riot," 390, 391f
Nevermind, 447, 538–539, 544–545
Never Mind the Bollocks, Here's the Sex Pistols, 96, 223, 441, 445, 447–448, 465
New Crimes, 275
New Hollywood movement, 419–420, 423
New Hormones, 34, 272
Newman, Thunderclap, 488
New Order, 34, 271
New Romanticism, 267–269, 271, 486–487
"New Rose," 1, 76, 439
Newton, Adi, 266
New Wave, 429–430
New Winds, 325
New York Dolls, 7, 10, 33, 101
New York punk films, 426–429, 432–433
New York Rocker, 456
NF. *See* National Front
Nguyen, Mimi Thi, 57–58, 60–62, 173

Nichols, Mike, 423–424
Nieuwe Koekrand, 456
Nighthawks, 430
999, 389
"1977," 89
924 Gilman Collective, 154, 160
"99 Red Balloons," 493–497
Nipple Erectors, 117, 119
Nirvana, 364–365, 370, 374, 406–407, 434n5, 447, 529, 538–539, 541–545, 547–548, 550–551
Nissen, Melanie, 456
NME, 29, 32–34, 118, 125–126, 266–267, 269, 381*f*, 466, 468–469, 471–473, 481, 496
Nobakht, D., 15
No Code, 550–551
NOFX, 563
Noise Addiction, 222
Noisey, 76, 193
Nol', 285
"No More Sectarian Shit," 338
Northern Ireland, punk in, 332–349, 333*f*
No Skin Off My Ass, 208–209
"No somos nada," 317, 319
nostalgia, 46–49, 53–58, 334–336, 343, 349, 556, 558, 562–563
Nova Generatsia, 306*f*, 307–309
Novi Tsvetya, 295, 299–310, 301*f*, 304*f*
No Wave, 433n3
"Now I Wanna Sniff Some Glue," 455
NPR, 194
N.W.A., 161
Nyende, Jasmine, 224–225, 228
Nylon, 47

O'Brien, Lucy, 6, 11, 116, 119, 207
O'Brien, Susan, 249
O'Connell, H., 439–440
O'Connor, Hazel, 491, 492*f*
OC punk. *See* Orange County punk scene
"Ode an die Freude," 161
"O Death, Rock Me Asleep," 155, 156*f*
"Ode to Joy," 161, 164n6
"Off Duty Trip," 129
Offspring, 550
O'Hara, C., 4, 13–14

O'Hara, Frank, 58
"Oh Bondage, Up Yours," 128, 148–149, 409
Oi!, 4, 11, 13, 289–290, 342, 472, 505–507, 509–511
okupas, 326
Oldham, Andrew Loog, 272
O'Malia, James, 523
OMD. *See* Orchestral Manoeuvres in the Dark
O'Meara, Caroline, 123, 126
1 in 12 Club, 270–271
1000 Drunken Nights, 345–348, 345*f*
"On Kingsmill Road," 337
Ono, Yoko, 104
"Orange and Blue," 108
Orange County (OC) punk scene, 195–197
Orange County Strut, 189
Orchestral Manoeuvres in the Dark (OMD), 42, 491–492
"Orgasm Addict," 248
Orgazm Nostradamusa, 286–287
Orientalism, 154
Orwell, George, 433
Otherness and Others, 6, 8, 16n10, 225–226, 342, 532, 534–535
Outcasts, 333*f*
Out of the Blue, 424
Ovary Action, 157–158, 158*f*, 159*f*
"Overblown," 545

Paglia, Camille, 50–51
Paine, Thomas, 453
Palmolive, 121
Panov, Andrey "Svin," 283–284
Pansy Division, 209
Parents Music Resource Center (PMRC), 160
Park, MiRi, 408
Parker, James, 522
Parks, Rosa, 218
Parsons, Dave, 274
Partch, Harry, 441
Part of the Furniture, 273
Passions, 124
"Patriot," 307
Patterson, Fred "Phast Phreddie," 455
Pavitt, Bruce, 541–543, 551
Peach, Blair, 477

Pearl Jam, 538–539, 541, 544–545, 550–551
Peel, John, 30, 121, 267, 271–273
Peligro, D. H., 228
Pelly, Jenn, 64
Penetration, 129
Penis Envy, 106–107
Penman, Ian, 121
Pepi, Luci, Bom and otras chicas del montón, 319
Pere Ubu, 109
Performance, 88–89, 434n6
performance art, 107–110
Permanent Vacation, 425
Perry, Mark, 6, 10, 110, 274, 384, 455–457
Peterson, Charles, 542, 547
Peterson, Jordan, 400–401
Pfaff, Kristen, 550
Phranc, 206
Pickett, Dave, 41
Pilcher, Jane, 247–248
Pilkington, Hilary, 404
Pink Floyd, 440, 484
Pink Floyd: The Wall, 424, 429
Pink Turds in Space, 335, 338, 339f
"Pipes of Peace," 493
"Plastic Crap," 273
Plaza Sound, 441
PMRC. *See* Parents Music Resource Center
POC punks, 193–194, 196, 217–218, 223–224
pogoing, 187–198, 335
Pogues, 332, 343
Poison Girls, 118–120, 269
"Police Oppression," 509–510
political posturing, 410–411
"Politicians in My Eyes," 221
politics, punk and, 2, 12, 73, 75, 88, 256, 282–291, 302–303, 305
  alt-right movement and, 522–526, 529–535
  antiwar and antinuclear songs, 481–485, 482f, 487–489, 490t, 491–498
  fascism and, 3–4, 314, 343, 429–430, 465–467, 469–470, 472, 523, 526, 564
  identity politics, 170–175
  left-wing and, 78, 82, 471, 483–484, 524, 529
  libertarianism and, 5, 525, 530
  post-punk and, 486–489, 490t, 491–496
  progressivism and, 4–5

Pussy Riot and, 506, 509–510, 517
RAR and, 466, 471–474, 483–484
Polla Records, La, 317, 319
Polygram, 543–544
Poneman, Jonathan, 542–543
Pop, Iggy, 220, 398, 402–406, 405f, 409–410, 455
Pop Group, 276, 481
Popinjays, 254
Popov, Ivan, 301f
pop-punk, 529
Porcos Sujos, 324f
P-Orridge, Genesis, 101, 107–110
Portuguese punk, 234–235, 237, 318f, 320–328
posing and posers, 409–410
Postcard, 274
postfeminism, 50
Postman, Neil, 87
postmodernism, 366–367, 374–375, 404–405, 423, 527–535, 559–560
post-punk, 13–15, 76, 82, 83n3, 428
  Bulgarian, 297, 299, 303–304
  design, 390
  folk, punk and, 72
  in Liverpool, 37, 38f
  in Manchester, 37, 38f
  punk politics and, 486–489, 490t, 491–496
  Reynolds on, 483, 487
  slouching and, 406
posture, 397–412, 413n6
Powell, Enoch, 468
Power in the Darkness, 471
"Power in the Union," 291
PRB. *See* Punk Rock Bowling
Preslar, Lyle, 133, 135
Presley, Elvis, 219
Pressure, 429, 431
"Pressure Drop," 92
Price, Bill, 441, 445
Probe, 31, 35, 268
Profane Existence, 459–460
progressivism, 4–5
Proll, Astrid, 88
Pro Skater, 191, 194
proto-punk, 220–222, 423
provincial history, of UK punk, 265–277
PSN. *See* Punk Scholars Network

psychedelic rock, 232
psychoanalysis, 149
Public Enemy, 151, 161
Public Image Ltd., 96, 305, 487
pub rock, 390
Punk (docuseries), 222–223
Punk (zine), 29, 454–457
Punk 1976–1978 exhibition, 296
Punk and Post-Punk, 486
punk cinema, 421–433, 423*f*
punk generations, 238–240, 247–250, 249*t*
Punk Girl Diaries, 254
punk graphic design and visual style, 379–395, 386*f*, 391*f*
punk identities, 5–8, 12, 29, 207, 245–250, 255–256, 260, 379–380, 521, 524, 530–532, 535
Punk in Ireland 2006, 338, 340*f*
punk literature, 1–2, 15
Punk London exhibition, 240, 554, 556–558, 564
punk pedagogy, 154
Punk Planet, 458–459
Punk Renaissance, 2000s, 194
Punk Rock Bowling (PRB), 555, 560–564
Punk Rock Movie, The, 190, 430
Punk Scholars Network (PSN), 241
punk sonic aesthetics, 439–449
punk spaces, 10–12, 31, 75, 130n1, 171–175, 239, 269–272, 424–425
punk style and fashion, 6–7, 207, 227, 234, 241–242, 321
　of The Clash, 527–528
　clothes of punk women, 251–252, 255–256
　as cyclical, 363–365, 367
　gender and, 252
　grunge, 539, 545–546
　New York *versus* UK, 527–528
　NME advertisement for, 381*f*
　of Riot Grrrl, 177
　T-shirts, 359–375
　Westwood and, 8–9, 116, 203, 363, 365, 370, 375, 429, 528
punk worlds, 29–32, 37–41
　of Liverpool, 28, 30–43, 38*f*
　of Manchester, 27–28, 30–43, 38*f*, 40*f*
"Punky Reggae Party," 431–432

Pure Hell, 221–222, 227
Pursey, Jimmy, 472, 476, 478
Pussy Riot, 16n16, 502–517, 504*f*, 512*f*, 513*f*, 514*f*, 515*f*
Pussy Whipped, 506
Putin, Vladimir, 502–503, 505, 509–510, 513

QTPOC communities, 199–200
Queen, 447
Queen Elizabeth (band), 205
queer and feminist punk scenes, UK, 166–180
queercore, 7, 62, 199
　gender in first generation, 204–207
　G.L.O.S.S. and, 212–213
　Hedwig and the Angry Inch and, 209–211
　Jones, G. B., and LaBruce in, 202–205, 208–209, 214
　Riot Grrrl and, 166–173, 175–176, 528
　transgender punk and, 204–213
Queer Nation, 202, 208
queer style, aesthetics of, 177–179
queer theory, 202, 206
Queeruption, 209
Queeruption festivals, 168–169
Querelle, 424
Quoc Te, 204

race, 6–7, 143–145, 220, 222–224, 402
　Riot Grrrl on class and, 51–52, 57, 60–62, 64
Race Riot, 61
Rachmaninoff, Sergei, 513–514
racism and racist violence, 4, 6, 173, 226, 254, 429, 468–470, 472, 478–479, 523–524
Radar Records, 387
radical media, punk as, 87–88
Radkey, 560
Radway, Janice, 53, 65n6
Raincoats, 116–117, 123, 126–127, 129–130, 406, 434n5, 486
Ramírez-Sanchez, R., 6
Ramone, Joey, 398
Ramone, Marky, 223
Ramones, 1, 222–223, 361, 363, 369, 371, 389, 441, 448, 455–456, 521, 527–528
Ramones, 441, 448
Rana, Azhar, 473
Rancid, 529

Ranger, Terence, 76
Rankine, Claudia, 218
"Rape Victim," 129
RAR. *See* Rock Against Racism
RAR's Greatest Hits, 465
Ratledge, Miles, 276
Rattus Norvegicus, 390
Raw Power, 220
Razorcake, 458–459
Razorlight, 365
Reading Festival, 545
Reagan, Ronald, 49, 150–151, 197, 421, 503, 526, 542, 545, 549, 559
"Real Judas Syndrome, The," 325
"Rebel Girl," 509
Record Business, 393–394
recording and production, 438–449
record shops, provincial UK, 269–270
Red Album, 285
Red Card, 289
Reddington, Helen, 6, 12, 14, 120, 167, 250
Red Rhino, 270
Reed, Lou, 319, 455
Refill, 392
Refused, 535
reggae, 6, 93, 430–432, 432f, 439, 469, 474, 478–479, 492, 494, 523
Reid, Jamie, 8, 101, 104, 110–111, 364–365, 379, 382–385
Rejected Records, 338
"Religious Dictator," 273
"Remote Control," 92
Replacements, 545
reproductive rights, music education and, 153–156
resistance, punk and, 296–298
Revolution Goes On, The, 309
Revu, 295, 299, 306, 310
Reyes, Ron, 196–197
Reynolds, Simon, 13, 15, 46–47, 73, 76, 83nn3–4, 110, 267, 275, 411, 465, 483, 487, 496
Rhodes, Bernard, 35, 90–91, 96
rhythm and blues, 219, 468–469
Richards, Sam, 81
Rider, Alan, 276
Rimbaud, Penny, 74, 101, 104–105, 107, 387
Riot Grrrl, 5–7, 12, 130, 130n1

Bikini Kill and, 45–46, 49–50, 57, 59, 62–64, 224
DIY and, 45, 63, 168–170
feminism and, 45–46, 48–58, 62–64, 173, 179, 506, 544
historiography, place of music in, 62–65
legacy of, archives and absences in, 58–62
in 1990s, 49–53
nostalgia and, 46–49, 53–58
Pussy Riot and, 505–506, 509
queercore and, 166–173, 175–176, 528
on race and class, 51–52, 57, 60–62, 64
style and aesthetics of, 177
UK, 169–170
whiteness and, 173
zines, 53, 57, 60–64, 457
Riot Grrrl Collection at New York University's Fales Library and Special Collections, 58–63, 66n15, 66n23, 68n52
Riot Grrrl Convention, 1992, 61
Riot Grrrl Manifesto, 62, 168–169
"Riot in Russia— Putin Zassal," 504f
Ripped & Torn, 274, 456
Rise Above: The Tribe 8 Documentary, 207–208
Ritchie, Karen, 546–547
Rivett, Miriam, 7
Riviera, Jake, 387
Robb, John, 9, 274–275
Robertson, Scott, 151
Robin, Corey, 524
rocanrol, 191–193
Roche, Judith, 253–254
Rock Against Racism (RAR), 6, 271, 429, 465–479, 483–484, 494
rock and roll, 219, 224
rock clubs, provincial, 270–272
Rockin Devil's, Los, 192–193
"Rock N Roll Nigger," 225
Rock On, 455
rock radikal vasco, 319–320, 322
Rock Rendez Vous, 320, 329n10
rock siniestro, 319
"Rock the Casbah," 94
Rocky Horror Picture Show, The, 209
Rodel, Angela, 440
Roe v. Wade (1973), 150
Rogers, E., 365

INDEX

Roiphe, Katie, 50–52
Rolling Stone, 52, 162
Rolling Stones, 232
Rollins, Henry, 223, 241, 405
Rollins Band, 544
Romano, Renee C., 47
Rombes, Nicholas, 423
Rondarev, Artem, 288
Ron Johnson, 274
Roper, Dee Dee, 161–162
Rose, T., 233
Ross, A., 233
Rotten, Johnny. *See* Lydon, John
Rotz, 458
Rough Trade, 30, 269–270, 273
Roxy, 12, 121, 190, 430
Rude Boy, 430–432
Ruefrex, 337–338, 344
Rumble Fish, 423, 434n5
Rumours, 447
Rum Runner, 271
"Running Riot," 506
Runnin' Riot, 342
Russian punk, 281–291, 404
Rutherford, Paul, 495–496
Ruts, 473
Rybin, Alexei, 283

Sabin, Roger, 3–4, 88, 241, 470, 474
safe(r) spaces, 173–175
Saicos, Los, 193
Said, Edward, 154
Salazar, António, 314–315
Salnikov, Vladimir, 284
Salt-N-Pepa, 148–149, 151, 153, 161–164
Samiof, Steve, 456
Samutsevich, Katya, 503–504
Sandbrook, Dominic, 260
Sandinista!, 93
Sassy, 50
Saturday Night Fever, 418–420, 419f, 423, 425
Saturday Night Live, 545
Saunders, Red, 468
Saussure, Ferdinand de, 522
Savage, Jon, 4, 75, 87–90, 96, 100–102, 125, 130, 272, 275, 485, 523, 562
Saville, Peter, 37, 41–42, 383

Scafidi, Susan, 374
Schill, Brian James, 103
Schilt, Kristin, 52
Schoenberg, Arnold, 106
Schumann, Clara, 154
Schumann, Robert, 154
Schwartz, Andy, 456
Scott, Joan Wallach, 48
Scratch Acid, 541
Scream, The, 439
"Screaming at a Wall," 136–138, 144
Screaming Life, 542
Screaming Trees, 544–545, 551
Scritti Politti, 260
Search and Destroy, 454–456
Second Annual Review, The, 109
"Second Coming, The" (Yeats), 406–408
second-wave feminism, 48, 50, 54–55, 171
Secret Public, The, 275
Sedgwick, Edie, 426, 427f
Seeger, Pete, 298
Seeger, Ruth Crawford, 80
"Seeing Red," 135–138
Sektor Gaza, 285–286
self-reflexivity, 245
Sellberg, Karin, 210–211
Sent from Coventry, 276
Sepulveda, Susana, 196
Sergeant, D. C., 136–137
Severin, Steven, 109
Severnoe bugi, 285
sex, 148–150, 152, 156, 158–164, 167
SEX, 32–33, 203, 363, 429–430, 528
Sex Discrimination Act of 1975, 115, 248
sexism, 123–125, 167–168, 205, 429
Sex Pistols, 1, 3–4, 14, 16n16, 78, 80, 82, 97, 117, 305, 328, 564
    "Anarchy in the UK" by, 3, 78, 82, 102, 190–191, 234, 332, 385
    the Clash and, 90–91, 96–97, 231, 272, 304
    class and, 282
    Coon on, 29
    in *D.O.A.*, 425
    EMI and, 471
    fashion of, 528
    Filthy Lucre Tour, 234

Sex Pistols (*cont.*)
   "God Save the Queen" by, 305, 385, 421, 528, 554, 556–557
   in *The Great Rock 'n' Roll Swindle*, 430
   Grundy and, 469, 525
   Hard Rock Cafe and, 553
   Hebdige on, 429
   "Holidays in the Sun" by, 96, 439, 486
   in Manchester, 266
   McLaren and, 3, 10, 32–33, 90–91, 96, 101, 110–111, 384–385, 553
   La Movida and, 319
   Never Mind the Bollocks, Here's the Sex Pistols by, 96, 223, 441, 445, 447–448, 465
   noise and, 96
   in origins of UK punk, 27
   Reid and, 379, 382, 384–385
   in rock canon, 440
   SI and, 101–104, 110–111
   in *Sid and Nancy*, 190–191
   on *So It Goes*, 250
   Spencer, N., on, 29, 32–35
   on *Top of the Pops*, 96, 488
   visual style of, 379, 382, 384–385
   in *Who Killed Bambi?*, 429
sexual assault, 190, 198, 208, 506, 516
sexuality, gender and, 171–172, 178
Shahan, Cyrus, 485
Sham 69, 466, 472–473, 476, 478, 505–506
Shape of Punk to Come, The, 535
Shapes, 273
Shapiro, Peter, 433n1
Shaw, Greg, 454
Shawna Virago and the Deadly Nightshade Family, 206–207
Shirlow, Peter, 350n7
Shnurov, Sergei "Shnur," 288
shoegaze, 408
SI. *See* Situationist International
Sid and Nancy, 190–191
"Silence Equals Death," 213
Simonelli, David, 281
Simonon, Paul, 89–91
Simply Red, 42
Sinatra, Nancy, 221–222, 227
Sincero, Jen, 401
Singh, G., 375
Singles, 545

Sinker, Dan, 458
Siouxsie and the Banshees, 80, 117, 126, 439, 557
Siouxsie Sioux, 4, 109, 121–122, 126–127, 485, 527
Situationist International (SI), 3, 9, 97n2, 100–104, 110–111, 248, 260, 383, 385
ska, 116, 474, 492
ska-punk, 529
Skids, 489
skinheads, 4, 116–119, 430–431, 472, 506
Skin Yard, 541
Sklar, Monica, 254–255, 362, 529
Slacker, 547
slam, 189, 194–198, 526
Slash, 456
Slate, 55
Slaughter and the Dogs, 27, 29, 34
SLC Punk!, 194–195
Sleater-Kinney, 46, 63, 66n25
Slimane, Hedi, 365, 370
Slits, 2, 13, 116–119, 121, 125–127, 129–130, 557
slouching, 400, 403, 406–408
"Slug Bait," 109
Small, Adam, 30, 197
"Small Man, Big Mouth," 134–135, 139–140
Small Wonder, 273
Smart Studios, 446–447
Smash, 550
Smashing Pumpkins, 447, 544
"Smells Like Teen Spirit," 544–545
Smell the Magic, 544
Smith, Bill, 389
Smith, Erin, 57
Smith, Kyle, 502
Smith, Mark E., 41
Smith, Patti, 109, 225, 398, 439
Smith, Robert, 424
Smith, Sadie "Switchblade," 212–213
Smith, TV, 14, 32, 485
Smithereens, 421, 425–426, 427f, 428, 432–433
"Smokescreen"/ "Handlebars," 392
Smyth, G., 334
Sniffin' Glue, 10, 110, 274, 384, 454–457
Snow, George "God," 389
social conservatism, 150–153
Social Distortion, 197
socialism, 77–79, 248, 505
Socialist Workers Party (SWP), 470

Sofa Records, 273
So It Goes, 42, 250, 528
Sokoloff, Irving, 362
Sokologorskaya, Lyubov, 514
Solidarity Not Silence, 180
"Something in the Air," 488
"Song of Anarchist Workers, The," 290
Sonic Youth, 538, 541, 544
Sontag, Susan, 123
Soundgarden, 538–539, 541–545, 550
Sounds, 117, 121, 123, 127–128, 267, 269, 468, 472
Southern Studios, 443, 446
Soviet-Afghan War, 489
Soviet punk, 282–286
Spanish punk, 317, 319, 322–328
Spare Rib, 122–123, 129
Sparks, Donita, 223
Specials, 445–446
Spencer, Amy, 169
Spencer, Herbert, 383
Spencer, Neil, 29, 32–35
Spheeris, Penelope, 422, 525
Spice Girls, 53–54
Spiders, 270
Spiral Scratch, 34, 37, 272, 392
Spitfire Boys, 36, 495–496
Spooner, James, 6, 227
Sprechstimme, 106
Spungen, Nancy, 190
SST Records, 443–444, 544
Stalag 17, 337, 337f, 342
Staley, Layne, 550
"Stand Down Margaret (Dub)," 492–493
Stanford Rivers Quartet, 105
Starr, Ringo, 191
Stations of the Cross, 106
Station to Station, 467
Stearns, Peter N., 402, 407–408
Stein, Arlene, 123
Steinholt, Yngvar, 4, 11
Sterling, Linder, 36–37, 116, 167, 248
Stern, Shawn, 564
Sterne, Jonathan, 149
Stevenson, Nils, 120–122
Stewart, Francis, 342
Stewart, Jon, 488
Stewart, Mark, 481
Stiff Little Fingers, 332, 336–337, 489

Stiff Records, 272, 387, 394, 493
Still Birth, 338, 342
Stockhausen, Karlheinz, 104
Stolper, Paul, 385
Stonehenge People's Free Festival, 119
Stooges, 10, 32–33, 220–221
Stooges, The, 220
"Stop the Cavalry," 493
"Straightedge," 135–137
straight-edge movement, 405, 530
"Straight to Hell," 93–95
Stranglers, 117, 390
Straw, W., 28
Street, John, 260, 467–470, 487–488, 493, 497
Strength Through Oi!, 472
Strummer, Joe, 80, 89–92, 94–95, 248–249, 431
Stryker, Susan, 212
Stuart, Peter, 197
Studios, Mobius, 441
Stupidity, 390
Styrene, Poly, 121, 125, 127–128, 148, 252, 256, 409
subcultural capital, 539, 548–550
subculture, 28–29, 361, 539–540
Sub Pop, 538–544, 551
Sub Pop 100, 541–543
Subterranean Pop, 541
Suburban Press, 385
"Suburban Rebels," 506
Suburbia, 425
Subversa, Vi, 118, 122
"Suck My Left One," 506
Suicide, 441
Sumner, Bernard, 33–34
Sussenbach, Donna, 258, 258f, 259f
swastikas, 4, 117–118, 194, 469–470, 485, 525, 528
Swift, Taylor, 398, 409, 412
SWP. *See* Socialist Workers Party
Synth Punk Fest LDN 2017, 175

TAD, 543–544
Talking Heads, 527
Tampio, Nicholas, 533
tampon flute, 161
Taxi Driver, 424
Taylor, Diana, 188–189
Taylor, Frederick Winslow, 413n10
Taylor, Todd, 458–459
Taylor, Vince, 92

Taylor, Yuval, 391–392
Taylor Swift: Miss Americana, 409
Team Dresch, 169
Teddy Girls, 119
Teds, 2, 116
Teenage Depression, 390
"Teenage Kicks," 335
Teen Idles, 144
Temple, Julien, 92, 430, 553
Temple of the Dog, 544
Ten, 545
Testi, Ken, 31
Thatcher, Margaret, 107, 130, 275, 421, 432, 467, 473–474, 479, 492, 559
That Petrol Emotion, 337–338
"There are no Spectators," 276
"These Boots Are Made For Walkin'," 221–222, 227
third-wave feminism, 46, 48, 50, 54–55, 58
"This Is Radio Clash," 93–94, 97
Thomas, Chris, 441, 445
Thomas, Clarence, 50
Thompson, Dave, 76
Thompson, E. P., 497
Thornton, Sarah, 539
Thrasher, 366–367
Thrills, Adrian, 125
Throbbing Gristle, 101, 109–111
"Thrush," 129
Tigre, Le, 59, 63
Times Square, 422, 425–427
Tolokonnikova, Nadya, 503–507, 513, 516–517
Tomlinson, M., 347–348
"Tommy Gun," 91
Tom of Finland, 204
Tom Robinson Band (TRB), 466, 471–473, 478
Toothpaste, Lucy, 16n8, 116, 119, 129, 429
Toots and the Maytals, 92
Top of the Pops, 96, 487–488, 494–495
torero rock, 325
To the Declassed Elements, 284–285
"Touch Me I'm Sick," 542
Toxic Waste, 337–338, 337f, 342
Traber, Daniel S., 16n10, 531
Trafford, Howard, 32–35
"Training," 303
transcore, 204
Trans Day of Revenge, 212–213

Transgender Dysphoria Blues, 211
transgender punk, 204–213
Transición period in Spain, 314–315, 317, 320, 322, 327
trans music scene, UK, 176–177
transphobia and transphobic violence, 203–204, 208, 211–212, 215n10
Trash, 319
Trask, Stephen, 209
Travers, Brian, 492
Travis, Geoff, 30
Travolta, John, 418
TRB. *See* Tom Robinson Band
Tremblay, M., 7
Tribe 8, 206–208
Triggs, Teal, 9, 275, 439–440
Triumph, 272
Troitsky, Artemy, 283
Troubles, 332–334, 336–341, 337f, 344, 350n7, 483, 497
"Troubles and Beyond, The" exhibition, 332, 333f
True, Everett, 543
True Trans, 211
"True Trans Soul Rebel," 211
Trump, Donald, 66n16, 150, 502–503, 505, 517, 522–523, 532–535, 563
Truth Will Be Heard, The, 337–338, 337f
T-shirts, 359–375, 484, 496, 525, 528, 543
Tsurt, 367
"Tug of War," 338
Turbonegro, 561
Turner, Steve, 541
Turner, Tina, 128
Tutti, Cosey Fanni, 108, 110
Twain, Mark, 64
two-tone, 129, 275–276
"Two Tribes," 493, 495–497, 495f
"Typical Girls," 129

U 2, 496
UB 40, 492
UCR Punk Conference, 2019, 191–192
UK Subs, 489, 491f
UltraSound, 195–196
U-Men, 541
Uncle Anesthesia, 544

Undertones, 269, 332, 335
Up, Ari, 126–127
"Up Against the Wall," 471
Ure, Midge, 494

Vaginal Penetration of an Amelus with a Musty Carrot, 342
Vague, Tom, 91, 97n2, 103
Vail, Tobi, 49, 64, 544
Vale, V., 456
Vanity Fair, 545
Van Leeuwen, Johan, 456
Vasko the Patch, 308
Vaucher, Gee, 14–15, 104–105, 107, 116, 387–389
Vault, 12
Vazaleen, 209
Vedder, Eddie, 544
Vega, Arturo, 363
Velvet Underground, 33
"Very Friendly," 109
Vicious, Sid, 190, 424, 528
Vietnam War, 488
Vig, Butch, 446–447
Ville, Nicholas de, 389
Ving, Lee, 525–526
Vinyl Drip, 274
Virgin Records, 270
Vital Disorders, 129
"Vítimas do sistema," 321
Vive Le Rock, 363
Vmeste k pobede!, 289
Voev, Dimitar, 309
Voice of The Turtle, The, 74
Von Brücker, Jena, 205
Von Dirke, Sabine, 494
Vs., 550
Vulpes, Las, 322
Vulture, 95

Wailoo, Keith, 401–402
"Waiting Room," 188
Wakelin, Dave, 492–493
Wald, Gayle, 52, 457
Walker, Rebecca, 48
Walkerdine, Valerie, 125
Waller, Don, 455
Waller, Johnny, 275

War, 496
"Warhead," 489, 491*f*
Warhol, Andy, 319, 426, 427*f*, 432, 559–560
War Requiem, 106–107
Warzone Collective and Warzone Centre, 334–336, 335*f*, 341–342, 344, 346–349, 347*f*, 348*f*
Waters, John, 424
Watson, Paul Joseph, 523
Watt, Fiona, 256, 258
Webb, Peter, 268
Weber, Max, 236
"We Don't Need the English!," 191–192
Weiner, Nathaniel, 527
Weinstein, Deena, 560
Weitzer, R., 338
Weller, Paul, 489, 491
Wellington-Lloyd, Helen, 384–385
Werle, Dan, 460
Weschler, Lawrence, 558
Wessex Studios, 441, 445
Westwood, Vivienne, 32–33, 90, 120–121, 167, 282
  punk style and, 8–9, 116, 203, 363, 365, 370, 375, 429, 434n5, 528
Whalley, Boff, 268
Whalley, Chas de, 127
Wharf Chambers, 179
"What'd I Say," 219
What We Feel, 290
"Where Have All the Flowers Gone?," 298
White, Edmund, 420
White, Emily, 51–52, 67nn32–33
White, Jack, 221
Whiteley, Sheila, 425, 439, 447
White Mandingos, 227–228
"(White Man) in Hammersmith Palais," 89, 93
white nationalists, 523
whiteness, 173, 195–196, 199, 225
white punk, 193–196, 219, 224–227, 466
"White Riot," 89–90, 94, 190, 472
Whitman, Lucy, 122
WHO. *See* World Health Organization
Who, 232
Who Killed Bambi?, 429
Widdicombe, S., 373
Widgery, David, 465, 469
"Wild Colonial Boy, The," 337
Wilde, Oscar, 410

Wild Ram, 34
Wilkinson, David, 5, 8, 167
Williams, Alan, 444
Williams, Paul, 454
Williams, Tim, 274
Williams, Willie, 92
Willis, P., 232–233
Willsteed, J., 240
Wilson, Andrew, 385
Wilson, Dee, 346
Wilson, Tony, 31, 34, 41–42, 274
Winge, T., 361
Wipers, 541
Wobble, Jah, 429
Wobensmith, Matt, 62
Wolfe, Allison, 49, 57, 457
Wolfen, 421
women
    classical music composers, 154–155
    healthcare for, 148–153, 156, 160
    in hip hop, 148–150, 161–164
    in pop and rock, 117
    reproductive rights, music education and, 153–156
    in *rocanrol*, 192
    on Woodstock '99, 198
    See also feminism
women, in punk rock, 5–6, 12, 116–124, 130, 557
    all-female punk bands, dangers to, 116–120
    anger and violence of, 120–124
    clothes and, 251–252, 255–256
    on fear, 252–253
    female rap collectives and, 148–149
    feminism of, 249–250, 249t, 256, 260
    gender nonconformity and, 207
    generations of, 247–250, 249t
    hair and, 250, 251f
    hardcore scenes, 167
    hip-hop and, 148–150
    identities and, 245–250, 255–256, 260
    Latina and Chicana, 187–189, 199
    mosh pits and, 189–191
    1970s female punks today, 245–260
    noise and, 124–129
    "Oh Bondage Up Yours" and, 148
    on power, 253–254
    punk cinema and, 425
    See also Riot Grrrl

Women of Rock Oral History Project, 187
women's movement, 150
Wood, Andrew, 541, 543–544
Woods, Lesley, 117, 120, 126
Woodstock '99, 189–190, 197–198
Wooffitt, R., 373
Woolner, Christina, 57
"Wooly Bully," 390
Workers' Music Association, 78
working class, 282–291, 419–420, 472, 506, 543
World Health Organization (WHO), 151
World War II, 362, 402, 485
Worley, Matthew, 2, 4, 11, 83n3, 281, 486–487, 506
"Wot's For Lunch Mum? Not Beans Again!," 273
Wuelfing, Howard, 144
Wylie, Pete, 36, 41
Wyman, Bill, 93, 95

X-Ray Spex, 121, 127–129, 148–149, 245, 252, 557
XTC, 491

Yates, Paula, 494
Yeastie Girlz, 148–149, 151, 153, 157–161, 158f, 159f
Yeats, W. B., 406–408
Yes Sir, I Will, 106–107, 442
Yiannopoulos, Milo, 525
Yield, 550–551
Yohannan, Tim, 460
Yosifon, David, 402, 407–408
Young, J. O., 372, 374
Young, La Monte, 105
Young Americans, 467–468
Youth Brigade, 197
YouTube, 503, 512–513
Yugoslavian punk, 302, 309

Zappa, Frank, 160
Zeimbowicz, Eric, 366–367
zines, 9–10, 30, 265–266, 274–276, 384
    DIY and, 276, 452–453, 456, 458–459
    history of, 453–454
    Riot Grrrl and, 53, 57, 60–64, 457
    rise and importance of, 454–461
Zoo Records, 31
Zulueta, Iván, 319
Zverstvo, 286